RESEARCH HANDBOOK ON LAW AND ETHICS IN BANKING AND FINANCE

RESEARCH HANDBOOKS IN FINANCIAL LAW

Series Editor: Rosa Lastra, *Queen Mary University of London, UK*

This important new *Research Handbook* series presents high quality, original reference works that cover a range of subjects within the evolving field of financial law. National, regional and global financial markets are at the epicenter of economic, political and social developments. They are shaped by their own intrinsic dynamics, but are also at the receiving end of potent external forces, including monetary developments, state regulation and policies towards international and regional financial integration and free trade areas.

Under the general editorship of Rosa Lastra, these *Research Handbooks* are edited by leading scholars in their respective fields, and comprise specially commissioned contributions from distinguished academics, who critically, innovatively and substantially analyze a wide range of current issues in financial law.

Each of the individual *Research Handbooks* is a definitive reference work, essential for both scholars of financial law as well as for practicing lawyers. The comprehensive coverage and thorough examinations of the significant topics and ideas in financial law signify the *Research Handbooks'* position as authoritative and scholarly information resources.

Titles in the series include:

Research Handbook on Securities Regulation in the United States
Edited by Jerry W. Markham and Rigers Gjyshi

Research Handbook on Secured Financing in Commercial Transactions
Edited by Frederique Dahan

Research Handbook on Crisis Management in the Banking Sector
Edited by Matthias Haentjens and Bob Wessels

Research Handbook on International Financial Crime
Edited by Barry Rider

Research Handbook on State Aid in the Banking Sector
Edited by François-Charles Laprévote, Joanna Gray and Francesco De Cecco

Research Handbook on Central Banking
Edited by Peter Conti-Brown and Rosa Lastra

Research Handbook on Shadow Banking
Legal and Regulatory Aspects
Edited by Iris H-Y Chiu and Iain MacNeil

Research Handbook on Cross-Border Bank Resolution
Edited by Matthias Haentjens and Bob Wessels

Research Handbook on Law and Ethics in Banking and Finance
Edited by Costanza A. Russo, Rosa M. Lastra and William Blair

Research Handbook on Law and Ethics in Banking and Finance

Edited by

Costanza A. Russo

Senior Lecturer in International Banking Law and in Business Ethics, Centre for Commercial Law Studies, Queen Mary University of London, UK

Rosa M. Lastra

Sir John Lubbock Chair in Banking Law, Centre for Commercial Law Studies, Queen Mary University of London, UK

William Blair

Professor of Financial Law and Ethics, Centre for Commercial Law Studies, Queen Mary University of London, UK

RESEARCH HANDBOOKS IN FINANCIAL LAW

EE Edward Elgar
PUBLISHING

Cheltenham, UK • Northampton, MA, USA

Published by
Edward Elgar Publishing Limited
The Lypiatts
15 Lansdown Road
Cheltenham
Glos GL50 2JA
UK

Edward Elgar Publishing, Inc.
William Pratt House
9 Dewey Court
Northampton
Massachusetts 01060
USA

A catalogue record for this book
is available from the British Library

Library of Congress Control Number: 2019945340

This book is available electronically in the **Elgar**online
Law subject collection
DOI 10.4337/9781784716547

MIX
Paper from
responsible sources
FSC
www.fsc.org   FSC® C013604

ISBN 978 1 78471 653 0 (cased)
ISBN 978 1 78471 654 7 (eBook)

Printed and bound by CPI Group (UK) Ltd, Croydon, CR0 4YY

Contents

Contributors

Clara Barbiani is a Compliance Manager in the field of wealth management; previously, she was a Compliance Officer at Societe Generale in London, working on policy review and coordination. Before that, she worked for the steel multinational company Danieli, undertaking compliance tasks and legal assignments. On the academic side, Clara graduated in International and European Law at The Hague University. She has been studying financial law and regulation extensively between LSE, Queen Mary University and the University of Hong Kong. Throughout the years, Clara has been undertaking research in different areas of financial law with a focus on market abuse, conduct of business regulation and derivatives misuse.

Thomas C. Baxter, Jr., is a member of Sullivan & Cromwell's Financial Services Group, where he focuses his practice on advising clients in the financial services, insurance, securities and FinTech spaces. Mr Baxter's advice relates to complex issues arising from supervision and regulation, investigations and enforcement actions, governance, compliance and risk management, crisis management and organisational culture. He also brings extensive experience dealing with central banks from around the world, and with sovereigns and their instrumentalities, as they address sovereign debt and dollar-liquidity issues. Mr Baxter's deep knowledge in these areas comes from more than 35 years at the Federal Reserve Bank of New York, mostly in senior leadership roles.

Mr Baxter is active in the legal community as a member of the American Bar Association and the International Law Association. He is a Member of the American Law Institute, and has been recognised for his work in the legal community. Mr Baxter has published numerous articles about the legal aspects of bank supervision, cheque collection, securities transfers, electronic transfers of funds and the financial services industry. Mr Baxter is a frequent lecturer at programmes sponsored by various organisations.

William Blair is Professor of Financial Law and Ethics at the Centre for Commercial Law Studies (CCLS), Queen Mary University of London (QMUL). Sir William is a former High Court Judge in England and Wales, and before appointment to the bench practised as a Queen's Counsel specialising in the law of domestic and international banking and finance.

He served as a member of the Board of Trustees of the British Institute of International and Comparative Law until July 2015, and is a member of London's Financial Markets Law Committee.

He chairs the Monetary Law Committee of the International Law Association (MOCOMILA), which brings together leading people in the financial law field.

He is a judge of the Qatar International Court and an Associate Member arbitrator of 3 Verulam Buildings.

He served as Chairman of the Qatar Financial Centre Regulatory Tribunal until March 2011. He became President of the Board of Appeal of European Supervisory Authorities in 2012.

He is a Member of the Ethics Committee of Digital Catapult's AI Machine Intelligence Garage, the International Commercial Expert Committee of the Supreme People's Court of the People's Republic of China, and is Chair of the Bank of England's Enforcement Decision Making Committee.

Sir William Blair graduated from Oxford University.

Alan Brener completed his PhD at Queen Mary University of London. Alan is Deputy Director of the Advisory Board of the Centre for Ethics and Law and a Teaching Fellow in banking law at University College London. He is also a qualified Chartered Accountant and a Fellow of the Chartered Banker Institute in Scotland. Prior to starting his PhD, Alan worked in senior roles for Santander UK and the retail banking divisions of Natwest and RBS banks. In the 1990s, Alan was a financial services regulator and most recently has helped set up the Banking Standards Board with the objective of improving standards of conduct and professionalism within the banking industry.

Lee C. Buchheit is a Non-resident Fellow in the Center for Contract and Economic Organization at Columbia University. He is also an Honorary Professor at the University of Edinburgh Law School and a Visiting Professor at Queen Mary University of London. During Mr. Buchheit's 43 year career as a practicing lawyer he participated in the sovereign debt restructurings of over two dozen countries.

Andromachi Georgosouli is a senior lecturer at the Centre for Commercial Law Studies (CCLS) at Queen Mary University of London (QMUL). Her research focuses on the regulation of financial crisis prevention and management, and on the normative foundations and policy implications of financial resilience and adaptability. She is the co-Academic Director of the QMUL-UNIDROIT Transnational Commercial Law Institute, and in 2016 she became the holder of a prestigious scholarship under the European Central Bank (ECB) Legal Research Programme. In spring 2015, she was a visiting scholar at the George Washington University Law School and at the International Monetary Fund (IMF), where she conducted research on the EU legal framework of bank resolution.

Miriam Goldby is Reader in Shipping, Insurance and Commercial Law at the Centre for Commercial Law Studies (CCLS) at Queen Mary University of London (QMUL). She is also Deputy Director of the Centre's Insurance Law Institute, and Deputy Editor of the British Insurance Law Association Journal. Prior to joining Queen Mary, Miriam conducted research as a Visiting Scholar at George Washington University in Washington DC, USA. Between September 2007 and December 2010, she held a lectureship post at the University of Surrey where she taught Contract Law, Commercial Law and Banking Law. She read for her PhD degree at University College London where she also held the post of teaching fellow between January 2004 and August 2007, and taught on the LLM Banking Law and LLM International Trade Law courses. She has published extensively on various areas of commercial and financial law.

Katherine Hunt is a leading expert on the topic of financial inclusion via microfinance, particularly regarding microfinance regulation. Katherine approaches challenges in banking from a multidisciplinary perspective, ensuring that aspects of psychology, finance, development studies, commerce, law and economics are incorporated to develop practical recommendations. Ever the pragmatist, Katherine holds degrees in Psychology, Commerce and Finance from Griffith University, Australia. Additionally, Katherine holds a European Doctorate in Law and Economics from Erasmus University, the University of Bologna, and the University of Hamburg. Katherine's current research explores banking in Bhutan, Nicaragua, Europe, and Australia.

Marco Lamandini is Professor of Corporate and Capital Markets Law at the University of Bologna. He also sits on the Board of Appeal of the European System of Financial Supervisors (ESFS) and on the Appeal Panel of the Single Resolution Board (SRB). He is a member of the European Commission Informal Group of Company Law Experts (ICLEG). He is a Vice-Chair on the Academic Board of the European Banking Institute (EBI-Frankfurt) and an Academic Member of the European Capital Market Institute (ECMI/CEPS-Brussels). His publications include the books *EU Financial Law. An Introduction* (WoltersKluwer, 2016), *Il controllo* (Milano: Giuffrè, 1995), *Le concentrazioni bancarie* (Bologna: Il Mulino, 1998), *Struttura finanziaria e governo nelle società di capitali* (Bologna: Il Mulino, 2001) and a number of articles, primarily on the law of financial markets, company law and antitrust law. He lives in Bologna and Milan with Vesna and Tancredi.

Rosa M. Lastra holds the Sir John Lubbock Chair in Banking Law at the Centre for Commercial Law Studies (CCLS), Queen Mary University of London. She is a member of the Monetary Committee of the International Law Association (MOCOMILA), a founding member of the European Shadow Financial Regulatory Committee (ESFRC), an associate of the Financial Markets Group of the London School of Economics and Political Science, and an affiliated scholar of the Centre for the Study of Central Banks at New York University School of Law. From 2008 to 2010 she was a Visiting Professor of the University of Stockholm. She has served as a consultant to the International Monetary Fund, the European Central Bank, the World Bank, the Asian Development Bank and the Federal Reserve Bank of New York. From November 2008 to June 2009 she acted as Specialist Adviser to the European Union Committee [Sub-Committee A] of the House of Lords regarding its Inquiry into EU Financial Regulation and responses to the financial crisis. In 2015 she became a member of the Monetary Expert Panel of the European Parliament. Since 2016 she has been a member of the Banking Union (Resolution) Expert Panel of the European Parliament.

Manuel Monteagudo is the General Counsel of the Central Bank of Peru and principal professor at the Pontificia Universidad Católica del Perú (PUCP). He earned his law degree from the PUCP, his LLM from the University of Houston and his Doctorate in Laws from the University of Paris I, Panthéon Sorbonne. His doctoral thesis was devoted to central banks' independence (published in 2010). He is member of the Monetary Commission of the International Law Association (MOCOMILA), the Society of International Economic Law (SIEL) and the Latin American Section of SIEL. He has published articles and participated in book editions in the area of international economic law.

David Ramos Muñoz is a Senior Lecturer in Commercial Law at Carlos III University of Madrid, and the University of Bologna. He is a major in Law and Business Administration, and a PhD. He has published extensively in the field of the Law of Finance, the Law of International Contracts and Arbitration, and the Law of Fundamental Rights, is the author of *The Law of Transnational Securitization* (Oxford University Press), co-author of *EU Financial Law* (Kluwer), and of numerous other publications in peer-reviewed journals and books, and his research has received various prizes and distinctions. He co-directs the Master in International Advocacy, is the director of the programme in Financial Compliance at Carlos III University, and one of the organisers of the international legal competition Moot Madrid.

He is a lawyer at the Madrid Bar, an arbitrator in commercial and financial cases, and acts as a consultant for European and international bodies, as well as private firms. He is a member of the European Banking Institute (EBI), and the European Law Institute (ELI). Apart from Spanish, his mother tongue, he is fluent in English, Italian and French, and is improving his Mandarin. He lives in Madrid with his wife and two children.

Ruth Plato-Shinar is a Professor of Banking Law and Financial Regulation at the Netanya Academic College, Israel, where she also serves as the Director of the Center for Banking Law and Financial Regulation.

She is the author of the book *The Banks' Fiduciary Duty*, on which a few important precedents of the Israeli Supreme Court are based; as well as of the book *Banking Regulation in Israel: Prudential Regulation versus Consumer Protection*, which was translated into Mandarin.

She is a member of the Advisory Committee of the Israeli Minister of Finance, the Advisory Committee of the Governor of the Bank of Israel, the Advisory Board of the Commissioner of Capital Markets, Insurance and Savings; and a former Board Member of the Governmental Fund for Class Actions.

She also serves on the Academic Advisory Councils of the Asian Institute of International Financial Law (AIIFL) at Hong-Kong University, and the Center for Commercial Law Studies (CCLS) at Queen Mary University, London.

David Rouch is a partner in Freshfields Bruckhaus Deringer, specialising in financial regulation. He works with the full range of financial market participants, dealing with some of the market's greatest regulatory bodies. He is particularly known for his work on law and institutional culture, and has helped a number of firms with their culture-change programmes. He has run two joint projects between Freshfields and the London School of Economics exploring this area and has also participated in the work of the Law and Ethics in Finance Project.

Costanza A. Russo is the Senior Lecturer in International Banking Law and Business Ethics at the Centre for Commercial Law Studies (CCLS), Queen Mary University of London, where she teaches several post-graduate modules in ethics and in banking and finance. She is also the Director of the CCLS Institute for Regulation and Ethics and the Director of the CCLS LLM in Banking and Finance in Paris. More recently, she has been working for the Committee on Standards in Public Life (CSPL), a UK Cabinet Office Committee, in conducting a review of the ethics of UK banking and financial regulatory authorities, as part of the CSPL broader review 'Ethics for Regulators'. She also sat on a steering committee of the UK Banking Standards Board (BSB) for a research project investigating the relationship between law, regulation and ethics in finance. Since 2016, she has been a member of the Banking Union (Resolution) Expert Panel of the ECON Committee of the European Parliament.

She holds a Masters Degree in Law and a PhD in Economics.

Marcelo J. Sheppard holds a Law Degree (Doctor en Derecho) from Universidad de Montevideo (UM), Uruguay. Marcelo also holds an LLM (with Distinction) in Corporate and Commercial Law from the Centre for Commercial Law Studies (CCLS), Queen Mary University of London and is a PhD candidate at CCLS, Queen Mary University of London. He is in charge of the Law and Strategic Planning Department of Universidad de Montevideo (UM).

Before joining the UM, he worked as a lawyer in two prominent law firms in Uruguay and was a Country Manager of a multinational Corporate and Trust Services firm in Uruguay.

Marcelo is also Associate Professor of Commercial Law in Universidad de Montevideo and has been a Research and Teaching Associate at CCLS, Queen Mary University of London during the academic year 2018/19.

Kara Tan Bhala is President and founder of the Seven Pillars Institute for Global Finance and Ethics, the world's only independent think tank for the research, education, and promotion of financial ethics. The Institute was shortlisted in the Prospect Think Tank Awards 2016. Kara has over 23 years of work experience in global finance and is lead author of *International Investment Management: Theory, Ethics and Practice*. She was named by Ingram's in 2017 as one of the '50 Kansans You Should Know'. Kara has five degrees across three disciplines and has lived and worked in London, Oxford, Singapore, Hong Kong, New York, and Washington, DC.

Simon Thompson was appointed Chief Executive of the Chartered Banker Institute in 2007, and led the Institute's work to establish the Chartered Banker Professional Standards Board. Simon chairs the Global Education Standards Committee established by a group of leading international banking institutes, and is a former Vice President of the European Bank Training Network.

He is the editor and co-author of the forthcoming *Principles & Practice of Green Finance.*

Philip R. Wood CBE, QC (Hon), BA (Cape Town), MA (Oxon), LLD (Lund, Hon) was formerly Head of Allen & Overy Global Law Intelligence Unit, Special Global Counsel at Allen & Overy, Visiting Professor in International Financial Law, University of Oxford, Yorke Distinguished Visiting Fellow, University of Cambridge and Visiting Professor, Queen Mary University, London.

Philip is one of the world's leading experts in comparative and cross-border financial law and an experienced practitioner. He has written about 23 books. The latest edition of the nine volumes in his series on the law and practice of international finance was in the course of being published in mid-2019. In 2016, he published a book for the general reader called *The Fall of the Priests and the Rise of the Lawyers.*

He pioneered a method of measuring financial law according to key indicators and is particularly well known for his colour-coded global law maps. He has developed a methodology for legal risk ratings of the jurisdictions of the world with regard to both their written law and the application of the law.

He completed the London Marathon in 2005, the Berlin Marathon in 2011 (at age 69) and the Paris Marathon in 2014. He climbed Mount Kilimanjaro in 2009.

He was born in Livingstone, Zambia and is married with four children.

Philip was awarded an honorary QC in 2010 and CBE in the Queen's New Year honours list in 2015 for services to English and Financial Law.

Mark Yallop is an Independent Member of the Board of the Prudential Regulation Authority at the Bank of England and Chair of the FICC Market Standards Board. The Prudential Regulation Authority is responsible for ensuring the safety and soundness of the major UK-based banks and insurance companies and the UK financial system, and the protection of depositors and policy holders. The FICC Market Standards Board is an industry body, established in 2015 by HMT, the Bank of England and the FCA to improve standards in wholesale fixed income, currency and commodity markets.

Prior to this, Mark was, from March 2013 to September 2014, UK Group CEO for UBS, responsible for overseeing all UBS's Investment Banking, Wealth Management and Asset Management activities in the UK.

From 2005 to 2011 Mark was Group COO and main board director at ICAP plc. During his time there he built the electronic markets and post trade businesses of the firm, managed the Group's infrastructure and contributed significantly to the firm's growth and diversification of its business strategy. From 2009 to 2011 he also led a number of initiatives to develop industry and regulatory responses to the 2008 financial crisis.

From 1984 to 2004 Mark was at Morgan Grenfell and then Deutsche Bank, where he was one of the architects of its expansion in investment banking, built and ran as Global Head a number of trading and sales businesses, and served as Global Markets and Corporate and Investment Banking Chief Operating Officer. From 2002 to 2004 he was Deutsche Bank AG Group COO, responsible for managing the Group's infrastructure and its business rationalisation programme.

Mark serves on the Board of OpenFin, the US technology firm and is a Partner in Illuminate Financial Management, a fintech venture capital business. Previously, Mark served on the board of the International Swaps and Derivatives Association (ISDA) as well as numerous other financial services industry bodies and working groups, and on the Board of the Centre for Social Justice, as well as the Create the Change campaign board for the Francis Crick Institute, and also chaired the Development Board for University College, Oxford.

Mark read Chemistry at University College, Oxford from 1978 to 1982.

Basil G. Zotiades read Jurisprudence at Hertford College, Oxford (MA, 1983) and Philosophy of Law at University of Paris II (DEA, 1985). He qualified as a solicitor (England and Wales) in 1988 and as an 'avocat' at the Paris bar in 1994. He is a former partner of Linklaters and Latham & Watkins and former Global Head of Group Dispute Resolution at BNP Paribas. In private practice, he advised banks, asset managers and insurance companies on a broad range of financial markets transactions, including the securitisation or repackaging of financial assets ranging from loans, debt securities and OTC derivatives to commercial receivables and interests in funds.

Foreword: Research handbook on law and ethics in banking and finance
Andrew Bailey

It is a great pleasure to be able to make a small contribution to such an important piece of work. I am grateful to the contributors, not just for their work on this volume but more broadly for the leadership they show in such an important field. Unfortunately, we can say this with so much more certainty and passion having witnessed in the global financial crisis what can go wrong.

As a financial regulator, I am all too aware that we cannot place our faith in, and reliance on, contractual relationships alone. The same goes for statutory law: on its own, it is not enough. There are a number of reasons underpinning this state of affairs. Pure reliance on contracts flowing from statute does not deal well with the unequal distribution of power and influence. We have to recognise that many people in any society are vulnerable. Also, the application of contracts can often be opaque, and can thereby create an imbalance of power and influence, and harm to one or more parties.

So, it is not surprising that from at least the time of Ancient Greece, ethics have stood alongside jurisprudence, and there has been a continuous need to infuse the more abstract concepts of law with ethics. The system conveys both rights and duties, and we have to recognise and pursue the latter in order to uphold the former.

But history tells us that we cannot, and should not, expect the balance of law and ethics, and rights and duties, to remain constant. Over time there have been changes, for better and worse, and we can expect this pattern to go on. Before the financial crisis, there was a loss of anchoring in a broad moral tradition of ethics. It was supported by a re-assessment, and in my view misinterpretation, of history. How otherwise could the Adam Smith of the Theory of Moral Sentiments be so ignored in favour of an interpretation of Smith that did not fit with his work. But such things happen, and recent history would tell us that the area of finance is one of the fields most susceptible to such re-interpretation. The ethics of finance were compromised for a crucial period of time before the crisis.

There will no doubt be arguments of the 'This Time is Different' sort, namely that in view of the scale of the crisis we won't make that mistake again. But the authors are correct not to take that for granted. Maintaining the balance of law and ethics requires that we have an environment and culture which supports open debate and intellectual vitality. This debate has to be constantly invigorated. And, of course, times change, and the context of the debate needs to move on.

There are new forms of ethical challenge always appearing. Let me give a very pertinent example. A colleague recently reminded me that according to the 1982 original version of the film *Blade Runner*, in 2019 synthetic humans are engineered. I think we can be fairly sure that has not happened, but in financial markets we are seeing the rapid growth of the use of artificial intelligence, machine learning and the use of personal data on a much larger scale. When things go wrong – and like any activity they can and do – at the FCA we are not impressed by the type of excuse that goes under the heading of 'it was the machine that did it'.

Unlike the dystopia of *Blade Runner*, machines, however complicated, are ultimately controlled by humans, and that is where the responsibility and accountability resides. But, of course, along the way the ethical questions are many and various. Ultimately it is possible for us to outsource tasks, but not responsibility and control.

Let me thank the authors for such a thought-provoking set of contributions. Please read them, and be prepared to re-read them, because as the world around us changes we have to come back repeatedly to law and ethics.

Preface

In the foreword to its March 2018 discussion paper on 'Transforming Culture in Financial Services', the Financial Conduct Authority writes that 'Culture in financial services is widely accepted as a key root cause of the major conduct failings that have occurred within the industry in recent history, causing harm to both consumers and markets. For markets to work and firms to be successful, it is critical that they are seen as trustworthy.'[1]

These ideas have become widely accepted in recent years, not least because of the lead given by central banks, regulatory agencies such as the FCA, and leaders of financial institutions themselves. The challenge after the global financial crisis – which has heightened the discontent that arises from income and wealth inequality – is how to reconnect the interests of bankers and financiers with the interests of society. At the heart of the debate is an understanding that the law, in the form of financial regulation, and in the form of soft as well as hard law, can never by itself raise standards in the industry. Furthermore, in a globalised financial industry, where problems in one country or group of countries quickly spread to other countries, there is a need to achieve a degree of convergence to avoid opportunities for regulatory arbitrage or a rush to the bottom in the search for profit.

The law is concerned to establish minimum obligations, a legal floor if you will. The role of standards, culture, incentives, ethics, trust – whatever term is used – is to build on that floor. The aim is to encourage the pursuit of business in a manner which pays due regard to 'doing the right thing', as well as societal needs, without imposing a further raft of obligations and complication on already burdened financial business. This is in the interest of the business of finance, which overall has made such a major contribution to the contemporary world, as well as to its multiple users.

This is however, also in the interest of financial markets as a whole, whose integrity is premised upon existing trust among participants. Therefore, any breach of that trust harms its proper functioning.

More recently, instances of interest rate rigging and mis-selling of payment protection insurance exposed how lack of integrity can have harmful repercussions on both banks' financial health and on the industry's reputation as a whole. Equally important is the impact that misbehaviour can have on the trust society places in the sector. Therefore, given that the positive role finance plays in society finds no easy substitutes, it is imperative that industry and regulatory efforts are successful in rebuilding that trust and creating a financial system which is fair and effective for all.

Of course, such an approach raises many questions. What do we mean by 'doing the right thing'? How can one quantify trust? Can these ideas be practically implemented? Will they make a difference?

---

[1]   FCA, Transforming culture in financial services, DP 18/2, March 2018, 2, available at www.fca .org.uk/publication/discussion/dp18-02.pdf.

This Research Handbook investigates five main aspects of the debate. Its underlying theme though relates to the role as well as the (inherent) limitations that law, regulation and standards have in changing conduct and behaviour.

Part I explores the philosophical, legal and soft law foundations of ethical behaviour in finance. To this end, Tan Bhala's contribution considers deontology, virtue ethics, and the utilitarian and justice theories to explain why financial ethics has been largely absent from the financial discourse. She also argues that the two main reasons for the neglect and outright dismissal of financial ethics are Ethical Relativism and the findings of Modern Finance Theory.

Blair and Barbiani's chapter shifts the focus to the recognised role of standards in enhancing ethical culture and questions whether the new architecture may be producing inconsistencies and confusion due its complexity. Their work considers the interaction between industry-based and regulatory-driven initiatives and identifies the limits posed by the existence of different instruments aimed at regulating conduct, with distinct implications in terms of enforceability. While the significance of the role of standards has been broadly recognised, what remains unclear is whether the new framework created to enhance their role is being shaped adequately, or whether it is producing inconsistencies and confusion due to its complexity.

This chapter also focuses on the rise of a regulatory framework enhancing ethical values such as honesty, integrity and fairness. The new emphasis shows a move towards the recognition of the importance of these values, but, at same time, the process of placing them in the regulatory framework also raises new questions: how is it possible to expect people to respect these values and translate them into ethical conduct? And, also, how can we ensure that people develop a common and clear understanding of them?

Lastra and Sheppard consider how after the Great Financial Crisis, one of the relevant issues that has emerged in the design of financial regulation is the question of the *telos* or end of financial law.

Drawing on the Aristotelian tradition and the notion of the common good, they identify the principles of justice, prudence (underlying both macro- and micro-supervision) and integrity (underlying the conduct of business regulation) as key foundations of the relevant regulatory framework, one in which the interests of bankers and financial market participants (in particular, those in senior management) are realigned with the interests of society.

The second part of the book delves into the regulatory and self-regulatory framework governing ethical behaviour to investigate its efficacy as well as its potential to nudge institutions towards sustainable finance.

In this section, the chapter by Hunt et al. highlights how regulation and self-regulation could and should bolster a shift towards ethical finance which pays attention to sectors of society normally excluded from banking services. This in turn means, first, 'nudging' ethical niche banks towards self-sustainability choices, and, second, helping all other banks to pilot a transition towards more socially responsible and inclusive banking.

Rouch gives substance to a concept recently advocated by regulators and academics alike, namely the idea that financial institutions need a social licence to operate. Yet, can that be found in the law, regulation or standards? By using a 'written standards map' of financial sector laws, rules and codes of practice, this contribution considers the extent to which each category of written standards could be thought of as being part of a social licence; how they might express the substance of a social licence and how they might help to realise its aspirational dimension.

Standards applicable to the sector often come from professional bodies, such as the Chartered Banker Institute and from newly created bodies, such as the Fixed Income, Currencies and Commodities Markets Standards Board (FMSB).

The CEO of the Chartered Banker Institute, Simon Thompson, brings in the practitioner's perspective on the establishment, challenges, development and implementation of professional standards. However, he also covers the almost unchartered territory as to whether banking as a whole can or should be considered a profession.

Wood's contribution clarifies how the rule of law applies to money, finance and banks, where the principles often seem so remote from ordinary rule of law principles.

Finally, the Chair of the FMSB, Mark Yallop throws us back to a remote past to discuss some historical cases of market abuse. This puts the current debate into a wider context by discussing the serious limitations in using regulation and legislative measures to cure the problem and how newly introduced standards and markets codes can help alleviate it.

The third part of the book deals with some inherent limitations of the law in counteracting unethical behaviour. The scope is also enlarged to include ethical matters that may arise at sovereign level.

For instance, Buchheit discusses the tensions faced by a lawyer defending an insolvent state with regards to the fairness of intergenerational debt.

The author draws from his own experience as a leading lawyer in sovereign debt litigation to acknowledge how identifying the client in a sovereign engagement raises issues of fundamental political philosophy. In particular, it calls into question the relationship of a government to its citizens and what duties, if any, are owed by one generation of citizens to succeeding generations.

In this regard, discussion revolves around several questions, such as 'which citizens?', the existing body of citizens or future citizens as well? May a lawyer ethically assist a government in borrowing so much money that successor generations of citizens in the country must either default on the repayment of those loans or significantly impair their own standard of living in order to honour the debts? Or is the moral choice to withhold assistance today, even if it means increasing the suffering of the current citizens, in order to hasten the day when they and their successors can throw off the incubus? Finally, accepting that some degree of government corruption exists in most countries, what are the ethical implications for lawyers seeking to advise those sovereign clients?

Plato-Shinar's contribution deals with the thorny issue of the applicability of fiduciary duties to the banking sector. Fiduciary duties are the strictest duties that exist in the realm of private law. The fiduciary must act in the best interests of his principal, and prioritise these interests over every other interest – including his own. Hence, the reluctance to apply a fiduciary duty to banks, whose goal is to make profit. However, the fiduciary duty of banks should not be construed as an altruistic duty, but rather as a legal instrument designed to ensure a basic level of professional ethics in the activities of the banks. Based on this perception, the chapter calls for imposing a wide fiduciary duty on banks towards retail customers, due to the disparity of power between the parties and the fear that the bank could exploit its power to the detriment of the customer. The chapter examines the implications of establishing the fiduciary duty as a general guideline for the behaviour of the banks, and outlines the recommended format for ethical and legal implementation of such duty.

In concluding the third part of the book, Zotiades vividly analyses the trading malpractices affecting open-ended funds known as 'late trading' and 'market timing'. The author's aim is twofold: first to shed light on what these practices are (and are not); and second, to review the regulatory response to them in Europe and reflect on its adequacy and on how that response fits with our treatment of other forms of what we now call market abuse. The chapter illustrates how an incomplete perception of these practices, exemplified also by the use of the term 'market timing' to refer to them, has led to loopholes which are still being exploited today.

Part IV investigates the effectiveness of regulatory and supervisory actions in tackling unethical behaviour and lack of individual liability.

Brener's chapter discusses the recently enacted Senior Managers Regime (SMR) in the United Kingdom. The regime originates from the FCA and the PRA and applies to all firms operating in the financial sector. The SMR has three components: the clear allocation of responsibilities on a senior manager (with a mapping of their functions), the corresponding manager's liability in case of regulatory breaches within their functions, and the certification regime.

The aims of the SMR are: to change behaviour in financial services firms by clearly setting out regulatory expectations; making individuals personally accountable; and helping to assuage public anger by taking regulatory actions against those individuals who fail. However, the author argues that the efficacy of the regime may be hampered by the existence of individual psychological limitations and institutional structures. Financial regulation will never be fully effective if there is no substantial change in the culture of financial services in order to ensure that individuals acquire an ethical understanding of their own actions. This requires leadership and action by both the regulators and more importantly the firms themselves. Equally important is the need for professionalism, which is an aid to both improving competence and to developing and sustaining ethical behaviour. All these aspects can be buttressed by the regulators but require firms in the industry to act themselves, as the remedy rests with the industry in the end.

Georgosouli discusses one of the objectives of enforcement, namely credible deterrence. According to current orthodoxy, deterrence is credible when it is visible and visibility calls for enforcement action that is harsh enough to be taken seriously by the industry.

In this chapter, the author argues that the focus on enforcement is misplaced because, when it comes to the question of credibility, at best it tells half the story. The credibility of deterrence is contingent on a multitude of factors. In the chapter, she considers three of them, all of which are closely inter-related: the regulator's capacity to attain a congruence of minds and a congruence of hearts with the regulatees, and the regulator's ability to harness its profile as a credible enforcer.

To conclude Part IV, Goldby critically analyses UK regulators' approaches to breaches of anti-money laundering (AML) reporting obligations by bankers.

The need to ensure a high level of compliance with reporting requirements is key to the achievement of the objectives of AML legislation, however the author argues that failure to use enforcement measures that involve criminal prosecution may be precluding the change in corporate culture required to reduce the prevalence of money laundering through the UK financial system. She concludes by outlining the reasons why reform might be desirable as well as some possibilities for reform.

The last part of the book covers an aspect usually absent in the debate, namely the extent to which regulators behave ethically and how do they deal with apparently conflicting ethical principles in their supervisory actions.

To this end, Baxter examines whether central banks need to be mindful of their ethical culture. This contribution concludes that they face significant adverse consequences if they fail to do so. After establishing the factual predicate that central bank officials do occasionally engage in misconduct, it turns to the related topic of central banks and legitimacy, and offers the view that the objective of legitimacy and the related need for public trust makes it especially important for central banks to pay careful attention to misconduct risk. The chapter identifies some of the techniques that central banks use to mitigate misconduct risk, and the principal measures that may be employed to accomplish this objective.

Monteagudo discusses the specific tension between transparency and confidentiality of central bankers. Transparency is considered a crucial component of central bank independence as a means to make up for its 'democratic deficit'; and central bank intervention during the global financial crisis has reinforced this general perception. International organisations and domestic legislation have developed transparency standards to communicate policy objectives and results, in addition to a general evolution in favour of free access to the information in the hands of public bodies. But the 'transparency revolution' has not swept away central banks' confidentiality mandate, based upon professional secrecy, private rights protection of privacy and trade secrecy, and the need to protect central banks' capacity to continue collecting statistical data.

Discernment on when to be transparent or confidential requires a high level of wisdom and experience; but mostly, it requires a significant dose of ethical considerations to determine when the public interest prevails over the private interest and to explain the reasons for making one or another choice.

The legislation and case law show that the assurance of monetary policy effectiveness (as a public interest) is a significant consideration.

Finally, Russo covers some past concerns that have arisen from enforcement action as well as the importance of an appropriate legal framework to establish public trust in regulators.

The current FCA enforcement framework has been repeatedly amended to reflect and address those concerns. Yet enforcement is not a straightforward process and there may be a difficult balance to strike between different regulatory actions. After discussing this tension and the recent amendments to the Decision Procedure and Penalty Manual and to the Enforcement Guide, the chapter analyses ethical problems associated with enforcement, particularly with respect to settlement and private warnings. It is then argued that FCA efforts to become more transparent and to actively address criticisms certainly represent the right course of action. Regulators enjoy a vast amount of power and discretion, and should be held tightly accountable. They should also be responsive to well-founded concerns.

However, excessive responsiveness has its drawbacks. Furthermore, even though transparency is widely – and in most cases rightly – seen as an indicator of ethical behaviour, doubts may arise as to its efficacy in delivering its intended aims.

Credibility and effectiveness of action by enforcement authorities also require an institutional framework which is supportive of the efforts, of the activities, and of the exercise of discretion by the regulator.

Acknowledgements

First of all, we wish to thank our stellar group of distinguished contributors. Each of them has given up much time to make their contributions, and we are truly grateful to them. We consider ourselves very fortunate in having attracted such a high calibre and diverse group of scholars, which include academics, practitioners and current and former regulators. They have supported this project throughout the years with our same enthusiasm and have been a source of encouragement many times.

We are also privileged to have Andrew Bailey (who has made a big personal contribution to this subject) writing the foreword to this book.

We would like to thank our colleagues at the Institute for Regulation and Ethics of the Centre for Commercial Law Studies for the lively discussions and for all the assistance provided in organising the meetings that preceded this publication. We are also thankful to our students, especially those in the module on 'Law and Ethics in Finance' for their stimulating intellectual challenges throughout the years. Last but not least, we are greatly indebted to our publisher, Edward Elgar Publishing Ltd, for including the book in their successful Research Handbook series and particularly to Laura Mann, Iram Satti, Catherine Cumming and Stephanie Tytherleigh for their patience, enthusiasm and support for the project. We would also like to thank Clara Barbiani for valuable editorial assistance and Alvaro Castro Lora for his contribution.

Costanza A. Russo
Rosa M. Lastra
William Blair

Queen Mary University of London,
Centre for Commercial Law Studies,
67–69 Lincoln's Inn Fields,
London
2019

PART I

THE FOUNDATIONS OF ETHICS IN BANKING AND FINANCE

1. The philosophical foundations of financial ethics

Kara Tan Bhala

The foundation of financial ethics is moral philosophy, a profound subject with a majestic canon going back two and a half millennia. This canon guides us to right actions in life as it does in finance. The purpose of this chapter is to give a reasonably detailed overview of these philosophical foundations and propose that the established moral theories are relevant and applicable in the practical field of finance. There are reasons why financial ethics has lost its place in academic finance, and therefore in the practice of finance, and this chapter will elaborate on the causes. It is not overly optimistic to state that the rediscovery of ethics in finance has already begun.

DEFINING ETHICS

The reader should not get too mired in the difference in meaning of the terms "ethics" and "morality" because this abstruse problem is only a concern for professional philosophers. For the rest of us, the terms may be used interchangeably. Ethics derives from the Greek word, "ethos" which means traditional practice. Morals or morality derives from the Roman "mores" denoting custom. Morality has come to be associated with heavy-handed religion of the impositional variety. Hence, the term has fallen into disuse in modern parlance as it has negative connotations.

The term ethics as used today means to do the right thing. Rachels' more formal definition of ethics is "at the very least, the effort to guide one's conduct by reason – that is, to do what there are the best reasons for doing – while giving equal weight to the interests of each individual affected by one's decision."[1] Clearly, the proper practice of ethics requires three elements: a moral agent, reason and action.

First, ethics requires a moral agent, the individual who is doing the moral act. The moral agent does not necessarily have to be a human person. The agent may, arguably, be a corporation. The characteristic presumed in moral agency is freedom. We have to be free to choose to act ethically. Otherwise, if we act badly and do the ethically wrong thing, then we are not morally blameworthy. If we did not have free will, our moral actions cannot either be blamed or praised because we are not responsible for our actions.

Secondly, ethics requires reasoning. Ethical judgments must be backed by good reasons. It is usually unwise to allow emotions as ethical guides because ethics will simply become a preference such as liking the color red over the color yellow. Emotions may be irrational, products of prejudice, or cultural conditioning. For instance, people used to feel it was ethi-

---

[1] James Rachels and Stuart Rachels, *The Elements of Moral Philosophy* (7th edn, McGraw Hill 2012) 13.

cally right if women could not vote. Therefore, to discover the truth, it is best to let emotions be guided by reason. The ethically right thing to do is always supported by sound arguments.

Thirdly, the contemporary use of "conduct" when referring to ethical behavior in banking and finance finds its roots in the word "action". Ethics requires action. For Aristotle, a person does not become virtuous simply by thinking about virtue. She must choose a virtuous action and then carry out that chosen act.

Humanity has been concerned with doing the right thing for millennia and philosophers over the centuries have given us comprehensive and well thought out theoretical frameworks to help in this quest.

A SHORT HISTORY OF ETHICS

Ethics is one of the five fields of classic philosophical exploration. Each of the five specialties, with a succinct description, are given below:

1. Epistemology: How and what do we know?
2. Metaphysics: What is the nature of being?
3. Politics: How shall we govern ourselves?
4. Ethics: How shall we live?
5. Aesthetics: What is beauty?

Clearly, moral philosophy has an impressive lineage. This segment of philosophy is the attempt to understand the nature of human values, of how we ought to live and what constitutes right conduct.[2] Ethics perhaps, begins with Socrates asking the celebrated question, "How shall we live?" For Socrates and the Ancient Greek philosophers, the way to happiness or eudaimonia was to live a life of virtue. Eudaimonia is perhaps best described as flourishing or a well-lived life. Socrates sketched out a theory of what we now call virtue ethics, but it was Aristotle who took the theory to higher levels of sophistication and detail. In virtue ethics, whether an act is right depends on the character of the moral agent who performs the act. A person who possesses virtues such as courage, justice and generosity, is a virtuous person. There is a fuller discussion of virtue ethics later in this chapter.

Skipping ahead a few centuries to the medieval philosophers, St. Thomas Aquinas and the scholastics incorporated Aristotle's virtue ethics into their Christian moral theology. The Natural Law approach of Aquinas attempts to bring together Aristotle's idea that everything should fulfill its natural end or purpose. In fulfilling our purpose we achieve the supreme good. For Aquinas, God gives purpose or telos and instills in humanity a comprehensive view of what is natural and right. According to Natural Law, human reason endowed by God is a starting point for morality. The use of reason allows us to arrive at the same moral truths as are given through divine revelation. There should be no contradictions. The Natural Law approach dominates Catholic moral thinking. Yet, as Natural Law is based on reason, it is in principle discoverable by anyone, whether religious or not. For the same reason, it is universal, rather than culturally conditioned.

---

[2]   Richard Norman, *The Moral Philosophers: An Introduction to Ethics* (2nd edn, Oxford University Press 1998) 1.

A number of centuries later, during the Enlightenment, the most influential moral philosophers to arise at that time were Thomas Hobbes (1588–1679), David Hume (1711–76), Jeremy Bentham (1748–1832), John Stuart Mill (1806–73) and of course, Immanuel Kant (1724–1804). Hobbes thought ethics should be based on a contractual agreement between people, hence the creation of the idea of a 'social contract'. Hume proposed that ethics is based on sentiment rather than reason because people are able to have a natural sympathy for others. Bentham was the founder of modern utilitarianism and Mill later refined the theory by differentiating between the different pleasures. The utilitarians propose that ethics should be based on the expected results of action. In response to Hume and his emotivist ethics, Kant developed a magnificent moral system that is described as "deontological" or duty based. According to Kant, fundamental ethical principles can be based on pure reason alone. Kant stands at the pinnacle of the Enlightenment period. Other moral philosophers of note followed that period when human reason and the idea of human progress were idealized. In the nineteenth and twentieth centuries, Friedrich Nietzsche and Jean Paul Sartre, often labeled as existentialists, considered ethics in the light of the self-development of individuals, or the personal questions people ask. Their methods of moral philosophy fall within the category of the continental tradition.

A different ethical discourse was taking place in the US and UK. For much of the twentieth century ethical theory in the so-called Anglo-Saxon tradition was dominated by arguments about whether ethical language was meaningful. The predominant type of ethical inquiry during the post-modern period is called meta-ethics, a branch of analytic philosophy that focuses largely on the language of moral discourse. So, while the past couple of millennia were devoted largely to normative ethics that was concerned with the question, "What kinds of action are good or right?" the past century or so of meta-ethics focused on the question, "What is it to say of an action that it is good or right?"[3]

In the last three decades, there has been a revival of interest in applied ethics. Scholars now work on theories of social contract, virtue ethics and re-examining earlier ethical arguments. It became clear that meta-ethics was interesting mostly to academic philosophers and did not help people with practical ethical problems. Thus, meta-ethics in particular and philosophy in general were marginalized in society due to a large measure of irrelevance.

DEFINITIONS OF TERMS

To avoid confusion, the ethics terms in common usage and in this chapter ought to be defined.

Ethical – To behave ethically is to conform to a set of ethical norms, whether personal, religious or established by a society, group, or profession.

Unethical – An act is unethical if it goes against a professed set of norms. We use reason to assess whether an act is unethical.

Amoral – An act is amoral with respect to the entity that performs it. For the entity, there is no reference to any moral perspective or to any values that may result in a moral perspective. For example, a cat does not (debatably) have a sense of right and wrong. A person suffering from a mental condition and incapable of understanding right from wrong is

---

[3]   Norman (n 2), 1.

amoral. A human person of normal mental capacity, embedded in a group or culture, who does something wrong has acted unethically, in that instance, not amorally.

FINANCIAL ETHICS

Ethics in finance is applying moral norms to financial activity broadly conceived. It is crucial that finance be conducted according to moral norms because of the vital role "financial activity plays in the personal, economic, political, and social realms but also because of the opportunities for large financial gains that may tempt people to act unethically."[4] Unfortunately, while ethics is two-and-a-half millennia old, the subject of financial ethics is relatively young, less than a couple of decades. One of the first academics to devote a textbook to financial ethics is John Boatright. His book, *Ethics in Finance* is now in its 3rd edition and a fine reference for practitioners and students. Yet, his is one of a handful of books on the subject taught in a handful of business schools. Business ethics became a required core course for accreditation of MBA programs after the Enron scandal. Oddly, financial ethics courses have not been similarly mandated after the much more damaging Global Financial Crisis (GFC) of 2008.

Financial ethics falls into the area of applied ethics. We mentioned normative ethics and meta-ethics in the previous section. The other two sub-categories of ethics are descriptive ethics and applied ethics. The former describes the moral choices and values in a particular society. For example, we may describe the veiling of women in certain societies or how some societies allow girls younger than 16 years to be married. A key feature of this form of ethics is its complete lack of examination or questioning of issues of right and wrong. It describes but does not prescribe. Thus, descriptive ethics does not help with finding the right ethical choice in any ethical issue.

The other category, applied ethics, advanced as various fields of human endeavor flourished. For example, distinct and recognized areas of applied ethics include medical ethics, environmental ethics, feminist ethics and legal ethics. It is therefore, surprising that finance as a long and well-established undertaking should only recently have an association with ethics. There are several reasons for this peculiarity. They can be classed under two sections: (1) reasons inherent in moral philosophy itself and (2) reasons found in standard orthodox finance theory.

(1)   Issues Inherent in Ethics

The problem of objectivity
One reason for the emergence of meta-ethics in the twentieth century is the fear philosophers had of being arbiters of values and the best way to live for others. They feared being labeled preachers. Behind this fear is the view that moral philosophy cannot establish correct theories about how a person ought to live or act because no one can do so. According to this view, there is no one correct view about how we ought to live because beliefs about such matters cannot properly be said to be true or false. People and cultures differ from one another in their basic attitudes towards good or right. Philosophy cannot in principle resolve the disagreements. Thus, arose the doctrine of ethical relativism and the problem of objectivity (or lack thereof).

---

[4]   John R. Boatright, *Ethics in Finance* (3rd edn, Wiley Blackwell 2014) 14.

Ethical relativism

When philosophers threw in the towel on moral philosophy developing an objective theory of ethics, most of the learned and the leaders of society seemed to do so as well. Hence, the teaching of ethics in public schools was in large measure, abandoned. The problem was deciding which ethical tradition to teach because school authorities did not wish to privilege one culture or group's moral system over another. Yet, this wholesale discarding of ethics training and education is too extreme. Relativist arguments are not indefeasible and there are ways to refute cultural relativism.

The basic proposition of cultural relativism is, different cultures have different moral codes. There is not a way to decide which is right or wrong. There is no sub specie aeternitatis – a view from the eternal or simply put, a universal perspective. Thus, the moral codes across cultures are simply different, none are right and none are wrong. The idea of universal truth in ethics is fallacious.

The cultural relativism proposition has, paradoxically, become accepted truth in the West. Of course, the proposition cannot be true because according to cultural relativism, there is no objective truth in ethics. Therefore, the proposition that there is no objective truth in ethics cannot be an objective truth but merely one of many moral statements out there that are neither wrong nor right. Just by this logical move, the cultural relativism argument is defeated. However, this glaring logical flaw has not stopped the spread of the idea there is no objective moral code. Consequently, its popularity has led to the decline of ethics education and discourse. This line of (faulty) thought, more than any other, has persuaded people to be skeptical about ethics.

There is another way to refute the cultural relativism argument. Here is the general logical structure of the cultural differences argument:[5]

1. Different cultures have different moral codes.
2. Therefore, there is no objective truth in morality. Right and wrong are only matters of opinion, and opinions vary from culture to culture.

This argument is not valid. Valid arguments require the conclusion (2) must logically follow from the premise (1). In the cultural relativism argument, the conclusion does not follow from the premise. Even if the premise is true, the conclusion is still false. Just because two cultures disagree, it does not follow that there is no objective truth in the matter. The objective truth may be out there but we have not found it. The objective truth may be a moral code of one of the cultures, but we do not know that yet. The argument tries to derive a substantive conclusion (there is no objective truth in morality) from the mere fact that cultures differ. This is impossible. The conclusion does not follow from the premise. The cultural relativism argument is invalid. Thus, the argument fails.

Suppose the cultural relativism argument is true. This means that:

1. We cannot criticize morally egregious acts such as torture, female infanticide and cultural genocide.
2. The idea of moral progress is called into doubt, see for example equality for women. For most of history (and even now in many parts of the world), women were subjugated,

---

[5]   Rachels and Rachels (n 1), 18.

oppressed and lacked equal rights with men. If cultural relativism is correct, can increasing equality for women be viewed as progress? Moral progress is to replace old ways with new, improved ones. By what standard do we judge the new ways better?

These straightforward arguments against cultural relativism should lead to its rejection. After all, slavery is wrong wherever it occurs, and a culture can make fundamental moral progress. Because cultural relativism implies these judgments make no sense, the idea cannot be right.

The influence of scientism

Despite the refutations to relativism, people are still attracted to ethical subjectivism. One reason is that people think ethics, unlike science, does not have proofs. In an age of science, people expect scientific-like proof to solve important problems. Yet, the methods of science and the methods of ethics are different. Science uses the empirical method that involves experimentation and observation. The researcher gets data to support or refute a theory.

Even though ethics does not use the scientific method it is no less rigorous. The method of ethics is discursive which means to proceed by argument and reason. We used the same method in the previous section where we refuted the cultural relativism argument. From that process, the discursive method can be generalized as follows:

1. Give reasons to support a proposition about an act being right or wrong.
2. Analyze arguments.
3. Justify principles.

In the end, there may be good reasons to support an argument but it may be difficult to persuade some people to agree with the opinion. It is unlikely most arguments will receive unanimous agreement. It is particularly vexing when the examples given to support that "proof" in ethics is impossible are the ones involving supremely difficult moral issues such as abortion or euthanasia. In practice, ethical issues are far more quotidian and uncomplicated.

(2)   Issues Inherent in the Orthodox Finance Model[6]

Finance views itself as a positive science and as such, value neutral. The subject also has been influenced by the reverence for the methods of science. Accordingly, finance in its current state, is confined to facts, drawing empirically testable propositions from them. Neither academics nor practitioners endeavor to offer normative, that is, value-based prescriptions.

The separation of facts from moral values in economics is called the "separation thesis." Milton Friedman, the Nobel Laureate for Economics, propounded and popularized this theory. He is known for saying "Positive economics is in principle independent of any particular ethical position or normative judgments."[7] Finance is an offspring of economics and it follows finance scholars and professionals apply the separation thesis to their specialty. Consequently, since Friedman, a period of roughly 60 years, there has been little or no space for ethics in the theory and thus, the practice of finance.

---

6   Kara Tan Bhala, "Mission" (*Seven Pillars Institute for Global Finance and Ethics*, March 17 2010) https://sevenpillarsinstitute.org/mission, accessed on September 17 2015.

7   Milton Friedman, "The Methodology of Positive Economics" *Essays in Positive Economics* (Chicago, IL: University of Chicago Press 1966).

The orthodox model of finance is Modern Finance Theory or MFT. This theory is based on what is often termed, neo-liberal economics. Essentially, MFT comprises three models:

1. The Efficient Market Hypothesis.
2. The Capital Asset Pricing Model.
3. The Options Pricing Theory.

MFT makes five major assumptions:

1. Economic agents are always rational.
2. Rational agents are purely self-interested.
3. Rational agents aim only to maximize utility.
4. Utility is distilled to economic utility, i.e. profits.
5. Therefore, rational agents aim to maximize profits.

These are mere assumptions and were originally made to simplify a complex world in order to develop predictive quantitative models. Naturally, the assumptions do not capture the richness and complexity of the real world. For example, numerous experiments show people are not motivated purely by economic profit but also by values such as fairness and trust.

Over time and constant habitual use, the assumptions have evolved from:

a. "assume" (*assume* agents are rational, self-interested and aim to maximize profits) to,
b. "is" (agents *are* rational, self-interested and *do* aim to maximize profits) to,
c. "ought" (agents *ought to be* rational, self-interested and *ought to* aim to maximize profits.)

The assumptions of profit maximization behavior and an efficient market have replaced any need for ethical discourse to resolve ethical questions in theoretical finance. Hence, the conventional wisdom has been that markets decide efficiently and ethics is meaningless in finance.

MFT has served us well in systemizing a broad field and providing a simple framework but the theory and its assumptions have become entrenched and attained a vaunted status as the orthodox ideology. Since the GFC, questioning the primacy of neo-liberal economics-based finance theory has begun. Practitioners are more willing to speak of ethics in finance, urged on, no doubt by regulators and the public.

PURPOSE IN FINANCE

The first step in establishing ethics in finance is to borrow a doctrine of Natural Law and state a purpose for finance. Purpose is the end towards which actions are directed. Purpose guides actions. A noble purpose is more likely to engender good acts, although it does not guarantee every act will be good.

Finance aspires to be a profession but all professionals seek purpose in their work. Most professions have well-articulated, aspirational purposes. For example, doctors and nurses help people to be healthy. Lawyers help obtain justice. Teachers help people learn. Priests help people spiritually. The finance profession should therefore, profess a purpose. One suggestion for a statement of purpose is:

The purpose of finance is to help people save, manage, and raise money.[8]

Finance should have its purpose enunciated and accepted. Students in finance should learn it in their business education. Perhaps the purpose should be taught even at elementary school. Practitioners should be comfortable with the purpose of finance, knowing it implicitly and speaking it unabashedly. This acceptance and acknowledgement is a first step towards improving the culture of finance. Yet another step in the progress towards an ethically educated finance culture is the understanding of the main ethical theories.

ETHICAL THEORIES

What is an ethical or moral theory? "Moral theories attempt to systematize ordinary moral judgements, and to establish and defend basic moral principles."[9] We need ethical theories because simply listing a series of rules of dos and don'ts is not sufficient. The theories give us clarification and a decision procedure for resolving difficult or complex cases, or in other words, a working framework for ethical practice. In new situations of financial practice the theories help to explain and give justifications for a chosen act that is deemed ethically right. Using these frameworks and standard techniques allows us to practice and hone our moral reasoning. We become more adept at moral argumentation, which enables us to "take part in corporate discussions or public policy discussions in an intelligent way, with knowledge of how to present and evaluate moral arguments."[10] In sum, think of ethical theories as tools for solving ethical problems.

This chapter describes four major ethical approaches: (1) Utilitarian Theory, (2) Deontological Theory, (3) Justice Theory, and (4) Virtue Ethics Theory.

UTILITARIAN THEORY

Jeremy Bentham is the father of modern utilitarian theory. This form of ethical theory is a branch of ethics called consequentialism, which proposes the consequences of an action are all that matter when taking an ethical decision to act. The rightness or wrongness of an action depends on the consequences of the act. Consequentialist theories have been around for a long time. Elizabeth Anscombe coined the term "consequentialism" in her essay "Modern Moral Philosophy" in 1958. Utilitarianism is by far the most widely known form of consequentialism, and there is often confusion when distinguishing the two.

Teleological is the classical term for ethical theories that focus on outcomes, or ends, to determine correct ethical action. Teleology comes from the Greek words, "telos" meaning, "end" and "logos" meaning, "science." Before Anscombe, utilitarianism was the more general term for teleological ethical theories. Today, consequentialism is the most widely accepted

---

8   Kara Tan Bhala, "The Purpose of Finance" (*Seven Pillars Institute for Global Finance and Ethics*, January 22 2013) http://sevenpillarsinstitute.org/mission/the-purpose-of-finance, accessed on September 16 2015.

9   Richard T. De George, *Business Ethics* (6th edn, Pearson Prentice Hall 2006) 49.

10   De George (n 9), 50.

umbrella term, containing distinguishable sub-categories with a broad variety of desired outcomes.

For classical utilitarianism the desired outcome is creating the most good for the most people or maximizing the overall good. Both Bentham and Mill had the idea that good is associated with pleasure or happiness, which is a hedonistic view. Classical utilitarianism guides ethical decisions that bring the most pleasure or happiness for the greatest number of people. In sum, the Principle of Utility is:

> In all circumstances we ought to produce the greatest happiness or well-being for the greatest number.

In assessing the outcomes of an action the only thing that matters is the amount of happiness or unhappiness created. Everything else is irrelevant. Notably, each person's happiness counts equally and we cannot privilege our happiness or that of loved ones above the happiness of others. This makes the utilitarian approach universalistic.

Bentham was a pure and simple hedonistic utilitarian. In his view, happiness should be measured in terms of duration, intensity, how near, immediate and certain it is and how free from pain and how likely it is to lead on to further pleasure. These considerations are measured in 'The General Utilitarian Analysis' below. Bentham also thought that acting according to the Principle of Utility would itself bring pleasure and happiness. The principle can be followed for the intrinsic pleasure as well as for the benefit to others.

Mill refined Bentham's model to distinguish between higher and lower qualities of well-being. According to Mill's form of utilitarianism, we should seek to maximize higher forms of well-being rather than lower ones. There is a ranking of the value of various pleasures. The Millsian hierarchy of pleasures places sensual pleasure at the bottom and the pleasures of the mind at the top, so moral and intellectual pleasures are best while sensual pleasures are least good. Mill's utilitarianism has both a qualitative as well as a quantitative aspect. An obvious criticism of this refinement is one person's higher pleasure is another's lower pleasure and not everyone thinks listening to Beethoven's fifth piano concerto constitutes a higher form of well-being. Mill also goes beyond Bentham when he gives a positive place for rules within the overall utilitarian approach.

Rule Utilitarianism

The chief exponent of modern rule utilitarianism is Richard Brandt. After countless utilitarian evaluations of certain acts, it is possible to frame general rules. The rules may then be used in assessing a similar type of act because these rules apply to classes of actions. When evaluating the ethics of say, lying for personal economic gain, we can determine that lying under these circumstances is wrong simply by observing the consequences in the past. Thus, we may apply this rule, "Lying for personal gain is unethical" to a conduct that falls into this category without the need for performing the steps of a utilitarian calculation.

We also can make a distinction between strong rule utilitarianism and weak rule utilitarianism. The former holds that a person should never break a rule that is established on utilitarian principles. The latter states there may be circumstances when the outcome of a particular act may take precedence over the general rule in a utilitarian assessment, although that rule still needs to be taken into account.

The idea of rule utilitarianism is to remove the arbitrary aspects of the utilitarian analysis. It provides a measure of universality by introducing a rule of behavior between the individual and the conduct. The system separates the individual agent more from assessment of the morality of the act because she merely has to conform to some rules handed down on authority. Some argue this characteristic makes rule utilitarianism even more objective in use.

Act Utilitarianism

In contrast to rule utilitarianism, act utilitarianism does not approve of rules to assess the consequences of acts. Each individual action with its own specific details and facts should be subjected to utilitarian analysis. Utilitarian rules are generalizations of past examples, and some particular future instance may prove to be an exception to the rule. Consider the case of insider trading. In each case, the set of information and circumstances may be different. To determine the ethics of the conduct we should calculate the effects of a particular trade on a particular set of insider information. The effects will be, in part, similar to those of any trade on insider information, but they also will be in some measure, different. If we do not do a utilitarian analysis, we may not discover there are non-conventional facts about a particular insider trading case. Insider trading, as a rule, is unethical. However, some future instance may not fall under this rule. In that particular case, the act utilitarian claims that insider trading may, in fact, be morally permissible.

Other Forms of Utilitarianism

Another form of utilitarianism is preferential or preference utilitarianism. This approach takes into account the preferences of individuals involved, except where those preferences come into direct conflict with the preferences of others. Right action, in this case, is determined by maximizing the satisfaction of the preferences of those involved. This method overcomes the criticism that people have different ideas of happiness.

Critics argue both hedonism and preferentialism present subjectivist notions of well-being. To counter the subjectivism, the perfectionist form of utilitarianism is said to have a more objectivist notion of well-being. In this system, there is some type of objective list of properties that characterize a good life. Among the items on the list are knowledge, close relations, friendship and achievements of various kinds. According to perfectionism, well-being increases when a person acquires vital knowledge, friends or achievements.

These systems, while subtly different from the original, all take from Bentham the idea that utilitarianism starts with facts and claim only consequences of pleasure are to be admitted to an objective system of ethics. The finessed system, if consistent and coherent, must look something like Bentham's. Attempts to change it without changing the first principles result in systems less coherent and no better for providing a foundation for ethical obligation. So it is that Bentham remains the most consistent utilitarian.[11]

---

[11]   Montague Brown, *The Quest for Moral Foundations* (Georgetown University Press 1996) 62.

The General Utilitarian Analysis

Using the utilitarian approach, a decision-maker faced with an ethical choice proceeds along these general steps.[12]

1. Consider the conduct to be evaluated. In stating the conduct, it is best to state it in as morally neutral language as possible so as not to bias the evaluation.
2. Identify those directly and indirectly affected by the conduct. The evaluator should try to spread the net as widely as practicable. Many of our actions affect society as a whole. For example, insider trading has systemic effects. If the public realizes that individuals have access to non-public information, then the integrity of the market is compromised.
3. Evaluate the good and the bad outcomes of the conduct on the individuals and entities identified in (2) above. Start with the consequences on those immediately affected. Identify the most striking consequences first. Sometimes these may be so profound that further analysis is unnecessary because these outstanding consequences clearly show the act is unethical or ethical.
4. Extend the outcomes as far into the future as possible. Judgment is of course required because the further the forecasts go into the future, the less reliable they become.
5. Weigh the total good versus the total bad outcomes with due consideration given to the quantity, duration, propinquity, intensity and purity of each value and the relative importance of these values.
6. Sum up all the good and bad consequences. If the conduct produces more good than bad, then the conduct is ethical. If the conduct produces more bad than good then the conduct is unethical.
7. Consider an alternative action or actions.
8. Perform a utilitarian assessment of the alternative or alternatives.
9. If the evaluation demonstrates one of the alternatives produces more good than bad, then choose this action.
10. If the evaluation demonstrates the alternatives all produce more bad than good, then choose the conduct that produces the least bad.

It is important to stress we cannot expect mathematical precision in the utilitarian calculation and approximations are acceptable especially if they are noted explicitly. The evaluator should be as objective as possible but need not convince herself of the objectivity of her analysis. Still, some find the analysis above to be complex and difficult in terms of getting the accurate facts.

Criticisms of Utilitarianism

One common criticism of utilitarianism is that no one has the time to calculate all the consequences of an action prior to acting or refraining from acting. As humans, we are constantly faced with ethical decisions, especially in the workplace. In finance, professionals encounter a myriad of situations that require ethical choices. It is not practical to expect people, particularly busy professionals to take time to weigh utilitarian choices.

---

[12]   De George (n 9), 67–70.

This criticism is taking utilitarianism to the extreme because utilitarianism does not require we calculate all the consequences before we act. There is an ethical history of humankind on which we can rely. For instance, we know murder is wrong. We need not keep doing a utilitarian analysis to determine the ethics of murder. What the utilitarian method does provide the practitioner is an analytical framework to support the argument that murder is morally wrong. We know what to investigate and the analysis to undertake to determine if an act is right or wrong. When the ethics of an action is uncertain, there is a system to help analyze and resolve the issue. While there are not a plethora of moral problems, when one does arise, we can use the principles of utilitarian theory to arrive at a solution.

Another common criticism of utilitarian theory is that we cannot know the full results of any action. There are many individuals and parties who may be affected by an action and it is unrealistic to expect a decision-maker to include every affected entity. The consequences of actions may persist for an almost indefinite period of time. In addition, the calculation is likely to be inaccurate because we are unable to precisely assign values to the good and bad outcomes and weigh them correctly.

Most utilitarians concede it is impossible to give exact measures in practice. However, we can do a lot in practical life to arrive at reasonable approximations. As reasoned above, in judging most actions there is the benefit of knowing the consequences of similar actions done in the past. The utilitarian approach does not require mathematically precise calculations. This usually is not possible in cases dealing with the morality of actions. In the more standard cases the consequences are sufficiently obvious. The good or bad is sometimes so clear that accuracy is not necessary. In complex cases, where accuracy is in doubt, the evaluator should be ready to revise the analysis if she discovers the calculation is flawed. This characteristic is not a defect of the theory but a statement of the human condition and the nature of morality.[13] As stated earlier, the expectation of precision is an outcome of scientism and the incorrect imposition of the scientific method on ethics.

A third criticism of utilitarianism is the theory does not account for justice and may even give a different conclusion than one from the perspective of justice. John Rawls argues that utilitarianism does not take seriously the distinction between persons. The impersonal approach championed by utilitarianism may trample the rights of individuals in the name of some greater good.

Criticisms of ethics in general and distinct ethical theories in particular usually use examples of extreme moral quandaries to prove the shortcomings of both. Yet, ethical issues are usually rather standard and not of the "moral dilemma" category. In most cases, both justice and utilitarianism will agree on which actions are just. It is only when there is divergence of results that these cases should be treated separately, as special cases. A moral analysis using justice theory or utilitarian theory results in similar moral judgments in most cases. This conclusion should not be surprising because utilitarianism is an attempt to systematize and provide reasons for moral judgments based on rationality. The same can be said of the next system of ethical thought, deontological theories.

---

[13]   De George (n 9), 70.

DEONTOLOGICAL THEORIES

The term deontology derives from the Greek world deon, meaning duty. Deontological theories are duty based. The duty here is to our moral obligations. We are duty bound to act in accordance with our moral obligations, which are enunciated in moral principles. In contrast to utilitarianism, deontology denies an action is judged good or bad depending on its consequences. Deciding an act is ethical or unethical depends instead on whether it follows or violates a moral principle. Therefore, some acts are always wrong, even if the act leads to a positive outcome.

There are two major steps in the deontological framework:

1. Determine the moral principles, an example of which is, "it is wrong to kill."
2. Act according to these moral principles because it is your duty to do so.

Logically therefore, there must be a way of determining these moral principles to which we are obliged to adhere. There are so far, two main ways to determine moral principles. The method depends on the specific deontological system. Examples of the main deontological moral systems are:

1. The Judeo-Christian tradition.
2. The Islamic tradition.
3. The Greek Stoic tradition.
4. Kantian Ethics.

In the religious traditions of Judaism, Christianity and Islam, moral principles derive from God who reveals these principles to followers. Moses received the Ten Commandments, Jesus Christ gave his moral teachings during the Sermon on the Mount and the Prophet Muhammad (Peace Be Upon Him) received Allah's moral laws over the course of 23 years. In the religious deontological tradition, morality ultimately rests on God who reveals the moral law (consisting of moral principles) to followers.

Greek Stoic philosophy maintains that moral principles are found in natural law. For Stoics, god is in nature and, primarily, the immanent principle governing the world. Good is inherent in human nature and it is through human rationality that we are able to recognize the good. This doctrine, described earlier, defines the Natural Law approach to ethics. According to the Stoics, the universe has a rationality and a purposeful order. Human lives harmonize with this purpose and as such, humans have a divine spark that helps them to live in accordance with natural law. Moral principles, therefore, are part of the natural law but recognizable through human reason.

The religious deontological tradition is grounded on the divine while the Stoic tradition is grounded in natural law. Immanuel Kant formulated the most influential secular approach to deontological ethics. Kantian moral principles are given not by a divine being, but are grounded in human reason. Kant was influenced by science and stands at the height of European Enlightenment, an intellectual period famous for the attempt to go beyond authority and superstition and deal with the world on the basis of human reason.

Kant gives three propositions that delineate his ethical system:

1. A moral agent's action is moral only if the agent does it from a sense of duty.
2. A moral agent's action is moral only if the agent acts on the basis of a principle or maxim.

3.　It is a moral agent's duty to act out of reverence for the moral law.

Clearly, three elements are crucial in Kant's ethics. First, the moral agent is a person who performs an action and has the capacity to act morally. Normally, we say an agent needs to be free to be able to make moral choices, otherwise she cannot be blamed or praised for the act she chooses. Freedom is a prerequisite for morality. In contrast, Kant points out that the experience of the moral law leads to an awareness of freedom. A person experiences freedom when she reflects on the ability she has to make a moral choice.

Secondly, a maxim is a principle or general rule governing the action of a rational person. For instance, "It is wrong to commit murder" is a moral principle. Maxims are critical in Kant's ethics because they are the basis on which the will operates.

Thirdly, the desire to do one's duty in upholding and acting on moral principles comes out of the will. This is the faculty of deciding, choosing and acting. Kant's moral theory starts with the phenomenon of "good will" and celebrates what can be achieved by the application of human reason. We exercise good will when we act according to moral principles and the autonomous will is the source of moral action.

For Kant, in the realm of moral obligation, morality implies a categorical imperative. We do what we must because of our duty to follow the moral law. A categorical imperative tells us to do something without any reference to the likely result. In contrast, a hypothetical imperative tells us to do something in order to reach a desired end. An example of a hypothetical imperative is, if you are thirsty, then you should drink some water. All hypothetical imperatives come in the form of an "if . . . then" statement. Kant did not think there was anything moral in acting to achieve a particular end. Kantian ethics is a priori and is established apart from the consideration of consequences. This approach is diametrically opposed to utilitarianism.

The Categorical Imperative

Kant uses the categorical imperative to test if moral principles or acts are right. He gives three formulations of the categorical imperative.

> First Formulation: act only according to that maxim whereby you can at the same time will that it should become a universal law without contradiction.[14]

Put simply, Kant means that something is right only if you can, without contradiction, wish it to become universal law. This formulation provides a simple logical test. If we are content that everyone else should be bound by the same principle upon which we are acting, then what we are doing is logically consistent and therefore, right. Kant illustrates this using the example of keeping promises. Suppose X needs a loan from Y but will only get the loan if she promises to repay it. However, she knows she will not be able to repay the loan. Should X then promise to repay Y with this knowledge? Kant argues we would be right to make a promise we cannot keep only if this principle – "make promises you cannot keep" – can be made into a universal law. Yet, this principle involves a contradiction, because promise-making becomes nonsense

---

[14]　Immanuel Kant, *Groundwork of the Metaphysics of Morals* (Cambridge University Press 2012) 44.

if everyone is entitled to break their promises. Thus, Kant says it is always wrong to make a promise we know we cannot keep.[15]

> Second Formulation: act in such a way that you treat humanity, whether in your own person or in the person of any other, never merely as a means to an end but always at the same time as an end.[16]

We have a perfect duty to not use others or ourselves merely as a means to some end. Each human is a rational being who is valuable, possesses dignity and is worthy of respect. Therefore, we should treat each person as an end, with respect and dignity. Rational beings are not objects to be used as a means to someone's subjective ends. Take the example of X and promise keeping in the loan situation given above. If X takes the loan and makes a promise she intends to break, then X does not treat Y, the creditor, as an end but as a means to an end – which is to get funds.

> Third Formulation: therefore, every rational being must so act as if he were through his maxim a legislating member in the universal kingdom of ends.[17]

The 'kingdom of ends' is the society of rational beings. Rational beings also are autonomous and must be treated as such. Morality cannot be imposed on others but must be self-imposed. In other words, the third formulation tells we are rational beings capable of conceiving and understanding the moral law and as rational beings we knowingly and willingly act in accordance with the moral law. Because reason is the same for all rational beings, we each give ourselves the same moral law.

Going back to the example of promise keeping given above, X should not make a promise she intends to break to Y. In doing so, X does not treat Y as an autonomous person. Y is a rational being who does not wish to be on the receiving end of a broken promise. The moral principle, "make promises you cannot keep" would not be legislated by Y. Nor would it be legislated by X. The test of the morality of a principle is not whether people accept it but whether all rational beings should accept it regardless of whether they are agents or receivers of the actions.[18]

Moral Law versus Moral Principles

Note the categorical imperative does not tell you the content of your moral obligations. It is a first order principle of pure practical reason or reason as applied to action. The categorical imperative provides the criteria against which we can test whether an action or a second-order principle is moral. A second-order principle is for example, the moral principle that states "Lying is wrong." This principle proposes a moral norm or rule, applicable to all and binding on all unconditionally. However, this second-order principle has content and is in accord with the categorical imperative, which Kant calls the moral law.

As first stated in the beginning of this section, deontology requires two elements: moral principles and a duty to follow them. The moral principles derive from two main sources,

---

[15]   Mel Thompson, *Ethical Theory* (2nd edn, Hodder Murray 2005) 92–7.
[16]   Kant (n 14), 54.
[17]   Kant (n 14), 59.
[18]   De George (n 9), 84–6.

Table 1.1   *The foundations of moral principles in deontological ethics*

Moral Principle	Christian Deontology	Islamic Deontology	Kantian Deontology
Do not steal	The principle(s) is (are)	The principle(s) is (are)	The principle(s) conform(s) to the three formulations
Do not cheat	revealed by God so we	revealed by Allah so we	of the categorical imperative (moral law):
Do not lie	are obliged to follow the	are obliged to follow the	- It can be made a universal principle without
	principle(s)	principle(s)	contradiction
			- It does not treat others as means
			- It respects the autonomy and dignity of rational
			beings and will be legislated as a principle by all
			rational beings

a divine, supreme being or human reason. We need to know if a particular principle is moral and can test the principle or principles as shown in the Table 1.1. The principles probably most relevant in financial ethics are, "Do not steal," "Do not cheat" and "Do not lie." If we test these principles against religious deontological systems, we find God and Allah issue these commandments and adherents to these faiths should obey them. If we test these three principles against the three formulations of Kant's categorical imperative or what he calls his moral law, then we observe the principles are all in accord with the formulations. Therefore, these principles are morally correct norms. It is our duty to practice these principles. In sum, deontology is an ethical system that proposes we have a moral obligation to follow the commands of moral principles.

Criticism of Deontological Theories

A common criticism made against deontological theory, particularly against the Kantian version, is that there will be regularly in practice conflicts between moral principles. When such conflicts arise, we find ourselves in a moral dilemma.

A common example of a conflict of moral principles is the dilemma of the battered wife and her murderous husband. The wife runs away from her husband whom she believes will kill her. She tells you she is going to her mother's house to hide. The husband comes to you and asks you where his wife is. You believe if you tell the truth, the husband will kill his wife. However, if you lie, you will be breaking the moral principle of not lying. What should you do?

There are two ways to resolve the dilemma. The first is to make an exception to one of the principles in conflict so as to give a resolution to the conflict. For instance, we construct the principle of allowing a person to lie to save the life of a person. We test the principle with this exception against the three formulations of the Categorical Imperative. If the principle passes the tests, then it is moral. We may make exceptions in both the conflicting principles and test both with their exceptions to find out which is right. However, the answer may not always be obvious and we may need to give arguments to justify the correct principle.

The second way out of a moral dilemma is to view each of the conflicting principles as prima facie moral rules.[19] A prima facie rule is one that is in general binding. When there is only one prima facie rule that applies in any particular situation, then we are morally bound to obey the rule. However, when several prima facie rules apply, or when we cannot fulfill every one of them, then not all of the rules are morally binding. The actual moral duty that is binding

---

[19]   De George (n 9), 88–9.

in the multiple rule situation is the one appropriate in that particular case. We decide which is the morally binding rule by seeing which takes precedence. Reasons must be given why one rule takes precedence over the other or others.

In the case of the murdering husband, the moral principle, "Do not aid in murdering a person" trumps, "Do not lie." The reason is clear: a human life is measured against harming someone in a non-life-threatening way. The principle that takes precedence, "Do not aid in murdering a person," therefore, is the one we have a moral duty to follow.

When moral principles clash, it is often difficult to decide which takes precedence. In these cases the individual and society should carefully and as objectively as possible consider the various arguments in support of opposing views. When a clear decision is not possible, then the position with the strongest argument should be chosen.

JUSTICE THEORIES

Justice is an ancient concept. Plato's Republic is concerned with what is meant by justice. For Plato, justice is to find that right balance of emotions, reason and appetites within the human person and to know the right place of oneself and others in society. It is better to be just than unjust because, as Plato explains, a person who is unjust is driven by desires, which are usually numerous and somewhat unsatisfiable. The unjust are swayed by their appetites, which are temporary means of staving off loss and discontent. Consequently, the unjust person is invariably frustrated. It also is better to be just than unjust because the just are ruled by reason and reason deals with eternal values. Therefore, the just person possesses greater satisfaction even if he seems a failure in the conventional sense.

For Plato's most eminent student, Aristotle, justice is the supreme and complete virtue because it is the sum of all virtues. For instance, a coward is unlikely to be just, nor is a miser. Instead, a brave, generous person is more likely to be just. Aristotle distinguishes two forms of justice: distributive and corrective justice. Distributive justice concerns the distribution of honor, wealth and other items. Distributions count as just if equal persons receive equal shares. Clearly, just distributions require a determination of worth of the persons and worth of the thing being distributed.

Distributive justice concerns the distribution and burdens by the state, so that everyone receives her due. The great debate is over what is considered fair distribution. Some, such as Thrasymachus, an interlocutor in Plato's renowned dialogue, the Republic, argue that justice is in the interests of the stronger. So the strong, the rich, the powerful should receive a larger proportion of benefits. In contrast, some argue that everyone should be treated equally. John Rawls (1921–2002) an American moral and political philosopher developed a well-respected theory of distributive justice.

Corrective justice is concerned with restoring the equality between people when one has wronged the other. In corrective justice, the worth of the person does not matter. What does matter is correcting the difference of what is lost by the victim to the perpetrator. Corrective justice seeks to restore equality by taking away the perpetrator's gain and restoring it to the victim.

From the descriptions above, we observe a definition of justice, in the broadest sense, it is giving each person her due, treating equals as equals, and unequals unequally.[20] We often think of the term as synonymous with law or lawfulness. A broader sense of the word is closer to fairness. Behavioral finance studies show that people have an inherent sense of justice or fairness. This view of human nature clashes with the classical economic view of "homo economicus", which views humans exclusively as self-interested.

There are other forms of justice besides the two Aristotle describes. Compensatory justice requires compensating someone for a past injustice or making good some harm suffered in the past. People should be fairly compensated for their injuries by those who have injured them. This kind of justice may be and often is served through monetary compensation.

Retributive justice is punitive because it is the punishment due to someone who breaks the law or has committed harm to others. The punishments must be fair, just and in proportion to the wrongdoing. In general, relevant criteria for deciding the level of punishment are the seriousness of the crime and the intent of the criminal.

Commutative justice belongs in the sphere of transactions and is, therefore, particularly relevant to finance and business. This form of justice calls for fundamental fairness in all agreements and exchanges between individuals or private social groups. In the exchange of goods and services, sellers should set fair prices and not practice price gouging. To ensure fair pricing in transactions, there must first be full informational disclosure to both buyer and seller. Crucially, both parties in the transaction must enter it freely and not be forced to do so. In commutative justice both parties also should see some benefit from the transaction.

Procedural justice concerns fair decision procedures, practices or agreements and is relevant in the fair resolutions of disputes. There must be fairness and transparency in the processes by which such decisions are made. Fair procedures are necessary for equitable outcomes. This form of justice is important in the concept of due process in law.

Principles of Justice

Rawls is well known for his theory of distributive justice. His theory uses social contract theory and is Kantian in its approach in applying the third formulation of the categorical imperative. The social contract theory, first put forward by Thomas Hobbes, is a theoretical concept. Its basis is the need of the individual to be secure and to maximize necessities and aspirations through cooperation with others. Individuals decide to live together in a society and cooperate to better provide for everyone's needs. The members of the society agree on certain rules everyone must observe, and on ways to enforce these rules. It is this agreement that is called the social contract. The social contract underlies an individual's obligation to act with benevolence towards the others in the group and to follow the rules designed to ensure unselfish behavior.

The principles of any society are ones that all rational beings would agree to, as the third formulation of the categorical imperative proposes. Rawls agrees with Kant that individuals in a society are rational beings with autonomy. As such they will freely agree to adhere to the principles upon which they have legislated as rational beings. The members of a society decide on the principles in a Rawlsian hypothetical situation, which he calls the "original position."

---

[20]   De George (n 9), 97.

The original position is not an actual fact at any time, but is one we adopt by putting on the "veil of ignorance." To wear the veil of ignorance is to pretend not to know one's actual position in society, whether one is rich or poor, young or old, healthy or sick, Chinese or Hispanic, male or female and so on. Self-interest, operating behind the veil of ignorance, leads to the formulation of Rawls' two principles of justice.

First principle of justice
This is the principle of equal liberty. "Each person is to have an equal right to the most extensive basic liberty compatible with a similar liberty for others."[21] This principle is not chosen because of the belief that everyone should be treated equally. Rather, the members of the society legislate it because behind the veil of ignorance no one knows her position in society. She would want therefore, to be treated equally with people in higher stations in life if she finds herself in a lower place. This first principle is prior to the second and must always be considered the ideal.

Second principle of justice
This is the principle of equality. "Social and economic inequalities are to be arranged so that they are both (a) to the greatest benefit the least advantaged and (b) attached to offices and positions open to all under conditions of fair equality of opportunity."[22] This principle concerns the distribution of wealth and power. Inequalities are inevitable and can actually lead to improved conditions for all. These inequalities are acceptable to all only if the least advantaged group is better off as a result of them. In addition, the second principle ensures the least advantaged should not be denied equal opportunity. For example, take two financial institutions A and B. A is more unequal than B but the least disadvantaged in A has an income of 100. This is because the company hires and pays for the best people in the business in order for the business to be a great success. B is a financial company that is admirably equal, where every member has an income of 80. Clearly, the least advantaged in A is doing better economically than the least advantaged in B. Thus, from the point of the least advantaged, it is still better to be a member of company A than B.

Another example to consider is insider trading. This activity can be a violation of Rawlsian distributive justice in regards to the right of equal information for all traders. Under the veil of ignorance, traders will agree not to engage in insider trading because they do not know if they will be the least advantaged in the market, the ones without inside information. Non-insider traders will avoid being at the mercy of someone else with insider information. Therefore, if the principles of the market are determined using Rawls' original position and veil of ignorance, insider trading violates the principle of equality of information access.

Justice concerns fairness and giving individuals what is due to them. Questions of justice occur when one person is treated differently from another. The ethics of insider trading emerges from the question of fairness: should someone profit because she has privileged access to information while others in the market do not? These others may work hard on doing fundamental equity research. Yet they are outdone simply because of their unprivileged positions, lack of wealth or deficiency in connections. Many tend to think that in a just society, people can improve their circumstances through hard work.

---

[21]   John Rawls, *Theory of Justice* (Belknap Press 1971) 60.
[22]   Rawls (n 21), 83.

VIRTUE ETHICS

Virtue ethics dates back to the Greeks (again). The tradition was the dominant philosophy during the classical period. The most celebrated virtue ethicist and perhaps the starting point of discussion for most virtue ethicists is Aristotle. In the Nicomachean Ethics, Aristotle refines and formulates a sophisticated theory that is a prototype for contemporary virtue ethics.

Virtue ethics refers to an approach to ethics that has as its central focus the judgment of character. A person's character is made up of all her virtues and vices. A person who is honest will generally act honestly even if tempted to do otherwise. Virtues are character traits Aristotle calls dispositions. A disposition to be honest is instilled when young through regular practice. By constantly choosing to act honestly, the disposition to be honest eventually forms into a habit. This habitual honesty develops into a character trait and becomes part of a person's character. This same process of habituation applies to other virtues such as generosity, courage and moderation. The person who possesses the virtues and practices them is the virtuous person.

The focus on a person's character means the virtue ethics approach is agent-centered (the decision on whether an act is right or wrong depends on the person who does the act) rather than act-centered (the rightness of the act depends on the act itself and does not take into account the character of the person performing the act). The alternate focus on the agent differentiates virtue ethics from utilitarian and deontological ethics, both of which are act-centered. There are three versions of this agent-centered focus.[23] First, the moderate version views most of morality as connected with character, although some actions can be evaluated independently of virtue. Secondly, the reductionist version has all judgments of rightness being reducible to judgments of character. Lastly, there is the replacement version, where the virtuous notions gain priority by default, after the deontic concepts have been eliminated.

All three versions of virtue ethics are formulated through the idea of a virtuous character – the moral goodness of persons is determined by the virtues they possess. Instead of asking, "what should I do?" as deontological and utilitarian ethics do, virtue ethics considers what sort of person the moral agent should be and what sort of life she should lead. This question is not answered by consulting principles, norms or policies that apply to situations. Rather, the question is answered by considering the person's character along with other morally salient features of the situation. According to most virtue ethics theories, the virtuous do not act virtuously for the sake of being virtuous. Rather, an honest person, say, tells the truth because she loves the truth.[24]

The virtuous express who they are when they act, and in acting, they develop their characters. While the moral evaluation of the person is different from the moral evaluation of an action, nevertheless, the evaluations are related. A virtuous person refrains from immoral acts. So, for instance, a truthful person does not lie, and an honest person does not cheat.

Deontological and utilitarian theories have the notion of right and wrong acts. The theories represent our legalistic approach to ethical thinking. There is an emphasis on rules and laws, implying correct answers to ethical questions. By contrast, according to virtue ethics, especially in the replacement version, the recommended method in ethics is an Aristotelian one,

---

[23]   Daniel Statman, "Introduction to Virtue Ethics," in Daniel Statman (ed), *Virtue Ethics: A Critical Reader* (Georgetown University Press 1997) 7.

[24]   Stan Van Hooft, *Understanding Virtue Ethics* (Acumen Publishing 2006) 11.

in the sense that we can expect no precise answer to practical questions. Virtuous people may therefore, arrive at different answers to the same practical problem.

Virtues

Arete is the Greek word for virtue and can also be translated as "excellence." Aristotle's definition of virtue is that it is a state (hexis) of one's character.[25] This is equivalent to the definition with virtue being a "character trait." A hexis or character trait is a settled state that involves reason and emotion. A person is honest and does honest deeds "readily, eagerly, unhesitatingly, scrupulously, as appropriate."[26] Each of the virtues involves getting things right, for each involves practical wisdom (or in Greek, phronesis), which is the ability to reason correctly about practical matters. For Aristotle (some contemporary philosophers disagree), all virtues are morally good.

For Aristotle a virtue is the "mean between extremes," something more than the Greek emphasis on moderation. Aristotle is clear that the excess or deficiency of a virtue is not the virtue itself. Virtue is the mean between excess and deficiency. Courage is the mean between timidity and recklessness. Temperance is the mean between gluttony and prudishness. To judge what is the mean requires reason and knowledge – these excellences are the guides to our virtues.

David Hume is one of the two important modern virtue theorists. The other, who has special significance to business and the free enterprise system, is Adam Smith (1711–76). Both defended a portrait of human nature in which "sympathy" and "fellow-feeling" play roles as important as self-interest. For Hume and Smith, virtues are important because they are both useful and pleasing. In Smith's *Theory of the Moral Sentiments*, published before the (currently viewed) capitalist manifesto, *Wealth of Nations*, he places great store on the two basic virtues of modern market society – justice and benevolence. Followers of Adam Smith's economics often ignore his ethics, but the economics is not workable without the ethics.

There is another ancient virtue ethicist who may have been more influential than Aristotle, Hume, or Smith. Confucius (551–479 BCE) is the foremost Chinese proponent of virtue ethics, emphasizing virtues such as good upbringing, good habits and good instincts. Confucius taught the way to universal harmony (Tao) through right action (Jen) in harmony with others (Yi). The virtues, particularly the virtue of "filial piety," are central to this vision.

According to Aristotle, Confucius, Smith and Hume, virtues are cultivated responses and actions, which may, at the time require no deliberations whatsoever.[27] While deontology may require some reasoning for us to act on principle and utilitarianism encourages the calculation of utilities, the manifestation of virtue seems to require little or no thought. A virtuous person acts on a virtue naturally as the circumstance arise. The truly honest person for example, does not need to think about acting honestly. She never even considers lying. The virtues, accordingly, do not require deliberation. Indeed, too much deliberation, for example should I give a loan to a friend who needs monetary assistance, is evidence one does not have the virtue of generosity. Virtues may blur the distinction between altruism and selfishness, a duality

---

[25]   Rosalind Hursthouse, *On Virtue Ethics* (Oxford University Press 1999) 28–9.
[26]   *Ibid.*
[27]   Robert C. Solomon, "Business Ethics and Virtue," in Robert E. Frederick (ed), *A Companion to Business Ethics* (Blackwell Publishing 2003) 35–6.

often discussed by moral philosophers. A generous person may act generously not because of concern for the well-being of others but because she may simply be generous and/or take pride in being generous. To be generous is to act and be motivated by generosity, but no further claim needs to be given to distinguishing self-interest, altruism and concern for others.[28]

Hursthouse, who is an adherent of the Aristotelian version of virtue ethics, gives a general way to determine virtues. She neatly summarizes the premises that underlie the virtue ethics approach to right action in the following way:[29]

P.1.   An action is right if and only if it is what a virtuous agent would characteristically (i.e. acting in character) do in the circumstances.

P.1a.   A virtuous agent is one who has, and exercises, certain character traits, namely, the virtues.

P.2.   A virtue is a character trait that . . .

The second premise, P.2., is completed by giving a list or a criterion. In the Second Enquiry Concerning the Principles of Morals, David Hume completes P.2 such that: 'A virtue is a character trait that is useful or agreeable to its possessor or to others. Hursthouse completes P.2. in an Aristotelian manner: a virtue is a character trait that a human being needs for eudaimonia, roughly translated as happiness.'

Eudaimonia

Hursthouse says, "a virtue is a character trait a human being needs for eudaimonia, to flourish or live well."[30] Eudaimonia is a Greek word that roughly translates as "happiness," "flourishing" or "well-being," although each translation has its drawbacks. Happiness, in its contemporary understanding, connotes something subjective. Flourishing does not have this subjectivity problem but its drawback is that we may have a mistaken idea of what flourishing consists of, pleasure for instance. Well-being does not have a corresponding adjective, and is therefore clumsy to use. Hursthouse proposes that the notion of eudaimonia is close to the idea of "true (or real) happiness," or "the sort of happiness worth having."[31] We would want this sort of happiness for our children for their own sakes.

Eudaimonia is an expression of a form of naturalism. In other words, we can (to a certain extent) use an account of human nature to base our understanding of virtue on. The virtues are those character traits that make a human being a good human being. "Ethical evaluations of human beings as good or bad are taken to be analogous to evaluations of other living things as good or bad specimens of their kind. The analogy is instructive, because it reveals that several features of ethical evaluation thought to be peculiar to it, and inimical to its objectivity, are present in the quasi-scientific evaluation even of plants."[32] Human beings need those character traits to live well as human beings, to live a good, characteristically human life.

---

[28]   Solomon (n 27), 35.
[29]   Hursthouse (n 25), 28–9.
[30]   Hursthouse (n 25), 10.
[31]   Hursthouse (n 25), 12.
[32]   Hursthouse (n 25), 21.

Criticism of virtue ethics

Virtue ethics generally begin within an established tradition or culture that uphold traits which are admired in that tradition or culture. This cultural aspect of virtues gives rise to the criticism that virtue ethics is relativistic. Relativism is the idea that there may be very different virtues in different societies. How are we to decide which virtues are true?

Indeed, different virtues are praised in say, Homeric Greece versus the medieval period of Thomas Aquinas, versus the Confucian era and contemporary corporate Asia. However, it does not follow that there are not some non-relative virtues. These virtues are found in every human society or institution, just because, as Hursthouse argues, we are human. Thus, we consider trustworthiness and honesty to be virtues because they are crucial to almost any human interchange. The non-relative virtues are essential in all societies because we require them in order to cooperate and live together. We need to supply society with the necessities of life, protect society from others who would do harm and from natural disasters. All this suggests there are non-relative virtues, perhaps with local variations and interpretations, such as courage, honesty, generosity and congeniality. In finance, trustworthiness, fairness and cooperation are particularly important non-relative virtues because they undergird any form of market or non-market society.

CONCLUSION

The moral philosophical canon dates back 2,500 years. In contrast, Modern Finance Theory is about 60 years old. With 2,500 years of research, analysis, rigorous criticism and scholarship it seems reasonable to conclude that the discipline of ethics is more fully formed than the nascent field of finance. Why then, should the methods of ethics be ignored when issues of right and wrong invariably arise in financial practice? Indeed, the integration of ethics into the field of finance is more than likely to improve financial theory and increase the understanding and application of frameworks and concepts that moral thinkers have designed and refined in the last two millennia.

2. Ethics and standards in financial regulation

William Blair and Clara Barbiani[1]

I. FRAMING THE CONTEXT AND THE SCOPE

1.1 The Context

The context is the continuing interest in culture, standards and ethics together with financial regulation as providing a more effective overall scheme than financial regulation alone. This has arisen because of the global financial crisis of 2007–8, followed by the Eurozone sovereign debt crisis of 2011–12, and continuing problems arising out of behaviour in the financial sector such as that relating to the fixing of the London Interbank Offered Rate (LIBOR) and other benchmarks. The latter gave rise to a UK Parliamentary Commission on Banking Standards established in 2012. It issued its final report in 2013[2] making recommendations (to quote the Government response)[3] 'around sanctions, standards and remuneration in order to strengthen accountability and incentives for bankers to behave ethically and in a way that supports the long-term sustainability of banks'. Following the report, the UK banking industry set up the Banking Standards Review, which reported in 2014.[4] This recommended the establishment of a Banking Standards Review Council setting standards of good practice in the industry.[5] The Governor of the Bank of England endorsed the role of ethics in finance, saying that through a range of measures (including codes that are 'seeking to re-establish finance as a true profession, with broader societal obligations') 'finance can help to deliver a more trustworthy, inclusive capitalism – one which embeds a sense of the systemic and in which individual virtue

---

[1] This chapter develops themes published in the Stockholm Centre for Commercial Law publication, number 22 *'Functional or Dysfunctional – The Law as a Cure? Risks and Liability in the Financial Markets'*, and in *Reconceptualising Global Finance and Its Regulation*, eds Ross P Buckley, Emilios Avgouleas and Douglas W Arner, Cambridge University Press, 2016, chapter 21.

The authors would like to thank Sir Robin Knowles CBE for his valuable input into this paper through the Law and Ethics in Finance Project.

[2] Parliamentary Commission on Banking Standards, *Changing Banking for Good* (5th Com Report HC 175, 2013) www.parliament.uk/business/committees/committees-a-z/joint-select/professional-standards-in-the-banking-industry/news/changing-banking-for-good-report/ accessed on 5 February 2018.

[3] HM Treasury and Department for Business, Innovation and Skills, *The Government's Response to the Parliamentary Commission on Banking Standards* (Cm 8661, July 2013) www.gov.uk/government/uploads/system/uploads/attachment_data/file/211047/gov_response_to_the_parliamentary_commission_on_banking_standards.pdf accessed on 5 February 2018.

[4] Richard Lambert, *Banking Standards Review* (*Banking Standards Review*, 19 May 2014) www.bankingstandardsreview.org.uk/assets/docs/may2014report.pdf accessed on 5 February 2018.

[5] The Banking Standards Review Council has been reframed and renamed, lately, with the establishment of the Banking Standards Board in April 2015, which is taking forward the work initiated by Sir Richard Lambert in 2014. See: BSB, 'BSB Starts its Work and Announces Line-up of New Board' (*Banking Standards Board*, 2 April 2015) www.bankingstandardsboard.org.uk/bsb-starts-its-work-and-announces-line-up-of-new-board/ accessed on 5 February 2018.

and collective prosperity can flourish'.[6] That is the theme of this chapter, and the approach of the authors to the subject of discussion.

Meanwhile, new forms of ethical challenge have been identified which do not revolve so specifically around misconduct. Concern about financial exclusion in vulnerable communities, and even States themselves by virtue of de-risking by major financial institutions, have prompted interest in new ways of promoting financial inclusion. For example, there are issues concerning how well-adapted the UK anti-money laundering regulations are to the emerging realities of financial crime control, and the ever-increasing potentialities of reliance by the private sector on big data and machine learning technologies to detect and prevent suspicious transactions. The implementation by financial institutions of automated anti-money laundering (AML) systems is widespread. But the emergence of RegTech developing AI-based financial crime solutions has the potential to take the technology to a different level – and raises questions as to the adequacy of the existing AML framework, currently founded on the responsibility of banks and their employees to identify and report suspicious transactions. AI may help both to make AML regulation more effective, and at the same time minimise the financial exclusion which is sometimes its practical effect, to the benefit of business, regulators and people who are otherwise excluded unnecessarily from the use of the financial system.

Overall, there is a growing acceptance that standards of a non-legally binding nature have an important part to play, and that the culture of a financial business is something in which society has a legitimate interest. This in turn has sparked debate on the relationship between law (principally but not solely in the form of financial regulation) and broader ethical principles. These issues are international in nature, since in most if not all parts of the world, finance plays a significant role, and financial systems are axiomatically interconnected.

Is it not enough to obey the law? If standards need changing, the law can be changed. Why should financial institutions aspire to meet some further indefinite moral standards? One answer is that senior management of financial institutions internationally have also themselves been arguing for higher standards post-global financial crisis. A sound business case can be made for encouraging what may be called an ethical approach to the conduct of banking business. As used in the context of culture, ethics connotes shared standards of appropriate behaviour that are not in the form of legal rules. These standards are absolute in one sense, but also have to adapt to changing markets. As Governor Carney has put it: 'UK authorities have used their convening powers to encourage market participants to establish standards of market practice that are well understood, widely followed and, crucially, that keep pace with market developments.'[7]

On the other hand, there is an important question as to how effective statements of intent by business leaders who follow the lead of central bankers and regulators really are. That is not to call into question their sincerity. But in the highly competitive business of finance, particularly perhaps international finance, an avowed commitment to higher standards may mean little in itself without something to back it up.

---

[6]   Mark Carney, 'Inclusive Capitalism: Creating a Sense of the Systemic' (Conference on Inclusive Capitalism, Bank of England, London, 27 May 2014) http://www.fsb.org/wp-content/uploads/Carney -Inclusive-Capitalism-Creating-a-sense-of-the-systemic.pdf accessed on 5 February 2018.
[7]   Mark Carney, 'Worthy of Trust? Law, Ethics and Culture in Banking' (Speech at the Banking Standards Board Panel, 21 March 2017) https://www.bankofengland.co.uk/speech/2017/banking -standards-board-worthy-of-trust-law-ethics-and-culture-in-banking accessed on 7 February 2018.

For example, many financial institutions have for some time had codes of conduct that attempt to enshrine these standards. This is a development to be welcomed. On the other hand, these codes are not universal, their effectiveness is as yet unproven, and ethical principles are not easy to calibrate in a competitive market context. There is also a fundamental issue: are these codes to be treated as purely exhortatory in nature, or do they require something else to give them traction? As this article will consider further, financial institutions have also adopted concrete initiatives to bring the Code of Conduct alive; whether these initiatives are going to shape the internal culture remains a question unanswered or, maybe, it is just too early to say. But there is at least a good chance that they will.

1.2　The Scope

This chapter considers the interaction between industry-based initiatives and regulatory-driven ones with reference to enhancing the ethical culture within financial institutions. The purpose of this is: highlighting the importance of furthering a continuous move towards ensuring standards of conduct both within and outside financial institutions; and, at same time, identifying the limits posed by the existence of different instruments aimed at regulating conduct, with distinct implications in terms of enforceability. In other words, reconceptualising the role of standards is considered here within the current perspective: the financial industry a decade after the global financial crisis. The significance of the role of standards has been broadly recognised; however, what remains unclear is whether the new framework created to enhance the role of standards is being shaped adequately, or whether it is producing inconsistencies and confusion due its complexity.

Then, consideration is given to the rise of a regulatory framework enhancing ethical values such as honesty, integrity and fairness. The new emphasis shows a move towards enhancing the importance of these values, but, at same time, the process of placing them in the regulatory framework also raises new questions: how is it possible concretely to expect people to respect these values and translate them into ethical conduct? And, also, how can we ensure that people develop a common and clear understanding of each of them? Hence, the topics tackled are in line with a current shift of focus. Establishing a regulatory framework to ensure the presence of an ethical culture within financial institutions was the concern which arose immediately after the global financial crisis. Now, the interest has moved to defining how the new regulatory framework should be shaped to best address concerns in this area, and identifying the function of different key stakeholders in supporting the current transition towards the concrete establishment of a culture which can be described as 'authentically ethical' within financial institutions in a competitive marketplace.

II.　THE LIMITS OF THE LAW

2.1　The Reform of Financial Regulation

The response to the financial crisis has principally been to address perceived shortcomings in financial regulation with a view to avoiding the kind of systemic risk which necessitated public intervention in 2008. In other words, the law in the form of financial regulations is seen as the principal means to avoid recurrence. One view is that this is a sufficient response, and that codes of ethics and the like belong in the realm of the purely voluntary.

The law is clearly central. Law has always played a role in regulating financial activity. But whilst its principal purpose has been to prescribe the enforcement of financial transactions, it has also traditionally sought to alleviate the effect of such transactions, for example by outlawing abusive practices by creditors of various kinds. Such rules develop over long periods of time, and primarily have to do with protecting individual debtors. A feature of contemporary financial regulation, which is much more recent in origin,[8] is that it has to do with promoting the interests of society in general. Changes in relation to financial regulation may not avoid financial crises arising in the future,[9] but the reform process is nevertheless essential. At a time of globalisation and complexity in finance, the system is being made more robust in important ways.

2.2   The Limits of Regulation

Equally, it has to be recognised that there are limits as to what further regulation can achieve. Two examples will be given from prudential regulation and conduct of business respectively.

As regards capital adequacy, the reform of the Basel rules has been a necessary adjunct to strengthening financial institutions. But defining let alone measuring capital is a complex and inexact exercise, a point which has been made by Andrew Haldane of the Bank of England.[10] As the European Banking Authority (EBA), an objective of which is to provide a single set of harmonised prudential rules for financial institutions throughout the EU, stated, 'significant implementation challenges remain ahead'.[11] This statement remains valid. Its findings of November 2017 confirm that, notwithstanding the EBA's acknowledgement of the strengthening of capital positions across the EU banking sector, structural challenges persist: the level of non-performing loans remains a source of concern and the overall quality of assets shows only a slight improvement.[12]

The second example regards disclosure. As it is known, the global financial crisis affected different parts of the world in different ways, leading to concerns about the regional effects of the new rules.[13] As example, in Asia the global financial crisis had a substantial impact in jurisdictions such as Hong Kong, in which complex financial products were sold to retail clients on the basis of a prospectus which gave disclosure, but in a way which was not easily under-

---

[8]   The United Kingdom did not have a formal statutory regime governing banking until 1979, when the Banking Act was enacted to implement the First Banking Directive of what was then the European Economic Community. The primary objective of European legislation at that time was to encourage a single market in banking services.

[9]   Charles Kindleberger writing in 2005 lists his 'top ten' financial bubbles, beginning with the unlikely Dutch tulip bubble of 1636–7. The crisis of 2007–8 would certainly make it into any list of the top ten, probably right at the top. See: Robert Z Aliber and Charles P Kindleberger, *Manias, Panics, and Crashes: A History of Financial Crises* (7th edn, Palgrave Macmillan UK, 2015).

[10]   Andrew G Haldane, *The Dog and the Frisbee* (6th Economic Policy Symposium 'The Changing Policy Landscape', Federal Reserve Bank of Kansas City, Wyoming, 31 August 2012) 10.

[11]   European Banking Authority, *Risk Assessment of the European Banking System* (July 2013) 4.

[12]   European Banking Authority, *Risk Assessment of the European Banking System* (November 2017) 9.

[13]   Peter J Morgan and Victor Pontines, *An Asian Perspective on Global Financial Reforms* (August 2013) Asian Development Bank Institute Working Paper Series No. 433, 3.

standable by the target clients to whom the financial products were sold.[14] The identification of these mis-selling practices represented something which regulators did not address within the pre-existing regulatory framework,[15] showing the inadequacy of previous norms and driving financial reform in this area, led by the Securities and Futures Commission (SFC) of Hong Kong, in response to these events.[16] The emergence of an issue over the limits of disclosure as a *real* safeguard, which the experience of retail investors in Hong Kong emphasises, can be applied more generally to the framework for the conduct of business rules.

Thus, what the example of mis-selling shows[17] is that whilst disclosure may be necessary, it is often not sufficient. This is due to the complexity of modern financial markets. It has been said that accurately valuing even a single collateralised debt obligation (CDO), for example, demands a multifaceted analysis of an enormous volume of legal and financial data. The information costs associated with valuing a portfolio of these instruments are orders of magnitude higher. Viewed from this perspective, what matters is not just the *availability* of information in a strictly technical sense, but also the amount and complexity of this information and, consequently, the human capital and other endowments necessary to *process* it in any meaningful way.[18]

Finally, there is the problem of complexity in financial regulation itself.[19] This problem has been recognised for a long time and was an early driver of attempts to move towards principle-based regulation. The problem is difficult to deal with, and with the sheer volume of rule-making since the crash, has become more so.[20]

---

[14]   Specific reference is made to the purchase of Lehman 'Minibonds' by retail investors in Hong Kong and Singapore and elsewhere. Linked to this, it has been acknowledged that even professional intermediaries could not have understood these complex products' profile based only on disclosed available information (prospectus and marketing material) See: Douglas W Arner and others, *The Global Financial Crisis and the Future of Financial Regulation in Hong Kong* (February 2009) AIIFL Working Paper No. 4, 46–7.

[15]   'Retail structured notes became noticeable in Hong Kong after the SFC relaxed certain prospectus rules for unlisted securities in February 2003.' See: Paul Lejot, 'Dictum Non Meum Pactum: Lehman's Minibond Transactions' (2008) 38(3) Hong Kong Law Journal, at 2.

[16]   The SFC SIP Code of 2010 is intended to address major issues arising following the Lehman Minibonds crisis. The SIP Code sets a three-pillar structure, under which pillar one is concerned with disclosure enhancement, referring in this case to both the provision of offering documents and continuing disclosure obligations. See the *SFC Code on Unlisted Structured Investment Products* Sec IV 2010.

[17]   For a good discussion in the context of derivatives, see: Commodity Futures Trading Commission, *Business Conduct Standards for Swap Dealers and Major Swap Participants* (Federal Register, Vol. 77, No. 33, 17 February 2012).

[18]   Dan Awrey, William Blair and David Kershaw, 'Between Law and Markets: Is There a Role for Culture and Ethics in Financial Regulation?' (2013) 38 Del. J. Corp. L, 191 at 200–1. It is said there that ultimately it is the asymmetrical distribution of these endowments which renders disclosure, in and of itself, a relatively ineffective strategy for addressing opportunism within the context of bilateral counterparty relationships.

[19]   There is an interesting debate in this respect: 'While I recognize that to some degree complexity in financial structure breeds complexity in regulation, often the causality is reversed. Complexity in regulation leads to complexity in financial structures and systems, particularly in light of the efforts of market participants to mitigate the costs and complications induced by regulation, including attempts to engage in regulatory arbitrage.' See: Chester S Spatt, 'Complexity of Regulation' (2012) 3 Harvard Business Law Review Online, www.hblr.org/2012/06/complexity-of-regulation/ accessed on 5 February 2018.

[20]   The effects are tangible. Barclays Bank had approximately 1,500 compliance staff in 2012, up from 600 in 2008. See: Salz Review, 'An Independent Review of Barclays' Business Practices' (April 2013) para 3.13.

A further example is disclosure, in particular in the context of establishing rules for public disclosure in respect of security-based swaps in the US. These disclosure requirements appeared to represent a source of difficulty in implementation for swap dealers due to the way in which the regulatory framework was updated: the Commodity Futures Trading Commission (CFTC) requirements adopted in 2012[21] were supplemented in 2015 by the Securities and Exchange Commission's (SEC) enactment of two final rules in this area. However, these two rules show substantial divergences compared to the terms of the norms established by the CFTC. Consequently, it has been said that this raises the scope for: technical complexity for investment firms which have already built systems and processes in order to comply with CFTC rules; increased operational risk in the markets; and legal uncertainty on the cross-border application of rules, considering that SEC reporting requirements, for example, have a broader extra-jurisdictional application than CFTC ones.[22] Thus, it can be argued that the way in which the regulatory framework is shaped itself can represent an additional source of problems, or at least increased complexity, for financial institutions that are seeking to implement new requirements.

In Philip Wood's phrase, 'The law has power. But the law can also be another bubble.'[23] There will come a time when the volume of financial regulation becomes counterproductive. In any case, apart from inevitable issues as to interpretation and application, regulatory perimeters will always be susceptible to arbitrage.

Private law is open to the same limitations. The courts of London and New York tend to take a *caveat emptor* attitude to the sale of complex derivatives products. In particular, standard terms disadvantageous to the user may be given full effect. Where there is no real parity between seller and buyer the result may be that lawful selling is seen as inequitable in a wider sense, with an attendant loss of trust.

III.   THE IMPORTANCE OF AN ETHICAL RISK CULTURE

3.1   Enhancing Values, Promoting an Ethical Culture

These well-understood limits of the law and regulation mean that it is important to encourage an appropriate corporate culture to support the legal framework. The importance of values has also been advocated at the top of the banking industry,[24] and the financial crisis has made it manifest. There is a growing literature on the subject of ethics specifically in the context of financial services.

---

[21]   Ibid. note 16.

[22]   PWC, 'First Take – A Publication of PWC 's Financial Services Regulatory Practice: SEC's Swaps Reporting and Disclosure Final Rules' (PWC, February 2015) https://www.pwc.com/us/en/industries/financial-services/regulatory-services/library/sec-swap-reporting-and-disclosure.html accessed on 5 February 2018.

[23]   Phillip Wood, 'Can the Law Prevent Another Financial Crisis?' (Allen and Overy, 17 December 2008)   www.allenovery.com/publications/en-gb/Pages/Can-the-law-prevent-another-financial-crisis-.aspx accessed on 5 February 2018.

[24]   For example, Stephen Green (former Group Chairman of HSBC) stated: 'Everyone knows about the importance of truth and honesty for a sustainable business.' See: Stephen Green, *Good Value: Reflections on Money, Morality and an Uncertain World* (1st edn, Allen Lane, London, 2009).

Financial institutions have had to react to these sentiments, and this has been very pronounced in the United Kingdom. The case of Barclays Bank (whose Chairman and Chief Executive resigned following the bank's LIBOR settlement with regulators) may show what went wrong, but it also shows the efforts that have been made at redress. In January 2013, the new CEO announced five values that the bank will seek to embed throughout the bank. At the time of writing, these five values have not changed;[25] they are respect, integrity, service, excellence and stewardship. By 'integrity' is meant that the bank should 'act fairly, ethically and openly in all we do'.[26] It would be short-sighted to dismiss this kind of action as window dressing forced on the institution by scandal.[27] The theme is that legal rules need to be supplemented by a clear set of values that are understood through discussion and application, and that develop into a culture that tends to ensure good rather than bad behaviours.[28]

Thus, the move towards the establishment of an ethical culture within financial institutions has been increasingly recognised as meaningful, as stated by Governor Carney in one of his latest speeches: 'To maintain social capital, finance ultimately needs to be seen as a vocation, an activity with high ethical standards, which in turn conveys certain responsibilities. Those responsibilities recognise that finance is not an end in itself but a means to promote investment, innovation, growth and prosperity.'[29] Reflections like this from leading figures have helped create a climate of encouragement for financial institutions to realise that it is in the interest of their businesses to prove to be trustworthy by enhancing values internally and promoting an ethical culture which is clear and well-known to staff.

3.2   Implementing a Risk Culture

While considering culture within financial institutions, it is not only the establishment of values which is important or, at least, not in isolation. Internal culture can be seen as a barometer of two important factors, namely: *ethical conduct*, that is, the way in which employees behave in following both the firm's values and regulatory standards, and in their specific role, where it imposes a higher level of accountability;[30] and, *risk awareness*, in other terms, the perception that employees have of the risk their conduct may be originating or spreading, and,

---

[25]   Barclays, 'Purpose and Values' (Barclays website) www.home.barclays/about-barclays/barclays-values.html accessed on 5 February 2018.

[26]   Barclays Strategic Review, '*Barclays PLC: Becoming the Go-To Bank*' (Barclays, 12 February 2013) www.barclays.com/content/dam/barclayspublic/docs/InvestorRelations/IRNewsPresentations/2012News/antony-jenkins-presentation-to-investors-12-february-2012.pdf accessed on 5 February 2018.

[27]   Barclays also commissioned an independent review of its business practices and culture, which reported in April 2013. The review made a number of recommendations as to the bank's culture and business model, and was led by Sir Anthony Salz, Executive Vice-Chairman of Rothschild, and former senior partner of Freshfields Bruckhaus Deringer. See: Salz Review (n. 20).

[28]   Ibid., Salz Review at para 3.14.

[29]   Mark Carney, 'Reflections on Leadership in a Disruptive Age' (Speech at Regent's College, 19 February 2018) https://www.bankofengland.co.uk/speech/2018/mark-carney-speech-at-regents-university-london accessed on 20 February 2018.

[30]   In broad terms, reference is made here to the fit and proper assessment and the linked higher regulatory expectations on conduct which are placed on a limited number of individuals. For general reference, see: European Central Bank, *What is Fit and Proper Supervision?* (18 March 2016) https://www.bankingsupervision.europa.eu/about/ssmexplained/html/fap.en.html accessed on 28 February 2018.

potentially, reducing through their conduct. For this reason, there is now increased emphasis on the development of what is referred to as *risk culture*.

The significance of establishing a solid risk culture has been highlighted by regulators: for example, the Financial Conduct Authority (FCA) report on the failures of HBOS expressly mentions the ineffectiveness of the bank's risk management framework as the consequence of a culture which was not sufficiently risk sensitive.[31] Within the EU legal framework, the legislation which best reflects the cardinal function which the concept of risk culture plays within EU financial institutions' internal organisation is the Markets in Financial Instruments Directive II (MiFID II).[32] In fact, MiFID II establishes a clear requirement on the compliance department's side to perform risk assessments on a regular basis and determine risk-based monitoring activities.[33]

There is a strong rationale for this move, as established in the MiFID I Guidelines, which represented the first milestone for these amendments under MiFID II: 'The compliance function's objectives and work programme should be developed and set up on the basis of this compliance risk assessment.'[34] This new regulatory expectation of enhancing risk culture, combined with the imposition of a different and equally important requirement, that is, ensuring the independence of the compliance function from the operation of other business units, and establishing a direct reporting line between compliance officers and the management body,[35] shows that financial institutions should seek to engage compliance officers who bear this increased responsibility not only with reference to ensuring respect for the values embraced by the financial institution itself, as the example of Barclays shows, but also in connection to maintaining an adequate risk culture – which is a fairly new concept and one which is intended to gain a greater degree of significance within investment firms in the post-MiFID II world.

At this moment of transition, what can be observed already is that some investment firms are reframing their internal organisational structure to comply with the requirement that compliance should become a fully independent function, mostly in connection with the firm's performance of its MiFID II-related activities, and to further adherence to other related regulatory requirements within linked legal instruments such as the Capital Requirements Directive IV (CRD IV): Article 9(1) of MiFID II expressly sets a duty for firms to comply with the CRD IV framework on internal governance.[36]

---

[31]   FCA and PRA, '*The Failure of HBOS plc (HBOS) – A Report by the Financial Conduct Authority and the Prudential Regulation Authority*' (November 2015) para 91, Sec 1.5.4 www.bankofengland.co .uk/-/media/boe/files/prudential-regulation/publication/hbos-complete-report accessed on 5 February 2018.

[32]   Council Directive 2014/65/EU on markets in financial instruments and amending Directive 2002/92/EC and Directive 2011/61/EU [15.05.2014] OJ L 173/349 (MiFID II).

[33]   Ibid MiFID II, Article 22(2).

[34]   ESMA, *Guidelines on Certain Aspects of the MIFID Compliance Function Requirements* (28 September 2012) ESMA/2012/388, para 17 (MiFID I Guidelines) www.esma.europa.eu/sites/default/ files/library/2015/11/2012-388_en.pdf accessed on 5 February 2018.

[35]   The management body is also vested with the power of appointing and replacing compliance officers. See: MiFID II, Article 22(2.c; 3.b); MiFID I Guidelines, para 58.

[36]   The difference of approach under these two EU legal frameworks can be described as: deductive (in the case of CRD IV) v. inductive (with reference to MiFID II), as MiFID II sets governance rules in order to ensure compliance with the specific kind of risks presented under MiFID II, whereas CRD IV sets a more general and comprehensive framework to ensure sound internal governance. See: Directive

Accordingly, as may be inferred from these new expectations placed on financial institutions, the cultural change is seen not only as part of proper business practice, but as an essential aspect of effective regulation: regulators need healthy bank cultures to enable them to do their work effectively. They can never have sufficient resources to monitor every part of an institution's work. So, culture is the crux to ensuring that organisations comply not just with the law, but with the spirit of the law too. Markets rely on rules and laws, but those rules and laws in turn depend on truth and trust. Better cultures should ideally require less regulation, fewer laws and fewer regulators, which is a desirable direction of travel for finance generally.[37]

IV.   PRINCIPLES AND CODES

4.1   Principles Inspiring Regulation

So, we need more than just regulation. But what do we need? How can better standards be defined? Can they ever be underpinned by some form of sanction, other than reputational? These are not new questions. There have been various statements of principle, before and after the crisis. In 2004, the respected central banker Eddie George drafted succinct Principles for Good Business Conduct for international financial services providers. These principles say that compliance with rules must be 'underpinned by behaviour that is rooted in trust, honesty and integrity', which is a common lodestone in this field.[38]

In the wake of the crisis, the *Principles for Enhancing Corporate Governance* set out by the Basel Committee on Banking Supervision (*BCBS Principles*) in 2010 stated that a demonstrated corporate culture that supports and provides appropriate norms and incentives for professional and responsible behaviour is an essential foundation of good governance.[39] The *BCBS Principles* also specify that a bank is expected to have in place a code of conduct, or comparable policy document. Such a code or policy should 'articulate acceptable and unacceptable behaviours'. It 'should also discourage the taking of excessive risks as defined by internal corporate policy'.[40]

The *BCBS Principles* were reviewed and re-published in 2015. The principles now reflect the rise of a more stringent expectation on the regulatory side towards the establishment of

---

2013/36/EU of the European Parliament and of the Council of 26 June 2013 on access to the activity of credit institutions and the prudential supervision of credit institutions and investment firms, amending Directive 2002/87/EC and repealing Directives 2006/48/EC and 2006/49/EC [27.06.2013] OJ L 176/338 (CRD IV).

[37]   Salz Review, Appendix B.

[38]   John Thirwell, 'The Worshipful Company of International Bankers – A Short History of Its Formation' *The International Banker* 19 https://internationalbankers.org.uk/wp-content/uploads/2014/07/company-history.pdf accessed on 5 February 2018.

[39]   Basel Committee on Banking Supervision, *Principles for Enhancing Corporate Governance* (Bank for International Settlements, October 2010) 8 www.bis.org/publ/bcbs176.pdf accessed on 5 February 2018 ('BCBS Principles').

[40]   At [26–27] and at [92]: 'Sound corporate governance is evidenced, among other things, by a culture where senior management and staff are expected and encouraged to identify risk issues as opposed to relying on the internal audit or risk management functions to identify them. This expectation is conveyed not only through bank policies and procedures, but also through the "tone at the top" established by the board and senior management.'

a sound framework of corporate governance within banks. In fact, referring back to the point previously made on risk culture, it is worth mentioning that this concept has been included in this framework in the following terms: 'In order to promote a sound corporate culture, the board should reinforce the "tone at the top" by: . . . promoting risk awareness within a strong risk culture, conveying the board's expectation that it does not support excessive risk-taking and that all employees are responsible for helping the bank operate within the established risk appetite and risk limits.'[41]

Another aspect which is fairly new is the stronger emphasis placed on senior management's role, including in enhancing corporate governance. Notably, the previous reference to senior management being encouraged, together with staff, to identify risk issues[42] has been changed into: 'Senior management contributes substantially to a bank's sound corporate governance through personal conduct . . . Members of senior management should provide adequate oversight of those they manage and ensure that the bank's activities are consistent with the business strategy, risk appetite and the policies approved by the board.'[43]

This change witnesses the transition towards a new era with the development of a new emphasis on the role played by senior management in establishing a risk culture and a sound corporate governance framework, and raising regulatory expectations towards senior individuals who are considered empowered to change internal culture and a firm's accountability – but at same time these individuals are vested with a greater degree of individual liability in relation to the performance of their tasks within the risk management function. Starting with this general principle, the concept of placing responsibility on senior management attracted the interest of regulators in the United Kingdom, which transformed it into something more prescriptive through the establishment of the Senior Managers Regime (SMR).

This development started with the Parliamentary Commission on Banking Standards publishing its Final Report – *Changing Banking for Good* – in June 2013.[44] Commenting on the publication of this report, the Chairman, Andrew Tyrie, stated: 'Recent scandals, not least the fixing of the LIBOR rate that prompted Parliament to establish this Commission, have exposed shocking and widespread malpractice . . . A lack of personal responsibility has been commonplace throughout the industry. Senior figures have continued to shelter behind an accountability firewall.' Thus, chronologically speaking, the UK approach in this area moved in parallel to the BCBS approach rather than *ex post*, though as the global financial crisis showed, these shortcomings were certainly not exclusive to the United Kingdom.

The action taken by the UK authorities to translate this concept into the Senior Managers Regime shows a commitment on the regulatory side which can be compared to initiatives on the side of investment firms. The FCA and the Prudential Regulation Authority (PRA) published the final rules on the new framework to enhance individual accountability in July

---

[41]   Basel Committee on Banking Supervision, *Corporate Governance Principles for Banks* (Bank for International Settlements, July 2015) 9, para [30] https://www.bis.org/bcbs/publ/d328.pdf accessed on 5 February 2018 (*BCBS Principles*).

[42]   Basel Committee on Banking Supervision (n. 39), para [92].

[43]   Ibid. note 40, para [91].

[44]   Parliamentary Commission on Banking Standards, *Changing Banking for Good* (5th Com Report HC 175, 2013) www.parliament.uk/business/committees/committees-a-z/joint-select/professional -standards-in-the-banking-industry/news/changing-banking-for-good-report/ accessed on 5 February 2018.

2015.[45] The Senior Manager Regime represents one of the main focuses together with the Certification Regime and the new Conduct Rules.[46] The SMR replaced the Approved Persons Regime from March 2016 and it is therefore a fairly new process for investment firms. In March 2017, the FCA issued on its website an informative note with the title 'Senior Managers and Certification Regime: one year on'. This acknowledged that improvements have been made in the way in which the investment firms operate, but also that there is substantial work still to be done. Cultural change, of course, demands time.[47]

The significant change that the establishment of the SMR underpins will become tangible at some point in the future: 'The SMR re-establishes the link between seniority and accountability. Senior Managers are now held accountable if they fail to take reasonable steps . . . to prevent or stop regulatory breaches in their areas of responsibility.'[48] The UK experience in this context is good evidence of how principles have a role in making a difference when there is a regulatory commitment behind them. This gives investment firms a stronger incentive to comply, and also a more concrete point of reference in determining how changes should be made in practice. However, the question which remains in this context is whether regulatory intervention of this kind always provides the best solution in terms of bringing cultural change.

The answer to this question is, probably yes. Nevertheless, it is also important to recognise that changes through regulation have their limits. They oblige banks to fulfil new sets of criteria and continuously alter their internal structures to comply with these new requirements. Because each investment firm represents its own micro financial ecosystem,[49] the well-known issue of *one size fits all* can pose challenges to internal procedures and systems which are inherently likely to be developed to reflect a particular firm's inner culture, geographical scope and specific business aims.

The combination of these factors, of course, tends to be unique in each financial institution, driving tailor-made solutions, internally and externally. Notwithstanding this, voluntary-driven initiatives, compared to regulator-driven ones, have not been shown to be as successful as the latter in practice.

---

[45]   FCA, *CF15/22 Strengthening accountability in banking: Final rules (including feedback on CP14/31 and (IP15/5) and consultation on extending the Certification Regime to wholesale market activities* (July 2015) https://www.fca.org.uk/publication/consultation/cp15-22.pdf accessed on 5 February 2018.

[46]   FCA, 'FCA publishes final rules to make those in the banking sector more accountable' (Press Release, 7 July 2015) https://www.fca.org.uk/news/press-releases/fca-publishes-final-rules-make-those -banking-sector-more-accountable accessed on 5 February 2018.

[47]   FCA, 'Senior Managers and Certification Regime: one year on' (Press Release, 7 March 2017) https://www.fca.org.uk/news/news-stories/senior-managers-and-certification-regime-one-year accessed on 5 February 2018.

[48]   Mark Carney, 'Worthy of Trust? Law, Ethics and Culture in Banking' (Speech at the Banking Standards Board Panel, 21 March 2017).

[49]   This reference here is to the conceptual framework which acknowledges the existence of a financial ecosystem which constitutes 'a system-of-systems, in which every sub-system has its own sub-systems. Species of all kinds act as "agents" within each sub-system, and their relationships with one another constitute countless networks of different sizes. Each sub-system has self-similar patterns with other micro-level systems, and with the macro-level system'. See: Cheng-Yun Tsang, 'Rethinking Modern Financial Ecology and its Regulatory Implications' (2017) 32 Banking 8; Fin. L.R. 461. In this framework, domestic and transnational regulators as well are considered part of the ecosystem. See: Lawrence G Baxter, 'Betting Big: Value, Cautions and Accountability in an Era of Larger Banks and Complex Finance' (2012) 31 Rev. Banking & Fin. L. 765, 857.

There remains an important and different question with reference to enhancing corporate governance through principles – what is the evidence that these principles have been acted on?

4.2   Regulatory Expectations Driving Banks' Internal Changes

In answering this question, it is convenient to look at the principles that firms adopt on a voluntary basis and in adherence to the prudential regulatory framework. What is the nexus between conduct and prudential requirements? As provided in a recent Financial Stability Board (FSB) report of May 2017: 'For prudential regulators, misconduct . . . can become a prudential issue for three reasons. First, fines and redress payments are losses that deplete the loss-absorbing capacity of a financial institution. Second, misconduct cases can be a reflection of underlying weaknesses of the governance framework. Third, misconduct . . . suggests that some financial institutions may be unwilling or unable to get their employees to adhere to proper standards of conduct. This may further indicate that they are also unable to get their employees to adhere to other standards, including those for sound risk management.'[50] It is in this light that we discuss here the role of high-level regulatory expectations in driving the endorsement of principles of corporate governance within financial institutions.

In November 2012, the Financial Stability Board published an updated list of 28 global systemically important banks (G-SIBs), using a methodology developed by the BCBS. The number of G-SIBs which are the object of this assessment has moved to 30, as confirmed in the list issued in November 2017.[51] The rationale is that the changes made in terms of allocating institutions to 'buckets' reflects the combined effect of changes taking place in underlying activities and the use of supervisory judgment. The interest in looking at G-SIBs lies in the higher regulatory expectation placed on these institutions, expressly stated as follows: 'G-SIBs are required to meet higher supervisory expectations for risk management functions, data aggregation capabilities, risk governance and internal controls.'[52]

Rather than looking at this in the context of regulatory rules, the discussion here is on a regulatory expectation of change which allows financial institutions to take a more active role in designing and implementing change, leaving space for setting priorities and strategies which fit best the institution's internal environment. However, this regulatory expectation for setting a risk governance framework does not exist in a vacuum. The reference to the use of supervisory judgement as a weighted element shows the emphasis placed on qualitative data

---

[50]   FSB, *Stocktake of Efforts to Strengthen Governance Frameworks to Mitigate Misconduct Risks* (23 May 2017) http://www.fsb.org/wp-content/uploads/WGGF-Phase-1-report-and-recommendations -for-Phase-2.pdf accessed on 5 February 2018.

[51]   In particular, the 2017 list includes: under bucket 1, Agricultural Bank of China, Bank of New York Mellon, Credit Suisse, Groupe Credit Agricole, ING Bank, Mizuho FG, Morgan Stanley, Nordea, Royal Bank of Canada, Royal Bank of Scotland, Santander, Société Générale, Standard Chartered, State Street, Sumitomo Mitsui FG, UBS, Unicredit Group; under bucket 2, Bank of China, Barclays, BNP Paribas, China Construction Bank, Goldman Sachs, Industrial and Commercial Bank of China Limited, Mitsubishi UFJ FG, Wells Fargo; under bucket 3, Bank of America, Citigroup, Deutsche Bank, HSBC; under bucket 4, JP Morgan Chase. See: FSB, *2017 List of Global Systemically Important Banks* (21 November 2017) http://www.fsb.org/wp-content/uploads/P211117-1.pdf accessed on 5 February 2018.

[52]   FSB, *2013 Update of Group of Global Systemically Important Banks (G-SIBs)* (11 November 2013) http://www.fsb.org/2013/11/r_131111/ accessed on 5 February 2018.

Table 2.1   *Ethical code/code of conduct for the top ten banks of the 2017 Banker's Top 1000 World Banks ranking*

	BANK	COUNTRY	ETHICAL CODE/CODE OF CONDUCT
1.	*Industrial and Commercial Bank of China (ICBC)*	China	A Code of Conduct (not publicly accessible) for the staff has been adopted and is effective from 1999
2.	*China Construction Bank Corporation*	China	Annual CSR report, core values (Integrity, Impartiality, Prudence, and Creation) latest version available dated 2016; a staff behaviour standard manual (not publicly accessible) also exists
3.	*JP Morgan Chase & Co.*	US	Code of Ethics supplements the Code of Conduct (latest version 12 June 2017)
4.	*Bank of China*	China	Annual CSR report; a Code of Conduct (not publicly accessible) exists; and Codes of Conduct are in place in some jurisdictions (e.g. Canada)
5.	*Bank of America*	US	Code of Ethics has 11 key themes (including 'We act ethically'): the latest version of the Code is dated 2018
6.	*Agricultural Bank of China*	China	A Staff Code of Conduct (not publicly accessible); and, reference in the Annual CSR report
7.	*Citigroup*	US	Code of ethics for financial professionals dated December 2016, which supplements 2017 Code of Conduct
8.	*Wells Fargo & Co*	US	Code of Ethics and Business Conduct
9.	*HSBC Holdings*	United Kingdom	There are set Values, Business Principles, specific codes (i.e. for suppliers), a Code of Ethics applying to Senior Financial Officers and, Codes of Conduct in place in some jurisdictions (e.g. Germany)
10.	*Mitsubishi UFJ Financial Group*	Japan	Principles of Ethics and Conduct

Source: The authors of this table are the authors of the present chapter.

to complement quantitative data.[53] Firms which are G-SIBs are allowed to act as they wish in creating their own risk governance framework, but they are overall bound to show, for the purpose of the annual assessment, that their risk management function is organised in a way which matches the higher regulatory expectation.

This expectation seems to be a trigger to drive each of these financial institutions to become the real 'champions of compliance' in comparison to their 'less systemically important competitors'. It is of interest therefore to understand what these G-SIBs are doing, in practice, to enhance corporate governance and risk management internally.

The first and probably foremost legal instrument which offers a benchmark in this context is the code of conduct. Although it is reasonable to expect a degree of uniformity of approaches because G-SIBs are subject to the same regulatory expectation, a comparison shows that there is still a strong divergence of approaches in this field, which probably reflects the jurisdictional framework with which they are mainly associated. The approach differs from country to country, with US banks in particular having codes of ethics linked to codes of conduct. In

---

[53]   Financial Stability Institute, 'Reading Material: G-SIBs, D-SIBs and Contingent Capital' (BIS) https://www.jvi.org/uploads/tx_abajvicoursemanager/Reading_List_14BI40_01.pdf   accessed   on   5 February 2018.

other countries, ethical issues appear to be dealt with in the context of employee conduct and/ or corporate responsibility.

Taken from their websites, the position as regards the top ten banks in The Banker's Top 1000 World Banks ranking published in 2017[54] can be expressed in tabular form in Table 2.1 as at the time of publication.

As appears from comparing this list with the FSB list of G-SIBs in 2017, the top ten banks listed here are all within the 30 G-SIBs, not surprisingly. The sequence is, however, shaped under The Banker's list to put the banks in an order which reflects their financial strength in terms of tier 1 and assets capital, rather than the 'bucket' thresholds. The order would be further re-shaped if the denominator chosen was the perception of trust which retail investors place in the firms. According to surveys, China and India would be at the first place with a level of investors' trust at 89 per cent and 90 per cent respectively. On the other side, the most sceptical investors seem to be those in the United Kingdom and in Germany, showing a level of trust at 44 per cent and 40 per cent respectively. The United States is also close to these results at 54 per cent.[55] A second observation on the basis of the table is that there is a clear lack of homogeneity in approaches undertaken to codify ethics and conduct, and substantial differences in the way in which different G-SIBs address this subject.

4.3   Country's Culture and Firm's Culture in Interaction

As previously anticipated, on the face of it, Table 2.1 shows compliance particularly by US banks, but a somewhat different approach as regards banks in China. However, that may not present the full picture for China. It is thought that the introduction of a wide CSR provision into China's *Companies Law 2006* may have had a significant impact in relation to professional ethical standards in the financial services industry. This Act, which was further amended in 2013, provides that '[w]hen conducting business operations, a company shall comply with the laws and administrative regulations, social morality, and business morality. It shall act in good faith, accept the supervision of the government and general public, and bear social responsibilities'.[56]

In general, it seems that ethical requirements of the kind under discussion have been built into professional conduct rules in three tiers.[57] The first is at the watchdog level through the China Banking Regulatory Commission (CBRC). The Commission issued *Guidance on Professional Conduct for Staff of Banking and Financial Institutions* in 2009, which has been further revised in 2011;[58] *Guidelines on Internal Control of Commercial Banks* in 2014, which under Article 31 sets professional ethics as an important factor that banks should

---

[54]   The Banker, 'Top 50 Banks in Top 1000 World Banks by Tier 1 and Assets 2017'.

[55]   CFA Institute and Edelman Berland, 'From Trust to Loyalty – A Global Survey of What Investors Want' (2016) https://www.cfainstitute.org/learning/future/getinvolved/Documents/trust_to_loyalty _executive_summary.pdf accessed on 5 February 2018.

[56]   See: William Blair, 'CSR in Finance: The Development of International Norms' in J Lou (ed.), *Studies on Corporate Social Responsibility* (Peking University Press, Beijing, 2009) 559–66.

[57]   We are indebted to Dr Xuelian Jiang, Lecturer in Law, Beijing Institute of Technology, for her comments on this section and on the table under Section 4.2 of this chapter.

[58]   Notice of the China Banking Regulatory Commission on Issuing the Guidance on the Professional Conduct of Practitioners of Banking Financial Institutions (2011 Revision).

take into account while recruiting;[59] the *General Office Notice on Further Strengthening the Construction of Integrity in the Banking System* in 2016, setting an expectation for the establishment of 'in-depth integrity management' processes within banks;[60] *Guidance Opinions on the Standardisation of the Banking Sector's Provision of Service to Enterprises Expanding Abroad and the Strengthening of Risk Prevention and Control* in 2017, which sets a requirement for banks to align themselves to international standards as part of the Belt and Road initiative, and thus to set a solid compliance culture and abide by commercial ethics while dealing with foreign clients and counterparties;[61] and, most lately, in February 2018, the *Banking Sector Financial Institution Professional Conduct Administration Guideline*, which for the moment represents a draft for consultation but is expected to bring a significant change, if endorsed, in terms of standardising the professional standards of conduct expected within Chinese financial institutions.[62] The text, in fact, provides reference to the imposition of a duty on a Chinese bank to ensure that there are adequate internal rules to discipline employees' conduct and that the latter behave in good faith in their working interactions.[63] Reference is also made to the need for employees to comply with rules on anti-money laundering, anti-bribery and corruption, and insider trading. Given the generic character of these statements, it may be inferred that the CBRC is currently keen to ensure: that banks in China are currently developing procedures to ensure that employees behave according to the rules and in good faith; and, potentially, that the internal Code of Conduct is relied on for this purpose. This suggests that, for Chinese banks, the process of codification of conduct rules under a Code of Conduct and the bank's policies and procedures is relatively new, notwithstanding the existence of Codes of Conduct in several banks dating from the 1990s.

The second is at the industry association level, in that the China Banking Association issued *Guidance on Professional Conduct for Staff of Banking and Financial Institutions* in 2007. This association has not issued further relevant guidelines yet; notwithstanding that, there is a reasonable expectation that this will happen once the *Banking Sector Financial Institution Professional Conduct Administration Guideline* starts becoming applicable to banks' practice in China, considering the large impact that this is expected to have, and its capacity to bind Chinese banks and be enforced by the regulator for sanctioning purposes.

The third is at the institutional level, in that the major banks have produced their own sets of employee codes of professional conduct, codes of compliance requirements, etc. It seems that the principles and rules set out in these documents are similar to those in other international banks.

There are two other points. The first is that CSR of the kind now embraced by major financial institutions covers wider ground than what is usually regarded as ethics in business, but

---

[59]   Article 31 states: 'A commercial bank shall develop human resources policies conducive to sustainable development, regard professional ethics and professional competence as the major criteria for promoting and recruiting employees, ensure that employees have the necessary professional qualification and practicing experience, and strengthen employee training.'

[60]   General Office of the CBRC Notice No. 89 [2016].

[61]   CBRC Guidance Opinions [2017] No. 1.

[62]   Chinese Banking News, 'Regulator Seeks to Standardise Conduct of Banking Sector Professionals' (12 February 2018) http://www.chinabankingnews.com/2018/02/12/regulator-seeks-standardise-conduct -banking-sector-professionals/ accessed on 5 February 2018.

[63]   Article 4, Banking Sector Financial Institution Professional Conduct Administration Guideline (draft, 2018).

it can be seen as part of the same picture.[64] The other is that though a good business culture is often framed around client service, it is not only about client service, but has a wider meaning.

A further explanation as to why the comparison of Codes of Conduct may not represent the full picture in China is based on a factor which is often underestimated – customary and traditional influences on business ethics. For China and for some other countries in Asia this is represented by Confucianism. It has been said that this produces an inclination towards relationship-based forms of governance rather than rule-based ones.[65] It has also been said that the establishment of an ethical culture within China's banks and the linked expectation in terms of standards of conduct towards professionals is a matter which is addressed differently depending on the situation and context.[66] The Confucian director is therefore conceived as someone holding the principles of rightness and integrity as 'dear to the heart' and, for this reason, not likely to engage in fraudulent activity.[67]

On the other hand, the recent move of the CBRC towards setting an expectation for the standardisation of banking standards of conduct shows that China has an interest in aligning to international practices in this field, which can be justified in the light of financial complexity, financial innovation and the desire to improve risk management processes within banks,[68] a challenge which is also linked to the request of establishing a solid risk culture under the Basel framework.

Another example of that is offered by Italy: in order to understand Italian business culture and ethics it is important to acknowledge the essential role which family-based forms of organisation play in the internal economy, something which shows that the concept of *pater familias* is intrinsically embedded in the Italian system. Within this conceptual paradigm, there are considerations applicable to business ethics:

> at the most elementary degree of institutionalization, the head of the family, the *pater familias*, the eldest, most senior member, is tacitly recognized as the only person entitled to speak on behalf of the family group in all official circumstances . . . The institutionalized delegation, which ensures the concentration of social capital, also has the effect of limiting the consequences of individual lapses by explicitly delimiting responsibilities and authorizing the recognized spokesmen to shield the group as a whole from discredit by expelling or excommunicating the embarrassing individuals.[69]

This is not the whole picture, and for Italian financial institutions the framework is partially different – Italian banks have mostly developed their compliance practice in reaction to the decisions taken at EU level, as one would expect. They interact with Italian corporate culture in which family companies represent a reality that cannot be disregarded or underestimated. When we think about family companies, the first image is one of a small sustainable activity with limited costs and profit; the world of family companies in Italy is far more financially

---

[64]   Shuguang Wang, *Financial Ethics* (Peking University Press, 2011).

[65]   Angus Young, 'Conceptualising a Chinese Corporate Governance Framework: Tensions Between Tradition, Ideologies and Modernity' (2009) I.C.C.L.R. 235–44.

[66]   Say Goo and Charles Lam, 'Confucianism: A Fundamental Cure to the Corporate Governance Problems in China' (2014) 35(2)Comp. Law. 2014, , 52–56.

[67]   Ibid.

[68]   Jing Bian, 'Enhancing financial System Stability – A Case Study of the Chinese Banking Industry' (2012) 23(11) I.C.C.L.R. 365–73.

[69]   Pierre Bourdieu, 'The Forms of Capital' in J Richardson (ed.), *Handbook of Theory and Research for the Sociology of Education* (Greenwood Publishing Group, Westport, CT, 1986).

significant than that. Some of these family-owned businesses are ranked among leading companies worldwide in their field of business. They are listed mostly active on various financial markets and have their own private banks in Italy or in other States such as Luxembourg.

It is this internal reality with which Italian banks interface. Each family sets its own internal rules; a family-owned multinational company also functions like that and the *pater familias* is, ideally, the CEO of the company and most often is also the majority shareholder and ultimately the person in whom decision-making power is concentrated, which includes setting internal values and the tone of the firm's internal culture. A firm's culture is, therefore, an extension of the CEO's vision of what ethical conduct means and which values should be respected; the ethical culture of a family-owned multinational private bank is therefore found more in the Code of Ethics of the company rather than in the bank's Compliance Manual, as the latter one rather reflects a need to comply with applicable rules and licensing requirements.

It is difficult to understand this simply by reading the code of ethics of an Italian private bank or company. The statements made by Pri.Banks, the Italian association of private banks, are in line with the view which places personal accountability at the top of the chain. In fact, the 32 private banks which are currently part of this association and are 'banks held by one family or with strong reference shareholding', are described as holding a common interest in guaranteeing 'ethical governance based on personal accountability'.[70] Thus, in Italy, business ethics hold a personal dimension which is mostly allocated to the top of the pyramid and which, as a consequence, spreads and influences the whole operation.

Some Italian firms became famous for their enlightened shareholders and CEOs setting an internal culture[71] of 'actions based on values',[72] an example being 'Ferrero Women and Men',[73] which is aimed at promoting a heterogeneous environment in which there is fair gender representation at all levels including senior management. Instead, other companies manifest poor values and insufficient consideration towards ethical concerns.[74]

Within this framework that ranges from G-SIBs like Unicredit to other large banks like Intesa San Paolo and Monte dei Paschi di Siena and large private banks, it is important to acknowledge the existence of small banks in Italy which are less exposed to international challenges but which pooled together represent quite a significant part of the Italian banking reality. Here, it is useful to refer to Sabrina Lautenschlager's statement at European Central Bank level for considering the application of a different set of rules for smaller banks in adherence to the principle of proportionality.[75]

---

[70]   Pri.Banks – Associazione Banche Private Italiane (*Pri.Banks*, Website – Associazione – Chi Siamo) http://pribanks.it accessed on 15 February 2018.

[71]   Ferrero, 'Global Care: Corporate Social Responsibility – Summary of 2016 Report' (*Ferrero,* July 2017) https://s3-eu-west-1.amazonaws.com/ferrero-static/globalcms/documenti/2805.pdf accessed on 15 February 2018.

[72]   Ferrero, Code of Ethics (*Ferrero,* Website) https://www.ferrero.com/social-responsibility/code-of-ethics/a-renewed-commitment accessed on 15 February 2018.

[73]   Ferrero, 'Ferrero Women and Men' (*Ferrero*, Website, CSR Section) https://www.ferrerocsr.com/our-responsibility/women-and-men/ferrero-employees/?lang=EN accessed on 15 February 2018.

[74]   Selected Italian companies rely on a system of awarding negative ethical points for non-compliance with internal behavioural expectations.

[75]   Sabine Lautenschlager, 'Is Small Beautiful? Supervision, Regulation and the Size of Banks' (ECB, 14 October 2017) https://www.ecb.europa.eu/press/key/date/2017/html/ecb.sp171014.en.html accessed on 15 February 2018.

The question is, do smaller banks trigger the risk that, since they may be subject to a lower regulatory burden, they will be less encouraged to set a risk culture which is ethically sound as well? This re-connects to the point previously made that risk culture and ethical culture are becoming increasingly related, and potentially the higher the expectation on having a sound risk culture in place, the higher the chances that the ethical culture will be considered to have improved as well.

In summary, the Code of Conduct is a good benchmark to understand where countries are placed in terms of setting ethical culture within banks, but it is certainly not the only indicator. What the above discussion shows is that the cultural background of a society plays a role in determining which values are upheld within banks in that society, and perhaps the extent to which what is stated in the Code reflects the actual culture within the financial institution.

4.4   The Role of Codes of Conduct

It has been said that 'new codes are seeking to re-establish finance as a true profession, with broader societal obligations'.[76] As has been commented, it is difficult to assess whether financial institutions have concretely moved towards that ideal. On the basis of insights provided by compliance officers working in some of the EU G-SIBs, what can be observed is that some Codes of Conduct envisage ethical standards as relevant only in the jurisdictions in which the staff members covered by the Codes are active. In this sense, we may argue that, for these financial institutions, the expected move towards re-establishing societal obligations is not yet there. It is not acceptable to limit good behaviour to a geographical perimeter or a temporal setting.

Notwithstanding this, many other initiatives within banks testify to the existence of a concrete move towards bringing the Code of Conduct alive by, for example, organising workshops aimed to test in an informal and friendly setting not only the staff's knowledge about their Group's core values, but also their reactions in different dilemma scenarios, testing their capacity to take decisions ethically. The questions discussed range from theoretical to practical and are phrased in a way that highlights the benefits and limits of the system. This encourages critical reflection on the significance of the Code among staff.

This represents a good way of ensuring that responsibility for compliance with the Code of Conduct is considered at a truly individual level and results so far as possible in a true commitment. There is the risk of having the threshold set intentionally low or too generically, on the employees' side. This is a concern that often arises with reference to setting behavioural objectives, an exercise which line managers in many financial institutions are now required to do each quarter, semester or on an annual basis for their subordinates. The more the behavioural objective is generally framed, the less are the chances that the person will comply with it.

Evidencing a further move towards staff familiarising themselves with these commitments, and again in the context of internal workshops, a visualisation method is now sometimes used within financial institutions aimed to discover what the Code of Conduct means to staff. This requires employees to draft in a group an image that symbolises what the Code of Conduct means for them: no words are allowed, only images. This recourse to the imagination can be effective – the Code of Conduct is as good as in our imagination it can be. It is for the staff

---

[76]   Mark Carney, 'Inclusive Capitalism: Creating a Sense of the Systemic' (Conference on Inclusive Capitalism, Bank of England, London, 27 May 2014).

to ensure that what they visualise as being in the Code becomes part of it and gets respected. In practice, it has the potential of increasing internal awareness and leading towards cultural change originated from inside the financial institution's environment on the basis of individual initiatives which share a common vision. All this shows why financial institutions should recognise that the scope of re-shaping culture does to a real extent start with their Code of Conduct, with the workshops they conduct internally on it, the communication they foster on the subjects within the Code, and optimally a move towards mapping the potential ethical dilemmas that each team within the institution may have, analysing these dilemmas and framing suggestions on how to address them.

It is human to face ethical dilemmas, and we all know that we are meant to understand each other in these terms more than we are ready to admit. This is something which is part of the collective patrimony.[77] It is also human sometimes to fail to acknowledge that our capacity to recognise ethical dilemmas is inadequate, which in turn drives a failure in addressing them adequately. That is why proactive commitment of the kind under discussion can ultimately make a real contritbution to the cultural change that society is asking of financial institutions.

As the FCA Director of Supervision, Jonathan Davidson, stated in an FCA Discussion Paper issued on March 2018: 'regardless of individual motivation, firms' cultural initiatives may be in vain unless firms also foster an environment where employees can "speak up" and learn from mistakes'.[78] This statement not only proves that the establishment of firms' initiatives cannot be an end point for financial institutions, but also that regulators are expecting the firms' concrete endorsement of this higher commitment in fostering a healthy culture.

In this light, it is also worth noticing that the regulatory authorities have been increasingly moving towards enforcing this broader scope of applicability for standards of conduct, an example of that is the the 2014 FCA decision to ban for life a former Asset Management Managing Director at Blackrock UK on the basis of evading his train fare on several occasions.[79] The FCA's director of enforcement and financial crime at the time stated: 'Approved persons must act with honesty and integrity at all times and, where they do not, we will take action.'[80] The significance of this statement is twofold. It shows a clear move towards a demand for greater individual accountability within this sector, especially towards persons who have a leadership role within the institution and thus are expected to be accountable not only for their own conduct but for that of others and for the accountability of the institution itself. As Governor Carney has put it: 'leadership is the acceptance of responsibility rather

---

[77]   Terentius, 'Homo sum: humani nihil a me alienum puto' (I am a human being, so nothing human is extraneous to me). For further context, see: Vito R Giustiniani, 'Homo, Humanus, and the Meanings of "Humanism"' (1985) 4–6(2) Journal of the History of Ideas.

[78]   FCA, 'Transforming Culture in Financial Services' (Discussion Paper, March 2018) https://www.fca.org.uk/publication/discussion/dp18-02.pdf accessed on 12 March 2018.

[79]   FCA, 'Former Blackrock Asset Management Managing Director Banned' (Press Release, 15 December 2014) https://www.fca.org.uk/news/press-releases/former-blackrock-asset-management-managing-director-banned accessed on 5 February 2018.

[80]   FT Adviser, 'FCA Bans "Foolish" Manager for Life After Train Scam' *Financial Times* (Regulation section, 14 January 2015) https://www.ftadviser.com/2015/01/14/regulation/fca-bans-foolish-fund-manager-for-life-after-train-scam-SxKvuaU3Np1cdF1M1THxaI/article.html accessed on 5 February 2018.

than the assumption of power. True leadership is not an end in itself but rather as a means to accomplishing a worthwhile goal.'[81]

It also shows that the Code of Conduct does not apply only within the financial institution's business perimeter. Acts which fall outside the perimeter of business relationships may be essential in making or diminishing trust towards financial institutions, trust being the fundamental principle on which financial markets are based. As Onora O'Neill affirmed: 'without trust we cannot stand'.[82] The process of trust of course engages far more than the institution's own Code of Conduct, as is now explained.

4.5   The Role of Industry-Written Codes

More or less in parallel to the endorsement of codes of conducts at the level of financial institutions, initiatives have been undertaken to introduce industry-written codes: an example of that is the Global FX Code which establishes global principles of good practice in the foreign exchange market.[83] Of course, the Global FX Code may be more the exception than the rule in this framework. Based on an initiative led by the Bank for International Settlements, the Code reflects a commitment taken at central bank level.[84] The drafting work was substantially performed by the industry[85] but the level of regulatory supervision over the process was high; it is this arrangement that legitimates the Global FX Code in the eyes of the regulator, something which does not necessarily apply to all other industry-written codes.

However, these codes are not intended to impose any legal and regulatory obligations but rather function as a supplement to local rules.[86] The position of a regulator on the role which such industry-written codes should have may vary from one jurisdiction to another, creating discrepancies in interpreting applicable standards, and even generating uncertainty for financial players active in transnational contexts. The latter point is of course only relevant to codes which are global in scope.

The FCA has acknowledged that there is a rationale for setting higher standards through recognising the value of industry-written codes, and that reliance on these codes may extend the expectation of proper market conduct to unregulated markets.[87] But rightly in the authors' view, the FCA considers that these codes remain voluntary and are aimed at encouraging firms

---

[81]   Mark Carney, 'Reflections on Leadership in a Disruptive Age' (Speech at Regent's College, 19 February 2018).

[82]   Onora O'Neill, 'Lecture 1: Spreading Suspicion in a Question of Trust' (Reith Lectures, 2002).

[83]   Global Foreign Exchange Committee, *FX Global Code* (December 2017) https://www.globalfxc .org/fx_global_code.htm accessed on 5 February 2018.

[84]   Patrick Graham, 'Central Banks Launch Forex Market Code of Conduct' *Reuters* (25 May 2017).

[85]   James P Bergin, Senior Vice President of the Legal Group of the Federal Reserve Bank of New York, clearly explains in his speech the role of industry FX committees in this context: 'Generally composed of private sector market participants, these committees advise central banks on developments in the FX markets and engage on matters regarding the effective functioning of the market.' See: James P Bergin, 'The Launch of the FX Global Code' (Federal Reserve Bank of New York, 25 May 2017) www .newyorkfed.org/newsevents/speeches/2017/ber170525 accessed on 5 February 2018.

[86]   Ibid. Foreword, at 1.

[87]   The FCA, in fact, acknowledges that lack of appropriate standards of conduct in unregulated markets may also harm confidence on regulated markets: see FCA, *Consultation Paper on Industry Codes of Conduct and Discussion Paper on FCA Principle 5* (CP 17/37, November 2017) https://www .fca.org.uk/publication/consultation/cp17-37.pdf accessed on 5 February 2018.

to adopt higher standards that go beyond the minimum prescribed by binding regulations.[88] The link with principle 5,[89] however, is clear enough. The FCA intends to refer to these codes in order to clarify the scope of proper market conduct by issuance of a public statement, with the intention of triggering adherence to codes by firms. In the context of rules on senior managers and the certification regime, the FCA intends to rely on the industry codes to fill in the gaps with reference to areas in which it does not have an established framework of rules, effectively imposing general requirements for firms to look to these codes to determine proper market conduct,[90] thereby providing industry-written codes with a function which resembles a *lex specialis*.[91]

There is therefore something of a question as to how far codes are being relied on to fulfil a function which goes beyond the one traditionally expected of them. This new trend risks originating legal uncertainty over the effect of a regulatory framework composed of norms bearing different levels of prescriptive nature. Nevertheless, a clear and strong benefit linked to furthering the progressive creation of industry-written codes has been identified: 'Total regulation is bound to fail because it promotes a culture of complying with the letter of the law, not its spirit, and because authorities inevitably lag developments in fast-changing markets.'[92]

This offers a source of reflection and encourages us to think whether the main discussion on industry-written codes should rather be directed to examine how to make them progressively effective and, in practice, increasingly applicable to the specific issues which the targeted market is experiencing or may reasonably be experiencing in the near future. In other words, there is scope for leveraging on their uniqueness: they are particularly suitable to adapt to change and react time-wise, compared to other instruments which have a greater level of enforceability.

V.   HOW TO GIVE EFFECT TO THESE VALUES

5.1   Defining and Recognising Ethical Values

Before entering into the discussion as to how it is possible to give effect to ethical values, it is important to clarify the preliminary question: 'what are these values?' The problem also lies in the fact that ethical values often tend to be taken for granted in the business setting. This

---

[88]   Ibid. at 1.11–1.12.

[89]   Principle 5 refers to the rule 'You must observe proper standards of market conduct' set under the FCA Handbook, see: FCA Handbook, COCON 2.1.5 https://www.handbook.fca.org.uk/handbook accessed on 3 January 2018.

[90]   Ibid. note 87, at 3.18.

[91]   There is a substantial debate surrounding the choice of applying a specialised set of rules in a context by deviating from the way in which the same situation has been addressed in the past, advocating that the new scenario differs from the past one. The issue has been considered in detail under international law, an area which, similarly to financial law, shows scope for fragmentation due to its continuing evolving nature: see Martti Koskenniemi, 'Study on the Function and Scope of the Lex Specialis Rule and the Question of "self-contained Regimes": Preliminary Report: Addendum' (2004) UN 1-44.

[92]   Mark Carney, 'Turning Back the Tide' (Speech at FICC Markets Standard Board for its 2nd anniversary, 29 November 2017) https://www.bankofengland.co.uk/-/media/boe/files/speech/2017/turning-back-the -tide-speech-by-mark-carney.pdf?la=en&hash=E6DC8F0093FF3ED65C249C0B5A7968A453567CCE accessed on 7 February 2018.

observation applies alike to financial institutions as well as corporate firms, especially within business contexts in which the direct clients are not retail investors or consumers, as is the case within investment banks or multinational companies with no consumer dimension.

An FCA principle provides: 'A firm must observe proper standards of market conduct.'[93] The imposition of this duty from a firm's perspective is not self-explanatory. However, the underlying concept is powerful and finds its legitimation on the recognition of the important role that markets play: 'Though markets can be powerful drivers of prosperity, markets can go wrong. Left unattended, they are prone to instability, excess and abuse. Markets without the right standards or infrastructure are like cities without building codes, fire brigades or insurance.'[94] Thus, the interest in ensuring proper market conduct appears as twofold: on one side, it is a mutual expectation for counterparties that transact business with each other; on the other side, it represents a societal imperative, as the invisible hand theory in finance proved its limits in recent financial crises. There is a collective recognition, therefore, of the need for regulatory norms and control mechanisms to oversee financial market conduct in practical terms.

The current focus is on codifying the expectation for proper market conduct in a way which is detailed enough to be prescriptive and enforceable within specific areas, as in the fixed income, currency and commodities (FICC) markets. The purpose of the Fair and Effective Markets Review (FEMR) is to: 'Ensure proper market conduct is managed in FICC markets through monitoring compliance with all standards, formal and voluntary, under the Senior Managers and Certification Regimes.'[95]

Proper market conduct, of course, imposes a duty which may not appear as straight-forward as integrity or fairness; this is probably because proper market conduct is not *per se* an ethical value. In our minds, we may all have a vision of what integrity and fairness mean to us; but we develop an understanding of proper market conduct only by knowing the context in which it is expected. However, proper market conduct shares with these ethical values a common feature: it is often defined in interaction with other values.

Effective markets mean, in this context, undertaking transactions in a predictable way and in support of a broader non-financial economy; fair markets provide confidence that participants will behave with integrity.[96] Of course, the definition of fair and effective markets in the Review includes many other determinations, but these examples show that adding the connotations gives definition to the principle. With reference to fair markets, the definition of fairness may require inserting another ethical value into the picture, for example integrity. This highlights the fact that ethical values are not standalone; they do not work in isolation: they are inherently interrelated.

However, ethical values such as integrity and fairness have a stronger abstract dimension than proper market conduct and this can make them difficult to define. Each of us has an idea of what they represent but if we compare our individual perception, we may discover that the

---

[93]   FCA Handbook, PRIN 2.1.1 [5]. See also the matching principle applicable at the individual's level: FCA Handbook, COCON 2.1.1.

[94]   Mark Carney, 'Building Real Markets for the Good of the People' (10 June 2015) https://www.bankofengland.co.uk/speech/2015/building-real-markets-for-the-good-of-the-people accessed on 5 February 2018.

[95]   Fair and Effective Markets Review, *Final Report* (10 June 2015) at 7 https://www.bankofengland.co.uk/report/2015/fair-and-effective-markets-review---final-report accessed on 5 February 2018.

[96]   Ibid. at 18.

ideas diverge to a greater or lesser extent.[97] The attempt to give them a definition is both useful and misleading at same time: the benefit is that it encourages us to develop a common view of what we intend by these concepts; the limit is that there may be cases in which the definition is so narrow as to exclude fundamental aspects of what a certain ethical value should represent.

If we take the concept of integrity, the first principle of the FCA Handbook is: 'You must act with integrity.'[98] But what does this mean, in practice? And, how do you measure or determine the existence of integrity at both individual and firm level? There can be no firm answer to this at present, and probably never will be. Further, integrity represents one of those things you notice by its absence rather than presence: we have heard of situations showing lack of integrity, but we have not heard so much about regulators finding it. There is a professional standard under the PSB Chartered Banker Code of Professional Conduct which clearly prescribes: 'Treating all customers, colleagues and counterparties with respect and acting with integrity.'[99] Thus, this ethical value is setting professional standards as well.

The courts also expect to find adherence to this ethical value within the banking industry, as the following extract demonstrates: 'What this case has shown is the absence of that integrity that ought to characterise banking.'[100] Mr Justice Cooke placed honesty with integrity, and defined these values by reference to the standards set by ordinary reasonable and honest people. He referred to the 'maintenance of ordinary standards of honesty and integrity that are essential to the conduct of business and markets'.[101] This approach links good conduct with what is expected by ordinary reasonable people.

It again shows the interaction between ethical values, which seem engaged in a process of reciprocal definition: integrity and honesty are here presented as essential to ensure proper market conduct. To revert to the Review, proper market conduct in the FICC markets, in turn, means fair markets.

The best framework of regulation will not *per se* be sufficient to bring cultural change: 'integrity can neither be bought nor regulated. Even with the best possible framework of codes and principles, the soundest compensation schemes, and the most committed efforts to improve transparency, financiers – in both the public and private sectors – must consistently challenge themselves and the standards they uphold.'[102] The recognition that the solution does not lie with imposing rules was highlighted by Christine Lagarde, Managing Director of

---

[97]   This is consistent with Onora O'Neill's reflection on values and the problems they raise: 'The term "value" has risen in popularity but lost a lot of its point and weight during the last century . . . "Values" are now often seen as subjective, as something that individuals choose or reject, as projections of self or of individual autonomy, rather than as objective. Values are indeed commonly equated with preferences.' See: Onora O'Neill, 'What is Banking For?' (Federal Reserve Bank of New York, 20 October 2016) https://www.newyorkfed.org/medialibrary/media/governance-and-culture-reform/ONeill-Culture -Workshop-Remarks-10202016.pdf accessed on 5 February 2018.

[98]   FCA Handbook, COCON 2.1.1. See also the matching principle applicable at the firm's level: FCA Handbook, PRIN 2.1.1 [1].

[99]   Chartered Banker – Professional Standard Board, *The Chartered Banker Code of Professional Conduct* ('PSB Chartered Banker Code of Professional Conduct'), rule 1 https://www.charteredbanker .com/filemanager/root/site_assets/governance/the_chartered_banker_code_of_professional_conduct _47494.pdf accessed on 7 January 2018.

[100]   *Regina v. Tom Alexander W. Hayes* [2015] EWCA Crim 1944 [88].

[101]   [2015] EWCA Crim 1944 [32].

[102]   Mark Carney, 'Worthy of Trust? Law, Ethics and Culture in Banking' (Speech at the Banking Standards Board Panel, 21 March 2017).

the International Monetary Fund, who said: 'Yet, regulation alone cannot solve the problem. Whether something is right or wrong cannot be simply reduced to whether or not it is permissible under the law. What is needed is a culture that induces bankers to do the right thing even if nobody is watching.'[103]

This shows the shift of interest in considering ethical values. The rules of the game have been re-shaped, and a move towards expecting value-based behaviour within financial institutions has been made. How to deal with this move? The response of some investment firms is to begin the process of setting up an internal Ethics Committee. Others have it in place already.

5.2   Ethical Values and Firm's Values

In parallel with the ethical values that have been acknowledged in recent years, as discussed so far with particular reference to integrity, honesty and fairness, there are a firm's particular values, which may include other more business-oriented values such as team spirit, openness or commitment. These values are often contained in the Code of Conduct. The advantage of a voluntary approach of this kind is that it has the potential of encouraging good business practice without the disadvantage of further regulation, and without detracting from necessary competition and innovation. On the debit side, since it is voluntary, it may become a paper exercise.

A fair criticism of this approach is that without sanctions, there is no substance. As Daniel Tarullo, former Governor of the Federal Reserve Board, pointed out: 'one important determinant of behaviour is the shared expectation as to which of the stated values and rules of an organization will be supported and reinforced by management action, and which are generally regarded as window dressing.'[104] In other terms, it is often difficult for an external observer to understand what the actual culture is within a financial institution. What can we do to make these standards and values more real and visible? The standards are vital as a first step but not as an end point.

5.3   Establishing Leaders Within Firms

Governor Carney has said:

> As a leader you also need to be humble about success and honest about failure. Humility and honesty are essential to authenticity . . . Being authentic means doing what you say, and people knowing who you are . . . Authenticity is intimately connected with trust. People may not agree with all of your decisions, but they deserve to know why you made them. And your decisions will be easier to follow if people know what you stand for.'[105]

---

[103] Christine Lagarde, 'Ethics and Finance – Aligning Financial Incentives with Societal Objectives' (Speech at the Event hosted by the Institute for New Economic Thinking 'Finance and Society', 6 May 2015) https://www.imf.org/en/News/Articles/2015/09/28/04/53/sp050615 accessed on 5 February 2018.

[104] Daniel K Tarullo, 'Good Compliance, Not Mere Compliance' (Speech at the Federal Reserve Bank of New York Conference 'Reforming Culture and Behavior in the Financial Services Industry', New York, 20 October 2014) https://www.federalreserve.gov/newsevents/speech/tarullo20141020a .html accessed on 5 February 2018.

[105] Mark Carney, 'Reflections on Leadership in a Disruptive Age' (Speech at Regent's College, 19 February 2018). The qualities that leaders should have are stated as: 'Ambition. Purpose. Clarity. And Humility. Not all of these qualities are ever visible in any leader, certainly never at the same time.'

The inference is that leaders that instil trust are in the position to develop teams which are more motivated and inclined to observe the rules rather than cheat. Of course, whether it is possible to instil humility is an open question, and for this reason, cultural changes remain the key.

5.4   Reputational Sanctions

There is a price to pay for behaviour perceived as unethical in reputation terms. Reputational sanctions may be real. On the other hand, as the financial crisis recedes, there can be no guarantee that the effect of this will continue. One reason that pre-crisis behavioural lapses were not treated with the attention they deserved was that, overall, the financial system was seen as working well, with markets such as the derivative, market seen as distributing risk. Notwithstanding the changes in this field undertaken at international level after the global financial crisis, it has been said that: 'despite regulations, supervisory focus, and firms' own efforts, misconduct risk persists. In recent years, for example, high profile incidents of misconduct emerged related to reference rates, foreign exchange trading, and retail banking sales practices.'[106]

Of course, the penalties may go far beyond merely reputational damage. In aggregate, large financial firms have in recent years paid fines in excess of $320 billion worldwide in connection with employee misconduct,[107] which is a huge figure. It shows that reputational sanctions are certainly not *per se* considered as a solution to misconduct risk. On the other hand, the two are linked in that the size of the sanction can itself engender reputational damage.

5.5   Banks Undertaking Practical Steps

There are a number of concrete means to provide support for a more ethical culture and avoid these outcomes. There are practical steps that can be taken within institutions, some of which are already in place. US banks typically have ethics 'hot-lines' that can give the caller anonymity.

The Salz Review commissioned by Barclays Bank (see previous section) makes a number of recommendations. These include learning programmes for staff, targets against which to assess progress on embedding the values necessary to build a strong ethical culture, regular updates to the code, and annual attestation by employees as to their compliance with the code. The Review recommends that in all recruiting, but particularly for senior managers, the bank should look beyond a candidate's financial performance and include an assessment of their fit with its values and culture.

As previously anticipated, there may also be merit in having a board-level ethics committee, perhaps with a broader CSR remit, as is already in place in a number of institutions.

As regards remuneration, the UK FSA's Remuneration Code requires taking into account non-financial criteria to assess individual performance for the purpose of remuneration, including 'metrics relating to conduct, which should comprise a substantial portion of the

---

[106]   Gary Gensler, 'Remarks of Chairman Gary Gensler on Libor before the Global Financial Markets Association's Future of Global Benchmarks Conference' (23 February 2013).

[107]   Stephanie Chaly and others, 'Misconduct Risk, Culture, and Supervision' (Federal Reserve Bank of New York, December 2017) https://www.newyorkfed.org/medialibrary/media/governance-and -culture-reform/2017-whitepaper.pdf accessed on 5 February 2018.

non-financial criteria'.[108] The identified non-financial risk metrics include 'effective risk management and compliance with the regulatory system'.[109] Some financial institutions have voluntarily gone further than this. Morgan Stanley, for example, has altered the provisions in senior banker remuneration to enable claw-backs where, inter alia, there are violations of the firm's ethical standards.[110]

5.6   Promoting Regulatory Intervention

Another approach is to involve regulators by focusing on the two areas of behaviour within the banking industry that have come in for particular adverse comment since the crisis. One has to do with the unfair treatment of counterparties in financial transactions, whether based on information asymmetries, or otherwise; and the other has to do with socially excessive risk-taking.

In these respects at least, there is a case for financial regulators to engage with banks' internal systems and processes, not with a view to prescribing the content of codes of ethics, and certainly not adding a further layer of rules and regulations, but with a view to monitoring how ethical considerations are carried forward within organisations.[111] This approach would allow bodies to develop their own solutions, with the regulator concerning itself with broad objectives and the adequacy of the processes in place to achieve them. Such an approach has been suggested by one of the two authors (and others) elsewhere.[112] The initiatives undertaken by the FCA in this area show a concrete move towards this process of engagement: in fact, the FCA has been establishing, on the basis of industry-based feedback which steps financial institutions are taking to identify conduct risk within their organisation'.[113] On the other side, the FCA has also engaged actively in the process of randomly testing the knowledge that firm's employees have within business lines, of the notion of conduct risk endorsed by their financial institution.

This kind of intervention is in line with what other jurisdictions have been doing. The Netherlands represents a good example. De Nederlandsche Bank (DNB), which is the Dutch central bank and the financial authority for prudential regulation in the Netherlands, has been undertaking an initiative which started in 2010 and is aimed at taking into account behavioural patterns and the cultural aspects of financial institutions while assessing them. The premises on which this initiative has been based are three and each is consistent with what has been said above; increasing rules and regulations is not enough, the importance of assessing behaviour and culture is its connection with public trust and financial stability, and behaviour and culture are part of sound business operation.[114] The report that the DNB issued in 2015 testifies to the success of the initiative:

---

[108]   FCA Handbook, Remuneration Code SYSC 19A.3.37 G 03/05/2017.

[109]   Ibid.

[110]   SEC, *Schedule 14A: Proxy Statement Pursuant to Section 14(a) of the Securities Exchange Act of 1934 – Morgan Stanley*, at 28–29 (Washington DC, 5 April 2012) DEF 14A.

[111]   In a different context see: Julia Black, *Rules and Regulators* (Clarendon Press, 1997).

[112]   Awrey et al (n. 18).

[113]   FCA, 'Conduct risk programs' (Questions feedback, April 2017) https://www.fca.org.uk/firms/5 -conduct-questions-feedback/conduct-risk-programmes accessed on 18 December 2017.

[114]   De Nederlandsche Bank, *Supervision of Behaviour and Culture – Foundations, Practice & Future Developments* (Eurosysteem, 2015) 30.

Since we started this type of supervision in 2010, we have developed and tested a method for supervising behaviour and culture at financial organisations that has proved to be successful. We have been able to identify and assess risks relating to behaviour and culture, and – in most cases – mitigate them.[115]

Whether this success is quite as substantial and whether it could be replicated in other jurisdictional settings is hard to assess without analysing the methods used and the extent of concrete change linked to the outcomes to which reference is made. But the Netherlands' experience is valuable nevertheless.

5.7   Addressing the Transactional Perspective

In financial transactions, behavioural objectives could include a commitment to treat counterparties fairly, and as well as sophisticated and retail customers. This would involve the fair disclosure of relevant information about products and refraining from marketing products that even sophisticated market participants would be unlikely to understand and price accurately. Such objectives would go well beyond what is currently required. The FCA Principles for example provide that the duty is towards clients and is expressed as: 'You must pay due regard to the interests of customers and treat them fairly.'[116] As has been pointed out, the fact that counterparties may not be considered as clients constitutes an issue itself.[117] There is no clarity over this point.

5.8   Moving Towards a Solid Risk Culture

As regards risk taking, the emphasis would be on taking externalities seriously, that is, paying regard to the adverse effects of particular activities on particular institutions and more generally on society. The objective would be to foster a culture in which systemic risk taking is identified and avoided, and the consequences are better understood. As previously discussed, moving towards a solid risk culture represents a regulatory expectation in this context which is real and difficult to ignore on financial institutions' side, especially in light of: the endorsement of regulatory norms which place strong emphasis on individuals' accountability, as is the case with the introduction of the Senior Managers Regime in the UK; and, across Europe, the establishment of a legal framework under CRD IV and MiFID II ,which requests that firms have, as second line of defence, a compliance function which acts independently from the business, bases its activities on risk-based assessments, and reports directly to the management board.

---

[115]   Ibid., at 16.

[116]   FCA Handbook, COCON 2.1.4. See also the matching principle applicable at the firm's level: FCA Handbook, PRIN 2.1.1 [6].

[117]   Thomas Baxter, 'The Rewards of an Ethical Culture' (Remarks at the Bank of England, London, 20 January 2015) https://www.newyorkfed.org/newsevents/speeches/2015/bax012015 accessed on 5 February 2018.

5.9   Enhancing Culture with Industry-Based Initiatives

In jurisdictions like the United Kingdom, it can be observed that substantial and valuable work in this field has been carried on by private bodies which do not have statutory powers, and which while to a greater or lesser degree representing the financial industry, maintain a level of independence and impartiality.[118]

The UK Banking Standards Board (BSB) was established in 2015 and does not act as a lobbyist for the banks and the building societies that are members. It does not attempt to do the work of the regulators, and it does not handle customer complaints. It issues annual reviews which identify challenges on the basis of its own assessments. These reports provide a useful benchmark to identify the shift of concerns within financial institutions in the previous year. For example, one of the BSB's original objectives consisted in encouraging the adoption of whistleblowing protocols, and the 2016–17 annual review reports that 'Nearly three in ten employees across all firms would be worried about the negative consequences for them if they raised concerns.'[119]

It is this link between the aims and the facts and data collected through insight from the industry that allows the BSB to provide the public with a practical viewpoint.[120] The findings under the report are then used to develop the BSB's objective of the following year. In this context, 2017 objectives included, for example: 'understanding and helping to address an apparent mismatch between the values espoused by the firm and the way that some employees see business being done'; and 'helping to develop a culture within the banking sector of responsibility and accountability rather than of blame'.[121]

Similarly, the FICC Markets Standard Board (FMSB) was established in 2015 as a private sector response to the conduct problems revealed in global wholesale FICC markets after the financial crisis. FMSB has only one ambition: to help raise standards of conduct in global wholesale markets and thereby make those markets more transparent, fair and effective. It is the subject of another chapter of this book written by its Chair, Mark Yallop.

---

[118]   BSB, 'What is the BSB' (*Banking Standards Board*, Website) https://www.bankingstandardsboard .org.uk/what-is-the-bsb/ accessed on 5 February 2018.

[119]   Banking Standards Board, *Annual Review 2016/2017* https://www.bankingstandardsboard.org.uk/ annual-review-2016-2017/ accessed on 2 December 2017.

[120]   In this context, the 2016–17 findings on ethical and honest conduct within banks are of interest: 'Nine out of ten employees across firms say that their colleagues act in an honest and ethical way. At the same time, however, 12% see instances where unethical behaviour is rewarded, 13% see it as difficult to get ahead in their careers without flexing their ethical standards, and 18% see people in their organisation turn a blind eye to inappropriate behaviour.' See: ibid., *Annual Review 2016/17* at 18.

[121]   Ibid., *Annual Review 2016/17* at 28–9.

VI.   CONCLUSIONS

The issues raised in this chapter are current issues, not theoretical ones. A number of conclusions can be expressed.

(1) The idea that ethics, and in particular an ethical culture, has a place in finance, is widespread. It is seen to be an essential adjunct to the law as it applies in the form of financial regulation, and has the support of national and international institutions.

(2) Financial institutions seem increasingly comfortable with his idea. Whether this is an involuntary response to public pressure or is the result of corporate social responsibility principles mandated by the law or is simply a reflection of a good business case, does not matter, because the potential for improved standards is there.

(3) It is widely recognised that promoting ethical behaviour within an institution is a matter of culture. This cannot be legislated for, and comes through adoption by example, particularly from a bank's leadership. The importance of fostering values implies real leadership.

(4) One means by which banks have sought to do this is through 'codes of ethics' or documents having similar effect. The significance of these documents is that they represent an attempt by institutions to articulate their own view of what is meant by 'ethical conduct'. This is important, because what conduct is ethical is not always easy to pin down in the highly competitive commercial environment of international finance. It is important that employees take ownership of the firm's codes, and there are standard means of encouraging this.

(5) These codes should not however be treated in the same way as legal obligations or seen as quasi-binding as is the case with formal guidance issued by regulators. The reasons for this are twofold. First, the duties are necessarily expressed at a high level, and can be difficult to define. Second, they are properly treated as aspirational in nature, in that they implicitly acknowledge that standards aimed for are not necessarily achieved.

(6) Common themes appear to revolve around fair treatment and the avoidance of socially excessive risk-taking.

(7) There are reputational incentives for institutions to seek to implement the values expressed in such codes. There are also practical steps that can be taken within institutions to promote an ethical culture.

(8) There is a case for financial regulators to engage with banks' internal systems and processes, not with a view to prescribing the content of codes of ethics, and certainly not by adding a further layer of rules and regulations, but with a view to monitoring how ethical considerations are carried forward within the organisation.

(9) An example of practical support for such standards is to be found in the United Kingdom's Banking Standards Board and the FICC Markets Standard Board.

According to the CFA Institute/Edelman '*Investor Trust Study 2013*',[122] investors cited compliance with a voluntary code of ethics and maintaining independence and objectivity as the actions that matter most. The President of the CFA Institute commented on the 'significant

---

[122] CFA Institute and Edelman, 'Investor Trust Study 2013' http://www.cfainstitute.org/learning/future/getinvolved/Documents/cfa_institute_edelman_investor_trust_study.pdf accessed on 5 February 2018.

opportunity for investment professionals and firms to actively build a culture where ethical practices are valued as highly as investment performance'.[123] As the CFA Institute/Edelman Investor Trust Study 2016 says: 'Ethical standards matter. Institutional investors, with their complex constituencies and a clear focus on risk management, hold their investment managers to the highest ethical standards.'[124] This point, read in conjunction with that which says that acting in an ethical manner represents the most important attribute of a firm,[125] shows that for financial institutions promoting an ethical culture is not optional. It has always been the hallmark of good business.

---

[123] CFA Institute and Edelman, 'CFA Institute/Edelman, Study: Only Half of Investors Trust Investment Firms to Do What is Right' (Press Release, New York, 14 August 2013) www.edelman .com/news/cfa-instituteedelman-study-only-half-of-investors-trust-investment-firms-to-do-what-is-right accessed on 5 February 2018.

[124] CFA Institute and Edelman, 'From Trust to Loyalty – A Global Survey of What Investors Want' (2016).

[125] Ibid.

3.   Ethical foundations of financial law

Rosa M. Lastra and Marcelo J. Sheppard

INTRODUCTION

The aim of this chapter is to understand the ethical foundations of financial law, drawing on legal and philosophical considerations. The chapter is divided into six sections. Section I examines justice and financial law. Section II briefly reviews the notion of common good and the principles of social life. Section III analyses the behavioural causes of the Great Financial Crisis (GFC) and how regulators issued financial standards based on the principle of integrity. Section IV examines the concept of prudential supervision (micro and macro) from the perspective of prudence. Section V considers the nature of human rights in the context of financial law. Section VI recommends a regulatory framework for the financial industry based on the principles of justice, prudence and integrity.

I.   JUSTICE AND FINANCIAL LAW

After the Great Financial Crisis one of the relevant issues that has emerged for financial actors is the question of the telos or end of financial law. As Christine Lagarde wrote in 2015:

> The theme of ethics in finance is one that we have pushed for some time now. The goal? To revive the telos of the financial sector – its purpose and broader responsibility to society. After all, the goal of the financial sector must be not only to maximize the wealth of its shareholders, but to enrich society by supporting economic activity and creating value and jobs – to ultimately improve the well-being of people.[1]

In order to reach or rediscover the telos of financial law we need to understand which are the ethical foundations of financial law. Teleology is the 'The explanation of phenomena in terms of the purpose they serve rather than of the cause by which they arise'.[2] According to Aristotle a right action would be that which conduces to the attainment of the human's own good or telos (end), while the action which does not conduce to one's own good would be a wrong action.[3] In Book 1 of *The Nicomachean Ethics* (Ethics) he states 'Every art and every inquiry, and similarly every action and pursuit, is thought to aim at some good; and for this reason the good has rightly been declared to be that at which all things aim'.[4] What is good for man is

---

[1]   C. Lagarde 'The Role of Personal Accountability in Reforming Culture and Behavior in the Financial Services Industry', IMF (2015) http://www.imf.org/en/News/Articles/2015/09/28/04/53/sp110515 accessed 2 March 2018.

[2]   Oxford Dictionaries https://en.oxforddictionaries.com/definition/teleology accessed 2 March 2018.

[3]   F. Copleston *A History of Philosophy, Vol 1 Greece and Rome* (Continuum 1946) 332.

[4]   Aristotle *The Nicomachean Ethics of Aristotle* Sir D. Ross (Translator) (OUP 1963) 1.

generally accepted to be happiness.[5] And laws are just when they tend to produce happiness to the community: 'we call those acts (laws) just that tend to produce and preserve happiness and its components for the political society'.[6]

The Aristotelian tradition emphasises the importance of intellectual[7] and moral virtues. The latter need to be exercised by repetition of the corresponding acts and come as a result of a habit.[8] Virtue is a mean between two extremes. In one extreme there is an excess and in the other there is a defect. For instance, with regard to feelings of fear and confidence, courage is the mean, while fearlessness and being a coward are defects.[9]

For Aristotle, virtues are dispositions to act in 'specific ways for specific reasons. Education into the virtues involves the mastery, the disciplining and the transformations of desires and feelings. This education enables one to exercise the virtues . . . enjoying that kind of life which constitutes the good and the best life for human beings.'[10]

In Book Five of the Ethics, Aristotle talks about justice. Under justice he distinguishes on the one hand the 'just' as what is lawful or universal justice and, on the other hand, the 'just' as the fair and equal or particular Justice. 'Justice is often thought to be the greatest of virtues, and "neither evening nor morning star" is so wonderful'; 'proverbially in justice is every virtue comprehended'.[11] And it is 'complete virtue in its fullest sense because it is the actual exercise of complete virtue. It is complete because he who poses it can exercise his virtue not only in himself but towards his neighbor also'.[12]

Justice in a universal sense is used 'for the exercise of all the citizens in their relations with other citizens'.[13] Justice in a particular sense is distributive and corrective or rectificatory.[14] Corrective justice has the function of restoring the unjust action,[15] while distributive justice has the function of fulfilling the means by geometrical proportion: 'The just is the proportional; the unjust is what violates the proportion.'[16] According to Aristotle, equity is a corrective of legal justice. 'The reason is that all law is universal but about some things it is not possible to make a universal statement which shall be correct . . . And this is the nature of the equitable, a correction of law where it is defective owing to its universality.' Also, he explains that because

---

[5]   The US Declaration of Independence in 1776 refers to the pursuit of happiness: 'We hold these truths to be self-evident, that all men are created equal, that they are endowed by their Creator with certain unalienable Rights, that among these are Life, Liberty and the pursuit of Happiness.' *Declaration of Independence: A Transcription*, National Archives https://www.archives.gov/founding-docs/declaration -transcript accessed 2 March 2018.

[6]   Aristotle above note 4, II29b 17 108.

[7]   Intellectual virtues are Science, Art, Practical Wisdom, Intuitive Reason, Philosophical Reason, Goodness in deliberation, Judgement. Ibid 137–158.

[8]   Some special moral virtues listed and analysed by Aristotle are: Courage, Temperance, Liberality, Magnificence, Good temper, Friendliness, Truthfulness, Ready wit, and Justice. Ibid 28.

[9]   Aristotle above note 4, II06 b36 39.

[10]   A. MacIntyre *Whose Justice? Which Rationality?* (University of Notre Dame Press 2003) 101.

[11]   Aristotle above note 4, II29 b13 108.

[12]   Ibid.

[13]   A. MacIntyre above note 10, 101.

[14]   Ibid.

[15]   Ibid 104.

[16]   Aristotle above note 4, II31 b14 114.

of this there is a need for not only laws but decrees, 'since the rule adapts itself to the shape of the stone and is not rigid, and so too the decree is adapted to the facts'.[17]

In Book I of Politics, Aristotle discusses the role of money in human life. He states it is an error to search for more and more money without limit since those skills 'are eager for life, but not for the good life . . . For where enjoyment consists in excess, men look for that skill which produces the excess that is enjoyed . . . [they] turn their skills into skills of acquiring goods, as though that were the end and everything had to serve that end'.[18] In Ethics Aristotle identifies two vices on the extremes of justice, which are 'that of acting as to aggrandize oneself, whether one's desert entitle one to it or not', and 'acting so as to suffer injustice voluntarily'.[19] The former is named pleonexia.

Pleonexia 'denotes an excessive desire to get more, which violates canons of distributive fairness within self-conscious communities'.[20] Hobbes was the first to translate and define the term as 'a desire for more than their share'.[21] MacIntyre believes that in most cases the injustice would imply taking more that one's share, but the real meaning of pleonexia is just 'no less than simple acquisitiveness'.[22] According to McIntyre the translation of pleonexia as 'greed' is misleading since that word denotes a type of desire, whereas pleonexia 'names a disposition to engage in a type of activity'.[23] David Ross refers to pleonexia as 'grasping', which according to the Oxford Dictionary is defined as 'avaricious' that is: 'Having or showing an extreme greed for wealth or material gain.'[24]

Acting with pleonexia has a wide impact on society as a whole. 'In Aristotle's presentation, greed for wealth is an important feature of social strife, but must be appropriately located within the web of other concerns that animate civic conflict.'[25] When financial sector actors behave with pleonexia in general they take a share that belongs to others, to the detriment of the common good. To withstand this temptation financial actors need to have fortitude or courage.[26] Fortitude implies a certain degree of pain 'for it is harder to face what is painful than to abstain from what is pleasant'.[27] Only the vulnerable that acknowledge their limitations can be brave.[28]

The late Aristotelian tradition interpreted by Aquinas emphasises the importance of temperance, which also complements justice. *Temperantia* means *quies animi* or 'serenity of spirit'.[29] As Pieper says 'the purpose and goal of temperantia is man's inner order, from which alone, this "serenity of spirit" can flow forth'.[30]

---

[17] Ibid 133.

[18] Aristotle *Politics* 1257 b40 (Penguin Classics 1992) 85.

[19] A. MacIntyre above note 10, 111.

[20] R. Balot 'Aristotle's Critique of Phaleas: Justice, Equality, and Pleonexia' Hermes, 129. Bd., H. 1 [2001], 32–44.

[21] T. Hobbes, *Leviathan* (first published 1651 Penguin, 1985) 15.

[22] A. MacIntyre above note 10, 111.

[23] Ibid 112.

[24] Oxford Dictionaries https://en.oxforddictionaries.com/definition/avaricious accessed 2 March 2018.

[25] R. Balot above note 20, 32–44.

[26] Aristotle above note 4, III9 48.

[27] Ibid.

[28] J. Pieper *The Four Cardinal Virtues* (Notre Dame 2010) 117.

[29] T. Aquinas *Summa Teologica* II, II, 141, 2 obj 2.

[30] J. Pieper above note 28, 147.

The implications of this for modern financial markets remain most relevant. Indeed, while the social status of bankers, fund managers, and other financiers grows in part due to talent and in part due to high earnings, exercising humility and magnanimity (which derive from this *temperantia*) is vital in order to serve clients and the society as a whole.

II.   COMMON GOOD AND PRINCIPLES OF SOCIAL LIFE

Common good in a political community can be identified as the 'securing of a whole ensemble of material and other conditions that tend to favour the realization by each individual of the community, of his or her personal development'.[31]

Martin Rhonheimer advocates the benefits of market economics for the common good:

> [D]uring the last two centuries, the capitalist free market economy and free trade without tariff barriers have continuously improved the conditions of life of all social levels, always and everywhere. Conversely all kinds of state interventionism, bureaucratic planning of the economy and socialism have deteriorated conditions of life and welfare of all social levels, always and everywhere.[32]

However, he suggests that 'we need a vision of the common good that is not simply economic, but much more integral'.[33] This vision requires a re-evaluation of the relationship between the state and the market, a defining issue in political and economic theory, which determines the role of law and regulation in the financial sector.

The state is 'an association [community[34]] intended to enable members, in their households and the kinships, to live well, its purpose is a perfect and self-sufficient life . . . not for the purpose of living together but for the sake of noble actions'.[35]

In Politics, Aristotle affirms that 'man is by nature a political animal *[zoon politikon]*'[36] which implies the need of the community to fulfill its happiness.

Maritain explains:

> There is a correlation between this notion of the person as social unit and the notion of the common good as the end of the social whole. They imply one another. The common good is common because it is received in persons, each one of whom is as a mirror of the whole . . . The end of society, therefore, is neither the individual good nor the collection of the individual goods of each of the persons who constitute it. Such a conception would dissolve society as such to the advantage of its parts, and would amount to either a frankly anarchistic conception, or the old disguised anarchistic conception

---

[31]   J. Finnis *Natural Law and Natural Rights* (Second edition, OUP 2011) 154.

[32]   See M. Rhonheimer 'Capitalism, Free Market Economy, and the Common Good: The Role of the State in the Economy', Chapter 1 in Martin Schlag and Juan Andrés Mercado (eds.) *Free Markets and the Culture of Common Good* (Springer 2012) 23.

[33]   Ibid 38. 'Liberalism is not a political and economic doctrine aiming at money making, maximum productivity and profit. It is part of a vision of society based on freedom and which sees in freedom an essential part of the common good'.

[34]   J. Finnis *Aquinas: Moral, Political and Legal Theory* (OUP 2004) 222.

[35]   Aristotle above note 18, 1281 a2-4, 1992 198.

[36]   'The real difference between man and other animals is that humans alone have perception of good and evil, just and unjust, etc. It is the sharing of a common view in these matters that makes a household a state.' Aristotle ibid, 1253 aI-3, 1253 a18-22.

of individualistic materialism in which the whole function of the city is to safeguard the liberty of each; thus giving to the strong full freedom to oppress the weak.[37]

In order to respect human dignity and human initiative, the law should let different groups (family, societies, clubs, associations, local governments, etc.) fulfil their own initiatives without being oppressed by a superior or centralised organisation. In this sense it can be said that 'the principle of subsidiarity is a principle of justice'.[38] 'Subsidiarity is the process by which the state helps private and intermediate groups attain their legitimate ends, never supplanting their initiative, only facilitating it.'[39] An example of this principle can be found in the principle of subsidiarity in the European Union.[40]

An expression of subsidiarity is the principle of participation, where every member of the political community is not only invited but has the right to participate in the construction of the community they live in. This is a corollary of man being a *zoon politikon*.[41]

Another dimension of the social dimension of human beings is the principle of solidarity. According to Booth, 'The concept of solidarity is important because individuals are born into societies with a duty to care for other members of society. Solidarity is a virtue which involves a deep-seated concern for others.'[42] However, this should not be an excuse to create 'over-arching welfare states' since 'solidarity is first and foremost a sense of responsibility on the part of everyone with regard to everyone, and it cannot therefore be merely delegated to the State'.[43]

III.   BEHAVIOURAL CAUSES OF THE GFC AND ADOPTION OF FINANCIAL ETHICAL STANDARDS IN RESPONSE TO THE CRISIS

Complex situations rarely have unique causes.[44] The 2007–9 GFC is no exception. It is possible to divide the explanations for the crisis into ten groups. These are not mutually exclusive. It is conceivable that they all played a part: (1) Macro-economic imbalances; (2) Lax monetary

---

[37]   J. Maritain *The Person and the Common Good* John J. Fitzgerald (Translator) (Charles Scribner's sons 1947) https://maritain.nd.edu/jmc/etext/CG.HTM accessed 2 March 2018.
[38]   J. Finnis above note 31, 169. Aristotle states that the law should be able to 'make citizens good and just'. Aristotle *Politics*, 1280 b11 (Penguin Classics 1992) 197.
[39]   P. Booth 'The Environment, the Common Good and the Economic Way of Thinking' in P. Booth (ed.) *Catholic Social Teaching and the Market Economy* (The Institute of Economic Affairs 2007).
[40]   'The principle of subsidiarity means that action should only be taken at EU level when the desired objectives cannot be effectively achieved by means of action taken at national or regional level'. UK Parliament, Lords Select Committee (2017) https://www.parliament.uk/business/committees/committees-a-z/lords-select/eu-select-committee-/committee-work/parliament-2017/subsidiarity/ accessed 2 March 2018. According to O'Brien, 'This (principle of subsidiarity) is different from the concept of subsidiarity that is supposed to operate within the European Union, where the higher governmental structures determine aims and then are supposed to require the lower structures to pursue those aims', P. Booth above note 39, 52.
[41]   Aristotle above note 18, 1253aI-3.
[42]   P. Booth above note 39, 37.
[43]   Ibid.
[44]   This section of the chapter draws on R. Lastra and G. Wood 'The Crisis of 2007–09: Nature, Causes, and Reactions', Journal of International Economic Law [2010].

policy; (3) Regulatory and supervisory failures; (4) Too big to fail doctrine and distorted incentives; (5) Excesses of securitisation; (6) Unregulated firms, lightly regulated firms and the shadow banking system; (7) Corporate governance failures; (8) Risk management failures, excessive leverage and excessive complexity; (9) The 'usual suspects': greed, euphoria and other human traits; (10) Faulty economic theories.[45] The first four groups put the blame on the authorities – governments, regulators, central bankers. The second five blame mainly the markets – financial products, managers, risk, greed, leverage. The last group (faulty theories) blames economists.[46]

As regards 'the usual suspects': greed, euphoria, human frailty are always factors in both crisis and non-crisis situations. But the 'boom' phenomenon with which euphoria often gets associated (inevitably followed – as history teaches us – by a 'bust') is dangerously associated with excessive 'group think' and 'herd behaviour'.

The 'unbridled greed' – or pleonexia to which we referred above – the system of incentives that rewarded the pursuit of excessive profits, while not appropriately internalising the costs of losses was partly at fault. The 'too big to fail' doctrine (and its variants of too interconnected, too complex, etc.) contributed to this. While it is beyond the domain of this chapter to discuss corporate governance issues, suffice it to say that shareholders must surely take responsibility for management decisions.

As Christine Lagarde emphasises:

> Reckless behavior was followed by episodes of misconduct that persisted well after the onset of the crisis – from rigging of interest rates and exchange rates to malfeasance and governance failures . . . These actions tear at the very fabric of the financial industry. In the process, the financial industry's most valuable asset – trust – became its biggest casualty. Public opinion as regards the integrity of the financial system is still the lowest in a very long time. According to a 2014 Harris Poll, up to 45 percent of the people rated the overall reputation of the industry as negative. The industry ranks third from the bottom after government and tobacco. This is cause for serious concern.[47]

Following the GFC, there has been a multiplicity of regulatory responses at the national, regional and international level. For the purposes of this chapter it is worth recalling a few. In 2012, the UK Parliament established a Commission as a result of the LIBOR scandal, to examine the professional standards and culture in the UK financial sector and to make recommendations that would help to build new legislation on the matter.[48] The Chairman of the Parliamentary Commission on Banking Standards, Andrew Tyrie MP, stated in the final report:

> Taxpayers and customers have lost out. The economy has suffered. The reputation of the financial sector has been gravely damaged. Trust in banking has fallen to a new low . . . Prudential and conduct

---

[45]   Ibid.

[46]   'There is nothing worse than an economist who only knows economics – except perhaps a moral philosopher who knows no economics at all', P.J. Boetke *Living Economics. Yesterday, Today and Tomorrow*, AEI (The Independent Institute 2012) 32.

[47]   C. Lagarde above note 1.

[48]   See UK Parliament, Joint Select Committee 'Banking Commission publishes report on changing banking for good' https://www.parliament.uk/business/committees/committees-a-z/joint-select/professional-standards-in-the-banking-industry/news/changing-banking-for-good-report/ accessed 2 March 2018.

failings have many shared causes but there is no single solution that can restore trust in the industry . . . A lack of personal responsibility has been commonplace throughout the industry. Senior figures have continued to shelter behind an accountability firewall . . . Risks and rewards in banking have been out of kilter. Given the misalignment of incentives, it should be no surprise that deep lapses in banking standards have been commonplace . . . It is not just bankers that need to change. The actions of regulators and Governments have contributed to the decline in standards . . . Governments need to get on with the job of implementing these reforms. Regulators and supervisors need rigorously to enforce them.[49]

The Commission recommended some changes in regulation including: (1) A new 'Senior Persons Regime', replacing the 'Approved Persons Regime', reinforcing the ownership of responsibility by senior individuals, based on enhanced personal accountability; (2) 'A new licensing regime underpinned by Banking Standards Rules'; (3) 'A new criminal offence for Senior Persons of reckless misconduct in the management of a bank, carrying a custodial sentence'; and (4) A new remuneration code, among others.[50]

In the UK, in 2014 the Financial Conduct Authority (FCA) published the Financial Conduct Handbook, which includes the Principle for Business (PRIN) standards: (1) Integrity; (2) Skill, care and diligence; (3) Management and control; (4) financial prudence; (5) Market conduct; (6) Customers' interests; (7) Client communications; (8) Conflicts of interests; (9) Customers and relationships of trust; (10) A firm must arrange adequate protection for clients' assets when it is responsible for them; and (11) Cooperation with regulators.[51]

The same Financial Handbook includes standards for Senior Management Arrangements and Control Systems (SYNC), The Code of Conduct for Staff sourcebook, part of the Handbook in High Level Standards (COCON) and the Statements of Principle and Code of Practice for Approved Persons (APER).[52]

The Prudential Regulation Authority (PRA) adopted in 2014 eight Fundamental Rules:

1) A firm must conduct its business with integrity; 2) A firm must conduct its business with due skill, care and diligence; 3) A firm must act in a prudent manner; 4) A firm must at all times maintain adequate financial resources; 5) A firm must have effective risk strategies and risk management systems;

---

[49]   Ibid.

[50]   Ibid.

[51]   (1) Integrity – a firm must conduct its business with integrity; (2) skill, care and diligence – a firm must conduct its business with due skill, care and diligence; (3) management and control – a firm must take reasonable care to organise and control its affairs responsibly and effectively with adequate risk management systems; (4) financial prudence – a firm must maintain adequate financial resources; (5) market conduct – a firm must observe proper standards of market conduct; (6) customers' interests – a firm must pay due regard to the interests of its customers and treat them fairly; (7) client communications – a firm must pay due regard to the information needs of its clients and communication information to them in a way which is clear, fair and not misleading; (8) conflicts of interests – a firm must manage conflicts of interest fairly both between itself and its customers and between a customer and another client; (9) customers and relationships of trust – a firm must take reasonable care to ensure the suitability of its advice and discretionary decisions for any customer who is entitled to rely upon its judgement; (10) a firm must arrange adequate protection for clients' assets when it is responsible for them; and (11) relations with regulators – a firm must deal with its regulators in an open and cooperative way and disclose anything that would be reasonably expected. See *FCA Handbook. Principles for Businesses* Financial Conduct Authority (2018) https://www.handbook.fca.org.uk/handbook/PRIN/2/?view=chapter accessed 2 March 2018.

[52]   Ibid.

6) A firm must organize and control its affairs responsibly and effectively; 7) A firm must deal with its regulators in an open and cooperative way and must disclose to the PRA appropriately anything relating to the firm of which the PRA would reasonably expect notice; 8) A firm must prepare for resolution so, if the need arises, it can be resolved in an orderly manner with a minimum disruption of critical services.[53]

In April 2017 the Bank of England issued the UK Money Markets Code which supersedes the NIPS Code.[54] It states: 'The ethical and professional behaviour of UK Market Participants underpins the fairness and integrity of the market . . . Applying judgement is fundamental to acting ethically and professionally, and both firms and individuals acting as UK Market Participants should be guided by the high-level principles'. UK Market Participants should: (1) Act honestly in dealings with other participants; (2) Act transparently with other participants; and (3) Act with integrity, not participating in, and fighting 'questionable practices and behaviours'.[55]

It also states that 'Maintaining high standards of behaviour is the responsibility of: (a) firms . . ., (b) senior and front-line management . . ., and (c) individuals, who when dealing in the UK Markets should expect to be held accountable for unethical behaviour, and, if in any doubt, should seek advice where appropriate'.[56]

The integrity principle is now a key principle of inspiration of positive ethical financial standards. Integrity – which means acting honestly – is horizontal to every virtue. In the financial sector, the virtues of justice (especially avoiding pleonexia) and prudence are key both to authorities and financial market participants, while prudence is crucial for regulators.

IV.   PRUDENCE AND REGULATORY RESPONSES

One of the causes of the crisis was the failure by regulators and supervisors before 2007 to address the safety and soundness of the financial system as a whole. A revised framework for micro prudential supervision and the adoption of macro prudential policies or macro prudential supervision to complement micro prudential supervision constitute some of the most significant responses to the financial crisis. The emphasis is on prudence.

Aristotle defines prudence or 'practical wisdom' (*phronesis*) as the virtue that enables one to 'deliberate well about what is good and expedient for himself . . . and about what sorts of things (that) conduce to the good life in general'.[57] Prudence is a virtue necessary for leaders[58] and authorities since prudent men 'can see what is good for themselves and what is good for

---

[53]   See *PRA Rulebook* Bank of England (2018) http://www.prarulebook.co.uk/rulebook/Content/Part/ 211136/02-03-2018 accessed 2 March 2018.

[54]   See *UK Money Markets Code* Bank of England (2017) http://www.bankofengland.co.uk/ publications/Pages/news/2017/037.aspx accessed 2 March 2018.

[55]   See *The UK Money Markets Code* Bank of England (2017) https://www.bankofengland.co .uk/-/media/boe/files/markets/money-markets-committee/uk-money-markets-code.pdf?la=en&hash= C7854B22B681B65244EE35A8CC306288454B4506 accessed 2 March 2018.

[56]   Ibid.

[57]   Aristotle above note 4, II40a24-31 142.

[58]   W. Walker Moskop 'Prudence as a Paradigm for Political Leaders' Political Psychology, Vol. 17, No. 4 [1996] 619–42.

men in general; we consider that those who can do this who are good at managing households and states'.[59]

The Aristotelian tradition applies the virtue of prudence not only to individuals but also to politics. "The wisdom concerned with the city, the practical wisdom which plays a controlling part is legislative wisdom, while that which is related to this as particulars to their universal is known as 'political wisdom'". The virtue of prudence should inform laws and decrees that seek the public good or good life in general.[60] Aristotle emphasizes the role of experience in acquiring practical wisdom: 'such wisdom (practical wisdom) is concerned not only with universals but with particulars, which become familiar from experience'.[61]

'It is not possible to be good in the strict sense without practical wisdom, or practically wise without moral virtue.'[62] As Finnis states, 'Prudentia is nothing other than the disposition to guide one's choices and actions by practical reasonableness. So it is informed and directed at every stage by every relevant practical principle and moral norm'.[63] The test of reasonableness is one that has always inspired the judicial review of administrative decisions.

'Every immorality involves a failing in prudentia, and every failing in prudentia involves a deviation from one or more of the relevant moral norms.'[64]

Historically, the term prudence has been reduced at times to the equivalent of 'discretion' or 'caution'.[65] Pieper identifies, following Aquinas, three kinds of imprudence. The first is thoughtlessness. This kind of imprudence manifests when a person acts 'without proper consideration and without well-founded judgement'.[66] A second type of imprudence is irresoluteness or indecisiveness which implies a lack 'of vigorous final decisiveness'.[67] Another form of false prudence is 'cunning': 'the insidious temperament of the intriguer who has regard only to tactics, who can neither face things squarely nor act straightforwardly'.[68] Pieper pinpoints

---

[59]   Aristotle above note 4, II40b9-12 143.
[60]   'Perhaps one's own good cannot exist without household management, nor without a form of government' Aristotle above note 4, II42a9-11.
[61]   Ibid II42a18-21 148.
[62]   Ibid II44b33-36 158.
[63]   J. Finnis above note 34, 168.
[64]   Aquinas, *Summa Theologica*, II-II q. 53 a IC; ibid. q. 57 a V: 'Prudence is a virtue most necessary for human life. For a good life consists in good deeds. Now in order to do good deeds, it matters not only what a man does but also how he does it; in other words it matters that we do it from the right choice and not merely from impulse or passion.'
[65]   R. Cessario *The Moral Virtues and Theological Ethics* (Second Edition, University of Notre Dame Press 2008) 79. As Ratzinger explains 'Here it is necessary first to eliminate a misunderstanding. Prudence is something other than shrewdness. Prudence, according to the Greek philosophical tradition, is the first of the cardinal virtues. It indicates the primacy of the truth which, through "prudence", becomes a criterion for our action. Prudence demands humble, disciplined and watchful reason that does not let itself be blinded by prejudices; it does not judge according to desires and passions but rather seeks the truth, even though it may prove uncomfortable. Prudence means searching for the truth and acting in conformity with it.' See J. Ratzinger, Homily Benedict XVI, 12 September 2009 http://w2.vatican .va/content/benedict-xvi/en/homilies/2009/documents/hf_ben-xvi_hom_20090912_ord-episcopale.html accessed 2 March 2018.
[66]   J. Pieper above note 28, 13.
[67]   Ibid 19.
[68]   Ibid 19–20.

foresight as a requisite of the man who issues imperatives. Foresight is the capacity 'to estimate whether a particular action will lead to the realization of the goal'.[69]

Proportionality is a dimension of prudence, which has important implications for judicial review and for the imposition of adequate sanctions. Prudence is the virtue by which one rightly discerns the proportionate reasons for acting or not acting, and for selecting one action in preference to another.

The principle of proportionality embedded in the EU Treaty is a guiding principle of the jurisprudence of the Court of Justice of the European Union, recently applied – in the context of monetary and financial law – in the *Gauweiler* case, where the Court assessed that the action in question (the OMT programme) was both suitable and necessary to achieve its goals (monetary objectives).[70]

Macro Prudential Policy After the GFC[71]

As stated above, regulatory and supervisory failures were one of the causes of the GFC. Before the GFC, the foresight (to which Pieper referred as a requisite of prudence) was manifested mainly in micro prudential supervision, while after the crisis emphasis has turned on macro prudential policies (as a complement – not a substitute – to enhanced micro prudential supervision).

The GFC challenged many pre-existing conceptions about systemic risk. One of these is the so-called 'composition fallacy'[72] which contends that the safety and soundness of any financial system is the aggregate soundness of all its participating institutions.[73] This fallacy assumed that if individual entities were robust, then the whole system would be resilient. This assumption proved to be misguided. Using an analogy with forest management, the safeguarding of the health of the forest requires a different type of strategy than the safeguarding of the health of each individual tree. Ecological considerations would also warn us against excessive reliance on a 'static' notion of stability. Andromachi Georgosouli has pointed out[74] the notion of systemic risk control requires an understanding of resilience as adaptability, thus a dynamic consideration.[75]

---

[69]   Ibid 18.

[70]   Case C-62/14 *Peter Gauweiler and Others v Deutscher Bundestag* [2014] OJ C129/11.

[71]   This sub-section of the chapter draws generally on R. Lastra 'Systemic Risk and Macro-prudential Supervision' in N. Moloney, E. Ferran, and J. Payne (eds.) *The Oxford Handbook of Financial Regulation* (OUP 2015).

[72]   M Brunnermeier, et al. *The Fundamental Principles of Financial Regulation*, Centre for Economic Policy Research (CEPR) and International Center for Monetary and Banking Studies (ICMB), Geneva Reports on the World Economy 11 [2009] 15.

[73]   J. Osiński, K. Seal and L. Hoogduin 'Macroprudential and Microprudential Policies: Toward Cohabitation' International Monetary Fund (IMF), Monetary and Capital Markets Department [2013] 6.

[74]   Andromachi Georgosouli, in an unpublished manuscript entitled 'Financial Resilience' (cited with the permission of the author) addresses the problem of financial vulnerability, shifting away from the financial stability metaphor towards a resilience-oriented scheme of regulation. She defines financial resilience as 'adaptive capacity to change', which 'is measured in terms of one's ability to learn, prepare and, where appropriate, cope and recover from future contingencies'. A. Georgosouli 'Financial Resilience' (2012) unpublished manuscript.

[75]   N. Taleb *Antifragile: Things That Gain From Disorder* (Penguin 2012).

Systemic risks pose a threat to financial stability. And, as the crisis evidenced, these types of risks are not confined to the banking system: they can also affect securities and derivatives markets. Such was the case of international insurer AIG and investment banks such as Lehman Brothers and Bear Stearns. During the economic meltdown, systemic risks stemmed from non-bank institutions and from financial instruments that traditionally fell outside the regulatory perimeter. Furthermore, systemic risks are not bounded by territorial borders; they have a tendency to spread across geographical borders. The dichotomy between global markets and institutions on the one hand and national law and national policies on the other hand is particularly acute in the management of systemic risk and in the design of adequate institutional solutions to deal with its negative spillover effects.[76, 77]

The absence of a clear-cut definition of financial stability entails that the 'notion of financial stability is often discussed in terms of the concept of systemic risk and its sources'.[78] Systemic risk management – and consequently, macro prudential policy – aims to contain the 'build-up of systemic vulnerabilities over time'.[79]

Macro Prudential Policy[80]

As we have already pointed out, before the crisis, supervision was mostly concerned with the safety and soundness of individual institutions (micro prudential supervision).[81] Since the crisis, the focus has widened to encompass the macro dimension. For example, the Basel Committee on Banking Supervision (BCBS) enhanced the scope of risk-based supervision in its *Core Principles for Effective Banking Supervision* to include:

> [T]he need for greater intensity and resources to deal effectively with systemically important banks; the importance of applying a system-wide, macro perspective to the microprudential supervision of banks to assist in identifying, analysing and taking pre-emptive action to address systemic risk; and the increasing focus on effective crisis management, recovery and resolution measures in reducing both the probability and impact of a bank failure.[82]

Although a relatively recent phenomenon, macro prudential policy has already sparked many academic papers, high-level discussions and policy reports. This progress notwithstanding,

---

[76]   J. Golden 'The Courts, the Financial Crisis and Systemic Risk', Capital Markets Law Journal, Vol. 4 [2009] S141–S149.

[77]   E Greene, et al. 'A Closer Look at "Too Big to Fail": National and International Approaches to Addressing the Risks of Large, Interconnected Financial Institutions', Capital Market Law Journal, Vol 5, No. 2 [2010] 117–40, 118.

[78]   G. Galati, and R. Moessner 'Macroprudential Policy – a Literature Review' BIS Working Papers No. 337 [2011] 13 http://www.bis.org/publ/work337.pdf accessed 2 March 2018.

[79]   International Monetary Fund (IMF), Key Aspects of Macroprudential Policy [2013] 7. See also R. Lastra 'Systemic Risk, SIFIs and Financial Stability', Capital Markets Law Journal, Vol. 6, No. 2 [2011] 197–213.

[80]   This sub-section of the chapter draws generally on R. Lastra 'Systemic Risk and Macro-prudential Supervision' in N. Moloney, E. Ferran and J. Payne (eds.) *The Oxford Handbook of Financial Regulation* (OUP 2015).

[81]   See R. Lastra 'Defining Forward-looking Judgment-based Supervision', Journal of Banking Regulation, Vol. 14, No. 3 [2013] 221–7.

[82]   Basel Committee on Banking Supervision, *Core Principles for Effective Banking Supervision* [2012] 2. See also ibid *Core Principles* 8 and 9.

'[w]e are in the early days of macroprudential policy, akin perhaps to where monetary policy stood in the 1950s'.[83]

The macro prudential perspective can be a murky concept to grasp, somewhere in between micro prudential supervision and monetary policy. The contours are not always easy to demarcate. The European Systemic Risk Board (ESRB) states that:

'[t]he ultimate objective of macro-prudential policy is to contribute to the safeguard of the stability of the financial system as a whole, including by strengthening the resilience of the financial system and decreasing the build-up of systemic risks, thereby ensuring a sustainable contribution of the financial sector to economic growth'.[84]

Before the macro prudential paradigm shift, 'the broader financial system was steered by a combination of monetary policy and microprudential regulation'.[85] With the onslaught of the crisis, the focus has now expanded to take into account of the bigger picture: the safety and soundness of the whole financial system as well as the global interconnectedness of systems and infrastructures across borders.[86]

Macro prudential policy looks to provide a backstop for systemic risk containment and must not be confused with other forms of micro prudential management, like consolidated supervision. While consolidated supervision focuses on the related entities within a financial group, macro prudential supervision is concerned with the relationship between any individual institution (or financial group) and the safety and soundness of the system as a whole.

One of the major challenges of implementing a system-wide supervision is the understanding of the policy interaction between macro prudential policy and other economic policies. Additional levels of complexity arise when considering that micro and macro prudential supervision are not only limited to the commercial banking sector – but span across other financial subsectors (insurance, investment banking, shadow banking) on a domestic and transnational level.

With the implementation of macro prudential supervision, the authorities should engage in a more robust exercise of the virtue of prudence, mainly by strengthening foresight, knowing that the scope of their supervisory actions has broadened from the supervision of the individual financial institutions to the safety and soundness of the entire financial system. At the same time, the authorities should exercise thoughtfulness since the repercussions of their acts may have a systemic repercussion. And they should beware of the dangers of inaction, insufficient action or irresoluteness, since a delayed decision may be as disastrous in a crisis situation.

---

[83]   D. Elliott 'Macroprudential Policy: Time to Start Experimenting' *The Economist*, 4 June 2013. A similar view has been stated by A. Haldane 'Macroprudential Policies – When and How to Use Them' (2013) http://www.imf.org/external/np/seminars/eng/2013/macro2/pdf/ah.pdf. accessed 2 March 2018.

[84]   European Systemic Risk Board (ESRB), Recommendation of the European Systemic Risk Board on Intermediate Objectives and Instruments of Macroprudential Policy, ESRB/2013/1 2013/C170/01 (2013) Art. 1.

[85]   D. Schoenmaker and P. Wierts 'Macroprudential Policy: The Need for a Coherent Policy Framework' DSF Policy Paper Series Paper No. 13 [2011] 2.

[86]   R. Lastra above note 79, 198.

V.   HUMAN RIGHTS AND FINANCIAL LAW[87]

In order to exist and prosper, financial institutions and markets need to establish and maintain their legitimacy in the eyes of those they affect. Often this sense of legitimacy is founded on the legal concepts of justice and human rights.

'The concept of human rights derives primarily from international law, which in turn took it from the philosophy of natural law.'[88]

In a revisionist account of the history of human rights, Freeman persuasively argues that the 17th-century concept of natural rights developed by Grotius, Hobbes and Locke derived from late-medieval controversies and from the Spanish thinkers of the 16th century,[89] particularly from the so-called 'School of Salamanca'.[90] According to their understanding, 'natural rights were what were commanded by natural law'.[91] Domingo de Soto and Francisco de Vitoria in particular developed the association between rights and freedom.[92] Freeman uses this revisionist account to show that the concept of natural rights – anchored in the Christian tradition of respect for the dignity of human beings[93] – pre-dated by a few centuries the concept of capitalism and that the concept of human rights has 'transcended the debate between capitalism and socialism to become a post-socialist instrument for the critique of capitalism'.[94] Indeed in his opinion, international human rights embody, on the one hand, some of the most important concessions capitalism has made and, on the other hand, they signify an erosion of the concept of state sovereignty.[95]

Finnis argues: 'The fact is that human rights can only be securely enjoyed in certain sorts of milieu – a context or framework of mutual respect and trust and common understanding, an

---

[87]   This section draws extensively on R. Lastra 'Global Financial Architecture and Human Rights', in Juan Pablo Bohoslavsky and Jernej Letnar Černič (eds.) *Making Sovereign Financing & Human Rights Work* (Hart Publishing 2014) 129–38, and Rosa M. Lastra and Alan H. Brener 'Justice, Financial Markets and Human Rights' in Lisa Herzog (ed.) *Just Financial Markets? Finance in a Just Society* (OUP 2017).

[88]   M. Freeman 'Beyond Capitalism and Socialism' in J. Dine and A. Fagan (eds.) *Human Rights and Capitalism: A Multidisciplinary Perspective on Globalisation* (Edward Elgar Publishing 2006) 3.

[89]   Ibid 7–26.

[90]   The 'School of Salamanca' is the name applied to a group of Spanish jurists, theologians and philosophers who created a body of doctrine on natural, international and economic law, rooted in the intellectual work of Francisco de Vitoria, who started teaching in Salamanca in 1526 in the *catedra de prima*, the most important chair of theology at the University. Other distinguished members of this school were Domingo de Soto, Fernando Vázquez de Menchaca, Diego de Covarrubias, Luis de Molina, Juan Ginés de Sepúlveda and Francisco Suárez. The role of the School of Salamanca in the development of early monetary theory has been documented in the work of Marjorie Grice-Hutchinson. While at the LSE, Marjorie came under the influence of Friedrich von Hayek, who urged her to study the manuscripts of this group of Spanish scholars from the 16th and early 17th century. Her monograph, *School of Salamanca: Reading in Spanish Monetary Theory, 1544–1605*, was published by Clarendon Press, Oxford in 1952.

[91]   M. Freeman above note 88, 9.

[92]   Ibid 10. Freeman also argues (13) that 'The historical record of the liberal-democratic West . . . has given inordinate emphasis to individual property rights'. He argues that medieval debates about property (24–5) can help understand the current debate about the relations among rights, property and justice.

[93]   These Christian origins can actually be traced back to St Augustine, ibid 23.

[94]   Ibid 6–7.

[95]   Ibid 25–6.

environment which is physically healthy and in which the weak can go about without fear of the whims of the strong.'[96]

One can draw historical parallels between the development of the market, both in practice and as a concept, and the understanding of rights and freedoms.[97] Issues relating to markets, setting value and the freedom of exchange and money and the effects on the poor concerned at least two thinkers of the 'School': Domingo de Soto and Francisco de Vitoria, who considered and developed their thinking on the need to promote relief for the poor, not as an act of charity but, rather to '[uphold] the poor man's right to liberty of person and action'.[98] This was set out in a treatise by de Soto and submitted to Spanish King Phillip II in 1545. Thus, theories on natural law resulted in important parallel developments in the concepts of markets and human rights. However, the economic analysis of markets subsequently took a different path and a gap in this relationship developed.

The subsequent development by Grotius and others of a modern school of international law was reassessed in the 20th century in the context of the legal responses to the atrocities – violation of human rights and the genocide of the Jewish people[99] – perpetrated by Nazi Germany. This led to a re-examination of the justification of positive law when it becomes dissociated from natural law. These debates clearly showed that legal positivism, which had been influenced by the work of Hans Kelsen[100] and taken up by thinkers such as H. L. A Hart in its contrasting form of Anglo-American legal positivism, has its limits.[101]

A recent book by Philippe Sands[102] weaves together the contributions by a generation of outstanding scholars – including Hersch Lauterpacht and Rafael Lemkin – to illuminate this recent chapter in the development of international law in response to the Nazi atrocities. Lauterpacht, a Cambridge Professor of International Law and one of the outstanding legal scholars of the 1940s, became a key figure in the development of the international rights regime. Rafael Lemkin, a Polish Jewish lawyer, coined the term 'genocide'.[103]

What is at stake is the fact that the state cannot suppress human rights, and that the recognition and protection of human rights is inviolable. This led to the adoption of the Universal Declaration of Human Rights by the General Assembly of the United Nations on 10 December 1948 (UDHR 1948).

---

[96]   J. Finnis above note 31, 216.

[97]   O. Gelderblom *Cities of Commerce: The Institutional Foundations of International Trade in the Low Countries* (Princeton University Press 2013) 1250–650; M. Grice-Hutchinson *School of Salamanca, Reading in Spanish Monetary Theory* (Clarendon Press 1952) 40–2; H. Kamen *Philip of Spain* (Yale University Press 1997) 27.

[98]   M. Grice-Hutchinson ibid 1544–605; H. Kamen ibid 24.

[99]   The Nazi regime targeted many groups for extermination, including Gypsies, Slavs, the disabled and homosexuals. However, the persecution and murder of Jews were on a scale without comparison. More than six million Jews were killed in the Holocaust.

[100]   H. Kelsen *Pure Theory of Law* (first published 1934, University of California Press Berkeley 1967).

[101]   See D. Bodansky, and J. Shand 'State Consent and the Sources of International Obligation' Proceedings of the Annual Meeting (American Society of International Law 1992) 86, 108–13 on the limits of state consent.

[102]   P. Sands *East West Street: On the Origins of Genocide and Crimes Against Humanity* (Weidenfeld & Nicolson 2016).

[103]   R. Lemkin *Axis Rule in Occupied Europe* (Carnagie Endowment for International Peace 1944) 79.

Economics, Financial Markets, Human Rights and Justice in Today's World

While the recognition and protection of human rights is widely recognised as an intrinsic element of the rule of law in a democracy, the debate about the relationship between markets (including financial markets) and the state continues to evolve. It frames current and historical policy debates and influences the electoral agenda of diverse political parties. Issues of social justice cannot be disentangled from questions about markets in the construction of a fair and just society. This has important consequences in terms of the design of adequate national and international policies and institutions.

An innate and intensely felt sense of injustice after the Great Financial Crisis triggered protests around the World, from New York ('Occupy Wall Street') and London to Spain ('Indignados') and the subsequent development of political movements/parties that have gained prominence in some countries in the Eurozone (for example, Syriza in Greece and Podemos in Spain). What lies underneath this development is a re-examination of the relationship between justice and markets (in particular financial markets) from the perspective of equality/inequality.[104]

While this debate has contemporary manifestations, the issues at stake are not new. Indeed, debates about social justice, solidarity, social policy and social security permeate the history of the design of the welfare state in Europe in the 20th century.

Nowadays, many of social security systems (based in the 'Welfare State') have been downsized and are now endangered in their very existence, given the fiscal necessities of nation states across the developed world, in particular in the aftermath of the GFC, but also considering the demand of public pensions and defined benefit systems in the light of demographic, financial and fiscal developments.[105]

Coming back to the debate about human rights, Hohfeldian contends that they exist at the level of the nation state, since the latter owes or grants rights to its citizens in exchange for correlative duties such as obligations to obey the laws of the state, pay taxes etc.[106] However, financial markets and institutions cross borders and operate internationally. Consequently, there is an issue concerning to what extent, if any, there is an interaction between human rights and global financial markets and institutions. This problem is exacerbated by the development, in economic thinking, of 'homo economicus'.

While it is possible to view man as a purely economically oriented being,[107] and it is useful for economic modelling purposes to construct the 'homo economicus' as a representation of

---

[104] 'Rousseau's *Discourse on Inequality* and many others since (Thomas Piketty's "Capital in the Twenty-first century" being a significant contemporary contribution) emphasize how wealth and income inequality feed popular discontent. Those that feel disenchanted, with little to lose, will vote, rebel or protest against the "political establishment". There is a widespread feeling that the skilled jobs in manufacturing, and elsewhere, have been lost, outsourced to China or overtaken by robots'. See C. Goodhart, and R. Lastra 'Populism and Central Bank Independence' *Open Economies Review* (2017) https://doi .org/10.1007/s11079-017-9447-y accessed 2 March 2018.

[105] E. P. Davis and R. Lastra 'Pension Provision, Care and Dignity in Old Age: Legal and Economic Issues', Working Paper No. 16-06 (Brunel Economics and Finance 2016).

[106] W. Hohfeld *Fundamental Legal Conceptions as Applied in Judicial Reasoning* (Yale Law Review 1917) 710–70.

[107] For example, John Stuart Mill holds that 'political economy . . . is concerned with [man] solely as a being who desires to possess wealth, and who is capable of judging the comparative efficacy of means for obtaining that end' J. Stuart Mill *Essays on Some Unsettled Questions of Political Economy*

some aspects of reality, it is also necessary to stand back and to consider the human being as a whole.[108] With this perspective comes the concept of 'human dignity', the view that each person has a range of potentialities and that society has a responsibility to develop these both for the benefit of the individual and of the community as a whole.[109]

The global dislocation experienced in the wake of the GFC created failure perceptions of previous economic certainties and a growing distrust in financial institutions and markets, not least because of the failure of financial markets to create wealth for society as a whole.

In part this may be seen as a failure of a technocratic approach to economics and markets in communicating with and engaging a wider population. Hitherto trust had been placed in a relatively small group of experts to guide and manage these areas. The GFC and its aftermath revealed severe deficiencies in this approach, which were made worse by a number of political failures. There is a growing concern that many financial markets have lost touch with the societies to which they belong. It is likely that trading securities has become an end in itself; failing to satisfy societal needs.[110] The result has been manifest in a perception of increasing inequality, injustice and the failure to engage and develop a sense of community.

Taking this forward and connecting it to the previous discussion, it is important to consider which human rights are most relevant for this analysis. Human rights are often classified into two main groups: those that are absolute (e.g. rights to life, freedom and fear of physical violence) and those that are relative (e.g. rights to free education, access to clean water, adequate food, etc.) (see e.g. Raz,[111] in which he questions whether the second group are actually 'human rights'). This second group has been described as requiring 'compossible duties' as the counter-party to rights, in that absolute rights can be satisfied by forbearance and restraints while relative rights require 'positive actions' on those that bear the duty.[112] This latter set of rights may be described as 'aspirational' and the duty to satisfy these rights as dependent on the relative ability of the authorities involved to achieve the satisfaction of these rights. However, this form of conceptualisation may be too limited. It seems to be grounded in a form of economic analysis that obscures both what is important and what is possible.[113]

This view has also been expressed by Amartya Sen, who is critical of a narrow economic focus on income and wealth; although these are important, he views the creation of 'capabilities of people to lead the kind of lives they value' as more relevant.[114] Individual and

---

(first published 1836, Kitchener 2000) 97. 'Homo economicus' is and remains a prevalent concept in economic theorising.

[108]   It is possible to view economic analysis as 'consequentialist' in that economic policies can be assessed by empirical evaluations of the results (i.e. 'outputs focused'). However, concepts such as human rights are seen as 'strongly deontological' in that they are based on absolute principles. M. Freeman above note 88, 22.

[109]   These concepts can be traced back to Aristotle and Aquinas. See, for example, M. Nussbaum 'Aristotle, Politics, and Human Capabilities: A Response to Antony, Arneson, Charlesworth, and Mulgan', Ethics, Vol. 111, No. 1 [2000] 102–40 at 106 and 112. See also P. Lee and R. George 'The Nature and Basis of Human Dignity', Ratio Juris, Vol. 21, No. 2 [2008] 173–93.

[110]   A. Turner *Between Debt and the Devil* (Princeton University Press 2016).

[111]   J. Raz *The Morality of Freedom* (Clarendon Press 1986) 225 and 229–31.

[112]   O. O'Neill 'Response to John Tasioulas' in S. Cruft, Matthew Liao and Massimo Renzo (eds.) *Philosophical Foundations of Human Rights* (OUP 2015) 71.

[113]   Contrary views have been expressed by, for example, J. Nickel *Making Sense of Human Rights* (Wiley-Blackwell 2006) 7 and J. Griffin *Well-being* (Clarendon Press 1986) 284–312.

[114]   A. Sen *Development as Freedom* (OUP 1999) 18.

community capabilities are increased by a number of 'freedoms', including the alleviation of disease and improved health, education opportunities and an ability to participate in the economic and political world.[115] It is about giving people choices: increased capabilities provide opportunities for individuals and societies, as a whole, to help themselves in accordance with their human dignity. If they are able to participate in developing these capabilities they, in turn, influence the areas to which they are connected.[116] Being able to participate in a market is in itself a 'freedom' and an aspect of a human right and can be viewed as liberating.[117]

Consequently, the right, and ability, to engage with markets, both financial and otherwise, is fundamental to individual capabilities and human rights. The failure of markets to engage both individuals and communities and to support the development of their capabilities may breed distrust and alienation. As mentioned earlier, this is particularly true of financial markets following the GFC. Markets need to be perceived as fair and connected and supportive of the society in which they operate. This means that individuals in markets need to operate ethically, and the culture of markets needs to include clear and understandable explanations of their social purposes, their transparency and their relevance to society with clear lines of accountability.

VI.   A NEW FRAMEWORK FOR THE FINANCIAL INDUSTRY BASED ON JUSTICE, PRUDENCE AND INTEGRITY

Christine Lagarde explains that education on ethical values is essential for cultural change. 'This calls for individuals to be educated in values that not only respect the rules but also seek to pursue the public good. Individuals should base their actions not only on "what can I do," but above all on "what should I do".' She adds: 'In essence, what is needed is a culture of greater virtue and integrity at the individual level in the financial industry . . . So by promoting and instilling "virtuous" norms in individuals within the firm, a cultural renewal within the industry can be induced.'[118]

The test of the 'man of practical wisdom'[119] in finance would be expressed by the need to act with integrity. Aristotle treats integrity in a horizontal way since it 'disperses honesty among the other virtues'.[120] As Christine Lagarde affirms 'promoting individual integrity is crucial for inducing a cultural change at the firm level'.[121]

It is critical that the responsibilities of all financial sector stakeholders be clearly identified. While the causes of the crisis are always multifactorial, there is a special responsibility that rests upon financial industry leaders, and the authorities in charge of supervising them.

---

[115]   Ibid 15–17. See also M. Nussbaum above note 109, 69, where she expands the use of the term 'capabilities' as a way to measure 'what people are actually able to do and to be in a way informed by an idea . . . of life that is worthy of the dignity of the human being'.

[116]   Ibid 15.

[117]   Sen discusses this in the context of female education and work force participation, ibid 115–16. See also R. Claassen 'A Capability Framework for Financial Market Regulation' in (ed.) L. Herzog *Just Financial Markets? Finance in a Just Society* (OUP 2013).

[118]   C. Lagarde above note 1.

[119]   Aristotle above note 4, II06b36 39.

[120]   H. J. Curzer *Aristotle and the Virtues* chapter 10 (OUP 2012).

[121]   C. Lagarde above note 1.

Leaders must after all lead by example. 'All good principles and intentions on ethics and integrity will only be effective if there is buy-in at the top. After all, the most important internal choices are made by management under oversight of the board of directors'.[122] 'Regulation . . . has the ability to affect individuals' behaviors.'[123] The competent authorities should be capable of translating prudence into 'legislative wisdom' through adequate laws, as well as through effective micro and macro supervision.

Ethical standards must become enshrined in the law or in codes of conduct, accompanied by an adequate system of incentives and sanctions in the case of violation of the rules.[124] Since personal accountability (responsibility) is a direct consequence of freedom, the repercussions of individual actions should be clearly known by all those who operate in the financial industry (transparency) and applied consistently.

A regulatory framework for the financial sector based on the exercise of the virtues of justice, prudence and integrity will result in a changing culture. While justice should be the overriding principle, prudence (the principle underlying micro and macro prudential supervision) and integrity (the principle underlying much of the conduct of business supervision) complement justice. Such a framework would go a long away towards addressing the misgivings of those who feel rightly disappointed by the effects of the GFC, and would help the general public better understand the 'telos' of the financial industry. After all, a well-functioning financial sector is a key element of economic development, aimed at the pursuit of the common good. It is time to reconnect the interests of bankers with the interests of society.

---

[122] Ibid.

[123] Ibid.

[124] 'A recent survey conducted in the U.S. and the U.K. among senior professionals working in the financial sector (including fund managers, bankers, analysts and asset managers) found that over a quarter of respondents observed or had firsthand knowledge of unethical behavior in their organization.' See M. Pitesa 'The Psychology of Unethical Behavior in the Finance Industry' in P. O'Sullivan, N. F. B. Allington, M. Esposito (eds.) *The Philosophy, Politics and Economics of Finance in the 21st Century: From Hubris to Disgrace* (Research Collection Lee Kong Chian School of Business 2015) 344–69 http://ink.library.smu.edu.sg/lkcsb_research/5030 accessed 2 March 2018. The survey to which Pitesa refers to is Labaton Sucharow (2012) http://www.labaton.com/en/about/press/upload/US-UK -Financial-Services-Industry-Survey-July-2012-Report.pdf accessed 2 March 2018.

PART II

THE ROLE PLAYED BY LAW AND STANDARDS

4. Nudging inclusive banking and micro finance towards self-sustainability

(The ethical role of regulation and self-regulation)

Katherine Hunt, Marco Lamandini and David Ramos Muñoz

1. A BRIEF INTRODUCTION ON VALUES AND ON AN INSTITUTIONAL DESIGN COMMITTING TO VALUES

As the societal tide moves towards social and environmental sustainability, the legal framework, historically focused on profit-maximising corporations, has needed adjustment. An example is offered by Benefit Corporations in the United States, now available in more than 30 States, following the Benefit Corporation Model,[1] and Benefit Companies ('società benefit')[2] in Italy, reportedly the first two jurisdictions to have used regulation to nudge businesses towards a re-balanced calibration of profit-seeking and social involvement.

The financial sector has not been exempt from a rising trend that seeks to re-balance profit and social involvement. Financial institutions across the world have started to incorporate, albeit with a wide array of variations, social and environmental sustainability principles into their business models and product offerings[3] and customers have responded positively.[4] Socially responsible investment law[5] and microfinance have become popular subjects in their own right. Some banks and credit unions have long been targeting community financing and socially or environmentally responsible lending; however, now some entrench this as a core mission. UmweltBank in Germany, Triodos Bank[6] in the Netherlands, Banca Etica and Banca Prossima in Italy, the Co-operative Bank in the United Kingdom, and some large 'conventional' banks, like CaixaBank in Spain, although not being 'ethical banks' *per se*, have

---

[1] Compare, for an updated state of the art, Winston, E. (2017), 'Benefit corporation and the separation between benefit and control', (2017) *Cardozo Law Review*, 1783.

[2] ESELA (2016), *The first European benefit corporation: blurring the lines between 'social' and 'business'*, available at http://esela.eu/news/the-first-e; De Ricco, G. and Mazzeschi, M. (2017), *The Italian benefit corporation: to profit and .... beyond!*, available at http://www.lawyerissue.com/italian-benefit-corporation-profit-beyond/; The ECCLBlog (2017), *The legacy of B Lab: Italy's Società Benefit*, available at http://www.ecclblog.law.ed.ac.uk/2017/03/31/the-legacy-of-b-lab-italys-societa-benefit/.

[3] Loorbach, D., Avelino, F., Haxeltine, A., Wittmayer, J., O'Riordan, T., Weaver, P., and Kemp, R. (2016), 'The economic crisis as a game changer? Exploring the role of social construction in sustainability transitions', *Ecology and Society*, 21, 5–7.

[4] Pérez, A., and Rodríguez del Bosque, I. (2014), 'Customer CSR expectations in the banking industry', *International Journal of Bank Marketing*, 32(3), 223–44 (at 235–40). See also: Yusof, J. M., Manan, H. A., Karim, N.A., and Kassim, N.A.M. (2015), 'Customer's loyalty effects of CSR Initiatives', *Procedia – Social and Behavioral Sciences*, 170, 109–19 (at 117–18).

[5] Richardson, B.J. (2008), *Socially Responsible Investment Law: Regulating the Unseen Polluters*, Oxford University Press, Oxford and New York (at 73 ff. for an overview of SRI growing since the eighteenth century).

[6] www.triodos.co.uk.

inserted ethical investment as part of their group strategy, with specialised subsidiaries.[7] These individual examples stand alongside the other members of FEBEA, the European Federation of Ethical and Alternative Banks,[8] which exemplify this trend.[9] Thus, Socially Responsible Investment (SRI) gains traction in Europe and the developing world.[10]

Furthermore, according to FEBEA ethical banks are a new generation of social banks, originated through a bottom-up process, which reclaims the traditional idea that banks should contribute to the development of their territory.[11] The 29 ethical financial institutions which are members of FEBEA are present in 14 European countries. Despite the fact that they represent a very small segment of the overall European banking and financial system they are quite heterogeneous among themselves. More importantly, they aspire to act, in their own words, as a 'prophetical minority'. Their numbers are encouraging so far:

> 29 members in 17 countries (13 banks and 16 financial institutions); more than 3,300 employees, more than 250 branches, more than 200,000 shareholders, more than 240,000 depositors; total assets: 30.5 billion euros, more than 670,000 clients, more than 18 billion euros in loans, more than 9.8 billion euros in TBL (people, planet, prosperity) assets; more than 33 million euros obtained in EU funding; members implementing practices to assess non-economic benefits of loans' requests: 70%; members offering convenient conditions to socio-environmental projects: 75%; bank members offering social financial products: 82%; members implementing practices to verify the origin of funds, beyond the mandatory standard (2014): 81%; bank members disclosing information on allocation of assets (2014): 87.5%; average highest wage/lowest wage ratio (2014): 3.75; members having ethical principles included in articles of association or internal regulations: 95%

They, together with many other initiatives worldwide in microfinance and microcredit, are part of a wider movement towards what has rightly been described as 'a new age of responsibility in banking and finance'.[12]

---

[7] A model to be taken as an example: MicroBank – Banco Social La Caixa from 2007 to end 2012 granted 169,282 microcredits for a value of €1,045,000,000 (only in 2012, 11,185 microloans productive type for a value of €116.5 million and 29,599 social microloans for a value of €119 million). See http://www.microbanklacaixa.com/informacioncorporativa/datosbasicos_es.html.

[8] www.febea.org.

[9] Compare again Richardson B.J., *Socially Responsible Investment Law*, 75–6.

[10] '[W]ith its traditions of stakeholders capitalism and relatively high awareness of environmental challenges, Europe will likely lead such changes in the social responsible investment . . . [In turn] SRI is gaining traction [also] in emerging and rapidly industrializing economies. Microcredit institutions for community development and poverty reduction are the strongest element of SRI in the developing world, epitomized by the successful Grameen Bank in Bangladesh'. Richardson B.J., *Socially Responsible Investment Law*, 80–8.

[11] 'These have the objective of achieving a positive impact on the collection and use of money. They invest in new activities such as organic farming, renewable energies, the Third sector (or nonprofit sector), Fair Trade. They respond more and more to the needs of those who are excluded from the banking system, and to the needs of savers and investors who are increasingly interested in the way their savings are used. Thanks to ethical banks, the "banking institution" returns to a path interrupted at the beginning of the twentieth century, and it becomes again an instrument of development for the territory and for new social and environmental initiatives.' Compare www.febea.org/.

[12] Kenadjian P.S. and Dombret A. (eds.) (2016), *Getting the culture and the ethics right. Towards a new age of responsibility in banking and finance*, Institute for Law and Finance Series, de Gruyter, Berlin, Boston (in particular at 32 the acknowledgment that this expression is borrowed from Mark Carney).

Ethics and culture are indeed key in rebuilding people's trust in the financial sector,[13] something that, according to some, may take a generation.[14] However, this requires redirecting financial activity to better target the underprivileged, address poverty challenges and self-employment in the transition from unemployment, and sustainable development in local communities.[15] In other words, 'values' need to be credible and operational, and this requires them to be *institutionalised*. A change in culture, in other words, is transient and not enduring absent a change in institutional arrangements.[16] These help to bridge the gap between values and goals[17] and warrant that, once a specific code of values is adopted, these values are respected at all times and not traded off against more profitable goals when convenient.

We intend to explore some of these institutional arrangements looking at the sub-cluster of financial institutions represented by ethical niche banks and microfinance institutions (MFIs). Although these offer case-specific peculiarities, there are some useful broader lessons to be drawn from their experience, which may prove interesting for all banks and for policymakers in this process of adaptation to the 'new age of responsibility'.

After the financial and social crisis originated by sub-prime mortgages unfolded all its dramatic feedback effects, an avant-garde of financial institutions turned its attention to the market segment which traditionally had been considered financially unsustainable and was historically left – at very high and ethically disturbing social costs – to shadow or informal financiers.[18] Our query is whether *inclusive niche ethical banks and MFIs which build business models around serving the previously financially excluded can be helped, or 'nudged' into building business models that are also financially robust*. We posit that they can, and that once this is achieved, the sector can tap resources that may dwarf corporate social responsibility

---

[13]   Group of Thirty, *Banking Conduct and Culture (2015): A Call for Sustained and Comprehensive Reform*, at http://group30.org; FSB (2014), *Guidance on Supervisory Interaction with Financial Institutions on Risk Culture* (at http:/www.fsb.org/2014/04/140407); compare Raaijmakers, M. (ed.) (2015), *Supervision of Behavior and Culture: Foundations, Practice & Future Developments*, De Nederlandsche Bank, Amsterdam.

[14]   Kenadjian P.S., 'We ignore Culture at our Peril', in Kenadjian P.S. and Dombret A. (eds.), *Getting the culture and the ethics right. Towards a new age of responsibility in banking and finance*, 23.

[15]   For the impressive number of US citizens in need of better financial inclusion in the face of weak social and health protection schemes, compare recently Servon L. (2017), *The Unbanking of America. How the New Middle Class Survives*, Houghton Mifflin Harcourt, Boston-New York, in particular at 166 ('in a study of US financial health, CFSI [The Center for Financial Services Innovation] found that 57% of Americans – 138 million people – are struggling financially, more than double the number of adults the FDIC categorized as unbanked or underbanked in its most recent survey').

[16]   'First, recognize that culture exists and it matters. Second, explicitly define the ideal culture for your institution. Here I would add that it needs to conform both to your business strategy and to society's expectation of how people in your position should behave. To the extent your business strategy calls for activities which go beyond what society understands or finds appropriate, that strategy may have to be altered to suit the expectations of the people on whose sufferance you are allowed the substantial privileges you enjoy, including deposit insurance and access to the lender of last resort, both of which allow you to operate with a degree of leverage unheard of in other sectors. Third, institutionalize mechanisms for shaping culture, including instilling clear values' Kenadjian P.S., 'We ignore Culture at our Peril', at 41.

[17]   On values and goals in ethical finance, Guiso, L., Sapienza, P., and Zingales, L. (2013) 'The Determinants of Attitudes toward Strategic Default on Mortgages' *The Journal of Finance*, LXVIII(4), 1473–515.

[18]   Islam, A., Nguyen, C., and Smyth, R. (2015) 'Does microfinance change informal lending in village economies? Evidence from Bangladesh', *Journal of Banking & Finance*, 50, 141–56 (at 153).

(CSR) programmes in terms of social impact. Today, these financial institutions are still marginal, but they *clearly represent one of the greatest opportunities of our times: to achieve financial inclusion (also) via the private sector*. In fact, their still diminished role may be partly due to a regulatory environment that has been tardy to respond to their challenges.

In the present chapter, we argue that regulation and self-regulation in this sector could and should bolster this shift, and that rules should be designed to help achieve this purpose. This, in turn, means, first, 'nudging'[19] ethical niche banks and MFIs towards self-sustainability choices, and, second, helping *all* other banks to pilot a transition towards more socially responsible and inclusive banking. We consider herein two aspects of the problem:

(a) organisationally, a special prudential and transparency rule-set (at a minimum, in the form of an ethical bank and MFI regulatory sandbox) under the aegis of 'proportionality';
(b) functionally, the institutionalisation of a fair coexistence of profit-seeking and financial inclusion as an ethical choice available for opt-in.

To be clear from the very outset, we certainly acknowledge that ethical niche banks and MFIs also pose micro-prudential and transparency challenges that need to be duly addressed by appropriate rules: nudging towards ethical involvement should not come at a cost for the micro-soundness of institutions, or the macro-stability of the system. Yet we are also convinced that (i) tailor-made solutions are needed, and (ii) recalibration experiments between profit-seeking and financial inclusion may help self-sustainability, and offer useful lessons for the banking industry as a whole. Another fundamental point is that these solutions should 'nudge', rather than prescribe. The remainder of this section presents the main ideas that will structure the subsequent discussion and recommendations.

1. First, we argue that ethical niche banks and MFIs should be offered, *as a default regime unless they opt for the traditional banking or financial licences*, a special and proportionate set of prudential and transparency rules, at a minimum in the form of an EU regulatory sandbox. Disproportionate regulation can undermine banks' basic function as financial intermediaries,[20] and 'induce arbitrage within the banking system if, for any reason, regulation impacts disproportionably on some types of banks' by making it harder for instance for small players 'to compete with more established players'[21] and prevent newcomers from entering the market.[22] This general idea also applies to niche ethical banks and MFIs,

---

[19] Compare Thaler, R.H. and Sunstein, C.R. (2008) *Nudge: Improving Decisions About Health, Wealth and Happiness*, Yale University Press, New Haven and London, 4; for the same conceptual reference to nudging in SRI, recently, Herwig, P. (2017) 'The Choice Architecture of Sustainable and Responsible Investment: Nudging Investors Towards Ethical Decision-Making', *Journal of Business Ethics*, 140(4), 743–53.

[20] BSG, *Proportionality in the Bank Regulation*, EBA, London 2015, 9.

[21] BSG, *Proportionality in the Bank Regulation*, 15; European Commission, *Economic Review of the Financial Regulation Agenda*, SWD (2014) 158 final, at 260.

[22] The UK debate on challenger banks vividly portrayed this. Compare CMA, *Retail Banking Market Investigation*, Summary of Challenger Roundtable, 3 July 2015, where it is argued that in the United Kingdom it has been calculated that – due to the differences in the risk weights under the IRB and standardised models – 'for every £1 of capital set aside to cover credit risk, a large bank can do 10 times more low LTV mortgage lending than a small bank or a building society. Put another way, for taking exactly the same credit risk, the smaller lenders have to set aside ten times more capital that the 6 biggest firms that [in the United Kingdom] control 80% of the mortgage market'. Since capital is a bank's most

for which non-proportionate requirements carry a 'knock on effect'.[23] The problem is particularly acute in Europe, where Basel prudential requirements[24] still pivot around the over-simplistic idea that EU implementation of these standards ought to be the same for *all* European banks and other regulated financial institutions to bolster safety, soundness and stability, whilst the United States and, especially, Japan see Basel rules as a blueprint only for the largest, internationally-active banks.[25] This approach, misguided as it is for all small banks with a simple business model, is truly damaging for ethical niche banks and MFIs, *unless a choice is given to these institutions*, among several possible approaches within the Banking Union.[26] First, a series of *special* exceptions and adjustments for individual rules of the Single Rule Book could be introduced. Second, a new regulatory package could be designed 'from scratch'. A third way, though, would in our view be at point here. Rather than providing for exceptions, exclusions and calibrations from the Single Rule Book, the special (and optional) regulatory framework for ethical niche banks and MFIs should pick from the Single Rule Book provisions that are *explicitly* made *applicable* to them, with the necessary adjustments and calibrations. This would counter the creeping and inertial expansion of the 'one-size-fits-all' approach,[27] and, at a minimum, should amount to an 'ethical banks and MFI's regulatory sandbox'.

For this purpose, we develop a financial self-sustainability strategic matrix, relying on selected comparative experiences in microfinance. In most countries, regulation of inclusive banks and MFIs is identical to those of regular banks, meaning that they do not have enough capital to qualify for savings mobilisation, and are reliant on donations to fund expansion and working capital.[28] A tailored regulatory environment which is supportive and nudges towards self-sustainability ensures that inclusive banks and MFIs can innovate

---

scarce and most expensive resource, this is not only a quite impressive competitive disadvantage. In reality, the 'one-size-fits-all' approach hides – in the clothes of and under the false pretence of equal treatment – a fatal discrimination against small banks in two concomitant ways: (a) it denies the potential for a *reasonable* calibration of capital requirements for small banks, adjusted to take into account the relative simplicity of their business model, and (b) it requires small banks to set aside much more capital to take exactly the same risk that big banks are weighing in a different and more favourable way through IRB models. As it has been noted, this generates disturbing markets effects because small banks are pushed to write proportionally higher LTV mortgages (since they have to charge more than large banks for low LTV mortgage lending), whereas the biggest banks write proportionately more lower LTV mortgages and their profitability is materially higher than that of the small banks. This is clearly paradoxical, because 'the banks taking the lowest risks and setting aside the least capital to support these risks [appear to] generate the highest levels of profitability'.

[23]   BSG, *Proportionality in the Bank Regulation*, 28.

[24]   This includes the revisions under discussion. Compare Coen W. (2016) *The global policy reform agenda: completing the job*, Keynote speech at the Australian Financial Review's Banking and Wealth Summit, Sydney, 5 April 2016 (available on the BIS website), 2.

[25]   Coen, W. (2016), *Finalising Basle III*, Introductory remarks at the ECON Committee, Brussels, 12 October 2016 (available on the BIS website), 1.

[26]   Compare Dombret A. (2016) *Banking diversity and regulation – do we need more proportionality in banking regulation?*, speech at the Banking Industry Conference of the People's Banks and Raiffeisen Banks, Berlin, 8 June 2016, 5.

[27]   Tarullo ,D.K. (2014) *Rethinking the Aims of Prudential Regulation*, Speech at the Federal Reserve Bank of Chicago, Chicago, 8 May 2014 (available online), 5.

[28]   Kiweu, J. M. (2011) 'Relaxing Financing Constraint in the Microfinance Industry: Is Commercialization the Answer?' *Journal of Business & Economics Research*, 9(10), 87–104 (at 102).

in the way they access capital, and in the products that they offer, such that they are financially self-sustainable. *This type of environment ensures that long-term financial inclusion can be achieved without reliance on donors.* Within a supportive regulatory environment, MFIs can achieve profitability or operational self-sustainability (OSS) while providing financial services to those most vulnerable.[29] Hence, regulation has the power to provide an environment where financial institutions are able take the next step in reflecting the increasing societal focus on social good, while blending profit and impact.

2. Second, we claim that self-regulation, possibly assisted by a fiscal nudging, and, where needed, regulation inspired by Benefit Corporations, should help in re-orienting value creation towards financial inclusion, in a partial departure from profit maximisation. In our view, the key is to focus on the bottom line, in a way that targets profitability and social engagement through the institutionalisation of internal reinvestment policies in activities directed at those financially excluded, in a way that indirectly expands the company's client base. This type of institutionalised inclusive banking has been tested for example in Italy throughout the last decade and will be discussed in detail in section 3.

In order to explore the impact of regulation on the financial self-sustainability of inclusive banks and MFIs, both hard and soft regulation will be discussed with direct relevance to this sector. Further, a specific regulatory comparison will be made between India, Bangladesh, Pakistan, Italy and Spain to highlight the different paths that regulators take in pursuing their financial inclusion goals.

2.   NUDGING TOWARDS INCLUSIVE BANKING AND FINANCE THROUGH PROPORTIONATE REGULATION

Inclusive finance is about facilitating access to financial services to those without them, and a large part of this typically concerns the extension of micro-loans to these people or socially-committed institutions.[30] Inclusion occurs when financial institutions make use of credit scorings and judgmental methodologies to supplement, and often override ordinary commercial banking standards, e.g. the Italian Banca Etica's social indicators, or resort to other corrective tools that expand the lending spectrum without impairing the institution's soundness and safety.

Inclusive finance has become a popular, albeit controversial,[31] method of facilitating development, not only in poor countries but also in the poorer segments of the richest soci-

---

[29]   *Ibid.,* 101–2; Kyereboah-Coleman, A., and Osei, K. A. (2008), 'Outreach and profitability of microfinance institutions: the role of governance', *Journal of Economic Studies*, 35(3), 236–48 (at 246); Obamuyi, T. M. (2009) 'Credit delivery and sustainability of micro-credit schemes in Nigeria', *Journal of Enterprising Communities*, 3(1), 71–83 (at 81).

[30]   European Commission, *A European initiative for the development of micro-credit in support of growth and employment*, COM (2007) 708 final, Brussels, 13 November 2007.

[31]   For a critical assessment of micro-credit as a suitable development instrument for developing countries, see for example Dyal-Chand R. (2007) 'Reflection in a Distant Mirror: Why the West has Misperceived the Grameen Bank's Vision of Microcredit', Northeastern University School of Law, Working Papers Series no. 13, 2007 (available at http://ssrn/abstract=962374); on the failure of the Canadian Calmeadow Metrofund Williams T. (2001) 'Requiem for microcredit? The decline of a romantic ideal', available at http://ssrn/abstract=976211 (showing how peer lending does not work

eties, by providing financial support to start-ups, microenterprises, non-profit organisations and disadvantaged persons. Mainstream commercial banks have traditionally failed to adequately meet the demand for credit by those who cannot offer sufficient collateral and do not possess a regular income.[32] This significantly restrains entrepreneurial risk-taking and self-employment, especially in the transition from unemployment to self-employment, and the financing of non-profit organisations. The means to bridge this gap are so far insufficient, but have rapidly grown in the past 30 years, with the expansion of targeted financing through niche ethical banks and MFIs,[33] often encouraged by public support mechanisms, including

---

in the United States and Canada and advocating for 'the imposition on financial institutions of strictly regulated duties to serve disadvantaged communities'). See also: Al-Mamun, A., Malarvizhi, C. A., Hossain, S., and Tan, S.-H. (2012), 'Examining the Effect of Microcredit on Poverty in Malaysia', *ASEAN Economic Bulletin*, 29(1), 15–28 (at 25–6); Block, W. E. (2010) 'A critique of Yunus and his micro-finance', *Economics, Management and Financial Markets*, 5(2), 57–75 (at 73); Brett, J.A. (2006) '"We Sacrifice and Eat Less": The Structural Complexities of Microfinance Participation', *Human Organization*, 65(1), 8–19 (at 17); de Mel, S., McKenzie, D., and Woodruff, C. (2011) 'Getting Credit to High Return Microentrepreneurs: The Results of an Information Intervention', *The World Bank Economic Review*, 25(3), 456 (at 461); Gloukoviezoff, G. (2016) 'Evaluating the impact of European microfinance: The foundations', EIF Research & Market Analysis, Working Paper, 33 (at 8); Hamdani, S. M. Q. and Naeem, H. (2012) 'The Impact of Microfinance on Social Mobility, an Empirical Evidence from Pakistan', *Interdisciplinary Journal of Contemporary Research In Business*, 3(9), 81–9 (at 87); Holvoet, N. (2004), 'Impact of Microfinance Programs on Children's Education', *Journal of Microfinance*, 6(2), 27–49 (at 45); Hossain, M. K. (2012) 'Measuring the Impact of BRAC Microfinance Operations: A Case Study of a Village', *International Business Research*, 5(4), 112–23 (at 119–21); Hunt, K. (2013) 'Microfinance: Dreams and Reality', *International Review on Transitions in Corporate Life, Law and Governance*, 2(1), 62–77 (at 73); Karlan, D. and Goldberg, N. (2007) 'Impact Evaluation for Microfinance: Review of Methodological Issues', *Poverty Reduction and Economic Management: Thematic Group on Poverty Analysis, Monitoring and Impact Evaluation, November 2007*, 1–37 (at 31); Kyereboah-Coleman, A. and Osei, K. A. (2008) 'Outreach and profitability of microfinance institutions: the role of governance', *Journal of Economic Studies*, 35(3), 236–48 (at 243); Mallick, I. (2012) 'Major impacts of microfinance on the poor: snapshots from Bangladesh', *Munich Personal RePEc Archive, MPRA*(39038), 1–18 (at 15); Mosley, P. (2001) 'Microfinance and poverty in Bolivia', *The Journal of Development Studies*, 37(4), 101–32 (at 128); Pollinger, J. J., Outhwaite, J., and Cordero-Guzmán, H. (2007) 'The Question of Sustainability for Microfinance Institutions', *Journal of Small Business Management*, 45(1), 1–23 (at 19); Schrauwers, A. (2011) '"Money bound you – money shall loose you": Micro-Credit, Social Capital, and the Meaning of Money in Upper Canada', *Comparative Studies in Society and History*, 53(2), 314–43 (at 339); Sharma, M. (2005) 'Emerging Contours of Micro Finance: Where Do We Go From Here?' *The Business Review, Cambridge*, 4(1), 288–95 (at 294); Yoong, F. J., See, B. L., and Baronovich, D.-L. (2012) 'Financial Literacy Key to Retirement Planning in Malaysia', *Journal of Management and Sustainability*, 2(1), 75–86 (at 84).

   [32]   Chakravarty, S., and Scott, J. S. (1999) 'Relationships and Rationing in Consumer Loans', *The Journal of Business*, 72(4), 523–44 (at 535–42); Stiglitz, J. E. and Weiss, A. (1981) 'Credit Rationing in Markets with Imperfect Information', *The American Economic Review*, 71(3), 393–410 (at 406–9); Williamson, S. D. (1987) 'Costly monitoring, loan contracts, and equilibrium credit rationing' *Quarterly Journal of Economics*, 102(1), 135–45 (at 143).

   [33]   The literature is extremely rich: compare for instance *Microfinance for Poverty Reduction: Building Inclusive Financial Sectors in Asia and the Pacific*, UN ESCAP, Development Paper no. 27, New York, 2006; ABI – Fondazione Giordano Dell'Amore (2006) *Banche e microfinanza*, Bancaria Editrice, Roma; Novak M. (2005) *Non si presta solo ai ricchi – la rivoluzione del microcredito*, Einaudi, Torino; Schreiner M. (2004), *Rural Microfinance in Argentina After the Tequila Crisis*, Edwin Mellen Press, Lewiston, NY; Uddin N. (2003), *Regional Rural Banks and Development*, Mittal Publications, New Dehli; Midgley J. (2008), 'Microenterprise, global poverty and social development', *International Social Work*, 467–79; Mendoza R. and Thelen N. (2008), 'Innovations to Make Markets More Inclusive

the EU supranational level, with EU PHARE, European Investment Fund and European Bank for Reconstruction and Development programmes, and the European Regional Development Fund (ERDF) and European Social Fund (ESF).

Basel II and III force microfinance institutions, along with other credit providers, to hedge against credit risks via insurance, guarantee funds, or securitisation, and these instruments are supported by various institutions within the European governance and funding environment.[34] However, the nature, size, operational features and economic and financial outcomes of these ethical niche banks and MFIs are extremely heterogeneous. This is not new in Europe, which has witnessed the birth of early English lending charities, Irish Loan funds, saving banks and credit cooperatives.[35] History shows two points of particular interest. First, financial exclusion is back, and large in developed economies due to the financial crisis. Lisa Servon's look at the US financial system, notes that banks have been gradually turning away from consumers, while the gap has been filled by other types of institutions with no incentive to increase social inclusion: ordinary people lack access to finance when they need it most, and the picture is

for the Poor', *Development Policy Review*, 427–58, especially at 444–8. See also: Al-Mamun, A., Malarvizhi, C. A., Hossain, S., and Tan, S.-H. (2012), 'Examining the Effect of Microcredit on Poverty in Malaysia', *ASEAN Economic Bulletin*, 29(1), 15–28 (at 25–6); Amoako-Kwakye, F. Y. (2012), 'Background Characteristics and Determinants of Performance of Women's Business Operations in Agona and Asikuma-Odoben-Brakwa Districts, Ghana', *Journal of Management Policy and Practice*, 13(3), 129–48 (at 145); Arora, S. (2012), 'Microfinance interventions and customer perceptions: a study of rural poor in Punjab', *Decision*, 39(1), 62–76 (at 74); Das, S. K. (2012), 'Entrepreneurship through Micro Finance in North East India: A Comprehensive Review of Existing Literature', *Information Management and Business Review*, 4(3), 168–84 (at 181); Gloukoviezoff, G. (2016), 'Evaluating the impact of European microfinance: The foundations', *EIF Research & Market Analysis, Working Paper*, 33 (at 8); Hamdani, S. M. Q. and Naeem, H. (2012), 'The Impact of Microfinance on Social Mobility, an Empirical Evidence from Pakistan', *Interdisciplinary Journal of Contemporary Research In Business*, 3(9), 81–9 (at 87); Hossain, M. K. (2012), 'Measuring the Impact of BRAC Microfinance Operations: A Case Study of a Village', *International Business Research*, 5(4), 112–23 (at 119–21); Mallick, I. (2012), 'Major impacts of microfinance on the poor: snapshots from Bangladesh' *Munich Personal RePEc Archive, MPRA*(39038), 1–18 (at 15); Nwaokoro, A. N. (2012), 'Sources, Stigmatization, and Alleviation of Poverty in Albany/Dougherty, Georgia'. *Journal of Applied Business Research*, 28(2), 155–70 (167); Oncioiu, I. (2012), 'Small and Medium Enterprises' Access to Financing – A European Concern: Evidence from Romanian SME', *International Business Research*, 5(8), 47–58 (at 54); Parvin, L., Rahman, M. W., and Jia, J. (2012), 'Determinates of Women Micro-entrepreneurship Development: An Empirical Investigation in Rural Bangladesh', *International Journal of Economics and Finance*, 4(5), 254–60 (at 252); Randøy, T., Strøm, R. Ø., and Mersland, R. (2015), 'The impact of entrepreneur-CEOs in microfinance institutions: A global survey' *Entrepreneurship Theory and Practice*, 39(4), 927–53 (at 948); Wilson, T. A. (2012), 'Supporting Social Enterprises to Support Vulnerable Consumers: The Example of Community Development Finance Institutions and Financial Exclusion', *Journal of Consumer Policy*, 35(2), 197–213 (at 210); Yoong, F. J., See, B. L., and Baronovich, D.-L. (2012), 'Financial Literacy Key to Retirement Planning in Malaysia', *Journal of Management and Sustainability*, 2(1), 75–86 (at 80).

[34] For an overview in Europe, Viganò, L. (2004), *Microfinanza in Europa*, Fondazione Giordano dell'Amore, Milano, Giuffrè Editore; Leone, P. and Porretta, P. (2014), 'Introduction' (1–21) in *Micro Credit Guarantee Funds in the Mediterranean* Palgrave Macmillan, Basingstoke, UK.

[35] Hollin, A. and Sweetman, A. (1998), 'Microcredit: What Can we Learn from the Past', 26 *World Development*, 1875. As opposed to the US experience of credit unions, European credit cooperatives are generally subject to general banking law and supervision: see however, for an exception, the historical legacy of 163 'casse peote' (informal credit associations) still existing in the Italian Veneto and Friuli Venezia Giulia.

even more sombre for African Americans or Latino households.[36] Second, financial institutions relying on donors were more fragile than deposit-taking institutions,[37] which stresses the importance of self-sustainability for inclusive banking.

Significant differences in the patterns of inclusive banking and micro-finance caution against any unwarranted generalisation, however. The literature on micro-credit in Europe illuminates several aspects of this difference: in Europe (i) the average number of clients of each institution is often much lower; (ii) group lending and other peer lending practices based on community control are hardly effective; (iii) loans are usually of a significant amount (up to €25,000,00); (iv) average interest rates are much lower than the usual 20–60 per cent range in developing countries;[38] (iv) operating and transaction costs are high.[39] *Under these conditions, only a small fraction of institutions are self-sustainable, and thus most of them are associated with Non-Government Organisations (NGOs) and/or rely on support from public or private donors.*

Against this factual background, proportionate regulation of inclusive banking has the potential to help correct some vulnerabilities in the *current scenario, where most of the potential of ethical niche banks and MFIs is strangled in the cradle by regulatory costs, while profit-seeking banks are not nudged towards financial inclusion.* In the past, government initiatives have not been matched by regulation that fosters self-sustainability, which has made donations necessary, and crippled levels of outreach growth.

We turn first to the reasons why the regulation that is appropriate for traditional banks is inappropriate for inclusive banks and micro-finance institutions, and how a special set of rules can nudge towards financial self-sustainability, while preserving financial stability and promoting financial inclusion.

(a)   Why General Regulation Does Not Fit

Regulation for banks and MFIs are like shoes: one size does not, and cannot, fit all. There are vast differences in size, ethical banks and MFIs are typically smaller in loan and deposit size, individually or as a cluster. Yet, and more significantly, the goals are different. For

---

[36]   Servon, L., *The Unbanking of America. How the New Middle Class Survives*, XIII and XVII.

[37]   Hollin, A. and Sweetman, A., 'Microcredit: What Can we Learn from the Past', at 1877; Al-Azzam, M. D., Mimouni, K., and Ali, M. A. (2012), 'The Impact of Socioeconomic Factors and Financial Access on Microfinance Institutions', *International Journal of Economics and Finance*, 4(4), 61–71 (at 68); Hamdani, S. M. Q. and Naeem, H. (2012), 'The Impact of Microfinance on Social Mobility, an Empirical Evidence from Pakistan'. *Interdisciplinary Journal of Contemporary Research in Business*, 3(9), 81–9 (at 87); Kiweu, J. M. (2011), 'Relaxing Financing Constraint in the Microfinance Industry: Is Commercialization the Answer?' *Journal of Business & Economics Research*, 9(10), 87–104 (at 100); Mbogo, M. and Ashika, C. (2011), *Factors Influencing Product Innovation in Micro Finance Institutions in Kenya: A Case Study of MFIs Registered with the Association of Microfinance Institutions*, Washington, United States (at 8).

[38]   See: Block, W. E. (2010), 'A critique of Yunus and his micro-finance'. *Economics, Management and Financial Markets*, 5(2), 57–75 (at 70); de Mel, S., McKenzie, D., and Woodruff, C. (2011), 'Getting Credit to High Return Microentrepreneurs: The Results of an Information Intervention' *The World Bank Economic Review*, 25(3), 456–85 (at 456); Mayer, R. (2012), 'Loan Sharks, Interest-Rate Caps, and Deregulation', *Washington & Lee Law Review*, 69(2), 807–49 (at 844).

[39]   Hunt, K. (2014), 'The Law and Economics of Microfinance', *Journal of Law and Commerce*, 33(1), 1–79 (at 72–3).

example, while a large bank such as Standard Chartered may have the motivation of being the world's best bank and operating at the highest standards,[40] MFIs have goals of meeting social objectives and operating efficiently.[41] Their mission is to fight poverty, they often operate as non-profit entities without private owners,[42] and are often promoted by international NGOs, despite the concern this raises about their sustainability,[43] but their goals do not change when MFIs are established as a regulated Microfinance Bank: empowerment, education, health care and other goals are poles apart from those of profit-seeking banks. Thus, one can surmise that rules based on assumptions of risk-taking driven by short-term profit maximisation will prove inadequate for institutions with a different set of goals, and thereby incentives.

Consider, first, capital requirements. These try to ensure the soundness of banks, which are deposit-taking and deposit-mobilising institutions. Banks guaranteeing access to liquidity are intrinsically risky, because they are subject to 'runs', which makes deposit insurance necessary, which in turn, increases the banks' incentive to increase risk, since profits will stay at the bank, while losses will be 'socialised' through the Deposit Guarantee Scheme. Now consider MFIs. They sometimes take micro-deposits, and mobilise those deposits to deliver loans, but many of them do not, or do so in low amounts, which means that an insolvency priority for depositors and the Deposit Guarantee Scheme, and the corresponding subordination of other investors, would be easy to achieve with lower levels of capital. This without mentioning the fact that the same type of management risk-taking cannot be simply taken for granted in institutions that do not only seek to maximise profit. Changes in capital requirements impact lending programmes across the board,[44] and although, in principle, increasing capital requirements positively impacts welfare over the long term[45] and simultaneously decreases consumption,[46] this only applies when those requirements are needed to correct a defined set of incentives, not in the case of those incentives are different.

Second, capital requirements encompass two relevant components: 'micro' risks, e.g. credit risk, market risk and operational risk, and 'macro' systemic risk. Credit risk is higher in inclusive banks, and the Basel accords already require hedging via insurance, guarantee funds, or securitisation.[47] The result of hedging for inclusive banks is a long-term reduction in the price

---

[40]   Standard-Chartered (2017), Our Brand and Values. Retrieved from https://www.sc.com/en/about -us/our-brand-and-values/.

[41]   See, e.g. KIVA, a large MFI. Kiva (2017), About Us: Mission Statement. Retrieved from http:// www.kiva.org/about.

[42]   Spahr, R. W., Ashraf, M., Scannell, N., and Korobov, Y. I. (2011), 'The governance of non-profit micro finance institutions: lessons from history', *Journal of Management & Governance*, 15(3), 327–48 (at 344).

[43]   Spahr, R. W., Ashraf, M., Scannell, N., and Korobov, Y. I. (2011), 'The governance of non-profit micro finance institutions: Lessons from history, *Journal of Management & Governance*, 15(3), 327–48 (at 345).

[44]   Bridges, J., Gregory, D., Nielsen, M., Pezzini, S., Radia, A., and Spaltro, M. (2014), 'The impact of capital requirements on bank lending', Working Paper No. 486, Bank of England, London (at 12).

[45]   Nguyen, T. T. (2014), 'Bank capital requirements: A quantitative analysis' at https://papers.ssrn .com/sol3/papers.cfm?abstract_id=2356043 (at 12).

[46]   Van den Heuvel, S. J. (2008), 'The welfare cost of bank capital requirements', *Journal of Monetary Economics*, 55(2), 298–320 (at 317).

[47]   Leone, P. and Porretta, P. (2014), 'Introduction' in *Microcredit Guarantee Funds in the Mediterranean*, in particular 15–19.

of micro-credit, increased sustainability and increased outreach.[48] The factors relevant to the capital requirements of micro-finance are as different as the borrowers are – micro-finance borrowers are small scale, and have limited financial collateral.[49] Micro-finance banks are similarly different in that they generally serve clients through small-scale loans, and charge higher interest rates to recover the cost of servicing such an expensive population.[50] In turn, as pointed out in the literature *inappropriate regulatory caps on interest rates likely result in the withdrawal of MFI funding, reduced MFI scale, increased loan sizes, and at the end of day increases in effective interest rates for the poor[51] (as there will be a shift towards informal lenders who charge higher interest rates than MFIs).*

Yet with regard to 'macro' risk, inclusive banks pose no systemic problems, which suggests that it is not appropriate for the regulation to be the same. Studies addressing MFI regulation in Tanzania[52] recommend internal rules for board governance and auditing for non-deposit-taking MFIs, rather than stringent requirements to ensure financial stability, as the law would for a deposit-taking MFI.

Another example is reporting. One way that regulation ensures financial stability is by monitoring financial institutions through mandated reporting of financial indicators in a comparable format. This ensures the regulator is in control of understanding the benchmarks and trends for each financial institution and for the industry as a whole. This reporting requirement is as suitable for inclusive banks and MFIs as it is for traditional banks, *but in different forms*. Calibrations are appropriately available in some jurisdictions but not across the board. The reporting requirements of MFIs range from the usual one for financial institutions in Italy to an annual balance sheet in India, to an internal audit and annual report and a weekly financial summary in Pakistan, to a list of requirements to be provided half-yearly in Bangladesh. There are very significant operating costs associated with reporting: when reporting regulation is overly demanding, this will add another cost to MFIs' operational structure and stand in the way of self-sustainability. One way to achieve the desirable level of information in a way which allows MFIs to have long-term financial self-sustainability could be to follow the lead of Pakistan: the State Bank of Pakistan (SBP) requires weekly reporting from Microfinance Banks (MFBs), but only of key indicators. This provides a nudge to the MFBs to keep their financial records up to date while staying within benchmarks of financial soundness, and allows timely monitoring of trends by the regulator.

---

[48]   Leone, P., Mango, F. M., Panetta, I. C., and Porretta, P. (2014), 'Regulatory Framework and Supervisory Authorities in Microcredit Sector: A Comparative Analysis' in *Microcredit Guarantee Funds in the Mediterranean*, in particular 22–62.

[49]   Agyapong, D., Agyapong, G. K. Q., and Darfor, K. N. (2011), 'Criteria for Assessing Small and Medium Enterprises' Borrowers in Ghana', *International Business Research*, 4(4), 132–8 (at 134).

[50]   de Mel, S., McKenzie, D. J., and Woodruff, C. (2009), 'Measuring microenterprise profits: Must we ask how the sausage is made?', *Journal of Development Economics*, 88(1), 17.

[51]   Di Bella, G. (2011), 'The Impact of the Global Financial Crisis on Microfinance and Policy Implications, Western Hemisphere Department', IMF Working Paper 11/75 (at 37).

[52]   Satta, T. A. (2004), 'Microfinance regulation influence on small firms' financing in Tanzania', *Journal of Financial Regulation and Compliance*, 12(1), 64–75 (in particular at 72–3).

(b)   How Self-regulation Could Help

Self-regulation can remove part of the burden of rule-making from the government, while still ensuring a high level of industry quality. In order to explore in detail how self-regulation has helped and not helped inclusive banks, interviews were conducted by one of us with MFIs, Inclusive Banks, regulators and self-regulators in Italy, Pakistan, Bangladesh and India in 2013 and 2015. *The interviews in countries with self-regulatory institutions (namely MFIN in India and PMN in Pakistan) revealed that the role of these bodies is much more important than research previously considered.* The interviews revealed that the self-regulatory body not only ensures MFIs are able to set their own industry standards and keep each other in line, but it also serves as a forum for sharing ideas, and a powerful lobbying body to get changes in the legislation that would have otherwise been impossible. Indeed, these institutions have indicated many particular changes in the law have been a direct result of their negotiations with the government, which are uncomplicated because the government has overlapping goals with the MFIs. Even more importantly, *in instances where the self-regulatory body has power because it is a funder of MFIs, such as PKSF in Bangladesh and PPAF in Pakistan, it is a very efficient regulatory system for the smaller MFIs – which are the ones that seek funding from these bodies.* This is especially the case in Bangladesh where the regulator has opted for paper-based reporting (and manual entry into an electronic system to monitor MFIs), and thus does not have the resources to monitor all of the MFIs in a detailed manner. *Government organisations which simultaneously fund and oversee to keep MFIs accountable to reporting and operational standards are effective soft regulatory tool which show that 'money talks' in 'nudging' MFIs to operate in a way which can be financially self-sustainable in the long term.*

An additional aspect which illustrates the positive effect of self-regulation is found in credit bureaus. The establishment of a Credit Information Bureau (CIB) which MFIs are required to report to is an example of soft regulation that works. Some initiatives, such as a credit database and disclosure regulation, have the potential to promote micro-finance in a '*softly, softly*' manner, which does not have many potential disadvantages, but has many potential benefits.[53] A study[54] focussed on 'second wave' Indian financial reforms suggested that the government can do things to reduce the risk of over-borrowing other than caps on interest rates, such as a credit database.[55] In a sense, credit bureaus are institutions built also for consumer protec-

---

[53]   Research on CIBs in the less-developed context can be found in papers by: Bumacov, V., Ashta, A., and Singh, P. (2014), 'The use of credit scoring in microfinance institutions and their outreach', *Strategic Change*, 23(7–8), 401–13 (at 411); McIntosh, C., Sadoulet, E., Buck, S., and Rosada, T. (2013), 'Reputation in a public goods game: Taking the design of credit bureaus to the lab', *Journal of Economic Behavior & Organization*, 95, 270–85 (at 282); Pandit, A. (2013), 'The Role of Credit Bureaus in the Commercialized Indian Microfinance Sector: A Catalyst or An Obstacle to Financial Inclusion?' (at 6); Serrano-Cinca, C., Gutiérrez-Nieto, B., and Reyes, N. M. (2016), 'A social and environmental approach to microfinance credit scoring', *Journal of Cleaner Production*, 112, 3504–13 (at 3511).

[54]   Herd, R., Koen, V., Patnaik, I., and Shah, A. (2011), 'Financial Sector Reform in India: Time for a Second Wave?', Economics Department Working Papers No. 879, 1–37 (at 32–5).

[55]   Research on CIBs has often considered general areas, such as the work by Herd, Koen, Patnaik, and Shah (2011) (ibid.) in an OECD working paper who analyse the financial reforms of India and develop recommendations for micro-finance regulation to promote micro-finance. The authors based an analysis on the law of micro-finance in India with the aim of avoiding the consequences such as were seen in Andhra Pradesh in 2010 with interest rate caps introduced by the state parliament. The paper established the situation of micro-finance in India in 2010, and theoretically discussed the effect

tion.[56] These institutions compile borrower data from all of the different MFIs in order to make sure that borrowers do not become over-indebted by obtaining loans from different companies, and ensure there are inherent incentives for loan repayments in that borrowers who default cannot obtain loans from any MFI in the future. In this way, the credit bureaus enforce the rules about the maximum number or value of micro-finance loans per borrower. Regulation which requires reporting to a CIB is a very low-cost way of ensuring country-wide portfolio quality and consumer protection. From the perspective of MFIs, credit bureaus play a dual role. Not only do the credit bureaus ensure that clients self-select into microfinance only if they take the loans seriously enough to repay them; the credit bureau also serves as an industry apex of information sharing to make sure that borrowers are given incentives to repay their loan, because if they do not repay they will not be able to access any loans from other MFIs. Hence the credit bureau plays a role throughout the loan process. *Discussions with MFIs in Pakistan and India revealed that their portfolio quality and repayment rate has increased since the credit bureaus have been active. This lends some support for the 'law matters' principle where regulation nudges versus market solutions capable not only of supporting MFIs in increasing portfolio quality, but also of protecting consumers from over-indebtedness.* Research has commented in the past on the ability of microfinance borrowers to take multiple loans, with each loan being used to repay the previous one, being responsible, for example, for the crisis in Andhra Pradesh.[57] Obviously, portfolio quality has the potential to impact MFI operating sustainability. A question particular to Europe is whether niche ethical banks and MFIs should rely on sector-specific CIBs duly linked with traditional banking ones on with the latter, duly expanded to encompass also this segment of the market.

(c)   A Matrix for Strategic Decision-Making in Regulating MFIs Nudging Towards Self-sustainability

In this chapter we are not putting forward a specific proposal for rules of one kind or another on niche ethical banks and MFIs in Europe but rather we start laying down the conceptual foundations for a tiered approach to their co-regulation. Regulation shall follow an in-depth impact assessment and a much wider debate; here we simply claim that a European experiment of a regulatory sandbox would appear quite at point to nudge European ethical niche banks and MFIs towards self-sustainability.

To support this, we considered that a strategic decision-making matrix could prove useful and we started to develop it, looking at the comparative experiences of MFIs in selected

---

of financial sector reforms on financial sector efficiency and the spill-over effects on the rest of the economy. In particular it was found that 13 out of 14 of India's largest MFIs were regulated as non-bank financial companies and were not allowed to take deposits. The result of this is understandably that there is lower micro-finance penetration (as found by: Hartarska, V., and Nadolnyak, D. (2007), 'Do regulated microfinance institutions achieve better sustainability and outreach? Cross-country evidence', *Applied Economics*, 39(10), 1207–22 (at 1219)).

[56]   This is the case in Pakistan, India and Italy. However, in Bangladesh there are a variety of credit bureaus, which compete for data from MFIs, who are reluctant to pass on information as a result of competition fears. Interviews in Bangladesh revealed that MFIs would prefer lower portfolio quality rather than the perceived risk of increased competition if they report borrower data to a CIB.

[57]   Das, S. K. (2012), 'Entrepreneurship through Micro Finance in North East India: A Comprehensive Review of Existing Literature', *Information Management and Business Review*, 4(3), 168–84 (at 181–2).

countries. Identifying countries to compare on this topic can take one of two main perspectives. Some authors have indicated that the most beneficial legal comparison can be made between countries which have large contextual differences.[58] On the other hand, some authors have attempted to compare similar countries. Both perspectives are important for establishing a sound empirical methodology. A key consideration is also the availability of data, as although micro-finance is present in many countries, the availability of data on micro-finance laws differs widely.

Considering this, and without any pretention of being exhaustive, five key countries have been identified hereunder for consideration – Bangladesh, India, and Pakistan and Italy, as leading jurisdictions in ethical banking and investment, to which we add another, Spain, where such types of investments are still low. Indeed, from a historical perspective, the first three countries were administered by Britain as one country until less than 70 years ago. India, Pakistan and Bangladesh have been chosen as comparable countries for a number of key reasons. In particular, these countries have a similarity in history and culture, despite different dominant religions. There is also relative similarity across geography, language and established micro-finance presence. Although the countries have distinctly different cultures, religions and regulatory conditions now, it can be argued that these differences are smaller than would exist between a geographically diverse set of countries. Italy and Spain have been included to compare how two developed countries, where nonetheless ethical banking is in different stages of development, have reacted to micro-finance by trying to adapt their banking regulatory framework to include also MFIs. They are also included to illustrate how they can learn, in this process of adaptation, from the developing countries when it comes to the regulation of inclusive banks. The Italian experience is also useful to discuss existing European strategies and the most desirable future course of events. In a nutshell, the 2010 Italian reform on micro-finance has identified MFIs as a new class of financial intermediaries ('micro-credit operators') which, provided that certain minimum requirements are met, are licensed and can operate as non-deposit-taking micro-finance providers. Under Article 111 of the Italian Banking Act, as introduced in 2010, they are listed in a register, provisionally held by the Bank of Italy, until there are enough of them present in the market to warrant the establishment of a specialised supervisory office responsible for this class of intermediaries only. Micro-credit operators can provide financing for the purpose of promoting 'the taking up or pursuit of autonomous work activities or of micro-enterprises' ('entrepreneurial micro-credit') or of supporting 'individuals in conditions of particular economic and social vulnerability' ('social micro-credit').[59] The granting of loans must be accompanied by the provision of ancillary

---

[58]   Marr, A., and Tubaro, P. (2013), 'The microfinance wholesale lending market: A comparative study of India, Peru and Tanzania', *International Journal of Economics and Business Research*, 5(1), 33–54 (at 49–52 and 45–8).

[59]   In this way, micro-finance is normatively bifurcated in Italy: when it takes the form of 'entrepreneurial micro-credit', micro-financing must be (i) for amounts not exceeding €25,000 and without collateral; (ii) aimed at the establishment or development of entrepreneurial initiatives or inclusion in the labour market; (iii) accompanied by the provision of ancillary assistance and monitoring services. When it takes the form of 'social micro-credit', i.e. social welfare loans that can cover the costs of health care, education and job placement, or expenses arising from a situation of sudden and temporary vulnerabilities, financing must be (i) up to €10,000; (ii) unsecured; and (iii) accompanied by the provision of ancillary services to family budgeting; and (iv) on terms more favourable than those prevailing in the market. Note that some micro-finance can still be exercised, but at 'rates adjusted to merely allow the

mentoring services. Ministerial Decree No. 176/2014[60] implemented Article 111 and detailed all technical aspects related to lending in micro-finance. In turn, Bank of Italy issued on 3 June 2015 rules[61] governing the registration and reporting of MFIs, including also reports on ancillary services. However, Bank of Italy has limited supervisory powers over micro-credit operators; these powers are listed in Article 113 of the Banking Act, which confers upon the supervisory authority the power to request information and documents, carry out inspections, prohibit new operations, impose a reduction in assets and order cancellation from the register in extreme circumstances.

The Spanish case sits in contrast with the Italian one, and even more with that of developing countries, due to the almost non-existent regulation, and the preponderance of self-regulation. INVERCO (the association of fund management institutions) issued a circular in November 1999, which was approved by the Spanish securities Commission (CNMV) but only applied to mutual funds, differentiating between ethical funds, green funds and sharing funds. This was supplemented by the standards launched by the Spanish Association for Standardization and Certification (AENOR) on Socially Responsible Financial Products.[62] These standards have been updated to account for the developments at an international level, e.g. UN Principles and procedures, and a European level, e.g. the Regulation on Social Entrepreneurship Funds, and thus a new Circular was adopted by INVERCO in 2014, and a new standard was adopted in 2012 (UNE 165001). The legislature, however, has been reluctant to adopt mandatory regulation. The extreme case is that of MFIs, which lack any specific rules. The Spanish Association of Microloans has tried to bridge the vast gap by adopting a Code of Good Practices, which can operate as a sort of framework for principles,[63] but these are very broad, and focus on the bank-customer relationship.[64]

The picture has only worsened since the financial crisis. In Spain the banking market was traditionally divided between ordinary banks and *cajas*, or saving banks. The latter originated as partly 'social' institutions, and had to dedicate a percentage of their annual profits to social works.[65] Spanish *cajas* experienced an extraordinary expansion in pre-crisis years, which led

---

recovery of the costs incurred by the creditor', by certain non-licensed non-profit organisations, recorded in a separate section of the register referred to in paragraph 1 of art. 111. However, they can offer only 'social' micro-credit. Compare Pellegrini, F., 'Microcredit in Italy: Searching for a Model', in (2015) ESD 9th Conference, *Book of Proceedings*, eds. Vrankic, I., Kozina, and G. E Kovsca V., Istanbul, 329, noting also that since 2012 the European Microfinance Network (EMN) has adopted a similar differentiation 'as a first step towards a more focused discussion on institutional blueprints and lending models for microfinance in Europe'. See: *Overview of the microcredit sector in the European Union* (2012), 14 and 39. The EU recognises this distinction, for example in the report of the European Commission COM (2012) 769 final, 18 December 2012, 4.

[60]   Legislative Decree 17 October 2014, no. 176, *Disciplina del microcredito, in attuazione dell'articolo 111, comma 5, del decreto legislativo 1° settembre 1993, n. 385.*

[61]   Banca d'Italia, *Disposizioni per l'iscrizione e la gestione dell'elenco degli operatori di microcredito*, 3 June 2015, available at http://www.bancaditalia.it/compiti/vigilanza/normativa/archivio-norme/disposizioni/disposizioni-microcredito/Disposizioni.pdf.

[62]   UNE 165001:2002 (AENOR).

[63]   AEMIP *Código de buenas prácticas para la concesión de micropréstamos* 10 December 2015.

[64]   One of the most specific contributions is the access to a mediator in case of over-indebtedness. See Code no. 6.7, and the framework agreement available at https://www.aemip.es/agentes-mediadores/.

[65]   See, e.g. Fundación de Estudios Financieros 'Las Cajas de Ahorros: Modelo de Negocio, Estructura de la Propiedad y su Gobierno Corporativo' *Papeles de la Fundación* no. 218 (2007) 21.

them to accumulate around half of the loans originated in the country,[66] and, despite that this may have come at the price of a gradual 'bankarisation' of their model and practices, they still had more social roots than pure banks. The most damning side effect of the expansion, however, was the reckless accumulation of risky loans, which eventually led to restructuring the whole banking sector.[67] Despite the fact that the lack of prudent management can be traced back to deficiencies in the *cajas'* governance model, which had led to rampant political meddling,[68] subsequent reforms have tended to paint the whole model with the broad brush of suspicion, and to separate savings 'banks', turning them into ordinary banks, and non-bank activities, which can be exercised through foundations, still socially active, but with more constraints on accessing the bank's financial muscle.[69] Some institutions continue to see social lending as part of their company purpose due to institutional path-dependence, like Caixabank, which was originally a (solvent and sound) *caja*, and now accumulates a large volume of micro-credit in Spain. However, it is telling that Caixabank turned into an ordinary bank years before the crisis, and runs its micro-credit operations through Microbank, which is also registered as an ordinary bank, and is also a fully-owned subsidiary,[70] which poses no issues with minority shareholders seeking to maximise profits.

The field of SRIs, on the other hand, has seen some timid developments, after a larger social security reform introduced (i) a requirement for managers of pension funds to make explicit their investment policies, which, in the case of employment pension funds, must include a reference to extra-financial risks, including ethical, social, environmental or governance issues; and (ii) the obligation for the fund's manager, or control committee to include a reference to the implementation of such criteria for socially responsible investment.[71] The single text establishing specific rules is the EU Regulation 346/2013 on Social Entrepreneurship Funds.

There are therefore no controls on sound and prudent management tailored to the specific needs of these institutions, which makes a cross-country comparison more pertinent.

The criteria for such a comparison have been identified based on the aspects of regulation likely to have the largest impact on MFI financial sustainability, which relate to business activities, including provisions for capital requirements, corporate governance, reporting and consumer protection via credit bureaus. Table 4.1 offers the relevant data of the comparison and some of the results which in our view stand out are commented overleaf.

Two findings, in our view, stand out from this matrix, for careful consideration for future developments.

First, the central role of suitable, but *ad hoc*, risk management provisions. Particularly of interest in this context is the finding that both internal funding via retained profits and external guarantee funds are present in the matrix, and they appear effective, and complementary,

---

[66]   Illueca, M. Norden, L. and Udell, G. (2014), 'Liberalization and risk-taking: evidence from government-controlled banks' *Review of Finance*, 18(4), 1217–47.

[67]   *Ibid.*

[68]   *Ibid.* See also Cuñat, V., and Garicano, L. (2010), 'Did Good Cajas Extend Bad Loans? Governance, Human Capital and Loan Portfolios' *FEDEA* Working Paper (February 2010).

[69]   See Royal Decree-Law 11/2010, and Act 26/2013, on Saving Banks and Bank Foundations.

[70]   https://www.microbank.com/conocemicrobank/quienessomos/nuestramision_es.html.

[71]   New art. 14(7) of the Royal Legislative Decree 1/2002, which establishes the Single Text on the Regulation of Pension Funds, introduced by the Final Provision Eleventh of Act 27/2011, of 1 August, on the Updating and Modernization of the Social Security System, and art. 69(5) of Royal Decree 304/2004, on the regulation of pension commitments, as modified by Royal Decree 681/2011.

Table 4.1   Cross-Country Regulatory Comparison

Criteria	India	Pakistan	Bangladesh	Italy	Spain
Regulatory environment					
Relevant legislation	MFI Bill, 2012; RBI/2012-13/161; DNBS(PD) CC.No.300 /03.10.038/2012-13; Marr and Tubaro (2013); Nair, Sathye, Perumal, Applegate and Sathye (2014).	Prudential Regulation for Microfinance Banks (2014); Microfinance Institutions Ordinance, 2001; AC&MFD Circular No. 02 of 2015; AC&MFD Circular No. 05 of 2015; the Societies Registration Act, 1860, The Voluntary Social Welfare Agencies Ordinance, 1961, The Trust Act, 1882, and the Companies' Ordinance, 1984 (for MFIs and Rural Support Programs (RSPs)).	Financial Reporting Act (2015); Grameen Bank Ordinance (1983); Microcredit Regulatory Authority Rules (2010) SRO No. 394-Law/2010; Microfinance Regulatory Act (2006).	Articles 111 and 113 Banking Act; Legislative Decree 176/2014 and Provisions of Bank of Italy 3 June 2015.	Article 14(7) Royal Legislative Decree 1/2002 on Pension Funds, article 69(5) Royal decree 304/2004 (SRI-specific), Act 10/2014 on Supervision of Credit Institutions, circulars 2/2016, 2/2014 (capital requirements, Act 16/2011 on Consumer Credit (not MFI-specific) self-regulation.
Regulator	RBI (Reserve Bank of India) and Self-Regulatory Organisations (SROs). Most MFIs are registered as non-bank financial companies (NBFCs) or under Acts for Societies, Cooperatives and Trusts.	SBP (State Bank of Pakistan) with a Microfinance Division established in 2001. The Microfinance Consultative Group was also created in 2001 and is chaired by the SBP.	Microcredit Regulatory Authority (MRA): 'Independent' body with Central Bank representation on board.	The Minister of Economy and Finance, after consulting with the Bank of Italy.	Bank of Spain for banks, CNMV for funds. No differentiated treatment.
Self-Regulation	All MFIs must be a member of a Self-Regulatory Organisation (SRO) recognised by the RBI. MFIs must comply with the Code of Conduct of the SRO. Responsibility for compliance with the regulations lies with the NBFC-MFIs.	Various industry bodies have been created to provide a level of on-going self-regulation, the peak of which is the Pakistan Microfinance Network (PMN).	No relevant industry bodies established with the purpose of self-regulating MFIs have been established.	Not relevant.	Most important source of criteria, but focussed on transparency and investor protection.

Criteria	India	Pakistan	Bangladesh	Italy	Spain
Tiered Approach to MFI Regulation	MFIs of different sizes (based on loans outstanding) are regulated differently in the stipulation regarding business activities. MFIs are either 'large' or 'small'.	MFBs are regulated differently to MFIs (NGOs) and informal micro-finance providers. This table will consider MFBs only.	No. There is one set of regulations for MFIs and a separate legislation for the Grameen Bank under the previously stated Ordinance.	No	No
Tier thresholds	The benchmark is that a large MFI is one with more than Rs. 100 crore (1 crore = 10 million) loan portfolio (approx. €14 million).	MFBs need €7.7 million in paid up capital to be regulated as such. Each MFI has the ability to decide under which regulatory code they are regulated. There is no clear tier structure with defined thresholds.	No thresholds.	No thresholds, just benchmarks for what microcredit is.	No
Capital Requirements					
Initial Capital Requirements	All NBFC-MFIs need to have NOF (Net Owned Funds) of Rs. 5 crore (approx. €700,000). There is an exception for the NE Region for Rs. 2 crore (approx. €280,000). If they do not have the required capital, they are restricted to lending only 10% of funds in micro-finance loans, but can still be registered as an NBFC-MFI.	Rs. 1 billion (approx. €7.7 million) in paid up capital to be regulated as an MFB. The RSPs and other regulatory tiers have other capital requirements, and they are not directly regulated by the SBP.	No requirements from the MRA. Requirements are from the regulation under which NGOs were created (of which there are four).	Legislative Decree 176/2014 (Article 6.1.c)	Act 10/2014 on the Supervision of Credit Institutions, Bank of Spain circulars 2/2014 and 2/2016, hereafter Banking rules (not specific to MFIs).
On-going Capital Adequacy Requirements	Capital Adequacy of 15% of Risk Weighted Assets.	Capital Adequacy of 15% of Risk Weighted Assets.	All NGO-MFIs maintain CAR of above 10%.	Banking Act – not specific to MFIs.	Banking rules – not specific to MFIs.

Criteria	India	Pakistan	Bangladesh	Italy	Spain
Risk Management Provisions	Must provide a percentage of profits as a reserve fund to the RBI each year (which will be used for MFI training etc.).	Cash reserve requirement (5% of deposits); statutory liquidity requirement (10% of demand and time liabilities); statutory reserve (20% of annual profits); depositor's protection fund (5% of annual profit); provisioning requirements (100% loss declared on arrears of 180 days); exposure against contingent liabilities (= 5 times equity). Standards for board composition are documented.	10% of total income surplus (accumulated surplus or profits) must be maintained in a reserve fund (a separate bank account). The remaining profits can be used for operational activities or poverty alleviation activities (if approved by the MRA). Liquidity of 15% (previously 10%) required (5% in cash and 10% in term deposits) balanced half-yearly. MFI to classify loans as 'Regular', 'Watchful', 'Sub-standard', 'Doubtful' and 'Bad Loan' on an annual basis and provision based on the percentage indications provided in the rules. Bad debts are classified as an expenditure in accounting.	Banking Act – not specific to MFIs.	Banking rules – not specific to MFIs.
Savings Mobilisation	Can mobilise deposits if the MFI has capitalisation of US$400,000 and a CAR of 12–15%.	MFBs can mobilise deposits if the risk management guidelines are followed.	Grameen Bank is permitted to accept deposits from the general public. Under the MRA, MFIs are allowed to intermediate deposits from members (up to 80% of loan portfolio), but that is different to deposit mobilisation.	Banking Act – not specific to MFIs.	Banking rules – not specific to MFIs.

Criteria	India	Pakistan	Bangladesh	Italy	Spain
Access to finance – debt	Can mobilise deposits if benchmarks above are met. Of the lenders to MFIs, 21% are international (compared with 55% in Peru and 75% in Tanzania (Marr & Tubaro, 2013)).	Microfinance Credit Guarantee Fund (MCGF): GBP 10 million (USD 16.47 million) is available to the microfinance industry as guarantees to access commercial debt. This fund is also part of the Financial Inclusion Program (FIP).	MFIs can take loans from financial institutions. For loans from international institutions Government authorisation must be obtained. Securitisation is allowed. Loans from people other than clients are allowed with a well-defined contract. Grameen Bank can sell bonds and debentures guaranteed by the Government.	Legislative Decree 176/2014 (Article 14.1)	Banking rules – not specific to MFIs.
Access to finance – equity	Foreign investment in MFIs is automatically approved. Being a regulated NBFC allows them to attract commercial investment.	Investment in MFBs has no restrictions. Other providers of micro-finance have investment restrictions, such as RSPs, thus giving incentives to move up the tiered regulation structure.	MFIs are structured as NGOs, therefore the ownership of the NGO is subject to the specific regulations under which it was founded.	Legislative Decree 176/2014 (Article 7); Provisions of Bank of Italy 3 June 2015 (Article 3)	Banking rules – not specific to MFIs.
Governance					
Legal Form requirement	No requirement.	Legal form restrictions are placed on MFIs regulated by other supervisors than the SBP.	Depends on the regulation under which the NGO was formed.	Legislative Decree 176/2014 (Articles 6.2 and 11.1)	No requirement
Ownership	No restrictions. Can be NGO owned or private companies.	No restrictions. Can be companies which allocate profits to shareholders and receive investments.	Depends on the regulation under which the NGO was formed.	Legislative Decree 176/2014 (Article 7); Provisions of Bank of Italy 3 June 2015 (Article 3)	No requirement
Management board				Legislative Decree 176/2014 (Articles 6.2.e and 8); Provisions of Bank of Italy 3 June 2015 (Article 2)	No requirement

Criteria	India	Pakistan	Bangladesh	Italy	Spain
Asset (Loan Portfolio) Guidelines	85% of assets must be 'Qualifying Assets' (applies to post-2012 assets only) to receive eligible bank funding. In addition, 70% of loans must be for income generation purposes (as opposed to for housing repairs, education, medical emergencies).	The MFB must determine that the borrower has the ability to repay the loan. Hence, loans for business purposes are easier to verify, and many MFBs only provide loans for business purposes. MFBs can provide loans for any purpose that are backed by gold collateral up to 35% of the loan portfolio.	Loans for micro-enterprises must be less than 50% of the total loan portfolio. Regulatory guidelines from July 2011 ban unofficial deductions by lenders for so-called saving schemes (forced deposits from borrowers), limit charges for administration fees and set a 15-day mandatory grace period for repayment, and borrowers must pay back their loans in 46 instalments.	Legislative Decree 176/2014 (Article 5.7)	Banking rules – not specific to MFIs.
Reporting					
Reporting	Must provide P&L and BS to RBI annually.	Weekly report of summary (one page of financial indicators). Annual audit to SPB. Need an internal audit department which reports to the board. Annual audit rating.	Abstract of results of internal audits must be published. MRA must be informed of the interest rate, duration and repayment schedule of all loans on a half-yearly basis. Send to the MRA annual reports of the BS, CF, Income-Expenditure, Change in Capital, Portfolio Statement.	Article 113 Banking Act; Provisions of Bank of Italy 3 June 2015 (Articles 6 and 7)	Banking rules – not specific to MFIs.
Accounting Standards	Interest rate calculation (monthly and annual) certified annually by Statutory Auditors and reported in the BS.	Different types of MFI regulation result in different accounting standards for each type. However, the legislation refers to 'international accounting standards'.	Standard accounting procedures must be followed. Further, 'heads' of income and expenditure reports have been stipulated by the MRA for the financial management of accounts. Annual budget must be approved by the board.	Italian Accounting Standards – not specific to MFIs.	Spanish Accounting Standards – not specific to MFIs.

Criteria	India	Pakistan	Bangladesh	Italy	Spain
Interest rate caps	Loans under US$4,000 are subject to an interest rate cap. Interest rates are capped at 26% pa (with 4% pa +/- leeway). To calculate the cap, MFIs must use a calculation of the annual average borrowing cost plus the margin (max of 10% or 12% for 'small' MFIs). The aim of this is that in a low interest rate environment the borrower will benefit and in a high interest rate environment the NBFC-MFI will have enough leeway to maintain sustainability.	No restrictions.	Microfinance interest rates are capped at 27%pa.	Legislative Decree 176/2014 (Articles 5.6 and 11.5)	Act of 23 July 1908, on Usury – not specific to MFIs.
Legislated loans to micro-finance	Domestic banks must lend 40% of lending portfolio to 'weaker sectors' (including micro-finance).	No restrictions.	70% of clients must be borrowers	No	No
Deposit taking – Regulatory framework to allow (EIU)	Regulated MFIs can take 'thrift', but not mobilise the savings for business activities.	MFBs can receive deposits as outlined in the regulations.	Grameen Bank can take deposits, and in 2009 had a ratio of 142% for client savings to loan portfolio. Total deposit balance will not exceed 80% of total loans outstanding at any time. There are conditions which need to be followed in order to receive voluntary deposits (including that they cannot exceed 25% of the total capitalisation of the organisation). Detail is given about how to administer deposits and the conditions to follow.	No allowance for MFIs to take deposits. Banking Act – not specific to MFIs.	Banking rules – not specific to MFIs.

Criteria	India	Pakistan	Bangladesh	Italy	Spain
Credit Bureaus					
Credit bureaus	Every MFI must be a member of a Credit Information Company (DiCicco-Bloom & Crabtree) created under the CIC Regulation Act 2005. Each MFI must share information with the CICs about indebtedness and source of borrowing.	MF-CIB, a micro-finance specific credit bureau was released in June 2012 to reduce the likelihood of microfinance defaults for over-indebtedness.	Luoto, McIntosh and Wydick (2007) indicates that the World Bank planned to establish a credit bureau in Bangladesh, but no evidence has been found.	Banking Act – not specific to MFIs.	Banking rules – not specific to MFIs.

tools to address risk, and achieve inclusion and self-sustainability. MFIs offer loans without financial collateral. *An institutional framework supporting suitable forms of credit market guarantees*[72] *nudges towards inclusive banking because it allows inclusive banks to lend, offering to the loan provider some security of the loan capital. Government-funded guarantee funds could also display useful market discipline in terms of better MFI governance*: as we noted above, commenting on PKSF in Bangladesh and PPAF in Pakistan, organisations which simultaneously fund and oversee to keep MFIs accountable to reporting and operational stand-ards 'nudge' MFIs to operate in a way which can be financially self-sustainable in the long term. We will discuss this issue in some detail in the following sections.

Second, innovation seems to be key for inclusive finance. Government support for innova-tion through regulation has direct flow-through effects on MFI operations and subsequently on financial inclusion in each country. Regulation has the ability to allow companies to form equity partnerships with international firms to share knowledge, to create innovative products, or to seek to leverage off technology in increasing outreach to the poorest. As Lisa Servon[73] put it recently:

> a confluence of forces has created a moment ripe for innovation and wholesale change in the consumer financial-services industry, with a slew of innovators posed to seize the opportunities. Enormous advances in technology, significant changes in consumer behaviour and a radically revised regulatory environment are coming together in ways that offer hope for more efficient, effective and equitable provision of consumer financial services. This moment is notable for its rarity.

It is surprising thus that some governments – for instance those of India and Bangladesh – did not seem to support adequately innovation in micro-finance, nor leverage off technology to come up with a more accurate credit-scoring model. The regulation of these countries reflects that MFIs are not encouraged to innovate in product design. In interviews with one of us, the Indian government explicitly communicated its willingness to avoid the use of mobile phones in banking, to avoid the creation of 'eMoney' outside of fiscal control. Yet, mobile phones have already revolutionised financial services in Kenya, where 19 million people (90 per cent of the adults) manage their money through M-PESA. Furthermore, regulations can introduce specific licensing and reporting requirements which make e-money easier to track than cash, rather than the opposite. Furthermore, some studies, including by one of us, point out that legal solutions do not need to simply 'bankarise' mobile e-money companies, e.g. rules that focus on the insulation of customer funds through a trust or fiduciary arrangement[74] can protect

---

[72]   In Pakistan, MFBs are well capitalised, but they need to prove to the market that they are able to operate as efficient businesses, and according to interviews with the Pakistan Institute of Management they are incompetent as they are just SMEs themselves, learning to operate efficiently. The DIFID Guarantee fund has helped 27 loan contracts take place by guaranteeing the loans accessed by MFBs on the Pakistani capital markets. According to the VIS Ratings Agency, this is effectively a 'credit enhance-ment'. It is critical that inclusive banks have diversified sources of credit. Although they cannot access the interbank overnight credit markets, they should be supported by regulation to access the capital markets. One effective mechanism to facilitate this is a guarantee fund, as exists in Pakistan.

[73]   Servon L., *The Unbanking of America. How the New Middle Class Survives*, 143.

[74]   Ramos, D., Solana, J., Buckley, R.P., and Greenacre, J. (2016), 'Protecting Mobile Money Customer Funds in Civil Law Jurisdictions' *International and Comparative Law Quarterly*, 65(3), 705–39; Greenacre, J. and Buckley, R.P. (2014), 'Using Trusts to Protect Mobile Money Customers' *Singapore Journal of Legal Studies*, 59–78.

customers, while avoiding onerous prudential requirements, which are conceived more for entities that, unlike payment institutions, have an important recourse to leverage and maturity transformation. In turn, in Pakistan Telecommunications Companies (TelCos) are investing in MFBs in a strategic way because the innovations in branchless banking mean that the poor are now a potential market for financial services. These investments in MFIs are profit motivated, in terms of increasing the potential market for TelCo products and services.

Once the poor are treated as a promising market, financial inclusion will increase through MFI growth. Interviews in Pakistan with leading MFI 'Tameer' illustrated how MFI regulation directly affects their business operations and model. Tameer's equity partner is TeleNor (a Norwegian Telecommunications Company) which allows the MFI to increase outreach using phone banking for certain services, as well as capital to invest in innovative infrastructure and market research. This equity partnership also provides TeleNor with an entry point into the Pakistani mobile phone sector, one of the most innovative and advanced in developing countries. This equity partnership is directly supported by enabling rules, unlike rules in India and Bangladesh, which explicitly deny equity partnerships of this nature. Tameer also benefits from a partial waiver on gold-backed loans,[75] which means that gold-backed loans do not require as large an amount of capital reserves as unsecured loans do.

Also Italy and Europe offer interesting examples of the necessary interplay between innovation and inclusive banking and on the difficulties that regulators face to keep abreast of technological and societal developments, if only one considers social lending on specialised online platforms (Terzo Valore, a peer-to-peer social lending platform developed in Italy by Banca Prossima being an excellent example).[76] EBA issued guidelines[77] and the Bank of Italy adopted in November 2016 the relevant implementing provisions (covering soundness and stability concerns; the 'transparency leg' of such initiatives being governed by the Prospectus Regulation and its exemptions).[78] Although this was an endeavour to set out a comprehensive framework for such innovative initiatives granting also some leeway to deposit taking (limited to small amounts), the regulatory approach still does not give full justice to innovation and insufficiently 'nudges' towards social financing since an overhang of concerns of a path-dependent nature (e.g. on yearly quantitative limits to public offerings and no clear exemptions for personalised social financing via platform) constrain innovative platforms from delivering the full potential of their social impact.

---

[75]   Tameer is well known in Pakistan for its 'gold-backed' micro-finance loans, which, despite only serving those with some gold investments, increase the flexibility of collateral, and allow the firm to have 100% repayment of gold-backed loans. Interviews with both Tameer and the State Bank of Pakistan revealed that the gold-backed products are a direct result of the regulation which provides a partial waiver to the 'general conditions' for gold-backed loans. The State Bank of Pakistan has released instructions entitled: *Financing against Gold Backed Collateral-Instructions for MFBs* which can be found at: http://www.sbp.org.pk/acd/2015/C2-Annex.pdf.

[76]   https://www.terzovalore.com/terzovalore/.

[77]   EBA, Opinion of the European Banking Authority on lending-based crowdfunding, EBA/Op/2015/03, 26 February 2015.

[78]   Compare C.O.N.S.O.B. (Italian Securities Commission), 10 December 2010, No 10101143.

(d)   What Next for Europe? The Path Towards a Regulatory Sandbox Nudging Niche Ethical Banks and MFIs Towards Self-sustainability

Europe has already devoted considerable attention and resources to micro-finance and inclusive finance in the last decade. For instance, the European Commission, following its Staff Working Document of 2004 on 'Microcredit for European small businesses'[79] and the works and recommendations of its Expert Group[80] issued in 2007 a Communication on 'A European initiative for the development of micro-credit'[81] acknowledging that 'micro-credit can play an important role in the realisation of the Lisbon strategy for growth and jobs and the promotion of social inclusion'. It also recognised that 'evidence suggests that banks engage in micro-credit activities (directly or more often in partnership with non bank institutions) where they are encouraged to do so by public support mechanisms' and that there is scope for EU action in the field, first of all, because 'the institutional framework in the Member States appears to be often ill-suited to the development of micro-credit'. The European Commission supported therefore (i) a wider provision of loan guarantees and, as portfolios develop, securitisation; (ii) relaxation of interest caps for micro-credit operations; (iii) access to banks' CBIs for MFIs; and (iv) favourable tax schemes. The Commission correctly underlined in its Staff Working Document of 2004 that inclusive banks are not just about funding, but also *implied 'the provision of non-financial services, in particular mentoring, [which] is essential to increase the chance of survival of start-ups and small enterprises'. Business support services help both sides of the loan agreement to reduce their transaction costs and information asymmetry.* In turn, it also implied,[82] more appropriate credit scoring techniques for assessing the credit risk of microloans.[83]

As to prudential regulation, the EC approach was in favour of a bifurcation between deposit-taking institutions (for which general prudential requirements should apply) and non-deposit-taking institutions, for which regulation could be simplified 'so that it does not put a brake on the supply of micro-credit and the growth of specialist MFIs'. It is also important to note that the Commission acknowledged that 'methods developed for providing

---

[79]   SEC (2004) 1156 of 11 September 2004.

[80]   Expert Group Report, *The Regulation of Microcredit in Europe*, Brussels, April 2007.

[81]   Communication from the Commission to the Council, the European Parliament, the European Economic and Social Committee and the Committee of the Regions, *A European initiative for the development of micro-credit in support of growth and employment*, COM/2007/0708 final. Compare also: *A European initiative for the development of micro-credit in support of growth and employment*, European, Parliament resolution of 24 March 2009 with recommendations to the Commission on a European initiative for the development of micro-credits in support of growth and employment (2008/2122(INI)).

[82]   Bhatt N. and Tang S. (2001), 'Making Microcredit Work in the United States: Social, Financial and Administrative Dimensions', *Economic Development Quarterly*, 15, 229, at 236.

[83]   *Ibid.,* 236 ('such methods could include landlords references, savings records, and proofs of car payments or utility bill payments. Although it may somewhat increase program administrative costs to access such records, the strategy may help to identify low-income individuals who lack a strong credit history but have demonstrated reasonable repayment discipline in the recent past. In addition, programs might secure their loans with items such as television sets, stereo units, furniture, pieces of equipment or cars. Although such non-traditional or creative collateral might not have significant market value compared to the loan amounts disbursed, they are often important to individual borrowers and have been known to serve as effective security against wilful default for some of the more prominent US programs').

and recovering micro-credit differ from traditional banking techniques. This exchange of know-how would allow *inter alia* better integration of quantitative methods such as credit scoring, which are beginning to extend to micro-credit and trust-generating contacts, on which the micro-project and its reimbursement depends'. To this purpose the Commission identified the need for a 'central body with financial and social expertise and the ability to monitor and coordinate action in support of micro-credit and to act as a permanent discussion partner for those in the field'. The tricky side, however, is how to implement those principles.

The European approach is multi-faceted, and needs to combine measures directed at encouraging prudent management with others to enhance capacity building.[84] The matrix developed in the previous section offers, in our view, some initial insights into the most desirable course of action for Europe on the best way to combine prudent management with a different mission.

However, in addition to those rules, a central feature to ensure the success of MFIs has been programmes of financial support centred around guarantee funds. And for good reasons, for financial institutions regard micro-loans as risky if there is no financial collateral. The risk of having no collateral is mitigated by a guarantee consortium or a guarantee fund.[85] Therefore, the operating model in the provision of micro-credit in Europe often includes three main actors: (1) a no profit organisation, which identifies and assesses the needs and demands for micro-credit, presents the potential beneficiary to the bank or financial intermediary that will provide the credit and follows the beneficiary through several *tutoring* activities; (2) the bank or lending financial institution; and (3) an (often publicly funded) guarantee fund. Authors have found that MFI guarantee funds contributed to lower financial exclusion, and that regulation to this aim is key.[86] These guarantee funds must operate, however, according to rules and practices and be duly supervised, which should be directed at minimising moral hazard from the side of the borrowers. In our view, thus, one of the main challenges in supporting self-sustainable inclusive banking in Europe revolves around the role of guarantee funds. If appropriately designed, they couldhelp in fostering networking in inclusive banking,[87] in the

---

[84]   'At the European level the situation is also highly heterogeneous due to the differences between the legal and institutional frameworks of the Member States as well as the variety of entities operating in the microcredit field. The joint initiative of the European Commission, the European Central Bank and the European Investment Fund called JASMINE (Joint Action to Support Microfinance Institutions in Europe), in particular through the adoption of the European Code of Good Conduct for microcredit provision, attempted to establish principles of governance and prudent management consistent with best practices in the industry, with the aim of establishing a set of rules approved in the European Union and recognized as essential to the operations and financial reporting of entities operating in microcredit . . . Despite support from the European Commission in recent years to the Microfinance sector through several programmes (CIP, EPPA, JEREMIE, JASMINE, EPMF, etc.) there is still a clear need to invest in the capacity building and refinancing of microfinance institutions in Europe over a sustained period of time, allowing them to improve their institutional capacities and providing them with access to sustainable funding sources. And this seems to be the way that the European Commission wants to carry on.'

[85]   Leone, P. and Porretta, P. (2014), 'Introduction' in *Micro Credit Guarantee Funds in the Mediterranean*, Palgrave Macmillan, Basingstoke, UK (1–21, at 20).

[86]   See Cozarenco, A. (2015), 'Microfinance Institutions and Banks in Europe: The story to date' Working Papers CEB, 15 (at 4); Lorenzi, M. (2016), 'Microcredit in the European Union: A Feasible Means for Business Growth and Fair Access to Credit' *Innovation (EaSI)*, (at 20); Marakkath, N. and Attuel-mendes, L. (2015), 'Can microfinance crowdfunding reduce financial exclusion? Regulatory issues', *International Journal of Bank Marketing*, 33(5), (at 632).

[87]   Lamandini, M. (2009), 'What Community Action for Microcredit?', *Rivista di Diritto Societario*, 4/2009, 903.

first place, and act as a central coordinator with financial and social expertise and the capacity and powers to monitor the decentralised action of a multiplicity of MFIs, in the second place – two functions which in our view are key for the long-term self-sustainability of micro-finance. This is just an example, but one which illuminates how adapting the regulatory environment might prove effective in nudging towards inclusive banking.

3.   NUDGING TOWARDS AN INTERNAL GUARANTEE FUND: FAIR COEXISTENCE BETWEEN PROFIT SEEKING AND SOCIAL ENGAGEMENT AS A PATH TO SELF-SUSTAINABILITY

In the previous section we showed that guarantee funds are key for developing inclusive finance. In this section we discuss an experiment of an 'internally funded' guarantee fund, i.e. a fund set up through retained profits, as a suitable and complementary self-regulatory response to promote inclusive banking, to nudge ethical banks and MFIs towards self-sustainability and traditional banks towards more inclusive banking as part of their commitment to ethics and corporate social responsibility. This is in line with the movement which recently led to the regulatory recognition of Benefit Corporations and one which could help to traditional banks to restore the bond of trust with society which seems currently broken.

Banca Prossima s.p.a. was established in Italy in 2007 by Intesa San Paolo (ISP) as a fully owned bank intended to operate as a niche ethical bank for inclusive banking, mainly servicing non-profit organisations; it offers, in our view, an interesting case study.[88] This bank, despite its strong social focus on inclusive banking, was designed as self-sustainable. After 10 years of operations, the experiment looks successful. Its specialty is reflected in the special provisions of its articles of association. Under Italian company law, whilst profit-seeking is a mandatory requirement, profit *maximisation* is not. The articles of association can therefore calibrate. Such calibration, in the case of Banca Prossima, was (mostly) made with a special provision concerning the allocation of yearly profits,[89] by which yearly disposable profits are used in part

---

[88]   Lamandini, M. and Steiner, I. (2007), 'Social Banking in Practice: an Italian Case for Corporate Social Responsibility in Banking', *Rivista di Diritto Societario*, 4, 174–94.

[89]   'The net profits shown in the accounts, net of the legal reserve and of any other provisions which the Company is required to set aside under the applicable laws in force at the time, shall be distributed as follows: a) a share equal to the cost of capital invested by the Bank shall be allocated to a non-distributable statutory reserve to be calculated in accordance with the accounting methods generally employed by the market; b) the net yearly dividend allocated to shareholders shall not exceed 50% of the profits approved by the shareholders' meeting, net of the provisions set out under letter a) above; c) *all remaining profit shall be set aside for solidarity and development initiatives and allocated to a specific Fund for Development and the Social Enterprise. This risk and contingency Fund shall be employed – according to the procedure described here below – to cover losses arising from solidarity and development loans granted by the Company at below-market rates or to persons who do not have, or have only limited access to traditional credit facilities. If at the end of the financial year the Company should record losses attributable, in full or in part, to solidarity and development programmes, any such losses shall be fully covered by the Fund for Development and the Social Enterprise.* If the above losses cannot be covered by the above Fund, the net profit generated by the Company in the following financial years shall be set aside, after the mandatory legal reserve provision, to bring the shareholders' equity back to its previous level, net of the above Fund. If, conversely, the operating losses are due to other causes and do not arise

for *the accumulation of a specific reserve working as an internal guarantee fund.* The fund is without segregation and remains under the management of the bank's board of directors. *It is to be used, however, specifically to 'face the risks and cover the losses' stemming from inclusive banking.*

In particular, as specified by implementing the internal rules, when the bank lends to borrowers whose credit scoring is below the minimum (classes 'R4' and 'R5', together constituting the so-called 'portfolio Gamma') under the usual eligibility standards of the ISP group, specific provisioning is made against the fund in a percentage of 2.5 per cent of the gross value of the loan, as long as the loan is performing, and 40 per cent if it is defaulted. This is meant to ensure that the fund can make good those realised losses derived from loans extended to borrowers who, under normal credit scoring standards, would not be eligible for the loan, but who are nonetheless financed by the bank based upon a complementary 'social assessment', using different methodologies for inclusive banking (and who are also often receiving mentoring assistance by a specialised task force set up by the bank as part of the loan monitoring exercise). The provisioning against the fund is statistically calculated to prevent a misalignment between the fund's resources and the stock of insured portfolio Gamma loans. The functioning of the fund is such that it insures the additional risk for the bank associated with the difference in performance between the portfolio Gamma (credit scoring classes R4 and R5) and the last class (R3) of eligible borrowers under usual credit scoring standards applied within the ISP group. In so doing, once such additional risk is covered by the fund, R4 and R5 borrowers can be treated, for any other aspect, as if they were eligible borrowers. The increased risk associated wiyj the portfolio Gamma is neutralised by the fund (on a rotated basis, with yearly computations) once the loss is realised, making good such loss (ideally, in net terms and to the extent it is attributable to the differential risk of portfolio Gamma), but at the same time the group reaches a much wider client base and delivers a measurable social output in terms of inclusive banking.

This example, in our view, is quite illustrative of the virtues of nudging towards self-sustainability in inclusive banking. It offers a functional self-regulatory model of profit distribution (inspired by an ethics of moderation) which draws a balance and satisfies both profits and social expectations, and which is optional but could be further nudged through fiscal incentives (if for instance realised profits allocated to the solidarity fund were totally or partially exempted from taxation). At the same time, it adopts a long-term view of value creation, whereby the present use of part of the short-term profits is justified to internally subsidise social engagement and enlargement of the client base in view of the mid-to-long term returns associated, both in economical and reputational terms, with these investments.

We are aware that this experiment may invite all sort of arguments usually adopted against multi-stakeholders' governance. Sacrificing (part of the annual) profits in the social interest is extremely controversial. It raises important questions, normative as well as positive. On a normative level, there is disagreement over the question whether corporations *should* and/or *could*

---

from solidarity and development initiatives the Fund under point c) above may be used to cover such losses only after all other voluntary and statutory reserves have been used to this end, including the reserve under point a) above. If the Fund under point c) above is used to cover losses which do not arise from solidarity and development programmes, the net profit of the next two financial years, net of any legal reserve provisions, shall be used to bring the above Fund back to its previous level' (article 28 of the articles of association, emphasis added).

sacrifice parts of their profits in the social interest to begin with, and under what conditions they may do so. Yet, as nicely put, recently, by Robert Bartlett and Eric Talley,[90] even in the United States the issue is much less black and white than we usually care to admit:

> notwithstanding longstanding judicial equivocation about corporate purpose, courts (especially Delaware courts) have been far less hesitant in indicating that, absent special provisions in a company's charter, the corporate maxim should at least involve some form of profit maximization. This vision appears clearly in the Delaware Chancery Court's 2010 opinion in *eBay v. Craigslist* [eBay Domestic Holdings, Inc. v. Newmark, 16 A.3d 1, 34: Del. Ch. 2010]. There, the Chancery Court was asked to determine whether the founders of Craigslist could dilute eBay's ownership interest in the company in the name of preserving a corporate culture that explicitly avoided maximizing corporate profits. According to Chancellor Chandler: Having chosen a for-profit corporate form, the Craigslist directors are bound by the fiduciary duties and standards that accompany that form. Those standards include acting to promote the value of the corporation for the benefit of its stockholders . . . Thus, I cannot accept as valid . . . a corporate policy that specifically, clearly, and admittedly seeks *not* to maximize the economic value of a for-profit Delaware corporation for the benefit of its stockholders.

This means that, in principle, 'individuals who wish to subordinate profit maximization to other goals should accordingly look to non corporate forms of organization that are more accommodating of these objectives such as the non-profit corporation and, more recently, the Benefit Corporation'. At the same time, however, several states outside Delaware have promulgated statutes that grant boards the immutable right to account for a variety of non-shareholder interests – such as those employees, debt holders, and even surrounding communities – in discharging their fiduciary obligations. And even in Delaware, a more recent Delaware Chancery decision *In re Trados, Inc.*, 73 A.3d 17, 41 n.16 (Del. Ch. 2013) found that:

> [W]hile tolerably clear in the abstract and sometimes in real-world settings, the enterprise value standard ultimately complicates rather than simplifies the difficult judgments faced by directors acting under conditions of uncertainty . . . The enterprise value standard compounds the number of valuation alternatives that must be solved simultaneously and the resulting multivariate fiduciary calculus quickly devolves into the equitable equivalent of a constituency statute with a concomitant decline in accountability.

As one of us already discussed in a different paper[91] several years ago, together with Ilan Steiner,[92] from a social welfare perspective, how could we determine whether the social benefits compensate for the forgone profits? In our view, the problem lies in the methodology used to cope with the abovementioned questions: it cannot be confined to the framework of corporate governance, law, finance or economics. The context of the normative debate over the inclusion of social benefits within the scope of corporate action and the role of business

---

[90] Bartlett, R.P. and Talley, E.L. (2017), 'Law and corporate governance', *The Handbook of the Economics of Corporate Governance, Volume 1,* Hermalin & Weisbach, eds, 2017, UC Berkeley Public Law Research Paper (2017). Available at: https://scholarship.law.columbia.edu/faculty_scholarship/2047

[91] Lamandini, M. and Steiner, I. (2007), 'Social Banking in Practice: an Italian Case for Corporate Social Responsibility in Banking', *Rivista di Diritto Societario*, 4, 174–94.

[92] Steiner, I. (2014), *Law and Economics of Corporate Social Responsibility in Israel: Towards a Social Norms Theory*, Thesis submitted for the degree 'Doctor of Philosophy', University of Haifa, Faculty of Law.

corporations in society is by far broader. Today, however, so much water has passed under the bridge from the time when this issue could be reduced to two seemingly conflicting poles:

1. On one side of the spectrum, Nobel laureate Milton Friedman and his followers claimed that the social responsibility of corporations is to increase their profits and maximise shareholders' value.[93] According to this view, under the assumptions of a perfect market, shareholders' value maximisation would result in an increase in social welfare, since shareholders are the residual claimants. Put simply, corporations ought to focus on what they do best, which is maximising shareholder value rather than attempting to satisfy the interests of multiple stakeholders. Consistent with this view, social concerns are best left for the government or the non-profit sector to deal with. This belief is based on the assumption that managers cannot be held accountable if they are told to pursue multiple objectives, rather than simply maximise shareholder value. In the context of inclusive banks this would encourage separate institutions, as opposed to banks expanding operations to achieve financial inclusion.
2. On the other side of the spectrum were the proponents of the stakeholder theory.[94] This approach rejected the neo-classical assumptions about perfect markets and zero externalities and further suggested that value maximisation is not a value in itself. In line with this approach, corporations ought to have a moral commitment towards society in return for their so-called 'licence to operate' which allows shareholders to enjoy corporate profits.

In the last decade or so, many steps have been taken to converge some of the conflicting approaches.[95] And many European member states, as well as several US states, reflected this approach in their regulation. This is no surprise. In reality, more and more people have come to realise that the price associated with various corporate externalities has become too high; financial exclusion is for sure one of these, and it is exacting a very big toll on society. Using state authority, such as command and control regulation, is only partially effective, due to information asymmetries, regulatory capture, enforcement problems and high transaction costs. The challenge is to find further ways to also make market actors voluntarily bind themselves, through self-regulation, to this principal effort. Nudging has the potential to deliver some good results, helping corporate insiders (such as dominant shareholders and senior managers), in internalising the right social norm. Indeed,

> in the minds of millions of people all over the world the image of the corporation is shifting and more emphasis is given to corporate citizenship as well as social and environmental performance. There is extensive evidence that shows how powerful social norms could be in this context . . . The rationale behind this argument is straightforward – the human beings who navigate the corporate entity are

---

[93]   Friedman M. (1970), 'The Social Responsibility of Business Is to Increase Its Profits', *The New York Times Magazine*, September 13, 1970.

[94]   For an overview of the fundamentals of stakeholder theory see Freeman, R.E. (1984), *Strategic Management: A Stakeholder Perspective*, Pitman, Boston; Blair, M. M. (1995), *Ownership and Control: Rethinking Corporate Governance for the Twenty-First Century*, Brookings Institution, Washington; Blair, M. M and Stout, L. (1999), 'A Team Production Theory of Corporate Law', *Virginia Law Review*, 85(2).

[95]   Jensen, M. (2001), 'Value Maximization, Stakeholder Theory, and the Corporate Objective Function', *European Financial Management Review*, No. 7.

not immune to social norms by which they are surrounded. *Therefore, the road to change the way corporations act passes in the minds and hearts of those who run them.*[96]

---

[96] Lamandini, M. and Steiner, I. (2007), 'Social Banking in Practice: an Italian Case for Corporate Social Responsibility in Banking', 194.

5. The social licence for financial markets, written standards and aspiration

David Rouch

Real markets are resilient, fair and effective. They maintain their social licence.[1]

INTRODUCTION

The Governor of the Bank of England's annual Mansion House speech is a notable event in the City of London's calendar. The Governor generally uses it to give a view on the state of the finance sector and to share policy thinking. In as much as any speeches make an impact across the UK financial markets, this is usually one of them. However, those reading the *Financial Times* on the morning of 11 June 2015 will have remained ignorant of one aspect of the previous night's speech, so significant to the Governor, Mark Carney, that he referred to it on five occasions – the social licence for financial markets. The *Financial Times* did not mention it once.[2]

Talk of a social licence for financial markets has only emerged relatively recently.[3] While the concept has certainly attracted some attention, engagement has so far been limited when compared, for example, with the intense industry and media interest generated by some parts of the post-crisis regulatory reform agenda.[4] Why is that? Some might be tempted to dismiss the idea of a social licence for financial markets as 'mere metaphor', forgetting that the use

---

[1]   'Building real markets for the good of the people', speech by Mark Carney, Governor of the Bank of England, at the Mansion House, London 10 June 2015, available at http://www.bankofengland.co.uk/publications/Pages/speeches/2015/821.aspx, accessed 1 December 2017.

[2]   Caroline Binham and Martin Arnold, 'Bank of England governor Mark Carney to extend market abuse rules', *Financial Times* (London 11 June 2015).

[3]   The extractive industries have for some years worked with the concept of a 'social licence to operate' in relation to the communities in which they are active. More recently the idea has also been applied to the relationship between society and other forms of economic activity (see in particular, John Morrison, *The Social License: How to Keep Your Organization Legitimate* (Palgrave Macmillan 2014)). However, the idea of a social licence for financial markets is largely novel. It was not mentioned in the final report on the UK Fair and Effective Markets Review published in June 2015 by the Bank of England, HM Treasury and the FCA following an extensive assessment of how to re-establish confidence in the fixed income, currency and commodities markets. However, it subsequently became a key topic for discussion at the Bank of England's Open Forum in November 2015, held as a result of the Fair and Effective Markets Review.

[4]   See for example Justin O'Brien et al., 'Professional standards and the social licence to operate: a panacea for finance or an exercise in symbolism' (2015) Law and Financial Markets Review 9(4), 283; Pamela Hanrahan, 'Corporate governance, financial institutions and the "social licence"' (2016) Law and Financial Markets Review 10(3), 123. However, a word search of the *Financial Times* (accessed 1 December 2017) discloses almost no discussion of the topic and nor does it seem to have occasioned much debate in the context of the main financial industry associations.

of a metaphor tends to confirm the existence of its primary subject. Others might consider the concept as too theoretical. However, governors of the Bank of England cannot generally afford themselves the luxury of theoretical flights of fancy, not in their public role at least. The *Financial Times* certainly did not accuse the Governor of that on the morning of 11 June 2015. There is also a third, much more intriguing, possibility: perhaps the Governor's remarks on the social licence did not attract more attention because they were largely congruent with the way in which many who heard or who have read the speech see the world. They might not have used the expression 'social licence', but perhaps they nonetheless recognise the reality it seeks to illuminate – one of a relationship between society and those who engage in market activity within it, with the activities of the latter in some sense contingent on the former. This third possibility is the departure point for what follows: talk of a social licence for financial markets seems to refer to something that can be seen operating in practice and to draw on commonly held aspirations that are relevant to the future relationship between financial activity and the communities within which it takes place.

Yet, even if the idea of a social licence has resonance, that does not mean it is well under-stood or that the relationship between society and finance of which it speaks is in good health. The relationship remains troubled, and it is clear from the Governor's speech that he was advancing the idea of a social licence to help address precisely that. From this perspective, two of the most important characteristics of the social licence framework he described are its aspirational nature and the emphasis on cooperation and co-dependency[5] in the context of which public and private interests can begin to be reconciled. However, for the idea of a social licence for financial markets to have that effect, it needs to be approached purposively and, as a first step, requires greater definition. The aim of this chapter is to help move that process forward. It should be treated as no more than a sketch from the perspective of a lawyer who has been involved in the interaction between law and behaviour in the financial markets first hand over many years. Because of that, its principal focus is the relationship between the idea of a social licence and what will be described as 'written standards', in particular, those that apply in the UK financial markets. However, its significance to other financial markets, and to the relationship between economic activity and society more generally, will be clear.

What is meant by 'written standards'? This is considered further in Part 2, but it is helpful to provide a preliminary indication. There are many ways in which groups of people seek to change the behaviour of those within and beyond the group, so that it is consistent with the group's aspirations for the way in which intra-group and external relationships should operate. However, one of the most obvious is by defining in writing standards of behaviour and the frameworks within which behaviour can take place and then enforcing them. Written statements of this sort are not restricted to legal rules and regulations. They also include behav-ioural codes published by private bodies.[6] Like the idea of a social licence, written standards concern the ordering of relationships and involve an aspiration for the way in which those relationships should function. It is therefore reasonable to suppose that there may be a close

---

[5]   See Part 1 below.

[6]   See Part 2 below. Where these standards are in the form of law, the main focus of this chapter is on what can be described as 'primary rules' that require people to do or refrain from doing something (or have a similar effect by defining the context for action) rather than 'secondary rules' which concern the making, administration and enforcement of the primary rules (see H.L.A. Hart, *The Concept of Law* (3rd edn, OUP 2012) at Chapter 5).

connection between the idea of a social licence for financial markets and the written standards that are applied to those markets. The idea of a social licence is not restricted to its interaction with written standards, and written standards alone do not change behaviour. However, in view of the vast reliance placed on written standards in regulating the financial services sector, they must be a prime area for attention in seeking to understand the idea of a social licence for financial markets.

The chapter is organised as follows. Part 1 starts by considering why it is meaningful to talk of a social licence for financial markets and its possible terms. Some written standards may have a claim to be articulating the terms of a social licence. However, they also need to be seen in the broader aspirational context voiced by talk of a social licence. Part 2 then turns to the different sorts of written standards operating within the financial markets in the United Kingdom. It looks more closely at the extent to which each category of written standards could be thought of as being part of a social licence; how they might express the substance of a social licence and how they might help to realise its aspirational dimension. It identifies what appears to be both substantive and aspirational common ground between the idea of a social licence and written standards directed at participants in financial markets, especially in the case of written standards that operate by reference to other-regarding values. Both seem to concern the pursuit of just ends by just means in financial markets. The chapter concludes by briefly highlighting some of the implications of this for the use of written standards.

As noted, I approach the subject principally as a lawyer. However, the definition and application of a concept described as 'social' cannot be confined to particular groups. There has already been significant activity across a range of academic disciplines that is relevant, but it has not generally been connected with the idea of a social licence and there is still some way to go in bringing the streams together. Where I stray into their specialist territory in what follows, it is in the hope of advancing that process, not as an expert. Importantly, attempts to change what happens in financial markets, and between markets and the communities in which they operate, need to involve those on the ground: that is ultimately where practice emerges and gets changed. Because of the need for this broad-based engagement, the following is designed to be accessible to a wide range of readers. I hope it will support the developing cross-sectoral dialogue and provide further coordinates from a legal perspective for charting the way.

PART 1: THE SOCIAL LICENCE FOR FINANCIAL MARKETS AND ITS TERMS

Why Talk of a Social Licence for Financial Markets Makes Sense

Is it at all meaningful to talk about a social licence for financial markets? In other words, is it possible to say that financial markets operate, in some sense, with the permission of the communities in which they are situated?[7] Particularly in broadly democratic societies, if we can see government at some level representing the interests of the community, the answer to this question is 'yes'. Most obviously, it is not possible to engage in financial business in most

---

[7]   This puts to one side for the present the international dimension of financial markets which transcends particular communities, but raises an important question for those who wish to assert the presence of a social licence.

jurisdictions without being authorised to do so by a governmental agency: this is commonly referred to by those in the market as being 'licensed'. In many parts of the financial market, there are also regulatory regimes for market operators, such as the London Stock Exchange, requiring them to be recognised before they can provide a framework within which market participants can trade. These licences and approvals do not attach to whole markets, but are nonetheless necessary for a market and its infrastructure to function – no market operator and no participants, no market. Further, the corporate vehicles through which market activity is generally conducted are the gift of the state, vesting the benefit of limited liability on their shareholders. This can be thought of as a form of licence:

> Today it almost seems to have been forgotten that the word 'Limited' was intended as a red danger flag . . . That this should be so is a tribute to the morality of the English commercial community and indicates the very small extent to which they have abused the privileges of incorporation. Nevertheless, the possibilities of abuse are plain and abuses do occur. In this respect freedom may have amounted to license – and a remarkably cheap license at that.[8]

Finally, financial activity involves using a series of social constructs: the very 'raw materials' of financial business, such as money, shares and debt, are not natural resources, but creations of human communities, underpinned by law and regulation. A banking licence is, among other things, a licence to create money, the meaning of which is culturally determined.

Statutory licensing recognises the importance of these cultural constructs, both the benefits that can accrue when they are used properly and the damage that can flow when they are not. The idea of a social licence may incorporate statutory licencing regimes. However, ultimately it also reaches beyond them: the talk is of 'social licence', not simply, for example, authorisation under section 19 of the UK Financial Services and Markets Act 2000 (FSMA).[9] From that perspective, statutory licensing can be seen as a token of something broader: a recognition that ends sought by those involved in financial activity and those of the communities within which that activity takes place are in some ways shared and inter-dependent; an understanding that society and financial markets need each other, and that both can be damaged if participants in the latter do not operate in a way that recognises the interests and expectations of the former. This is not the result of a detached, rational calculation by either element in the relationship. It has been a dialogic process, perhaps as old as humanity itself. The contemporary financial services licensing and company law regimes made a relatively late entry into pre-existing financial markets, but rules on lending appear in some of the world's earliest extant legal texts.[10] Financial activity, the recognition of its desirability and its dependence on ordered relationships, and steps by societies to regulate it consistent with that, have grown up cheek by jowl over centuries. In view of that inter-dependency and the fact that financial activity

---

[8]   L.C.B. Gower, 'The English private company' (Fall 1953) Law and Contemporary Problems 18, 535–45.

[9]   FSMA establishes the UK authorisation regime for firms wishing to engage in investment or financial business.

[10]   See, for example, the Code of Hammurabi, a collection of rules complied towards the end of the 42-year reign of Hammurabi, sixth ruler of the first Dynasty of Babylon (1792–1750 BC); Martha T. Roth, *Law Collections from Mesopotamia and Asia Minor* (Scholars Press, Atlanta 1995) 71.

is socially contingent, it makes sense to talk of society in some sense 'licensing' financial markets.[11]

The Social Licence and Observed Reality

Social licences for financial markets cannot be acquired in the same way as a driving licence. Even if they could, it is not clear how a market as a whole could acquire one as compared with the multiple participants that comprise those markets. It is important, therefore, to acknowledge that the social licence for financial markets is in part a metaphor; it uses the two concepts of 'society' and 'licence' to try to understand and influence the relationship between participants in financial markets and the societies in which they operate and upon which they rely.

However, talk of a social licence is not just metaphorical, nor is it simply a theoretical exercise. As noted, the licence of society for participants in financial markets is reflected in law, which lends substance to the idea that the markets themselves are also in some way being licensed. Further, the current discussion of the idea of a social licence grows from mounting evidence that the relationship of which the licence speaks is increasingly strained – where a perception has emerged that financial activity is conducted in a way that does not recognise broader interests and expectations. That strain was noted, for example, by the United Kingdom's Parliamentary Commission on Banking Standards in 2013 when it spoke of 'a profound loss of trust born of profound lapses in banking standards'[12] and by the Bank of England in preparatory work for its Open Forum in November 2015.[13] A continuing sense of fragmentation has also been picked up in a multitude of surveys.[14] Most recently, public debate in the context of elections and referenda in the West suggests that public mistrust towards business in general and the financial services sector in particular has lost none of its edge,[15] lending the current discussion immediacy and urgency.[16] It is an issue that a growing number of investors and senior business people seem to recognise.[17]

This apparent connection with the realities of financial and social life suggests that talk of a social licence should not be viewed in the same way as a contractarian thought experiment

---

[11]   'What is banking for?', remarks by Baroness Onora O'Neill, Federal Reserve Bank of New York, 20 October 2016 available at https://www.bankingstandardsboard.org.uk/remarks-by-baroness-onora -oneill/, accessed 1 December 2017.

[12]   *Changing Banking for Good*, Report of the Parliamentary Commission on Banking Standards, Volume I: Summary, and Conclusions and Recommendations 2013.

[13]   See video of Open Forum Breakout Session 1, Panel 2: https://www.youtube.com/watch?v=dUE _opd011A, accessed 15 December 2017.

[14]   See, for example, the 2017 Edelman Trust Barometer, produced by the Edelman marketing group, available at http://www.edelman.com/trust2017/, accessed 1 December 2017.

[15]   See for example, the 2017 Labour Party manifesto at page 4: 'Britain is the fifth richest country in the world. But that means little when many people don't share in that wealth. Many feel the system is rigged against them. And this manifesto sets out exactly what can be done about it.'

[16]   Jim Pickard, 'Corbyn lashes out at financial sector "speculators and gamblers"', *Financial Times* (London 1 December 2017).

[17]   Patrick Jenkins, 'Greed and tax dodges leave capitalism ripe for reform, say business leaders', *Financial Times* (London 23 October 2017). See also the annual letter from the CEO of Blackrock, Larry Fink to the CEOs of companies in which Blackrock invests on behalf of its clients (https://www .blackrock.com/corporate/en-no/investor-relations/larry-fink-ceo-letter, accessed 22 January 2018).

in the style of a Hobbes, Locke or Rawls. Rawls' *Theory of Justice*[18] certainly gave impetus to 'social contract' theories as a way of approaching the relationship between business and society, and aspects of those may be helpful in understanding the nature of any social licence.[19] However, the use of the expression 'social licence' rather than 'contract' seems to distance the current discussion from that. Rather, there is a sense in which, with the social licence, we start with reality and work backwards to understand the nature of the licence instead of beginning with a notional contract and theorising forwards based on concepts such as fairness, reasonableness, bounded rationality and an 'original condition' of humanity. It is concerned with things as they are and motivations as they are experienced.

Nonetheless, there is no single definition of what is meant by the 'social licence for financial markets'. It follows from the idea that it is a 'social' licence that its terms are socially, not privately, defined. Financial businesses and their staff are not excluded from the definitional process: they are, or at least are capable of being, part of the social mix from which an understanding of what is being licensed must flow.[20] Regulatory licensing and associated rules are particularly significant because of their public status. However, they can only be a partial expression. A consent given by society as a whole is not ultimately within the control of any one element of it. Rather, talk of a social licence concerns the role of financial markets considered proper by a particular community of people having, at some level, shared cultural characteristics and expectations. The most obvious community from which such an understanding might be thought to grow is the nation state. However, in a globalising and increasingly inter-connected world, the concept could also be connected with regions such as the EU or even a 'global community'. Global financial institutions operate in ways that reflect each of these social groupings and the boundary between the national, the transnational regions and the global is far from fixed.[21]

The idea that the licence is social also suggests that understanding its scope needs to involve a process of engagement within and careful listening to the relevant community. However, the recent experience of political pollsters in Western election processes should make us cautious about thinking that we can hear with any precision what a community is really saying at any given time and even more that we can discern a consensus. Further, the complexity of financial market activity presents an obvious barrier to developing a social consensus given the technical knowledge and experience required to make judgements; it is an area where even specialists can struggle to discern what is prudent. The interplay between local, regional and global communities and changing circumstances means that attitudes can sometimes seem as if they are in a constant state of flux, although the discussion of values below suggests that there may

---

[18]   John Rawls, *A Theory of Justice* (1st edn, Harvard University Press 1971) in which he advanced a theory of justice based on the concept of fairness.

[19]   Thomas W. Dunfee and Thomas Donaldson, 'Social contract approaches to business ethics: bridging the is-ought gap' in Robert E. Frederick (ed.), *A Companion to Business Ethics* (Blackwell 1999).

[20]   The idea that a body corporate, a legal person as opposed to a natural person, can be involved in this process and the basis of its participation raises a number of important questions which fall outside the scope of this chapter.

[21]   As noted, this chapter focuses on the position in the United Kingdom. It is not feasible here to do more than draw attention to the relationship between local understandings of what might be involved in the idea of a social licence for financial markets and notions of a social licence for financial markets that transcend national communities.

be some important continuities.[22] There is also an emotional dimension to the expectations of a community, introducing additional instability.[23] Further, there is no single 'voting chamber' in which the voice of society can be heard. The ways in which beliefs, attitudes and values are expressed has become increasingly fragmented.

What are the Terms of the Licence?

With these important qualifications, what can we deduce about the possible substance of the social licence for financial markets from the way the expression has been used? The most notable references to a social licence have been those of the Governor of the Bank of England. While it is beyond any one person to provide a comprehensive definition, as discussed in the introduction, there is reason to suppose that what he has said may resonate with a broader constituency. This is therefore a good place to start.

The way the Governor has used the expression suggests that he understands it as extending both to the outcomes of financial activity and the processes by which those are achieved. For him, the licence is the 'consent of society' that is needed by markets if they are to function: that consent can be called into question by repeated misconduct but, in the words at the start of this chapter, markets that are resilient, fair and effective retain their social licence.[24] In isolation, this might appear to suggest that the social licence solely concerns good conduct in financial markets. However, Carney's use of the concept has gone beyond that, linking it to the under-lying purpose of financial activity: 'Markets are not ends in themselves, but powerful means for prosperity and security for all. As such they need to retain the consent of society – a social licence – to be allowed to operate, innovate and grow.'[25] Carney's description of the social licence therefore situates financial market activity in the context of the need to realise social goods – prosperity and security for all. The goods will be lost if financial activity is conducted as if it were an end in itself – in other words, detached from its social context. The goods iden-tified can be seen as 'social' goods in at least two senses: first, because the outcomes benefit society as a whole ('security for all', for example, cannot be individually realised but speaks of a state of social relations) and, secondly, because they can only be realised in a way that relies upon a social framework.

Logically, this association between social licence and social goods makes sense. Communities cannot prevent everything they do not like. However, a community could not be expected to allow and even facilitate activities anticipating that the result would be social damage. Yet it is implicit in the notion of a licence that the activities concerned are, nonethe-less, capable of causing damage if not conducted as contemplated by the licence; they need to be pursued within parameters consistent with the relevant goods. Consequently, while talk of a social licence may well incorporate hard regulatory structures such as licensing regimes, it is also profoundly aspirational: it recognises the opportunity for private and social goods, but also the possibility for business to be conducted in a way that means that these are not achieved and expresses an aspiration for the former without the latter. This idea of realising private and

---

[22]   Pages 115–16 below.
[23]   Hans Bernhard Schmid, 'The feeling of being in a group: corporate emotions and collective con-sciousness' in Christian von Scheve and Mikko von Salmela (eds), *Collective Emotions* (OUP 2014).
[24]   See Carney, note 1 above.
[25]   *Ibid.*

social goods seems to connect talk of a social licence with notions of what is just (substantive justice, in the sense of what is right, not just formal justice, in the sense of the proper administration of law): 'A just society distributes . . . goods in the right way; it gives each person his or her due.'[26] Indeed, if the idea of a social licence can be regarded as extending both to the ends and means of financial activity, one way to view it might be as a permission to pursue just ends in a just manner in the financial markets.[27]

Clearly, the nature of what is just is highly contested and it is not possible to do more here than draw attention to its apparently foundational presence. However, is it possible to be any more specific about the substance of the licence – the ends for which permission is given and the expectations that apply to the process of their realisation? Up to a point. As discussed, references to a 'social licence' draw attention to something that can, to some extent, be seen operating in practice. At least in a democratic society, one would expect it to find partial expression in the law and regulation applied to financial market activity. Law and regulation will be considered more fully in Part 2. However, as noted already, it is necessary to be licensed in order to conduct financial services activities in the United Kingdom. Those licences are given by regulators who are appointed by government to grant or withhold permission, acting, in some sense, on behalf of society as a whole.[28] Further, those who are licensed are required to carry on their business in accordance with certain prescribed standards, especially (but not exclusively) in the form of the laws and regulations society makes through its institutions of government and courts to order the role of the financial markets in social life.[29]

However, as noted, while talk of a social licence may in some sense incorporate the black letter of law and regulation it also reaches beyond them – otherwise, it would only be necessary to talk of people pursuing purposes defined by law in the manner prescribed by law. Indeed, if it is correct to think of a social licence for financial markets as a permission to pursue just ends in a just manner in financial markets, this aspiration dovetails with the limits of positive law.[30] The creation and application of law and regulation can be understood by reference to justice but is not a full articulation of it.[31] Consistent with that, the highest duty of English and Welsh solicitors when working with their clients in the financial markets or otherwise is not simply to apply law and regulation, but to 'uphold the rule of law and the proper administration of

---

[26]   Michael J. Sandel, *Justice* (1st edn, Farrar, Straus and Giroux 2009) 19.

[27]   There is a question as to whether the concept of 'legitimacy' also helps to make sense of the idea of a social licence. It may well do so. However, a more fundamental connection between talk of a social licence and justice seems consistent with the apparently aspirational dimension of the former on the basis that justice involves an aspiration about the ordering of social relations whereas legitimacy is arguably more concerned with perception.

[28]   This puts to one side for the present the question of how far regulators are pursuing the public interest and the extent to which power structures can be dominated by particular interest groups; see for example Mike Feintuck, 'Regulatory rationales beyond the economic: in search of the public interest' in Baldwin et al., *The Oxford Handbook of Regulation* (OUP 2011).

[29]   Again, putting to one side the question of how far these rules represent societal interests or more confined interests within society.

[30]   In other words, law that has been formally articulated.

[31]   The nature of the relationship between law and justice, and morality more generally, has been a subject of prolonged debate, most famously perhaps in the exchanges between H.L.A. Hart (see especially *The Concept of Law* note 6 above), Lon Fuller (see especially *The Morality of Law* (2nd edn, Yale University Press 1969)) and Ronald Dworkin (see especially *Law's Empire* (Harvard University Press 1986)). There is not the scope to explore those discussions here.

justice'. Where there is any conflict between this and the other conduct principles that apply, 'the principle that takes precedence is the one which best serves the public interest in the particular circumstance, especially the public interest in the proper administration of justice'.[32] Whether they are used to thinking of their role in these terms in practice is another matter.

Is it possible to identify what the social licence for financial markets might mean in this area beyond what is recorded in the black letter of the law? Here, it is inevitably necessary to be more tentative. However, the following four suggestions ought to avoid the charge of being overly speculative.

First, on the basis that the purpose of regulators is, in some sense, to pursue the public interest,[33] arguably the practical behavioural understandings that emerge from the relationships between regulators and the regulated reflect at some level the terms of a social licence. These may be partially articulated in writing, for example, in the form of regulatory guidance and statements of supervisory practice and in the precedent of regulatory enforcement cases. However, the process of regulatory supervision also involves many judgements and compromises as a result of which standards of acceptability get set, for example, as to the level of Pillar 2 regulatory capital that it is appropriate for firms to hold[34] or how many non-executive and independent non-executive directors financial groups should have on the boards of significant subsidiaries. There is also a sense in which standards get set by reference to what the regulator is 'thought to want' based on what comes out of these processes. Discussions take place between industry associations and firms on the one hand and regulators on the other, there are supervisory dialogues, there are speeches and consultations in which regulatory commentary is given, regulatory guidance is issued, and so understandings of what is and is not acceptable emerge.[35]

Secondly, democratic societies tend to generate statements about what they consider appropriate or just that are not necessarily reduced to law or regulation; these may have some claim to be expressing the substance of a social licence for financial markets. Examples would include the proceedings of the highly active House of Commons Treasury Committee (the remit of which is, among other things, to examine the administration and policy of the UK regulatory authorities, which draws the Committee into assessing and commenting on the activities of the regulated); the Parliamentary Commission on Banking Standards, a commission appointed by the House of Commons and the House of Lords to consider and report on professional standards and culture in the UK banking sector, which published its report in June 2013; and the work of the European Union High-Level Experts Group on Sustainable Finance formed by the European Commission in 2016 to advise on enhancing the sustainability of finance within the European Union.[36]

---

[32]   Solicitors Regulation Authority Principles 2011 contained in the SRA Handbook.

[33]   Subject to the caveats in note 28 above.

[34]   An amount of capital that a firm is required to hold which exceeds a statutory minimum. The amount is based on the firm's own assessment of the risks in its business, but is agreed with its regulator. See in particular Directive 2013/36/EU of the European Parliament and of the Council on access to the activity of credit institutions and the prudential supervision of credit institutions and investment firms OL L176/338, art 73.

[35]   As to how far the resulting standards can be thought of as 'social', this again puts to one side the possibility of regulators developing their own agendas or being unduly influenced by interest groupings, or simply not understanding their own rules or the activities they are seeking to regulate.

[36]   https://ec.europa.eu/info/system/files/161028-press-release_en.pdf, accessed 1 December 2017.

Thirdly, a case can also perhaps be made for industry, professional and corporate codes as potentially articulating the terms of a social licence. This is particularly the case where they represent an attempt to respond to wider social expectations so that they could be seen in some sense as a statement of the originator's understanding of the terms of a licence,[37] or the code has in some way been 'enlisted' into the regulatory project.[38] Indeed, codes of this sort are sometimes introduced with the encouragement of central banks and regulators[39] or otherwise relied upon by them in pursuing their statutory agenda.[40] However, industry and corporate codes are made by private actors, rather than on behalf of society as a whole, and a range of motivations is at work. In that sense, while they can be thought of as 'social' within the more confined social contexts from which they emerge, any claim to be social by reference to society as a whole is qualified.[41]

Yet, ultimately, references to a social licence seem to reach beyond these sources as well. Law and regulation and other forms of written standards and understandings about the way they are applied by regulators can only ever be a partial articulation of the aspirations of a community. The considerable challenge involved in identifying the precise nature of these aspirations at any given time has been noted. Nonetheless, it is reasonable to suppose that they would incorporate an expectation that financial activity will be conducted in a way that accords with commonly accepted social values and that it should produce outcomes consistent with those. This, then, is the fourth area where we might look to understand references to a social licence.

Work on the nature and operation of values is a field in its own right. Values can be thought of as having various characteristics. Among other things, they have motivational force, since they are closely related to the outcomes that people desire or aspire to (such as individual survival, or justice); they transcend specific situations, not stipulating precisely how to act, but guiding behaviour in any given set of circumstances; pursuing one value may not be consistent with acting in accordance with another (for example, the pursuit of power as compared with

---

[37] For example, in relation to professional codes, see Donald Nicholson, 'Making lawyers moral? Ethical codes and moral character' (2005) Legal Studies 25(4), 601, 604.

[38] Julia Black, 'Mapping the contours of contemporary financial services regulation' (2002) Journal of Comparative Law Studies 2(2), 253. See for example, Consultation Paper on Industry Codes of Conduct and Discussion Paper on FCA Principle 5, FCA CP17/37, November 2017.

[39] See for example, The Basel Committee on Banking Supervision Principles for the Sound Management of Operational Risk, June 2011 and The Model Code of Ethics, a report of the SRO consultative committee of IOSCO, June 2006. See also the UK Money Markets Code, the Global FX Code and the Global Precious Metals Code.

[40] At the time of writing, the FCA is consulting on a proposal for it in some cases to 'recognise' codes of conduct that apply to unregulated financial markets, with the intention of giving those codes greater force (CP17/37, see note 38 above). Similarly, a list of privately originated codes and guidance that apply to regulated activities and that has been 'confirmed' by the FCA (so that compliance will help to establish compliance with FCA regulations) is at https://www.fca.org.uk/about/rules-and-guidance/confirmed-industry-guidance. See also the ABI Code to Good Practice for Unit Linked Funds (2014) which it describes as having been revised by an ABI working group in consultation with the FCA and a wide range of stakeholders and which addresses an area where the FCA has not made detailed rules (https://www.abi.org.uk/news/news-articles/2014/05/abi-publishes-guide-to-good-practice-for-unit-linked-funds/ accessed 7 December 2017).

[41] Significantly, the Global FX Code and the UK Money Markets Code have been described as 'one form of licence'; 'In codes we trust – redefining the social licence for financial markets', speech by Sarah John, Head of the Sterling Markets Division of the Bank of England, 13 June 2017 available at https://www.bankofengland.co.uk/speech/2017/in-codes-we-trust, accessed 21 December 2017.

the well-being of others); and people do not hold all values with equal strength, so that the relative dominance of a particular value for a person will affect how that person behaves.[42]

Consistent with common sense and experience, research on values held by different societies, particularly that of Shalom Schwartz, has consistently identified a similar hierarchy of prioritisation between different values, on average within those societies, across most of those societies.[43] This suggests a universal organisation of human motivations. By way of contrast with what we might expect from the *Wolf of Wall Street*[44] genre of commonly rehearsed greed stories about financial life, at the top of that hierarchy are other-regarding values, that can be described as 'benevolence' (preserving and enhancing the welfare of those with whom one is in frequent personal contact) and 'universalism' (understanding and regard for the welfare of all people and for nature). Individuals and groups within a society can differ substantially in the relative importance they attribute to those values; they may prioritise values differently from the societies in which they operate. This helps in understanding the potential for mismatches between the attitudes of participants in financial markets and those of the communities in which they operate. Further, the notion of 'benevolence' clearly does not need to be understood by reference to the same community as the one associated with talk of a social licence; it could, for example, operate by reference to a trading team within a bank. However, the research nonetheless appears to support the expectation that a set of other-regarding values is likely to be an important feature of any social licence for financial markets, both in terms of market behaviour (be it between firms and counterparties or firms and their clients) or the relationship between markets and society.[45] Apparently consistent with this, much academic research in the field of ethical behaviour in organisations begins with the premise that ethical (broadly, other-regarding) behaviour is good and unethical behaviour bad, with the objective of helping organisations produce more of the former and less of the latter.[46] Significantly for the preceding discussion of the social licence, and especially its apparently aspirational dimension, other-regarding values have long been associated with justice. While it may have a self-regarding dimension, 'justice, alone of the virtues, is thought to be "another's good", because it is related to another; for it does what is advantageous to another'.[47]

---

[42]   Based on the description of values developed by S.H. Schwartz for the purposes of his theory of basic values: Shalom H. Schwartz, 'Les valeurs de base de la personne: théorie, mesures et applications' (2006/4) Revue Française de Sociologie 47, 929, 931.

[43]   Shalom H. Schwartz and Anat Bardi, 'Value hierarchies across cultures: taking a similarities perspective' (2001) Journal of Cross-Cultural Psychology 32(3), 268. There is an obvious question as to why this might be. However, that falls outside the scope of the current exercise. For the present, it is sufficient to note the apparently consistent ordering of values.

[44]   The film of the rise and fall of US stockbroker Jordan Belfort, Paramount Pictures 2013.

[45]   Shalom H. Schwartz and Anat Bardi, note 43 above. See also Jesse Graham et al., 'Mapping the moral domain' (August 2011) Journal of Personality and Social Psychology 101(2), 366 and Joseph Henrich et al., '"Economic man" in cross-cultural perspective: behavioural experiments in 15 small-scale societies' (2005) Behavioural and Brain Sciences 28, 795.

[46]   L.K. Treviño et al., '(Un)ethical behavior in organizations' (2014) Annual Review of Psychology 65, 635, 637.

[47]   Aristotle, *The Nicomachean Ethics*, Book V, trans. David Ross, revised by Lesley Brown (OUP 2009).

PART 2: WRITTEN STANDARDS AS PART OF A SOCIAL LICENCE AND THE ROLE OF ASPIRATION

Discussion of a social licence for financial markets seems to express an aspiration about the ends and forms of behaviour in those markets. One of the main ways in which communities seek to influence behaviour so that it reflects aspiration is by using written standards.[48] A connection between written standards and talk of a social licence has been noted above and it is now time to look at that more closely. What written standards have been advanced in relation to financial market activity in the United Kingdom, to what extent can they be thought of as articulating a social licence and how might they help in realising the aspirations which talk of a social licence seems to express? In particular, what is the role of written standards that require or encourage behaviour by reference to other-regarding values – written standards which could therefore be viewed as most closely aligned with the aspirations that seem to lie behind references to a social licence?

Behavioural Norms and Written Standards

In approaching this topic, it is important to make a fundamental distinction between: (1) the regular behavioural patterns of firms and individuals in the financial services sector (behavioural norms); and (2) written standards in the form of law, regulation and codes of practice which are deliberately advanced to influence that behaviour towards what is aspired to by the originators of those written standards.

Behavioural norms concern the substance of financial life as it can be seen operating day-to-day: the objects of transactions, the way in which they are struck, and the manner in which staff are employed and promoted, market participants relate day-to-day, conflicts emerge and get resolved, and financial life proceeds. Most of these norms are not formally enforced by any external body. They simply represent 'the way things are'. Behavioural norms emerge and are shaped by a range of factors, including the cultural environment and, within that, 'market forces'.[49] Written standards are only one of those factors.

What is described as the 'social licence for financial markets' is not a behavioural norm, nor is it a written standard. However, if it is right to regard it as an attempt to direct financial activity towards just ends pursued in a just manner, it does express an aspiration about what behavioural norms should be and the outcomes they should produce. Written standards are advanced to influence behavioural norms. Because of that, and because of their social context, we could expect there to be some alignment between written standards that apply in the financial markets and notions of a social licence in the place of difference between existing behavioural norms and the aspired ends and practices of financial market activity. Put another way,

---

[48]   Written standards are by no means the only means of seeking to change behaviour, but they are the principal focus of this chapter for the reasons given. In particular, the activities of regulators can be a hybrid affair with written standards often advanced to support the use of other regulatory techniques. However, even in the context of these processes, expected standards are frequently articulated in writing in one form or another.

[49]   Social and emotional factors can be deeply involved in assessments of 'value' (for example, by affecting a person's sense of need) and consequently what someone is prepared to pay in a particular market.

a possible connection between talk of a social licence and concepts of justice is noted above: securing justice is also the stuff of law and regulation, if not written standards more widely.

In view of the vast expansion in regulatory rules in the UK financial services sector in the 30 years since the 'Big Bang' of 1986,[50] it is not surprising that there has been considerable attention to the forms, types and uses of regulatory rules in the financial markets and their relationship with other regulatory instruments. The literature is now extensive.[51] What follows draws on but is not intended to rehash that work. Rather, it seeks to place regulatory rules in the context of the full range of written standards operating in or applicable to the UK financial markets in order to clarify how different sorts of written standards might be related to the idea of a social licence for financial markets.

Types of Written Standard and Their Relationship with a Social Licence

There are various ways of categorising the written standards that apply in the UK financial markets. This chapter has already relied upon one of them in determining its scope: as noted above, it does not address what could be described as 'secondary rules' concerning the creation, administration and enforcement of rules with more primary behavioural intent. None of the available categorisations offers a single authoritative basis for looking at written standards, and all of them depend upon the perspective of the person undertaking the categorisation and the reasons for the exercise. Even where categories of written standards can be identified, they are rarely rigid, but overlap and display interdependencies.[52] It is nonetheless necessary in understanding the relationship between written standards and talk of a social licence to distinguish between some of the broad categories of relevant written standards.

An overview of the written standards operating within or applicable to the UK financial markets is therefore set out in the Appendix to this chapter (the Written Standards Map). Together with what follows, the Written Standards Map highlights a number of features that help in understanding how written standards relate to the idea of a social licence: first, by distinguishing between the originators of those standards (i.e. those who promulgate them) and those to whom the standards are addressed; and secondly, by seeking to indicate the extent to which the written standards it covers could be thought of as 'aspirational' in nature. It does the second in three ways, reflecting the manner in which written standards can draw on aspirations based on other-regarding values: it applies a rating based on the extent to which standards in the relevant category expressly reference other-regarding values (an 'aspirational rating'); it rates standards based on the extent to which they rely upon enforcement administered by a public body to secure compliance (a 'legal hardness rating'); and it indicates the way in which public and private enforcement mechanisms are available to enforce the relevant standard. The basis for these ratings is described further below.

---

[50]   It now seems ironic that this was ever referred to as 'deregulation', although it did involve a form of structural deregulation of the financial markets.

[51]   Starting with Julia Black, *Rules and Regulators* (OUP 1997).

[52]   See for example, Bronwen Morgan and Karen Yeung, *An Introduction to Law and Regulation*, (Cambridge University Press 2007) Chapter 3. While they discuss a broader range of regulatory instruments and techniques than just written standards, many of them involve written standards and the issues are similar.

Because the Written Standards Map is intended to provide no more than an overview, it comes with any number of health warnings and qualifications. However, for current purposes it is hoped that none of these is material. In particular, it will be clear that the aspirational and legal hardness ratings do not depend upon an especially scientific process. It is challenging to apply a single rating to some of the categories of written standards covered in the map because some categories are comprised of a mixture of written standards that fall at various points along each spectrum. The ratings should therefore be regarded as providing no more than an indication of the extent to which a given category of written standards has characteristics of the sort concerned. It would certainly be possible to debate the ratings assigned to each of the categories of written standards in the map – indeed, there might be merit in doing so to develop a better understanding of the role and operation of each. However, for current purposes this looser guide must suffice.

The Originators of Written Standards

As noted in Part 1, the source of written standards affects the extent to which they can be regarded as part of a social licence. Those with the closest connection to public authorities arguably have the strongest claim. The Written Standards Map helps to show the 'polycentric' dimension to the promulgation of written standards for financial markets. A multitude of what can loosely be described as 'public' and 'private' actors is involved, with the first being more dominant in terms of output. Distinguishing between the different originators of written standards is important: the involvement of democratic, or at least public, bodies is not only relevant in assessing how far each sort of written standard can be regarded as part of the social licence, but also affects the way in which formal legal enforcement powers attach to them. That, in turn, has a bearing on the extent to which the effectiveness of a given set of standards is likely to rely upon alternatives to the state-sanctioned use of force and, in particular, an ability to inspire particular sorts of behaviour.

Public originators of written standards

Governments and public authorities articulate and enforce written standards (commonly referred to as laws and regulations) principally through the legislature, the courts (subject to judicial independence) or regulators. These written standards can broadly be divided into two groups:

1. public law standards – very loosely, these are legal standards created by public bodies such as governments and regulators, usually in the form of statutes and regulations, which concern the relationship between individuals and the state or relationships between private individuals which are of wider public interest; and
2. private law standards (i.e. those arising at common law and which rely upon the courts): these include contractual standards (whether under standard form documentation created and maintained by industry associations such as the International Swaps and Derivatives Association (ISDA) or entirely private arrangements between two or more parties),

tortious standards (e.g. negligence, negligent misstatement) and equitable standards, especially fiduciary duties (the duty of loyalty to a principal).[53]

The role of the first group of written standards is principally to protect society at large. The role of the second is to protect individuals and other entities and allow them to regulate their relationships bilaterally, but this function also serves socially desirable ends such as the need for relational certainty and social stability.

A further category of 'public' standards is derived from international governmental and regulatory organisations. These can also be thought of as falling into two categories. First, there is a body of standards promulgated by the United Nations that are relevant to business activities of any sort, known as the United Nations Guiding Principles on Human Rights.[54] Secondly, there are sets of standards issued by international regulatory committees (comprised of representatives from participant countries) such as the Basel Committee on Banking Supervision and the International Organization of Securities Commissions. Their standards are principally intended as a means of coordinating the activities of national regulators both in response to and to further the internationalisation of the financial markets, rather than directly regulating market participants. Not only do these standards apply to different subjects from those outlined above, they are also 'enforced' differently, for example, through the operation of Financial Sector Assessment Programmes.[55] Nonetheless, since the standards set by these international regulatory bodies are ultimately directed at financial market activity and are sometimes taken into account by market participants in deciding how to act, they are included in the Written Standards Map. Their inclusion is for completeness and they are not considered further in what follows.

Private originators of written standards
Private bodies may also seek to articulate and enforce written standards. In spite of their private origins, there are three broad ways in which they could be viewed in some sense as partially articulating the terms of a social licence: where they represent an attempt by the group concerned to align its behavioural standards with social expectations; where they have been specifically required or adopted by public sector bodies for that purpose; and where they reflect and seek to apply commonly accepted values of the sort discussed above.[56] Elements of all three can be seen in written standards promulgated by all of the five main categories of private bodies below.

First, there are industry bodies. In the case of industry associations, these will be generally acting in the interests of their members, for example, to lobby on behalf of the relevant industry on regulatory reform and to maintain its good standing with its client base and other interested parties. However, the United Kingdom's FICC Markets Standards Board is an example of an

---

[53]   Although the distinction between public and private law originates from civil law jurisdictions, it has increasingly been made in common law jurisdictions such as England and is helpful for current purposes.

[54]   Available at http://www.ohchr.org/Documents/Publications/GuidingPrinciplesBusinessHR_EN.pdf, accessed on 7 December 2017.

[55]   These involve an in-depth analysis of the stability and operation of a country's financial sector. They are the joint responsibility of the International Monetary Fund and World Bank in developing economies and emerging markets and of the International Monetary Fund alone in advanced economies.

[56]   See pages 115–16.

industry body that was established, with regulatory encouragement, specifically as a private standard-setting body in the fixed income, currency and commodities markets. Written norms promulgated by this sort of originator include, in particular, codes of conduct and statements of good practice (particularly in areas of regulation that involve a significant element of judgement or where the rules are uncertain) and, in some cases, industry standard contractual documentation such as the standard form derivatives documentation, mentioned above, produced and maintained by ISDA (highlighting the potentially close relationship between public and private promulgation of written standards). Over-arching industry association codes of conduct are less common where the industry sector concerned is heavily regulated, as compared with unregulated or lightly regulated markets. For an example of a code governing unregulated markets, see the FX Global Code, a set of global principles of good practice in the largely unregulated foreign exchange markets. However, strictly, that was the product of a joint project between public sector regulators, central banks and market participants.[57]

Secondly, there are professional bodies comprised of individual members. Their role is essentially two-fold: helping their membership to achieve standards of professional competence and seeking to advance professional conduct standards. They do this largely by offering professional training and qualifications programmes. Their existence is therefore based around commonly agreed standards of professional competence and behaviour, the latter usually articulated in codes of ethics or conduct. At present, professional bodies have a relatively low profile in the financial services sector, and significant areas of financial services activity are not covered by a professional body. Because of that, it is questionable whether they have had a material role in shaping behaviour in the financial services sector in recent years, even for those parts of the sector they cover.[58] However, it is possible that they could assume a more prominent role in future as a result of the phased introduction of the United Kingdom's Senior Managers and Certification Regime, among other things, requiring regulated firms to certify the fitness of staff carrying on the firm's core activities.[59] Just how material any change will be remains to be seen.

The third group of standard-promulgating private bodies is comprised of firms operating in the financial services sector. These may use written standards (1) as a compliance and risk-management tool and to comply with specific regulatory requirements to maintain policies in areas such as conflict management; (2) to establish their credentials with their potential customer-base; and (3) to define their relationship with those with whom they deal (i.e. the contractual terms on which firms choose to transact, whether with counterparties, clients, suppliers or staff, highlighting once again the blurred boundary between public and private standard setting). Written standards in the first and second categories can take many different forms including codes of behaviour, codes of ethics, statements of good practice and internal policies of various sorts (for example, remuneration schemes, appraisal standards and policies on such matters as risk management, outsourcing, which clients to take on and which mandates

---

[57]   https://www.globalfxc.org/docs/fx_global.pdf.

[58]   Jim Baxter and Chris Megone, *Exploring the Role of Professional Bodies and Professional Qualifications in the UK Banking Sector*, a report prepared for the Banking Standards Board, October 2016, available at https://www.bankingstandardsboard.org.uk/wp-content/uploads/2016/10/160928-Professionalism-in-banking-publication-FINAL-WEB.pdf.

[59]   See further below at pages 123 and 132.

to accept, conflict management, trade execution and allocation, product development and staff discipline).

Fourthly, investment exchanges and trading platforms, and market infrastructures such as payment systems, depositaries and clearing houses also generate written standards in the form of membership agreements, rules and operating manuals governing access to, operation of, and conduct within the relevant market or infrastructure. In many cases, the relevant platforms are directly or indirectly required to maintain these by law, as a condition of being permitted to operate. For example, EU-regulated exchanges are required under 'MiFID II' to maintain, 'transparent and non-discriminatory rules and procedures that provide for fair and orderly trading and establish objective criteria for the efficient execution of orders'.[60] Once again this serves to highlight the close relationship between publicly and privately originated written standards, and consequently their potential proximity to the idea of a social licence.

Finally, there is a loose category of private bodies that could be described as public interest groupings. These would include organisations such as Tomorrow's Company[61] or Transparency International[62] which are seeking to encourage changes in market behaviour, among other things, by promoting 'score cards' and other forms of ratings. The rating criteria therefore arguably constitute a form of written standard. They would also include an organisation known as the PRI, an independent body set up with the encouragement of the United Nations to advance thinking and practice in the area of sustainable investment. As part of that, the PRI has advanced six 'voluntary and aspirational' principles of responsible investment which now have nearly 2,000 signatories.[63]

Although a distinction has been made between 'public' and 'private' originators of written standards, it will be clear from this brief overview that the threshold between the two is porous. In particular, private actors may rely upon private law, enforced in the courts, in setting standards (for example, by using contract law) and in setting their own internal standards (for example, investment firm conduct codes intended to secure compliance with public law standards). However, private standards may also affect the application of public standards (for example, in determining whether a duty has been properly discharged), or even be enlisted in public law regimes (for example, the United Kingdom's Corporate Governance Code, promulgated by the Financial Reporting Council but used as part of the United Kingdom's listing regime).[64] There are also standard-setting bodies, such as the United Kingdom's Takeover Panel, that started life as essentially private sector initiatives, but whose role has progressively become adopted by the public sector.[65] As noted, this interaction is one factor in assessing the extent to which the standards originated by private bodies can be viewed as, in some way, articulating a social licence. However, it is also relevant in understanding the behavioural force of the standards they promulgate, which will be considered further below – in particular, the extent to which compliance with the standards concerned rests on the deployment of negative incentives (in the form of legally enforced sanctions), or draws on other-regarding aspirations.

---

[60]   Directive 2014/65/EU of the European Parliament and of the Council on markets in financial instruments OJ L173/349, art 47(1)(d).

[61]   Tomorrow's Company describes itself as an independent non-profit think tank that inspires and enables businesses to be a force for good in society: http://tomorrowscompany.com.

[62]   The international anti-bribery and corruption organisation: https://www.transparency.org.

[63]   See https://www.unpri.org/about, accessed on 7 December 2017.

[64]   FCA Handbook, LR 9.8.6R.

[65]   Part 28 of the Companies Act 2006.

The Subjects of Written Standards

To whom are these standards addressed? The first thing to say is that they are not aimed at 'markets'. As discussed in Part 1, markets are comprised of market participants and those who operate the markets. Market participants and operators are the principal subjects of written standards. However, an important distinction needs to be made between written standards that apply to regulated firms (including for these purposes, market operators) and those that apply to individuals working for regulated firms. Written standards that are specifically addressed to individuals are shown in the Written Standards Map in italics. It will be clear that most of the written standards in the map apply to firms rather than individuals. However, professional and firm codes of conduct generally apply to individuals (the latter, in part, designed to help the firm to comply with its own legal and regulatory obligations by applying, as noted above, a form of 'private' regulation). The conduct codes associated with the UK Financial Conduct Authority (FCA) Approved Persons Regime[66] and the UK Prudential Regulation Authority's (PRA) and FCA's Senior Managers and Certification Regimes also apply to individuals;[67] the Senior Managers and Certification regimes are designed to increase 'individual accountability' for the compliance of regulated firms. Written standards in this category are potentially particularly important in seeking to realise aspired behaviours because individuals are not only responsible for their own conduct, but also that of the firms for which they work: ultimately, companies can only make decisions and act through the individuals who run and work for them. Further, while it is clearly possible to talk of organisations having values and aspirations, ultimately these can only be held and experienced by individuals, although group context can influence the way that happens. Until relatively recently, this dimension of financial market behaviour received relatively little regulatory attention from the public sector. The introduction of the Senior Managers and Certification Regime, mentioned above, is an attempt to redress the balance, as is the current regulatory emphasis on the need for firms that operate in the financial markets to establish a robust culture.[68] However, the impact of these initiatives may still be limited since their emphasis upon accountability and control does not obviously operate within a broader concept of character formation.

---

[66]   FCA Handbook, Statements of Principle and Code of Practice for Approved Persons. The FCA has stated that its approved persons regime will be replaced by an extended version of the Senior Managers and Certification Regime (which already applies to banks and insurers) during the course of 2019; Individual Accountability: Transitioning FCA firms and individuals to the Senior Managers & Certification Regime, CP17/40, FCA, December 2017. See further at page 132 below.

[67]   FCA Handbook, Code of Conduct; PRA Rulebook, Banking and Investment Rules Conduct Rules and Insurance Rules Conduct Standards.

[68]   Regulatory work on firms' culture falls outside the scope of this chapter, but is potentially significant in the context of talk of a social licence for financial markets. The extent to which the FCA is now placing an emphasis upon individual accountability is illustrated by its consultation on recognising industry guidance in unregulated financial markets (see note 40 above), which concentrates on the relationship between industry guidance and individuals' compliance with the Senior Managers and Certification Regime and only addresses the question of conduct by firms as a subsidiary matter.

Written Structural and Behavioural Standards

Not all written standards can be seen as articulating a social licence. Some set the context within which licensed activities can take place, or define their subject matter. At the highest level, written standards tend to affect or seek to affect behaviour in one of two ways: first, by establishing or formalising structures within which or by reference to which behaviour takes place (written structural standards)[69] and secondly, by prescribing or proscribing behaviours (written behavioural standards). This could be described as a functional categorisation of written standards.

Written structural standards typically take the form of law or regulation, or contract-based arrangements, and are used to establish or facilitate structures that affect behaviour, intentionally or otherwise. First, they can set the framework within which behaviour takes place. Examples of this in the financial markets would include arrangements such as ring-fenced banks,[70] clearing houses,[71] the limited liability company, and recognised investment exchanges. Secondly, structural standards can be used to establish or formalise structures by reference to which behaviour takes place. Common examples in the financial markets would include the notion of private property, money, shares, and debt and security interests. These structures are defined, supported and operated in accordance with a network of legal and regulatory rules. In view of this, written structural standards should not generally be thought of as articulating a social licence for financial markets. Rather, written structural standards *set the context* for what it is possible to do with a licence because they define the raw material of financial activity and establish the channels through which it is possible to engage in it. By analogy, a driving licence permits a person to drive a car, but different laws and regulations define what a car is and support the infrastructure necessary to enjoy the licence.[72] So it is with an authorisation to engage in financial activity. Take, for example, money. While money grew out of the behavioural norms of social exchange (and continues to mutate as a social mechanism, for example, as a result of the Fintech revolution), it now rests on an underpinning of structural law and regulation. Authorisation allows the person concerned to use money in various ways, and even to create it, but essentially takes money as a given.

---

[69]   John C Coates IV, 'The Volcker Rule as structural law: implications for cost–benefit analysis and administrative law' (2015) Capital Markets Law Journal 10(4), 447.

[70]   Bank ring-fencing refers to the requirement for banking groups to separate their retail banking activities from their wholesale banking and investment activities, so that the former will be less affected by a failure in the latter. Among other things, this involves the ring-fenced retail banking activities being run out of a separate legal entity with its own board of directors, subject to discrete liquidity and capital requirements.

[71]   Once two parties have entered into an investment transaction, clearing houses provide a standardised means for settling it, including making the necessary payments and delivering the relevant financial instruments. In addition, central counterparty clearing, which is now common in the derivatives markets, involves the clearing house being interposed between two parties to a trade thereby assuming an obligation to each of them to perform the other's obligations under the contract. The central counterparty is independently capitalised and operated, and must be provided with collateral to cover the exposures it assumes under cleared trades. The aim of this is to manage counterparty risk more effectively within the financial system, with the possibility of mutualisation should it crystallise. However, questions remain over the extent to which central counterparty clearing could be a source of new risks.

[72]   Speed limits, by contrast, concern the behaviour of a person when making use of the licence and are therefore more similar to behavioural standards, considered below.

Although written structural standards are principally concerned with upholding the relevant structure, they may nonetheless have a behavioural impact that goes beyond marshalling behaviour in support of the structure. That is because they define what is possible, and create and underpin structures which are also sometimes stores of cultural significance, so setting the parameters for, or establishing the objects of, behaviour. The behavioural implications of conducting business out of a limited liability entity are not the same as conducting it out of a partnership with unlimited liability; activity based on money subject to the gold standard is different from using fiat money; and the impact of a debt relationship on those involved (with the associated creditor controls applied to the debtor through security interests) is entirely different from a transaction between two people financed by cash. The claim of structural standards to be seen as articulating a social licence is therefore limited. However, it is important to recognise the way in which the structures they help to sustain can either support or undermine the sort of aspirations that lie behind talk of a social licence. Perhaps the most striking example of this is the 1986 'Big Bang'. This was a major structural change to the UK financial markets that involved, among other things, the abolition of fixed commissions and the distinction between client-facing stock brokers and market-dealing stock jobbers. However, at least in part, it lay behind the need for, and subsequent expansion of, written behavioural standards to govern the United Kingdom's financial markets.

The Form of Written Behavioural Standards and the Role of Aspiration

By contrast, written behavioural standards articulate accepted or desired behaviours or behavioural outcomes and can therefore more readily be associated with the substance of the behavioural aspirations that seem to lie behind talk of a social licence. In considering the relationship between written behavioural standards and the concept of a social licence for financial markets, it is helpful (1) to distinguish between the different sorts of written behavioural standards that are in operation in the UK markets; and (2) to explore the extent of any aspirational overlap between written standards and the idea of a social licence.

A common categorisation of written behavioural standards is between those that are prescriptive and those that are in the form of principles. However, it is also possible to approach written behavioural standards by reference to their aspirational force – in particular, the extent to which they either (1) reference, or (2) rely for their impact on other-regarding values.[73] Standards in the first category are often in the form of principles, but that is not necessarily the case for standards in the second category. All written behavioural standards are advanced with the aspiration of shaping behaviour in some way. For example, the regulatory requirement that firms should secure 'best execution' when entering investment transactions on behalf of clients is intended to ensure that firms act so as to obtain the best terms for the client,[74] and even a simple requirement to provide a notice to a client (for example, setting out the firm's

---

[73]   This distinction between prescriptive standards and aspirational standards is well established. See for example Mark S. Frankel, 'Professional codes: why, how, and with what impact' (1989) Journal of Business Ethics 8, 109; Judith Lichtenberg, 'What are codes of ethics for?' in Margaret Coady and Sidney Block (eds), *Codes of Ethics and the Professions* (Melbourne University Press 1996); Brian J. Farrell et al., 'Codes of ethics – their evolution, development and other controversies' (2002) Journal of Management Development 21(2), 152, 159; Donald Nicholson, note 37 above, 619.

[74]   FCA Handbook, COBS 11.6.

contact details) is intended to ensure behaviour consistent with that. However, the 'aspirational standards' considered in what follows are notable for the way in which they rely upon other-regarding values. This reliance can be viewed from two perspectives: the first concerns the content of the relevant standards (whether they explicitly reference other-regarding values), and the second the basis upon which people are expected to act in accordance with them (the extent to which this depends upon other-regarding values held by those to whom the standard is addressed). Aspirational standards are of particular significance in considering the relationship between written standards and the idea of a social licence for financial markets. If it is correct to regard the social licence as embedding an aspiration towards just ends pursued justly in financial markets, aspirational standards as described above most clearly expressly or implicitly reflect similar aspirations because of their relationship with other-regarding values. Aspirational standards in some way reach beyond individually prescribed behaviours to values that transcend and underpin them. There is therefore a sense in which aspirational standards could be regarded as the aspirational meeting-point between talk of a social licence for financial markets and the use of written standards in financial markets.

Turning first to standards with aspirational content, most written behavioural standards are largely descriptive (and in some way prescriptive) of specific behavioural standards: they hold out or reflect basic standards of good practice and either (1) guide, require or incentivise all to attain them or (2) ban behaviours that fall sufficiently short (prescriptive standards). An example of prescriptive standards would be regulatory rules on the prevention and detection of money laundering. Although these allow the subjects of the rules a significant degree of discretion on how to comply with them, they nonetheless apply precise requirements on, among other things, systems and controls to verify customer identity and detect and report money laundering.[75] However, within the broad category of written behavioural standards there is a smaller group of written standards comprising those formulated as foundational principles. Principles are less specific as to the action they require, but tend to operate by reference (1) to values that should be applied (or in the case of human rights, respected), or (2) broad outcomes that should be achieved (for example, that a bank is adequately capitalised[76]).[77] Principles in the first category tend to reference other-regarding values of a sort that would commonly be regarded as integral to just behaviour, such as a duty to 'act fairly', recalling the Schwartz categories of 'benevolence' and 'universalism' discussed above.[78] This seems to suggest a connection with the aspirational dimension of talk of a social licence for financial markets. It is this quality that Ronald Dworkin may have had in mind when describing legal principles as 'a standard that is to be observed . . . because it is a requirement of justice or fairness'.[79] In this chapter, principles (whether legal or non-legal) that reference values of this sort are treated as aspirational standards because they invite or require those to whom they are addressed to determine their behaviour by reference to over-arching values that express how people themselves generally desire to be treated. In other words, these are standards that could be equally

---

[75] Money Laundering, Terrorist Financing and Transfer of Funds (Information on the Payer) Regulations 2017, SI 2017/692, Part 3.

[76] FCA Handbook, PRIN 2.1.1R, Principle 4.

[77] Baldwin et al., *Understanding Regulation* (2nd edn, Oxford 2012), 302; Julia Black, 'The rise, fall and fate of principles-based regulation' in Kern Alexander and Naimh Moloney (eds), *Law Reform and Financial Markets* (Edward Elgar 2011).

[78] See pages 115–16 above.

[79] Ronald Dworkin 'The model of rules' (1967) University of Chicago Law Review 35(1), 14, 23.

applicable in a range of situations, whether in work or private life, because the standards they reference are understood to transcend any specific set of circumstances. They will be referred to in what follows as 'content-based aspirational standards'.

The Written Standards Map in the Appendix provides an indication of how content-based aspirational standards are distributed among the various categories of written standards that apply to the UK financial services sector by including an 'aspirational' rating (in column 4) for each category of written standards covered by the map. The rating is based on the extent to which standards in each category involve content-based aspirational standards. The map treats a standard as a content-based aspirational standard where it references an other-regarding value used in the FCA's Principles for Businesses: integrity, due care, proper standards of conduct and fairness (the last being particularly prominent in the Principles because it appears in three of them and is arguably implicit in others).[80] The FCA Principles are taken as a base-line because, in the context of talk of a social licence, public regulatory standards probably have the greatest claim to be part of the licence, as compared with written standards produced by private bodies. In addition to these four expressions, a standard has also been deemed aspirational if it references 'honesty' or 'ethics'. The reason for including the first is that it appears in another over-arching FCA rule, which the FCA refers to as the 'client's best interests rule'.[81] The second is included on the basis that references to 'ethics' in written standards generally seem intended to encourage other-regarding behaviour based on commonly understood values.[82] The Written Standards Map uses a rating of A1–A3: categories of written standards that, on their face, make material use of content-based aspirational standards have a rating of A1 whereas those that tend to be based on prescriptive standards receive a rating of A3.

The second basis upon which written behavioural standards (whether prescriptive or content-based aspirational) could be regarded as aspirational standards turns not on their content, but on the way they are applied in practice. In particular, it concerns the extent to which behaviour consistent with the relevant standard has to be incentivised by punishment or reward, or relies upon the other-regarding values of those to whom the standard is directed. Essentially, mechanisms that are used to encourage compliance with a particular written standard tend to fall into one of three categories: (1) deterrence (relying upon negative self-interest, especially in the form of sanctions for those who breach the standard); (2) positive incentive (relying upon self-interest, for example, in the form of enhanced remuneration for those who follow the standard); and (3) inspiration to comply with the standard by appealing to other-regarding sentiments – i.e. an aspiration on the part of the subject concerning how they should treat others.[83] The first and second are familiar. An example of a standard that relies upon the third is the Lord George Principles for Good Business Conduct of the Worshipful Company of International Bankers of the City of London, the introduction to which seeks to inspire adherence to the standards by rehearsing the critical role of international financial ser-

---

[80]   FCA Handbook, PRIN 2.1.
[81]   FCA Handbook, COBS 2.1.1 which requires firms to act, 'honestly, fairly and professionally in accordance with the best interests of their clients'.
[82]   However, written standards requiring a person to behave 'ethically' are somewhat empty without an understanding of which ethic is involved, and cynics might suggest that this is precisely the reason the word is used. Indeed, it would be possible for an ethic to be far from other-regarding.
[83]   Tom R. Tyler, 'Reducing corporate criminality: the role of values' (2014) American Criminal Law Review 51, 267.

vices activity in maintaining social well-being.[84] The more that adherence to a written standard is secured using positive and negative incentives, the more likely it is that adherence will be treated as a compliance exercise rather than the realisation of an other-regarding value. The use of positive and negative incentives certainly has a fundamental role in realising the sort of aspirations that seem to lie behind talk of a social licence. However, it is also important to recognise that it involves the subject of the standard in a very different deliberative exercise – one based more on self-interest and less dependent upon other-regarding motivations.[85]

It is not especially easy to provide a simple snapshot of how every category of written standards in the map gets enforced. However, as a proxy, column 5 of the Written Standards Map applies what is described as a 'legal hardness' rating. This is intended to give an indication of the extent to which formal legal enforcement tools are available to incentivise compliance with each category of written standards, or whether the standards rely upon something else for their force, in particular, positive self-interest or their inspirational power to motivate behaviour. It is important to recognise that this rating can only provide one perspective on the question of enforcement: the way written standards are enforced in practice does not just depend upon the formal enforcement powers of the standard originating body, but also the style and approach of that body to enforcement. The hardness ratings take no account of regulatory style and activism (for example, the well-publicised move towards 'credible deterrence' by the FCA in the aftermath of the Global Financial Crisis, heralding a period of more intense enforcement activity). Financial services regulators have a considerable range of methods available to them to seek to secure compliance on the part of the regulated and, most of the time, their activities involve softer tools such as supervisory dialogue, advice and persuasion rather than a resort to sanctions.[86] Separately, there is also the matter of positive incentives used privately by firms in seeking to shape staff behaviour; even though firms' incentive frameworks will generally be supported by a series of private law rights and obligations, these do not have the same characteristics as a regulatory enforcement regime. It is beyond the scope of the standards map to seek to indicate all of the different public and private enforcement mechanisms in operation or show the sometimes-complex interplay between them. However, some indication of this is provided in column 3 of the standards map. Essentially, it is important to bear in mind that the availability of hard enforcement powers does not mean that those powers will be used, nor should it lead us to assume that regulators will ignore other-regarding aspirations on the part of those to whom standards are addressed to change behaviour.[87]

The legal hardness rating distinguishes between H1 (written standards enforced using legal powers given to public authorities), H2 (written standards which can be enforced using private law remedies in the hands of the parties affected by a breach where restitution in the context of a business relationship may be at least as important as the enforcement of a particular standard) and H3 (those that do not seem heavily reliant upon any legal or regulatory enforcement mechanism, or are not reliant at all). A rating of H2 has also been given to official guidance on the meaning and application of standards rated H1 since the guidance itself is generally

---

[84]   https://internationalbankers.org.uk/about-the-company/principles-for-good-business-conduct/.

[85]   Iris Bohnet et al., 'More order with less law: on contract enforcement, trust, and crowding' (2001) The American Political Science Review 95(1), 131.

[86]   See for example the enforcement pyramid in Ian Ayres and John Braithwaite, *Responsive Regulation* (OUP 1992) 35.

[87]   Neil Gunningham and Peter Gabrosky, *Smart Regulation* (OUP 1998).

not enforceable, but may have a bearing on the outcome of enforcement of the underlying standard. H1 represents standards with the highest legal hardness rating and H3 the lowest. Category H1 is further split into H1.1 and H1.2, the former being applied to standards that can be enforced using criminal sanctions and the latter to standards that are subject to civil enforcement tools. However, note that aspiration can still be seen operating at H1.1 (for example, the prospect of feeling shame at having failed to behave in an other-regarding manner) and positive and negative enforcement can still be seen operating within H3 (for example, in the form of expulsion from membership of an association or 'cold shouldering'). Consequently, it is not necessarily the case that just because a category of standards has been given a particular rating, enforcement relies exclusively upon only one of the three factors mentioned above.

Aspirational standards – observations based on aspirational and legal hardness ratings
What becomes clear from the aspirational ratings in the Written Standards Map is that content-based aspirational standards (i.e. those making express reference to other-regarding values) are ubiquitous. This ubiquity seems to be consistent with what one might expect from the values prioritisation work of Schwartz referred to above. Aspirational standards of this sort are associated with all types of originator, whether public or private, and apply to both sorts of subject, whether firms or individuals. What the Written Standards Map does not show, but is nonetheless relevant in thinking about aspirational overlap between aspirational standards and talk of a social licence, is that content-based aspirational standards promulgated by the FCA in the form of its Principles for Businesses tend to be referenced to the interests of customers and market users (associating them closely with firms' transactional activities), whereas the drafting of some of the more private aspirational standards (with, ironically, perhaps less of a claim to be articulating a social licence) appear to acknowledge a broader social remit, closer to the apparent scope of the social licence. For example, Barclays Bank's code talks of 'creating a virtuous link between our services and society's progress, not discounting one or the other'.[88] Others, while not expressly referencing society hold themselves to a very high standard, such as Morgan Stanley which states that it strives to adhere to 'the highest standards of ethical conduct' and JP Morgan Chase which describes itself as being committed to 'the highest level of integrity and ethical conduct'.[89]

The legal hardness ratings provide an additional insight into the operation of content-based aspirational standards: standards of this sort are associated with all categories of legal hardness, except for H1.1 (since, in view of the broad drafting of aspirational standards, it would not be appropriate to apply criminal sanctions in the event of a breach). This means that content-based aspirational standards originated by public regulatory bodies are associated with harder enforcement powers (but noting comments above concerning the range of regulatory enforcement approaches and the possibility that reliance on the motivational power of other-regarding values could also be a factor for a regulator in deciding which to adopt). By contrast, content-based aspirational standards originated by private bodies, especially professional associations, are usually subject to softer legal enforcement powers. This would appear

---

[88]   The Barclays Way (https://www.home.barclays/content/dam/barclayspublic/docs/Citizenship/BAR_TheBarclaysWay%20final.pdf, accessed 22 January 2018).
[89]   Morgan Stanley Code of Conduct 2017 (https://www.morganstanley.com/about-us-governance/code-of-conduct); JP Morgan Chase & Co Code of Conduct 2017 (https://www.jpmorganchase.com/corporate/About-JPMC/document/code-of-conduct.pdf, accessed 22 January 2018).

to create a risk for content-based aspirational standards associated with harder enforcement powers since legal enforcement could detract from their aspirational force, with the broad drafting of the standard operating more like a regulatory backstop to catch behaviours not covered by prescriptive rules. If so, it raises a question as to whether, where a content-based aspirational standard appears in one context associated with 'hard enforcement' mechanisms and a similar standard is promulgated by another originator that places more reliance on its intrinsic inspirational force, the former could tend to crowd out the aspirational aspect of latter.[90] Apparently consistent with that, as noted above, it is less common for industry associations to promulgate broad codes of conduct, including content-based aspirational standards, where the part of the industry they cover is heavily regulated (although industry codes have an important and potentially growing role in unregulated markets).[91] This may suggest that the role of industry associations in the regulated sector in aspirational standard setting has been largely crowded out by regulatory intervention.[92] Nonetheless it raises a question as to whether industry codes could play a valuable role in future in the regulated sector, much as is hoped for in the unregulated sector,[93] particularly in the area of aspiration that talk of a social licence seems to address.

What else can be learnt from the legal hardness ratings? Unsurprisingly, standards that can be thought of as aspirational because of the way they rely for their force upon the other-regarding values of those to whom they are addressed have a limited role among written behavioural standards promulgated by public bodies (since these are automatically associated with the legal enforcement powers of the relevant originator). For similar reasons, written standards of this sort (whether prescriptive or content-based aspirational) are more prevalent among written standards promulgated by non-public originators of standards. However, where they are advanced by firms, they are likely to be associated to some degree with contractual private law enforcement mechanisms which use remuneration and disciplinary processes to incentivise compliant behaviour. For this reason, standards of that sort have been rated as H2 rather than H3 in the Written Standards Map. As with the use of sanctions by regulators, the precise impact of those mechanisms on the way staff relate to the standards is likely to depend materially upon how the firms concerned deploy them. However, the use of remuneration structures as a means of managing the risk of negative behaviours and incentivising behaviours thought desirable by firms or regulators is widespread. The relationship between remuneration and behaviour has received considerable attention in the period since the Global Financial Crisis. To what extent this has taken account of the possible impact of incentivising compliance on the power of other-regarding values to motivate behaviour and the potential for different outcomes in terms of character formation is less clear.

---

[90]   For example, both the FCA's Principles for Approved Persons and Code of Conduct and the Lord George Principles for Good Business Conduct state that those to whom they are addressed should act honestly, fairly and with integrity.

[91]   The possibility of this crowding out effect seems to be recognised by the FCA. See for example, CP17/37 (note 38 above) at paragraph 1.12.

[92]   Industry associations covering more heavily regulated sectors of the financial services markets do issue various pieces of guidance and codes of good practice. However, these often concern how to comply with technical legal and regulatory rules, and can therefore be thought of as related to the enforcement regimes attached to those rules.

[93]   FCA CP17/37, see note 38 above.

Aspirational standards – observations based on experience
There is a further question which cannot be addressed in the Written Standards Map: to what extent have written behavioural standards in practice helped to support the sort of behaviours which seem to be involved in talk of a social licence, especially aspirational standards which have been identified above as an aspirational meeting point between the two? Further, has there been any difference in effect between aspirational standards that are associated with hard enforcement tools (i.e. H1) as compared with those which are associated with softer forms of enforcement? Clearly, it is impossible to know what would have happened had the relevant standards not been there. However, from the available indications, the picture seems mixed. The clearest example, touched on further below, of aspirational standards having a material behavioural impact involves standards originated by the public sector and applied to firms (rather than individuals), combined with the possibility of regulatory sanction. Yet, as noted above, recourse to enforcement to procure 'compliance' potentially undermines the inspirational dimension of standards to motivate particular behaviours. If so, there seems to be an inherent tension: at the point at which written standards might be thought of as most closely aligned with aspirations that seem to lie behind talk of a social licence, it has apparently been necessary to rely upon negative self-interest in the form of enforcement in order to secure compliance, with the risk of undermining the same aspirations. The following considers briefly the available evidence on the use and operation of aspirational standards – first, those originated by public bodies and, secondly, those promulgated by private bodies.

Aspirational standards emanating from the public sector and addressed to firms active in the financial markets have been a feature of the UK regulatory regime since 1990 when the United Kingdom's Securities and Investments Board published the precursor to the current FCA Principles for Businesses.[94] There have been numerous behavioural failures over that period: some aspirations have not been met, but whether the shortfall would have been more marked without the presence of those aspirational standards is unknown. There are certainly examples of aspirational standards originated and enforced by public bodies being associated with changed behaviour in the financial markets during this period. In particular, there is little doubt that the regulatory initiative known as 'treating customers fairly' or 'TCF', based on the aspirational standard in Principle 6 of the FCA's Standards for Businesses, has had a considerable impact on behaviour in parts of the UK financial services sector.[95] That said, the part of the TCF initiative concerning the manufacture and distribution of investment products has now been converted from regulatory guidance on Principle 6 into a rule-based regime as a result of MiFID II,[96] which suggests that the regulatory community was still not satisfied that reliance upon the Principle combined with guidance was sufficient to generate behaviours consistent with their aspirations. In the case of public sector aspirational standards directed at individuals, there is greater reason to believe that these have not hitherto been working as intended. The United Kingdom's Parliamentary Commission on Banking Standards in its final report in 2013 concluded that the Approved Persons Regime (including its aspirational Code

---

[94]   Julia Black, 'Forms and paradoxes of principles-based regulation' (2008) Capital Markets Law Journal 3(4), 425, 433.

[95]   Dan Awrey et al., 'Between law and markets: is there a role for culture and ethics in financial regulation?' (2013) Delaware Journal of Corporate Law 38, 191.

[96]   MiFID II, arts 16 and 24 and Commission Delegated Directive (EU) 2017/593 OJ L87/500, arts 9 and 10.

of Conduct) had been materially defective.[97] The response has been a new set of rules and content-based aspirational standards – the Senior Managers and Certification Regime including new conduct codes, mentioned above.[98] The Senior Managers and Certification Regime requires greater accountability from key individuals within a business ('senior managers') for their own conduct and for the activities of the part of a firm's business for which they are responsible. As a result, there is heightened regulatory enforcement risk for senior managers where they fail to discharge their responsibilities. The content-based aspirational standards that had applied to staff under the approved persons regime have been largely replicated in a new Conduct Code.[99] However, the Conduct Code now covers nearly all staff within a firm – a much wider constituency than previously. In addition to the Code being directly enforceable by the regulator,[100] senior managers will be responsible for ensuring that it is adhered to, so that the arrangements for the Code's indirect enforcement have also been strengthened. The new regime does not prescribe how firms and their senior managers should seek to align behaviour with the Code. They are free to decide how far to rely upon positive and negative incentives, reward and sanction (as inevitably they must to some degree) and how much upon steps to strengthen the aspirational force of the Code. It is unclear to what extent firms appreciate that this is one of the choices confronting them, and the potential significance of that choice.

It is also challenging to assess the impact hitherto of aspirational standards promulgated by private bodies – whether content-based aspirational standards or otherwise. As noted above, it is not especially common for industry associations covering regulated markets to publish codes of conduct, except on matters of technical compliance. However, the effectiveness of those issued to cover the unregulated fixed income, foreign exchange and commodities markets was heavily criticised by the United Kingdom's Fair and Effective Markets Review following its review of behavioural and operational failures in those markets.[101] Notably, one of the criticisms was that the mechanisms for ensuring that code signatories complied with the codes were insufficient; apparently, aspiration combined with market forces was not enough.

Aspirational standards are more prevalent in the codes of professional bodies such as the Chartered Banker Code of Professional Conduct[102] and firms operating in the financial markets. However, there is a material question as to the impact of written standards promulgated by the former, at least in the banking sector.[103] Indeed, the striking finding of a survey for the Banking Standards Board (BSB) was that fewer than 25 per cent of respondents to the banks and building societies survey thought that 'to improve their ethical standards' was an advantage of membership of a professional body, and fewer than 40 per cent saw 'to earn the trust of the public' as an advantage, most viewing the main benefit of professional associations

---

[97]   *Changing Banking for Good*, Report of the Parliamentary Commission on Banking Standards, Volume II: Chapters 1 to 11 and Annexes, together with formal minutes, 2013, 283.

[98]   See page 123 above.

[99]   See note 67 above.

[100]   Financial Services and Markets Act 2000, section 66.

[101]   HM Treasury, Bank of England and FCA, Fair and Effective Markets Review, Final Report, June 2015, available at https://www.bankofengland.co.uk/-/media/boe/files/report/2015/fair-and-effective-markets-review-final-report.pdf.

[102]   https://www.cbpsb.org/code/, accessed 22 January 2018.

[103]   '[A]ll professional bodies have a code of ethics, but it was not always clear whether members engaged seriously with the code, or whether there were serious consequences for those who breached the code', *Exploring the Role of Professional Bodies*, note 58 above, at paragraph 76.

as technical training.[104] In the case of financial services firms, in practice there rarely seems to be any express reference to their codes of conduct in considering the impact of legal or regulatory standards upon a proposed course of action; discussions can tend to proceed on the assumption that legal and regulatory standards are determinative. This may partly reflect the fact that one function of corporate codes is to reinforce messages about the need to comply with law and regulation, so managing what is commonly called 'enforcement risk'.[105] If so, it lends weight to the idea that the presence of legally enforceable regulatory rules may impair the operation of aspirational standards. However, as noted, content-based aspirational standards in private codes not infrequently express an aspiration for standards of behaviour that are higher or broader[106] than the legal and regulatory base line; if they did not, there would be little obvious point to them, since firms could simply replay existing legal standards or give guidance to staff on how to comply with law and regulation. The apparent absence of reference to corporate codes in daily practice does not necessarily mean that they have no role in setting the corporate 'mood music' in some way. However, the BSB 2016 assessment of culture in 22 of its members seems to hint at tensions between what employees feel under pressure to do and firms' espoused values.[107] It found that only 65 per cent of employees responding to the BSB assessment agreed that there is no conflict between their firm's stated values and the way the firm does business, and 14 per cent claimed that they did see such a conflict.[108] Of those who perceived a conflict, almost half said they did not believe that senior leaders in their organisation mean what they say when they espouse values. Further, 12 per cent of employees had seen instances where unethical behaviour was rewarded and 13 per cent considered it difficult to get ahead in their careers without 'flexing' their ethical standards.[109] This picture seems consistent with the findings of studies on the effectiveness of corporate codes of conduct more generally. An assessment of these suggests at best a mixed picture. However, some caution is needed since the studies concerned were undertaken in a variety of contexts by different individuals and did not use the same methodology.[110]

Aspirational standards may be aligned with the sort of aspirations that seem to underlie talk of a social licence for financial markets and may support their realisation. However, whether originated by public or private bodies, the indications to date do not seem entirely encouraging

---

[104]   *Exploring the Role of Professional Bodies*, note 58 above, at paragraph 32.

[105]   However, it is important to distinguish between corporate codes of conduct and the various compliance policies that firms maintain specifically to comply with aspects of the regulatory regime, such as policies on customer verification, trade execution and allocation, and managing conflicts of interest.

[106]   In particular, because they sometimes reference social purpose rather than the narrower focus of regulatory rules on relations with customers and within markets.

[107]   BSB Annual Review 2016/17.

[108]   The percentage was higher in systemically important institutions.

[109]   One 2013 report put the figure rather higher: 'While respondents admit that an improvement in employees' ethical conduct would improve their firm's resilience to unexpected and dramatic risk, 53% think that career progression at their firm would be difficult without being flexible on ethical standards.' *A Crisis of Culture – Valuing Ethics and Knowledge in Financial Services*, Economist Intelligence Unit 2013, 4. However, it is not clear whether the difference in numbers represents an improvement or simply reflects a different sample of firms and set of questions. The BSB states, for example, that some of the percentages noted above were higher in larger financial institutions.

[110]   Muel Kapetein and Mark S. Schwartz, 'The effectiveness of business codes: a critical examination of existing studies and the development of an integrated research model' (2008) Journal of Business Ethics 77, 111.

for those who favour the use of aspirational standards as a way of bringing behaviour in the financial markets into line with those aspirations. This is particularly the case where the aspirational standards are not directly underpinned by the power of formal public sector enforcement. Yet, as noted, the introduction of legal enforcement powers then risks undermining their aspirational force by reducing the exercise of responding to them into one of determining what is needed to secure a reward or avoid a punishment more than what aspiration might demand.

CONCLUSION

Talk of a social licence for financial markets has more substance than we might think. It is not simply theoretical and it is more than metaphor. Among other things, the idea of a social licence can be seen in the written standards that apply within the financial services sector. The idea of a social licence and written standards are both advanced in an attempt to shape behaviour, and embed an aspiration for the way behaviour should be and the results it should produce. Both the social licence and written standards seem connected at some level with notions of justice – just ends pursued justly in financial markets. However, for the idea of a social licence to have its intended effect, it requires greater definition and the current chapter has sought to advance that process. Taking it further needs to involve a broader constituency of parties to the licence. The need is pressing in view of the evidence of continuing low levels of public trust in financial institutions touched on in Part 1.

Giving effect to the idea of a social licence relies in part on written standards. Aspirational standards appear to represent the point of greatest overlap between written standards and the aspirations involved in the idea of a social licence. In view of that, they deserve greater attention – not just those originated by public bodies, but also those published by private bodies which have so far tended to operate in the shadow of the former and may to some extent have been crowded out by them. It is not clear how effective these aspirational standards have been in practice to shape behaviour in a manner consistent with the idea of a social licence. However, the challenge with seeking to enhance their effectiveness is that evidence to date suggests that aspirational standards are taken most seriously when associated with legal enforcement whereas reliance on legal enforcement may weaken the 'inspirational force' of aspirational standards to shape behaviour. A particular area for attention is where publicly originated aspirational standards cover (or could be perceived as covering) the same ground as privately originated aspirational standards, since the hard law enforcement of the former could potentially undermine the inspirational force of the latter. As noted above, work on industry codes of conduct being undertaken by the FCA at the time of writing suggests that it recognises a risk of this sort although it does not articulate it in quite the same way.[111] Market participants are ranged across a broad behavioural and aspirational spectrum. Because of that, it is not possible to do without some element of legal enforcement. However, approaches based upon process regulation may help to manage the risk, since they require those to whom the standards apply to engage with the relevant standard and to be in a position to show how they have done so, rather than sanctioning or rewarding compliance with the standard itself.[112] This could be considered, for example, in the context of a heightened focus on the way in which

---

[111]   See note 91 above.
[112]   Awrey et al., see note 95 above.

firms create and operate their own behavioural codes, where practice is currently mixed. As noted above, industry associations could also have a role to play, for example in helping to reduce 'first mover' concerns between their members. However, the idea of a social licence for financial markets may itself be one of the most important means of strengthening the operation of aspirational standards, by clarifying the ends of aspiration.

Appendix 5a   The Written Standards Map[a]

1. Category of written standard	2. Application to UK market participants	3. Extent to which reliant upon public or private legal enforcement mechanisms	4. Aspirational rating	5. Hardness rating
International				
United Nations The Principles of the UN Global Compact, United Nations Guiding Principles on Business and Human Rights.	Not legally binding, except to the extent enshrined in national law, but businesses can voluntarily subscribe to the principles, e.g. through joining the Global Compact. Principles operate as a framework for national and international legislative initiatives, and as a way for society to monitor companies' sustainability impact, especially in the area of human rights.	Public: not enforceable except where enshrined in national law (see further below). Private: no private law enforcement (unless incorporated in some way by the parties into their relationship). However, the Guiding Principles are sufficiently specific to facilitate monitoring (e.g. by NGOs) so encouraging compliance.	A1–2[b]	H3
International standards for regulators set by bodies such as the Financial Stability Board, Basel Committee on Banking Supervision, the OECD, the International Organization of Securities Commissions, International Association of Insurance Supervisors and the Financial Action Task Force to coordinate legal and regulatory standards globally.	Not directly applicable to market participants, but assumed to be relevant to: The way other directly applicable regulatory standards may be interpreted or applied; The future shape of the regulatory regime. Hence, larger firms pay attention to emerging policy and statements at this level.	Public: not enforced against market participants since they define standards for regulators, but belief that they could influence the enforcement of rules identified below that are directly applicable. Private: no private law enforcement (unless incorporated in some way by the parties into their relationship).	A2	H3
International private law coordination in particular the Hague Convention, UNIDROIT and UNCITRAL – principally focussed on harmonisation of standards relating to property, contract and insolvency rights and the elimination of legal uncertainty.	Only applicable to the extent adopted into or incorporated in national law or contractually adopted by the parties.	Public: no direct enforcement against market participants. Private: no private law enforcement (unless incorporated in some way by the parties into their relationship).	A3	H2
European Union				
EU Regulations (Level I/Level II)	Apply directly to businesses. Must be enforced by relevant UK authorities and applied by English courts and ultimately the ECJ.	Public: generally enforced at UK level using public enforcement tools although EU trend to stipulate minimum requirements. Private: limited, but could be taken into account in private law actions. May rely upon market forces to secure desired result.	A2–3	H1.2

1. Category of written standard	2. Application to UK market participants	3. Extent to which reliant upon public or private legal enforcement mechanisms	4. Aspirational rating	5. Hardness rating
EU Directives (Level I/Level II)	Implemented by UK authorities in rules that apply to businesses. Enforced by relevant UK authorities and applied by English courts and ultimately the ECJ.	Public: generally enforced at UK level using public enforcement tools although EU trend to stipulate minimum requirements. Private: limited, but could be taken into account in private law actions. May rely upon market forces to secure desired result.	A2–3	H1.2
Regulatory Technical Standards and Implementing Technical Standards	Detailed implementing rules made under Regulations or Directives. Enforced by relevant UK authorities and applied by English courts and ultimately the ECJ.	Public: as for framework legislation. Private: limited, but could be taken into account in private law actions.	A3	H1.2
EU Commission guidance	Relevant principally because it expresses the EU Commission's view on the meaning and application of EU legislation.	Public: no direct sanction, but may influence the enforcement of EU Regulations or rules implementing EU Directives. Private: limited, but could be taken into account in private law actions.	A2–3	H2
EBA/ESMA/EIOPA' (ESAs) guidance and recommendations	To promote supervisory convergence the ESAs have the power to issue guidelines that are addressed to individual member state regulatory authorities or, less frequently, to market participants. ESAs may also address an individual decision to a market participant where a member state authority has failed to act. Need not be specifically related to the application of Regulations and Directives but often will be.	Public: in most cases ESAs do not currently have direct enforcement rights, but should influence member state enforcement of EU rules or those implementing relevant EU legislation. Private: limited, but could be taken into account in private law actions.	A2–3	H2
EU Commission Q&A/ EBA/ESMA/EIOPA Q&A	Provides the views of the EU Commission/ESAs on the meaning and application of EU legislation, but is not legally binding.	Public: not directly enforceable against market participants, but could be used by member state courts and regulators in assisting in the interpretation and enforcement of EU legislation. Private: limited, but could be taken into account in private law actions.	A2–3	H2

1. Category of written standard	2. Application to UK market participants	3. Extent to which reliant upon public or private legal enforcement mechanisms	4. Aspirational rating	5. Hardness rating
Commission and ESA consultations, feedback documents and other commentary	No direct legal effect, but is sometimes referenced by industry participants in seeking to understand the purpose and effect of the resulting provisions in Regulations and Directives.	Public: not directly enforceable against market participants, but could be taken into account in assisting in member state and judicial interpretation and enforcement of EU legislation. Private: limited, but could be taken into account in private law actions.	A3	H3
United Kingdom				
Private law, especially contract law and fiduciary duties	Directly applicable, as a minimum, to those located and conducting activities in the United Kingdom. Contractual rights are a particularly important feature of the financial markets, especially under industry standard documentation such as the master documentation maintained by the International Capital Market Association or ICMA (bond market documentation and repurchase agreements), ISDA (derivatives), the International Securities Lending Association or ISLA (securities lending) and the Loan Market Association or LMA (lending).	Public: enforced by the courts using the full range of private law sanctions. Private: may be used as a basis for enforcing written norms promulgated by private bodies.	A1–2	H2
UK Statute/Statutory Instruments	Directly applicable to all persons within their jurisdictional reach – i.e. very broadly, those carrying on activity with a UK connection. (Also implement EU regulatory standards – see above.)	Public: will depend upon the relevant statute, but generally apply criminal sanctions for breach of the primary legislation. See regulatory regimes below for sanctions upon breach of rules made by regulators under the legislation. Private: not generally applicable save to the extent the legislation makes use of private enforcement mechanisms or market forces.	A2–3	H1.1–1.2

Prudential Regulatory Authority (PRA) – prudential regulation of UK incorporated banks and insurers

1. Category of written standard	2. Application to UK market participants	3. Extent to which reliant upon public or private legal enforcement mechanisms	4. Aspirational rating	5. Hardness rating
PRA Fundamental Rules technically PRA 'General Rules' (see below), but in the form of high-level principles rather than precise targeted requirements.	Directly applicable to all PRA authorised firms. (Also implement EU regulatory standards – see above.)	Public: full range of PRA sanctions applies if breached. Could also have other consequences such as increased capital requirements. Private: limited, but could be taken into account in private law actions. Breach could affect attitudes of counterparties and clients and therefore the firm's commercial position.	A1	H1.2
PRA General Rules (under s 137G of the Financial Services and Markets Act 2000 (FSMA)), specialised rules and various other rules made under other powers.	Directly applicable to all PRA authorised firms. (Also implement EU regulatory standards – see above.)	Public: full range of PRA sanctions applies if breached. Could also have other consequences such as increased capital requirements. Private: limited, but could be taken into account in private law actions. May rely upon market forces to secure a given result. Breach could also affect attitudes of counterparties and clients and therefore the firm's commercial position.	A2–3	H1.2
PRA Evidential Rules (s 138C FSMA).	Apply to all authorised firms except inward business under an EU cross-border passport. However, indicative only. Compliance with these will tend to establish compliance with another specified rule and breach will tend to establish non-compliance.	Public: no sanction for breach, but may be relevant to whether a binding rule is breached – see above. Private: limited, but could be taken into account in private law actions.	A2–3	H2
PRA Guidance including guidance statements in the PRA Handbook **PRA Supervisory Statements** **Other materials such as PRA letters**[d]	Guidance on the operation of specified parts of FSMA and on the PRA rules and the PRA's functions, therefore relevant to authorised firms in complying with the above.	Public: may be taken into account by the PRA in considering whether a standard has been breached. Private: limited, but could be taken into account in private law actions.	A2–3	H2
PRA Directions/Requirements given under various Acts (including a 138A FSMA) and statutory instruments	Binding on the persons or categories of persons to whom they are addressed. Relevant to the way particular rules apply to those persons.	Public: as for the rules to which the direction relates. Private: as for the rules to which the direction relates.	A3	H1.2

1. Category of written standard	2. Application to UK market participants	3. Extent to which reliant upon public or private legal enforcement mechanisms	4. Aspirational rating	5. Hardness rating
PRA Senior Managers Regime[c]	*Requirement for PRA individual approval for those managing aspects of the firm's affairs relevant to regulated activities which could involve a risk of serious consequences for the firm or business or other interests in the United Kingdom.*	*Public: a range of PRA sanctions can be applied under the PRA Conduct Rules to an individual who fails to discharge responsibilities.* *Private: limited, but could be taken into account in private law actions including between an individual and their employer. Could also be taken into account in the context of membership of professional bodies and by future potential employers.*	A2	H1.2
PRA Conduct Rules	*Applies to all PRA and FCA senior managers and PRA certified persons and others involved in the business of the firm.*	*Public: a range of PRA sanctions can be applied to an individual who is in breach.* *Private: limited, but could be taken into account in private law actions. Could also be taken into account in the context of membership of professional bodies and by future potential employers.*	A1	H1.2
FCA – conduct of business regulation for all firms in the UK market, prudential regulation of non-PRA UK firms, listing authority				
FCA Principles for Businesses technically FCA 'General Rules' (see below), but in the form of high-level principles rather than precise targeted requirements.	Increasing use made of these. Directly applicable to all authorised firms except inward business under an EU cross-border passport. (Also implement EU regulatory standards – see above.)	Public: full range of FCA sanctions applies if breached. Could also have other consequences such as increased capital requirements. Private: limited, but could be taken into account in private law actions. Breach could affect attitudes of counterparties and clients and therefore the firm's commercial position.	A1	H1.2

1. Category of written standard	2. Application to UK market participants	3. Extent to which reliant upon public or private legal enforcement mechanisms	4. Aspirational rating	5. Hardness rating
FCA General Rules (under s 137A–F, H, O–R and T FSMA), specialised rules (under s 140–7 FSMA), listing rules under s 73A and various other rules.	Directly applicable to all authorised firms except inward business under an EU cross-border passport. (Also implement EU regulatory standards – see above.)	Public: full range of public enforcement mechanisms used. FCA sanctions apply if breached. In some circumstances, can also lead to an action for damages from those who suffer loss as a result of the breach. Could also have other consequences such as increased capital requirements. Interplay with Financial Ombudsman complaints process for firms dealing with private individuals. Private: limited, but could be taken into account in private law actions. May rely upon market forces to secure a given result. Breach could also affect attitudes of counterparties and clients and therefore the firm's commercial position.	A2–3	H1.2
FCA Evidential Rules (s 138C FSMA) – applicable to firms.	Apply to all authorised firms except inward business under an EU cross-border passport. However, indicative only. Compliance with these will tend to establish compliance with another specified rule and breach will tend to establish non-compliance.	Public: no sanction for breach, but may be relevant to whether a binding rule breached – see above. Private: limited, but could be taken into account in private law actions.	A2–3	H2
FCA General Guidance (s 139A FSMA). Generally set out in the FCA Handbook or in a separate 'Regulatory Guide' or, in an emergency, in a Guidance Note.	Guidance on the operation of specified parts of FSMA and on the FCA rules and the FCA's functions therefore relevant to authorised firms in complying with the above. Must generally be consulted upon in the same way as rules. Not binding on the courts.	Public: not binding and does not have evidential effect. Enforcement action would turn on breach of a binding rule to which the guidance relates. However, FCA has indicated that where a person acts in accordance with general guidance, FCA will proceed as if the person has complied with the requirement to which the rule relates. Private: limited, but could be taken into account in private law actions.	A2–3	H2

1. Category of written standard	2. Application to UK market participants	3. Extent to which reliant upon public or private legal enforcement mechanisms	4. Aspirational rating	5. Hardness rating
Other FCA material informal guidance/expressions of view – in consultation papers, feedback statements, discussion papers, speeches.	Potentially relevant to all authorised firms except inward business under an EU cross-border passport to the United Kingdom.	Public: not binding and does not have evidential effect, but taken by the industry as providing a further gloss on the way the FCA is likely to enforce particular Principles or Rules. Private: limited, but could be taken into account in private law actions.	A2–3	H2
FCA Statements of Principle for approved persons *(s 64 FSMA)* *Will be merged into the Code of Conduct (see below).*	*Apply to individuals conducting 'controlled functions' in authorised firms.*	*Public: a range of FCA sanctions can be applied to the individual who is in breach.* *Private: limited, but could be taken into account in private law actions including between an individual and their employer. Could also be taken into account in the context of membership of professional bodies and by future potential employers.*	*A1*	*H1.2*
FCA Code of Practice for approved persons *(s 64 FSMA)* *Will be replaced by the Code of Conduct (see below).*	*Apply to individuals conducting 'controlled functions' in authorised firms.*	*Public: compliance with the Code will tend to establish compliance with the relevant Statement of Principle and vice versa.* *Private: limited, but could be taken into account in private law actions including between an individual and their employer. Could also be taken into account in the context of membership of professional bodies and by future potential employers.*	*A2*	*H1.2–2*
FCA Senior Managers Regime[f]	*Requirement for FCA individual approval for those managing aspects of the firm's affairs relevant to regulated activities which could involve a risk of serious consequences for the firm or business or other interests in the United Kingdom.*	*Public: a range of FCA sanctions can be applied under the FCA Code of Conduct to an individual who fails to discharge responsibilities.* *Private: limited, but could be taken into account in private law actions including between an individual and their employer. Could also be taken into account in the context of membership of professional bodies and by future potential employers.*	*A2–3*	*H1.2*

1. Category of written standard	2. Application to UK market participants	3. Extent to which reliant upon public or private legal enforcement mechanisms	4. Aspirational rating	5. Hardness rating
FCA Code of Conduct	*Applies to all employees in a firm other than those performing a role not specific to the financial services business of the firm, such as drivers.*	*Public: full range of FCA sanctions applies if breached. Could also have other consequences such as increased capital requirements.* *Private: limited, but could be taken into account in private law actions including between an individual and their employer. Could also be taken into account in the context of membership of professional bodies and by future potential employers.*	*A1*	*H1.2*
Regulated markets				
Membership rules of UK regulated markets (London Metal Exchange, ICE Futures Europe, London Stock Exchange, CME Europe, Euronext London, NEX Exchange, BATS Europe)ᵃ	Apply to market participants that need membership of the relevant markets to carry on business, and may have an impact on the terms on which those market participants can transact in the market. Concern the operation of and conduct within the relevant markets.	Public: regulated markets are required to maintain these as condition of being permitted to operate. Breaches by market participants could affect the exercise of regulatory discretion or even involve a breach of regulatory rules. Private: generally enforceable against members as a private law matter under the terms of membership; may also involve rights between members. Breach could affect market perception.	A2–3	H2
Infrastructure providers				
Membership and operating rules of market infrastructure providers (i.e. payment systems such as CHAPS, central securities depositaries such as Euroclear UK & Ireland and central counterparties such as LCH Limited)ᵇ	Apply to market participants that need membership of the relevant organisations to carry on business (i.e. effect payments, clear transactions and hold UK securities), and may have an impact on the terms on which those market participants can transact with third parties.	Public: the relevant infrastructures are required to maintain these as a condition of being permitted to operate. Breaches by market participants could affect the exercise of regulatory discretion or even involve a breach of regulatory rules. Private: generally enforceable against members as a private law matter under the terms of membership; may also involve rights between members.	A3	H2
Other UK Codes with a legal footing				

1. Category of written standard	2. Application to UK market participants	3. Extent to which reliant upon public or private legal enforcement mechanisms	4. Aspirational rating	5. Hardness rating
The Corporate Governance Code (FRC)	Sets out standards of good practice in relation to board leadership and effectiveness, remuneration, accountability and relations with shareholders. All companies with a Premium Listing of equity shares in the United Kingdom are required under the Listing Rules to report on how they have applied the Code in their annual report and accounts. Tends to be regarded as relevant by other authorised firms because it is believed that the PRA and FCA refer to it in setting governance standards.	Public: 'comply or explain' for UK listed firms. Otherwise, no direct sanction. Private: relevant to assessment of company by potential investors/clients. Could be taken into account in private law actions.	A1–2	H2–3
The Stewardship Code (FRC)	A statement of good practice to which the FRC believes institutional investors should aspire. It also describes steps asset owners can take to protect and enhance the value that accrues to the ultimate beneficiary.	Public: all UK-authorised Asset Managers are required under the FCA's Rules to produce a statement of commitment to the Stewardship Code or explain why it is not appropriate to their business model. Private: 'comply or explain'. Could be taken into account in private law actions and by potential clients.	A1–2	H2–3

1. Category of written standard	2. Application to UK market participants	3. Extent to which reliant upon public or private legal enforcement mechanisms	4. Aspirational rating	5. Hardness rating
The Takeover Code (Takeover Panel)	Intended to reflect collective opinion of those professionally involved in takeovers as to appropriate business standards, fairness to offeree company shareholders and an orderly framework for takeovers. While the Takeover Panel was originally a private body, it has been designated as the authority to carry out certain regulatory functions in relation to takeovers under the Directive on Takeover Bids (2004/25/EC) and its statutory functions are set out in and under Chapter 1 of Part 28 of the Companies Act 2006. Following the implementation of the Directive by means of the Act, the rules set out in the Code have a statutory basis in relation to the United Kingdom.	Public: may issue a private or public censure, suspend or withdraw any exemption, approval or other special status which the Panel has granted. May report conduct to a regulatory authority particularly the FCA to decide whether to take action (including fines), e.g. where firm fails to observe proper standards of market conduct. May publish a Panel Statement indicating that the offender is someone who is not likely to comply with the Code. FCA rules and certain professional bodies oblige their members, in certain circumstances, not to act for the person in question in a Code transaction (cold-shouldering). May issue directions (enforceable through the courts) and order the payment of compensation. Certain breaches of bid documentation rules constitute a criminal offence. Private: Panel grew from the private not public sector but now placed on a statutory footing. Regime is intended to reduce scope for recourse to the courts in matters covered by the Code.	A2	H1.2–3
The Joint Money Laundering Steering Group Guidance Notes	The JMLSG is comprised of the leading UK financial services trade associations. Its aim is to promulgate good practice in countering money laundering and to give practical assistance in interpreting the UK Money Laundering Regulations, principally by publishing guidance.	Public: no sanction for not complying with the guidance, but potentially relevant to whether the primary money laundering prohibitions, the Money Laundering Regulations or other regulatory rules have been breached. Courts required to take account of behaviour in accordance with the guidance in certain circumstances. FCA has regard to whether conduct complied with the guidance in determining whether requirements breached.[i] Private: limited.	A2–3	H2

Private UK codes 'confirmed' by the FCA.[1]

1. Category of written standard	2. Application to UK market participants	3. Extent to which reliant upon public or private legal enforcement mechanisms	4. Aspirational rating	5. Hardness rating
LIBOR Code of Conduct	Adopted by ICE Benchmark Administration Limited for benchmark submitters to ICE LIBOR. Intended to provide a framework within which contributing banks can operate, and to assist users of LIBOR rates when deciding whether LIBOR is an appropriate rate to use in contracts.	Public: the FCA will regard firms following the guidance as complying with the relevant FCA Handbook rule. But failure to comply with the guidance does not indicate failure to comply with the rule.[k] (Knowingly or deliberately making false or misleading statements in relation to benchmark-setting is a criminal offence under the Financial Services Act 2012 and the FCA's rules on benchmark submission are in Chapter 8 of its Market Conduct Sourcebook.) Private: limited, but could be taken into account in private law actions and impact market perception.	A2–3	H2
Other private UK/international industry codes for financial services firms				
Codes produced with the active involvement of regulators, especially the Bank of England and other central banks: (a) the UK Money Markets Code (a voluntary code of good practice for the money and securities financing markets facilitated by the Money Markets Committee which is chaired by the Bank of England); (b) the FX Global Code (a voluntary code of good practice in the global FX markets developed by the FX Global Committee comprised of central banks and FX market participants); and (c) the London Bullion Markets Global Precious Metals Code (standards and best practice expected of participants in the global wholesale precious metals markets).	Voluntary, but regulators take a keen interest in adherence. Central banks (through the FX Working Group) have published a 'blueprint' on adherence to the FX Global Code.[l] The Bank of England is involved in key oversight committees. See also FCA work on industry codes of conduct.[m]	Public: not directly enforceable, but levels of compliance could influence the exercise of regulators' supervisory powers and could be relevant to whether other rules have been complied with, whether by firms or individuals. Private: limited, but could be taken into account in private law actions and impact market perception	A1–2	H2–3

1. Category of written standard	2. Application to UK market participants	3. Extent to which reliant upon public or private legal enforcement mechanisms	4. Aspirational rating	5. Hardness rating
Industry association conduct standards produced by, for example, the Alternative Investment Management Association, the Asset Backed Finance Association, the Association of British Insurers, the British Private Equity and Venture Capital Association, the International Capital Markets Association, the International Forum Investment Association, the International Forum of Sovereign Wealth Funds, the Lending Standards Board, the Standards Board for Alternative Investments, the Wolfsburg Group. See also the Equator Principles.	Generally voluntary in that firms usually have a decision as to whether or not to join the relevant body or on the extent to which they will adhere to the relevant written norms. Codes issued by industry bodies in areas of the financial markets that are heavily regulated generally concern matters of technical compliance with regulatory rules whereas codes concerning conduct in more lightly regulated parts of the market are more likely to be in the form of over-arching conduct codes.	Public: no direct sanction, but in some cases these standards could be referenced by regulators in deciding whether standards under their rules have been met. Private: in some cases, private bodies may rely to some degree upon Court-enforced contracts (such as membership agreements) to secure compliance. Otherwise, generally rely upon a mixture of private enforcement mechanisms. Could affect market perception if not followed.	Lightly regulated market sectors: A1–2 More heavily regulated market sectors: A1–3	H3
Other private UK codes for individuals working in the financial services sector				
Codes produced by The Chartered Banker Institute, The Chartered Financial Analysts Institute, The Chartered Institute for Securities and Investments, The Chartered Insurance Institute, the London Institute of Banking and Finance, The Worshipful Company of International Bankers	*UK professional and other membership bodies. Codes voluntary, but could affect continued membership.*	*Public: no direct sanction.* *Private: generally rely upon a mixture of private enforcement mechanisms. Breach could be relevant to whether employment contracts breached and employment decisions by employers and potential employers.*	*A1*[n]	*H3*
Firms' own codes of conduct				
Firm-specific	*Frequently apply group-wide within international financial services groups, including to UK staff who are expected to comply as part of the terms of their employment.*	*Public: no direct sanction, but the extent to which a firm has complied with its own standards could be relevant to the exercise of regulatory discretion. Private: privately enforced within the firm, including under the terms of employment contracts, but also using career progression and remuneration decisions.*	*A1–2*	*H2 3*

Notes:

[a] As at 1 January 2018. It has therefore not been possible to reflect any changes in the relationship between UK and EU law that might emerge from the on-going negotiations for the United Kingdom to leave the EU.

[b] Although the Principles do not contain many of the expressions described in Part 2 as being associated with content-based aspirational standards, they have nonetheless been rated as highly aspirational because of their profound connection with issues of justice, whether in the form of human rights, environmental justice or otherwise.

[c] European Banking Authority, European Securities and Markets Authority and the European Insurance and Occupational Pensions Authority.

[d] Mainly relevant to firms, but potentially also relevant to individuals in relation to the Conduct Rules.

e Strictly, the Senior Managers Regime applies to firms rather than individuals. However, the effect of the Conduct Rules is that senior managers have heightened responsibility for that part of the firm for which they are allocated responsibility as a result of the Senior Managers Regime, which therefore defines their duties under the Code.

f See note e above.

g Financial Services Register (https://register.fca.org.uk/ShPo_HomePage) accessed 19 December 2017.

h For an overview, see https://www.bankofengland.co.uk/financial-stability/financial-market-infrastructure-supervision, accessed on 19 December 2017.

i FCA Handbook, DEPP 6.2.3G, EG 12.2 and EG 19.82.

j See https://www.fca.org.uk/about/rules-and-guidance/confirmed-industry-guidance, accessed on 19 December 2017. The FCA lists four pieces of guidance, but only the LIBOR code has a confirmation expiry date of later than 31 December 2017.

k FCA Handbook, DEPP 6.2.1(4)G.

l Report on Adherence to the FX Global Code, Foreign Exchange Working Group, May 2017.

m See note 38 above.

n The disciplinary powers of the professional associations are currently limited, and there seems to be confusion even within some of the associations themselves as to the extent of their disciplinary powers and the basis upon which they can be exercised (see *Exploring the Role of Professional Bodies*, note 58 above, at section 4.3.4.1).

6.   The development and implementation of professional standards for UK bankers: a practitioner perspective

Simon Thompson FCBI

1.   INTRODUCTION

In October 2011, nine leading UK banks[1] plus the Chartered Banker Institute[2] founded the Chartered Banker Professional Standards Board (referred to hereinafter as the 'CB:PSB') and published 'Our Commitment to Professionalism in Banking',[3] signed by Chairs and Chief Executives of the organizations involved. The founders of the CB:PSB recognized that, following the Global Financial Crisis of 2008–10, banks, bankers and banking needed to rediscover an organizational and individual culture of professionalism that had been in decline since the 1980s.[4] They agreed, therefore, to form the CB:PSB as a collective initiative to lead the re-professionalization of UK banking, with the aims and objectives of:

- Developing a series of professional standards to support the ethical awareness, customer focus and competence of those working in the banking industry;
- Facilitating industry and public awareness and recognition of the standards;
- Establishing mechanisms for the implementation, monitoring and enforcement of the standards; and
- Helping build, over time, greater public confidence and trust in individuals, institutions and the banking industry overall, and enhancing pride in the banking profession.

In the five years to December 2016, the CB:PSB succeeded in developing and publishing an industry-wide Code of Conduct, the Chartered Banker Code of Professional Conduct, which by December 2016 had been extended to cover nearly 600,000 bankers worldwide.[5] The CB: PSB developed and published its initial Professional Standards, the Foundation Standard for Professional Bankers and Leadership Standard for Professional Bankers in 2012 and 2014

---

[1]   Barclays plc, Clydesdale and Yorkshire Banks, HSBC Bank plc, ING Direct UK (since acquired by Barclays plc), Lloyds Banking Group, The Royal Bank of Scotland Group, Santander UK, Tesco Bank and Virgin Money.

[2]   The Chartered Banker Institute is the oldest institute of bankers in the world, established in 1875 as the Institute of Bankers in Scotland. For more information on the Institute, please see: www .charteredbanker.com.

[3]   Chartered Banker Institute, *Our Commitment to Professionalism in Banking* (2011, accessed via: www.charteredbank.com/employers/chartered-banker-professional-standards-board.html 5 May 2017).

[4]   This pre-dated the exposure of the LIBOR rate-rigging scandal (2012) and the subsequent Parliamentary Commission on Banking Standards (2012–13). For more on the reasons for the decline, see Section 2 below.

[5]   Chartered Banker Professional Standards Board, *Progress Report 2017* (Chartered Banker Institute, 2017).

respectively, followed by the Intermediate Standard for Professional Bankers in March 2017. Whilst a non-statutory initiative, achievement of the Foundation Standard in particular has been significant, with 168,079 individuals, representing 95 per cent of the CB:PSB member firms' in-scope population, meeting the Standard in 2016.[6]

This chapter sets out the background to, the development and implementation of, and the impact of the CB:PSB's professional standards from a practitioner perspective and will, I hope, be of interest and provide insight to others in banking and financial services in the United Kingdom and internationally and to those interested in professionalism and professional standards in other sectors.

2.   BACKGROUND TO THE DEVELOPMENT OF PROFESSIONAL STANDARDS FOR UK BANKERS

The publication of *Changing banking for good*, the report of the Parliamentary Commission on Banking Standards (PCBS) in 2013,[7] prompted by a series of revelations involving inappropriate, unethical and, at times, illegal behaviour by banks and bankers, most notably the LIBOR rate-rigging scandal, led to major regulatory reform and a succession of statutory and other initiatives designed to improve standards and culture in UK banking.

Whilst culture relates to the conduct and behaviour of banks and the banking industry overall, it is individuals working in the banking industry who make decisions, albeit informed by regulation, organizational policies and shaped by organizational and team cultures, who take decisions and follow courses of action that can result in either positive or negative outcomes for their customers, clients, counterparties, colleagues and the wider community. The PCBS, and other reviews including the Salz Review[8] and the Banking Standards Review[9] all noted a decline in professional standards and professionalism in banking, and proposed, to a greater or lesser extent, that this should be addressed. In its submission to the PCBS inquiry, the Chartered Banker Institute set out a number of reasons that, in its view, had led to the perceived decline in professional standards in banking:

1. the increasing career specialism of individuals employed in financial services and lack of demand for well-qualified, experienced, generalist bankers with all round experience;
2. a shift away from banking as a structured lifelong career;
3. changes in recruitment and onboarding practices;
4. recruitment of non-bankers (e.g. sales and marketing specialists) directly into senior roles;
5. increased use of technology (e.g. credit scoring) reduced the need for highly-skilled qualified professionals exercising professional judgement;
6. a regulatory focus on firms, rather than individuals;

---

[6]   *Ibid.*

[7]   Parliamentary Commission on Banking Standards, *Changing banking for good* (House of Commons, HC 175, June 2013).

[8]   *The Salz Review of Barclays Business Practices*, April 2013 (accessed via: http://online.wsj.com/ public/resources/documents/SalzReview04032013.pdf on 3 May 2017).

[9]   Richard Lambert, *Banking Standards Review* (2014, accessed via: http://1984london.com/ _banking-standards/pdf/banking-standards-review.pdf on 16 June 2017).

7. a 'tick box' approach to regulation and compliance which devalued professional judgement at all levels, from judging the appropriate amount of capital to set aside to 'Know Your Customer' rules;
8. lack of encouragement and support for professional banking qualifications and membership of professional banking institutes from employers, regulators and policymakers; and
9. a general change in banking culture from stewardship to sales.

The Institute also stated that, in its view, previous professional banking norms of thrift, prudence and professionalism were, in many cases, no longer valued or inculcated by senior banking executives and cascaded down through organizations to the same extent as they had been in the past.[10]

Whilst significant public and policymaker interest in banking standards and culture, including the PCBS, Salz Review and Banking Standards Review, was triggered by the LIBOR rate-rigging scandal in 2012, the Chartered Banker Institute had already identified these as key issues emerging from the Global Financial Crisis of 2008–10, and had sought, with (at that time) only limited success, to attract industry, regulator and policymaker attention to these. In April 2009, the Institute's governing Council noted there were many initiatives underway at national and international level aiming to rebuild confidence and trust in banking and financial services following the Global Financial Crisis. Most, if not all, focused on measures to improve financial stability through increasing capital and liquidity buffers, to improve national and international macro-prudential regulation, and to seek solutions to the 'too big to fail' problem. In considering the response of the Institute – a professional body focused on the education and professional development of individuals, rather than a trade association representing the industry – the Council agreed that, whilst measures to improve banks' capital ratios were important, so were measures to improve the banking industry's human capital.[11]

In the Council's view, standards of individual technical and professional expertise within banking had, self-evidently, been insufficient to prevent the Global Financial Crisis, and, in particular, severe problems at a number of UK institutions. Such standards must, it was argued, be enhanced and sustained if the banking industry were to regain the confidence and trust of customers, counterparties and the wider public. This would require, as a minimum, developing and embedding higher standards of technical skills and professionalism. Yet at that time (2009) there was no common agreement or industry framework for determining what minimum or higher standards should be attained. Banking was one of the few professional sectors in the United Kingdom where there were no existing professional standards. Thus, there was no definitive answer to the question 'what did an individual need to know to be a banker?'

The Council agreed the creation of industry-wide professional standards for bankers would help banks, bankers, regulators, policymakers and the public answer that question, and would represent a significant step towards rebuilding banking professionalism by, at the very least providing a definition of this and a foundation on which banking professionalism could be rebuilt. These professional standards would not be regulatory standards, and would not have statutory force; banks would voluntarily choose to implement the standards to demonstrate

---

[10]   Chartered Banker Institute, *Response to the Parliamentary Commission on Banking Standards* (2012, accessed via: www.charteredbanker.com/knowledgehub/policy--research/ on 8 May 2017).

[11]   Chartered Banker Institute Council paper, 17 April 2009.

their commitment to professionalism, and bankers would aspire to meet the standards in order to develop their careers. The professional standards would seek to complement, but go well beyond on basic standards of fitness and propriety set by regulators, and promote higher standards of knowledge, skill and expected behaviour for bankers.[12]

Furthermore, as the only remaining banking institute in the United Kingdom, the Council recognized that the Chartered Banker Institute was uniquely positioned to lead the work required to create professional standards for the UK banking industry, provided broad industry support for these could be gained. It was agreed, therefore, that the Institute would seek the support of the major UK banks for the development of a Professional Standards Board, or similar, which would oversee the development, publication and implementation of professional standards for UK bankers. Dame Susan Rice, CBE, an Institute Council member, and Simon Thompson, the Institute's Chief Executive, were asked to engage with the Chairs and Chief Executives of the major banks and seek their support for this work.

Initial responses from the majority of the UK banks approached were positive, and it was agreed, in December 2010, to establish a Development Group comprising representatives from each of the organizations expressing interest in the professional standards initiative, which would develop plans for the permanent establishment of a Professional Standards Board, or similar, for the UK banking industry. These would be set out in an initial prospectus, or similar document, seeking broad industry and other stakeholder support for the establishment of the Board, and its subsequent work programme.

By June 2010, the Development Group had developed its initial prospectus, setting out its proposals in 'Our Commitment to Professionalism in Banking' for the establishment of the 'Chartered Banker Professional Standards Board' (CB:PSB), supported by leading UK banks, which would develop and promulgate professional standards for bankers 'to support the ethical awareness, customer focus and competence of those working in the banking industry'.[13] The support of Chairs and Chief Executives of nine banks – Barclays Plc, Clydesdale and Yorkshire Banks, HSBC Bank plc, ING Direct UK (since acquired by Barclays Plc), Lloyds Banking Group, The Royal Bank of Scotland Group, Santander UK, Tesco Bank and Virgin Money – was secured, with a written and personally signed commitment from each[14] to:

- Endorse the initiative and commit their personal and organizational support;
- Provide a senior representative from their organization to join the CB:PSB Board;
- Provide a representative to join the CB:PSB's Professional Standards Committee, which would undertake more detailed standard-setting work;
- Subscribe to the Chartered Banker Code of Professional Conduct;
- Establish an internal working group, or similar, to support the development, embedding and monitoring of standards within their organization;

---

[12]   Subsequent research conducted by YouGov plc for the Chartered Banker Institute found that two-thirds of UK stakeholders, MPs and opinion formers considered professional standards as the key hallmark of a profession. See: Chartered Banker Institute, *Building Professionalism in Banking: CB:PSB Research 2012–17* (2017).

[13]   Chartered Banker Institute, *Our Commitment to Professionalism in Banking* (2011, accessed via: https://www.charteredbanker.com/employers/chartered-banker-professional-standards-board/cb-psb -publications.html on 5 May 2017).

[14]   It was decided that a 'wet signature' from the Chair and/or CEO of each founder member would best ensure their personal and organizational commitment to the initiative.

- Celebrate and encouraging employees' achievement of the standards;
- Report regularly on their organization's achievement of the standards; and
- Fund the initial work of the CB:PSB for three years.

These commitments enabled the CB:PSB to be launched publicly in October 2011, together with the Chartered Banker Code of Professional Conduct, an industry-wide code setting out, at a high level, the ethical and professional values, attitudes and behaviour expected of professional bankers by the CB:PSB. The CB:PSB's 'Framework for Professional Standards'[15] (subsequently revised in 2014) was also published at this time, setting out how the CB:PSB would develop, implement and monitor professional standards, and including a glossary of key terms. This included the key definition of a 'Professional Banker' as 'an individual who has met, and continues to meet, the requirements of the CB:PSB's Foundation Standard for Professional Bankers, or a higher CB:PSB standard', thereby defining for the first time the requirements for an individual to be able to describe themselves, and to be identified as, a 'Professional Banker'.

At the time of the CB:PSB's launch, the nine founder members employed approximately 350,000 individuals, representing at that time nearly 75 per cent of the UK banking workforce, giving the CB:PSB, via the Chartered Banker Code and its Professional Standards, the opportunity to influence the knowledge, skills, values, attitudes and behaviour of a significant majority of UK bankers.

3.   WHAT ARE 'PROFESSIONAL STANDARDS'?

In establishing the CB:PSB, the Development Group considered a wide range of professional standard-setting and similar activities in banking, and in other sectors, both in the United Kingdom and internationally, in order to propose a realistic remit, aims and objectives for the CB:PSB, and the likely scope and structure of its professional standards. In doing so, the Development Group identified considerable academic and industry debate around the meaning of terms such as 'professionalism' and 'professional standards', and what constitutes and defines a 'professional' in sectors such as accountancy, law, medicine and teaching. In particular, whilst some sectors seemed to relate professional standards to the achievement of particular qualifications (i.e. standards relating to the development and demonstration of specialist knowledge and skills), other sectors viewed professional standards in relation to expectations of conduct and behaviour, with professional standards boards and similar bodies in these cases assessing whether standards had been breached and imposing sanctions on individuals. The need to differentiate 'professional standards' (that is, standards relating to individual professional practice) from wider 'banking standards' (standards of organizational banking practice) was also identified.[16]

---

[15]   Chartered Banker Institute, *Framework for Professional Standards* (2011). The revised version (2014) of the Framework for Professional Standards may be viewed at: https://www.charteredbanker .com/employers/chartered-banker-professional-standards-board/cb-psb-publications.html.

[16]   This latter distinction can be understood in the UK banking context by the distinction between the roles of the *Banking Standards Board*, which, focusing on organizations, 'has been established to promote high standards of behaviour and competence across UK banks and building societies' and

It was decided, therefore, to agree a series of definitions, subsequently published in the Glossary to the CB:PSB's Framework for Professional Standards,[17] setting out how the CB:PSB understood terms such as 'professionalism' and 'professional standards' in the context of its work and of the UK banking industry more broadly. After much reflection, it was decided that the CB:PSB's professional standards should comprise both standards of professional conduct (values, attitudes and behaviours) and professional expertise (knowledge and skills). The standards would, therefore, set clear benchmarks for both conduct and expertise against which colleagues, customers and others could measure a banker's professional competence.

The definitions agreed by the CB:PSB in 2011, and still in use at the present time, are:

- *Professionalism:* the knowledge, skills, values, attitudes and behaviours expected of a professional.
- *Professional standards:* provide a framework for developing and demonstrating the appropriate professional values, attitudes and behaviours required to perform a professional role in banking.
- *Professional knowledge and skills:* the specialist body of knowledge and skills required to perform a professional role. In the context of the CB:PSB, this requires individuals to have the requisite technical knowledge of banking and related services to be able to perform their role in a manner consistent with the Chartered Banker Code of Professional Conduct.
- *Professional values and attitudes:* the moral principles and personal beliefs, supported by organizational and professional norms, that support the professional behaviours expected of all bankers by the CB:PSB as set out in the Chartered Banker Code of Professional Conduct.
- *Professional behaviours:* the day-to-day actions and conduct expected of all bankers by the CB:PSB as set out in the Chartered Banker Code of Professional Conduct.
- *Professional qualifications:* develop and demonstrate the acquisition of a specialist body of knowledge and skill required to perform a professional role within banking.
- *Professional Banker:* an individual who has met, and continues to meet, the requirements of the CB:PSB's Foundation Standard for Professional Bankers, or a higher CB:PSB standard.

It can be seen, therefore, that the CB:PSB has developed and has set a clear understanding of what 'professionalism', 'professional standards' and related terms mean within a banking context. By defining these terms the CB:PSB created a structure within which it could develop its professional standards of conduct and expertise, framed by the CB:PSB's expectations of individuals' values, attitudes and behaviours as set out in the Chartered Banker Code of Professional Conduct, and leading to the ultimate definition of a 'Professional Banker' as an individual who has met the requirements of one or more of the CB:PSB's professional standards.

---

the *CB:PSB*, which was established to develop a series of professional standards to support the ethical awareness, customer focus and competence of those working in the banking industry, i.e. individuals.

[17]   Chartered Banker Institute, *Framework for Professional Standards* (2011).

4.   STRUCTURE AND OPERATIONS OF THE CB:PSB

The CB:PSB, when launched in October 2011, comprised:

- The *CB:PSB Board* – comprising senior bankers appointed by each founder CB:PSB member firm;
- The *Professional Standards Committee* – comprising Learning & Development professionals, and others with relevant expertise, from CB:PSB member firms, which would be the 'working group' that would develop and draft standards for Board approval; and
- The *Advisory Panel* – representing the views of a small group of key stakeholders to the CB:PSB Board.

The Development Group recommended that the CB:PSB should be established as a quasi-independent body under the auspices of the Chartered Banker Institute. The CB:PSB member banks would pay an annual membership fee to the Institute, based on the size of their organization, but these would be paid to a restricted fund established by the Institute which could only be used to fund the CB:PSB's standard-setting and implementation activities. It was agreed that the CB:PSB would be governed by a Board, that would, formally, report to the Institute's Council via quarterly written reports, that the CB:PSB Board's Terms of Reference would be approved by Council, and that the Chair of the CB:PSB would be a Council member of the Institute. In practice, the CB:PSB Board would manage its own affairs and would exhibit a high degree of operational independence from the Institute. Dame Susan Rice CBE was appointed as the first Chair, and the nine founding member banks appointed senior executives to the Board.[18]

At the same time, the Professional Standards Committee was established, chaired by the Chief Executive of the Chartered Banker Institute, comprising representatives (mainly from HR and L&D) from the nine founding member firms, and including some individuals who had participated in the Development Group, ensuring familiarity with the aims and objectives of the initiative, and continuity. An Advisory Panel was also established to represent the views of stakeholders, particularly the 'end users' of banking services, to the CB:PSB Board.

Whilst the original structure of the CB:PSB proved sufficient to develop the original versions of the Chartered Banker Code of Professional Conduct and the Foundation Standard for Professional Bankers, over time the need to enhance the governance and operations of the CB: PSB became apparent, and the CB:PSB was developed to comprise:

- The *CB:PSB Board* of senior bankers appointed by each major CB:PSB member firm, plus two independent members and an independent Chair;
- The *Professional Standards Committee*, as detailed above;
- The *Implementation Group*, comprising L&D professionals from most CB:PSB member firms directly involved with the implementation of professional standards within their organization;
- The *Independent Monitoring Panel*, which oversees and provides assurance on the implementation and achievement of professional standards;

---

[18]   For a list of the Founder Board Members, see: Chartered Banker Institute, *Our Commitment to Professionalism in Banking* (2011).

- The *Stakeholder Forum*, which superseded the Advisory Panel, and engages with and represents the views of a much wider range of stakeholders; and
- A dedicated *Professional Standards Team* within the Chartered Banker Institute, supporting the CB:PSB initiative and each CB:PSB member firm.

The CB:PSB's approach to defining, developing and publishing professional standards was originally devised by the Development Group, set out in the original Framework for Professional Standards, and remains substantially unchanged:

1. The CB:PSB Board, in consultation with the Professional Standards Committee (PSC) and Stakeholder Forum, defines the area(s) in which a standard is required;
2. The PSC, supported by the Professional Standards Team (PST), develops an initial, draft standard, utilising appropriate industry and Stakeholder Forum expertise;
3. The CB:PSB Board approves an initial draft standard for consultation;
4. The PSC and PST consult with member firms and other stakeholders, via the Stakeholder Forum and, when required, via a wider public consultation;
5. The PSC, supported by the PST, re-drafts the standard based on industry and stakeholder feedback;
6. The CB:PSB Board approves the standard, or proposes further consultation; and
7. The final standard is published and promoted by the CB:PSB.

In most cases, it takes approximately 12 months for the CB:PSB to develop, consult on and publish a standard. Standards are reviewed by the CB:PSB approximately every three years to ensure that they remain fit for purpose, with the Foundation Standard for Professional Bankers (originally published in 2012) revised in 2016, and the Leadership Standard for Professional Bankers, published in 2014, revised in 2017.

From the outset, the CB:PSB Board was clear in its understanding that developing and publishing Professional Standards alone would not be sufficient if the initiative were to achieve its aim of enhancing and sustaining professional standards in banking. Effective implementation, monitoring, reporting and evaluation of the achievement of the CB:PSB's Professional Standards would also be required and, in fact, these account for the majority of Professional Standards related activity by CB:PSB member firms and the Institute's Professional Standards Team. The establishment and operation of these are discussed in detail elsewhere in this article but, in brief, implementation and monitoring are closely aligned, and work together to create a cycle of continuous improvement. A 'three lines of defence' approach has been adopted, enhanced in 2016 by the establishment of an Independent Monitoring Panel to provide greater assurance to the CB:PSB Board and the general public of the achievement of the Professional Standards.[19]

The CB:PSB reports achievement, implementation and impact of its Professional Standards to stakeholders and the wider public, on an annual basis, via the CB:PSB's annual review. From 2017 onwards, the Independent Monitoring Panel will publish a separate annual report providing a greater degree of assurance to the CB:PSB Board, stakeholders and the wider public as to the achievement of the Standards.

---

[19]   The remit and composition of the Independent Monitoring Panel, chaired by Dr. Ian Peters MBE, can be viewed at: https://www.charteredbanker.com/resource_listing/cpd-resources/independent -monitoring-panel---terms-of-reference.html

5. STAKEHOLDER ENGAGEMENT

Prior to the public launch of the CB:PSB in 2011, the founder CB:PSB member firms recognized that, whilst the initiative would aim to work primarily with banks and bankers on the development of Professional Standards, the views and insights of a wide range of stakeholders would ensure Standards were customer and client focused, and reflected society's expectations of bankers. A small Advisory Panel was, therefore, established, comprising representatives from academia, business representative organizations, consumer bodies, trade associations and others, seeking to reflect and represent, as far as possible, the views of the 'end users' of banks' and bankers' services.[20] The Advisory Panel played a key consultative role in the initial standard-setting process, in particular in the development and revision of the Foundation Standard for Professional Bankers, and also offered advice on the monitoring and evaluation of Professional Standards implementation, resulting in a sub-group of the Advisory Panel, the Monitoring Working Group, recommending the establishment of an Independent Monitoring Panel in 2016, as noted above and discussed in more detail below.

Over time, the CB:PSB's approach to engaging stakeholders and to reflecting their views in the development and implementation of Professional Standards has evolved. In 2015, two independent members were appointed to the CB:PSB Board, to represent the broad public interest, joining representatives of the CB:PSB's member firms and the Chartered Banker Institute. In 2016, a new and wider Stakeholder Forum, including trade union representatives, and representatives of other bodies working to enhance and sustain culture and standards in banking, replaced the Advisory Panel, whilst still including the 'end users' previously represented on the Panel.

Whilst the Stakeholder Forum is a relatively new part of the CB:PSB's structure, it has already had an impact on the direction and shape of the CB:PSB's standard-setting and other activities. Stakeholder Forum members contributed to the development of the Intermediate Standard for Professional Bankers, and feedback from the Forum on evaluation and measurement of the CB:PSB's impact against its overall aims was incorporated into the CB:PSB's annual surveys from 2016 onwards.

6. THE CHARTERED BANKER CODE OF PROFESSIONAL CONDUCT

When considering the potential role and activities of the CB:PSB, prior to its establishment in October 2011, the Development Group concluded that a valuable initial activity would be to publish a common ethical code, or similar, for the UK banking industry. The Group identified several professional body codes relating to parts of the banking industry,[21] and codes of

---

[20] The initial Advisory Panel consisted of representatives from the Confederation of British Industry, the Federation of Small Business, Citizen's Advice and Which, and was chaired by Professor Robin Jarvis, an expert in small business issues. The Stakeholder Forum, which replaced the Advisory Panel in 2016, comprises representatives from more than 20 organizations.

[21] Including the Lord George Principles promulgated by the Chartered Institute for Securities and Investment and Worshipful Company of International Bankers, the Chartered Institute of Bankers in Scotland's Code of Professional Conduct, and the Bankers' Oath.

conduct, or similar, published by UK banks, but noted that banking in the United Kingdom, unlike other professions such as accounting, medicine and law, had no recognized, common ethical code on which more detailed, codified standards of professional knowledge, skill and behaviour could be based.

Working with the senior executives appointed as the CB:PSB's first Board members, including a number of bank CEOs, the Development Group drafted what became the Chartered Banker Code of Professional Conduct (the Code), setting out the ethical and professional values, attitudes and behaviour expected of all professional bankers. It was agreed as part of the founder member banks' commitment that all CB:PSB member firms would subscribe to the Code, and would align and enhance their own codes of business and personal conduct, and similar, with the Code.

The Code was initially published in October 2011, at the time of the CB:PSB's launch, and formed the foundation of values, attitudes and behaviour on which the CB:PSB's first professional standards were developed (see below). At the time of its launch, CB:PSB member firms subscribing to the Chartered Banker Code employed in aggregate approximately 350,000 individuals, meaning nearly three-quarters of the banking workforce were, for the first time, covered by a common code.

The Code was revised in January 2016 to be consistent with the terminology in the new Financial Conduct Authority (FCA) Individual Conduct Rules,[22] introduced in March 2017, and exceeds these regulatory requirements by setting out how individuals should follow best practice and demonstrate their personal commitment to professionalism in banking, by:

1. *Treating all customers, colleagues and counterparties with respect and acting with integrity;*
2. *Developing and maintaining their professional knowledge and acting with due skill, care and diligence; considering the risks and implications of their actions and advice, and holding themselves accountable for them and their impact;*
3. *Being open and cooperative with the regulators; complying with all current regulatory and legal requirements;*
4. *Paying due regard to the interests of customers and treating them fairly;*
5. *Observing and demonstrating proper standards of market conduct at all times;*
6. *Acting in an honest and trustworthy manner, being alert to and managing potential conflicts of interest; and*
7. *Treating information with appropriate confidentiality and sensitivity.*[23]

The Development Group and initial CB:PSB Board recognized at an early stage, prior to the launch of the CB:PSB initiative, that without individuals developing and being able to demonstrate the appropriate technical knowledge and skill required for their role, they could not be expected to apply the principles enshrined in Code in a consistent and practical manner. The CB:PSB's planned Professional Standards, therefore, would set out how individuals might develop and demonstrate the knowledge, skills, values, attitudes and behaviour required to put the Code into practice on a daily basis.

---

[22]   FCA Handbook, COCON 2.1.
[23]   Chartered Banker Institute, *Chartered Banker Code of Professional Conduct* (2016, accessed via: https://www.charteredbanker.com/resource_listing/cpd-resources/chartered-banker-code-of-professional-conduct.html on 9 June 2017).

In addition, following the launch of the Code and the implementation of the CB:PSB's first professional standard, the Foundation Standard for Professional Bankers, CB:PSB member firms subscribing to the Chartered Banker Code were expected to put in place systems for monitoring, identifying, investigating and dealing with any breaches of the Code by individuals who have achieved the CB:PSB's professional standards, or are in the process of achieving these. The CB:PSB is, as discussed above, not a regulatory body and, unlike professional bodies in, for example, accounting, medicine and law has no statutory investigatory or disciplinary powers over individuals. It has to rely, therefore, on CB:PSB member firms as employers conducting investigations and taking action against individuals breaching the Code. As part of the CB:PSB's approach to monitoring and evaluation (see below), the operation and effectiveness of these systems is assessed. Since 2017, with the introduction of the FCA's Individual Conduct Rules, all UK deposit-taking institutions are required to have in place systems for monitoring, identifying, investigating and dealing with breaches of these. Given the alignment of the revised Chartered Banker Code with the Individual Conduct Rules, a breach of the latter would, *prima facie*, be a breach of the former, and CB:PSB member firms now have, therefore, their systems for dealing with these established on a firmer basis as a result of the new regulatory requirements.

7. THE CB:PSB'S PROFESSIONAL STANDARDS

The CB:PSB's Professional Standards describe the detailed Professional Conduct (values, attitudes and behaviours) and Professional Expertise (knowledge and skills) requirements expected of all professional bankers. The CB:PSB's professional standards define, therefore, the key components of banking professionalism (what it means to be and to be identified as a 'Professional Banker'); promote the improvement of banking knowledge, skills and competence; and enable benchmarking of organizations' learning and development activities against industry standards. The standards set clear benchmarks against which colleagues, customers, clients and others can measure bankers' professional competence.

The CB:PSB proposed, when the initiative was launched, and has since developed and published professional standards at three levels:

- The Foundation Standard for Professional Bankers[24] (published 2012, revised January 2016)
- The Intermediate Standard for Professional Bankers[25] (published March 2017)
- The Leadership Standard for Professional Bankers[26] (published September 2014, revised 2017).

As can be seen in Figure 6.1, in developing its Professional Standards at three levels, the CB: PSB has created pathways for Professional Bankers to develop and demonstrate their profes-

---

[24] Chartered Banker Institute, *Foundation Standard for Professional Bankers* (2012, accessed via https://www.charteredbanker.com/employers/chartered-banker-professional-standards-board/professional-standards.html.

[25] Chartered Banker Institute, *Intermediate Standard for Professional Bankers* (2017, accessed via www.charteredbank.com/employers/chartered-banker-professional-standards-board.html.

[26] Chartered Banker Institute, *Leadership Standard for Professional Bankers* (2014, accessed via www.charteredbank.com/employers/chartered-banker-professional-standards-board.html.

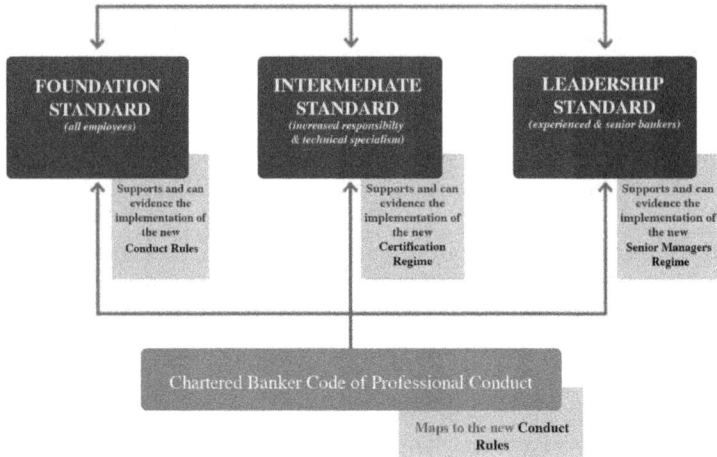

Figure 6.1   CB:PSB Standards Journey (Chartered Banker Institute, 2016)

sional conduct and expertise throughout their careers. The CB:PSB's Professional Standards are designed to complement and build on each other. For example, the similarities in focus of the Foundation and Leadership Standards mean that those meeting the Leadership Standard will be deemed to have met the Foundation Standard. For those who begin with the Foundation Standard, it may be expected that individuals will progress to the Intermediate Standard and ultimately to the Leadership Standard as their career and responsibilities develop.

The Foundation Standard for Professional Bankers sets out the CB:PSB's expectations of all individuals in relation to the Professional Conduct and Professional Expertise requirements for all those working in the banking industry. It details how all Professional Bankers can develop and demonstrate, in the context of their role, function and organization, the knowledge, skills, values, attitudes and behaviour required to support the principles enshrined in the Chartered Banker Code of Professional Conduct. The CB:PSB Board took the decision to develop the Foundation Standard as its first standard in order to provide the clear benchmark for conduct and expertise for all bankers that the UK banking industry, at the time of its publication in 2012, lacked.

The Intermediate Standard sets out the CB:PSB's expectations for Professional Bankers making a commitment to higher standards of expertise and conduct than those set out in the Foundation Standard. It is intended to provide a 'next step' for individuals who have achieved the Foundation Standard, and to support the continuing professional development of banking professionals. It is also intended to support the development of specialist knowledge and skills, reflecting the many functional specialisms within banking that a high proportion of bankers will spend a considerable proportion of their careers in.

The Leadership Standard is aimed at Professional Bankers with leadership responsibilities for developing, promoting and embedding a culture of customer-focused, ethical professionalism consistent with the values, attitudes and behaviour set out in the Chartered Banker Code of Professional Conduct. The CB:PSB believes this should always include the Chief Executive, members of the senior management team and their direct reports, as a minimum, although it recognizes that leadership is exhibited at many levels throughout an organization, and encourages CB:PSB member firms to consider implementing the Leadership Standard to as wide a leadership population as possible. Through the Leadership Standard, the CB:PSB aims to promote an appropriate 'tone at the top', the 'tone at the middle' and, potentially, the tone throughout many levels of an organization where Professional Bankers have leadership and managerial responsibility. Launched in 2014, implementation of the Leadership Standard by CB:PSB member firms has been slow because of the subsequent introduction of the PRA and FCA Senior Manager Regimes, which had the effect of changing organizational priorities and resources. Whilst some CB:PSB firms have begun to pilot the Leadership Standard, and to undertake benchmarking activity, none has, at the time of writing, fully implemented the Standard.

Structure and Content of the CB:PSB's Professional Standards

Each Professional Standard is structured in a similar fashion, and set out in two separate documents:

1. **Requirements** – outlines the Professional Expertise (knowledge and skills) and Professional Conduct (values, attitudes and behaviour) needed to meet the Standard and to ensure that an individual has the ability to perform their role. These are set out as a series of indicators and outcomes:
   - Professional Knowledge and Skills Indicators relevant to an individual's role, function and organization; and
   - Professional Performance Outcomes illustrating the required level of workplace competence.
2. **Guidance** – explains how the Requirements may be met in terms of learning and development activities, assessment and experience. The provision of Guidance seeks to ensure consistency, as far as possible, in the implementation of the Professional Standards by CB: PSB member firms.

Given the many technical specialisms present within the banking industry, and significant disparities in CB:PSB member firms' size, scale, scope and operations (e.g. a 'Risk Manager' working in a large member firm's corporate banking team will have a very different role from a 'Risk Manager' working in a smaller, 'challenger' bank's mortgage department), the Knowledge and Skills Indicators take account of these differences by requiring individuals to demonstrate the knowledge and skills required in a manner that is relevant to their role, function and organization. The Professional Performance Outcomes illustrating the required level of workplace competence are generic, however, as the CB:PSB believes these should form a common benchmark for Professional Bankers across the banking industry. For example, in the CB:PSB's Foundation Standard for Professional Bankers, these are set out as follows:

Expertise

1.   Professional knowledge indicators

Individuals should demonstrate a basic level of professional knowledge in the areas set out below by being able to describe and explain, in areas relevant to their role, function and organization:

1. The purpose and functions of a bank;
2. The economic and business environment;
3. Banking products and services and their suitability for different types of customer and counterparty;
4. Regulatory and legal requirements and how these factors influence the operation of a bank; and
5. The principles of credit and lending.

2.   Professional skills indicators

Individuals should demonstrate professional skills, as described below, relevant to their role, function and organization:

1. Exhibit an understanding of banking and the economic and business environment, applying it in day-to-day activities and interactions and effectively communicating how these factors may impact on customers' needs and plans;
2. Inform customers, counterparties and others of their banks' products and services in an effective and professional manner;
3. Identify and effectively communicate the basic and more complex needs of customers, counterparties, colleagues or others, and escalate issues where necessary;
4. Apply relevant regulatory and legal requirements; and
5. Effectively and accurately articulate decisions and the decision-making process.

3.   Professional performance outcomes

1. Individuals demonstrate the application of their general and role-specific knowledge through their day-to-day activities and decision-making in order to meet customers' and others' needs in a responsible and professional manner; and
2. Individuals take responsibility and accountability for ensuring they remain compliant with relevant regulatory and legal requirements, the Chartered Banker Code of Professional Conduct and other relevant employer or professional codes.

Conduct

1.   Professional knowledge indicators

Individuals should demonstrate a basic level of professional knowledge in the areas set out below by being able to describe and explain, in areas relevant to their role, function and organization:

1. The importance and key features of an ethical and professional approach, as set out in the Chartered Banker Code of Professional Conduct and other relevant employer or professional codes, in dealing with customers, counterparties, colleagues and others;
2. The Individual Conduct Rules;

3. Mechanisms for identifying, reporting and resolving ethical dilemmas, including conflicts of interest;
4. Legislation, regulation, policies and procedures relating to confidentiality and security;
5. Mechanisms for dealing with complaints effectively;
6. Approaches to risk management;
7. Banks' social responsibilities; and
8. Impacts on individuals, institutions, the banking industry and society of unethical and unprofessional behaviour.

2.   Professional skills indicators
Individuals should demonstrate professional skills, as described below, relevant to their role, function and organization:

1. Apply the core principles set out in the Chartered Banker Code of Professional Conduct and other relevant employer or professional codes;
2. Apply the Individual Conduct Rules;
3. Recognize dilemmas and conflicts of interest and communicate these to others who may be able to help resolve them;
4. Maintain information with appropriate confidentiality and sensitivity;
5. Deal with complaints in a fair, efficient and consistent manner, using internal processes and sign-posting external mechanisms as necessary;
6. Identify and mitigate risks; and
7. Exhibit an understanding of banks' social responsibilities and the impact of unethical and unprofessional behaviour, applying it in day-to-day activities and interactions.

3.   Professional performance outcomes
1. Individuals take responsibility for their day-to-day activities, decision-making and for acting ethically and professionally within the context of their work, including identifying and taking steps to resolve ethical dilemmas and potential conflicts of interest;
2. Individuals develop and maintain relationships with customers, counterparties, colleagues and others based on honesty, integrity, fairness and respect;
3. Individuals remain compliant with the Individual Conduct Rules; and
4. Individuals take responsibility for acting in a manner that is consistent with the Chartered Banker Code of Professional Conduct and other relevant employer or professional codes.[27]

8.   IMPLEMENTING THE CB:PSB'S PROFESSIONAL STANDARDS

The CB:PSB's member firms have voluntarily agreed to support the CB:PSB, to subscribe to the Chartered Banker Code of Professional Conduct and to implement the CB:PSB's professional standards. There is no regulatory requirement to implement the professional standards;

---

[27] Chartered Banker Institute, *Foundation Standard for Professional Bankers* (2016, accessed via: www.charteredbank.com/employers/chartered-banker-professional-standards-board.html on 26 May 2017).

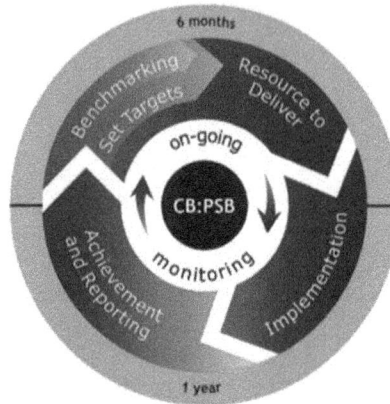

Figure 6.2   Professional Standards Implementation Overview (Chartered Banker Institute, 2016)

at the outset, member firms chose to do so to demonstrate their organizational commitment to professionalism and to rebuilding the banking profession. With the introduction of the PRA and FCA's Senior Manager and Certification Regimes (2016) and Individual Conduct Rules (2017), an additional benefit of implementing the professional standards is that they can help CB:PSB member firms demonstrate to the regulators that they meet the spirit, as well as the letter, of the new regulatory requirements.

In line with the commitment made by each CB:PSB member firm to support the initiative, organizations set targets for standards implementation and allocate sufficient resources to support the implementation process, in most cases identifying an individual as the Implementation Lead and, in larger member firms, establishing an Implementation Team or similar. Member firms are also required to establish a suitable internal monitoring and reporting mechanism to ensure that targets, once agreed, are met. The implementation, monitoring and reporting of Professional Standards are linked, and provide a mutually supportive framework for the development and demonstration of professionalism by individuals in CB: PSB member firms, as set out in Figure 6.2.

Implementation Targets

Collectively, CB:PSB member firms share a common vision for the continued development of professionalism in UK banking. The CB:PSB recognizes, though, that each member firm is a different organization facing different organizational challenges, and that it is, therefore, for each member firm to determine, supported by the CB:PSB Board and the Professional Standards Team, the extent to which professional standards will be implemented across the organization and the details of standards implementation.

In the early stages of implementing the CB:PSB's first professional standard, the Foundation Standard for Professional Bankers, initial Target Groups for the majority of CB:PSB member firms were small, as member firms wanted to pilot the implementation of professional standards, and identify and overcome challenges and practical difficulties. By 2014, however, the

Table 6.1　　Individuals achieving the Foundation Standard for Professional Bankers (2014–16)

	2013	2014	2015	2016[a]
Total Number of Individuals in Target Group	n/a[b]	198,316	265,363	176,158
Individuals Achieving Foundation Standard	66,500	187,326	245,986	168,079
Individuals in Target Group Not Achieving Foundation Standard	n/a	11,100	19,377	8,079

Notes:
[a] The number of individuals achieving the Foundation Standard for Professional Bankers fell from 2014 to 2016 as a result of (a) one large CB:PSB member firm restructuring its international operations, with the Standard no longer, therefore, being deployed to overseas colleagues, (b) one bank leaving the CB:PSB initiative, and (c) a general decline in the numbers of individuals employed in UK banking over the period.
[b] This information was not collected in 2013.

majority of member firms had successfully piloted the Foundation Standard, and the CB:PSB agreed to provide guidance that the member firms should seek to implement the Foundation Standard to all customer-facing staff in their UK operations. This had been substantially achieved by December 2015, with one member firm deciding to implement the Foundation Standard to all staff globally.

The number of individuals achieving the Foundation Standard is set out in Table 6.1.

As can be seen, not all individuals in the Target Group (the population of all individuals identified by CB:PSB member firms as being in scope for the implementation of the Foundation Standard) achieved the Standard. This could be for a variety of reasons, including that:

- They are new to the role/new to the organization, and have not had the time to develop the knowledge and skills required to meet the Standard;
- They have been assessed by their line manager or other as not achieving the requirements of the Standard;
- They have taken time away from work during the implementation and monitoring period (e.g. for a career break/maternity leave/illness); and
- Their employer has identified that they breached, or may have breached, the Chartered Banker Code of Professional Conduct and therefore have not demonstrated the values, attitudes and behaviour expected of Professional Bankers.

Where individuals within the Target Group fail to meet the requirements of the Foundation Standard, or other CB:PSB professional standards, CB:PSB member firms are expected to put in place remedial mechanisms for helping individuals develop and demonstrate the conduct and expertise required.

At the time of writing, only the CB:PSB's Foundation Standard for Professional Bankers has been implemented on a large scale by CB:PSB member firms. The Intermediate Standard for Professional Bankers was published in March 2017 and implementation of this Standard is just beginning. As discussed above, whilst member firm benchmarking activity has been undertaken, full implementation of the Leadership Standard for Professional Bankers, originally published in 2014, was delayed by the introduction of the PRA and FCA Senior Manager Regimes, and the Standard was revised in 2017 to ensure alignment with these.

Methods of Implementation

Whilst member firms' approaches to standards implementation may differ, the requirement to meet the requirements of the CB:PSB's Professional Standards in full is consistent. It was originally envisaged that the professional standards might be used in a number of ways by CB: PSB member firms, including:

1. Benchmarking organizational performance management mechanisms against professional standards;
2. Developing and benchmarking learning and development and talent programmes;
3. Supporting member firms' assessment of employees' ethical and professional competence;
4. Applying for accreditation of learning and development programmes by the Chartered Banker Institute;
5. Supporting employees' continuing professional development (CPD); and
6. Supporting the award of professional membership designations by the Chartered Banker Institute.

In practice, it has emerged that member firms have, for the most part, focused their implementation of the CB:PSB's Professional Standards on 1 and 2 above. Via benchmarking, led by the member firm's Implementation Lead and supported by the CB:PSB's Professional Standards Team, member firms align organizational mechanisms (including training and development programmes, competency and capability frameworks and assessment schemes) to meet the requirements of the CB:PSB's Professional Standards. Detailed guidance material has been developed for each CB:PSB Professional Standard, and ensures, as far as possible, consistency across member firms in the implementation of the Standards.

Benchmarking

As noted above, benchmarking plays a key role in the implementation of the CB:PSB's Professional Standards. This enables CB:PSB member firms to:

- Compare existing learning, development and performance management systems against the requirements of the CB:PSB's Professional Standards;
- Identify any gaps in the organization's existing practice or in supporting the development of individuals;
- Assist the scoping of new learning and development programmes, in addition to enhancing existing programmes; and
- Identify target groups and potential evidence sources to support the Annual Progress Review of professional standards implementation, carried out by member firms and the Professional Standards Team.

Whilst the details of each benchmarking exercise will differ for each CB:PSB member firm, in most cases this begins with an internal desktop review exercise supported by the Professional Standards Team to help a member firm understand which existing mechanisms may support the implementation of Professional Standards. This exercise involves the member firm's Implementation Lead benchmarking existing mechanisms against the Professional Conduct or Expertise Indicators set out in the relevant Professional Standard or Standards, and assessing alignment in conjunction with the Professional Standards Team. The CB:PSB provides a benchmarking template to member firms to assist in this process. Where gaps are identified, the Professional Standards Team will help member firms identify suitable methods to address these.

As the CB:PSB's Professional Standards need to be revalidated on an annual basis, to ensure that individuals continue to meet and demonstrate the Professional Conduct and Professional Expertise requirements, member firms are required to benchmark annual activities that support this. Activities which may support attainment and on-going validation of the CB:PSB's Professional Standards may include, but are not limited to:

- Learning and development programmes – e.g. mandatory training, certificated learning, experiential learning, employee journeys, accredited prior experience and banking qualifications already achieved by individuals;
- Elements of competency frameworks and role profiles, as appropriate;
- Performance management and similar processes – including balanced scorecards, initial and/or on-going competence assessments, behavioural frameworks, job specific performance, structured observations and personal development plans;
- An organization's mission, purpose, values and code of conduct;
- Risk Management frameworks and assessments, decision-making models and frameworks;
- Corporate policies and procedures including corporate communications and CSR; and
- Reporting/escalation mechanisms including whistleblowing.

Member firms are also encouraged to benchmark and align induction and on-boarding programmes to the CB:PSB's Professional Standards, in particular to the Foundation Standard for Professional Bankers to ensure as far as possible that new entrants are aware of and engaged in the process of attaining the Foundation Standard from the start of their banking career. The introduction of the Foundation Standard in 2012 has had a significant impact on on-boarding and induction programmes in CB:PSB member firms, bringing a degree of standardization to a significant proportion of the UK banking industry, and ensuring that these programmes contain elements of professional ethics and core banking skills including a basic understanding of credit and risk, which were by no means universal parts of such programmes prior to the introduction of the Foundation Standard.

Organizational Alignment

CB:PSB member firms are given considerable support and guidance by the Institute's Professional Standards Team to help them align their Learning & Development, Talent Management and other similar activities to enable their employees to meet the requirements of, and achieve, the CB:PSB's Professional Standards. Rather than have to develop and deploy new systems and programmes, CB:PSB member firms have found that it is often more cost-effective, and adds value to existing systems and programmes, if these can be adapted to meet the requirements of the Professional Standards. This may include, but is not limited to, aligning and/or incorporating some or all of the following with the Standards:

- Recruitment and assessment centres;
- Induction and on-boarding programmes;
- Employee/career journeys and similar;

● Elements of competency frameworks and role profiles;
● Initial and/or on-going competence assessments;
● Learning and development strategies and programmes; and
● Performance management and similar processes.

CB:PSB member firms have, in most cases, aligned relevant learning and development activities with the requirements of the Standards. These include, but are not limited to:

● Supported study for relevant academic, professional or vocational qualifications (including, recently, apprenticeship qualifications);
● Classroom-based training, distance learning, e-learning and blended learning programmes;
● Required reading and other regulatory training;
● Seminars, workshops and similar live or online events organized by employers, professional bodies, training providers and others;
● Discussing real-life ethical dilemmas and conflicts of interest with colleagues, line managers and others;
● Coaching and mentoring; and
● Self-reflection on personal and professional experiences.

As noted above, the CB:PSB's Professional Standards, particularly the Foundation Standard for Professional Bankers, have helped CB:PSB member firms develop and shape a significant proportion of their learning and development activities to align with the Standards. Not only has this enhanced the professional ethics and core banking content of many such programmes, it has enabled CB:PSB member firms to more accurately target learning and development expenditure, and make cost savings by developing joint training solutions in some cases.

9.   MONITORING AND REPORTING PROFESSIONAL STANDARDS' ACHIEVEMENT

As set out in Figure 6.2 above, monitoring of the CB:PSB's Professional Standards is closely aligned to the implementation process, with both working together to create a cycle of continuous improvement. This was enhanced, in 2016, by the establishment of an Independent Monitoring Panel to provide greater assurance to the CB:PSB Board and the general public of the achievement of the Standards, providing a 'three lines of defence' approach. The Monitoring Regime currently, therefore, consists of:

1. Internal monitoring by CB:PSB member firms;
2. External progress review conducted by CB:PSB Professional Standards Managers; and
3. The Independent Monitoring Panel.

Monitoring by CB:PSB Firms

CB:PSB firms are required to establish an Internal Monitoring Team comprised, for example, of internal audit, compliance or risk functions to monitor implementation of the CB:PSB's Professional Standards on an annual and on-going basis. As well as ensuring implementation is progressing effectively, monitoring helps identify best practice which can be shared across

CB:PSB member firms. The Internal Monitoring Team is expected to ensure that implementation and achievement of Professional Standards is carried out correctly and consistently. To do this, monitoring will usually include sampling or spot checks by the Internal Monitoring Team. It is, therefore, a very similar approach to internal audit.

In addition, as discussed above, CB:PSB member firms are expected to have systems for monitoring, identifying, investigating and dealing with any breaches of the Code by individuals who have achieved the CB:PSB's Professional Standards, or are in the process of achieving these. Member firms, in many cases through their internal monitoring and conduct risk teams, monitor the day-to-day activities and behaviour of individuals. Where individuals' behaviours fall short of those expected by the CB:PSB, firms are required to have systems and processes in place to identify these and, where appropriate, withdraw the achievement of a Standard or Standards.

External Progress Review

In addition to the internal monitoring of Professional Standards implementation described in the previous section, CB:PSB firms are required to take part in an annual, external progress review of implementation conducted by the Chartered Banker Institute's Professional Standards Team. This comprises (a) a self-evaluation completed by CB:PSB member firms' Internal Monitoring and Implementation Teams, and (b) a progress review completed by the Professional Standards Team:

(a)   Self-evaluation

1. A designated member of the Implementation Team (Implementation Lead) completes a survey which evaluates the organization's commitment and strategic approach, implementation of Professional Standards, monitoring and enforcement activity and support for the CB:PSB's overarching aims in general. The survey may be 'themed' in specific areas, to focus on areas of strength or weakness, to support effective embedding of Professional Standards.
2. The Internal Monitoring Team critically evaluates the survey, independent of the Implementation Team, to assess its accuracy.
3. The Implementation Lead, a representative from the Internal Monitoring Team and an authorized senior executive sign the completed survey confirming its content, and submit the survey to the Professional Standards Team.

(b)   Progress Review

4. The Professional Standards Team review the completed survey and advise the member firm of supporting evidence required. Evidence may come from organizational and/or individual sources.
5. The Professional Standards Team conducts a site visit to each CB:PSB member firm to review supporting evidence and sample data to verify individuals have met the requirements of the Standards.
6. The Professional Standards Team produce a detailed written report (Draft Report) for each member firm, highlighting any development areas and potential risks, and issue this to the firm.

7. The member firm and Professional Standards Team discuss the Draft Report and where development areas and risks have been identified, action plans are jointly agreed to support firms in implementing Professional Standards.
8. The Professional Standards Team issue an agreed Final Report to the CB:PSB firm.
9. An Executive Summary, setting out CB:PSB member firms' performance is prepared by the Professional Standards Team and circulated to the CB:PSB Board and the Independent Monitoring Panel. The Executive Summary describes the extent to which the member firm has implemented the Professional Standards and, more generally has contributed to the achievement of the CB:PSB's overall aims, identifies areas of good practice, highlights deficiencies and sets out agreed action plans.

Independent Monitoring

The CB:PSB Board and member firms recognize that it is important that Professional Standards are effectively implemented, and credibly and robustly monitored, if the initiative is to achieve its overall aims of rebuilding trust, confidence and pride in banking. Following the recommendations arising from the 2015 CB:PSB Monitoring Working Group, established at the behest of the stakeholders represented by the (then) Advisory Panel, an Independent Monitoring Panel (IMP) was established in 2016. The IMP will make recommendations to the CB:PSB Board within its remit, acting as a 'critical friend' to the CB:PSB, providing constructive internal (i.e. non-public) comment, challenge and advice to the CB:PSB Board on the extent to which the CB:PSB's aims are being achieved. It will also comment externally on the CB:PSB's progress on Professional Standards implementation and monitoring via its own independently published annual report, designed to provide a greater degree of assurance to the CB:PSB Board, stakeholders and the wider public as to the achievement of the CB:PSB's Professional Standards.

The IMP is fully independent of CB:PSB member firms, and, it is intended, will be recognized both by member firms and, crucially, by the public as having credibility and authority to report its views on the implementation of the CB:PSB's Professional Standards and progress towards the achievement of the CB:PSB's overall aims. That credibility and authority is derived from the skills and expertise, experience and character of the Panel Chair (Dr. Ian Peters, MBE, Chief Executive of the Chartered Institute of Internal Auditors) and the individual IMP members.[28]

The IMP is currently, at the time of writing, preparing its first independent report, which was expected to be published in autumn 2017.

Reporting

As noted above, the CB:PSB's Professional Standards Team produces a detailed report for each CB:PSB member firm, on an annual basis, evaluating the firm's commitment and strategic approach to the CB:PSB initiative, its implementation of Professional Standards, its

---

[28]   The composition of the Independent Monitoring Panel can be viewed at: https://www.charteredbanker.com/employers/chartered-banker-professional-standards-board/cb-psb-governance.html.

monitoring and enforcement activity and its support in general for the CB:PSB's overall aims. Key findings and data are summarized for the CB:PSB Board on an annual basis, with Board members seeing the data relating to other CB:PSB member firms in addition to their own.

Since 2012, the CB:PSB has published regular Annual Reviews[29] of the achievement of its Professional Standards, as well as progress towards the achievement of the CB:PSB's wider aims and objectives. Member firm data is aggregated to provide an overall picture of the achievement of the Standards, and is not set out firm by firm, as the CB:PSB is a collective initiative to enhance and sustain professional standards in banking. Member firms may, if they wish, publish their own data or statements on CB:PSB Professional Standards achievement, and some are increasingly choosing to do so,[30] believing that promoting their commitment to, and achievement of the CB:PSB's Professional Standards will resonate with customers, clients, analysts, regulators and wider stakeholders.

The CB:PSB's Annual Reviews are made available to the general public via the CB:PSB's website, and copies are sent to more than 100 individuals and organizations identified as key stakeholders. As noted above, from 2017 onwards, the Independent Monitoring Panel will publish a separate annual report on the achievement and monitoring of the CB:PSB's Professional Standards,

10.   EVALUATION AND IMPACT OF THE CB:PSB'S PROFESSIONAL STANDARDS

The CB:PSB seeks to evaluate its success against its aims and objectives, as set out in 'Our Commitment to Professionalism in Banking' and detailed in the Introduction above. As described above, it publishes, each year, data on the collective achievement of its Professional Standards, as well as information on progress towards the achievement of the initiative's wider aims and objectives.

With the publication of the Intermediate Standard for Professional Bankers in March 2017, the CB:PSB completed its initial suite of standards as envisaged when the initiative was launched in 2011, thereby achieving its aim of developing a series of professional standards to support the ethical awareness, customer focus and competence of those working in the banking industry. As set out in Table 6.1 above, as at 31 December 2016, 168,079 individuals,[31] representing 95 per cent of CB:PSB member firms' in-scope population, gained or retained the Foundation Standard in that year, exceeding the CB:PSB's target for the implementation of the Foundation Standard to all customer-facing bankers in the United Kingdom in CB:PSB member firms.

With all CB:PSB member firms subscribing to the Chartered Banker Code of Professional Conduct, and either adopting this or aligning their own internal codes with the Code, by

---

[29]   Available at: https://www.charteredbanker.com/employers/chartered-banker-professional-stan dards-board/cb-psb-publications.html.

[30]   See, for example, *RBS Group Annual Report & Accounts 2016*, p. 16 (accessed via: http://investors .rbs.com/~/media/Files/R/RBS-IR/results-center/annual-report-2016.pdf on 10 June 2017).

[31]   144,870 in the UK and 23,209 internationally. Figures from the Chartered Banker Professional Standards Board, *Progress Report 2017* (Chartered Banker Institute, 2017).

31 December 2016 nearly 600,000 bankers worldwide were covered by the Code,[32] a very substantial achievement. Despite the decision by one of the founder member firms (Lloyds Banking Group) to leave the initiative at the end of 2016, and the acquisition and subsequent disappearance of ING Direct UK, another founder member firm, by Barclays Plc, three new members have joined the CB:PSB in recent years: United Trust Bank, Sainsbury's Bank, and Shawbrook Bank. The successful and widespread implementation of the Code and Foundation Standard exceeded the CB:PSB Board's expectations, and those of many early observers. As noted above, however, the implementation of the Leadership Standard has been slower than anticipated because of the introduction of the PRA and FCA Senior Manager Regimes; however the Standard is currently being revised and a number of CB:PSB member firms are keen to align leadership development programmes and similar with the Standard.

As noted above, the CB:PSB's Professional Standards, particularly the Foundation Standard for Professional Bankers, have helped CB:PSB member firms develop and shape a significant proportion of their learning and development activities to align with the Standards – induction and on-boarding programmes in particular. It has now become 'business as usual' for CB:PSB member firms to include the development and demonstration of the knowledge, skills, values, attitudes and behaviour, including basic banking knowledge and an understanding and ability to apply professional ethics, set out in the CB:PSB's Professional Standards in many such programmes. It should be remembered, however, that these and related topics were often not included in learning and activities prior to the publication of the Professional Standards. The CB:PSB has, therefore, had a significant impact on the content of learning and development programmes across a substantial part of the UK banking sector; and, via the delivery of these programmes, on large numbers of individuals in the banking industry.

As well as developing, publishing and implementing the Professional Standards, the CB: PSB's aims and objectives include raising industry and public awareness and recognition of the Standards, and helping to rebuild greater confidence, trust and pride in the banking profession, although the CB:PSB recognizes that its work and the Professional Standards can only play a part in building public confidence and trust. In June 2017, the CB:PSB published an evaluation of its work and impact on banking employees, banking stakeholders and the general public for the five years from 2012 to 2017,[33] based on research conducted by YouGov plc, as well as the CB:PSB's own research. There were positive trends across all key measures in the report; in particular confirming that public confidence and trust in individuals working in the banking industry is increasing, and that professionalism, and the CB:PSB's Professional Standards in particular, are increasingly valued by the industry, by stakeholders, and by the public. Given that measures and perceptions of confidence, trust and professionalism were at very low levels when the CB:PSB was launched in 2011, despite the increases there is still clearly a great deal more to be done.

One of the CB:PSB's initial challenges, following its launch in 2011, was to raise awareness within the banking industry of the (then) new Professional Standards. In 2013, only 26 per cent of banking employees reported that they were aware of the CB:PSB and the Professional Standards; by 2017, awareness had increased to 43 per cent of banking employ-

---

[32] *Ibid.*
[33] Chartered Banker Institute, *Building Professionalism in Banking: CB:PSB Research 2012–17* (2017).

ees, demonstrating significant progress.[34] Importantly, in terms of the impact of the CB:PSB's Professional Standards on customers, the 'end users' of banking services, 52 per cent of banking employees believe that the Foundation Standard helps them provide a better service to customers.[35] Given that there has been very little promotion of the CB:PSB externally, it is unlikely that the majority of bank customers would be directly aware of the initiative. They should, however, feel the effects of the CB:PSB's Professional Standards via the service they receive from their banks and bankers. Whether this is, in fact, the case would be the subject of interesting further research.

11. CHALLENGES IN DEVELOPING AND IMPLEMENTING THE CB:PSB'S PROFESSIONAL STANDARDS

From a practitioner perspective, the development, publication and implementation of the CB:PSB's Chartered Banker Code and Professional Standards has been a significant, although not unqualified, success when measured against the initiative's original aims and objectives. The evolution of the CB:PSB since 2011 has not been without its challenges, however, and there have been a number of important lessons learned.

Perhaps the most important of these has been the need for adaptability in ensuring the CB:PSB's Professional Standards, and activities overall, align with and complement the work of regulators and other key stakeholders, and the CB:PSB member firms themselves. As discussed elsewhere in this chapter, when the CB:PSB was founded in 2011 it was a unique, collective industry initiative working to enhance and sustain professional standards in banking. Following the report of the PCBS in 2013 (see Section 2 above), UK banking regulators have introduced the Individual Accountability Regime, including the Senior Manager and Certification Regimes, and the Individual Conduct Rules. All have had a direct impact on the Chartered Banker Code of Professional Conduct, and the CB:PSB's Professional Standards, which have been revised to align with the new regulatory requirements. The introduction of the new regulatory regime also placed significant demands on CB:PSB member firms' HR, L&D, conduct risk, internal audit and similar teams, many of whom had less time to work with the CB:PSB on Professional Standards implementation and monitoring. From a member firm perspective, the demands of regulators had to take priority, and this has slowed the CB:PSB's progress at times, particularly in terms of the implementation of the Leadership Standard.

Similarly, the emergence of new organizations in the banking standards landscape, including the Banking Standards Board, established to 'promote high standards of behaviour and competence across the UK banking industry',[36] and the Fixed Income, Currencies and Commodities Markets Standards Board, 'a standards setting body for the wholesale Fixed Income, Currency and Commodities markets'[37] has created challenges for the CB:PSB in ensuring that such bodies did not, inadvertently, replicate or duplicate the CB:PSB's work. Continued liaison with these bodies, with the regulators, and with other organizations interested in issues of ethics,

---

[34]   *Ibid*, p. 12.
[35]   *Ibid*.
[36]   www.bankingstandardsboard.org.uk.
[37]   http://fmsb.com.

culture, conduct and standards in banking has placed significant demands on the CB:PSB's small resources in a manner that was not foreseen when the initiative was launched in 2011.

Another key challenge for the CB:PSB has been significant internal restructuring, reorganization and redeployment of individuals within CB:PSB member firms. Of the founder Board members representing the CB:PSB member firms, only Lady Susan Rice, the CB:PSB Chair, and one Board member remain. Some member firms have been represented on the CB:PSB Board by three or four individuals during the CB:PSB's six years of operation, and there have been similar high levels of turnover on the Professional Standards Committee and in member firms' Implementation Teams. Whilst the Chartered Banker Institute's Professional Standards Team provides an element of continuity, some of the repeated personnel and organizational changes within CB:PSB member firms have undoubtedly created practical issues for the implementation and monitoring of Professional Standards. One of the most significant of these has been the need to regain personal and organizational commitments from senior executives of CB:PSB member firms, when those making the original or subsequent commitments moved on. With further restructuring of the larger banks currently underway, in preparation for the introduction of the United Kingdom's ring-fencing regime in 2019, the CB:PSB anticipates this remaining a challenge.

Finally, it has proven more difficult than anticipated to explain the difference between professional qualifications (that develop and demonstrate the acquisition of a specialist body of knowledge and skill) and professional standards (which provide a framework for developing and demonstrating the professional values, attitudes and behaviour expected) to the banking industry, to stakeholders, and to the general public. There seems to be a general expectation, rooted in a traditional approach, that bankers should take banking exams to demonstrate their fitness and propriety. Whilst passing an exam may demonstrate the achievement of technical and professional knowledge and understanding, it does not, however, demonstrate that an individual can necessarily apply this in the workplace nor that individuals have developed and can demonstrate the values, attitudes and behaviour expected of Professional Bankers. Meeting the CB:PSB's Professional Standards requires both the development and demonstration of relevant knowledge and skill and acquiring and demonstrating the expected values, attitudes and behaviour set out in the Chartered Banker Code of Professional Conduct. This is, the CB:PSB believes, more likely to inculcate and embed the culture of customer-focused, ethical professionalism required. Yet, as the CB:PSB's approach is complex, compared with traditional qualifications and exams, there is still a widespread lack of understanding as to what it entails. This article, hopefully, will help counter this to some extent, but there is clearly a need, currently beyond the CB:PSB's resources, to do more to educate bankers, customers, stakeholders and the general public.

12.   PROFESSIONAL STANDARDS – THE NEXT STEPS

In December 2016, five years after the public launch of the CB:PSB, the CB:PSB Board considered its successes, challenges and impact to date, and considered how the initiative might continue to evolve beyond the further implementation of the Foundation, Intermediate and Leadership Standards for Professional Bankers, including the planned revision of the latter. The Board agreed that the importance of enhancing and sustaining professional standards in banking was now widely (at least within the industry) understood, not only as a result of the

CB:PSB's work but because of the post-LIBOR focus on banking standards by policymakers, regulators and others. There was a good opportunity, therefore, for the CB:PSB to accelerate the pace of the initiative, and a number of actions were agreed to do this.

With the Foundation Standard for Professional Bankers now, to a greater or lesser extent, 'business as usual' for the majority of CB:PSB member firms, except the most recent joiners, the next phase of the CB:PSB's work would focus on individuals moving beyond the Foundation Standard via 'professional pathways' developed for and embedded in each CB:PSB member firm. These pathways would map CB:PSB member firms' learning and development and other activities with the CB:PSB's Intermediate and Leadership Standards, together with relevant professional qualifications that might help individuals develop and demonstrate the knowledge requirements of the Standards. It was agreed that this approach would be piloted on a small scale in each CB:PSB member firm in 2017 and, if successful, would be implemented on a larger scale from 2018 onwards. This would then, in turn and over time, become 'business as usual' for CB:PSB member firms, with the CB:PSB's Professional Standards providing the framework for individuals' career development in banking.

13. CONCLUSION

This chapter has described, from a practitioner perspective, the establishment, development, achievements and challenges of the CB:PSB, a collective initiative formed by leading UK banks and the Chartered Banker Institute to develop and implement professional standards to support the ethical awareness, customer focus and competence of individuals working in the banking industry. As discussed above, the CB:PSB aimed, amongst other objectives, to answer the question 'What does it mean to be a professional banker?' Through the Chartered Banker Code of Professional Conduct, and the CB:PSB's Professional Standards, this has now been answered in some considerable detail.

When launched in 2011, the CB:PSB was a unique, collective initiative in the UK banking standards landscape, established at a time when issues of ethics, culture, conduct and standards were not widely prioritized by regulators, policymakers, and others. From 2012 and 2013 onwards, following the exposure of the LIBOR rate-rigging scandal, the banking standards landscape became increasingly complex, and, to some extent, the CB:PSB's progress was slowed by a series of inquiries and the emergence of other organizations and initiatives working, or potentially working, in similar areas. This undoubtedly dissipated, for at least some time, the CB:PSB's development and implementation of Professional Standards, and the initiative's overall impact. Despite these challenges, nearly 600,000 bankers worldwide were covered by the Chartered Banker Code, and nearly 170,000 individuals gained or maintained the Foundation Standard at 31 December 2016, representing very substantial progress and a collective achievement significantly exceeding the CB:PSB Board's early expectations.

When measured against its original aims and objectives, the CB:PSB has developed and implemented on a considerable scale a common professional code and series of professional standards, it has facilitated awareness and recognition of these (although there is more to be done in this area), it has established robust and credible monitoring and evaluation regimes, and it has played its part in rebuilding public confidence and trust in banks and bankers, and pride in the banking profession. It has, therefore, succeeded to a significant extent in meeting its aims and objectives, and has done so in a unique, collective and entirely voluntary manner that should be of interest to regulators, policymakers and bankers in other countries seeking to enhance and sustain a culture of customer-focused, ethical professionalism in banking, as well as to those with an interest in professional standards, qualifications and education in other sectors.

7.   What should we do about the law of money, finance, banks and the like?

Philip R. Wood CBE, QC (Hon)

SOME SAFE PROPOSITIONS

If we can accept the proposition – which I believe we safely can – that the law is the one universal religion everybody on the planet believes in, more or less, apart from a few anarchists, then we are making some progress in working out the solutions, or at least the principles which should guide our decisions as to what the law should be.

If we also accept the proposition – which I also believe we safely can – that, although you can have a society without this or that political philosophy and without its religions (which I do not necessarily celebrate), it must be fair to say that you cannot have a society without law. It is true that some challenge this claim, even though the claim would seem to me to be a platitude. It is often difficult to get consensus even on some really basic things, however obvious.

I do not say that the law is all good because plainly there are some laws which are misguided or even ridiculous. Nor do I say that lawyers perform some higher moral role like priests, but only that they have special responsibilities.

One can however advance the view that the law and religions do share one aspect, that is, they both have codes of survival, that is they have moral or ethical propositions which underlie their purposes.

THE DOMAINS OF MORALITY

So, if all the above points bear some resemblance to the truth, then we have a kind of methodology or set of principles to decide about the rule of law or the role of law or the reign of law in the fields of money, finance and banks. These subjects are drenched with a moral view, sometimes right, sometimes wrong. Morality is not confined to such topics as sex and murder, which may pervade the most primitive approaches to morality, but is also at the foundation of money, capital markets, taxation, bankruptcy, constitutions, the conflict of laws, contract, tort and all these other domains which have now proliferated so vastly in modern societies.

We can also advance some basic propositions about the nature of money, how it is stored, how it is used and what it is for. Certainly, the amount of money and its other invisible representations such as deposits and investments, have grown hugely in amount even over the last 20 years. Thus, in 1996 the amount of global money, investments and so forth, calibrated to some degree in the frequent statistical measure of GDP, was about three football fields of $10 trillion each. One football field of $10 trillion was the United States. The second football field was greater Europe. The third football field was the rest of the world, of which half was Japan and what were then called the tiger economics of the East, while the other half was mournfully occupied by the deprived and impoverished rest of the world. Africa only had 3 per cent of world wealth. But after the financial crisis in 2010 the GDP of the world was about five football fields of $10 trillion each, now including countries such as China which had changed direction in 1979.

At this rate, and assuming nothing terrible happens in the meantime, it is not unreasonable to contemplate a future where there will be 10, 12 or 15 football fields. This is gracelessly described as financialisation. More money, therefore more prosperity, we hope. And more mayhem probably.

Therefore if we go along with all of this, it is completely convincing that the law relating to money, finance banks etc. plays a crucial role and is a fundamental aspect of our societies now and of the planet in the future. It has direct consequences for how we live and the rules which govern our survival. Indeed if we did not have these things which I am talking about, there would be nothing on the plate for breakfast.

WHY MONEY IS MORE THAN JUST MONEY

When Galileo worked out that the earth was going round the sun, that was a stupendous discovery. Even though this was also a platitude and was obvious, nobody wanted to hear it, just as they do not want to hear that the law is the one thing we have to cling on to. Galileo died in 1642, which is the year that Isaac Newton was born (roughly, since there was a change in calendar about then). Newton was responsible for an even more stupendous invention, the remarkable gravity equation announced in his book published in 1687.

Long before these inventions, there was another great invention. This was the invention of money.

Without money, it would be impossible mechanically even to do something as simple as buying a loaf of bread. One would have to hand over something in return – eggs or a couple of flowers or some knitting one had done. Even the simplest transactions would not really be feasible.

Money connects us to other people who live abroad. It enables people to export and import so that the produce and manufactures of the world can be shared. It forms a vital link between peoples and societies.

Money also connects us to our future, once it is transformed into financial assets such as bank deposits, bonds and shares. These financial assets are the ultimate store of our work and labour, the fruits of our efforts, which we can keep for our future, especially when we are old. They are the product of the work of the people.

Money is a public utility of enormous importance in people's lives. It is the commons.

WHY BANKS ARE MORE THAN JUST BANKS

Once money was invented, there had to be somewhere to put it. Hence the invention of banks. When you switch on the light, the light comes on. This is because there is a power station. The power station has often been financed by the money which people put into banks which banks then lend to finance things like power stations. So the real creditor is the depositor, the citizen. The bank is just a conduit, an intermediary, which manages the money and connects with borrowers who need it, something that the original depositors would not be able to do on their own. The same applies to bond issues in the capital markets, except that the main lenders now include insurance companies as well as banks.

If you strip aside all the veils of incorporation of banks and companies and insurance companies, you end up with individuals as creditors. It is their money, their public utility, and they are the ultimate creditors of the ultimate borrowers on a see-through basis. Banks are therefore like lakes which gather the rain of the people and then use it to irrigate the land. A great deal of bank money is wasted. But then people waste their lives, and that is not unreasonable.

Like many great inventions, banks have a built-in defect. They are very prone to losses by contagion since if depositors lose confidence in their banks, they demand their money immediately and there is no way that banks can call in all of their power station loans in time to pay the stampeding depositors. So the bank is instantly insolvent.

Banks are also in the business of prophesy since they have to predict whether a borrower will be able to repay many years hence. They have to be able to predict economic depressions and the future financial condition of others. Accurate predictions are impossible and in addition banks are run by ordinary mortals who, like everyone else, are prone to making mistakes.

Nevertheless, banks play a fundamentally important role in modern economies since they pool the product of the work and labour of the people, the money of the people, in such a way as, hopefully, to help enterprise and prosperity.

REASONS FOR INVASIONS ON THE RULE OF LAW IN RELATION TO MONEY AND BANKS

Because money and banks represent wealth, and therefore power and control, it is not surprising that they should be the object of attention by governments and hence vulnerable to actions which might be said to prejudice the rule of law.

It is therefore worth identifying some of these intrusions and exploring why they can prejudice the rule of law and what the exceptions should be. It is hard to lay down absolute rules which apply in all circumstances and so virtually all the rules have exceptions, nuanced exemptions, when the rule has to be modified or disapplied. This often happens because the rule conflicts with another fundamental rule or because there is an emergency which threatens the whole system or survival.

INFLATION

For example, a common example of a questionable policy which engages the rule of law is inflation of money. Inflation has always been a favourite tool of despotic governments or of negligent governments from historical times, way before the Romans, back to the Greeks. Inflation is now much easier because in virtually all countries there is no longer any link between money and some tangible asset such as gold. The link with gold was weakened in the 1930s and was abandoned altogether in the early 1970s when the United States renounced the right of holders of the US dollar to convert it into gold at a fixed price.

John Kenneth Galbraith observed that it was repellent (or some word to that effect) how easy it is to create money. Nowadays, central banks do not even have to print it. They can just send an email to banks advising them that the central bank owes those banks several hundred billion or any figure the central bank cares to name or has time to type out. Those banks can lend out the money and it multiplies.

In very simplistic terms, if the central bank and the banking system double the amount of money available, then it will be worth half as much. One of the effects is that debtors only have to pay half as much and creditors only receive half what they are owed. There is therefore a massive redistribution from creditors to debtors and the taking away of the money of creditors or savers, simply by virtue of the fiat of the central bank.

In most countries, inflation is now recognised as being a corruption and a threat to the rule of law. This is because it functions like an expropriation without compensation. All of the main central banks in charge of the main currencies in the world are subject to an express or implicit duty to control inflation – or inflation above some modest level of 2 per cent. They can usually do this by virtue of their power to reduce the supply of money and by virtue of other powers, e.g. to fix interest rates, at least short-term interest rates.

There might be some circumstances where inflation is permissible. It is sometimes argued that inflation is permissible when a sovereign state is bankrupt because on bankruptcy creditors only get a dividend, not the full amount. Inflation in such a case is equivalent to just paying a reduced amount to creditors, such as 30 instead of a debt of 100. The detail of working out how and when this would be permissible on the ground that bankruptcy is recognisably not an expropriation would need meticulous delineation, even if there is a credible case for it at all.

PRICING OF MONEY

I mention inflation because it is an obvious example of a taking. Another analogous example is the low pricing of money.

Central banks have the power to manipulate the price of money, in other words, the interest rates which people pay to borrow money.

They can do this by virtue of their power to create money and lend it at whatever low price they like to banks, with the result that banks can borrow money from the central bank very cheaply, if the central bank so chooses. The banks can then lend it on at these cheaper rates plus a margin or spread to reflect the risk of the ultimate borrower and to give the banks a profit for their work.

This power to price money is most potent in relation to short-term deposits and borrowings. It is harder for the central bank to do this for longer-term loans, such as medium-term bonds of, say, seven to ten years. Nevertheless, it is still possible for central banks to manipulate long-term rates.

The pricing of money at a very low interest rate or at a negative interest rate after tax and inflation has a similar effect to inflation. The money which central banks are pricing does not belong to the central banks, even though they create it. The money belongs to depositors with banks, savers. It is their money that is being priced high or low.

Accordingly, pricing money very cheaply is to the advantage of borrowers and to the detriment of creditors including depositors with banks. It is no different from a coercive or forcible taking away of somebody's car or house by a governmental authority and selling it to somebody at half-price.

Effectively, there is a compulsory distribution from creditors to debtors, just as in the case of inflation.

THE PRICING OF MONEY AND THE FINANCIAL CRISIS

For example, from round about the year 2001, the Federal Reserve in the United States priced money at an interest rate of around 1 per cent. The reasons may have been that there was no need to control inflation and hence to raise interest rates, that the Fed wanted to encourage homebuyers and also to enhance the ability of US companies to compete with other countries by having cheap money and generally to boost the economy. Another reason may have been that low interest rates would make it cheaper for the US government to borrow from abroad, such as borrowings from China. All very sound and apparently beneficial policies economically.

One result was a borrowing spree as borrowers borrowed home money from banks for virtually nothing, ultimately leading to a bubble in the housing market. Every taxi driver in Manhattan knew there was a bubble, but not apparently anybody else.

Once one major country adopted a low interest policy, other major central banks had to fall in line to maintain the competitiveness of their economies. They may also have had similar motives for cheap money similar to those of the Fed.

What was wrong with that pricing policy was not just that it ignited a spark which was fanned by the banks, often irresponsibly. The fault lay in the fact that the pricing of money, the money of the people, was a forcible redistribution and, in particular, a redistribution otherwise than through the tax system, a redistribution which was opaque to the general public. Probably most borrowers did not appreciate that they were receiving somebody else's money at a coercively reduced price.

A further consequence was that the bursting of the bubble, resulting in the collapse of banks and a financial crisis, meant that interest rates had to be kept low in order to protect economies from the adversities of the economic crisis. So the people who were really paying to rescue countries from the crisis were the same creditors and savers whose money continued to be priced at nothing, the very people who had already been taxed and were now taxed again, except that this tax lasted longer and was higher in amount.

One cannot say that a low interest policy is wicked or evil. Indeed, it is possible for the authorities to advance materialistic arguments why money should be cheap and why this benefits everybody, not just debtors or homebuyers or the corporate sector as borrowers.

What was wrong in this particular case was that it seemed (at least as far as I could determine) that those involved at the Federal Reserve did not appear to give much weight to the ethical dimension, namely that this was a mandatory redistribution, like tax, a redistribution which should have been at the forefront in the consideration of policies. A lawyer would be aware of this, not necessarily an economist (they don't have a quant for justice or morality so they just leave them out).

The manipulation of money can have very adverse consequences. There is an ethical angle which springs from the rule of law and which should be considered by those responsible for pricing money, just as they must consider this in relation to inflation.

EXCHANGE CONTROLS

Exchange controls are regulations which typically prohibit residents of a country from holding foreign currency or foreign currency securities, or from paying for purchases in foreign currency or borrowing in a foreign currency. Residents must surrender all foreign currency proceeds to the central bank in return for the local currency at a prescribed rate of exchange.

The object is to give the central bank a monopoly of foreign currency and therefore to be able to ration it, control the supply of money and control the exchange rate between the local currency and foreign currencies.

Exchange controls are a significant intrusion on legitimate freedoms. If you cannot move your money, you cannot move and are a slave to the land. If you cannot pay for foreign things without some permission, then this impacts on freedom of trade. Exchange controls strike at the heart of freedom of movement, freedom of trade, freedom of business and freedom of capital. They fetter and manacle us. In the worst case, they are despotic.

However, there are situations where perhaps a case might be made out for the imposition of exchange controls. Such a case might be where the state is insolvent or where there is a run on banks so that the exchange control is in effect a bankruptcy moratorium. Again, the circumstances in which this kind of moratorium can be imposed would have to be meticulously delineated so as not to violate the rule of law. Exchange controls were ubiquitous until the 1980s, continue in many emerging countries, and were introduced by Iceland and Cyprus when they recently got into financial trouble.

THE PURPOSE OF THE RESTRICTIONS OF LAW

Law is inherently restrictive and impinges upon freedom in some way. The rationale of the limitations of the law is some higher purpose, such as the protection of harm to others, whether physical or economic. So the test is always whether a particular regulation is justified by some higher purpose which is of greater value than the impingement on freedom.

This test basically involves the question of whether the law restricts us so as to liberate us. Thus, on the famous raft which was built out of the planks of the shipwrecked frigate *The Medusa* 90 kilometres off the coast of Senegal (now Mauritania) in 1816, 147 people from the ship got on the raft but only 15 survived when they were picked up by another frigate which was out searching for them, the *Argus*. Almost all of the rest were killed in the fighting on the raft for the four barrels of brandy and biscuits. The captain and the crew had disappeared over the horizon in the six boats from the ship.

Contrast this with the entombment of the 33 Chilean miners in August 2010. They were down in the mine for 69 days. They all got out. What was the difference? Apart from some obvious difference of circumstance, the Chilean miners, when they discovered their terrible fate, appointed a leader. This leader made strict rules about the sharing of the available water and food. In other words they had an emergency constitutional government and they had a legal system. On the other hand, on the raft of *The Medusa* there was no government and there was no law. The Chilean miners were redeemed but the passengers on the raft were doomed. One had law, the other did not. The Chilean miners had law in order to survive. So the law restricted them in order to free them. The law controls so as to liberate.

FINANCIAL REGULATION

The regulation of banks is a particular example of the controversy which pervades this concept of restriction against freedom. It symbolises what is good about the law and also what is bad. In particular, financial regulation raises two acute issues affecting the rule of law.

The first is that a governmental authority which can make rules and enforce them is legislator, executive and judiciary rolled into one. There is therefore no separation of powers. The separation of powers is generally considered a fundamental constitutional proposition.

The second issue is that financial regulation, as in the case of other areas of regulation, such as the regulation of the environment or health and safety or free competition, criminalises the law, but often without the protections of the criminal law. The administrative sanctions do not include a sojourn in jail, but can involve enormous fines and effectively the ostracising of those involved, who are no longer able to participate in their chosen profession. But this criminalisation, although often simply called 'administrative' as a kind of disguise or mask, is typically without the protections of the criminal law. Regulation sometimes tends to offend some basic principles of criminal protections built up over centuries, such as the proof beyond reasonable doubt, specific offence (as opposed to some general principle), the conduct of an investigation, open justice as opposed to secret settlements, proof of dishonest intent, not just negligence and not just lack of supervision without proving actual complicity, and the right to silence. For example, banks are under duties to report delinquencies to the authorities, which is equivalent to a duty on motorists to report to the police every time they exceed the speed limit.

In some countries, the penalties in terms of fines imposed by the regulators for breaches are enormous and appear disproportionate when measured against the penalties imposed for ordinary criminal offences. It is not the job of government agencies to be the most zealous of the zealots.

Similar issues arise where governments introduce strong-arm bankruptcy statutes for the resolution of banks which sidestep the role of the courts and which give the authorities arbitrary discretions over the rights of creditors and other property rights. These statutes nationalise bankruptcy law. Bankruptcy law is probably the most fundamental of all private law domains because of its destructive force and because, if there is not enough money to go around, the law has to decide who is the victor and who is the victim, who drowns or who gasps the last bubbles of oxygen at the top of the ladder of priorities. Bankruptcy is a destroyer and spoliator. It fires passions and anger, crystallised by individual losses which sometimes can sap whole economies.

In these cases, there are unquestionably powerful arguments which support this or that specific regulation or which support this or that specific emergency power to deal with failing banks and which have sufficient safeguards to respect the rule of law principles involved.

Now that the dismay and passion have cooled and now that the structures of laws built with such ardent enthusiasm over the last ten years can be viewed as a whole, we can begin to attempt some assessments of what we have done.

One can summarise by saying that the law-makers after the financial crisis sometimes used the statute book to express their indignation at the financial crisis, whose origins lay in a cheap money policy which they cheered on at the time. There also is far too much of it. The statute book is a holy book, a sacred place. These scriptures should be measured and rational, they should be comprehensible.

At one time the financial regulatory authorities in Britain were said to have a 'light touch', a proposition which was sometimes criticised as if the regulators were being too tolerant. In fact, that 'light touch' recognised that financial regulation is on the borderline and has to be applied with caution. One cannot help agreeing with that caution. It reflected a desire to adhere to the rule of law and to moderate the powers the regulators were given. Nobody has ever said that US regulators have a 'light touch'.

I do not say that regulation is inherently unsafe. In the modern world we have to have these systems of regulation. They comprise vast fields of necessary law, ranging from the regulation of the environment to such matters as data protection, employee rights and even pensions. Nevertheless, in view of the potency of regulation, the authorities have powers that should be exercised with restraint in the normal case.

CONCLUSION

To the ordinary members of the public, it may often be hard to see how the rule of law applies to money, finance and banks where the principles often seem so remote from ordinary rule of law principles. It is considered that the ethical principles and the moral ideals embedded in the ideology of the rule of law are just as applicable to money and banks as any other realm of human conduct. They are just as relevant as any other case involving the relationship between the government and the governed. This must specially be the case where the situation is changing so quickly and where the quantity of invisible property is accumulating at such speed. The survival function of law should extend its domains to this property and apply the same principles of the rule of law as apply to older classes of property.

The law embodies the credentials of a society, its civilisation and its attitudes towards justice.

8. Rebuilding trust in financial markets: beyond the limits of law and regulation[1]

Mark Yallop

THE COST OF WHOLESALE MARKET MANIPULATION

The cost to the banking industry, and the wider global economy, of the global financial crisis has received much analysis. IMF[2] and other estimates[3] put total financial institution losses at more than $4 trillion and the total economic damage, including the impact of lower growth, at numbers significantly greater even than $20 trillion. The public support given to financial institutions in the form of direct bail-outs, government guarantees of bank liabilities and special central bank liquidity schemes during 2008/9 was $15 trillion.[4]

Less often commented on has been the cost of the market manipulation that was uncovered during and in the aftermath of the crisis. But this was very substantial as well. In direct terms, 50 per cent of the net profits of UK banks were disgorged in 2015 in fines and other penalties for market abuse of one sort or another. In the past six years, banks globally have paid $375 billion in conduct fines, about 80 per cent of which related to wholesale markets. The Bank of England has estimated[5] that if that money had been retained as capital it would have supported $5 trillion in bank lending to the real economy.

The fines, and the cost of the remediation work that went with them – which is not just financial – have not only been a problem for the short-term profits of a few banks. The penalties extracted have been of such a scale that they have hindered the recapitalisation of the banking system, and undermined the 'investability' of banks that have been struggling to generate dependable earnings in excess of their cost of capital. It is not without cause that

[1]   This chapter is based on a previous article by the author: *Bad apples, rotten barrels and rebuilding trust in financial markets*, in JFC vol 2:1, 2018, available at www.henrystewartpublications.com/jfc/v2. The author wishes to thank JFC for granting permission to reproduce part of that article.

[2]   International Monetary Fund, *'Global Financial Stability Report: Responding to the Financial Crisis and Measuring Systemic Risks'*, April 2009.

[3]   See for example: Dallas Fed Staff Paper *'How bad was it: The costs and Consequences of the 2007–09 Financial Crisis'* by Tyler Atkinson, David Luttrell, and Harvey Rosenblum. Better Markets Inc. (2011), *'The Cost of the Wall Street-Caused Financial Collapse and Ongoing Economic Crisis Is More than $12.8 Trillion'*, www.bettermarkets.com/cost-crisis, and the US Government Accountability Office, *'Financial Crisis Losses and Potential Impacts of the Dodd-Frank Act'*, Report to Congressional Requesters, 16 January, www.gao.gov/products/GAO-13-180 also contain analysis of this topic.

[4]   Mark Carney, *'What a difference a decade makes'*. Remarks at the Institute of International Finance's Washington Policy Summit, the Reagan Centre, Washington DC, 20 April 2017.

[5]   Minouche Shafik, *'From "ethical drift" to "ethical lift": Reversing the tide of misconduct in global financial markets'*. Remarks given at a Panel Discussion at the Federal Reserve Bank of New York Conference on 'Reforming Culture and Behaviour in the Financial Services Industry' 20 October 2016.

some regulators[6] have described grappling with misconduct problems in the banking industry as the 'second phase' of the recovery from the global financial crisis, equivalent in importance to the recapitalisation, de-leveraging and other de-risking measures taken in the 'first phase' of prudential regulatory intervention from 2008 to 2013.

Indirectly, given the vital transmission mechanisms that wholesale Fixed Income Currencies and Commodities (FICC) markets play in the global economy, market manipulation throws grit into the wheels of global growth with a multiplier effect much larger than just the damage to bank capital.

More seriously, manipulation of markets has also created long-term costs for the banking industry through the systemic damage it has done to trust in financial services – not just trust in banks and bankers but in many other actors too – and the erosion it has caused of the social licence to operate that banks and others in the financial system need.[7] Notwithstanding the huge financial costs already noted, this is probably the most damaging legacy of the recent crisis and the manipulative activity it revealed.

Strenuous efforts have been made, and are continuing, by lawmakers, regulators and the private sector to address these conduct and manipulation problems and their consequences. For anyone concerned with the health of the industry and the global economy the question nevertheless arises: will these measures deliver the desired outcome?

A SHORT HISTORY OF WHOLESALE MARKET MANIPULATION

Many people, observing the global financial crisis and the manipulation of asset-backed securities, LIBOR and FX markets that was identified in its aftermath, assume that wholesale market abuse is a modern phenomenon. In fact, it has a long history, stretching back to the earliest days of modern capital markets.

In 1792, just 16 years after independence, the nascent US government bond market suffered the first major manipulation of the modern age. At that time, George Washington was President and Alexander Hamilton had been appointed first ever Secretary of the Treasury three years earlier. William Duer, a native of Devon, England, who had arrived in New York via Antigua in the West Indies and was a prominent trader and speculator, was the first Assistant Secretary of the Treasury to be appointed.

Hamilton devised a plan, which was approved by Washington in 1790, to create a new Bank of the United States which would be capitalised partly with subscriptions of cash and partly by investors exchanging debt securities, including what was at that point near-worthless pre-War of Independence debt issued by the bankrupt Continental Congress and state governments to soldiers, farmers and others who had supported the revolution.

William Duer, who should really be recognised as the first great insider trader of the modern era, and some co-conspirator bankers, anticipated a re-rating of this pre-war debt. They devised a plan to corner the market, funding themselves with large loans from third parties

---

[6]   Andrew Bailey, Speech delivered at the City Banquet, London 16 October 2014, www .bankofengland.co.uk/publications/Documents/speeches/2014/speech763.pdf.

[7]   Mark Carney, '*Building real markets for the good of the people*'. Speech given at the Lord Mayor's Banquet for Bankers and Merchants of the City of London at the Mansion House, London, 10 June 2015, http://www.bankofengland.co.uk/publications/Pages/speeches/2015/821.aspx.

and by creating their own credit through endorsing each other's promissory notes. Initially the scheme was successful and the price of government debt rose substantially, supporting at the same time a significant rise in the price of shares in the Bank of the United States. On the back of this the bank expanded its balance sheet very rapidly.

But the Bank of the United States soon ran into liquidity problems, drastically curtailed lending and in so doing caused its over-extended borrowers to have to deleverage by selling, among other assets, the government debt securities that they had borrowed from the bank to buy. During the winter of 1791, this activity in turn created a liquidity crunch for Duer and his accomplices who were major holders of the government securities. Secretary Hamilton was able to contain the crisis by offering primitive 'lender of last resort' repo facilities to commercial banks in New York and the North East, but by March 1792 Duer and his co-conspirators were finally unable to repay their creditors. They were sued and imprisoned; the price of US government debt fell by 20 per cent in a few weeks, imposing losses that have been estimated at $3 million on the market and causing misery to many. Duer died, a disgraced man, in prison in 1799.[8]

Extreme calamity can motivate positive outcomes, and so it was in this case. In the aftermath of the disaster, dealers resolved that the market for debt and shares needed to be better controlled and in May 1792 they entered the 'Buttonwood Agreement', so called after the buttonwood tree under which they met at what is today 68 Wall Street, which laid the foundations for a formal market – the New York Stock Exchange – to be established for buying and selling shares and bonds.[9]

In February 1814, the port of Dover in England was on high alert for news from the Continent. Napoleon had been defeated in his disastrous Russian campaign in 1812, and again at Leipzig in October 1813, but was still at large with significant forces in Northern France. While no one in England seriously feared an invasion, Napoleon at the head of an army was nonetheless a potent threat. Indeed, Napoleon had thoroughly trounced the Coalition forces led by Blücher on six occasions in battles across Northern France in the previous three weeks. So, Britain waited news of Napoleon's next move with some anxiety.

Late in the evening of Sunday, 20 February a stranger, dressed in a soaked greatcoat over an unusual-looking, battle scarred and very muddy uniform, appeared in the town, stating that he was Lieutenant-Colonel du Bourg, just arrived from France with the most important news that had to be delivered immediately to Admiral Foley, Commander of the south coast naval forces at nearby Deal.

Had they looked more closely some of the surprised Dover residents might have noticed that the battle-stained uniform was in fact streaked with boot-black; and they would have been even more surprised some minutes earlier to have seen the stranger standing in the nearby millstream throwing water over his coat to simulate a sea-soaked Channel crossing.

But unaware of these details, the locals provided Du Bourg with the wherewithal to write to Admiral Foley, and his letter set out the remarkable news that Napoleon had been defeated in battle: 'Bonaparte was overtaken by a party of Sachen's Cossacks who immediately slayed

---

[8]   Among other accounts of Duer's activities see: Scott B. MacDonald and Jane E. Hughes, *Separating fools from their Money*, Transaction Publishers, 2009, Chapter 2.

[9]   Richard J. Teweles, Edward S. Bradley and Ted M. Teweles, *The Stock Market*, 1992 (6th edition), p. 97.

him and divided his body between them. General Platoff saved Paris from being reduced to ashes . . . an immediate peace is certain' he wrote.

Du Bourg's letter was delivered to Admiral Foley at 3am, but the poor weather prevented its transmission to London via the primitive mechanical telegraph system then available. Nevertheless, the sensational news started to spread by word of mouth, across and inland from the south coast, even at this early hour. And Du Bourg left for London personally, changing horses and carriage several times before arriving in the capital early on Monday, 21 February.

While Du Bourg was *en route*, two gentlemen claiming to be French officers of the pre-Napoleonic Bourbon government appeared in Dartford, with even more lurid details of the demise of the Emperor, also demanding transport to the capital.

The combined effect of the overnight rumours and the arrival in the early morning of two separate parties with news of impending peace created pandemonium among Londoners and on the Stock Exchange. Large crowds gathered outside the Mansion House hoping for an official announcement from the Lord Mayor. In the course of the day government stocks – gilts – rose in value by 20 per cent, anticipating the favourable transformation of government finances that an end to the war would signal.

Inevitably, as the day wore on with no further corroboration of this dramatic turn of events, suspicion mounted and disappointment grew. It was confirmed later in the afternoon that Napoleon was in fact alive and that Lieutenant-General Baron Sachen's Cossacks had been engaged elsewhere. Gilt prices fell sharply and many investors caught up in the frenzy of the morning lost large sums of money.

In the investigation that followed it transpired that four individuals had sold gilts on that Monday – Sir Thomas Cochrane (10th Earl of Dundonald, a distinguished Naval hero, MP and member of the Order of the Bath), Andrew Cochrane Johnstone (ex-Governor of Dominica, MP for a rotten borough in Cornwall and Thomas's uncle), Richard Butt (a stockbroker) and John Holloway (a wine merchant).

These four owned almost £1 million in holdings of gilts – equivalent to some £50 million today – at the start of the day's trading. They could have made profits of between £5 and £10 million in today's money on their trading, if things had gone well; as it was, long before the days of best execution rules, they only netted about £0.5 million.

The four of them, and du Bourg, whose real name turned out to be Charles Random de Berenger, were tried at the Old Bailey on eight counts including that they:

> did conspire and by diverse false and subtle arts, devices, contrivances, representations, reports, and rumours to occasion without just and true cause a rise and increase in the prices of the public Government Funds . . . and sell and cause to be sold for them divers other large parts of the said Government Funds at higher and greater prices than said parts would otherwise sell for with a wicked and fraudulent intention to thereby cheat and defraud . . . all his Majesty's subjects who should contract for or purchase part of the said public Government Funds . . . of diverse large sums of money.

They were found guilty, fined, placed in the public pillory at the front of the Royal Exchange and sent to prison for 12 months in the first ever successful prosecution in the English courts for market manipulation.[10]

---

[10]   I am indebted to Linda Stratmann's book *Fraudsters and Charlatans: A Peek at Some of History's Greatest Rogues*, The History Press, 2010 which contains a much more detailed account of this episode in Chapter 1, pp. 1–21.

In the early years of the 19th century, French government bonds were traded in Paris and on a number of regional bourses. Prices were transmitted from Paris by various means and the distances to the remoter bourses meant that the latter might only receive prices from Paris with a delay of several days if news travelled by the regular mail; the 360-mile trip from Paris to Bordeaux, for example, took five days. To reduce this delay, and improve the conduct of other government business, the French government installed the earliest type of optical tele-graph system on many such routes, cutting the time to transmit messages, and bourse prices, to a few hours. The system was very similar to the design used by the British Admiralty to communicate between London and the south coast of England and which had failed to transmit Admiral Foley's message in February 1814. It consisted of a series of towers with mechanical arms which could be moved to signify a series of characters and numbers. Each tower being spaced within visible distance of at least one other, a message consisting of a sequence of arm movements could ripple down a line of intermediary points, or routing stations, across long distances.

Despite its relatively crude design the system was felt to be very secure as all messages were encrypted before sending, only government business could be conducted on the system, and none of the operators knew the codes used for encryption.

But in 1834 two Bordeaux bankers, François and Joseph Blanc devised a way to break the system. They persuaded the telegraph operator near Tours, in the middle of the chain of towers to their local market, to insert additional control codes, which contained the latest market prices, into the messages being transmitted on certain days. Agents of the Blanc brothers then observed the mechanical arm signals arriving at Bordeaux, watched for the additional control codes, and prices hidden therein, and passed them on to the brothers. Under the protocols for operating the telegraph system, additional control codes were always deleted by the next operator in the line, so the brothers' insertions were deleted on arrival in Bordeaux, leaving no trace of their intervention. The brothers were then able to trade on the Bordeaux bourse with information about the prices that would in due course be revealed to be trading on the main market in Paris, but that was yet not known to their counterparts locally. Their agents and the corrupt telegraph operators were well rewarded for their cooperation and the Blanc brothers were able to sustain this deception for two years until they were uncovered in 1836. Interestingly, the French courts were unable to find any law that had been broken, all the oper-ators were acquitted and François and Joseph were ordered to leave France.[11]

Disguise has been a common factor in wholesale market frauds across the centuries. It was fundamental to these 18th and 19th century examples; but it was also key to the modern frauds perpetrated by the manipulators of LIBOR and FX. Where their predecessors dressed up, modern manipulators hide behind social media messaging applications and computer algorithms; but the fraud behind the disguise – manipulation of market prices by a group of collaborators – is almost identical.

Disguise has sometimes been turned to their advantage by regulatory authorities.

In 1987, in the Chicago futures markets, the exchange authorities were concerned about corruption in the trading pits, including pre-arranged trading, fictitious trades, 'out of hours' trades and the use of 'bagmen' (locals who would do favours for brokers and traders in exchange for cash payments). As these were floor-based, open outcry markets at that time,

---

[11]   See for example: Roy S. Freedman, *Introduction to Financial Technology*, Elsevier, 2006, p. 21.

a normal external investigation was impossible. So the authorities placed agents on the floors of the Chicago Mercantile Exchange (CME) and the Chicago Board of Trade (CBOT), disguised and working as traders, but wearing wiretaps. Ironically, one of the enforcement agents – 'Randy' Jackson – turned out to be a decent broker. What the agents observed and recorded resulted in 46 indictments for various trading abuses over the two years that followed.

But this success for the authorities was a case of 'careful what you wish for'. The following year, one Thompson Saunders, a former grains trader on the CBOT and a group of collaborators, wore wigs, make-up, glasses and fake trading identities, badges and trading jackets to gain access to the CBOT financials trading floors and conduct fictitious trades in Treasury Bond futures. One of the defendants in the trial that ensued explained to the court the difficulty he had had in finding the right shade of mascara to paint in his false moustache. In his defence, Mr Saunders claimed that he had been inspired to engage in covert trading by the actions of the authorities in the CME the year before, and to hide his trading activity from over-zealous lawyers representing his former wife.

Market manipulation is almost certainly as old as markets themselves. But while product innovation and new technologies have multiplied the opportunities for misconduct in markets many times over, they have not necessarily expanded the range of techniques employed by the manipulators.

MANIPULATION: THE INGENUITY OF MAN

The judges in *Cargill Inc v. Hardin*[12] remarked that: 'the methods and techniques of manipulation are limited only by the ingenuity of man', encapsulating a widely held notion there are a very large number of deceptive techniques used by those intent on manipulating markets.

Interestingly the evidence suggests otherwise. The FICC Markets Standards Board[13] ('FMSB') has recently undertaken a review of the history of market abuse across 26 jurisdictions over the past two centuries.

This study of some 400 representative cases of manipulation reached some interesting conclusions. Despite the regular interventions of lawmakers and regulators across many jurisdictions to defeat market manipulation, manipulators have in fact struck repeatedly over the past two centuries across debt, equity, currency and commodity markets. Further, and even more interestingly, those manipulators have used a relatively small number of distinct techniques, deploying them repeatedly across multiple asset classes, instruments, markets and geographies over the years.

The FMSB study suggests that there are about 25 fundamental manipulative practices (summarised in Figure 8.1) lying behind the thousands of reported instances of manipulation. These group naturally into seven categories, as shown below. Many of these techniques have

---

[12]   *Cargill, Incorporated, et al., Petitioners, v. Clifford M. Hardin, Secretary of Agriculture, Thomas J. Flavin, Judicial Officer by Appointment of The Secretary of Agriculture, and the United States Department of Agriculture, Respondents*, 452 F.2d 1154 (8th Cir. 1971).

[13]   See www.fmsb.com.   The FICC Markets Standards Board ('FMSB') is a private sector standard-setting body for the global wholesale fixed income, currencies and commodities markets. Established in London in 2015 it has 50 members who collectively account for a major proportion of activity in wholesale FICC markets. The study referred to here is currently private, but will be published later in 2018 on the FMSB website.

Price Manipulation	Circular Trading	Collusion & Information Sharing
Spoofing/Layering	Wash Trades	Pools
New Issue/M&A Support	Matched Trades	Information Disclosure
Ramping	Money Pass & Compensation Trades	
Squeeze/Corner	Parking/Warehousing	Improper Order Handling
Bull/Bear Raids	Reference Price Influence	Front Running
	Benchmarks	Cherry Picking and Partial Fills
Inside Information	Closing Prices	Stop Losses & Limits
Insider Dealing	Reference Prices	Misleading Customers
Soundings	Portfolio Trades	Guarantees
Research	Barriers	Window Dressing
		Misrepresentation

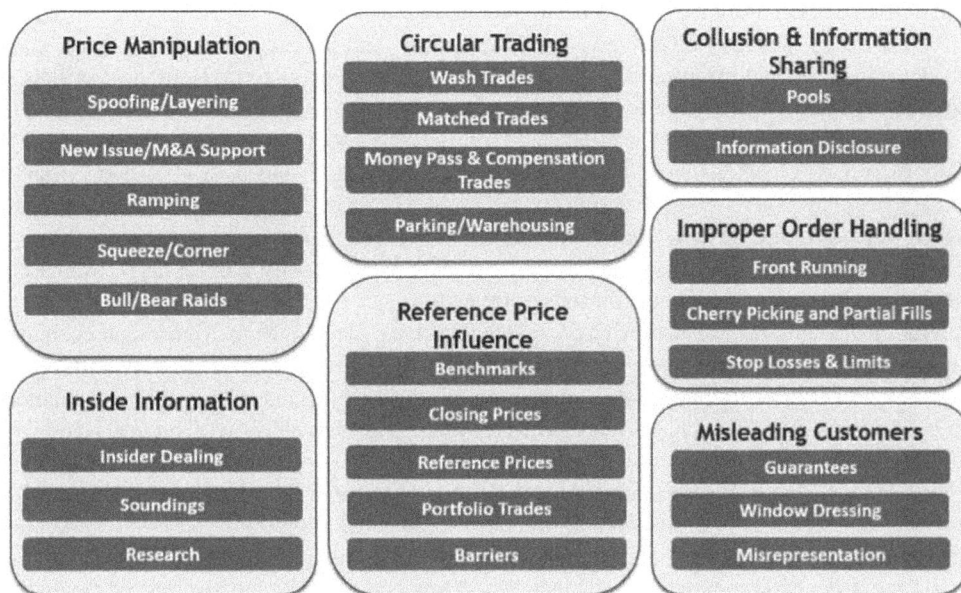

Figure 8.1   Categories of market manipulation

been declared illegal or have been banned by formal regulation. Why they keep recurring is an interesting conundrum, which is examined further below.

Equally interesting are the practical implications of this study for market participants and regulators. Focussing effort on this cluster of repeating patterns of behaviour should help both the private and public sectors to bear down more effectively on malpractice with greater efficiency. For example, firms can use these insights to develop a taxonomy of (mis)conduct risks (as they often do for other types of operational, credit and market risk), and use this to aid the design of surveillance systems, the training of staff in both front office and independent control functions, and the production of management information for senior management and governance fora.

The FMSB historical study and its conclusions clearly also provide a useful basis for regulators to design their supervision and intervention strategies.

When thinking about the root causes of manipulation and misconduct, it is helpful to distinguish between two types of force at work: structural issues with the way firms, markets and regulation are organised; and the personal motivations of individuals in markets. Naturally, these factors interact but it is useful to address them separately in the first instance.

RECURRING CONDUCT PROBLEMS: STRUCTURAL ISSUES

Markets activity has been at the core of investment banking, and their predecessor merchant banking businesses, for two-and-a-half centuries. In the earliest days, these firms were often commodity traders, who moved successively into the financing of those commodities and on into the underwriting, issuing and trading of purely financial instruments.

Conflicts of interest have always been inherent in the evolving business of these firms and they had to be managed effectively. Individual firms, and people within those firms, came to possess privileged information; and they had to develop ways to manage the conflicts of interest that came with this knowledge.

They did this in the way they organised themselves – generally as partnerships – through their recruitment methods, and in the way they developed their business models, concentrating on advisory businesses where relationships were highly valued. Capital was committed only when necessary and then fleetingly. Reputation, the maintenance of trust between firm and client, and ensuring good outcomes for those clients, was not only a necessity: it was a key source of competitive advantage for these firms.

But the development of widely traded capital markets, and the technological and economic modelling advances that supported the growth of derivatives from the 1970s onwards, made the investment banking business more commoditised, more reliant on formal legal relationships, and fundamentally changed the nature of trusting relationships in the industry and with its clients.

When more financial capital is at stake – and it is committed for much longer periods (as it is over many decades in derivatives transactions today) – through trading, capital market and derivatives activity, and technology has eroded information advantages, then the inevitable trend is for business to be ruled by 'black letter' law and formal contracts, not by reputation and standards.

There is another aspect to this evolution as well: economic advances and technological change also enabled individuals to build personal reputations in the industry as important as those of the firms they worked for. This has increased significantly the potential for conflict between the interests of the firm and its star employees, not just between the firm and its clients; and thereby further emphasised a contractual rather than reputation-based approach to business.

This reliance on formal contractual arrangements has had unfortunate, unintended consequences. A system based solely on the observance of legally-binding contracts creates incentives for legal arbitrage, as participants wanting to achieve goals that are forbidden by legislation develop ways to achieve their economic goals in forms that don't infringe the law.

Formal law is always open to interpretation; and those who look for creative loopholes will always be able to find them. As we have seen many times in recent years, however, when the business principle becomes 'if it's not illegal we can do it' and the first and most important question is 'how do I avoid breaking the law' then regard for others, and discussion of the fairness and effectiveness of customer outcomes, get crowded out.

Many in wholesale markets have been aware (even if dimly) of at least some of the opportunities for bad outcomes in markets long before the manipulation of benchmarks and other problems were revealed in recent years; although few of them can have envisaged the scale of what, for example, Tom Hayes was able to achieve with Yen LIBOR, which was met with genuine astonishment as the details emerged.

However, those individuals were caught in a bind: an extreme form of collective action problem in which market structure, coupled with huge short-term personal and corporate rewards derived from the *status quo*, meant that collaboration with others to change the system was never, or hardly ever, a viable strategy. The way in which career paths were managed also exacerbated already strong incentives to preserve the *status quo*. The result was that markets lacked any mechanism to unlock this collective action problem and provide a solution to the dilemma that kept market participants economic prisoners of their situation.

It is hard to see how the 'legalisation' of markets can be reversed and collective action problems are also hard to solve. But there is a third factor that is much easier to address, namely the natural limits on what conduct regulation can achieve.

Two broad approaches to regulation for financial markets have evolved in recent years: principles-based and rules-based. Most jurisdictions operate one or the other model and some (the United Kingdom being a prime example) try to combine both. Unfortunately, both approaches struggle to address the causes of conduct failure. On the one hand, the high-level 'principles' approach does not guide specific market practice at a granular enough level to show market participants the right approach to resolving the multiple conflicts of interest that they encounter every day. Unfortunately, neither, on the other hand, does the multiplicity of low-level, complex operational rules that the 'rule book' approach takes show market participants how to resolve these conflicts. Regulation has become increasingly refined in telling market participants 'what to do' and 'what not to do'; but doesn't tell them 'how to do' business. Two simple, everyday examples will illustrate the kind of challenges that market participants regularly face for which formal regulation doesn't provide the guidance they need:

How should a syndicate desk act in managing the allocation process for a new bond deal fairly, taking into account the separate views of the issuer, investor and lead manager? What information might the desk share with potential investors about the state of the book ahead of pricing? How might this advice change if the deal is being co-led by several banks acting together?

In what sequence should bids and offers reaching an electronic central order book be executed? First in first out? Largest orders first? On a randomized basis? How should work-up orders be treated in an electronic market? Is the proliferation of order types across multiple electronic trading platforms a good idea or not? How should parallel voice, hybrid and electronic markets operate when trading the same instruments?

Neither the general principles for the conduct of business promulgated by regulators, nor their detailed rule books, answer these questions at the level or with the specificity that market professionals require. There is a 'conduct void' between high-level principles and low-level rules which needs to be filled with better guidance for market participants; how this can be done is examined further below.

It is important to note that a world in which this conduct void was filled with detailed regulation would be very unattractive: if market participants were told by regulators 'how to' undertake every conceivable activity in markets there would be no innovation, unforeseen risks would likely bunch around business practices mandated by regulators; and market users would not necessarily be well served either.

One intended consequence of regulation after the crisis was that tougher prudential and conduct rules would prick the bubble of speculative trading activity, particularly by taxpayer insured banks. It is widely acknowledged that market liquidity has diminished in many asset classes as a result of these measures; but there is anecdotal evidence that the reductions in trading activity, and in market liquidity over the past eight years, have exceeded what was intended in the regulatory clamp-down, and that which would be expected as a logical result of the tougher prudential capital and liquidity rules.

'Conduct anxiety' is one important explanation of this observation. When institutions come to fear that their actions today may be reinterpreted in future with 20/20 hindsight, then they often conclude that it is just more prudent not to trade today. Unfortunately, the poorer liquidity that results hurts market users and makes markets less effective.

The challenge of making conduct regulation work within the confines of one jurisdiction is multiplied enormously by the fact that most wholesale markets trade globally, across national borders and legal and regulatory boundaries. Lawmakers and regulators across the key financial market jurisdictions have taken a variety of paths, at different speeds, following the global financial crisis. These differences have created an extremely complex web of policy initiatives which can contradict, overlap or underlap each other. The current juncture, at which it appears that EU and US market regulation are heading on divergent paths, is one example of the difficulty.

Sometimes, policy or political imperatives appear to have trumped a thorough analysis of foreseeable and undesirable market consequences. As a result, some regulatory initiatives have fragmented liquidity, increased the costs and impaired the effectiveness of markets for end users.

US regulation, for example, has since 2012 fragmented swap market liquidity, both domestically in the United States and internationally between the United States and Europe, to the detriment of all. As Chris Giancarlo, Chairman of the CFTC has said: 'Flawed and ill-suited swaps market regulation arbitrarily increases the cost of risk management, repels global capital, diminishes trading liquidity and stymies the legitimate use of derivatives causing the economy as a whole to suffer.'[14]

Further examples may include the proposal currently under discussion in Europe for a 'location' policy for euro denominated OTC derivatives clearing and the different requirements for charging for research in Europe under MiFiD 2 and in the United States under SEC regulations.

The structure of wholesale markets can also create, or conceal, actual or potential problems for market users. The privileged, private, over the counter ('OTC') 'inter dealer' professional market at the heart of the fixed income markets differs radically from the 'all to all' open, exchange or ECN-based structure of most cash equity markets. A full account of the ways in which these structural differences impact market users, potentially adversely, is beyond the scope of this chapter. But it is worth noting that both approaches can present problems as well as offer benefits. On the one hand, the OTC fixed income market is less transparent, and the competitive forces that might be thought to ensure 'fair' pricing and outcomes for users, may not always work well. But the OTC market is better suited to handling large orders and trading in illiquid instruments than is the exchange/Electronic Crossing Network (ECN) model. On the other hand, the exchange or central order book model is more transparent for simple, liquid products and hence by some measures 'fairer', but struggles to accommodate large transaction sizes and less liquid instruments.

Since the financial crisis, significant efforts have been made by regulators to change the structure of OTC fixed income markets, by obliging many of those markets to trade electronically in a public central order book format. While these measures have much to commend them it is essential to emphasise two things.

---

[14] Commodity Futures Trading Commission, *Pro-Reform Reconsideration of the CFTC Swaps Trading Rules: Return to Dodd-Frank* White Paper by J. Christopher Giancarlo, Commissioner US Commodity Futures Trading Commission, January 2015.

First, electronic exchange/ECN type central order book market structures are not immune to the kinds of market abuse discussed above. Indeed, the FMSB historical study already mentioned found that virtually every category of manipulation that developed originally in older, voice-based OTC markets also now has its equivalent in more modern electronic markets. Using machines and technology to trade does not eliminate malpractice (and can even make it easier to perpetrate).

Second, electronic exchange/ECN style markets can have new vulnerabilities not seen in the older voice-based OTC markets. For example, it is well known that many electronic markets incentivise market makers to compete on speed of order submission (because of the FIFO execution protocols in those market matching engines). It is less well understood that traders in possession of faster algorithms can operate trading strategies that take advantage of slower traders. Of course, not all fast traders do this; but this is just one example of the susceptibility of electronic markets. Electronic trading does not just allow known historical manipulations to continue, it also introduces new hazards that have not yet been well studied.

Ultimately, it is the users of wholesale markets in the wider economy who bear the cost of unfair and ineffective markets. But they also pay the price if the measures taken to improve fairness and effectiveness are themselves ineffective or extremely inefficient. Not enough debate has yet occurred about where the right balance lies between the costs and benefits of measures intended to protect the interests of market users, and the liquidity, cost and efficiency impact of those measures on the markets that users need to access.

PERSONAL MOTIVATIONS: BAD APPLES AND ROTTEN BARRELS

The small number of individuals charged with offences after the global financial crisis has encouraged some observers to portray market manipulation as a 'bad apple' problem: an issue confined to a very limited number of corrupt individuals, or renegade factions within firms who devised clever ways to outwit the system and who were able to have an outsized impact because of the huge size of the markets that they operated in and the financial leverage available to them.

For understandable reasons this has been the preferred narrative of many observers in the industry. Such an explanation by implication shares the responsibility for poor outcomes between the 'bad apples' and their supposedly incompetent counterparts who didn't take enough care to check what was being done to them. This explanation also perhaps forestalls the broad-based systemic regulatory response that might be felt necessary to deal with a 'rotten barrel' problem in favour of a more manageable, nuanced regulatory reaction targeted at some specific 'bad apple' issues.

Some sterner critics have raised objections to the 'bad apple' account. Among others, Minouche Shafik, then Deputy Governor for Markets and Banking at the Bank of England, observed in 2014[15] that the scale of problems being revealed rendered the bad apple theory implausible and that wholesale markets might have a 'rotten barrel' problem of widespread malpractice across many individuals and firms.

---

[15]   Minouche Shafik, Financial Times interview, 27 October 2014.

Psychologists have debated the explanatory power of the 'bad apple' and 'rotten barrel' theories for at least 70 years. Edwin Sutherland's work in the 1940s on white collar crime in the United States,[16] the infamous Milgram experiments of the 1960s[17] and Zimbardo's Stanford Prison experiments of the 1970s[18] are just some of the most celebrated of many attempts to understand the psychological effects of perceived power and the situational, as opposed to dispositional, drivers of individual behaviour.

More recent thinking[19] has developed the idea of 'normalised deviance' and emphasised the importance of social networks. The former suggests that deviant behaviour can become normalised in organisations, and be the cause of disastrous outcomes, when gradually, in the absence of adverse consequences, the unacceptable becomes acceptable and a blind eye is turned to those doing unscrupulous things. Among other industries the airline and aerospace industries have used this analysis to think about why breaches of standard operating procedure occur.

In January 1986, NASA pushed ahead with the 25th launch of the Challenger space shuttle in five years, despite having ample evidence that key components of the booster rockets were vulnerable, and in full knowledge that they were doing so well below the manufacturer-specified launch temperature. The evidence that emerged from the enquiry into the disaster that ensued, when all crew members were lost in a massive explosion 73 seconds after launch, revealed uncomfortable truths about how behaviour among well-meaning people in well-intentioned organisations can evolve. The amount of acceptable rocket booster damage had grown, incrementally, over the previous five years from none to complete destruction; the practice of waiving safety measures became normalised; and all the while NASA was actually following its own rules that allowed launch criteria to be waived by management who thought 'we know what we are doing'.

Consider the issue of LIBOR manipulation in wholesale financial markets in the light of the NASA tragedy. In markets, OTC derivatives dealing desks are understandably curious about where LIBOR might settle at 11am as this influences the value and risk of their portfolios. Money market traders who are also trading short dated swaps are intrigued about where these are priced relative to the cash rates that they are trading.

Gradually, over time, curiosity on both sides turns into regular dialogue between junior swap traders and their colleagues on money markets desks. Subliminal messages about the concerns of the derivatives traders start unconsciously to influence the actions of money markets traders and, in turn, their views of where LIBOR should be. All the while, senior management, eager to promote cross-selling to clients, explicitly encourage inter-desk collaboration.

It only requires someone seeking deliberate advantage to spot the opportunity that this situation presents and to set about colluding with and bullying other actors in the market to target LIBOR fixings that suit his positions and profits.

Social networks, not just those facilitated by social media applications, but relationships based on shared work or experiences in private life, can create communities whose members

---

[16]   Edwin H Sutherland, *White Collar Crime*, Yale University Press, 1949.

[17]   Stanley Milgram, *Obedience to Authority: An Experimental View*, Harper & Row, 1974.

[18]   Philip G. Zimbardo, *Stanford prison experiment: A simulation study of the psychology of imprisonment*, Austin ABC, 1972.

[19]   See for example, Diane Vaughan, *The Challenger launch decision: risky technology, culture, and deviance at NASA*, Chicago: University of Chicago Press, 1996.

feel stronger loyalty to other members of their tribe than they do to those for whom they work, and make employees more likely to transgress their employers' or regulators' codes of conduct.

These factors blunt any sharp distinction between the 'bad apple' and the 'rotten barrel'. The behaviour of individuals is never neatly driven solely by their genetic pre-disposition, or by the tempting situations in which they find themselves. There are multiple shades on the behavioural spectrum between the extremes. And each shade on the personal behavioural spectrum is influenced by external structural factors – the legalistic approach to business, the career and compensation motivations of individuals, gaps in regulation and the structure of markets.

The complexity of the mix goes a long way to explaining why market manipulation has been so persistent. Ever since the dawn of modern capital markets, manipulators have been active, a step or two ahead of the authorities. Of course, regulators and lawmakers have tried to adapt to, and keep up with, the repeating evidence of market abuse. But it is clear that regulation cannot fix the problem on its own because so many factors far outside the purview of regulation are relevant as well.

A full response to the problem of manipulation must therefore address a complex spectrum of interacting environmental and behavioural drivers. At first sight this seems to be an impossibly complex task. But there is an alternative way to formulate the problem and think about a solution; that is to ask how the biggest casualty of the crisis – the destruction of trust within the industry, between financial services and the users of markets, and between financial services and society – can be reversed.

If a way can be found to restore and maintain trust, then the act of doing so will also address the challenges described above.

REBUILDING TRUST IN FINANCIAL MARKETS: A CHALLENGE FOR MARKET PARTICIPANTS

It is doubtful whether all the efforts, which have been underway for nine years now (and have some way further to go), to rebuild capital and liquidity levels in the financial system and increase its resilience to crisis, will of themselves restore trust in markets. They are certainly a necessary, but they are not a sufficient, condition for re-establishing trust in markets. Without trust being restored, the transmission mechanisms that markets provide for global economic growth will remain fractured; and the improved stability that financial reform has brought may turn out to be the stability of the graveyard.[20]

Onora O'Neill, the eminent moral philosopher, said in 2012 when talking about the loss of trust in established professions[21] that the question is not 'how do we restore trust' but rather 'how do we make it easier to judge trustworthiness'. Those who are determined to be untrustworthy will always look for ways to conceal their true purpose; what the rest of us need are the

---

[20]   Mark Carney, 'The high road to a responsible, open financial system'. Speech given at Thomson Reuters, London, 7 April 2017, www.bankofengland.co.uk/publications/Documents/speeches/2017/speech973.pdf.

[21]   Onora O'Neill, *'How can we restore trust?'*, BBC Podcasts – A Point of View 2012.

tools to be able to interrogate our counterparts more thoroughly and to place trust intelligently where the evidence shows that this is justified.

So, the real challenge today is not for regulators, but for market participants. How do they change the way they operate and make it easier for others to judge their trustworthiness? Two steps seem to be indicated if Baroness O'Neill's challenge is to be answered for wholesale markets.

First, wholesale market participants need to take responsibility themselves for leading the process of fixing problems that have been uncovered – and particularly for demonstrating better outcomes for market users. To do this they have to be permitted this opportunity by their regulators, and to act in a credible framework; and crucially they have to be seen to be taking the lead, rather than simply reacting to regulatory pressure.

Second, those wholesale market participants need to find credible, granular ways to define what will be done differently in future. Changes in market practice need to be genuine, proof of change needs to be provided, and that evidence needs to engage judgement, not merely the ticking of boxes, in order to demonstrate accountability. Further, the 'proof of change' needs to be published, so that others can judge whether the change is real and actually demonstrates a new level of trustworthiness.

Of course, neither of these outcomes can simply be legislated or regulated into existence: wholesale market participants have to want them, and make them happen.

One obvious solution to the problem defined in these terms would be for participants in the wholesale markets to break with tradition; to work together to create the codes or standards that would fill the 'conduct void' and show how business should be conducted; to actually implement those codes or standards; and for them to devise a method for showing the world that business was in fact being conducted in a new way; and to do all this without being instructed at every turn on how to act by regulators.

SOME BENEFITS OF PRIVATE SECTOR STANDARDS

Private sector standards or codes have a number of important advantages for addressing the problems seen in wholesale markets.

First, such standards are less prone to suffer the 'unintended consequences' problem – of creating incentives to arbitrage the rules – that arise with formal laws and regulations. Standards determined by market practitioners eliminate this risk *a priori* because the creators of the standards feel ownership of them, and write them to avoid arbitrage.

Second, private sector standards reinforce professionalism. Participants in wholesale financial markets have highly asymmetric knowledge; some are considerably better informed about what is going on than others. How this privileged knowledge is acquired, maintained and acted on, defines the professionalism of market participants. Engaging market experts in formulating standards obliges them to think about, and document, what are acceptable behaviours and professional conduct.

Third, private sector standards can be calibrated to the express level of principle (or sometimes detail) that market participants need when trying to navigate the 'conduct void'. The principles on which such standards are based can be more granular and useful than the very high-altitude regulatory principles; and their detail can be more explicit, up to date and relevant to the day-to-day needs of market practitioners than the regulatory rule books.

Fourth, private sector standards can more easily reflect the global nature of wholesale markets. Laws and regulation are (generally) set nationally and have to operate within a defined jurisdiction. Individual countries, politicians and regulators inevitably have differing priorities. By contrast, wholesale financial markets – especially the fixed income, currency and commodities markets – are global and many of the firms working in them are organised and operate globally. It is much easier, and significantly more efficient, for standards to be developed and adopted internationally, to address the global nature of wholesale markets, than to rely on nationally-determined laws and regulation.

Public sector standards-setting bodies also have a role to play in this area; but the advantages of engaging the most influential actors in the private sector and binding them to a central role in building professional standards that improve the outcomes for market users are immense.

TURNING THEORY INTO PRACTICE: THE FICC MARKETS STANDARDS BOARD AND THE FX GLOBAL CODE

In the United Kingdom, a major review of the problems in wholesale markets was undertaken by the authorities in 2014/15, which culminated in the publication of one of the most authoritative analyses of the market conduct landscape: The Fair and Effective Markets Review.[22] One of the central recommendations of this Review was that wholesale market participants should take more responsibility for fixing conduct problems and improving the outcomes for market users; and thereby for rebuilding trust in wholesale markets. The Fixed Income Currencies and Commodities Markets Standards Board, or FMSB, is the markets' response to this challenge.

FMSB brings together representative users from all sides of the markets to agree solutions, publish them as Standards, and provide a 'trustworthiness gauge' for others to judge the effectiveness of those Standards.

It is practitioner-led, owned and operated by the major participants in wholesale markets, including both market makers and market users. It is independent of regulators both in the United Kingdom and overseas and has been established solely to develop and promulgate Standards that set out best practice in wholesale FICC markets. FMSB is prohibited by its constitution from lobbying or acting in any way as an industry trade association. This is a crucial restriction designed to eliminate both the perception, and the reality, of any conflict of interest between the quality of the Standards produced and the commercial interests of the FMSB membership.

It now has a membership of close to 50 institutions, most of them global, representing all sides of the wholesale markets: the sell side – UK and international commercial and investment banks; non-bank liquidity providers; the buy side – real money asset managers and hedge funds; corporations; exchanges and OTC trading venues; custodians and other market infrastructure providers.

FMSB members account for more than 80 per cent of all sell-side activity in wholesale markets, over $10 trillion in assets under management, over $100 trillion in custody and administration assets, over $100 billion in corporate new issue volumes in the past year, 60 per cent of global inter-dealer broker volumes and a very large share of exchange traded

---

[22] *The Fair and Effective Markets Review*, 2015 Final Report, HM Treasury, Bank of England, Financial Conduct Authority, www.bankofengland.co.uk/markets/documents/femrjun15.pdf.

volumes. The FMSB Board is made up of the most senior people in the markets industry: Chief Executives and Chairmen, Investment Bank CEOs and Global Business Heads.

FMSB has as its strategic goals: identifying and reporting on actual and emerging conduct vulnerabilities in FICC markets; developing market practice Standards to address those vulnerabilities; and promoting the adoption of these Standards in all major international wholesale FICC market locations. FMSB has reviewed the horizon of conduct problems and expects to address some 70 areas of ambiguity and potential abuse in the 'conduct void' – both those that have been problems in the past and those that can be foreseen as future concerns.

In its first 18 months, FMSB has published nine pieces of work on topics ranging across the entire FICC arena including: the resolution of trading errors; the hedging of binary options; the management of new issues in the Eurobond market; the training, surveillance and supervision of FICC businesses and staff; and the monitoring of written communications. At the time of writing, work is underway on a further four pieces including the governance of algorithmic trading platforms; the operation of trading rulebooks by electronic trading platforms; information sharing across FICC markets; and the reporting of suspicious transactions.

FMSB has also developed a simple, standardised adherence process under which its members lay out publicly each year how they will adhere to the standards published in the previous 12 months. This is a major step towards answering Baroness O'Neill's challenge 'have we made it easy to establish trustworthiness?' and hence to laying the foundations for re-establishing trust itself.

By enlisting all participants, and empowering market users to play a larger role in determining how markets operate, FMSB aims to strengthen market discipline and encourage a move away from continual reliance on regulation to provide answers to questions it is often not well equipped to deal with. FMSB Standards will however complement important regulatory initiatives such as the Senior Managers Regime in the United Kingdom and the accountability frameworks in other jurisdictions. To this end, great care is being taken to work with global market authorities to promote the adoption of FMSB Standards that are tuned to local market needs and regulation; and the early signs are encouraging.

In 2015, the Bank for International Settlements established an FX Working Group of Central Banks and private sector FX market participants from 16 jurisdictions to develop a Global Code for dealing in the foreign exchange markets.[23] FMSB, which had already been doing preparatory work on this topic in the early months of its existence, provided its preliminary conclusions and work-product into the FX Working Group, and FMSB members were instrumental in helping with the drafting of the Global FX Code which was published in May 2017. The Code sets out important principles for business conduct in FX markets including ethics, governance, execution, information-sharing, risk management and compliance as well as confirmation and settlement. While it is voluntary, the Central Banks involved in its production have made clear that they will use it in their dealings in the FX markets (other than for official market operations) and will expect their counterparties to do so as well.

While the genesis of the FX Global Code is subtly different from the FMSB's approach (notably by the involvement of Central Banks in the drafting and approval process for the Code), the inspiration behind the code, its intention to improve market discipline, and its status

---

[23]   For further information about the FX Global Code see http://www.globalfxc.org/.

are very similar to the FMSB's broader work on global fixed income and commodity markets; and the two initiatives are seen by the wholesale markets as highly complementary.

History shows that misconduct has been a repeating problem over a long time. Experience shows that it has complex root causes and enablers. But lack of clear guidance about how business should be conducted is without question one major contributor; and the FMSB initiative and the FX Global Code have the capability to solve that problem. These two initiatives also provide an important opportunity for the private sector to demonstrate its determination to fix the problems in markets and a novel 'test bed' for collaborative work by the private and public sector on issues that formal regulation and lawmaking cannot be expected to address.

PART III

CAN LAW COUNTERACT
UNETHICAL BEHAVIOUR?
SOME EXAMPLES

9. Ethical considerations in the representation of sovereign clients

Lee C. Buchheit

The author of an essay on legal ethics must tread cautiously among several yawning crevasses. On one side beckons the *amorphous*. Because moral compasses are so notoriously subjective, saying anything specific in such an essay risks alienating a significant part of the readership. A different misstep will plunge the ethicist into a warm, soapy vat of the *platitudinous*. Slip there and only a gurgle of sweet vacuities will ever reach the surface. Finally, there is the *preachy*. In few other genres of writing is the temptation to imitate a Burning Bush so strong as in an essay on ethical behavior. Accepting these hazards, this paper will discuss ethical issues that arise in the legal representation of a sovereign client.

INTRODUCTION – THE LIMITS OF SOVEREIGNTY

Sovereignty. The supreme, absolute, and uncontrollable power by which any independent state is governed . . .[1]

"The failure of generations of political scientists and lawyers to define 'sovereignty' with precision," wrote D.P. O'Connell, "has made this term the least exact of any in the literature of international law."[2] Whatever its precise meaning, the implication of the word "sovereign" is that within its own territory the sovereign is the source, not the subject, of the law. Outside its territory, the sovereign shares this planet with a limited number (about 195 at last count) of fellow sovereigns, each of which is by tradition bound to respect the sovereignty of all the others. In practical terms, this has meant that one sovereign does not inquire into, or interfere with, the "internal affairs" of another sovereign. Externally, this deference once manifested itself in a rule – dubbed "absolute" sovereign immunity – that shielded a sovereign from being sued in the courts of another sovereign without its consent.

Not much remains of these traditional notions of sovereignty in the 21st century. In most countries, foreign sovereigns can now be sued without their consent in connection with their commercial activities undertaken abroad. Even a sovereign's treatment of its citizens entirely within the sovereign's own borders is now thought to be a fit subject for international concern and inquiry. International human rights law unabashedly slices through many of the artificial barriers that traditionally cloaked sovereign conduct from scrutiny and censure.

Whatever may be left of the notion that sovereigns, within their own territory, are "uncontrollable" (to use the definition quoted above), a sovereign that elects to participate in international commerce forfeits any entitlement to demand that its conduct remain shielded from

---

[1] BLACKS LAW DICTIONARY (revised fourth edn 1968).
[2] D.P. O'Connell, INTERNATIONAL LAW, Vol. 1 at 319 (1965).

review by national courts in the jurisdictions where the conduct occurs. This has been the rule in most countries since the last quarter of the 20th century. Under modern notions of sovereign immunity, by acting in a commercial capacity abroad a sovereign subjects itself to both the laws and the judicial processes of the places where that action occurs or where the action may have a direct and significant effect. No vestige of the ancient notion of sovereignty allows a sovereign to draw a curtain over its commercial behavior conducted beyond its own borders.

Quite apart from subjecting itself to the laws and judicial machinery of the foreign juris-dictions in which it engages in commercial activity, a sovereign also implicitly undertakes to respect the ethical norms applicable to commercial conduct in those places. By ethical norms I mean those generally accepted standards of behavior that lie someplace between the formal requirements of positive law and the more gauzy guidelines of business etiquette. For example, the commercial law of a jurisdiction may proscribe outright misrepresentations by a party in the course of negotiating a commercial contract and may give the aggrieved party a remedy in damages for such behavior. But a duty affirmatively to correct an obvious mistake, oversight or misunderstanding on the part of a counterparty during the negotiation of a commercial contract will be mandated only by a sense of business ethics; something more compelling than mere etiquette or common courtesy among businesspeople but less demanding than judicially sanctionable conduct.

If the sovereign itself is subject to both the laws and the ethical norms applicable to commer-cial dealings in the places where it elects to do business, the foreign lawyer that the sovereign hires to assist in those arrangements is similarly bound by the standards of professional ethics prevailing in the relevant jurisdiction. In other words, the conduct of a lawyer does not benefit, derivatively, from any special deference or latitude that her client may enjoy as a consequence of its status as a foreign sovereign.

I.   WHO IS THE CLIENT?

The threshold question for a lawyer accepting an engagement with a sovereign is to identify the client.[3] For purposes of illustration, let's assume that the Minister of Finance of the Republic of Ruritania has contacted you, a foreign (non-Ruritanian) lawyer, seeking your assistance in resolving Ruritania's unsustainable external debt position. Although the name of the Republic will no doubt appear on your engagement letter, as a practical matter to whom should your professional loyalty be owed? The options:

1.   The Minister of Finance who is hiring you.
2.   The administration in which that Minister is serving.
3.   The current citizens of Ruritania.
4.   The current *and future* citizens of Ruritania.

Depending on how you answer this question, your advice on issues arising in the course of the debt workout may vary. For example, assume the Minister and the administration he serves

---

[3]   For an astute discussion of the subject in the context of sovereign debt disputes see Michael J. Lockman, *An Ethical Representation of Sovereign Clients in Debt Disputes*, 30 GEORGETOWN J. OF LEGAL ETHICS 73 (2017).

have eight months left in office and cannot, or in practice will not, be re-elected. If you chose options (1) or (2) as the focus of your professional loyalty, an offer by the country's creditors to defer the maturity of their claims for nine months should logically command your support, even if it leaves Ruritania still burdened with an unsustainable debt load after that period expires.

If you regard the current citizens of Ruritania as your client, however, a stretch-out of claims over the medium term, but with a sharp escalation in payments thereafter, might strike you as an acceptable outcome. But if your sense of professional responsibility extends to Ruritania writ large – that is, Ruritania today and tomorrow – you would perhaps feel yourself under an obligation to hold out in the negotiations with creditors for a long-term resolution of Ruritania's debt problem.

Identifying the client in a sovereign engagement raises issues of fundamental political philosophy. In particular, it calls into question the relationship of a government to its citizens and what duties, if any, are owed by one generation of citizens to succeeding generations.

A.   Governments as Agents

One legacy of the 18th-century enlightenment is the way we view those who govern us. Rulers are no longer divinely appointed to that role. In most Western societies at least, the prevailing view is that the legitimacy of a government derives from the consent of the governed. This explains our distaste for tyrannies and dictatorships of one stripe or another.

If those who govern do so at the request, or at least with the sufferance, of the governed, it follows that governments stand in an agent/principal relationship with their citizens. Modern political philosophy views the citizens of a country as the principal and the government *du jour* as the agent. In such a relationship, the government owes a duty of loyalty to its citizens, not – as Louis XIV would have argued – the other way around.

As a lawyer hired by the Ruritanian government your client will be that government, but only in its capacity as agent of the citizens of Ruritania. Viewed in this light, any actions by the government that breach the duty of an agent to its principal are not legitimate exercises of governmental authority and may not ethically be supported by you. Such actions would include, of course, any form of self-dealing such as official corruption. But they would also cover actions or policies that, while detrimental to the citizens of Ruritania in the short or long-term, may be useful in smoothing the path, or perpetuating the political life, of an incumbent administration.

To put the matter succinctly, although the state of Ruritania itself may be sovereign, the government officials who hire you are decidedly not so. Quite apart from being themselves subject to the criminal and civil laws of Ruritania, those government officials owe a duty of faithful service to the citizens of the country. They may not ethically be assisted in an action or policy which breaches that duty. Stated in this way, of course, the last proposition shades into the platitudinous. It conceals, however, a number of subtle issues. For example: a lawyer may not ethically assist a government official in a corrupt act. But what ethical duty, if any, is implicated when the government official decides upon a course of conduct that the lawyer believes is unwise, reckless or downright daft? All lawyers owe their clients the benefit of their best professional judgment. If an officer in a corporation elects to ignore a lawyer's advice, there are usually ways in which to engage others in the company to reconsider the decision. That avenue may not be available with a government client.

To take an exaggerated example, it would obviously be unethical to assist a government official in soliciting a $1 million bribe to approve a government procurement contract. What if, however, that same government official asked for your assistance in spending $1 million of public money on a proposal to locate, and expropriate for the public benefit, the pot of gold under every rainbow that appears in Ruritania? Is this an ethical issue or is the wisdom of a client's business decision entirely beyond a lawyer's purview?[4]

B.   Intergenerational Tensions

Even if you conclude that the citizens of Ruritania, and not just the Government of Ruritania, should be the objects of your professional loyalty, this will not entirely resolve the ethical questions that may arise during the engagement. The question is "which citizens?", the existing body of citizens or future citizens as well.[5] After all, a policy that is good for the current crop may be proportionally bad for the next generation.

"[T]he earth belongs in usufruct to the living,"[6] is how Thomas Jefferson summarized the problem. In Roman law, usufructuaries were entitled to the enjoyment of property to which they had no legal title. The usufructuary therefore could not sell, encumber or despoil the property. When Jefferson said that "the living" enjoy this planet in usufruct, he was implying that they were under an obligation to turn it over to the next generation without encumbrances or alterations that would destroy its value to the folks who would inherit it.

If Thomas Jefferson is correct that the residents of this planet at any given time are under an obligation to refrain from taking actions that will impair the ability of future residents to enjoy it, the last two generations have much to answer for – depleting natural resources, permanently altering climate patterns, perhaps irreversibly polluting great parts of both the land and the sea. Among these sins must also surely be counted the practice of borrowing staggering amounts of money that will fall to be repaid by our progeny. It would be one thing if the proceeds of these loans had been used to avert an existential threat to the debtor country (a war or a massive financial collapse), or even employed to build infrastructure that would benefit the people who will be compelled to repay the loans. Much of the borrowing in the last 40 years, however, has resulted from a simple desire of the incumbent generation to spare themselves the disagreeable choice of either paying more in taxes or receiving less in public services and entitlements.

---

⁴   The American Bar Association's *Model Rules of Professional Conduct* conclude that:
When constituents of the organization make decisions for it, the decisions ordinarily must be accepted by the lawyer even if their utility or prudence is doubtful. Decisions concerning policy and operations, including ones entailing serious risk, are not as such in the lawyer's province.
AM. BAR ASSN., *Model Rules of Professional Conduct* (2017 edn), Rule 1.13, Comment [3] (hereinafter "*ABA Model Rules*").
⁵   The philosophy is Burkean:
As the ends of such a partnership [society or the state] cannot be obtained in many generations, it becomes a partnership not only between those who are living, but between those who are living, those who are dead, and those who are to be born.
Edmund Burke, *Reflections on the Revolution in France*, 1790, in THE WORKS OF THE RIGHT HONOURA-BLE EDMUND BURKE, Vol. 3 at 359 (London, 1899).
⁶   "Letter from Thomas Jefferson to James Madison (6 September 1789)", in Philip B. Kurland and Ralph Lerner (eds), *The Founders' Constitution, Vol. 1* (Chicago, IL: University of Chicago Press, 2001), 68.

May a lawyer ethically assist the Ruritanian Government in borrowing so much money that successor generations of citizens in the country must either default on the repayment of those loans or significantly impair their own standard of living in order to honor the debts? As politicians have long known, rationalizing the intergenerational tensions in this situation is relatively easy. One might, for example, trust that the debts will *never* have to be repaid on a net basis, just rolled over until the Crack of Doom. Oil, or perhaps it will be gold, in fabulous quantities, may be discovered in Ruritania tomorrow; more than enough to repay the debts incurred today. Everyone knows that the Ruritanian economy will always expand. The size of the Ruritanian debt in the future, however large it may be, will thus always be manageable in light of the increasing size of the Ruritanian economy. And then there is the very real possibility that a Beneficient Providence will find a way to succor succeeding generations and shield them from the disagreeable prospect of having to tax themselves to repay liabilities inherited from their ancestors.

In the end, however, these are just rationalizations. One generation can exploit the next just as surely as one group of existing citizens can victimize another group.[7] Intergenerational ethical qualms disappear entirely if one regards the government of the day as the client. This is presumably how most lawyers see the relationship. A government decides its policy, whether about borrowing or any other matter. It is presumptuous, bordering on impertinent, the argument goes, for an outside lawyer to second-guess those policies, particularly on the grounds that they may injure future citizens of the country. All true, unless the lawyer regards those lives-not-yet-in-being as encompassed by the client entity called the Republic of Ruritania.

II.   REPUGNANT REGIMES

A government administration, even if not overtly corrupt and self-dealing, may be obnoxious for any number of reasons: an insensitivity to human rights or environmental protections; the infringement of free speech or religious liberty; the misprizal of women or minorities; a failure to respect property rights or the rule of law; international belligerency and bullying. These traits, among others, can render a regime distasteful, perhaps even odious, in the eyes of some observers. The principal ethical issue for the lawyer asked to represent such a regime is not that, by accepting the engagement, the lawyer is endorsing the policies or behavior of the regime. Although that aspect may occasionally raise reputational concerns for a lawyer, the representation of a client – any client – should not be construed as suggesting that the lawyer necessarily sanctions the entirety of the client's conduct.

An ethical concern may be raised, however, if a lawyer is asked to assist a contemptible government with an indisputably beneficial project. For example, what if a corrupt, dictatorial regime in Ruritania asks you to assist the government in securing much-needed debt relief from the country's external creditors. Arguing in favor of accepting the engagement is the fact that the Ruritanian people will benefit from the debt relief. Arguing against is the realization that a successful debt restructuring will probably forestall an economic crisis and thus tend to cement the regime's grip on power. Your professional services may therefore leave Ruritania

---

[7]   Thomas Jefferson put it this way: "[B]y the law of nature, one generation is to another as one independent nation to another." *Id.*

with the foreign exchange needed to import additional food and medicine for its people, but only at the cost of perpetuating on those people the incubus of a corrupt, dictatorial regime.

An element of intergenerational conflict may also be present in this situation. Consider the following illustration:

> A group of hungry children are in a room. They can only be fed by leaving a plate of food outside the door to the room once a day.
> On average, a very large rat eats about one-half of the food left outside the door before the children can get to it.
> More children are added to the room from time to time, and some get to leave.
> If the food plates stop coming, the rat will eventually starve and future occupants of the room will enjoy all the food when the process restarts. But if the food plates stop, some of the children now in the room may also starve.
> If the plates keep coming, the rat will get fatter and more voracious – making him an ever more serious problem for future occupants of the room.

What then is the ethical choice, to risk the starvation of some of the current occupants of the room in order to improve the lot of future occupants, or to endure the predations of the rat on both current and future occupants in order to safeguard the current occupants? In the sovereign context, is it better to assist a repugnant regime in a project that benefits the current citizens of the country but which will tend to perpetuate the tenure of the regime? Or is the moral choice to withhold assistance today, even if it means increasing the suffering of the incumbent citizens, in order to hasten the day when they and their successors can throw off the incubus.

This is not the classroom hypothetical it may appear to be. At the time of writing this (June 2017), a similar debate has been triggered by the efforts of the Maduro regime in Venezuela to sell state assets – including bonds of the Republic of Venezuela – at discounts of up to 80 percent of face value. The Maduro administration has elected to remain current on external debt service at the cost of vastly restricting imports, including imports of food and medicine. This has led some commentators to refer to Venezuelan Government bonds as "hunger bonds" and to brand all those who deal with the regime as morally compromised. As the *Wall Street Journal* reported:

> A crisis of conscience is rippling through emerging markets, where portfolio managers are asking: Dare we hold on to Venezuelan bonds, let alone buy new ones, knowing that the government of President Nicolás Maduro is choosing to pay lenders rather than feed its people?[8]

III.   THE PROBLEM OF CORRUPTION

Corrupt government officials are present in every country; in some countries they are omnipresent. Government corruption prospers because many of the people who prove to be corruptible – judges, law enforcement professionals, politicians – are also the individuals responsible for investigating and punishing government corruption. Any lawyer who refuses on principle to advise a government blemished by a tincture of corruption will enjoy a considerable amount of free time in which to contemplate those principles. Accepting that some degree of government corruption exists in most countries, what are the ethical implications for lawyers seeking to advise those sovereign clients?

---

[8]   Matt Wirz and Carolyn Ciu, *Venezuelan Bonds v. Conscience*, Wall St. J., June 19, 2017.

A. Scenario

For the purposes of illustration, consider the following scenario:

> Vulturefund, a hedge fund specializing in "distressed emerging market sovereign debt," buys a $100 million face value loan to the Republic of Ruritania (one of the poorest countries on earth), for a mere $4 million. The loan has been in default for a number of years.

Vulturefund sues Ruritania for the full $100 million (plus interest and legal fees) due on the loan in a US federal court.

The Ministry of Finance of Ruritania hires you to defend the lawsuit. The Minister himself calls you to arrange your retention. After nine months of discovery, it appears that Ruritania may have a good defense to the claim based on the applicable statute of limitations.

During that nine-month period, however, Vulturefund has hired private investigators to compile a dossier of documents and witness statements strongly suggesting that the Minister of Finance, the First Deputy Minister and the General Counsel of the Ministry were all personally involved in a corrupt (but completely unrelated) financing transaction several years ago. Vulturefund's representative in Ruritania is seen entering the Ruritanian Ministry of Finance clutching this dossier.

Forty-five minutes after that representative leaves the Ministry of Finance building you receive a telephone call from the Minister. The conversation proceeds as follows:

> **Minister** – "Counselor, we have decided to settle the Vulturefund case for 98 percent of the amount the plaintiff is claiming plus $5 million to reimburse their legal fees."
> **You** – "But Minister, there is a very good chance that we will win this case outright. And even if you don't want to take the risk of further litigation, I am morally certain that we can settle for a small fraction of what Vulturefund is claiming."
> **Minister** – "Counselor, I have just instructed you to settle this case and told you the final terms of that settlement. Through my negotiating skills, I have saved the Ruritanian taxpayer a full 2 percent of the amount claimed by the plaintiff. What part of my instruction do you not understand?"
> You hang up the telephone and do what . . . exactly?

B. Due Diligence

If the strong odor of corruption implied by the above scenario proves accurate, the poor citizens of Ruritania will have been sinned against twice. First, by the presence of larcenous bureaucrats. Second, by the blackmail of those bureaucrats when the discovery of their misdeeds induces them to accept an unnecessarily rich settlement of a defaulted debt instrument. The threshold ethical issue raised by this scenario is one of due diligence. To what extent, if at all, ought the lawyer hired to defend the Government in this litigation inquire into the Minister's motives for accepting such a rich settlement? Corrupt bureaucrats rarely proclaim themselves as such. Some explanation – even if risible under the circumstances – can always be proffered for a suspicious decision. Is a lawyer under any ethical duty to probe that explanation?

The temptation just to salute and carry out client instructions is stronger when a lawyer is representing a sovereign client than it is with a corporate client. Sovereigns are, at least within their own territory, sovereign. Decisions taken by public officials may affect the entire population of the country, not just the commercial interests of a business enterprise. The need for confidentiality in the formulation of governmental policies is accordingly very high. An outside lawyer engaged to represent a sovereign in a commercial matter will not have been hired as an anti-corruption campaigner. Most lawyers in that position will therefore refrain from unsolicited inquiries into the behavior or motivations of the government officials with whom they deal. That said, "a lawyer cannot ignore the obvious."[9]

C.   Remedy

In the above scenario, even if the evidence of the Minister's having succumbed to a blackmail threat is incontrovertible, what is the lawyer to do? Codes of professional responsibility may direct how the situation is to be handled in the legal representation of a business entity. Here, for example, is the American Bar Association's recommendation:

> If a lawyer for an organization knows that an officer, employee or other person associated with the organization is engaged in action, intends to act or refuses to act in a matter related to the representation that is a violation of a legal obligation to the organization, or a violation of law that reasonably might be imputed to the organization, and that is likely to result in substantial injury to the organization, then the lawyer shall proceed as is reasonably necessary in the best interest of the organization. Unless the lawyer reasonably believes that it is not necessary in the best interest of the organization to do so, the lawyer shall refer the matter to higher authority in the organization, including, if warranted by the circumstances, to the highest authority that can act on behalf of the organization as determined by applicable law.[10]

Transposing this rule to the context of a government client may not be easy.[11] In our hypothetical scenario, who is the "highest authority" to whom the lawyer should report the decision of the Minister to pay off (with public funds) a blackmailing debtholder rather than risk disclosure of the Minister's own malfeasance? The head of state (for example, the President or Prime Minister)? The local legislature? Local law enforcement? Moreover, the resulting dust-up from such a disclosure will almost certainly test the boundary between bad decisions by a client (which the lawyer must dutifully accept) and corrupt or illegal decisions (which might entail a duty of reporting to a higher authority).

If "reporting up" is not an option, the only other remedy would be for the lawyer to withdraw from the representation altogether. In practice, of course, this would probably result in the Minister hiring new counsel, someone who would presumably be ignorant of the background to the whole affair. Unless the replacement lawyer regarded her predecessor's abrupt departure as a red flag suggesting that something was amiss, she will no doubt carry out the Minister's instruction to settle the matter on the terms he agreed with Vulturefund. While this outcome may salve the ethical sensibilities of the withdrawing lawyer, it does nothing to help the ultimate victims in this situation – the Ruritanian taxpayers.

---

[9]   *ABA Model Rules*, Rule 1.13, comment [3].
[10]   *ABA Model Rules*, Rule 1.13(b).
[11]   Even the American Bar Association's *Model Rules* recognize this. In a comment to Rule 1.13, the *Model Rules* note that although the duty defined in Rule 1.13 applies to governmental organizations:

> Defining precisely the identity of the client and prescribing the resulting obligations of such lawyers may be more difficult in the government context and is a matter beyond the scope of these Rules.

ABA Model Rules, Rule 1.13, comment [9].

IV.   CONFLICTS

For lawyers practicing in large law firms, the representation of sovereign clients can raise acute conflicts of interest issues. Consider, for example, the situation of a lawyer representing a sovereign in a large restructuring of the external debt of that sovereign. The creditors caught up in such an affair may number in the thousands. If the lawyer retained by the sovereign client belongs to a large law firm, the rule of "imputed disqualification"[12] will give rise to conflicts with other clients of the firm holding debt obligations of the afflicted sovereign.

This situation raises both a technical problem involving a lawyer's duty of client loyalty[13] and a client relationship problem.

A.   Technical Conflicts

Most law firms deal with the former by soliciting advance waivers of conflicts from their clients, often embodied in the engagement letter that the client will be asked to sign at the outset of the engagement. The text of such an advance conflicts waiver might typically read this way:

> The Firm represents many other companies and individuals. It is possible that, during the time we are representing the Company, some of our current or future clients will have disputes or transactions with the Company. By retaining us now, you agree that we may continue to represent, or undertake in the future to represent, existing or new clients in any matter, including litigation or bankruptcy proceedings, even if the interests of those other clients in such matters are directly adverse to those of the Company, but only on the following terms: absent your explicit consent, we will undertake such matters for other clients only if we conclude in good faith that our Firm can properly represent the interests of each client, and if such other matter is not substantially related to the matters in which we are representing or have represented the Company.

B.   Client Relations

Addressing the technical conflicts problem may be the easy part; handling client relationship issues will be more delicate. Financial institutions, as institutions, tend to be mature, experienced and worldly-wise. The individuals they employ, however, will be human beings with human emotions. When the vigorous representation of one client (the sovereign debtor) forces

---

[12]   The rule of imputed disqualification . . . gives effect to the principle of loyalty to the client as it applies to lawyers who practice in a law firm. Such situations can be considered from the premise that a firm of lawyers is essentially one lawyer for purposes of the rules governing loyalty to the client, or from the premise that each lawyer is vicariously bound by the obligation of loyalty owed by each lawyer with whom the lawyer is associated.

[13]   The *ABA Model Rules* describe the duty of loyalty in these terms:

Loyalty to a current client prohibits undertaking representation directly adverse to that client without that client's informed consent. Thus, absent consent, a lawyer may not act as an advocate in one matter against a person the lawyer represents in some other matter, even when the matters are wholly unrelated. The client as to whom the representation is directly adverse is likely to feel betrayed . . . In addition, the client on whose behalf the adverse representation is undertaken reasonably may fear that the lawyer will pursue that client's case less effectively out of deference to the other client . . .

ABA Model Rules, Rule 1.7, comment [6].

other clients (the creditors of that sovereign) to lose money – an inevitable outcome in a sovereign debt workout – a lawyer assisting the sovereign may receive anguished expressions of displeasure from those other clients. Sometimes these come directly to the lawyer working on the debt restructuring but often they are transmitted through the medium of that lawyer's partners and colleagues in the law firm.

When these expressions of unhappiness are conveyed to the lawyer working on the sovereign debt restructuring by a colleague, the ensuing conversation is bound to be awkward. It would, of course, be improper for the colleague to attempt – on behalf of a creditor client with whom they have a close relationship – to influence the advice being given by another lawyer in the firm to another client of the firm. That said, relaying to one's colleague the complaints of an aggrieved creditor will, implicitly or explicitly, be intended to do just that – nudge the colleague into tempering her advice to the sovereign client. Whatever its status under the rules of professional ethics, such a call undoubtedly breaches a rule of law firm etiquette.

V.   DISCLOSURE

One area that may sorely test the patience and ethical sense of a lawyer engaged to represent a sovereign client in a foreign financial transaction is the question of disclosure. The laws of many countries place upon the issuer of securities an obligation candidly to disclose to prospective purchasers all material information that may be needed for the investor to make an informed decision about whether to purchase the security. This is sometimes described as an obligation to refrain from material misstatements of fact in the offering documents and a duty to ensure that there are no material omissions from the information that is included. Many securities laws establish an inverse relationship between the presumed sophistication of a prospective investor of the security and the extent of the disclosure that the issuer must provide. An offering targeted at very sophisticated institutional investors might require relatively light disclosure while an offering directed to presumptively *un*sophisticated investors such as the general public would entail much more extensive disclosure. Finally, the law frequently imposes on the professionals engaged to assist in a securities offering – the bankers, lawyers and accountants – an independent obligation to use their reasonable efforts to ensure that the offering documents contain no material misstatements or omissions.

Issuers of securities frequently bridle at the demands of full and frank disclosure. After all, the purpose of the transaction is to *sell* the paper, not frighten prospective investors by a public airing of dirty laundry in the offering documents. Corporate issuers will sometimes balk when their professional advisers recommend (read insist) that unflattering, but material, information about the company, its history, its business prospects or its management be included in the offering materials.

Sovereign issuers share these sensitivities. The preparation of a disclosure document for a sovereign issuer can be a particularly uncomfortable experience for the professional advisers. Even more than corporate executives, politicians are reluctant to acknowledge publicly their failings as stewards of the country and its economy. Politics, or more accurately political fragility, can be a uniquely sensitive subject for sovereign issuers. For example, the author once had occasion to prepare a disclosure document for a sovereign client whose government had come to power in what might euphemistically be described as an extra-constitutional process. To make matters worse, the new administration had endured six attempted *coups d'état* early in its tenure in office. None of the attempts had succeeded, but it was beyond the author's skill to craft a completely anodyne English sentence describing a situation that screamed political fragility. Discussing the issue with the relevant government authorities was also not pleasant. Although this transaction was completed (with the sensitive disclosure included), there are many examples of sovereign issuers opting to cancel securities offerings rather than disclose information that their lawyers insisted could not be omitted. There must surely be many more instances, however, in which sovereign clients have cowed their lawyers into accepting a latitudinarian view of the word "material" in the context of disclosure documents.

VI.   CONCLUSION

There is an old adage to the effect that newspaper headlines never trumpet "Plane Lands Safely at Local Airport." Only mishaps garner headlines. Based only on a perusal of newspaper headlines, however, a casual observer might conclude that the aviation industry is facing a deep crisis.

Something similar happens with lawyers and their clients. The headlines tend to report instances of professional misconduct and ethical lapses. A casual observer reading those headlines might conclude that the legal profession is similarly facing a deep crisis. What the headlines do *not* reveal are the innumerable instances when the advice of legal professionals causes their clients to refrain from conduct that, while perhaps not illegal as such, would nonetheless trespass on a common understanding of what is fair, appropriate, proportional, mature and responsible. In short, what is ethical.

Many of the ethical considerations arising in the representation of sovereign clients will have their analogues in the representation of corporate clients. There are three main differences. First, the codes of professional ethics in many jurisdictions will spell out in detail how lawyers should approach ethical issues arising in a corporate context. Those guidelines may not easily be transposed for an attorney/client relationship with a sovereign. Second, the duty of faithful service owed by government officials to their citizens is even more extensive than the responsibility of officers and directors of a corporation to shareholders and employees. To "advise a sovereign" is normally just a shorthand way of saying that one is advising a group of public officials who in turn stand in an agent/principal relationship with the citizen body as a whole. As discussed above, both ethical and practical issues must be confronted if the lawyer comes to believe that the agent (the public officials) are faithless to their principal (the state and people of the country). Finally, sovereigns are sovereign. To a degree – but only to a degree – their behavior is shielded from the kind of inquiry and reprimand that similar conduct by a corporation might attract.

10. Law and ethics: the bank's fiduciary duty towards retail customers
Ruth Plato-Shinar

1.   INTRODUCTION

The fiduciary duty is the strictest duty that exists in the realm of private law. It imposes a stringent duty of loyalty and fidelity. The fiduciary must act in the best interests of his principal (the beneficiary). He is obliged to protect the latter's interests, and must prioritize them over every other interest, including his own.[1] It is therefore no wonder that the duty was associated with altruism and described as a "duty of angels".[2] Hence, the reluctance to apply it to banks whose goal is to make a profit.[3] After all, as was noted by the UK Court of Appeal, banks are not charitable institutions.[4]

In this chapter, I would like to propose a different approach to the fiduciary duty imposed on banks. In my view, the fiduciary duty of banks is not an altruistic duty, but rather a legal instrument designed to ensure a basic level of professional ethics in the activities of the banks. Therefore, not only is there no hindrance to imposing a fiduciary duty on the banks, but in many cases it is precisely the tool which renders the just and moral result in the circumstances. This conclusion is especially evident as regards retail customers, in view of their dependence on the bank; the inequality of power between the parties which leads to the vulnerability of the customers; the trust and confidence that customers place in the bank; and their expectations that the bank acts in their best interests.

The necessity to raise the ethical standards of the banks has become acute in recent years due to a series of scandalous cases, which made it clear that banks acted unfairly and dishonestly towards their customers (and in some cases even fraudulently and illegally). Banks adopted unethical practices, whose sole objective was to maximize their profits, whilst harming the interests of their customers. Suffice to mention the sub-prime crisis in the United States, which began by providing housing loans to customers with doubtful or no repayment ability, included a problematic securitization process, and eventually resulted in a global financial crisis; the LIBOR affair of 2012 which involved the largest international banks;[5] and the widespread mis-selling of PPI in the United Kingdom that, as at the time of writing, has

---

[1]   See section 3(c) below.

[2]   Aharon Barak, "A Judge on Judging: The Role of a Supreme Court in a Democracy", 116 Harvard L. Rev. 19, 92 (2002). Ruth Plato-Shinar, "An Angel Named 'The Bank': The Bank's Fiduciary Duty as the Basic Theory in Israeli Banking Law", 36 Common Law World Review 27 (2007).

[3]   E.P. Ellinger, Eva Lomnicka and C.V.M. Hare, *Ellinger's Modern Banking Law* 128–9 (5th edn., 2011) and the references mentioned there.

[4]   *National Westminster Bank plc v. Morgan* [1983] 3 All E R 85, 91 (CA).

[5]   See, for example: Liam Vaughan and Gavin Finch, "LIBOR Lies Revealed in Rigging of $300 Trillion Benchmark", *Bloomberg* (6 February 2013), available at https://www.bloomberg.com/news/articles/2013-01-28/libor-lies-revealed-in-rigging-of-300-trillion-benchmark.

led to more than 18.4 million complaints and £27 billion in compensation, and the affair is far from being ended.[6]

The unethical behavior of the banks is reflected, inter alia, in their misconduct costs.[7] In recent years, there has been a dramatic increase in misconduct costs of banks all over the world. Results for the 20 major international banks show an accelerated increase of their misconduct costs: From £199.97 billion in the period of 2008–12, to £264 billion in the period of 2012–16.[8] Following the Global Financial Crisis of 2007–9, the banking sector around the world has experienced unparalleled regulatory fines and court rulings that have raised growing concerns about banks' behavior.[9] These huge figures have brought to the fore discussions on a range of contentious policy issues, including the central role of ethics and culture in financial markets.

The unethical conduct of the banks has led to wide erosion of trust and confidence in the UK banking system, reflecting both poor individual and corporate standards of conduct. This erosion is not the result of a misplaced public perception, which could possibly be addressed by a public relations campaign; it is based on observations of what happened. The industry was not merely revealed as incompetent, but appeared morally bankrupt.[10] The erosion of trust is the long-term result of the systematic and deliberate change in the culture of banks, derived from the constant desire to maximize profits, even when it came at the expense of the customers. In addition to the loss of trust, the public has developed an unfavorable – and even hostile – attitude towards the banks, whose reputation has been severely damaged.[11]

This situation has led to various initiatives aimed at restraining the behavior of the banks and restoring a level of ethics into their operation. On the legislative and regulatory levels, in the United Kingdom a new Senior Managers Regime entered into force in March 2016, replacing the old Approved Persons Regime, with a stronger focus on conduct and culture. The Senior Managers Regime aims to support better decision-making by the banks, and ensure that senior managers be held accountable for breaches of regulations by the banks that fall within their areas of responsibility, if they fail to take reasonable steps to prevent them. In addition, a new Certification Regime was established, according to which firms will have to certify certain employees as being fit and proper to perform certain functions. Furthermore, new conduct

---

[6]   Lindsay Cook, "PPI – Hundreds of Thousands Could Still Claim Compensation", *Financial Times* (29 June 2017), available at https://www.ft.com/content/2f03811a-5283-11e7-a1f2-db19572361bb. See also: FCA: Payment Protection Insurance Explained, available at https://www.fca.org.uk/ppi/ppi -explained (last retrieved 24 February 2018).

[7]   Ruth Plato-Shinar and Keren Borenstein-Nativ, "Misconduct Costs of Banks – The Meaning behind the Figures", 32 BFLR 495 (2017).

[8]   CCP Research Foundation: Conduct Costs Results, available at http://conductcosts .ccpresearchfoundation.com/conduct-costs-results.

[9]   Taku Dzimwasha, "20 Global Banks Have Paid $235bn in Fines since the 2008 Financial Crisis", *International Business Times* (24 May 2015), available at http://www.ibtimes.co.uk/20-global-banks -have-paid-235bn-fines-since-2008-financial-crisis-1502794#.

[10]   The Kay review of UK Equity Markets and Long-Term Decision Making – Final Report, section 6.1 (July 2012), available at https://www.gov.uk/government/consultations/the-kay-review-of-uk-equity -markets-and-long-term-decision-making. House of Lords, House of Commons: Changing Banking for Good – Report of the Parliamentary Commission on Banking Standards, Vol. 2 at 82–3, 85 (June 2013), available   at   http://www.parliament.uk/business/committees/committees-a-z/joint-select/professional -standards-in-the-banking-industry/news/changing-banking-for-good-report/.

[11]   Changing Banking for Good, ibid, at 85.

rules for senior managers and individuals covered by the certification regime, were issued.[12] These initiatives intend to ensure that staff at all levels be held to appropriate standards of behavior, and to improve standards of individual and market conduct across the industry.

Another measure was the launch, in June 2014, of the Fair and Effective Markets Review, whose goal was to examine the manner in which wholesale financial markets (FICC markets) operate, and recommend measures to restore trust in those markets. In June 2015 the Review published its final report, which contained recommendations aimed at raising standards, professionalism and accountability of individuals.[13]

In addition, voluntary measures have been taken by the industry itself. A good example is the establishment of the Banking Standards Board – a private sector body supported by Britain's banks and building societies, whose goal is to promote high standards of behavior and competence across the UK banking industry.[14]

Measures for increasing ethics and standards have been taken in other countries as well. In the Netherlands, the Dutch Central Bank now oversees banking culture as part of its supervisory assessment.[15] In July 2015, after conducting an extensive empirical research, the G30 issued a report which highlighted the main course of actions to change banking conduct and culture.[16]

These and similar measures may help improve banking standards, assuming they are actually implemented and strictly enforced. However, it is doubtful whether they can provide an effective-enough framework for ensuring the banks' fair and moral conduct towards their customers at the individual level, where a more concrete approach is required. Therefore, in addition, a solid legal instrument is required, that will prevent the banks from exploiting their power, forbid them from acting in conflicts of interests, and ensure that they act in the best interests of their customers. Such an instrument is the fiduciary duty.

The fiduciary duty is a legal concept. However, it stems from, and therefore strongly reflects, basic moral principles. Its concept, as a vague standard, left the courts with an extensive area for discretion and they applied it in a manner consistent with basic human and ethical attitudes. In those cases where a fiduciary duty was recognized, it constituted the desirable behavior from a moral perspective, and therefore justified its imposition. In other words, the fiduciary duty served as a legal tool for ensuring ethical behavior.

Indeed, in recent years, an increased recognition has evolved of the fiduciary duty as a vehicle for promoting moral standards in the financial sector. Thus, for example, the Kay

---

[12]   Financial Services (Banking Reform) Act 2013, Part 4. See also: PRA: Strengthening Accountability, available at http://www.bankofengland.co.uk/pra/Pages/supervision/strengtheningacc/default.aspx. FCA: Senior Managers and Certification Regime, available at https://www.fca.org.uk/firms/senior-managers-certification-regime. These changes are based on the recommendations of the report of the Parliamentary Commission on Banking Standards: Changing Banking for Good, *supra* note 10.

[13]   Fair and Effective Markets Review: Final Report (June 2015). In addition, in July 2016 it published an Implementation Report. Both reports are available at http://www.bankofengland.co.uk/markets/Pages/fmreview.aspx.

[14]   See their website at http://www.bankingstandardsboard.org.uk.

[15]   De Nederlandsche Bank: Supervision of Behaviour and Culture: Foundations, Practice & Future Developments, available at https://www.dnb.nl/binaries/Supervision%20of%20Behaviour%20and%20Culture_tcm46-334417.pdf.

[16]   G30: Banking Conduct and Culture, a Call for Sustained and Comprehensive Reform (July 2015), available at http://group30.org/images/uploads/publications/G30_BankingConductandCulture.pdf.

Review of UK Equity Markets and Long-Term Decision Making, whose final report was published in July 2012, recommended that all participants in the equity investment chain should observe fiduciary standards in their relationship with their clients and customers, and that contractual terms should not override these standards.[17] A comprehensive reference to fiduciary duties is also found in the Law Commission's report on Fiduciary Duties of Investment Intermediaries, which focused on fiduciary duties in the field of pensions.[18]

The aim of this chapter is to examine the nature of the fiduciary duty that should be imposed on banks towards their retail customers; to examine the implications of establishing the fiduciary duty as a general guideline for the behavior of the banks; and to outline a recommended format for ethical and legal implementation of this duty.

The structure of this chapter is as follows: In the next section, I present and analyze the nature of the fiduciary duty at the moral level, at the economic level of market activity, and at the managerial level of the banking business. My conclusion is that the fiduciary duty reflects basic business ethics which are expected from a bank as a professional body, and which also serves the interests of the bank itself. Hence, the rationale and legitimacy for applying it to the banks in their relationships with their customers.

In section 3, I examine the tests that have been developed in the case-law for recognizing fiduciary relationships. I claim that these tests are satisfied in the day-to-day relationship between the banks and their retail customers, and therefore justify the imposition of a general fiduciary duty on the banks towards retail customers. Section 3 continues with an examination of the contents of the bank's fiduciary duty, and claims that the duty includes not only prohibitions but also positive obligations. The section perceives the duty as a dynamic duty whose scope may vary according to the circumstances of each particular case.

Section 4 focuses on the ability to make stipulations in respect of the bank's fiduciary duty. It acknowledges such ability but conditions it on a few requisites. Section 5 concludes with insights about the bank's fiduciary duty, which may be applicable to other financial intermediaries as well.

2. THE FIDUCIARY DUTY

(a) The Nature of Fiduciary Duty

Fiduciary duty is the highest duty of loyalty.[19] The fiduciary must act with the utmost loyalty and fidelity vis-à-vis his principal (the beneficiary). The fiduciary must focus on the interest of the beneficiary, promote it and protect it. He must act in the beneficiary's "best interest".[20] Moreover, the fiduciary must prefer the interest of the beneficiary to any other interest. The

---

[17] Kay Report, *supra* note 10, Principle 5 at 65, and Recommendation 7 at 67.

[18] Law Commission: Fiduciary Duty of Investment Intermediaries (June 2014), available at http://www.lawcom.gov.uk/wp-content/uploads/2015/03/lc350_fiduciary_duties.pdf ("the Law Commission Report").

[19] In the past, the term "fiduciary duties" has been used in a broad sense to cover all the various duties a fiduciary owes. However, the courts ruled that this term should be confined only to the duty of loyalty, which is peculiar to fiduciaries. See: *Bristol & West Building Society v. Mothew* [1998] Ch 1, 16. The Law Commission Report, supra note 18, at 33, and the authorities mentioned there.

[20] Benjamin J. Richardson, *Fiduciary Law and Responsible Investment* 116–17 (2013).

duty of loyalty obligates the fiduciary to put the interest of the beneficiary first, ahead of the interests of third parties, and even ahead of the fiduciary's self-interest. Not only is it forbidden for the fiduciary to harm the interests of the beneficiary, but he must stifle and suppress his personal interests in order to promote the interests of the beneficiary.[21]

Because of the fear that the fiduciary may not resist temptation and prefer its personal interest or other extraneous interests over the interests of the beneficiary, the fiduciary duty includes a prohibition on conflicts of interest.[22] The prohibition on conflicts of interest can be divided into two main categories: The fiduciary must avoid acting where there is a conflict between his duty and his interest (a "duty-interest" conflict), and also where there is a conflict between duties that he owes to multiple beneficiaries (a "duty-duty" conflict).[23] An additional prohibition is the "no profit rule": A fiduciary should not make any profit by virtue of his position. The fiduciary duty does not prevent fiduciaries from being paid for their services on a commercial basis. Rather, it does prohibit the fiduciary from making a profit from the discharge of his duties.[24]

Requiring a person to act in the interests of another party and to prefer them over his own personal interests, is an extremely stringent duty. In fact, in the sphere of the private law, there is no obligation that sets a conduct threshold higher than the fiduciary duty.

The fiduciary duty is a stricter duty in comparison to the duty of care that arises in the law of tort. The duty of care merely requires reasonable care and skill. According to this duty, a person need not possess the highest tier of expert skill. It is sufficient he exercises the ordinary skills of an ordinary, competent, person, exercising that particular art.[25] In contrast, the fiduciary duty requires a different and much stricter behavior: It requires a person to act unequivocally for the interests of another, whilst acting in a reasonable manner would not suffice. Whereas, the duty of care guards against carelessness and incompetence, the fiduciary duty guards against abuse of power. It is intended to prevent the fiduciary from abusing its power to the detriment of the beneficiary. Whilst the duty of care is intended to prevent damages, the fiduciary duty considers the underlying motive or purpose of a decision[26] and is intended to

---

[21] *Bristol & West Building Society v. Mothew, supra* note 19, at 1, 16, 18. Deborah A. DeMott, "Beyond Metaphor: An Analysis of Fiduciary Obligation", Duke L. J. 879, 882 (1988). Plato-Shinar, *supra* note 2, at 29. Kay Report, *supra* note 10, section 9.6. On the notion of fiduciary duty as "self-denial" see: Sarah Worthington, "Fiduciaries: When is Self-Denial Obligatory?", 58 Cambridge L. J. 500 (1999).

[22] Rashid Bahar and Luc Thevenoz, "Conflicts of Interest: Disclosure, Incentives and the Market", in *Conflicts of Interest – Corporate Governance & Financial Markets* 1 (Luc Thevenoz and Rashid Bahar eds. 2007).

[23] M. Conaglen, "Fiduciary Regulation of Conflicts between Duties", 125 Law Quarterly Review 111, 140 (2009). The Law Commission Report, *supra* note 18, at 41–2. *Bristol & West Building Society v. Mothew, supra* note 19, at 18–19.

[24] Kay Report, *supra* note 10, at section 9.6. The Law Commission Report, *supra* note 18, at 42–3. *Regal (Hastings) Ltd v. Gulliver* [1967] 2 AC 135. S. Sealy, "Some Principles of Fiduciary Obligation", Cambridge L. J. 119, 128, 132–5 (1963). E.J. Weinrib, "The Fiduciary Obligation" 25 U.T.L.J. 1, 2. (1975). See also: J.R. Maurice Gautreau, "Demystifying the Fiduciary Mystique", 68 Canadian Bar Rev. 1, 26, 27 (calling for flexibility in the implementation of the non-profit rule).

[25] *Bolam v. Friern Hospital Management Committee* [1957] 1 WLR 582, 586.

[26] Law Commission: Fiduciary Duty of Investment Intermediaries – Consultation Paper No. 215 (2013) section 6.34, available at http://www.lawcom.gov.uk/wp-content/uploads/2015/03/cp215_fiduciary_duties.pdf.

prevent disloyal decisions and actions. It is therefore possible for a breach of fiduciary duty to occur without any breach of a duty of care, and without any damage being caused.[27]

The fiduciary duty determines a standard of conduct even higher than the duty of good faith, which is broadly used in civil law jurisdictions. The duty of good faith determines a minimum standard of appropriate behavior (*bona fides*), while the fiduciary duty requires a supreme standard of behavior (*uberrima fides*). The duty of good faith is based on rules of fair play between adversaries who act to advance their own self-interests. The fiduciary duty, on the other hand, is not based on rivalry, but on one single interest that the fiduciary must protect, which is the interest of the beneficiary.[28] While the duty of good faith requires a person to act fairly in the course of pursuing his own personal interest, the fiduciary duty requires him to act fairly for the best interests of his beneficiary, and to prefer the interest of the beneficiary over his own personal interest.

(b)   Fiduciary Duty and Altruism

Based on the above analysis, there is no wonder that the fiduciary duty was recognized as an altruistic duty,[29] and described by the metaphor "an angel's behavior".[30]

However, the metaphorical description of the fiduciary duty as an angel's duty and its association with altruism, have been intended to emphasize its uniqueness and severity, rather than characterize it as an altruistic duty in the accepted sense of this term. The association between fiduciary duty and altruism has given the duty some rhetorical power, visualizing an alternative approach to financial markets that is less driven by financial gain and more attuned to the needs of customers, investors and other stakeholders.[31]

The implication of presenting the fiduciary duty as an altruistic duty is particularly evident in the financial context, due to the ostensible contradiction between the definition of a financial institution as a profit-making institution, and the apparent requirement that it should deviate from its goal and ignore its own economic interest. This apparent contradiction is the reason for the exaggerated fear of those who are deterred from implementing the fiduciary duty in the financial markets. However, the fiduciary duty does not require financial institutions to discard their economic interest, as shall be explained below.

At first glance, phenomena such as altruism, cooperation and trust contradict the paradigm of classical economics, which places self-interest as the sole engine of market behavior. However, the fiduciary duty is not necessarily exogenous to the logic of business activity. Contemporary theoretical economists have challenged the identification of rational behavior with benefit-based considerations. They emphasized the existence of non-vested motives in

---

[27]   A question that exceeds the scope of this chapter is whether compensation should be awarded in such a case.

[28]   Barak, *supra* note 2.

[29]   Peter Birks, "The Content of Fiduciary Obligation", 34 Isr. L. Rev. 3, 14–22, 37 (2000). This description of the fiduciary duty can be found in various rulings of the Israeli Supreme Court. See: Ruth Plato-Shinar, *The Bank's Fiduciary Duty – the Duty of Loyalty* 22 (2010, in Hebrew).

[30]   Plato-Shinar, *supra* note 2.

[31]   The Law Commission Report, *supra* note 18, at 5. Anna Tilba and Terry McNulty, "Engaged versus Disengaged Ownership: The Case of Pension Funds in the UK", 21 Corporate Governance: An International Review 165, 172 (2013).

the operation of markets, and the contribution of trust to the efficiency of economic actions.[32] Laboratory studies have shown that, in many cases, considerations of fairness were stronger than considerations of benefit, and therefore they were the ones that ultimately directed behavior.[33] Game theory researchers have described situations in which a strategy guided by self-interest would lead to worse results than those that could be achieved through cooperation based on mutual trust.[34] The role of non-selfish considerations was particularly prominent in long-term relationships, in which mutual expectations developed, creating a nexus of commitment between the parties.[35] The consequence is that as measures intended to create trust, not only do they not contradict the nature of economic relations, they actually constitute an essential component in their construction.

The willingness to promote the interests of another person was also discussed in philosophical literature. Most appropriate here are the words of John Stuart Mill:

> When a person, either by express promise or by conduct, has encouraged another to rely upon his continuing to act in a certain way – to build expectations and calculations, and stake any part of his plan of life upon that supposition – a new series of moral obligations arises on his part towards that person, which may possibly be overruled, but cannot be ignored.[36]

From the above it appears that establishing a binary relation between an act for promoting a personal interest, and a concern for the interests of others, does not suit the concept of the marketplace as the meeting point for the expectations of the parties.

This conclusion is especially true in respect of the banks and their relationships with their customers. The banking system, which is the mainstay of an economy, is based on concepts such as trust, integrity and loyalty, and their absence endangers its existence. Therefore, it is not unreasonable to impose a fiduciary duty on the banks, a duty which is intended to promote these values.

The representation of the fiduciary duty as the absolute opposite of rational economic behavior is also incompatible with the prevailing concept of Corporate Social Responsibility (CSR). According to this concept, the fiduciary duty towards customers is not merely an abstract theoretical requirement, but a guiding principle in shaping the business strategy of the banking corporation operating in the free market. Many banks are no longer satisfied with the publication of financial statements as required by law, and voluntarily (as yet) also publish social responsibility reports. In the focus of these reports, we usually find the bank's credo which can be seen as a declaration of intent regarding its commitment to its customers, and

---

[32] Kenneth J. Arrow, "Social Responsibility and Economic Efficiency", 21 Public Policy 303 (1973). Amartya K. Sen, *On Ethics and Economics* (1987); Amartya K. Sen, "Does Business Ethics Make Economic Sense?", 3 Business Ethics Quarterly 45 (1993).

[33] Daniel Kahneman *et al*, *Rationality, Fairness, Happiness – Selected Writings* (Maya Bar-Hillel ed., 2005, in Hebrew). Robert H. Frank, *Passions within Reasons: The Strategic Role of Emotions* (1988). Richard H. Thaler, *The Winner's Curse: Paradoxes and Anomalies of Economic Life* (1992).

[34] Avinash K. Dixit and Barry J. Nalebuff, *Thinking Strategically: The Competitive Edge in Business, Politics, and Everyday Life* (1993). William Poundstone, *Prisoner's Dilemma: John von Neumann, Game Theory, and the Puzzle of the Bomb* (1993). David Gauthier, *Morals by Agreement* (1986).

[35] On parties' expectations in a long-term contract, see the text near note 30.

[36] John Stuart Mill, *On Liberty*, Chapter 5 "Applications", at paragraph 11 (originally published in 1869).

which shows the strategic nature of this commitment.[37] In addition, banks voluntarily publish ethical codes, purporting to show their commitment to ethical conduct in their relationship with their customers.[38]

It seems that the description of the fiduciary duty as the behavior of angels does not match the empirical reality of the market, since social responsibility is not only an external constraint on business operations, but also a growing strategic asset that promotes the business aspirations for success and profit. The flagship carriers of social responsibility emphasize its positive contribution to business success from various angles: Improving image and reputation, differentiation from competitors, strengthening consumers' satisfaction, increasing sales, rising stock prices, encouraging innovation, increasing productivity, ensuring good quality of services, strengthening the loyalty of veteran employees, and increasing the attractiveness for prospective employees.[39] The fiduciary duty, which requires social and ethical behavior, should therefore be seen as a vehicle for designing the business strategy of the bank, rather than an onus or burden.

An examination of the bank-customer relationship will lead to the conclusion that imposing a fiduciary duty is not an excessive requirement. The customer relies on the bank that, within the defined limits of its function, will act in his favor. The customer expects that the bank will exercise its power in the best possible professional manner, to guard his interests. The fiduciary duty is intended to ensure that these legitimate expectations are fulfilled by the bank as a professional body, and nothing more.

Based on the above analysis of the fiduciary duty, it seems that it would not be unreasonable to impose a fiduciary duty on the banks towards their customers. This conclusion is especially true in respect of retail customers, due to their special idiosyncrasies, as will be explained in the next section.

3. THE BANK'S FIDUCIARY DUTY TOWARDS RETAIL CUSTOMERS

(a) Recognizing Fiduciary Relationship

Fiduciary relationships arise under two main circumstances: Firstly, where a relationship falls within a previously recognized category, such as solicitor and client ("status-based fiduciaries"); and secondly, where the particular circumstances of a specific relationship justify imposing fiduciary duties ("fact-based fiduciaries").[40]

---

[37]   See, for example: Barclays Bank – Citizenship Report 2013, Strategy – at 8, The Way we Do Business – at 20–1. HSBC Holdings plc: Environmental, Social and Governance (ESG) Update 6–11 (April 2017), available at http://www.hsbc.com/our-approach/sustainability/sustainability-quick-read.

[38]   See, for example: The Barclays Way – How We Do Business, available at https://www.home .barclays/citizenship/our-approach/code-of-conduct.html. HSBC Statement on Conduct (April 2017), available at http://www.hsbc.com/our-approach/risk-and-responsibility/our-conduct.

[39]   Michael E. Porter and Mark R. Kramer, "Strategy & Society: The Link between Competitive Advantage and Corporate Social Responsibility", 84 Harv. Bus. Rev. 78 (2006). David Vogel, *The Market for Virtue: The Potential and Limits of Corporate Social Responsibility* (2005).

[40]   J. Edelman, "When do Fiduciary Duties Arise?" (2010) 126 Law Quarterly Review 302, 304–5. The Law Commission Report, *supra* note 18, at 34. Paul B. Miller, "A Theory of Fiduciary Liability", 56 McGill L. J. 235, 240–7 (2011).

According to English law, the bank-customer relationship has not been considered as falling within the first category of status-based fiduciaries. The reluctance to acknowledge the fiduciary relationship has even extended to retail customers, who might be considered more vulnerable when dealing with the bank.[41] The courts were only willing to acknowledge a fiduciary relationship between a bank and its customers in specific – and rather rare – cases, emphasizing the unique circumstances of the concrete case.[42]

In this section I argue that the relationship between the bank and its retail customers should be recognized as a status-based fiduciary relationship, imposing on the bank a duty of loyalty towards these customers.

The question of when a fiduciary relationship will be acknowledged is not easy to answer. Over the years, several tests have been developed in the case-law and legal literature to identify fiduciary relationships. Not only is there no single ultimate test for this purpose, the diverse tests applied have been stated in several distinctive ways, creating different variations; a situation that proves the difficulty of such a determination. Having said this, the major tests can be generally summarized as follows.

An undertaking to act for or on behalf of another person

According to one approach, a person would be subject to a fiduciary duty if he undertook to act for or on behalf of another person.[43] In the leading case of *Bristol and West Building Society v. Mothew*,[44] the idea of a voluntary undertaking was adopted in a similar – yet stricter – manner: "A fiduciary is someone who has undertaken to act for or on behalf of another in a particular matter in circumstances which give rise to a relationship of trust and confidence."[45] A similar definition suggested that "for a person to be a fiduciary he must first and foremost have bound himself in some way to protect and/or to advance the interests of another."[46]

Legitimate expectations

According to this test, a fiduciary relationship will be recognized where the circumstances of the relationship are such that one party is entitled to expect that the other will act in his interests and for the purposes of the relationship.[47] Ascendancy, influence, vulnerability, trust, confidence or dependence, undoubtably would be of importance in implementing this test.

---

[41]   Ellinger, Lomnicka and Hare, *supra* note 3, at 129, and the references mentioned there.

[42]   Ruth Plato-Shinar, "The Bank's Fiduciary Duty: An Israeli-Canadian Comparison", 22 BFLR 1, 7–12 (2006). Ellinger, Lomnicka and Hare, *supra* note 3, at 129.

[43]   Edelman, *supra* note 40. P.D. Finn, *Fiduciary Obligations* 201 (1977). A. Scott, "The Fiduciary Principle", 37 California L. Rev. 539, 540 (1948–9). Sealy, *supra* note 24, at 72–9. Margaret H. Ogilvie, "Canadian Bank Lender Liability: Semper Caveat Lender", in *Banks, Liability and Risk* 279, 289 (William Blair ed., 3rd edn., 2001). John D. McCamus, "Prometheus Unbound: Fiduciary Obligation in the Supreme Court of Canada", 28 Canadian Bus L. J. 107, 118 (1997).

[44]   *Bristol and West Building Society v. Mothew, supra* note 19.

[45]   Ibid, at 18.

[46]   Finn, *supra* note 43, at 9 (1977). J.C. Shepherd, *The Law of Fiduciaries* 64–71 (1981). In Canada: *Galambos v. Perez* [2009] 3 S.C.R. 247, at paragraph 66. *Alberta v. Elder Advocates of Alberta* [2011] 2 S.C.R. 261, at paragraph 28. *Scaravelly v. Bank of Montreal* (2004), 69 O.R. (3d) 295, [2004] at paragraph 33.

[47]   *Arklow Investments Ltd v. Maclean* [2000] 1 WLR 594, 598. The Law Commission Report, *supra* note 18, at 36, 38. Finn, *supra* note 43, at 46. DeMott, *supra* note 21, at 938–41.

However, it is not quite clear if they are vital elements for the creation of the entitlement, or only evidence a relationship suggesting that entitlement.[48]

Power and discretion
According to another prevailing approach, the power or discretion that one party has in respect of another party's affairs, may create a fiduciary relationship.[49] According to Canadian case-law, three elements are required in this regard: The fiduciary has scope for the exercise of some discretion or power;[50] he can unilaterally exercise that power or discretion, so as to affect the beneficiary's legal or practical interests; the beneficiary is peculiarly vulnerable to or at the mercy of the fiduciary holding the discretion or power.[51]

Trust and confidence/reliance
The trust and confidence that one party places in another party, or the reliance of one party upon the other, serve as a basis for recognizing a fiduciary relationship as well.[52] In *Lloyds Bank v. Bundy*,[53] a combined test of four elements was adopted in this regard: The bank provided advice or guidance upon which the customer relied; the bank was aware of this reliance; the bank derived a benefit from the transaction; and the relationship was one of a confidential nature, in the sense of a special relationship that "once it exists, influence naturally grows out of it."[54]

Although, from an analytical point of view, the different tests mentioned above can be presented as separate tests, their use in the case-law has usually been combined.[55] The courts very often use several tests in order to strengthen their conclusion,[56] or provide a complex argument which mixes elements of the different tests.[57] From a general survey of the main judgments, it

---

[48]   P.D. Finn, "The Fiduciary Principle", in *Equity, Fiduciaries and Trusts* (T. Youdan ed., 1989) 1, 46–8.

[49]   Shepherd, *supra* note 46, at 83–8 (1981). At 93, 96 he suggests: "A fiduciary relationship exists whenever any person acquires a power of any type on condition that he also receive with it a duty to utilize that power in the best interests of another, and the recipient of the power uses that power." Weinrib, *supra* note 24.

[50]   On the requirement of discretionary power, see: Robert Flannigan, "Fact-Based Fiduciary Accountability in Canada", 36 The Advocate's Quarterly 431 (2010).

[51]   *Lac Minerals Ltd. v. International Corona Resources Ltd.* [1989] 2 S.C.R. 574. *Hodgkinson v. Simms* [1994] 3 SCR 377 at 405. *Scaravelly v. Bank of Montreal, supra* note 46, at paragraph 32. Ellinger, Lomnicka and Hare, *supra* note 3, at 139 and the references mentioned there. The Law Commission Report, *supra* note 18, at 37.

[52]   Shepherd, *supra* note 46, at 56–60.

[53]   *Lloyds Bank Ltd v. Bundy* [1975] QB 326 (CA).

[54]   Ibid, at 341. See also: *Woods v. Martins Bank* [1959] 1 QB 55. In Canada: *Standard Investments Ltd v. Canadian Imperial Bank of Commerce* (1985) 22 DLR (4th) 410. *Scaravelly v. Bank of Montreal, supra* note 46, at paragraph 37. In the US: *Klein v. First Edina National Bank*, 196 NW 2d 619, 623 (1972) 623.

[55]   Edelman, *supra* note 40, at 317.

[56]   See, for example: *Scaravelly v. Bank of Montreal, supra* note 46.

[57]   See, for example: *Hodgkinson v. Simms, supra* note 51.

is not clear whether the different tests are equal to each other and may apply alternatively, or preside over each other.[58]

A motive that repeats in numerous rulings, albeit not as an independent test, is the issue of vulnerability, and not in vain. The vulnerability of a person may explain his reliance on the other party; the trust and confidence that he places in the other party; his subjection to the power and discretion of the other party; and the creation of legitimate expectations on his side that the other party would guard his interests or even act in his best interests. However, while some authorities considered vulnerability as "indispensable" or a key element for the identification of fiduciary duties; others reiterated that it is not an essential element, surely not the hallmark of the relationship.[59]

As we shall see below, the special characteristics of the relationship between the bank and its retail customers meet the tests mentioned above, thus giving rise to the recognition of this relationship as a fiduciary relationship.

(b)   The Special Characteristics of the Bank's Retail Customers

The idea of customers' classification is not new. It can be found in various legislative and regulatory instruments that require banks and financial firms to categorize their retail customers,[60] as well as in court decisions that have considered the type of customer in their rulings.[61] Indeed, the relationship between the bank and its retail customers is different from the relationship with other clients, due to the special idiosyncrasies of retail customers, as will be explained below.

(1)   The Customer's Inferiority and Vulnerability

The major idiosyncrasy of the relationship between the bank and its retail customer is the great inequality of power between the parties. There are huge disparities in the level of professional knowledge; in the technical methods of managing and monitoring financial activities; in the financial power of the parties; and in their bargaining power.

Another advantage that the bank has over its customer is that of information: The bank has a vast amount of information regarding the products and services it provides, whereas the customer is less well informed ("information asymmetries").[62] Since the products on offer are often complex and

---

[58]   For criticism on the unclear approach of the Anglo-Canadian Law, see: Plato-Shinar, *supra* note 42, at 9–12.

[59]   Shaunnagh Dorsett, "Comparing Apples and Oranges: The Fiduciary Principle in Australia and Canada after *Breen V Williams*", 8 Bond L. R. 158 (1996). See also: McCamus, *supra* note 43, at 122–3 (1997). Anthony Duggan, "Fiduciary Obligations in the Supreme Court of Canada: A Retrospective", 50 Canadian Buss L. J. 453, 458–9 (2011).

[60]   See, for example: FCA Handbook COBS 3.3, and the definition of a "retail client" in COBS 3.4.1R. Directive 2014/65/EU of the European Parliament and of the Council of 15 May 2014 on Markets in Financial Instruments and Amending Directive 2002/92/EC and Directive 2011/61/EU ("MiFID II"), Article 4(1)(11). Compare to the Kay Report, *supra* note 10, Recommendation 7 at 67, suggesting that fiduciary obligations should be "independent of the classification of the client".

[61]   The Law Commission Report, *supra* note 18, at section 10.11.

[62]   Peter Cartwright, *Banks, Consumers and Regulation* 16–17 (2004).

difficult to evaluate, customers are particularly vulnerable to unscrupulous offerings for services and products that do not necessarily suit their needs.[63]

In addition, customers tend to suffer from cognitive biases, such as over optimism, which lead to imperfect choices and financial mistakes. Such mistakes are particularly serious in the case of large transactions that extend over long periods of time, such as home mortgages, since even a small mistake can cumulate into large losses by the time the product matures.[64]

These differences between the parties lead to serious inferiority and the vulnerability of the customer.

The customer's inferiority and vulnerability in his dealings with the bank, characterizes every stage of their relationship: From the negotiation stage through to signing the banking contract, the execution period of the contract, and up until the termination of the relationship. The customer's vulnerability is also reflected in instances of legal disputes with the bank, given the existence of a great inequality in the financial ability to conduct legal proceedings, the difficulties of proof that stem from the lack of full information in the negotiation stage, and the lack of previous experience in legal conflicts.[65]

However, the inferiority of a party to a contract is not a sufficient reason for a regulatory intervention in the contractual relationship. The intervention is justified only where the inferiority is accompanied by a genuine concern that the weaker party may be unfairly taken advantage of by the party holding the power. Such concern has materialized in the banking reality more than once. The scandals that have happened over the years illustrate the risks inherent in the inequality of power between the bank and its customer, and the genuine fear of the abuse of the bank's power to the detriment of the customer.

In addition to the concern that power might be abused, inferiority becomes problematic when it creates a dependency of the weaker party on the stronger party. And when the dependency is related to vital services, as is the case with banking services, it becomes even more severe, as will be explained below.

(2) The Customer's Dependence on the Bank

The relationship between the bank and the retail customer creates a strong dependency of the customer upon the bank. The customer is dependent on the bank for the provision of the service, in the manner in which it is performed, in the determination of the price, as well as in the determination of the legal arrangement that applies to it.

The provision of the service
A discretion is conferred upon the bank to agree or refuse to carry out a banking transaction that the customer requests. A customer's dependence on a service provider is not exclusive to the banking sector and therefore it is insufficient, *per se*, to justify a regulatory intervention. However, what distinguishes it in the banking context is the fact that this is a dependency that relates to the provision of services that are vital for the public.[66] There is no person or entity today that does not

---

[63]   John Armour *et al*, *Principles of Financial Regulation* 55–7 (2016).
[64]   Ibid, at 206–12.
[65]   Orna Deutch, *The Legal Status of Consumers* 537 (2002, in Hebrew).
[66]   This argument on the vitality of the banking services was used by the Israeli courts to acknowledge the banks as "quasi-public" bodies. See Ruth Plato-Shinar, *Banking Regulation in Israel: Prudential Regulation versus Consumer Protection*, 40–4 (2016).

require banking services in one way or another: Credit for various needs, a housing loans, bank guarantees, investment counseling for small savings, or making payments by means of debit orders or bank transfers. Even those customers whose financial activities are limited to receiving a salary as an employee or receiving allowances from the government, need bank accounts where they cannot receive the payment in cash. This essentiality of banking services increases the customers' dependence on the bank.

The manner of the performance of the service

The customer is unable to effectively supervise the bank's activities because he lacks the professional know-how and technical means required. In addition, the customer usually receives information about what is happening in his account, only retrospectively. Thus, even hiring professional inspection services, which involve a high financial cost, will not solve the problem of supervision.[67] The customer is left with no alternative but to rely on the professionalism and integrity of the bank in performing its duties, which increases his dependence on the bank.

The prices of the banking services

In most countries, there is no supervision over bank fees, and the banks are free to determine the price of their services without any formal limit. In banking systems that are characterized by a lack of competition, these prices may be rather high and lead to unfair fee arrangements.[68] The retail customer has no actual power of negotiation regarding fees, and he very often has no choice but to pay the fee dictated by the bank. Indeed, in many other sectors the prices of products or services are pre-determined by the supplier. But here – as was previously mentioned – the service is vital, which creates dependency of the customer and no choice but to pay the dictated fees.

Determining the legal rule that applies to the relationship

The customer is dependent on the bank's power and discretion in this regard as well. The banking contract is a standard contract that is drafted in advance by the bank. Even if the bank agrees to conduct negotiations with a certain customer regarding the terms of the contract, the basis of the negotiations is the original document that was prepared by the bank and which clearly protects its interests. The banking documents usually include a long list of obligations that are imposed on the customer. If a reference appears therein to the bank, this usually deals with the rights of the bank vis-à-vis the customer. Past legislation that was aimed at protecting customers against unfair contractual terms[69] has been criticized as being highly reactive and

---

[67] Tamar Frankel, "Fiduciary Law", 71 California L. Rev. 795, 813 (1983). Robert Cooter and Bradley J. Freedman, "The Fiduciary Relationship: Its Economic Character and Legal Consequences", 66 N.Y.U.L.Rev. 1045, 1049 (1991).

[68] This was the situation in Israel, which led to the Bank Fees Reform of 2007 and the imposition of supervision over the bank fees. See: Ruth Plato-Shinar, "The Bank Fees Regime in Israel – A Political Economy Perspective", in *Perspectives in the Political Economy of Financial Regulation* (Emilios Avgouleas and David C. Donald, eds., Cambridge University Press, forthcoming).

[69] Unfair Contract Terms Act 1977. Unfair Terms in Consumer Contracts Regulations 1999 (implementing the EU Directive: Council Directive 93/13/EC of 5 April 1993 on Unfair Terms in Consumer Contracts [1993] OJ L95/29). On the difficulties in implementing the EU Directive, see: Mel Kenny and James Devenney, "The Fragility of Unfair Terms Law on Bank Charges: Towards a Complex

incapable of dealing with unfair contract terms on a systemic basis.[70] It remains to be seen if the Consumer Rights Act 2015[71] will materially change this situation.

The difficulty in switching banks

The customer's dependence on the bank is intensified, given the difficulties of moving from bank to bank.[72] Even if a customer has a strong incentive to move to another bank, such as a substantial difference in the prices of the banking services or a significant difference in the level of customer service, the technical difficulties associated with the move deter many customers. Moreover, even if the difficulties of the move were resolved, and customers could switch easily between banks, the move to another bank would not alter the customer's situation or his dependence on the bank much. The inequality of power between the bank and the customer would continue to exist even after his move to a new bank. The customer is not only a captive in the hands of the bank where he manages his account, but in the hands of the banking system as a whole, due to the monopolistic nature and the inability to receive banking services outside the banking system.

(3)   The Bank's Control and Discretion

Where one party has control over the affairs and the assets of another party, either *de jure*, as a result of a legally defined relationship, or *de facto*, due to physical control, there is concern that the controlling party may abuse its power to the detriment of the other party.[73] Hence the need for setting rules to restrain the controlling party.

Restraining the control is particularly important with respect to those that manage money on behalf of others. One who manages his own affairs, and through his own means, is entitled to manage them as he deems fit, provided that this is not to the detriment of others and that he does not cause them damage. However, this is not the case with the activities of a person or institution that manages the affairs of others and that deals with the money of others. Not only is it prohibited for him to cause harm to the person whose affairs he manages or to cause him damage, but he has a duty to act with the utmost fairness.[74]

This is also true in the banking context: The bank is granted power and control over the financial interests of the customer, with regard to the banking transactions that the customer decides to perform. This power stems not only from the control over the money that has been placed with the bank, but also from the discretion that the bank has as to how to perform its duties. For example, discretion is conferred on the bank as to whether to provide a customer

---

Re-Litigation in the UK?", in *Credit, Consumers and the Law after the Global Storm* 223 (Karen Fairweather, Paul O'Shea and Ross Grantham, eds. 2015).

[70]   C. Scott and J. Black, *Cranston's Consumers and the Law* 80 (2000), as cited in: Paul O'Shea, "Unfair Contract Terms Legislation: Is It Good Consumer Law?", in *Credit, Consumers and the Law after the Global Storm* 203, 210 (Karen Fairweather, Paul O'Shea and Ross Grantham, eds. 2015).

[71]   Sections 62–64.

[72]   Office of Fair Trading: Review of the Personal Current Account Market 94–99 (January 2013), available at http://webarchive.nationalarchives.gov.uk/20140402142426/http:/www.oft.gov.uk/shared _oft/reports/financial_products/OFT1005rev.

[73]   In Israel: CA 817/79 *Kosoi v. Feuchtwanger Bank Ltd.*, 38(3) PD 253, 277 (1984).

[74]   Moshe Bejsky, "Trust Relations Between a Bank and a Customer", in *Landau Book*, Volume 3 – Articles, Part 2, 1095, 1097, 1099 (Aharon Barak & Elinoar Mazuz, eds. 1995, in Hebrew).

who runs a current account with a credit facility on that account. In the event that the bank approves a credit limit for the customer, the bank may cancel the facility or reduce it according to its unilateral decision. A bank that provides a customer with a loan may, upon the fulfillment of certain conditions, demand early repayment of the loan (acceleration clause). The bank has a discretion regarding the realization of collateral that has been provided by the customer as security for his obligations. The bank has a discretion in whether to help a customer who has difficulty with the repayment of his debts, through debt restructuring and so on. The variety of measures at the bank's disposal, which are intended to exert pressure on the customer in order to ensure recovery of the debt, combined with the internal information that the bank has about the customer, strengthens even more the bank's control over a customer's financial affairs.

(4)   Trust, Confidence and Customers' Expectations

The inferiority of the customer and his dependence upon the bank, as was explained above, leaves the customer no choice but to rely on the bank and endow special trust in it, substituting the customer's actual knowledge, understanding and ability to supervise the bank. The customer places total trust and confidence in the bank and relies on the bank's judgment and discretion. Customers rely on the bank to such an extent that they generally neither seek another opinion before acting according to the bank's advice, nor examine the bank's activity with a discerning eye. The customer expects the bank to behave towards him with an exemplary level of professionalism, responsibility and good faith. Moreover, the customer perceives the bank official as someone who wishes the best for him, and expects the bank to act in his best interests. Needless to say, the bank is not only aware of this situation, but even encourages its customers to continue doing so.[75] After all, the banks cannot exist without public trust.[76] Indeed, past scandals have eroded the public's trust in the banks, as was mentioned above. Nevertheless, the individual customer, in his daily interactions with his bank, still continues to trust the bank. The result is reasonable reliance of the customer upon the bank, and justifiable expectations that the bank would act in his best interests.

These characteristics of the relationship between the bank and the customer led to classifying the banking contract as a "relational contract".[77] A relational contract is a long-term contract that creates a continuing and close relationship between the parties. It is characterized by a high level of trust and solidarity. The parties' expectations are for fairness, integrity, and ability to rely on each other. Moreover, the mutual expectations create a nexus of commitment

---

[75]   See, for example: HSBC Statement on Conduct, *supra* note 38, Pillar Culture and Behaviours, at 1: "Our culture supports our people and empowers them to consistently do the right thing for our customers ... Our people are competent and committed to the fair treatment of customers ... We reward and incentivise performance, behaviours and attitudes which deliver the fair treatment of customers". See also: HSBC Holdings plc Strategic Report 2016, Building Lasting Business Relationships at 22, available at http://www.hsbc.com/our-approach/sustainability/sustainability-quick-read.

[76]   Report of the Parliamentary Commission on Banking Standards, *supra* note 10, at 83. Plato-Shinar, *supra* note 66, at 7–8.

[77]   The banking contract was recognized as a relational contract by the Israeli Supreme Court: MA 195/97 *The Attorney General v. Bank Leumi Le-Israel Ltd*, at paragraph 4 (Nevo Database, 2010).

between the parties that goes beyond the formal contract and may lead to the imposition of additional obligations that are not expressly included in the underlying contract.[78]

(5)   The Bank's Undertaking

As we saw above, one of the tests for acknowledging the fiduciary relationship is an undertaking to act for or on behalf of another, in circumstances which give rise to a relationship of trust and confidence. Based on the relationship of trust and confidence that exists between the banks and their retail customers, it seems that this test is met as well.

A review of the Corporate Social Responsibility (CSR) Reports of the banks reveals statements of intent regarding the banks' commitment to act for the benefit of their customers. At the focal point of these reports we usually find declarations that reflect the commitment perception of the banks to their customers. For example, the SCR Report of HSBC states:

> Our goal is to connect [our customers] to opportunities that fulfil their hopes and realise their ambitions. We do this by getting to know our customers, supporting them when they need us most, listening to understand their evolving needs, and addressing their concerns . . . Our customers are at the heart of everything we do.[79]

Albeit such a statement does not include an express undertaking to act in the best interests of the customers, this is clearly what it means, evidencing the bank's commitment to do so.

In summary, the special characteristics of the relationship between the bank and its retail customers justify the imposition of a fiduciary duty on the banks towards these customers, in order to ensure ethical behavior and to prevent the bank from abusing its power to the detriment of the customers.

The perception of the bank's fiduciary duty as a vehicle for ensuring standards of ethics in banking activities, leads to the conclusion that the fiduciary duty should apply to the entirety of the relationship between the bank and its retail customer, and to the full range of services that the bank provides to the customer.[80]

In contrast, the approach of the English case-law is different. The English courts do not perceive the bank-customer relationship as a fiduciary relationship, and are reluctant to impose fiduciary duties on the banks. They are willing to do so only in rare instances, usually in situations pertaining to investment advice. In the past, the courts also used the doctrine of

---

[78]   Ian R. Macneil, "Relational Contract Theory: Challenges and Queries", 94 New U. L. Rev. 877, 881 (2000). Charles J. Goetz and Robert E. Scott, "Principles of Relational Contracts", 67 Virginia Law Review 1089 (1981).

[79]   HSBC Environmental, Social and Governance (ESG) Update, *supra* note 37, at 6. See also: RBS: Strategic Report 2016 – Creating a Simple, Safe, Customer Focused Bank, at 19 ("Our Ambition: No. 1 for customer service, trust and advocacy"), and at 31 (about customers trust), available at http://investors .rbs.com/annual-report-2016.aspx.

[80]   This is the approach of the Israeli Courts. See: Plato-Shinar, *supra* note 42. Plato-Shinar, *supra* note 29, at 71–97 (2010, in Hebrew). Ruth Plato-Shinar, "The Banking Contract as a Special Contract – The Israeli Model" 29 Touro Law Review 721 (2013). Ruth Plato-Shinar, "The Bank's Fiduciary Duty under Israeli Law: Is there a Need to Transform it from an Equitable Principle into a Statutory Duty?" 41 Common Law World Rev. 219 (2012). Ruth Plato-Shinar and Rolf Weber, "Three Models of the Bank's Fiduciary Duty", 2 Law and Financial Markets Review 422 (2008).

fiduciary duty in cases of receiving collaterals, but over the years they have moved to using the doctrine of undue influence, instead.[81] The fiduciary duty is also recognized in some common activities of the multifunctional bank, such as where the bank acts as a trustee for the customer, custodian, or investment portfolio manager.[82] However, in all other areas of activity, namely in most of the banking activities, the bank-customer relationship is not considered as a fiduciary relationship.

I believe that an overall fiduciary duty should be recognized, embracing the relationships between the bank and its retail customers in their entirety.

(c) The Content of the Bank's Fiduciary Duty

As was explained in section 2(a) above, the bank's fiduciary duty is underpinned by the duty of loyalty. The bank must promote the interest of the customer, protect it, and prefer it over any other interests including its own. By virtue of the fiduciary duty, the bank is subject to a prohibition on conflicts of interest: The bank must avoid acting where there is a conflict between the interest of the customer and the interest of the bank, or between the interest of the customer and a duty that the bank owes to a third party. In addition, the bank must refrain from making any profit by virtue of its position, and has to make do with receiving payment for its services from the customer.[83]

Due to the strict nature of the prohibition on conflicts of interest and the central role that it plays in fiduciary relationships, the fiduciary duty is traditionally considered as proscriptive rather than prescriptive: It tells the fiduciary what he should not do, rather than what he should do.[84] However, the perception of the bank's fiduciary duty as a vehicle for ensuring ethical banking conduct and for fulfilling the legitimate expectations of the customers for fairness and loyalty, obliges us to pour comprehensive content into the duty, and to include both restrictions as well as positive obligations in it.

For example, by virtue of the fiduciary duty, the bank is subject to a wide duty of disclosure and explanation.[85] When a customer encounters financial difficulties and has trouble repaying a loan, the fiduciary duty may oblige the bank to show flexibility and agree on a leeway, such as extending the loan over a longer period of time and reducing the repayment installments. The fiduciary duty may impose on the bank rules of responsible lending, such as to tailor a requested loan to the customer's needs and repayment capability. Needless to say, the bank should refrain from providing credit to customers who do not have repayment capability, or from "pushing" loans to customers who do not really need them, thus creating situations of over-indebtedness. Similarly, the bank must avoid offering other financial products to cus-

---

[81]   Ellinger, Lomnicka and Hare, *supra* note 3, at 131–6.

[82]   *Supra* note 11, at 129.

[83]   As we shall see in section 4, these prohibitions can be contracted out by the parties.

[84]   The Law Commission Report, *supra* note 18, at 45, and the authorities mentioned there. Richardson, *supra* note 20, at 106–7 (2013).

[85]   Ruth Plato-Shinar, "The Bank's Duty of Disclosure – Towards a New Model", 27 BFLR 427 (2012). Plato-Shinar, "The Banking Contract as a Special Contract", *supra* note 80. This approach of the author was adopted by the Israeli Supreme Court and a few legal precedents were based on it. See, for example: CA 8611/06 *Hapoalim Bank v. Martin* (Nevo Database, 2006). CA 8564/06 *Sultani v. Bank Leumi LeIsrael Ltd* (Nevo Database, 2008). CA 11120/07 *Simchoni v. Hapoalim Bank Ltd* (Nevo Database, 2009).

tomers which are not aligned with their needs. In any event, the bank should avoid aggressive marketing aimed at convincing customers to purchase a service or a product that they do not really need.

The fiduciary duty may be applied in respect of bank fees as well: If, for example, it is possible to conduct a banking transaction in two different ways, when the fee applicable to one of those ways is lower than the other, then by virtue of fiduciary duty the bank is required to inform the customer of such disparity and enable the customer to choose the option bearing the lower fee.[86]

The fiduciary duty may also impact on the contents of the banking contract: Since the bank has the power to design the contract as it wishes, it is subject to the duty to protect the legitimate interests of the customer within the framework of the contract.[87]

The bank's fiduciary duty in respect of investment services, including investment advice, is covered by regulatory provisions. The FCA's Conduct of Business Sourcebook (COBS) requires that: "A firm must act honestly, fairly and professionally in accordance with the best interests of its client."[88] However, most of the services that the bank provides to its customers are not covered by similar provisions. Instead, the regulatory approach makes do with softened principles such as: "A firm must pay due regard to the interests of its customers and treat them fairly";[89] or "A firm must manage conflicts of interest fairly, both between itself and its customers and between a customer and another client";[90] or "A firm must take reasonable care to ensure the suitability of its advice and discretionary decisions for any customer who is entitled to rely upon its judgment."[91]

In some specific issues, the regulatory instruments impose concrete obligations on the banks which reflect specific aspects that derive from the fiduciary duty, such as obligations aimed at ensuring the suitability of services to the customer's needs;[92] restrictions on providing an optional product for which a fee is payable, without the customer's informed consent;[93] restrictions in respect of financial promotions to customers;[94] etc. Nevertheless, these regulatory obligations cannot substitute for a comprehensive fiduciary duty that applies to the entirety of the bank-customer relationship and to the diverse range of services provided by the bank. The

---

[86]   In Israel, an application for a class action in this matter was approved by the District Court, but dismissed by the Supreme Court: CA 4619/08 *Mercantile Discount Bank Ltd v. Ezrat Israel Dormitories* (Nevo Database, 2012). On the conservative approach of the Israeli Courts in respect of class actions against banks, see: Ruth Plato-Shinar, "Class Actions Against Banks Under the New Israeli Law On Class Actions", 26 Annual Review of Banking and Financial Law 256 (2007).

[87]   In Israel: CA 6234/00 *Sh.A.P. Ltd. v. Bank Leumi Le-Israel Ltd*, 57(6) PD 769, 788 (2003).

[88]   FCA Handbook COBS 2.1.1(1). Implementing Article 24(1) of MiFID II, *supra* note 60, which replaces Article 19(1) of Directive 2004/39/EC of the European Parliament and of the Council of 21 April 2004, on Markets in Financial Instruments, amending Council Directives 85/611/EEC and 93/6/EEC and Directive 2000/12/EC of the European Parliament and of the Council and repealing Council Directive 93/22/EEC, OJL 145 ("MiFID I").

[89]   FCA Handbook PRIN 2.2.1R, Principle 6.

[90]   FCA Handbook PRIN 2.2.1R, Principle 8.

[91]   FCA Handbook PRIN 2.2.1R, Principle 9.

[92]   FCA Handbook COBS 9.

[93]   FCA Handbook BCOBS 2A.1.

[94]   FSMA 2000, section 21. FCA Handbook COBS 4. FCA Handbook BCOBS 2. FCA Handbook MCOB 3A.

significance of the fiduciary duty is particularly evident in those issues and cases that are not covered by regulatory provisions.

In addition, it should be noted that customers who have suffered a loss as a result of a breach of the FCA's Principles for Businesses (PRIN), have no right of action against the bank for breach of statutory duty under section 138D of the Financial Services and Markets Act 2000.[95] A breach of the FCA's Conduct of Business rules (COBS, MCOB, BCOBS) is actionable,[96] but under strict limitations rendering them difficult to implement.[97] Thus, for example, it is doubtful whether any claims have been successfully brought for the breach of the "best interest rule" under COBS 2.1.1.[98] In contrast, a breach of the "judge-made" fiduciary duty entitles the aggrieved customer to sue the bank and receive a wide basket of remedies.[99]

(d)   The Scope of the Bank's Fiduciary Duty

The bank's fiduciary duty, as explained in the previous section, is a general and broad duty that applies to the bank-customer relationship in its entirety, and to all of the services that the bank provides to its customer. The test of the fiduciary duty is, first and foremost, an objective test of fairness and loyalty. However, at the same time, it also involves concrete elements deriving from the special circumstances of the case under discussion. The concrete elements are of great importance in determining the level of the duty and the degree of its intensity in each particular case.

Several circumstances may have an influence when determining the level of the bank's fiduciary duty, such as:

The extent of the customer's (justified) reliance on the Bank: We saw in the previous section, that one of the rationales for imposing a fiduciary duty on the bank is the customer's reliance on it. However, there may be differences in the level of reliance of customers in various cases. These differences will have a bearing on determining the degree of the duty. The greater the trust and reliance of the customer on the bank, the deeper the duty of the bank.

The type of service or transaction: In general, the more complex the transaction, or the greater discretion it allows for the bank, the greater the level of the duty imposed on the bank. This condition is strongly connected to the issue of customer reliance, since the more complex the transaction or the more discretion that is exercised by the bank, the higher the level of reliance by the customer. Thus, for example, where the bank performs a simple payment order for the customer, the level of the duty would be narrower than in the case of providing advice or receiving collateral. Similarly, in the field of investments, the duty

---

[95]   FCA Handbook PRIN 3.4.4R and PRIN Sch 5. The Law Commission Consultation Paper, *supra* note 26, at 215 paragraphs 8.71 to 8.76 and Appendix B. The Law Commission Report, *supra* note 18, at 149.

[96]   FCA Handbook MCOB Sch 5. FCA Handbook BCOBS Sch 5. FCA Handbook COBS Sch 5.

[97]   The Law Commission Consultation Paper, *supra* note 26, at 128–9.

[98]   The Law Commission Report, *supra* note 18, at 149.

[99]   Indeed, as was noted in the Law Commission Report, *supra* note 18, at 206, there are difficulties in relying on "judge-made" law to control complex and fast-moving financial markets. However, from the point of view of the aggrieved customer, in contrast to market regulation, it is still the better – if not the only way – to gain redress.

may be narrower in the case of brokerage services, where the customer orders the purchase or sale of a security, in comparison to a case where he seeks investment advice (or – in the case of a multitask bank – in investment management).

The value of the transaction should not necessarily affect the level of the duty. Only in circumstances where the high-amount transaction was indeed complex; involved a wide scope of discretion on the part of the bank, or led to a special reliance by the customer, might it increase the level of the duty.

Customer's level of sophistication: Here, the main parameters are sophistication, understanding and the experience of the customer. The more sophisticated, knowledgeable and experienced the customer is, the lesser the degree of duty would apply. Auxiliary parameters for deciding on this matter may be the age of the customer, his level of education, his profession, etc. As to a corporation such as a small business: its size, the level and type of its business activity, and even the personality of its managers, should be taken into account. In contrast, the distinction between a long-term customer and a new customer, or between a customer with meager means and a wealthy customer, should generally have no impact. The customer's abilities will have greater relevance with respect to certain elements of the bank's fiduciary duty, and to a lesser degree – and even perhaps no relevance – with respect to other elements. For example, with regard to the duty of disclosure to a customer, the level of disclosure would be higher in a case of an unsophisticated or inexperienced customer. But if we take another element of the fiduciary duty, the prohibition on conflicts of interest, this prohibition obligates the bank to all its customers to the same degree and without taking into account the customer's personality.

The nature of the relationship between the customer and the bank: Here it is necessary to examine whether the customer is familiar with the bank and its officials; the relationship between the parties and the extent of the bank's involvement therein; the size of the branch; and the manner of handling the specific customer. The closer the relationship between the parties, the deeper the fiduciary duty owed to the customer by the bank.

In conclusion, the various circumstances of the transaction may have implications for the scope and level of the fiduciary duty, whereby in certain cases the duty may be limited in scope, but in other instances rather intensive.

4. THE ABILITY TO MAKE STIPULATIONS IN RESPECT OF THE BANK'S FIDUCIARY DUTY

As mentioned above, the fiduciary duty requires a bank to protect the customer's interest. The bank is obligated to consider the customer's interest as the overriding interest and to prefer it to any other interests, including its own personal interest, a particularly stringent requirement. The question is whether it is necessary to apply such a high standard of behavior by way of a *jus cogens*. Or, should we recognize contexts and circumstances where it would be more fitting to relax the duty and to allow the customer to waive it, in whole or in part?

Various considerations justify the view that the bank's fiduciary duty should be considered as a *jus cogens* that cannot be waived.[100] Because of the significant inequality of power between the parties, the dependency of the customer upon the bank and his vulnerability, it can be assumed that were the fiduciary duty not prescribed as a mandatory rule, it would be overridden by a contradicting stipulation made by the bank. In the absence of mandatory validity, the inferiority which essentially creates the need for a fiduciary duty, would be used by the bank in order to force a waiver of the duty.

Nevertheless, the rationale underlying the prohibition of a waiver of the bank's fiduciary duty – the protection of the customer – does not lead to the conclusion that the prohibition must be absolute.[101] Particularly because of its strict significance, it can be argued that classifying it as a cogent duty constitutes a severe violation of the freedom of contract and may have a negative effect on market mechanisms.

In addition, there could be circumstances where a waiver by the customer of a certain aspect of the bank's fiduciary duty would actually assist in the fulfillment of his personal interests. In such cases, not only would a transaction that is carried out in breach of the fiduciary duty not adversely affect the customer, but it would in fact benefit him. In such circumstances, the very waiver of the customer can act in his favor. An example of such a situation is where a bank advises a customer to purchase a particular security because this security is commensurate with the customer's needs, while, at the same time, the bank has a personal interest in the transaction. Yet, this is not the only case in which the customer's beneficial interest is accomplished even though the bank acts in a conflict of interest. If the customer is prepared to consent freely to assuming the risk of releasing the bank from its fiduciary duty, then, under specific conditions, he should be allowed to do so.

Indeed, the modern approach recognizes that banks and financial institutions cannot completely avoid situations of conflict of interest.[102] Various regulators around the world allow banks to act with a certain degree of conflict of interest. The banks are not required to completely avoid conflicts of interests, but rather to act to reduce potential conflicts, and to manage an unavoidable conflict in fairness and integrity.[103]

In view of all the above, a certain degree of leeway in respect of the bank's fiduciary duty should be allowed, either by receiving the customer's ad-hoc consent in a specific instance,

---

[100]   This is the approach of the Kay Review, *supra* note 10, Principle 5 at 12, 65.

[101]   This is the approach of the Law Commission Report, *supra* note 18, at 39–40, 43–5, 196. Bahar and Thevenoz, *supra* note 22, at 15.

[102]   Eddy Wymeersch, "Conflicts of Interest, Especially in Asset Management", in *Conflicts of Interest: Corporate Governance and Financial Markets* 261, 268 (Luc Thevenoz and Rashid Bahar eds. 2007). Bahar and Thevenoz, *supra* note 22, at 1, 15. Klaus J. Hopt, "Trusteeship and Conflicts of Interest in Corporate, Banking and Agency Law: Toward Common Legal Principles for Intermediaries in the Modern Service-Oriented Society", in *Reforming Company and Takeover Law in Europe* 51, 71–2 (G.A. Ferrarini, K.J. Hopt, J. Winter and E. Wymeersch eds. 2005).

[103]   See, for example: FCA Handbook SYSC 10.1.7R and 10.1.8R. MiFID II, *supra* note 60, Article 23 (replacing MiFID I, *supra* note 88, Article 18). Marc Kruithof, "Conflicts of Interest in Institutional Asset Management: Is the EU Regulatory Approach Adequate?", in *Conflicts of Interest: Corporate Governance and Financial Markets* 277, 320 (Luc Thevenoz and Rashid Bahar eds. 2007).

or by including the stipulation in the banking contract.[104] However, the following conditions should be met in order for the waiver to take effect:

1. The waiver does not harm the customer's best interests. This preliminary demand stems from the very essence of the fiduciary duty, which obliges the bank to act loyally and protect the interest of the customer.
2. The waiver would not allow acts of deceit, dishonesty, or wrongful acts knowingly committed.[105]
3. The waiver would only relate to a specific component of the fiduciary duty. A sweeping waiver of the fiduciary duty in its entirety should not be allowed.[106] For example, a customer may agree that the bank act in a particular transaction in a conflict of interest, or receive a fee from a third party in respect of a certain transaction.
4. The customer's consent to the waiver was obtained with free will and with full knowledge of all the relevant facts.[107] The bank bears the responsibility not only to provide the customer with full information, but also to ensure that the customer has understood the matter correctly. Where it is impossible or impractical to obtain the customer's fully informed consent, the bank should cease acting.[108]
5. The waiver is, naturally, subject to the law of contract. Thus, for example, a waiver clause may be considered as "unreasonable" under the Unfair Contract Terms Act 1977, and/ or "unfair" under the Unfair Terms on Consumer Contracts Regulations 1999 or the Consumer Rights Act 2015.[109] Similarly, a waiver clause may be interpreted according to the principle of *contra proferentem*.

The suggested approach projects a pragmatic attitude, according to which the cogent nature of the duty is not absolute, and the parties are permitted to limit it, although not to dismiss it altogether, under certain circumstances.[110] The conditions set forth above define the space in which the bank is permitted to make stipulations in respect of the fiduciary duty, in general,

---

[104] This technique has been endorsed by both the Privy Council and the House of Lords. See, respectively: *Kelly v. Cooper* [1993] AC 205, 214–15 (PC) and *Henderson v. Merrett Syndicates Ltd* [1995] 2 AC 145, 206 (HL). See also: *JP Morgan Chase Bank v. Springwell Navigation Corp.* [2008] EWHC 186 at paragraph 734 (Comm), affirmed [2010] EWCA Civ 1221.

[105] Compare: *Clark Boyce v. Mouat* [1994] 1 AC 428 (PC). FCA Handbook COBS 2.1.3G(1).

[106] Nili Cohen, "Interference with Performance of a Fiduciary Obligation", 17 Isr. L. Rev. 12, 16 (1982). Bahar and Thevenoz, *supra* note 22, at 8.

[107] According to Ellinger, Lomnicka and Hare, *supra* note 3, at 137, terms in the underlying banking contract that purport to exclude or modify the fiduciary duty, may serve as a substitute for seeking the customer's fully informed consent. My opinion is different, requiring the customer's consent even in such cases. In addition, according to English case-law, the customer's consent may be an implied consent. See: *Kelly v. Cooper, supra* note 104, at 214–15. My opinion is different, demanding only an express consent.

[108] Ellinger, Lomnicka and Hare, *supra* note 3, at 136. Such a situation might arise when the bank's duty of confidentiality to another customer precludes the bank from disclosing information relevant to a particular conflict of interest. Such a situation occurred, for example, in *Standard Investments Ltd. v. Canadian Imperial Bank of Commerce, supra* note 54. *Commonwealth Bank of Australia v. Smith* (1991) 102 ALR 453 (FCA).

[109] Part 2 of the Act, for contracts entered into after 1 October 2015. See also FCA Handbook COBS 2.1.3(2)G. FCA Handbook BCOBS 1.1.7G.

[110] Tamar Frankel, "Fiduciary Duties as Default Rules", 74 Or. L. Rev. 1209 (1995).

and the prohibition of conflicts of interest, in particular. This space expands between the minimum of good faith and fairness, to the maximum of prioritizing the interests of the customer over those of the bank itself.

In any event, it should be noted that the suggested approach may only apply to services and transactions in respect of which no legislative or regulatory arrangement exists, regarding the bank's ability to modify or exclude its duties. Thus, for example, with regards to investment services, the "best interests" duty under the FCA Handbook COBS cannot be excluded or restricted.[111]

5.   CONCLUSION

In this chapter I dealt with the bank's fiduciary duty towards its retail customers. As I explained, the fiduciary duty should not be perceived as an altruistic duty that demands self-sacrifice from the bank. Rather, it should be understood as a vehicle to ensure basic fairness in the relationship between the bank and its customers, and to realize the legitimate expectations of the customers for fair and loyal service from the bank. This perception of the fiduciary duty justifies imposing a sweeping duty on the bank towards its retail customers, which should apply to the relationship in its entirety and to the full range of services provided by the bank.

The fiduciary duty is a general duty whose test is an objective test of the best interests of the customer. However, at the same time, it also involves concrete elements derived from the special circumstances involved. There may be cases in which the bank will be subject to a broader duty, while in other cases the duty may apply in a narrower manner. Another conclusion emanating from a careful examination of the nature of the duty, is the recognition that a certain degree of stipulation in respect of the duty should be permitted, subject to certain restrictions.

Fiduciary obligations are imposed by private law, but their function is public and their purpose is social.[112] The need to provide customers with due protection, to preclude the banks from abusing their power to the detriment of the customers, and to restore public trust, are good enough public and social purposes that justify the imposition of fiduciary duty on the banks towards their retail customers.

The formulation of a clearer normative view of the fiduciary duty, as I proposed in this chapter, will enable policymakers to establish an orderly set of rules, whose main principle is prioritizing the interest of the customer over the advantage to the bank. From here, it will be possible to derive creative solutions to situations of conflict, to the extent and in such a manner as the hand of moral imagination will allow.

---

[111]   FCA Handbook COBS 2.1.2R. See also FCA Handbook COBS 2.1.3(1)G, and FCA Handbook BCOBS 1.1.6R.

[112]   Worthington, *supra* note 21, at 507.

11. Market timers, late traders and the ultimate insiders

Basil G. Zotiades

I. INTRODUCTION

Our subject relates to collective investment schemes, commonly known as funds; more precisely to a family of trading malpractices whose natural habitat lies in dealing in funds. The most prominent members of this family are known as 'late trading' and 'market timing'. Other terms abound: 'mutual fund timing', 'stale price arbitrage', 'time zone arbitrage', 'short-term trading', 'excessive trading', 'abusive fund trading' and 'known price arbitrage'. Confusion occasionally reigns, including, as we shall see, in some statements made by regulators.

Our aim is twofold: first, to shed light on what these practices are (and are not); and, second, to review the regulatory response to them in Europe and reflect on its adequacy and on how that response fits with our treatment of other forms of what we now call market abuse.

In light of our subject, we will focus on one category of funds. These are actively managed[1] open-ended[2] funds available to the public,[3] with portfolios invested primarily in publicly traded equity securities. Although many of the issues raised by these trading practices also affect to varying degrees other types of funds, it is in relation to this category that most, if not all, of the relevant ethical issues can be seen most clearly.

II. MARKET TIMING

Market timing is our point of departure. It is instructive to look at the original meaning of the term. Although that meaning is somewhat removed from the trading practice of the same name involving funds, the reasons for this semantic migration are, as is often the case, enlightening.

The fact that market prices for many financial assets fluctuate, at times wildly, sets the scene for market timing. The idea is to time both one's entry into, and exit from, a particular market (or individual asset) so as to attain, as perfectly as possible, a 'buy at the bottom, sell at the top' objective with a view to maximising gains. One attempts to predict future price movements in the markets and times purchases and sales accordingly.[4] To do this an array of different

---

*   Basil G. Zotiades completed this chapter on 17 April 2018.
[1]   As opposed to passive funds merely tracking an index, such as exchange traded funds (ETFs).
[2]   As opposed to closed-ended funds. See text to n 50.
[3]   As opposed to funds reserved to specific categories of clients meeting one or more requirements relating to income, net worth, investment portfolio size or investment expertise.
[4]   Market timing can be used, more or less aggressively, to speculate on the future direction of markets, including through merely adjusting the asset allocation of a diversified portfolio.

predictive tools can be used. They include analysis of economic data, technical indicators,[5] fundamental indicators[6] and behavioural data.[7]

The question whether such predictive tools can be used to 'time (one's exposure to) the market' so as to generate, consistently, risk adjusted returns superior to those of the equity market as a whole has attracted a lot of interest.

A. Market Timing as an Investment Strategy

An intuition, recurrent in financial theory, holds that this is not possible, at least in the case of regulated, large and liquid equity markets. This intuition, variously expressed over time through metaphors such as 'fair games',[8] 'random walks'[9] and 'martingales',[10] culminated in the efficient markets hypothesis.[11] This hypothesis and the modern random walk theory[12] associated with it claim that prices in such markets would quickly assimilate and reflect all, or most of,[13] the relevant information, including expectations as to the future, and that subsequent price changes will reflect future information, placing them therefore at the mercy of future developments and, in this sense, independent of historical price information. Apart from informational effects, there is no correlation between successive price changes. The evolution

---

5 For equities, metrics based on past market data (primarily prices and trading volumes), including moving average, mean reversion, relative strength, money flow and other quantitative indicators.

6 For equities, metrics thought to indicate companies' (i) fundamental (or intrinsic) value through their revenues, earnings, profit margins, cash flows and assets, or (ii) relative value compared to other assets.

7 Primarily, investor sentiment data interpreted through the lens of behavioural finance theories.

8 The concept can be traced to a study of gaming by Girolamo Cardano, *Liber de Ludo Aleae* (c. 1565). A fair game requires 'equal conditions', a (metaphorical) level playing field, so that it is not biased toward any player and each player's expected gain is the same. In financial theory, this evolved into an investment prospect that offers no opportunity to use an informational advantage to gain a superior return.

9 The random walk hypothesis (though not the term itself) can be traced to the doctoral thesis of Louis Bachelier, '*Théorie de la spéculation*' (1900) 3 17 *Annales scientifiques de l'Ecole Normale Supérieure*. In a study of exchange transactions in French government bonds, he postulated that, as in a fair game ('*jeu équitable*'), the 'mathematical expectation [expected return] of the speculator is zero' and modelled mathematically a random (step-by-step) fluctuation of prices.

10 In the (probabilistic) sense of a sequence of random variables where the expected value of the next observation, given all the past observations, is equal to the most recent observation. The term came from 18th-century betting strategies in France thought to originate from the town of Martigues and subsequent attempts to prove the impossibility of successful betting strategies.

11 One of its earlier and best-known statements is by Eugene Fama, 'Efficient Capital Markets: A Review of Theory and Empirical Work' (1970) 25 2 Journal of Finance 383. A discussion of the hypothesis, its history and subsequent criticism of it can be found in Stephen LeRoy, 'Efficient Capital Markets and Martingales' (1989) 27 4 Journal of Economic Literature 1583.

12 Although much older (see n 9), this theory was popularised by Burton Malkiel, *A Random Walk Down Wall Street* (W. W. Norton & Company, Inc. 1973). Probabilistically, a random walk is more restrictive than a martingale. Both exclude any dependence of each step in the sequence on the information available at the previous point in time but the former also excludes dependence of any future step in the sequence on any past information.

13 There are three forms of the hypothesis and the second (called 'semi-strong') excludes, unlike the first (called 'strong'), privately held information which is not publicly available. The third (called 'weak') postulates that future prices are independent of (cannot be predicted from) historic prices, and so corresponds to a random walk.

of prices over time resembles the random walk of a drunken man and cannot be foreseen or exploited through any predictive tools.

The hypothesis implied that, by quickly assimilating relevant information, prices always rationally reflect fundamental value. Subsequent research cast doubt on this implication. A weaker variant of the hypothesis emerged. This merely precludes the possibility of superior risk adjusted returns through persistent and exploitable pricing anomalies.[14]

Empirical studies support the weaker variant of the hypothesis, indicating that market timing, as an equities investment strategy, is unlikely to 'beat the market' consistently. A study by William Sharpe focused specifically on market timing.[15] Using a scheduled annual review model, it measured two variables: the likely gains from market timing over a 'buy and hold' equities strategy; and the degree of accuracy required for a market timer's predictions to achieve any such gains. For any given year, one could be fully invested in either equities (through the Standard & Poor's Composite Index plus dividends) or cash equivalents (through US Treasury bills).[16]

As regards likely gains, the conclusion was that 'Barring truly devastating market declines similar to those of The Depression, it seems likely that gains of little more than four per cent per year from timing should be expected from a manager whose forecasts are truly prophetic.'[17]

As regards predictive ability, an accuracy rate of at least 83 per cent in (annual) predictions was required to perform better than simply remaining fully invested in equities for the whole period. Even after adjusting for risk, an accuracy rate of at least 74 per cent was required to perform better than a static mixed portfolio of equities and cash equivalents presenting the same risk as the market timer's choices over the whole period.[18]

Further research identified another ground in support of Sharpe's conclusions. A study in 2008[19] looked at whether long-term returns accrue steadily over time or, instead, are determined primarily by a few 'outliers'.[20] The answer, based on a study of 160,000 daily returns from 15 international equity markets,[21] was that outliers have a massive impact on long-term performance. The results showed that missing just the best (or worst) ten days resulted in port-

---

[14] Burton Malkiel, 'The Efficient Market Hypothesis and its Critics' (2003) 17 1 Journal of Economic Perspectives 59. This weaker variant should not be confused with the 'weak' form of the original hypothesis (see n 13).

[15] William Sharpe, 'Likely Gains from Market Timing' (1975) 31 2 Financial Analysts Journal 60.

[16] Three sample periods were tested: 1929–72, 1934–72 and 1946–72. The first included the four years of the Depression and produced the most favourable results for perfect market timing (in terms of excess returns over a 'buy and hold' equities strategy). The third was the least favourable.

[17] Sharpe (n 15) 63. For the first period, including the Depression, the likely gains from timing were 5.50% (or 6.76% on a risk adjusted basis). For the third period, they were 2.26% (or 3.78% on a risk adjusted basis).

[18] Ibid 65. These results correspond to the middle period of 1934–72 selected by the author to provide a balanced view.

[19] Javier Estrada, 'Black Swans and Market Timing: How Not to Generate Alpha' (2008) 17 3 The Journal of Investing 20.

[20] In this context, the best days to be in and out of the market. The term was borrowed from Nassim Taleb, *The Black Swan: The Impact of the Highly Improbable* (Random House 2007).

[21] The length of the 15 sample periods varied and ranged from 31 to 79 years, in each case, to the end of 2006.

folios substantially less (or more) valuable than a 'buy and hold' investment.[22] The conclusion was that:

> black swans render market timing a goose chase. Attempting to predict the negligible proportion of days that determines an enormous creation or destruction of wealth seems to be a losing proposition. Of the countless strategies that academics and practitioners have devised to generate alpha, market timing seems to be one very unlikely to succeed. Much like going to Vegas, market timing may be an entertaining pastime, but not a good way to make money.[23]

In summary, theoretical and empirical studies suggest that market timing is not a viable long-term strategy for equity investment because it will fail to generate long-term risk adjusted returns superior to those of a 'buy and hold' approach. Put simply, this is due to the unpredictability of market movements. Their timing, direction and extent are for the most part (certainly most of the time for most of us) unpredictable. This reduces substantially the probability of timing correctly both the entry and the exit points, a prerequisite for superior long-term investment returns through market timing.

B.   Market Timing and Trading

Nevertheless, market timing is essential to many forms of short-term trading seeking serial gains from fluctuating prices by taking and then exiting positions. The aim here is not 'buy at the bottom, sell at the top'[24] but simply 'buy low, sell high and often'. The trader, armed with his predictive tools,[25] guided by his anticipation of future price movements, selects each position and the timing of each transaction. Although accurate predictions of the highest and lowest points during any given period are not required, the challenges are otherwise similar. It is no easy task. Even though the long-term investor need not worry about having to 'time the market', the trader in our example has no choice but to do just that. This is a function of their different objectives and time horizons.

As the US mutual fund scandal of 2003 and subsequent events revealed, trading strategies referred to as 'market timing' migrated to funds. As we shall see, there were good reasons why that occurred, but first we have to take a closer look at funds.

III.   FUNDS

The funds which concern us are open-ended equity funds available to the public. They are collective investment vehicles which, for a fee, pool together the cash contributions of a large number of clients and invest them in a common portfolio comprising primarily publicly traded equity securities. The portfolio is actively managed on a discretionary basis by an asset manager with a view to generating returns commensurate with those of a long-term investment in equities.

---

[22]   Estrada (n 19) 20. The figures are 50.8% less, and 150.4% more, valuable (see Exhibit 6, 28).
[23]   Ibid 32.
[24]   Within a defined investment horizon.
[25]   See text to nn 5–7.

The fund's clients, in effect, co-own the fund through the shares or units allocated to them in exchange for their cash contributions. Each share or unit represents a pro rata share in the value of the fund's assets. I will refer to these shares or units as fund interests.

From a regulatory perspective, these funds fall under the category of UCITS[26] in the European Union and that of 'registered open-end investment companies' in the United States (where they are known as 'mutual funds').

According to EFAMA,[27] at the end of the third quarter of 2017, there were 12,178 equity UCITS domiciled in Europe with assets of €3.576 trillion.[28] They represented by far the largest category of UCITS.[29] In the United States, according to ICI,[30] there were 4,706 equity mutual funds in December 2017 with total net assets of US$10.3 trillion, representing also the largest category of mutual funds.[31]

We will now explore three characteristics of these funds: first, the fact that they are investment vehicles designed primarily for, and widely held (whether directly or indirectly) by, retail clients; second, that they are designed for long-term investment in equities; and, third, that they are open-ended vehicles.

A.   An Investment Vehicle for Retail Clients

These funds are intended to provide the benefits of a professionally managed, diversified and cost-effective exposure to equities to retail clients, persons who for the most part do not have the knowledge, time or inclination to manage effectively the portion of their savings allocated to equities.

This is achieved by the mutualisation, through the fund, of its clients' cash contributions entrusted to the asset manager. This mutualisation is intended to confer on clients three benefits: lower investment risk through a diversified equities' portfolio actively managed by a professional; lower costs through economies of scale; and liquidity through the ability to convert, at the client's request, all or part of an investment into cash at short notice.

According to ICI's 2017 Investment Company Fact Book,[32] at the end of 2016, households held 89 per cent of total US mutual fund assets, either directly or indirectly through retirement accounts, variable annuities and similar savings products.[33] The number of those households

---

[26]   Undertakings for Collective Investment in Transferable Securities.

[27]   The European Fund and Asset Management Association is the representative association of the European investment management industry.

[28]   EFAMA, 'Trends in the European Investment Fund Industry in the Third Quarter of 2017' (Quarterly Statistical Release No. 71, December 2017) 5, tables 3–4. These numbers include equity ETFs and funds of funds established as UCITS. However, ETFs and funds of funds represent only 12% of all UCITS and 10% of all UCITS' assets, in each case (irrespective of the targeted asset class).

[29]   Ibid. Equity UCITS represented 39% of all UCITS by number and 38% by assets.

[30]   The Investment Company Institute is the principal association of regulated funds in the United States.

[31]   ICI, 'Trends in Mutual Fund Investing: January 2018' (27 February 2018) www.ici.org/research/stats/trends/trends_01_18 accessed 28 February 2018. These numbers (unlike EFAMA's) exclude ETFs and funds of funds.

[32]   ICI, '2017 Investment Company Fact Book' (57th edn, 2017) www.icifactbook.org accessed 28 February 2018.

[33]   Ibid 30, figure 2.3. This percentage relates to all mutual funds, irrespective of their target asset class.

was estimated to be 54.9 million, representing 43.6 per cent of US households.[34] The median amount invested by individuals in mutual funds stood at US$125,000.[35]

EFAMA's statistics do not yet provide equivalent detail on retail clients' direct and indirect holdings of UCITS in Europe. According to EFAMA,[36] it appears that in 2015 retail clients accounted for 27 per cent of total assets managed in Europe,[37] with insurance companies and pension funds each accounting for a further 27 per cent.[38] Most of the portion held by insurance companies and pension funds will in fact be held for the accounts of the retail clients.

More information can be gleaned from statistical releases from the United Kingdom and France. At the end of 2015, these two countries, with €2.673 trillion and €2.020 trillion of investment fund assets respectively, together represented 42 per cent of the total assets managed through investment funds in Europe.[39]

According to the IA,[40] the value of funds (whether domiciled in the United Kingdom or overseas) available for sale to retail investors in the United Kingdom and held by UK retail investors was £1.045 trillion, with equity funds being the largest category, accounting for 54 per cent of that amount.[41]

The IA also estimates the share of assets (including assets held by overseas clients) managed in the United Kingdom on behalf of various client types. On the basis of this methodology, 18.9 per cent of assets managed in the United Kingdom at the end of 2016 were managed on behalf of retail investors.[42] The shares of assets managed on behalf of pension funds and insurance companies were 44 per cent and 15.7 per cent, respectively.[43] As the IA admits, this breakdown understates the effective share of retail investors. The ultimate bearer of the investment risk in defined contribution pension saving schemes is the individual retail client (the underlying pension saver). Despite that, assets managed for defined contribution pension schemes are at the moment allocated either to pension funds, where these are the asset manager's direct client, or insurance companies, where the scheme is distributed through an insurance company via a wrapped product, such as a unit linked life policy.[44]

According to *Banque de France*, at the end of the third quarter of 2017, the French retail client sector (excluding non-resident investors) accounted for €227 billion or 19 per cent of assets managed through funds (other than money market funds) domiciled in France.[45]

---

[34]   Ibid 112, figure 6.1.
[35]   Ibid 113, figure 6.2.
[36]   EFAMA, 'Asset Management in Europe' (9th edn, May 2017).
[37]   Total assets managed include, in addition to funds (itself a broader category than UCITS), discretionary mandates.
[38]   EFAMA (n 36) 29, exhibit 33.
[39]   Ibid 25, exhibit 26.
[40]   The Investment Association is the trade body that represents UK investment managers.
[41]   IA, 'Asset Management in the UK 2016–2017' (September 2017) www.theinvestmentassociation .org/assets/files/research/2017/20170914-ams2017.pdf accessed 27 February 2018, 60. Of this amount, UK domiciled funds accounted for £940 billion and overseas funds for £105 billion (ibid 61).
[42]   Ibid 37, chart 6.
[43]   Ibid.
[44]   Ibid 37.
[45]   *Banque de France*, '*Panorama financier des OPC – France*' (release for the third quarter of 2017, 27 November 2017) www.banque-france.fr/sites/default/files/webstat pdf/panfinopc2163frsipanoramaf-inancieropct32017fr.pdf accessed 27 February 2018. These figures relate to all French funds and not just

Insurance companies accounted for €456 billion or 38 per cent of such assets.[46] The portion allocated to the insurance sector includes insurance companies' holdings of funds distributed to retail clients via wrapped products – in the case of France, unit linked life policies – where, again, the investment risk lies with the retail client (the policyholder). As unit linked policies represent a major part of French retail investors' savings,[47] this breakdown significantly under-states the share of retail clients, as was the case in the United Kingdom.

B.   A Long-Term Investment Vehicle

The primary economic function of these funds is to channel their clients' savings to (hope-fully) productive long-term investment through the equity capital of the companies in which the fund invests.

As equities produce greater returns than cash or debt securities over the long term but are subject to greater volatility, these funds were naturally conceived as long-term investment vehicles which would also satisfy retail clients' own needs to save for the long term.

This is reflected in the funds' investment objectives. These emphasise to clients that the aim is to generate returns (whether in the form of capital growth or income) over the longer term. Often, long term is defined for this purpose as five years or more.

Beyond their investment objectives, many of these funds emphasise that their own approach to investing is long term. Examples include statements that equities are bought to access the long-term future of a business or that the fund manager sees his role as that of a long-term investor in a business and not as a short-term trader of equities.

In relation to the United Kingdom and UK equity securities, these statements appear to be borne out by a study prepared for the IA in 2016. This suggests that UK asset managers hold UK equities for longer periods than other types of investor. Over the period from 2011 to 2014, the average holding period for asset managers (including active and passive strategies) was estimated to be 6.3 years, whereas it was 3.8 years for other investors (such as individuals, companies and institutional investors holding shares, excluding high frequency traders and banks in their role as liquidity providers).[48]

Consequently, the investment time horizon recommended to clients is also long term. Typical formulations are that the fund may be suitable for investors who look to set aside their capital for the long term or that the fund may not be appropriate for investors who plan to withdraw their money within five years.

Finally, the long-term nature of retail clients' own investments in funds appears to be con-firmed by statistical information. For example, in the United Kingdom the IA estimates the

---

those which are UCITS. They also allocate €152 billion (or 15% of assets) to other funds without looking through to ultimate ownership of the assets held through those other funds.

[46]   Ibid. According to the quarterly release for the fourth quarter, at the end of 2017, retail clients' share increased slightly to €235 billion and insurers' share decreased to €421 billion but no percentage breakdowns were given in that release.

[47]   The *Banque de France* estimated that, at the end of the third quarter of 2017, French households' indirect holdings of funds and other underlying assets through unit linked life policies stood at €298.8 billion. See *Banque de France*, '*Epargne et Patrimoine des ménages – France et étranger – T3–T4 2017*' (release for the third and fourth quarters of 2017, 6 February 2018) www.banque-france.fr/statistiques/epargne/epargne-des-menages accessed 27 February 2018.

[48]   Oxera, 'The contribution of asset management to the UK economy' (July 2016), 16 and 17.

average length of time that UK retail investors hold a particular fund. The average holding period stood at approximately three years in 2016 and has been fairly stable, between three and four years, since 2012.[49]

C.   An Open-Ended Investment Vehicle

The third characteristic of these funds is that they are open-ended. This means that, unlike closed-ended funds,[50] they do not have a set limit on the amount of fund interests which they can issue. Their capital (and size of their portfolio) is variable and fluctuates reflecting net demand for fund interests from clients.

So, one buys (subscribes) fund interests from the fund itself. The fund creates new fund interests and allocates them to the client in exchange for cash. Similarly, a client who holds fund interests can sell them to the fund, which buys them back (redeems them) for cash and cancels them. In this sense, unlike a closed-ended fund, the fund is the only counterparty facing clients who want to invest or withdraw money from the fund.[51]

The concept of an open-ended fund entails that its clients should be able to withdraw all or part of their investment by having their fund interests redeemed by the fund itself. With a view to protecting the interests of clients who, for various reasons, might need access to amounts invested, ensuring the liquidity of investments in such funds has been an objective of fund regulation. Almost all equity UCITS in Europe and all equity mutual funds in the United States provide daily liquidity to their clients enabling them to subscribe or redeem fund interests each business day.

IV.   PRICING FUNDS

The open-ended nature of these funds leads us to the question of how subscription and redemption orders for fund interests are priced.

A.   Net Asset Value

As these funds are pools of assets without any market (external to the fund) to determine the price at which their fund interests can be bought or sold, that price is necessarily determined on the basis of the value of the fund's assets minus the value of its liabilities. This is referred to as the fund's net asset value. A division of that net asset value by the number of fund interests outstanding at a particular time results in that fund's net asset value per fund interest (or 'NAV$_{FI}$') at that time. The NAV$_{FI}$ represents the value of a pro rata share in the fund cor-

---

[49]   IA (n 41) 60 and 78 (chart 79).

[50]   Closed-ended funds are launched with a fixed share capital, typically through an initial public offering, and their shares are traded on an exchange allowing investors to buy and sell shares from each other on that exchange.

[51]   See n 52 for certain UK 'dual-priced' funds which allow managers to deal in fund interests for their own account. In this case, the fund manager may be an alternative counterparty.

responding to one fund interest. It is used to price subscription and redemption orders for fund interests.[52]

In order to ensure fairness between a fund's clients, NAV_{FI} must at any time reflect accurately the actual value of the fund's portfolio at that time. If not, a redemption at a NAV_{FI} higher than the actual value of the fund's assets at that time would disadvantage the remaining clients of the fund. The payment by the fund of any amount in excess of the actual value of a redeeming client's pro rata share reduces or dilutes the value of the remaining clients' interests in the fund by an amount equal to the excess value received by the redeeming client.[53] Dilution would also occur if there were a subscription at a NAV_{FI} lower than the actual value of the fund's assets at that time. Conversely, a redemption at a NAV_{FI} lower, or a subscription at a NAV_{FI} higher, than the actual value of the fund's assets at that time would disadvantage the redeeming or subscribing client, respectively.

B.   Valuation and Dealing

In order to determine NAV_{FI} and use it to price orders while minimising dilution, each fund requires a valuation and dealing timeframe. This addresses the following questions:

1. How often should clients be able to deal in the fund's interests?
2. How often should the fund's net assets be valued?
3. At what point in time exactly on a valuation day should they be valued?
4. What prices for the equity securities in the fund's portfolio should be used for the valuation?
5. Once the valuation is complete and NAV_{FI} has been determined, which orders are to be priced at that particular NAV_{FI}?
6. By what time does an order have to be received for it to be priced at that NAV_{FI}?

The first question addresses a fund's dealing frequency; the second, its valuation frequency; the third, its valuation point; the fourth, its assets' valuation point (which may or may not coincide with the fund's own valuation point) and its price sources; the fifth, its valuation direction: will NAV_{FI} be used to price orders received before or after that NAV_{FI} is calculated; and, finally, the sixth, addresses a fund's dealing cut off point.

---

[52]   Depending on the fund and its jurisdiction, the price paid or received, although based on NAV_{FI}, may be adjusted. This is to reflect entry or exit fees, dilution levies or dilution adjustments (through swing pricing). In addition, in the United Kingdom, some funds are 'dual priced', have separate offer (issue) and bid (cancellation) prices and even allow managers to set subscription prices below the issue price and redemption prices above the cancellation price, deal in fund interests for their own account through a 'box' and retain 'box profits' from such dealing. A first, timid step to limit these opaque practices was recently taken by the FCA in proposing that managers should no longer retain some of those dealing profits, the 'risk-free box profits'. See FCA, *Consultation on implementing asset management market study remedies and changes to Handbook* (Consultation Paper 17/18, June 2017) s 5, 25–7.

[53]   Dual pricing and, for single priced funds, dilution levies or adjustments through swing pricing (see n 52) aim to address dilution. (Swing pricing allows a manager to switch the pricing of orders from an offer basis, when the fund is growing, to a bid basis, when the fund is contracting, so as to pass to redeeming or subscribing clients trading costs associated with their orders.) However, these are all imprecise tools which do not always fully compensate for dilution and can disadvantage some clients.

C.   Our Funds' Timeframe

In general, the funds which concern us, whether in Europe or the United States, have a fairly similar timeframe for valuation and dealing.

Their dealing and valuation frequency, with few exceptions, is daily. In the United States, daily dealing and valuation is a defining feature of mutual funds and has been entrenched in law since 1940.[54] In Europe, the UCITS regime only provides for a minimum dealing and valuation frequency of at least twice a month (and exceptionally once a month).[55] However, as regulators[56] expect funds to have a valuation and dealing frequency which is adapted to the nature of their assets, almost all equity UCITS are valued, and can be dealt in, daily.[57]

As a result, there is typically one valuation point each day, mostly at 4 pm (Eastern time) in the United States[58] and often, but not always, towards the middle of the day in Europe.

In order to capture the current market value of the underlying equity securities, these are generally valued on the basis of their latest prices from the relevant exchanges. Where these are not available or are considered unreliable, 'fair value' pricing is generally used instead. In the United States, these requirements are again mostly hardwired in law.[59] In Europe, the UCITS regime leaves valuation to the law of the member states.[60] In the United Kingdom, some basic principles are set out in the Collective Investment Schemes Sourcebook (known as 'COLL'),[61] while additional clarification is provided by the IA.[62] In France, detailed valuation

---

[54]   Mutual funds were conceived as entities continuously offering for sale redeemable securities entitling their holder to have them redeemed by the mutual fund at any time. The valuation frequency requirement (subject to very limited exceptions) is that NAV_{FI} be calculated at least once a day. It is set out in SEC rule 22c-1(b)(1) under the Investment Company Act of 1940 (ICA), 17 CFR 270.22c-1(b)(1).

[55]   Directive 2009/65/EC of the European Parliament and of the Council of 13 July 2009 on the coordination of laws, regulations and administrative provisions relating to undertakings for collective investment in transferable securities (UCITS) [2009] OJ L302/32 (UCITS IV Directive), art 76; see also, in relation to the UK, COLL 6.3.4 and, in relation to France, art 411-123 of the *Règlement général de l'AMF* (RG AMF).

[56]   Eg IOSCO, 'Principles for the Valuation of Collective Investment Schemes' (FR05/13 Final Report   May 2013) www.iosco.org/library/pubdocs/pdf/IOSCOPD413.pdf accessed 15 January 2018, fourth principle app A, 12.

[57]   By contrast weekly, fortnightly or monthly valuation is often used in certain European jurisdictions for funds invested in less liquid and less volatile assets, such as real estate.

[58]   This is the time when most major US exchanges close. The distant origins of this practice, from a time when US funds invested mostly in US domestic securities, lie in the laudable attempt to minimise pricing inefficiencies by ensuring that NAV_{FI} was set at the same time as the markets for the fund's securities closed and, therefore, reflected contemporaneous closing prices of those securities.

[59]   Section 2(a)(41)(B) of the ICA, 15 USC § 80a–2(41)(B) and SEC rule 2a-4 under the ICA, 17 CFR 270 2a-4. Mutual funds' financial statements are prepared in accordance with US GAAP, which provides comprehensive guidance specifically for funds.

[60]   UCITS IV Directive (n 55) art 85; Commission Directive (2010/43/EU) of 1 July 2010 implementing Directive 2009/65/EC as regards organisational requirements, conflicts of interest, conduct of business, risk management and content of the agreement between a depositary and a management company [2010] OJ L176/42 (UCITS IV Implementing Directive), art 8.

[61]   COLL 6.3.3A–D and 6.3.6.

[62]   IMA/IA, 'Statement of Recommended Practice: Financial Statements of UK Authorised Funds' (May 2014, as amended in June 2017) (SORP). The IA is recognised by the Financial Reporting Council for the purpose of issuing, through a SORP, clarification of UK accounting standards as they apply to authorised funds.

rules specific to open-ended funds are ultimately set by the *Autorité des normes comptables*,[63] the accounting standards authority.

Where the fund valuation point is set at a time when markets on which underlying securities are traded are open, the assets' valuation point for those securities will coincide with the fund valuation point. Where no such market is open, the last closing prices will be taken instead (unless fair value pricing is used,) resulting in an assets' valuation point falling earlier than the fund valuation point. Prices used will not be contemporaneous with the fund valuation point. In addition, whether or not the two valuation points coincide, for funds invested in 'small capitalisation' equities, which are often 'thinly traded', the most recent prices available may themselves already be out of date.

Once it is calculated, NAV_{FI} is used to price orders received *before* it was set. This is called 'forward pricing' (seen from the perspective of the client who has submitted an order). Orders are priced at the first NAV_{FI} calculated after the dealing cut off point. The aim is to ensure that fund interests are only bought or sold at prices not known in advance. The alternative is 'backward (or historic) pricing'. By allowing transactions at known prices, it would assist persons dealing in fund interests with a view to obtaining an advantageous NAV_{FI} (relative to the anticipated value of the fund's assets), thus diluting the interests of other clients. It would also encourage the use of funds as assets to be traded for short-term arbitrage, contrary to their function as long-term investment vehicles.

In recognition of these risks, forward pricing of mutual funds has been a statutory requirement in the United States since 1968.[64] The common UCITS regime does not address this point, leaving the issue to member states. In the United Kingdom, until fairly recently, historic pricing was possible subject to certain tests. On 1 October 2016, forward pricing at last became compulsory in the United Kingdom.[65] In France, this is dealt with at the level of the authorisation of an equity UCITS by the *Autorité des marchés financiers* (AMF), the local regulator. No equity (or bond) UCITS will be authorised if it is not 'forward priced'.[66]

Finally, given the use of forward pricing for these funds, it follows that the dealing cut off point is set not later than their fund valuation point.

This common timeframe shows that, even with a daily valuation point, a fund's NAV_{FI} will be static when compared to the prices of the equity securities held by the fund which fluctuate continuously on the exchanges or other venues on which they can be traded (including electronic communication networks on which premarket trading and after-hours trading takes place outside an exchange's regular hours).[67]

---

[63] *Autorité des normes comptables, Règlement* N° 2014-01 of 14 January 2014, JORF n° 0239 15 October 2014, as amended by *Règlement* N° 2017-05 of 1 December 2017, JORF n° 0304 30 December 2017.

[64] SEC rule 22c-1(a) under the ICA, 17 CFR 270.22c-1(a). For the reasoning (including that historic pricing 'encourages speculative trading practices'), see SEC Release No. 34-8429, IC-5519 (16 October 1968), 33 FR 16331 (7 November 1968).

[65] COLL 6.3.9.

[66] *Position AMF*, '*Les pratiques de* market timing *et de* late trading', DOC-2004-07, 23 July 2004, as amended on 1 August 2012 and 3 November 2015 (AMF Position), para 2.5, 4.

[67] This inertia of NAV_{FI} can be aggravated by other factors. In the United States, for example, mutual funds are allowed to (and most equity funds do) calculate NAV_{FI} on the basis of the assets held by them on the preceding business day. SEC rule 2a-4(a)(2) under the ICA provides that 'Changes in holdings of portfolio securities shall be reflected no later than in the first calculation on the first business day following the trade date' (17 CFR 270.2a-4(a)(2)). See also Peter Tufano, Michael Quinn and Ryan Taliaferro,

D.   Pricing Inefficiencies and Arbitrage Opportunities

Even before delving into the valuation and dealing arrangements of any particular fund, two general inferences may be drawn.

First, there will be price movements in equity securities held by a fund which will be reflected in its NAV_{FI} after a time lag. This will happen when a venue on which those securities are traded is open for trading at any time since the last daily assets' valuation point.

Second, changes in the prices of those equity securities may *otherwise* become apparent and, if they materialise, they too will only be reflected in that fund's NAV_{FI} after a time lag. This will happen when *other* price movements or events likely to influence the prices of those securities occur after the last daily assets' valuation point. Examples include price movements in future and option contracts on an equity index corresponding to a fund's securities (many such contracts are continuously traded across time zones); price movements in other equity exchanges or in their future and option contracts; movements in foreign exchange rates; major interest rate announcements; and significant corporate earnings announcements.[68]

At any given time for any fund, the length of that time lag will vary depending on the position of its assets' valuation point relative to its next dealing cut off point for orders to be priced at its next valuation point. This will itself be a function of a number of factors. The principal ones are: weekends and bank holidays in the markets where the underlying securities are traded but also in the city of the fund's operations; time zone differences between those markets and that city; and any early closure of the markets where the underlying securities are traded.

So, even when forward priced on a daily basis, these funds still present a pricing inefficiency. This can be exploited through arbitrage.[69] The arbitrage will aim to exploit new information, indicating a change in the value of a fund's equity portfolio, which becomes available during the interval between a fund's last assets' valuation point and the latest time at which one is still able to deal in that fund at a NAV_{FI} which will not yet reflect that change, and in that sense will be 'stale'.[70] It is this time interval which explains why some funds attracted the trading practices we will review.

V.   TIMING FUNDS

The two principal practices involving the exploitation of the pricing inefficiency inherent even in forward priced funds are called 'market timing' and 'late trading'. The issue had been identified by academics at least as early as the late 1990s.[71] However, it only came into

---

'Live Prices and Stale Quantities: T+1 Accounting and Mutual Fund Mispricing' (2006) HBS Finance Working Paper No. 881615.

[68]   Both inferences illustrate the predictability of a fund's NAV_{FI}.

[69]   In this context, transactions seeking risk free gains by exploiting price differences between assets representing similar exposures.

[70]   A fund's last assets' valuation point is the point where the clock, as it were, stops in terms of underlying prices to be reflected in the fund's next NAV_{FI}.

[71]   See, eg, Rahul Bhargava, Ann Bose and David Dubofsky, 'Exploiting International Stock Market Correlations with Open-End International Mutual Funds' (1998) 25 Journal of Business Finance & Accounting 765.

prominence in September 2003[72] with the eruption of what came to be known as the mutual funds scandal in the United States.[73] Most accounts of those events focus on the fact that asset managers and other mutual fund agents colluded, in breach of their fiduciary responsibilities, with third parties to facilitate mutual fund timing.[74] As the role of the 'facilitators' has been the focus of regulatory attention and was also extensively covered by commentators, our focus instead will be on the primary actors, those who have been described as 'predator-investors' and 'victim-investors'.[75] By the former, I mean the 'fund timer', whether a 'late trader' or not, and by the latter the 'buy and hold' long-term clients of a fund targeted by the trading activities of the former.

A.   'Market Timing'

There are many definitions of 'market timing' (in the context of funds) by both regulators and professional associations of asset managers. One which actually captures the essence of this trading practice was provided by the Securities and Exchange Commission (SEC) in 2004:

> Market timing may take many forms. In this release, we have used the term to refer to arbitrage activity involving the frequent buying and selling of mutual fund shares in order to take advantage of the fact that there may be a lag between a change in the value of a mutual fund's portfolio securities and the reflection of that change in the fund's share price.[76]

This definition highlights that the time lag can be used *systematically* in arbitrage solely aimed at exploiting it, through frequent buy and sell orders. Frequent transactions are inherent in such arbitrage. Each entry point into a fund merely crystallises the cost of the position taken (which is lower than it would have been had the time lag not been exploited). However, to realise a gain through the sale of that position, one also needs an exit point (which again, if the time lag is also exploited for the exit, will be higher than it would otherwise have been).[77] To maximise gains, one is tempted to 'invest' a large amount in this 'round trip' transaction and repeat the process.[78] The volatility inherent in equity markets coupled with NAV_{FI} inertia provides the backdrop against which a fund timer can keep on locking in meaningful serial short-term gains

---

[72]   The opening salvo was the filing on 3 September 2003 by the then Attorney General of the State of New York, Eliot Spitzer, of a civil complaint against Edward J. Stern and Canary Capital Partners, a hedge fund led by him.

[73]   An account of the scandal in the United States, its causes and the issues it raised for mutual funds and their regulation can be found in Tamar Frankel and Lawrence Cunningham, 'The Mysterious Ways of Mutual Funds: Market Timing' (2006) 25 Annual Review of Banking & Financial Law 235.

[74]   Eg 'In its pernicious sense, market timing describes mutual fund insiders' subtle use of the inherent structures of mutual funds and inside information to selectively provide benefits to favored participants at the expense of less-favored participants' ibid 236.

[75]   Ibid 236.

[76]   SEC Release No. 33-8408 IC-26418 (modified 20 April 2004) endnote 11 http://www.sec.gov/rules/final/33-8408.htm accessed 15 January 2018.

[77]   The time lag may, but need not, be exploited a second time, in the same way, for the exit if the price movement anticipated on entry is large enough. For example, the inertia of the fund's NAV_{FI} may allow the fund timer to exit at a profit the following day should he so wish.

[78]   The process can be repeated with the same or a different fund or through 'fund switching' between two or more funds (the ability, offered by distributors of funds, to transfer holdings from one or more funds to another or others through simultaneous exits and entries without any cash movement).

resulting from repeated 'round trips' in large amounts.[79] This explains why excessive trading, both in frequency and size of orders, is a feature of this practice.[80]

Due to an elongated lag caused by differences in time zones and bank holidays, funds established and managed in one continent but investing in equity securities of another present an ideal target. This is called 'time zone arbitrage'. Due to 'thin trading' resulting in exchange prices which are not current, funds focusing on the equity securities of small capitalisation companies also offer opportunities for stale price arbitrage.

Identifying the price movements and other events which will affect funds' NAV_{FI} is not difficult for a fund timer.[81] However, his success will be all the greater, if he is able to estimate accurately in advance the effect of market movements on the value of a fund's portfolio. Research, including analysis of funds' valuation and dealing timeframe,[82] helps identify optimal target funds for different types of market movements. Identifying the sensitivity[83] of a fund to market movements is not as challenging as it might seem (even in the absence of precise information as to the exact composition of a fund's portfolio at a given time).[84] Many actively managed funds are unfortunately little more than 'closet trackers' and others exhibit a fairly constant tracking error over time.[85]

Fund timers need not interact directly with a fund through an account in their name. They are able to hide their frequent trading from targeted funds. This can be achieved in different ways. There are complex arrangements, such as trading through different accounts over which the timer exercises investment control, but also simpler arrangements, such as trading through platforms offered by order aggregators.[86] These include 'fund supermarkets', providers of retirement savings plans (such as 401(k) plans in the United States and trust-based 'self-invested personal pensions' (SIPPs) in the United Kingdom) and insurers offering investment products.[87] A timer's order relating to a fund will be aggregated with the orders

---

[79]   Other variants may involve timing a fund while at the same time entering into an offsetting derivative transaction on a portfolio replicating the assets of that fund.

[80]   The following extract from an internal email sent by a portfolio manager illustrates this: 'In less than three months, the fund as [*sic*] had inflows of $91,991,193 (138% of assets) and outflows of $80,991,653. By my reckoning, we've had 14 round trips of massive flows in and out' (cited in Exhibit 2 to the Complaint by the Attorney General of the State of New York in *State of New York v J & Seligman & Co Incorporated*, 2 September 2006 http://ag.ny.gov/sites/default/files/press-releases/archived/Exhibits%201-10.pdf accessed 15 January 2018).

[81]   The two inferences referred to at n 68 illustrate the information which needs to be obtained.

[82]   Portfolio composition, top holdings, sector bias and net currency exposure (for international funds) will also be analysed on the basis of the fund's historical profile and information from funds' periodic reporting and fund rating agencies.

[83]   In this context, a measure of how NAV_{FI} responds to different types of market movements.

[84]   Selective portfolio disclosure by fund managers and others to favoured clients who used it for timing the relevant funds was one of the features of the 'market timing' scandal in the United States in 2003.

[85]   Tracking error is a measure of the deviation of a fund's return from that of its benchmark index. A 'closet tracker' (a supposedly actively managed fund which closely tracks its benchmark index) will have a low tracking error facilitating reliable estimates of its sensitivity to different types of market movements.

[86]   In the mutual fund scandal, the former were used primarily by hedge funds whereas the latter primarily by individuals.

[87]   Insurance products (including SIPPs) are discussed below. While both types of SIPPs involve order aggregation, in an insurance SIPP (unlike a trust SIPP) the underlying fund interests are benefi-

relating to that fund from all other clients of the platform. The aggregator will then pass to the fund, in its own name, either a single net (subscription or redemption) order or two orders (one for aggregate subscriptions and one for aggregate redemptions). In the United States, individuals trading mutual funds through their 401(k) plans featured in the scandal.[88] Despite reforms since 2003, the extent of frequent trading through 401(k) plans resurfaced as recently as 2015.[89] An audit by the US Government Accountability Office found a low prevalence of frequent trading through such plans. It cited two examples, a sponsor of a plan with 64,000 participants and a large record keeper responsible for more than 3 million participants. The former issued initial warning letters to 400 participants engaged in frequent trading and restricted from trading ten participants in 2013. The latter was reported as having issued 441 warnings and 253 restrictions since 2013.[90]

B.   'Late Trading'

A simple explanation of 'late trading' (in the context of funds) was provided in 2004 by the United Kingdom's Investment Management Association (now the IA):

> As the majority of UK investment funds are forward priced on a daily basis, the price an investor pays depends on when they place their order. If placed before the dealing cut off point, the investor will pay the price set that day. However, if the order is placed after the cut off point, the next day's price applies. Late trading is the illegal practice of managers accepting orders to buy or sell shares/units after the dealing cut off point and permitting the investor to pay the previous set price. This practice can be likened to betting on a horse race after the race has finished.[91]

Late trading is a violation of the forward pricing rule through a breach of a fund's dealing cut off point. As forward pricing is a legal requirement in the United States, the practice there was clearly unlawful.[92]

The late trader takes a step beyond the fund timer described in the preceding section. With the collusion of the fund's agents, he is able to deal in the fund at a known price in violation of forward pricing. Despite this obvious difference between the two practices, they are variations on the same theme.

---

cially owned by the insurer and not the client. The same applies to the other investment products involving funds offered by insurers.

[88]   Frankel and Cunningham (n 73) II. B. 6, 247 and III. C, 258; SEC Order relating to AEFC, Advisers Act Release No. 2451 (1 December 2005) III. 8, 3.

[89]   US Government Accountability Office, '401(K) Plans: Frequent and Collective Trading Are Uncommon and Not a Significant Concern for Plan Participants, Sponsors, or Mutual Funds' (GAO-15-427R, 14 May 2015).

[90]   Ibid Enclosure I, 17. The fact that some individuals still engage in frequent trading of mutual funds through their retirement plans is more noteworthy than the low prevalence of the phenomenon. It was to be expected that, following the 2003 scandal, only a small minority would continue to use a tax privileged long-term retirement plan for the purpose of frequently trading mutual funds.

[91]   IMA, 'Late trading and market timing' (Press Release, 18 March 2004) para 1, 1 www .theinvestmentassociation.org/assets/files/press/2004/20040318-01.pdf accessed 15 January 2018 (IMA Statement).

[92]   See text to n 64. In the mutual fund scandal, late trading also manifested itself through cancellations after the dealing cut off point (when NAV_{FI} was known) of orders previously given.

Modern late trading only emerged because trading gains can be made through arbitrage of funds' stale prices. Like the fund timer of the preceding section, the late trader exploits the interval between the time when changes in the value of a fund's equity portfolio become apparent and the time at which he is still able (in his case in violation of the dealing cut off point) to deal in that fund at a NAV_{FI} which does not yet reflect those changes. By breaching the dealing cut off point, he extends the time interval available to him to arbitrage the stale prices profitably and obtains the additional advantage of being able to deal at a known price, eliminating any residual uncertainty facing a mere fund timer as to the exact price at which his late order will be executed.

C.   Fund Timing through Insurance Products

Funds have become the underlying asset of choice for other financial products aimed at retail clients, primarily savings plans offered by insurers and other institutions to facilitate provision for long-term investment goals, particularly retirement. Amongst the insurance products, one finds variable annuity and variable life insurance contracts in the United States and unit linked life insurance policies and plans in Europe, including in the United Kingdom insurance SIPPs and 'single premium investment bonds'.[93] To encourage long-term saving, these products almost always offer a preferential tax treatment the form of which varies across jurisdictions and type of plan.[94]

A feature of these products is that, subject to any guarantees which their insurance 'wrapper' might add, their return is based on the performance of the investment options to which clients choose to allocate their cash contributions. Between clients and the underlying assets selected by them stands the insurer. It owns those assets. A client's claim under the policy fluctuates with the value of the underlying investments selected by it. Mutual funds in the United States and UCITS in Europe are the most common category of investment option.[95]

Although these products are substantially similar across jurisdictions, the way they are structured and regulated varies. Each investment option is a (more or less formalised)[96] separate account on the balance sheet of the insurer.[97] When the investment option corresponds to an actual fund, the separate account will be invested in fund interests of that fund.

The separate account is called a 'variable subaccount' in the United States,[98] 'unit linked fund' in the United Kingdom and '*unité de compte*' (unit of account) in France. In each case, the separate account is an identifiable pool of assets held by the insurer. In the United States and the United Kingdom that pool resembles in certain respects a managed fund, albeit one

---

[93]   See text to n 87.

[94]   Typically, tax is deferred while savings grow within the plan. This is often accompanied by reduced taxation on withdrawals after a number of years and sometimes also by tax relief on contributions.

[95]   Given how these products relate to our subject, this chapter will only focus on investment options which are mutual funds or UCITS.

[96]   In relation to our three jurisdictions, it is, as we shall see, most formalised in the United States and least formalised in France.

[97]   An account separate, and insulated, from the insurer's 'general account'.

[98]   Variable (as opposed to 'fixed') in the sense that the returns vary depending on the performance of that subaccount's underlying investments. By contrast, a fixed subaccount offers a fixed (or a minimum) rate of return and a client's cash contributions to it will usually be allocated to the insurer's general account.

that is invested exclusively or primarily in fund interests of an underlying fund. As a result, the separate account is, in substance, a clone of that underlying fund.[99] It has its own valuation and dealing framework for policyholders' orders and its own distinct net asset value calculation. By contrast, a French unit of account relating to a single underlying fund simply reflects the NAV_{FI} of that underlying fund. There is no intermediating 'fund clone' with its own operative provisions. Instead, provisions on policy transactions relating to each unit of account tend to appear in the general terms of the policy.

Another substantive difference is that in the United States, both variable annuities and the separate accounts through which they are offered are regulated also by the SEC.[100] Almost all variable annuities offering mutual funds use a dual investment company structure. The upper tier is the insurer's separate account structured as a 'unit investment trust' registered with the SEC.[101] The lower tier comprises the actual mutual funds offered as investment options. The upper tier is divided into subaccounts.[102] Each variable subaccount corresponding to a mutual fund is invested in shares of that mutual fund. Variable annuities are therefore redeemable securities issued by an investment company. As a result, all investments in, or redemptions from, a subaccount, and all transfers between subaccounts are subject to the forward pricing rule.[103] Unlike the position in the United States, neither unit linked funds in the United Kingdom nor units of account in France are regulated as 'collective investment schemes'.[104] As a result, forward pricing does not automatically apply to dealing in funds through UK or French unit linked policies.

Given that these policies allow policyholders to deal, albeit indirectly, in the underlying funds, they too were used extensively by fund timers to engage in short-term trading in funds, especially as they afford fund timers certain additional advantages.

As fund timing takes place within the policy, it is primarily implemented through transfers between investment options.[105] These include 'safe haven' options in the form of money market funds, short-term bond funds or a fixed subaccount or its equivalent.[106] As timing opportunities arise, a fund timer can make simple 'round trips' between one or more equity funds and one of these safe haven options. Alternatively, two distinct funds offered under a policy may both

---

[99]   In the United Kingdom, a unit linked fund which 'reproduces' a fund managed by a third party is often referred to as a 'mirror fund'.

[100]   The US Supreme Court held in 1959 that variable annuities were 'securities' and their separate accounts were subject to regulation under the ICA; see *SEC v Variable Annuity Life Ins. Co.*, 359 US 65 (1959). In addition, insurance regulation applies at the level of the state(s) in which an insurer is established and offers variable annuities.

[101]   A unit investment trust offers clients redeemable securities in a fixed, unmanaged portfolio held only for a specified period of time. In this context, redeemable securities in the unit investment trust are offered by the insurer to its variable annuity clients.

[102]   These can also include a fixed subaccount, see n 98.

[103]   See text to n 64.

[104]   However, both countries have asset eligibility rules on types of underlying assets that may be used in unit linked life policies and rules requiring insurers to match closely their liabilities under these policies with congruent assets. In addition, the United Kingdom requires insurers offering unit linked life policies to abide by certain fundamental (but vague) principles applicable also to asset managers.

[105]   This is often called 'fund switching'. See n 78.

[106]   In France, the equivalent would be a '*fonds garanti en euros*' offered as an option in almost all policies. In the United Kingdom, it could be a 'unitised with profits fund' offered as an option in some products (notably single premium investment bonds).

present at the same time a stale NAV_{FI} opportunity but in opposite directions. In that case, a fund timer can 'double dip', as it were, by switching out of the fund with the overvalued NAV_{FI} and into the fund with the undervalued NAV_{FI}. As these transfers take place within the policy, the capital gains realised through disposals do not give rise to a tax liability.[107]

Another advantage is that detection of frequent trading by the underlying fund is difficult. As for investment platforms, all orders by policyholders relating to a particular underlying fund are aggregated and the insurer passes to the fund either a single net (subscription or redemption) order or two orders (one for aggregate subscriptions and one for aggregate redemptions).[108]

As, unlike the United States, the forward pricing rule does not apply by operation of law to unit linked funds or units of account, there is a further advantage in the United Kingdom and France. The valuation direction and the valuation and dealing cut off points for transactions under the policies are contractually set between the insurer and the policyholders. This has resulted, especially in the case of older policies distributed in the last two decades of the last century, in historic pricing often being used for such transactions and in valuation frequencies, valuation points or dealing cut off points which do not match those of the underlying funds.[109] The effect of this can be to lengthen considerably the time lag which can be exploited by fund timers. An extreme example, which has attracted considerable press coverage, comes from France. Certain older policies there combine historic pricing with a weekly valuation frequency allowing policyholders to make transfers between units of account at a NAV_{FI} which can be up to a week old.[110]

VI.   THE EFFECTS OF TIMING FUNDS

Following the eruption of the scandal, the impact of these practices on funds and their long-term clients was recognised in quick succession by an array of regulators and asset manager associations. Among others, it was addressed (in chronological order) by the SEC,[111]

---

[107] In addition to tax deferral, fund timers can also benefit from a favourable tax treatment on cash withdrawals from policies after a certain number of years. For example, this is the case for most French unit linked life policies and SIPPs in the United Kingdom (to the extent of 25% of the value of the SIPP).

[108] See text to nn 86–88.

[109] In the United Kingdom, the mismatch would typically arise at the level of the provisions governing the operation of a specific unit linked fund, whereas in France at the level of the policy provisions relating to valuation and dealing in units of account.

[110] Dan McCrum (Alphaville), 'Meet the man who could own Aviva France' *Financial Times* (London, 27 February 2015) http://ftalphaville.ft.com/2015/02/27/2120422/meet-the-man-who-could-own-aviva-france/ accessed 5 February 2018; David Rose, 'Investor could be in line for one billion euros: Frenchman claims Aviva faces huge losses over "golden ticket" deals' (This is Money, 16 December 2017 as updated on 18 December 2017) www.thisismoney.co.uk/money/news/article-5186489/You-owe-ONE-BILLION-euros-investor-tells-Aviva.html accessed 5 February 2018.

[111] SEC Release No. 33-8343 IC-26287 (11 December 2003) Pt I.A paras 5 and 6 http://www.sec.gov/rules/proposed/33-8343.htm accessed 15 January 2018.

the FSA (now the FCA),[112] the IMA (now the IA),[113] the AMF,[114] CESR (now ESMA)[115] and IOSCO.[116] As some of these statements fail to distinguish adequately between different types of impact and the circumstances in which each arises, a simplified overview of how fund timing affects funds and their clients in different circumstances is set out below.

A.   The Dilution Effect

Any entry into, or exit out of, a fund timed to exploit a stale NAV_{FI} dilutes the value of the interests of the fund's other clients.[117] This would also be the case if the order was not part of a pattern of frequent trading by the relevant client but merely an informed timing decision when rebalancing a long-term investment portfolio. It would even be the case if the timing was purely coincidental, in that the order was not consciously timed so as to exploit that stale NAV_{FI}. However, the dilution intentionally caused by fund timers engaged in trading funds frequently and in large amounts is obviously of a different order of magnitude (ethically as well as quantitatively). While excessive trading is not a prerequisite of dilution, it exacerbates dilution.

I will refer to this impact as the 'dilution effect'. By diluting the value of the interests of the fund's long-term clients, it reduces the performance of that fund for those clients.

B.   The Effects of Disruption

Another consequence is the disruption of a fund's ability to manage its portfolio in the interest of its long-term clients and in accordance with its investment strategy and investment objective. This disruption is caused by excessive short-term trading, which, we saw, is a feature

---

[112]   FSA, 'Statement on Market Timing' (Press Release FSA/PN/024/2004, 18 March 2004) note 1 for editors www.fsa.gov.uk/library/communication/pr/2004/024.shtml accessed 15 January 2018 (FSA Statement). The FSA Statement (but without its notes for editors) is also appended to the IMA Guidelines cited in n 113 and future references to its paragraphs and pages relate to this appended version.

[113]   IMA Statement (n 91) last para, 1; IMA, 'Market Timing: Guidelines for managers of investment funds' (6 October 2004) 4th para, 2 and 2nd para, 3 www.theinvestmentassociation.org/assets/components/ima_filesecurity/secure.php?f=press/2004/20041006-02.pdf accessed 15 January 2018 (IMA Guidelines). A more recent, but substantially similar, version was published on 1 July 2008 www.theinvestmentassociation.org/assets/files/industry-guidance/20080701Markettiming.pdf accessed 15 January 2018.

[114]   AMF Position (n 66) para 1.5, 2. The initial reaction of the AMF in 2004 was in the form of a Recommendation published in the AMF's Monthly Review no. 5, July–August 2004. This became a Position in August 2012. The statements in para 1.5 of the AMF Position (as it currently stands) on the harmful effects of these practices first appeared in a '*fiche pédagogique*' (explanatory note) in the AMF's Monthly Review no. 15, June 2005.

[115]   CESR, 'Investigations of Mis-Practices in the European Investment Fund Industry – Report of the Investigations by CESR's members' (CESR/04-407, November 2004) 7th para, 2 www.esma.europa.eu/sites/default/files/library/2015/11/1-04_407.pdf accessed on 15 January 2008.

[116]   IOSCO Technical Committee, 'Final Report – Best Practices Standards on Anti Market Timing and Associated Issues for CIS' (October 2005) Pt I paras 8 and 13, Pt III para 9 www.iosco.org/library/pubdocs/pdf/IOSCOPD207.pdf accessed 15 January 2018.

[117]   See text to n 53. The term 'dilution' is sometimes used in this context restrictively to capture timed entries while excluding timed exits, eg McCabe (n 143) s 2, 4 and s 7.3, 24. I use the term to capture also the reduction in the value of the interests of other clients due to timed exits at a higher NAV_{FI}.

of fund timing used as a short-term trading strategy aimed at maximising trading gains.[118] Although fund timing is a cause of excessive trading in retail equity funds, disruption would also be caused if there were excessive short-term trading not motivated by fund timing. For example, derivative products using funds as their reference asset may cause frequent inflows and outflows through adjustments to the size of positions taken in those funds;[119] or short-term positions in funds may occasionally be taken either to hedge exposures to other market risks or, as the IMA stated, based on 'views, often resulting from quantitative analysis as to future market directions'.[120]

Disruption occurs because the fund manager is forced to modify the way it manages the fund's portfolio so as to deal with the liquidity pressures[121] caused by fund timers' excessive trading. That disruption in turn produces its own series of effects. I will refer to them as the 'effects of disruption'. These will vary for any given fund depending on how the manager chooses to deal with the disruption.

For example, a fund may be forced to stray away from its optimal asset allocation[122] by reducing its exposure to equities and increasing its allocation to cash. This is done so as to avoid having to invest transient cash inflows and then liquidate prematurely parts of the portfolio in order to meet cash outflows.[123] However, in a rising equities' market, this will impact (adversely) the fund through foregone performance. In order to limit the opportunity cost of carrying too much excess cash, the manager may also increase the allocation to equity index futures which could be liquidated easily, quickly and at a lesser cost than equity securities.[124] However, in the case of an actively managed equities fund priding itself on 'stock-picking', that would not be optimal.[125] In a similar vein, for funds authorised to invest across the spectrum of equities in a given region, country or business sector irrespective of the size of the relevant companies, fund timer activity may cause a fund to reduce its allocation to less liquid 'small- and mid-cap' equities in favour of 'large-cap' equities.

If due to net cash outflows[126] caused by fund timer redemptions the allocation to cash falls to zero or below the manager's minimum reserve level, the fund will be forced to replenish that

---

[118]   See text to nn 77–80.

[119]   Such products offer finance secured on a holding of fund interests or tailored exposure (leveraged or principal protected) to the performance of a fund. They rarely relate to retail equity funds.

[120]   IMA Guidelines (n 113) 3rd para, 2. This, of course, is market timing in the original sense of the term (see text to n 4). However, large and liquid ETFs, rather than actively managed funds, tend to be used for this purpose. To the extent that the latter are used, the profitability of such short-term trading is greatly enhanced if it is combined with stale price arbitrage. Contrary to the distinction drawn by the IMA, there is no reason to think that these two forms of trading are truly distinct in relation to the funds that concern us.

[121]   In this sense, the management of cash inflows that are unlikely to stay in the fund for long and cash outflows that are larger and more frequent than they would be absent fund timer activity.

[122]   As determined at any time by the fund manager in light of the fund's investment objective, market conditions and its own convictions.

[123]   The investment of fund timer cash inflows in equities only for a short period carries costs and risks. That investment, followed by a disposal in the near future, will generate two sets of trading costs and, if the disposal is at an inopportune time, may also generate a realised loss or otherwise result in foregone performance (irrespective of which assets are sold).

[124]   Assuming the fund is structured so as to permit investment in such futures.

[125]   If clients wanted passive equity index exposure, there are cheaper and more effective ways of obtaining it than investing in an actively managed fund.

[126]   These are caused by an excess of aggregate redemptions over aggregate subscriptions.

cash reserve through a sale of portfolio securities which is very likely to be for the most part involuntary and may also prove untimely. The manager will have to choose whether to sell part of the fund's most liquid equities at the risk of unbalancing the portfolio or a pro rata portion of all or most of the portfolio's holdings at the risk of incurring higher costs. Other factors may complicate the choice of which securities to sell. The sale of some may crystallise a gain, the sale of others a loss.[127]

To the extent that fund timer activity in relation to a particular fund causes involuntary sales, followed by purchases, of portfolio securities, these transactions expose the fund to adverse price movements between sales and purchases.[128] The same applies to purchases of portfolio securities due to fund timer inflows followed by forced sales.[129] The effect of any adverse price movements is exacerbated by the 'bid/offer spreads'[130] incurred in these transactions. In the case of less liquid securities, large orders by the fund may incur 'market impact cost'.[131] Finally, like all portfolio transactions, these purchases and sales give rise to transaction costs. These include brokerage fees, exchange, settlement and clearing costs, custody transaction charges and, depending on the fund and the countries in which it invests, also taxes and repatriation costs for local securities sold by a foreign investor.

It is in ways such as these that managing a fund is disrupted by fund timers' excessive trading. Whatever form the effects of disruption for a particular fund take, it is clear that, like the dilution effect, they too reduce the performance of a fund and, therefore, also its returns to its other clients.

C.   Certain Disruption and Dilution Distinctions

The magnitude of the effects of disruption, for any fund, will depend on the frequency and size of fund timer activity relative to the size of that fund and the level of concurrent inflows from, and outflows to, other clients. While modest trading could be absorbed, with minimal or no

---

[127] In the United States, net gains realised by a fund through a sale of portfolio securities have to be distributed to its clients and are potentially taxable upon distribution: 'Frequent trading also may result in unwanted taxable capital gains for the remaining fund shareholders', SEC Release No. IC-26782 (11 March 2005), 70 Fed Reg 13328 13329 (18 March 2005), 5.

[128] Eg if prices have risen generally since the sale, or if the price of any individual security purchased has risen since its previous sale.

[129] Eg if prices have fallen generally since the purchase, or if the price of any individual security sold has fallen since its prior purchase. The following extract from an internal email sent by a senior portfolio manager illustrates this graphically: 'I had to buy into a strong early rally yesterday, and I know I'm negative cash this morning because of these bastards and I have to sell into a weak market' (cited in the Complaint by the Attorney General of the State of New York in *State of New York v Invesco Funds Group, Inc. and Raymond Cunningham*, 2 December 2003 https://ag.ny.gov/sites/default/files/press-releases/archived/invesco_complaint.pdf accessed 15 January 2018).

[130] The difference in price at any time on an exchange between (a) the order offering a given security for sale at the lowest price, and (b) the order bidding for the purchase of that security at the highest price. If one wishes to sell (or buy) immediately, the highest bid (or the lowest offer) price available at that time for one's full volume is the best price one can usually get.

[131] Eg the order itself may, by virtue of its size, move the price against the fund, if only by consuming a number of different price levels in the order book and thus reducing the best price at which one can sell (or increasing the best price at which one can buy) the full volume of the fund's order.

disruption, by a large fund with regular inflows and outflows,[132] excessive trading that is not so absorbed will have a material impact on the fund through disruption. However, even modest trading by timers will cause dilution irrespective of the size of the fund and other inflows or outflows. Excessive trading by timers will exacerbate that dilution.

Another distinction lies in how dilution and disruption relate to timers' gains. Dilution results from the extraction of excess value from a fund by timers. In that sense, timers' gains are closely related, and are sometimes said to correspond exactly,[133] to the resulting dilution losses of the fund. By contrast, the losses due to disruption have been described as 'deadweight losses' in that no portion of timers' gains is derived from them.[134] They are just collateral damage.

Other distinctions relate to indirect fund timing through insurance products. Here, timing operates through the medium of separate accounts corresponding to underlying funds.[135] Fund interests held in separate accounts are owned by the insurer who is required to deal in fund interests so as to match its liabilities under these policies by congruent assets.[136]

First, impact on underlying funds and their direct clients should be distinguished from impact on policyholders investing in the corresponding separate accounts. Second, impact on those policyholders may be due to impact on underlying funds or separate accounts (or both).

As regards impact on underlying funds, fund timers' orders flow to underlying funds through insurers' aggregated orders. If fund timers' orders are frequent and large, they cause disruption in the usual way.[137] Any reduction in a fund's performance due to that disruption will affect all policyholders who have selected that fund as an investment option.[138] If the fund is not reserved to insurers, its direct clients will also be affected.

Whether an underlying fund is diluted will depend on whether the NAV_{FI} at which the insurer's order is priced reflects accurately the value of the fund's portfolio at that time.[139] For example, if the fund valuation point of the insurer's order coincides with the policy valuation point exploited by timers, dilution of the underlying fund is almost certain.[140] Conversely, if the insurer's order is issued after a lapse of time and is priced at a future NAV_{FI} which happens to accurately reflect the value of the fund's portfolio at that time, then there will be no dilution of the underlying fund.

Whether a separate account is itself susceptible to dilution or disruption depends on its structure. For example, a UK unit linked fund will be susceptible to both if its assets comprise

---

[132]   Where, on any given day, fund timers' in(out)flows are fully or substantially neutralised by other clients' out(in)flows.

[133]   Through a transfer of wealth effect, eg McCabe (n 143) s 2, 4 and s 7.3, 22–3, but see n 117 on McCabe's use of the term 'dilution'.

[134]   Ibid s 5.2.2, 16.

[135]   See text to nn 105–7.

[136]   See n 104.

[137]   To the extent they are not neutralised by other clients' orders. In this case, other clients are other policyholders and, if the fund is not reserved to insurers, also other direct clients. See n 132.

[138]   The value of their entitlement under the policy in relation to that investment option reflects that underlying fund's NAV_{FI}.

[139]   If it understates that value when the net order is a subscription, or overstates it when the net order is a redemption, there will be some dilution. (Any mismatch between the price at which a policyholder's *successfully timed* order is executed by the insurer and the NAV_{FI} at which the insurer's corresponding order is executed by the fund is likely to give rise to losses incurred by the insurer.)

[140]   In the absence of sufficient antidilutive measures.

both fund interests in the underlying fund it mirrors and cash, and if it has its own valuation and dealing framework for policyholders' orders, including its own distinct net asset value calculation. By contrast, a French unit of account which simply reflects the NAV_{FI} of a single underlying fund is not itself susceptible to any dilution or disruption apart from that suffered by that underlying fund.[141]

Where a separate account is so susceptible, it is exposed to disruption much as a fund would be in the case of direct fund timing.[142] The extent to which it is diluted will depend again on the extent of any mismatch between the prices at which fund timers' policy-level transactions are executed and the net asset value of the separate account at that time.

D.   Quantifying the Effects

The quantitative impact of fund timing on mutual funds in the United States was addressed by a number of studies prepared before and after the eruption of the scandal. Some, prepared before the scandal, attempted to measure only the dilution effect; others, prepared after the scandal, focused on differences in risk adjusted returns between funds, a measure that would in principle capture the effects of both dilution and disruption. The earlier studies were prepared before targeted funds were identified and tended to use as a sample international equity funds prone to dilution through timing. The later studies focused instead on funds managed by asset manager groups tainted by the scandal, but not always on individual funds known to have been targeted. The impact estimates of seven of these studies were summarised in a research staff working paper in the Finance and Economics Discussion Series (FEDS) of the Federal Reserve Board authored by Patrick E. McCabe and prepared in 2008, which also set out its own estimate of impact.[143] As one would expect, impact estimates vary between studies due to different methodologies, samples and periods. The summary below is based on the FEDS working paper.[144]

A 2002 study, using daily data on fund flows and returns to measure dilution, estimated that from 1998 to 2000 the average annual dilution effect for world equity mutual funds with above median flow volatility was 0.94 per cent of fund assets.[145]

---

[141]   It is in effect a mere notional accounting entry reflecting an underlying fund's NAV_{FI}.

[142]   To the extent timers' orders are not neutralised by other policyholders' orders (see n 137) or by the insurer dealing for its own account through a 'box' and taking the opposite side of the trade represented by those orders (see n 52).

[143]   Patrick McCabe, 'The Economics of the Mutual Fund Trading Scandal' (2009) Finance and Economics Discussion Series (FEDS 2009–06) www.federalreserve.gov/pubs/feds/2009/200906/ 200906pap.pdf accessed 15 January 2018

[144]   It omits four of the seven studies cited in the FEDS working paper: one earlier study of the dilutive impact (alone) on equity funds of late trading (alone); and three later studies, one concerned again with dilutive impact (alone) and two concerned with differences in returns (in one case simple average returns) of funds managed by groups tainted by the scandal (rather than specifically those funds which were targeted). It is interesting to note that the omitted earlier study found that the dilution effect of late trading alone was substantially lower than that of market timing as estimated by the same author in other studies. See McCabe (n 143) s 5.1 and Table 3.

[145]   Ibid.

A 2003 study, using futures data to identify timing opportunities more precisely than fund flow data does, found that from 1998 to 2001 the average annual dilution effect for equity funds focused on the Pacific region, Japan and Europe was 1.60 per cent.[146]

A 2006 study, focusing on differences in fund returns between targeted funds and other equivalent funds, found that from January 2001 to August 2003 the annual performance short-fall in risk adjusted returns for targeted funds was 1.95 per cent.[147]

The FEDS working paper included a sample comprising all known 'abused mutual funds'[148] irrespective of investment objective. The aim was to measure the difference in annual risk adjusted gross[149] returns between funds known to have been abused and equivalent 'untainted mutual funds'[150] for each of the three years preceding the scandal (September 2000 to August 2003). The result was that the relative returns[151] of abused funds were, on average, 4.86 per cent lower than those of untainted equivalent funds.[152] Three different methods for measuring risk adjusted returns were also used. Depending on the method, they show a lower, though still very high, annual performance shortfall of 4.37, 3.69 and 3.62 per cent.[153] A measure based on net (as opposed to gross) returns also shows a 3.62 per cent shortfall.[154]

Timers' gains from market timing and late trading of 'abused funds' in the same three-year period were estimated at $2.68 billion (an average of $894 million per year).[155]

VII.   THE REGULATORY RESPONSE

The initial response of the authorities to fund timing in 2003 came from the Attorney General of the State of New York in the form of legal action against fund timers.[156] Regulators around the world reacted soon afterwards. Their initial pronouncements on the impact of fund timing on funds and their long-term clients were cited in the first paragraph of Section VI. In this section, our focus will be on Europe and, in particular, the response to the issues raised by fund timing of regulators and professional associations in the United Kingdom and France.

A.   United Kingdom

Following the eruption of the scandal in the United States, the FSA launched an investigation. It found no evidence of late trading in UK authorised funds and attributed this in large part to

---

[146] Ibid.

[147] Ibid.

[148] A mutual fund was 'abused' if the fund manager had permitted the fund to be 'market timed' or 'late traded' or if it was abused by principals or employees of the fund manager, ibid 8.

[149] Returns before fees, ibid 13.

[150] A mutual fund was 'untainted' if it was neither abused itself nor 'operated by a mutual fund family that managed at least one abused fund', ibid 8.

[151] The relative return of a fund was defined as its total return less the asset weighted mean return of all funds belonging to its S&P mutual fund category. Relative returns, in this sense, were used as a simple measure of risk adjusted returns, ibid 11–12.

[152] Ibid s 5.2.2 and Table 4.

[153] Ibid s 5.2.1 and Table 4.

[154] Ibid.

[155] Ibid s 7.3, 24 and Appendix.

[156] See n 72.

the fact that orders are placed directly with fund managers before valuation points.[157] Some evidence of limited market timing activity was uncovered but 'no sign either that market timing is widespread or that it has been a major source of detriment to long-term investors'.[158] Most instances identified had been 'short lived with fund managers taking swift action to terminate relationships where clients have attempted to time funds'.[159]

When the scandal erupted, the FSA was in the process of revisiting certain aspects of fund regulation. A consultation paper had been issued in May 2003.[160] Two changes proposed in that paper, together with a clarification of the scope of an existing provision, formed, in the following year, the crux of the FSA's response to fund timing.

The first proposal was to allow fund managers to use fair value pricing as a means of addressing the problem of stale prices and the dilution risk they posed, particularly for international equity funds.[161]

The second proposal was to allow fund managers to set the dealing cut off point of a fund before its valuation point. The reason for this was to give fund managers more time to determine the number of fund interests to be created or cancelled at that valuation point.[162] After the eruption of the scandal, the utility of this as an anti-timing tool for international funds became apparent: an earlier dealing cut off point reduces the time interval available to exploit price movements and other market events since a fund's last assets' valuation point.[163]

Both changes came into force, subject to transitional provisions, on 1 April 2004.[164] The FSA also clarified that a provision in existing regulations which allowed fund managers to refuse subscription orders in certain circumstances could be applied to persons whose dealing activities may have a detrimental effect on the fund (and thus implicitly to fund timers).[165] This clarification did provide a useful tool in turning fund timers away and was apparently used for that purpose.[166]

Following its investigation, the FSA reached the conclusion that the existing regulatory framework 'provide[s] sufficient tools to enable firms to manage the conflicts of interest posed by market timers'.[167] The issue was passed on to asset managers to deal with.

---

[157] FSA Statement (n 112) penultimate para, 15. In 2003, the valuation point was also the dealing cut off point for UK funds.

[158] Ibid para 5, 15.

[159] Ibid para 2, 15.

[160] FSA, *The CIS sourcebook – A new approach* (Consultation Paper 185, May 2003) (FSA CP 185).

[161] Ibid paras 5.35–7, 31–2; Annex 2, paras 50–2, 10–11. Following coverage of the issue in academic literature (see text to n 71), the FSA was aware of the issue before the eruption of the scandal in the United States but, like others at the time, appears to have perceived fund price arbitrage in terms of dilution risk alone. See also FSA Statement (n 112) note 1 for editors.

[162] Ibid para 5.29, 30.

[163] FSA, *The CIS sourcebook – A new approach* (Policy Statement 04/7, March 2004), paras 2.16–17, 13. This policy statement was released simultaneously with the FSA Statement (n 112).

[164] Ibid App 1, 1.

[165] Ibid para 1.14, 5; para 2.23, 14. The provision in force in 2003 allowed managers to refuse a subscription order on reasonable grounds relating to the circumstances of the person submitting the order. It was amended to cover both subscription and redemption orders where the fund manager 'has reasonable grounds to refuse' them (without reference to the circumstances of that person). See ibid App 1, para 6.2.16(2)(a) and (3).

[166] FSA Statement (n 112) para 2, 15; IMA Guidelines (n 113) para 6.1, 14.

[167] FSA Statement (n 112) last para, 15.

In October 2004, the IMA issued its guidelines to asset managers.[168] These reminded asset managers that:

> Whilst Market Timing is not explicitly a breach of UK regulations, managers are subject to over-riding fiduciary responsibilities and should also take note of the FSA Principles, in particular Principle 6, 'A firm must pay due regard to the interests of its customers and treat them fairly' and Principle 8, 'A firm must manage conflicts of interest fairly, both between itself and its customers and **between a customer and another client**' Principle 8 would become especially relevant if managers were to contemplate offering privileged access to the Market Timer.[169]

The objective of the guidelines was to provide 'suggestions for a robust and demonstrably reasonable control framework that will give . . . comfort that managers are taking all reasonable steps to help ensure that funds are being protected from the activities of Market Timers'.[170]

The suggestions addressed the question of how to put in place 'a robust structure . . . to defend against, identify and deal with Market Timing'.[171] They included: measures on appropriate policies and procedures, staff training and assignment and acknowledgement of responsibility;[172] suggestions on how to identify market timing;[173] eight ways of attempting to make funds less attractive to market timers, including use of the two FSA measures implemented in April 2004;[174] and four ways of deterring identified market timers, including refusing to deal with them on the basis of the FSA's clarified and revised rule, implemented at the same time.[175]

The difficulty presented by order aggregators, in particular the manager's inability to look through an aggregated order, was identified.[176] The guidelines suggest that orders from aggregators could be subjected to appropriate monitoring and managers' terms of business with aggregators should set out managers' policies on market timing and the consequences of activity designed to circumvent them.[177] For managers who use dilution levies as part of their anti-timing tools, there was a specific suggestion. Managers should only waive dilution levies on orders from aggregators if they enter into an enforceable agreement obliging the aggregator to submit separately individual orders which would trigger the levy and allowing the manager access to the aggregator's records to monitor compliance.[178]

As regards unit linked funds, the FSA reminded insurers that the FSA Principles apply and encouraged them to adopt the tools available under the regulatory regime for funds 'to allow them to avoid potential detriment' to their policyholders from market timing.[179] In 2013, a thematic review by the FCA involving 12 insurers identified, among other issues, unit linked funds offered by four of them operating on a historic pricing basis with no, or very few,

---

[168] IMA Guidelines (n 113). The FSA saw and provided input to the production of the guidelines (penultimate para, 3).

[169] Ibid 3.

[170] Ibid 4. The guidelines are not binding and offer managers of funds liable to be targeted considerable latitude on how to address fund timing.

[171] Ibid Pt 2, 7.

[172] Ibid.

[173] Ibid Pt 3, 8.

[174] Ibid Pt 5, 10–13.

[175] Ibid Pt 6, 14.

[176] Ibid Pt 3, 8 and Pt 4, 9; see also FSA Statement (n 112) last para, 16.

[177] Ibid Pt 3.

[178] Ibid para 5.7, 13. For dilution levies, see nn 52–3.

[179] FSA Statement (n 112) penultimate para, 16.

controls to protect policyholders.[180] The FCA stated that historic pricing 'can be exploited by customers with market knowledge who can strategically deal to their own advantage – and potentially to the detriment of the fund and other customers'.[181] In response, the Association of British Insurers (ABI) revised its guide to good practice for unit linked funds.[182]

The revised guide, still in effect, certainly emphasises the need to address the impact of market timing on other policyholders and attempts to rise to the challenge by a series of suggestions.[183] These include, in relation to unit linked funds operating on a historic pricing basis, the deferral of policyholders' orders or even the temporary suspension of dealing rights for policyholders believed to be engaged in market timing.[184] However, the guide also states that any action taken should take into account relevant policy conditions.[185]

As regards the question of how fund timing was perceived in the United Kingdom and how the regulatory response was guided by that perception, the following points are noteworthy:

1. The FSA saw fund timing as just another form of 'arbitrage . . . of price imperfections' and considered that such arbitrage is a 'normal market activity' but one which, when applied to a fund, gives rise to a 'market imperfection' because 'the arbitrageur gains at the expense of the continuing investors'. This 'market imperfection' should be countered with tools provided to fund managers.[186]

   This early view was expressed before the eruption of the scandal in the United States and therefore before the magnitude of the effects of frequent fund timing on funds and their long-term clients had become clear. Nevertheless, the unstated assumption behind this view is that funds belong to the class of financial assets which it is appropriate to arbitrage (irrespective of their function as vehicles for retail clients' savings). If it were not so, their use for such arbitrage would not be seen as a 'normal market activity', and perhaps the unfortunate consequences of that use for other clients of the fund would no longer appear as an unavoidable 'market imperfection'.

2. Consistent with this early view, in 2004 the FSA perceived fund timing as a problem merely raising issues of conflicts of interest (primarily between timers and long-term

---

[180] FCA, *The governance of unit-linked funds* (Thematic Review TR13/8, October 2013) s 2.3.2, 17–18.

[181] Ibid.

[182] ABI, 'Guide to Good Practice for Unit-linked Funds' (May 2014) (ABI Guide). While ABI's guidelines are not binding, they were developed after consultation with the FCA, which indicated that it will take account of them in its supervision of insurers (ibid paras 1.8 and 1.11). It is incumbent on insurers to explain to the FCA the reasons for any failure to comply with them (ibid para 1.3).

[183] Ibid paras 5.10, 17, 19, 21 and 26.

[184] Ibid 5.22 and 23.

[185] Ibid 1.2, 2.1, 4.12, 5.24 and 5.27. For example, certain options may be contractually precluded by the terms of certain policies.

[186] FSA CP 185 (n 160) Annex 2, paras 51–2, 10–11.

clients)[187] and its own role as limited to ensuring that fund managers had sufficient tools at their disposal to deal with that problem.[188]

As it was assumed that it is appropriate to time funds in order to gain from their inherent price imperfection, the issue came to be seen as a conflict between two sets of legitimate interests, those of fund timers and those of the long-term clients of the fund. As such, it was relegated to fund managers to deal with through the IMA guidelines on market timing.

3. In the same vein, the IMA stated that, in the UK investment fund industry, market timing was 'generally regarded as being an unfair practice' or 'a sharp practice'.[189] In accordance with the FSA's approach, it framed its guidelines in terms of a conflict between the interests of timers and other clients.[190] The guidelines are mere suggestions, often accompanied by reasons, whether of cost or operational convenience, why managers may not be able to implement some of them.[191] The same applies to ABI's guidelines on fund timing through unit linked policies.[192] The implementation of the latter faces the additional obstacle of contractual provisions in older policies.[193]

Although the IMA and ABI guidelines issued on the basis of the FSA's approach are an insufficient response to fund timing, the measures proposed by the IMA in particular suggest that, at least, the interests of the fund's long-term clients should clearly take precedence over those of fund timers.[194] In addition, the IMA emphasised to fund managers that not affording any special treatment to fund timers is not sufficient – all reasonable steps to discourage them should be taken.[195] In doing so, it at least placed the issue beyond the narrow confines of conflicts of interests between different clients and into the sphere of investor protection. As we shall see, this step was not taken in France.

B.   France

In France, the AMF's response was set out in its 2004 Recommendation.[196] The main measure was a recommendation that equity (and bond) UCITS should operate on a forward pricing basis. Other recommendations related to asset managers having procedures in place to detect and avoid market timing and late trading (without specifying what these should be); being able to check that agents centralising orders respect the dealing cut off point of funds;[197] booking

---

[187] For this to raise also a conflict between the interests of the manager and those of the fund's long-term clients, collusion between the manager and the timers would be necessary (as occurred in the United States).

[188] FSA Statement (n 112) last para, 15; note 1 for editors.

[189] IMA Statement (n 91) para 2, 1; IMA Guidelines (n 113) para 2, 2.

[190] Ibid 3.

[191] IMA Guidelines (n 113) last para, 4; para 5.2, 10.

[192] ABI Guide (n 182) paras 1.2, 1.10, 1.13 and 5.20.

[193] See n 185. Guidelines of professional associations (or even regulators) cannot by themselves override contractual entitlements, however contrary to public policy the latter may be.

[194] See text to nn 171–175.

[195] IMA Guidelines (n 113) para 2, 3.

[196] AMF Position (nn 66 and 114).

[197] The recommendations aimed at late trading also clarified that the time specified in a fund's prospectus as the dealing cut off point relates to the latest time by which all orders must reach the agent centralising the orders rather than the intermediary receiving a client's order directly.

portfolio investments upon entering into the relevant trade;[198] not disclosing the composition of a fund's portfolio on a real time basis; requesting intermediaries receiving client orders to be particularly vigilant in relation to orders which by their frequency or size might indicate market timing; and checking that their own personnel do not engage in market timing or late trading.

In 2012, the status of these measures was elevated from that of mere recommendations to that of a 'position'[199] and they remain in place, essentially in the same form.[200]

As regards the manner in which the AMF apprehends these practices, the following points stand out:

1. The disclosure of the exact composition of a fund's portfolio to a 'market timer' is, surprisingly, a constitutive element of the AMF's definition of market timing.[201] This is surprising because, although such disclosure facilitates a timer's task, it is by no means a prerequisite to successful fund timing,[202] nor in any way a defining feature of the practice.
2. The culprits in the US scandal were hedge funds principally investing in Asian equities' funds.[203] This is a very narrow view not only of the mutual funds targeted at the time but also of the predator-investors involved. As is the case in France,[204] individuals had also engaged in fund timing.[205]
3. The AMF stated that fund timers' profits violate the principle of fair treatment of all clients because neither the exact composition of a fund's portfolio nor the ability to submit orders late is available to all.[206] This suggests that the AMF considers that, in the context of fund timing, it is only through late trading and selective portfolio disclosure to favoured clients that the principle is violated. In other words, an asset manager who does nothing to address variants of fund timing which resort to neither of these two extreme steps would appear, in the AMF's view, not to be in breach of the principle of fair treatment of a fund's clients or, in fact, of any other duty towards them.[207]
4. Favouring certain clients over others by facilitating such practices is contrary to the professional conduct rule that an asset manager should act solely in the interests of all clients, and could, therefore, result in an asset manager being sanctioned.[208] Although true, this final statement (which immediately follows the one cited in the preceding paragraph on

---

[198]   Presumably this is meant to apply also to sales of portfolio investments. See text to n 67.

[199]   A position of the AMF is an interpretation of legislative or regulatory provisions relating to matters within its competence. It ranks below an instruction but above a recommendation.

[200]   Subject to certain amendments made in 2012 and 2015 not relevant for our purposes.

[201]   AMF Position (n 66) para 1.1, 1.

[202]   See text to nn 83–85.

[203]   AMF Position (n 66) 1.4, 2.

[204]   See n 110. The use by individuals of unit linked life policies in timing funds may have been raised at the time of the AMF's investigation in 2004 by the French insurance regulator (see AMF, '*Rapport Annuel 2004*' (Annual Report for 2004), 1 June 2005, Ch 5 Pt 3, 176).

[205]   See n 88.

[206]   AMF Position (n 66) para 1.5, 2.

[207]   The AMF Position does not mention any other duty which could be breached by these practices. In particular (and surprisingly), there is no reference to any broader duty to protect investors in funds from fund timers.

[208]   AMF Position (n 66) para 1.5, 2.

fair treatment of all clients) confirms that the AMF saw its role as limited to ensuring that no clients received favourable treatment from the fund manager over others.

The regulatory provisions cited in the heading of AMF's Position as the ones to which it relates and which it interprets are all technical provisions relating to the processing and centralisation of orders, and as such are relevant to late trading rather than to fund timing in general.[209] The provisions relating to the principle of equal or fair treatment of clients, which forms the basis of the measures taken by the AMF is not cited. Similarly, other UCITS-inspired provisions which also came into force in France in 2011 relating to asset managers' duty to protect the interests of their clients specifically in relation to malpractices such as market timing and late trading were not cited when the Recommendation was elevated to a Position in 2012 or when it was amended again in 2015.[210]

AFG (*Association Française de la Gestion financière*), the professional body representing French asset managers, proceeded to transpose AMF's recommendations in its own code of ethics. In line with AMF's narrow perception of fund timing, the approach taken by AFG was much less detailed than that of the IMA. AFG's professional conduct principles (which are binding on member firms) simply provide that an asset manager should never disclose to certain clients or other parties any information about a fund's portfolio if this would infringe the principle of equal treatment of clients.[211] AFG's code of ethics also includes a separate set of recommendations to member firms.[212] As regards our subject, these reflect those of the AMF and are, on occasion, slightly more detailed. The main recommendation is that asset managers should identify those funds which present a significant risk of 'market timing' and take measures to 'manage that risk', including procedures and information tools to detect it and rules on dealing, booking transactions and valuation conducive to ensuring that subscriptions and redemptions are effected at an unknown price and on the basis of a 'fair value' for the fund.[213] There is nothing further on AMF's Position that asset managers should ask intermediaries receiving client orders to be particularly vigilant in relation to orders which by their frequency or size might indicate market timing.[214]

Finally, unlike the United Kingdom, no measures were taken to address the issue of fund timing through unit linked life policies even though equity funds which, on the basis of AMF's Position, are only available on a forward pricing basis can in fact be traded on a historic basis through such policies.

---

[209]   The provisions cited are those set out in the RG AMF (n 55) arts 411-65 -67 and -68 (in relation to UCITS funds).

[210]   See text to nn 217–20.

[211]   *AFG, 'Règlement de déontologie des OPCVM et de la gestion individualisée sous mandat – Dispositions'*, 10 December 2009 www.afg.asso.fr/en/publications-2/reference-texts/ (English translation) accessed 15 January 2018, Tl A, ch 1, para 13, 7.

[212]   *AFG, 'Règlement de déontologie des OPCVM et de la gestion individualisée sous mandat – Recommendations'*, 10 December 2009 www.afg.asso.fr/en/publications-2/reference-texts/ (English translation undated) accessed 15 January 2018.

[213]   Ibid ch 1, paras 8, 10 and 11.

[214]   Even though aggregation of orders is prevalent in France (beyond unit linked policies) because clients' fund interests are credited to securities accounts in their name held by intermediaries (typically banks) who submit consolidated orders reflecting clients' individual orders.

C.   The European UCITS dimension

The entry into force on 1 July 2011 of the UCITS IV regime presented an opportunity to European regulators to reinforce their response to fund timing.[215] The Directive set out the principles which, at a minimum, each member state should include in professional conduct rules binding on fund managers authorised by it.[216] A feature of these principles is that a manager should act 'in the best interests of the UCITS it manages and the integrity of the market'.[217] One of the implementing directives recognised that market timing and late trading may have detrimental effects on clients of funds, may undermine the functioning of the market and qualified them as 'malpractices'.[218] It provided that member states should require fund managers 'to apply appropriate policies and procedures for preventing malpractices that might reasonably be expected to affect the stability and integrity of the market'.[219] The same article provided that member states should require fund managers 'to act in such a way as to prevent undue costs being charged to the UCITS and its unit-holders'.[220] Finally, the special vulnerability of master feeder UCITS structures to market timing was recognised.[221] The Directive required that master and feeder UCITS should coordinate their valuation timeframe 'in order to avoid market timing . . . [by] preventing arbitrage opportunities'.[222]

The provisions of the implementing directive on the prevention of malpractices and undue costs being charged to funds were implemented, almost *verbatim*, both in the United Kingdom and France.[223] In the United Kingdom, following the approach of the directive,[224] FCA guidance cites market timing and late trading as examples of the malpractices referred to in the new rules.[225] There is also guidance that excessive trading (of the fund's assets) could be an example of undue costs referred to in the new rules.[226] In France, no express reference was made to market timing or late trading in the two new rules implementing the provisions on malpractices and undue costs.[227] In addition, the AMF did not seize the opportunity provided by this reform to update its Recommendation (as it still was in 2011) so as to provide its interpretation of the scope of the new rules and reflect the greater emphasis placed by the UCITS IV regime on investor protection.

---

[215]   UCITS IV Directive (n 55) and UCITS IV Implementing Directive (n 60).
[216]   UCITS IV Dir (n 55) art 14(1).
[217]   Ibid art 14(1)(a) and (b).
[218]   UCITS IV Implementing Dir (n 60) recital 18.
[219]   Ibid art 22(2).
[220]   Ibid art 22(4).
[221]   The UCITS IV regime permitted a UCITS to be a feeder fund to another UCITS. Without certain precautions, a feeder fund which is invested in fund interests issued by a master fund could be an ideal target for fund timers.
[222]   UCITS IV Dir (n 55), art 60(2).
[223]   COLL 6.6A.2R (3) and (5); RG AMF (n 55) art 314-3-1 3° and 5° (now art 321-101 3° and 5°).
[224]   See text to n 218.
[225]   COLL 6.6A.3G (1).
[226]   COLL 6.6A.3G (2). This is a reference to the costs borne by a fund as a result of the effects of disruption.
[227]   This omission, in conjunction with the use of the term '*malversation*' (for 'malpractice') in the RG AMF and the French version of the UCITS IV Implementing Directive, somewhat obscures the relevance of the new rules to fund timing in France.

VIII.   FUND TIMING REVISITED

By way of conclusion, the time has come to assemble the various pictures taken during our visit. There are pictures of fair games, random walks and martingales; pictures of funds seen as a tool designed for a purpose; pictures of those for whom this tool was designed and of how it was meant to be used, also of its intricate pricing mechanisms; pictures of how timers abuse it to a different end and of the consequences of that abuse; finally, pictures of how our rule makers perceive that abuse. Let us now draw these pictures together to see what emerges.

A.   What Fund Timing is and What it is Not

When we looked at 'market timing', we saw that it stood for the idea of timing one's purchases and sales on the basis of predictions of future price movements derived from analysis of a number of indicators with a view to maximising one's investment gains.[228]

Let us look at what *that* market timing has in common with the trading practice of the same name involving funds and what differentiates the two.

Like market timing, fund timing also aims at maximising gains through timing one's buy and sell orders on the basis of expectations as to future prices. However, the similarities end here. While the market timer is attempting to predict future price movements in the actual markets, the fund timer need not concern himself with anything as uncertain as that. He is only concerned with one predictable price, the level of the next NAV_{FI} at which he can deal. In respect of that price, he is primarily interested in how stale it will be in light of information he already has as to developments since the last assets' valuation point of the fund.

Put differently, faced with an uncertain future, a market timer is naked[229] or, at best, only lightly armed with his chosen indicators (be they economic, fundamental, technical or behavioural).[230] By comparison, the fund timer, targeting an appropriate fund at a suitable time, is armed with a valuable informational advantage on the level of the next NAV_{FI}.

For these reasons, 'market timing' when applied to timing funds is a misnomer which dissimulates the perverse nature of that practice. Timing funds regularly as part of a short-term trading strategy is neither about the markets and their future direction, nor about timing one's entry into, or exit from, different types of long-term equity exposure taken through funds as part of an occasional rebalancing exercise aimed at optimising one's long-term investment gains. In fact, it is not even about investment. It is all about locking in short-term trading gains through the ability to deal in certain funds, at opportune times, at prices that one knows are stale.

B.   Informational Advantages

After the scandal, commentators drew attention to the informational advantage used by timers when dealing in funds. It was described as 'market information known only to the privileged

---

[228]   See Section II (Market Timing).
[229]   If one believes in the Efficient Market Hypothesis.
[230]   See text to nn 5–7.

few'.[231] This presumably refers to market information about price movements or other events, since a fund's last assets' valuation point, which will impact its next NAV_{FI}.[232] Although not strictly 'market information', the term may also refer loosely to fund-specific information as to a fund's portfolio or the NAV_{FI} at which a late trader's order will be priced.

Taking the first type of (market) information, let us explore a parallel. Let us compare insider dealing with fund timing from the following perspectives: the nature and value of the insider's and the timer's informational advantage; how it is obtained; how and to what end it is used; and the effects of trading for personal gain on the basis of that informational advantage on other market participants.

In both cases, the information in question is not yet reflected in the price of the relevant financial asset at which one can deal, and it will, or is likely to, affect that price in the future. It is therefore valuable. In many, if not most, cases, the timer's information is of a higher quality than the insider's because its effect on NAV_{FI} is either inevitable or at least more certain.[233]

In both cases, the information can be obtained lawfully but is not available to all in any meaningful sense. For example, the insider may obtain it in the course and for the purpose of his employment, while the timer typically obtains it by using the services of market data providers to follow on a real-time basis certain price movements and other events occurring since a fund's last assets' valuation point.

Both the insider and the timer use their respective informational advantage to buy (or sell) financial assets at a price which will, or is likely to, rise (or fall). Both do so for personal gain and, more often than not, they succeed (at least initially, in the case of an insider that is actually caught).

If one compares the effects on other market participants of the use of their respective informational advantage in trading, the effects of fund timing seem, overall, more serious. Insider dealing has been described as a victimless crime. It may or may not be one depending on who (or what) counts as a victim but, in terms of *tangible* loss *directly* inflicted on *identifiable* others, timers seem to be comfortably in the lead over insiders. At the level of less tangible indirect effects, both seem to undermine confidence in the fairness and integrity of the financial markets to an equal degree. If anything, fairness and integrity when dealing with equity funds in which massive amounts of retail investors' long-term savings are invested seems a more pressing consideration than when dealing in some esoteric financial products reserved to professional investors. Finally, the inherent pricing inefficiency of certain funds, in conjunction with the volatility of equity prices, creates comparatively more opportunities for a timer to exploit through his informational advantage than any other financial asset offers to an insider, who is dependent on obtaining inside information each time.

Beyond the similarities, there are some differences. One is relevant from the perspective of financial ethics. The information of the insider, even though it may have been lawfully obtained, is almost always information obtained and held under a duty of confidentiality. The

---

[231]   Eg '[market timing] involves timing purchase and redemption orders of mutual fund shares in light of market information known only to the privileged few' Frankel and Cunningham (n 73) 236.

[232]   See the description in the two inferences referred to in n 68.

[233]   The price movements and other events since the fund's last assets' valuation point have already occurred. It only remains to submit an order just before the dealing cut off point. By contrast, the effect of the information on which an insider trades on the price of the relevant financial asset is, in many cases, contingent on future events (eg the completion of a transaction in the form anticipated and no other event occurring which would counteract its effect on that price).

information lawfully obtained by the timer on price movements and events since a fund's last assets' valuation point is not confidential and can be obtained by any experienced investor with superior access to market data. So, when an insider uses confidential information lawfully obtained by him for an extraneous purpose to trade for personal gain he is also acting in breach of confidence.

Other than that, both the insider and the timer seek to profit from information which is not available, in any meaningful sense, to all;[234] which will, or is likely to, affect the future price of a financial asset; and which they use to trade for personal gain (inflicting also, in the case of the latter, direct tangible loss to other clients of the relevant fund).

The insider's use of his informational advantage in trading for personal gain constitutes an offence attracting criminal sanctions, but the timer's use of his is only viewed as 'sharp practice',[235] which is neither prohibited nor sanctioned. If the difference in the treatment of the two practices is based on rational grounds, one may conclude that the treatment of insider dealing owes much more to 'breach of confidence' considerations than to other considerations, linked to the operation of the financial markets, often cited in defence of its treatment.[236] (However, other routes of redress and sanction were available for breaches of confidence committed through the use of confidential information for an extraneous purpose and personal gain). The alternative explanation is that this difference in treatment is not quite rational and that legislators and regulators have, in relation to these malpractices directed at funds, shied away from upholding the principles of 'market integrity' so loudly proclaimed.

C.   Beyond an Informational Advantage . . .

We saw in the previous section that the term 'market information known only to the privileged few' may also refer loosely to information as to the NAV_{FI} at which a late trader's order will be priced.

For a forward priced fund, this information can only be obtained unlawfully, providing certainty to the timer as to the price at which an order will be executed, and is therefore used, together with market information since a fund's last assets' valuation point, in deciding whether to submit an order after the dealing cut off point or withdraw an order previously submitted.[237] The informational advantage is reinforced illicitly by knowledge of the NAV_{FI} and the fund timer is now also a late trader and an insider.

Historically priced funds add a further permutation to the informational advantage. They provide timers lawfully with the very information as to NAV_{FI} which our US late trader could only obtain unlawfully. In doing so, they allow lawful dealing in fund interests at that known price. Seen in that light, historic pricing is, in essence, lawful late trading.

---

[234]   And certainly not to the average retail client of the funds that concern us.

[235]   See text to n 189. In France, it would even appear to be unobjectionable, in the absence of late trading, provided there the timer did not benefit from selective disclosure of a fund's portfolio composition.

[236]   Considerations such as undermining the integrity of financial markets and public confidence in them, see e.g. Regulation (EU) No 596/2014 of the European Parliament and of the Council of 16 April 2014 on market abuse [2014] OJ L173/1 (Market Abuse Regulation), recitals 2 and 23.

[237]   See text to n 92.

This explains why historic pricing was proscribed in the United States in 1968 and why European jurisdictions have belatedly started to abandon it.[238] As we saw, this process is not yet complete. For example, European equity funds subject to forward pricing are still available indirectly at historic prices through unit linked life policies and are still the target of timers engaging in frequent short-term trading and enriching themselves in the process at the expense of others.[239]

The informational and dealing advantage offered by a UCITS which uses historic pricing, even if abused only by timers, is at least offered equally to all existing and future clients of that fund. However, when a timer can lawfully deal in a forward priced equity UCITS through an insurance product at obsolete historic prices, his informational and dealing advantage is quite unique. All other investors in that fund may only deal in its interests on a forward pricing basis, precisely so as to discourage fund timing.[240] This violates the principle of fair or equal treatment of investors in that fund.

In addition, the timer in this case is uniquely able, lawfully, to take and exit equity market exposures through the policy at those obsolete prices. This violates the broader principle of a level playing field for all market participants, itself a prerequisite for fairness and integrity in financial markets.

We are in the presence of the ultimate insider, armed with certainty. There is no longer a need to obtain, lawfully or unlawfully, information and assess its likely impact on the future price of an asset so as to trade profitably at a price which does not yet reflect that information. One can just keep on dealing at obsolete prices. In doing so, one avoids the risk borne by other insiders that, due to future events, the price of the asset may not behave as one expected on the basis of the information on which the trade was previously made. Uncertainty has been eliminated. This unique, almost absurd, dealing advantage offers to these timers a shortcut to certain trading profits, which is unavailable to all other market participants to the detriment of others.

D.   Is there a Place for Fund Timing in Funds?

The funds which concern us are the vehicle of choice for mutual (or collective) investment by retail clients in the equity markets. Together with equity ETFs, they are in effect the only such vehicles available to most retail clients. Alongside their capital formation utility, their object is to offer those clients a means to invest, however modestly, in the equity markets and allow them to share in its superior long-term returns. This is achieved through a common pool of diversified equity exposures, which is meant to be professionally managed in a cost-effective way so as to generate investment gains in the long term.

Fund timers do not invest in, or through, funds; they merely use them as just another financial asset which can be profitably arbitraged for serial short-term gains. Amongst the myriad opportunities available for trading financial assets, a minority is attracted to timing funds because their pricing inefficiency, whether inherent or amplified by their insurance 'wrappers', offers an easy target that is free of risk. What was meant as a long-term investment vehicle accessible to financially unsophisticated persons requiring discretionary management

---

[238]   See text to nn 64–66.

[239]   See n 110.

[240]   Whether they are direct investors in the fund or have selected it as an investment option under their unit linked policy. (Modern policies do not have a historic pricing feature.)

services is treated by some as just another means to short-term trading gains at the expense of all other clients of the fund.

Unlike other means to trading gains, timing funds serves no useful economic purpose, whether in price formation or through the provision of liquidity. It merely enriches those who engage in it at the expense of others. Through the dilution effect, any trading gain from fund timing is extracted from the common pool and represents a loss for the fund's long-term clients. Extensive fund timing not only magnifies those trading gains and corresponding losses but also, through disruption, prevents the asset manager from performing properly the very task for which it is paid, managing the fund's portfolio for the long term in the interest of the fund's clients in accordance with the relevant investment objective. The effects of that disruption cause further losses to those clients which, as we saw, can exceed losses due to dilution.

The issue of fund timing can be viewed from a number of different perspectives: that of the uncertainty of future market prices and informational advantages; a teleological perspective focusing on the function of funds and the needs of those for whom funds were designed; the perspective of the timers' own motivations and their use of funds for a wholly different purpose; and finally from the perspective of the consequences of fund timing on those for whom funds were designed. However, one looks at the issue one can be forgiven for being puzzled by the fact that timing funds (other than through late trading) is neither prohibited nor sanctioned and that in at least one jurisdiction it appears to be tolerated and even, inadvertently, encouraged through regulatory inaction.

PART IV

THE EFFECTIVENESS OF REGULATION AND SUPERVISORY ACTIONS

12. Developing the senior managers regime

Alan Brener

INTRODUCTION

Financial services' rule books have increased in length but no amount of regulation can compensate for unethical behaviour by board members, senior executives and other individuals operating in financial services firms with the wrong culture. This was central to the recent financial crisis, and subsequently, to the mis-selling of financial products, extensive money laundering and the widespread abuse of financial indices. At the heart of many of these conduct problems was the lack of individual accountability. While regulators took successful action against many financial firms, senior individuals in these organisations largely escaped being held responsible. As a consequence, UK financial regulators recently introduced the Senior Managers and Certified Persons Regime (SMR), at first for banks and insurance companies. These regulations were extended to all financial services firms in 2019.

The new regulations are aimed at ensuring that senior management and other staff who are in a position to do significant harm to financial firms and their customers will, in future, each have their own documented areas of individual responsibility and will be held accountable, and hence liable to sanction, for regulatory failures within those areas. This is a major component in a series of regulatory changes which include better aligned remuneration and changes to market structures.

This chapter considers the conceptual underpinnings of the new regime, the barriers to success and possible additional steps to help transform the culture of financial firms and the ethics of individuals within these businesses. It also considers organisational and operational factors relevant to the success of the new rules and highlights the significant psychological barriers which may hinder both the identification of problems within a financial institution and the acceptance of responsibility in the event of failure.

Further, the new regulations operate in a Durkheimian sense, facilitating the public punishment of those who may have caused financial instability and loss, helping to reinforce societal cohesion with a focus on individual accountability and retribution. In another, and more positive sense, the new regime poses a challenge to the boards and executives of financial services firms. Its aim is to improve the culture within regulated firms to help foster public trust. Consequently, the SMR is not just another set of regulatory process requirements. With the right level of engagement the new regime does provide an opportunity to demonstrate a change in ethical behaviour.

The remainder of this chapter is organised as follows: after a brief historical account of the evolution of financial services regulation in the United Kingdom in section 1, section 2 examines the concepts of 'accountability' and 'responsibility' and the application of consequential liability for failure which underpins the SMR. Section 3 considers the moral and ethical collapse within UK banking and the role played by public outrage, which has yet to be ameliorated, the loss of social cohesion and the need for new regulations to render individuals responsible and, hence, accountable. Section 4 sets out key aspects of new rules and considers, more fully, the rationale behind the new requirements, which are, in many ways, conceptually innovative. Section 5 considers the factors which might militate against the effectiveness of these new arrangements in view of the fluid levels of actual accountability in most complex organisations, the culture and ethics evident in many banks and the current model for risk and compliance structures prevailing in these organisations. It also questions the effectiveness of the new regime based on the evidence that there are significant psychological barriers preventing both the identification of problems within a bank and the acceptance of responsibility in the event of failure. These impediments include: greed, hubris, tribal cultures, moral blindness and self-deception. This examination considers the role of bank boards in this context. Section 6 reviews the role of business culture and individual ethics, since many of the failures evident over recent years have at their heart deficiencies in culture and individual ethics. Finally, section 7 considers other methods to improve institutional culture and personal ethics including collective action by senior bankers for engendering cultural change and the need to improve professionalism and professional ethics, in the banking industry.

1.1   THE ORIGINS OF THE NEW REGIME

Financial services firms are the repositories of societal trust. The breakdown in public trust in banks following the 2007/8 financial crisis, coupled with the serious financial services scandals uncovered since then, has produced many strident calls for retribution. Political and public anger resulted in the establishment of the Parliamentary Commission on Banking Standards (PCBS). In 2013, the Commission issued a seminal report covering a wide range of issues relating to banking in the United Kingdom, its structure, governance and, in particular, its ethics and culture.[1]

The PCBS, the media and the general public have also been concerned about the general lack of punishment for senior bankers. Society had placed significant trust in these individuals. A number of them had been celebrated and honoured prior to the crisis.[2] In a significant number of instances this trust appears to have been abused.

Bankers have been subject to much greater criticism than those working in other problematic industries such as meat processing and distribution, and the automobile and extractive industries. Bankers, as a category, have been seen as venial, corrupt, incompetent, untrustworthy and generally unethical. The special opprobrium attached to bankers reflects the fact that, in many ways, 'banks are different from other corporate entities because public confidence is critical to their survival in a way and to an extent that does not arise even in the wake of serious brand damage sustained by a major consumer-oriented non-financial business. When depositor confidence is lost in a bank, its whole survival is put in jeopardy.'[3]

---

[1]   House of Lords House of Commons, 'Changing banking for good', Report of the Parliamentary Commission on Banking Standards, Volume II (2013, HL Paper 27-II HC 175-II).

[2]   For example, Forbes, 'Fred Goodwin "Forbes Global Businessman of the Year"' (1 June 2003) and The London Gazette, 'James Crosby was honoured with a Knighthood in 2006' (16 June 2006) No. 58014, Supplement No. 1.

[3]   David Walker, 'A review of corporate governance in UK banks and other financial industry entities: final recommendations' (November 2009), 23.

Public anger was exacerbated by the level of bonuses paid to bankers, particularly in a period in which banks needed to be rescued with public funds and some of this assistance was used to meet contractual bonus arrangements.[4] This has reinforced the general view that senior bankers were not held accountable and were not confronted with personal responsibility for their actions, and in many instances were rewarded for failure.

The financial crisis appears to have had two sets of intertwined causes. At one level it was the result of powerful economic and social forces, often difficult to understand, whose individual weight may still be disputed. At another level there were a number of individuals in important positions within banks who through incompetence or malfeasance, devastated the economy. The new regime for senior managers and certified staff seeks, primarily, to address this latter element.

The SMR needs to be seen in the context of the development of financial services regulation in the United Kingdom. The latter can be described as having three broad phases.[5] The initial approach, developed in the 1980s, was to trust the financial services industry with a system of self-regulation within a statutory framework.[6] Banks, at their own volition, could not be subject to regulatory fines under this arrangement, having elected to be supervised directly by the Securities and Investments Board.[7] The second phase commenced in 2001 with a statutory regulatory system operated by the Financial Services Authority (FSA) under the Financial Services and Markets Act 2000 (FSMA), where the most egregious breaches of conduct of business regulation were largely enforced by regulatory action against firms rather than individuals.[8]

The introduction of the SMR appears to introduce a third regulatory phase based on individual accountability. This is grounded on a number of issues. First, the apparent ineffectiveness of the earlier regulatory phases to influence corporate behaviour to prevent widespread product mis-selling and risk-taking in the run-up to the financial crisis. Second, public anger at what had happened and the failure to hold individuals to account. Third, regulators depend on the boards and senior management of regulated firms to ensure compliance with both the spirit and letter of the regulations. The new rules operate through setting up structures capable of bringing about the required outcomes such, as will be seen, regulator maps and statements of responsibility and setting standards of individual behaviour. These *ex-ante* measures are supplemented by the threat of *ex-post* regulatory action against those individuals who fail to meet those standards. This, it is hoped, will both encourage compliance and may satisfy public demands for retribution in the future.

---

[4]   For example, 'total compensation for employees at Wall Street's big five securities firms rose in 2007, to $66 billion from $60 billion in 2006', The Economist, 'The thorny issue of bankers' bonuses' (26 January 2008).

[5]   Philip Rawlings, Andromachi Georgosouli and Costanza Russo, 'Regulation of financial services: Aims and methods' (April 2014), http://www.ccls.qmul.ac.uk/media/ccls/docs/research/020-Report.pdf.

[6]   Ss 7–9, Financial Services Act 1986.

[7]   Andrew Large, 'Financial Services Regulation: Making the two tier system work' (May 1993), Securities and Investments Board, 72.

[8]   For example, enforcement was limited to firms' mis-selling of payment protection insurance: FSA Annual Report 2006/7, 29.

2.1   ACCOUNTABILITY, RESPONSIBILITY AND CONSEQUENTIAL LIABILITY

Accountability has been described as 'central to our understanding of justice' and has resulted in a demand for justice 'when things go wrong'.[9] However, the PCBS found that 'one of the most dismal features of the banking industry to emerge from our evidence was the striking limitation on the sense of personal responsibility and accountability of the leaders within the industry for the widespread failings and abuses over which they presided'.[10] As a consequence, both the Financial Conduct Authority (FCA) and the Prudential Regulatory Committee (PRC, formerly the Prudential Regulatory Authority (PRA)) have opted for a regime which imposes personal sanctions, since it appears clear that moral obloquy or, as Aristotle terms it, 'shame' is insufficient to encourage people to 'refrain from evil'.[11]

As a result of the regulatory failure to hold almost anyone to account, the PCBS recommended a new regulatory system fixing senior individuals in banks with personal areas of responsibility to which they would be held to account and would be liable to punishment for failure. Clearly, the terms 'responsibility', 'accountability' and 'liability' are interconnected but remain different. They do not exist in abstract, all having a subject who is responsible; and this person, or entity, must be subject to some obligation for which they are responsible and be held accountable for failures; and they must be liable to someone or something.[12] The new regulations seek to create this linkage by establishing individual responsibilities, holding managers accountable for inadequately controlling the exposure to risk of customers and business, and for any consequential harm and loss.

Accountability has been seen as 'requiring a person to explain and justify, against criteria of some kind, their decisions or acts, and then to make amends for any fault or error'.[13] It requires a number of elements. These include someone who takes responsibility under an obligation to someone else under which 'the former must give an account of, explain[ing] and justify[ing] his actions or decisions against criteria of some kind' and may be liable to some form of sanction for failure.[14]

The availability of sufficient information together with transparency of purpose, policy and implementation are the prerequisites of any system which upholds accountability. Thus may require the individual or body who is responsible for any decisions and actions to be transparent about what they propose – a form of *ex-ante* transparency. This would include setting out under what authority they are acting, the purpose of the planned action and, if appropriate, how

---

[9]   Mollie Painter-Morland, 'Redefining accountability as relational responsiveness' in Mollie Painter-Morland and Patricia Werhane (eds), *Cutting-edge issues in business ethics* (Springer, New York, 2008), 33.

[10]   Supra note 1 (PCBS report), 125.

[11]   Aristotle, *Nicomachean Ethics,* 1179b11 (Penguin Classics edition, London,1976), 277.

[12]   Nicolas Haines, 'Responsibility and accountability' (1955) Philosophy, Vol. 30, No. 113, 141–63, 143–7.

[13]   Dawn Oliver, 'Law, politics and public accountability. The search for a new equilibrium' (1994), Public Law, 238, 246.

[14]   Fabian Amtenbrink and Rosa Lastra, 'Securing democratic accountability of financial regulatory agencies – a theoretical framework' in R. V. De Mulder (ed), *Mitigating risk in the context of safety and security. How relevant is a rational approach?* (Erasmus School of Law & Research School for Safety and Security, Rotterdam, 2008), 115–32, 120.

the action will be undertaken and how success will be measured. Similarly, there needs to be *ex-post* transparency mechanisms measuring outcomes against a standard or benchmark. This may help in determining the degree of liability of those responsible and may result in some form of sanction.

An individual may assume responsibility for an action or it may be imposed upon them. However, to have significance there must also be accountability – at the very least to their conscience.[15] Accountability involves providing an explanation or rendering an account for ones' actions with the implication that they will be assessed and judged with some level of consequence. The relationship between those that take responsibility and those that hold them to account has been described as a means to permit and to control the exercise of power.[16] The application of responsibility, accountability and liability exists to control the exercise of power. 'Power must check power' operating within a set 'arrangement'.[17] These arrangements may take many different forms and exist for a wide variety of purposes.

What follows develops this further and considers the rationale for the new regime within the context of financial services regulation.

2.2   THE RATIONALE FOR THE CHANGES

The UK model of financial services regulation relies, inter alia, on firms having a good governance system overseen by their boards and senior management. It requires these individuals to interpret the regulations by applying their discretion and exercising judgement. Their judgement is mediated by systems of internal controls, which seek to achieve the regulatory objectives to satisfy both the letter and the spirit of the regulations.[18] This system of 'meta-regulation' has as its objective 'the connection of private internal justice' with the 'public justice of accountability'.[19] It requires that those working in the business, including senior management, internalise compliance with the regulations; that boards carry out effective oversight of the executive and that shareholders encourage market discipline and do not act as 'absentee landlords' or worse.[20] However, it became clear following the recent financial crisis that the regulatory foundation of 'reciprocity of interest' of bank boards, shareholders and regulators may have been overestimated.[21] These organisations are not faceless: strategy is set by individuals and systems of control are established and operated by real persons. The issue came clearly into focus following the 2007/8 financial crisis and was subsequently exacerbated by the manipulation of the Libor index. As mentioned, this resulted in the then

---

[15]   For example, St. Ignatius of Loyola, 'The Spiritual Exercises', 'To make a sound and good choice' (1522–4, printed by Nicolas Joseph Le Febvre, Saint-Omers,1736).

[16]   Supra note 14 (Amtenbrink and Lastra), 120.

[17]   , Charles-Louis de Secondat ,Baron de Montesquieu, *The spirit of the law* (published 1748, Cambridge University Press, Cambridge, England, 1989), Book II, 155.

[18]   Mads Andenas and Iris H-Y Chiu, *The foundations and future of financial regulation* (Routledge, London, 2014), 101.

[19]   Ibid, 101.

[20]   Paul Myners, 'Speech made to the Association of Investment Companies' (21 April 2009), para 38.

[21]   Supra note 3 (Walker), 25.

Chancellor of the Exchequer setting up the PCBS to review standards, including culture and ethics, in banking.

Upon examining the bankers' actions, the PCBS concluded 'that many bankers, particularly at senior level, have been allowed to operate with very little personal accountability. When things went wrong, individuals claimed ignorance or hid behind collective decision-making. Individual incentives were not linked to high conduct standards, and there was often little realistic prospect of enforcement action against senior individuals.'[22]

As mentioned above, this undermined a system of regulation which placed a heavy reliance on boards and senior management to understand and manage the business in the interests of meeting regulatory requirements[23] including moderating the expectations of shareholders.[24]

One theory of corporate retribution holds that it is fairer to sanction responsible individuals within the business rather than to impose collective punishment on the whole organisation which may have adverse effects on other innocent stakeholders.[25] Nevertheless, in many jurisdictions, regulators have rarely taken enforcement action against individuals and instead focused on disciplinary sanctions against regulated firms. There are usually two reasons given for this practice. First, regulated firms, in almost all cases, once presented with the evidence of a regulatory investigation accept the consequences without contesting the enforcement action. The evidence of rule breaches is usually overwhelming and there is little incentive to fight. This is cost effective for the regulator relative to the level of fine, extensive remediation activity and the reputation of the firm frequently attracting considerable publicity and demonstrating the effectiveness of the regulatory action. This is not the case when an action is brought against an individual. Normally, these are fiercely contested through all the layers of hearings and appeal for the individual has little to lose by doing so.[26] Moreover, the outcome for the regulator is not certain since they need to prove personal culpability and individuals are often insulated from judgement by layers of delegation, collective decision-making and a lack of clear evidence of fault pointing to one person.[27]

2.3   CONCEPT OF INDIVIDUAL ACCOUNTABILITY

The concept underlying the SMR indicates a regulatory move away from exclusive corporate responsibility and instead seeks to affix responsibility on the individual. The regime does this by requiring that senior individuals publicly accept duties in respect of certain aspects of a business. The history of the business, its pre-determined strategy, the relevant systems and

---

[22]   FCA, 'The FCA's response to the Parliamentary Commission on Banking Standards' (October 2013), 5. See also Tracey McDermott's answer to question 3015 to the Parliamentary Commission on Banking Standards, 29 January 2013, Minutes of Evidence, HL Paper 27-III/HC 175-III.

[23]   Guido Ferrarini, 'Understanding the role of corporate governance in financial institutions: a research agenda' (2017), ECGI Law Working Paper No. 347, 15.

[24]   Supra note 3 (Walker), 71–2.

[25]   Angelo Corlett, *Responsibility and punishment* (Springer, Dordrecht, Netherlands, 2013), 209–10.

[26]   'The estimated cost of the investigation of [Peter] Cummings (a HBoS Director) was over £2 million in external fees; and the investigation involved continuous work for around two years on the part of as many as 24 people' in the regulator's Enforcement Division, Andrew Green, 'Report into the FSA's enforcement actions following the failure of HBOS' (2015), 78 and n 44.

[27]   Supra note 22 (McDermott's answer).

processes, the context in which actions are undertaken or omitted are secondary, and may only be used to determine the degree of responsibility, not its existence. Ill-luck or being the wrong person present at the wrong time are, again, only relevant to determine the degree of culpability. The individual is seen as having placed themselves at personal risk by their own volition. This is not some 'Voysey inheritance' where the son inherits the father's fraud.[28] The expectations are that the incoming senior manager comes in with their eyes open and has a short time in which to uncover any significant issues and to disclose and resolve them before they are, themselves, deemed to 'own' the issues and will be held accountable for them.[29]

In practice, this means that the regulatory expectation is that 'the SMR re-establishes the link between seniority and accountability'.[30] If something goes wrong in their area of responsibility, the senior managers will be held accountable if they failed to take reasonable steps to prevent the issue. Success is likely to depend on a number of factors including individuals understanding and accepting their responsibility.

As with most areas of regulation the objective is to encourage individuals to do the right thing and therefore to prevent harm. This approach is based on the individual both internalising the risk to themselves and exercising their judgement accordingly. This is likely to be reinforced by regulatory public enforcement actions against senior managers who fail to take heed. This would both act as a warning to others in the industry and be a clear demonstration of regulatory seriousness – hopefully satisfying public calls for individual retribution.

Public anger mounted following the extensive public bank rescues, coupled with a general lack of contrition by senior banks who were often paid enormous sums even as their businesses failed and the consequential economic crisis unfolded. This outrage was reinforced by evidence of widespread mis-selling of financial products, money laundering and bench-mark indices' manipulation. The next section examines the cultural and ethical banking which underline these issues and the desire by the general public for retribution.

3.1   MORAL AND ETHICAL COLLAPSE, SOCIAL COHESION AND THE ROLE OF REGULATION TO ADDRESS PUBLIC OUTRAGE

In parallel with the investigation by the PCBS, the board of Barclays Bank commissioned a report on the culture and ethics of the bank from Anthony Salz. The Salz Report was published in 2013 shortly before the final report of the PCBS.[31] The two documents point to significant ethical and cultural failings within the major UK banks.

The report of the PCBS found that the behaviour and culture within banks had a significant role in the financial crisis and the various conduct-related scandals. 'However, under the statutory and regulatory framework in place at the time, individual accountability was often unclear

---

[28]   Harley Granville-Barker, *The Voysey inheritance* (first published 1906, Berg, Oxford, 2000).

[29]   *John Pottage v. FSA* (2012) Upper Tribunal, Reference number FS/2010/33, page 6, para 11.

[30]   Mark Carney, Remarks at the Banking Standards Board panel 'Worthy of trust? Law, ethics and culture in banking', at the Bank of England, 21 March 2017, 4.

[31]   'Salz review: an independent review of Barclays' business practices' (April 2013).

or confused. This undermined public trust in both the banking system and in the regulatory response.'[32]

'The public are angry that senior executives have managed to evade responsibility. They want those at the highest levels of the banks held accountable for the mis-selling and poor practice.'[33] The only other senior executive from a large UK bank to face any enforcement action in recent years was John Pottage, a UBS wealth management executive, whose fine for misconduct was overturned by a tribunal in 2012.[34]

The UK regulators see the SMR as a means of encouraging 'individuals to take greater responsibility for their actions' and of making 'it easier for both firms and regulators to hold individuals to account'.[35] At the launch of the new SMR, Andrew Bailey, at the time Deputy Governor, Prudential Regulation and CEO of the PRA, mentioned that 'holding individuals to account is a key component of our job as regulators of banks', and, in addition to assisting in this task, the new regulations 'should have a positive impact on behaviour and culture within banks'.[36] Martin Wheatley, at the time CEO of the FCA, expressed the view that the new regime would help meet public expectations of regulators holding individuals to account and 'also build on the cultural change we are beginning to see in the boardrooms of firms across the country'.[37] However, there is a darker side to the public desire to hold individuals to account. It is central to the history of public punishment used to assuage popular anger.

3.2   PUBLIC DESIRE FOR RETRIBUTION

As mentioned, an important part of the process of regulatory sanction is the need to satisfy public expectations that retribution has been visited on the guilty individuals and that this is explicit and highly visible.

Hart describes the response to an offence as one of 'resentment'.[38] However, following the 2007/8 financial crisis, the public response was much more than this. There was, and there remains, a very real sense of anger that little retribution has been visited on the senior executives and boards of the failed banks. The apparent powerlessness of the regulators was particularly significant. For example, a typical report had as a headline that 'Sir Fred [Goodwin, CEO of RBS] and RBS escape punishment over banking crisis and went on to state, 'In a move that will anger many . . . the FSA. . . . has concluded its investigation into RBS and said it has found no evidence of wrongdoing or "lack of integrity" by senior individuals at the bank in the run-up to its near collapse in 2008 . . . Rob MacGregor, national officer of the Unite union, said: "The report's conclusions are an outrage".'[39]

---

[32]   PRA and FCA Consultation Paper: FCA CP14/13/PRA CP14/14, 'Strengthening accountability in banking: a new regulatory framework for individuals' (July 2014), 5.

[33]   Supra note 1 (PCBS Report), 104,

[34]   Supra note 1 (PCBS report) 162.

[35]   Supra note 32 (FCA CP14/13/PRA CP14/14), 5.

[36]   News Release – 'Prudential Regulation Authority and Financial Conduct Authority consult on proposals to improve responsibility and accountability in the banking sector' (2014).

[37]   Ibid (SMR launch news release).

[38]   H.L.A. Hart, *Punishment and responsibility: essays in the philosophy of law* (first published 1967, 2nd edn, Oxford University Press, Oxford, 2008), 131.

[39]   Citywire, 'Sir Fred escapes punishment over banking crisis' (2 December 2010).

There appears to be a very real desire, in a Durkheimian sense, for the public punishment of the bankers in order to 'maintain inviolate the cohesion of society by sustaining the common consciousness'.[40] There 'is a retributivist method of corporate punishment' which seeks both a public acceptance of responsibility and penance followed by punishment in proportion to the perceived harm done and the extent of the wrongdoing.[41] In addition, there is the 'value of the authoritative expression, in the form of punishment, of moral condemnation for the moral wickedness involved . . . termed . . . a theory of reprobation rather than retribution'.[42] The actions of regulatory enforcement and punishment have a symbolic function, 'punishment generally expresses more than judgments of disapproval; it is also a symbolic way of getting back at the criminal, of expressing a kind of vindictive resentment'.[43] The failure of the regulators in this respect may have left a significant unresolved social wound bound in with feelings of unfairness and a lack of catharsis since 'punishment is deeply-rooted in the structure of society' and is 'sensitive to the political and economic dimensions of social cohesion'.[44] The alternative to this process of public adjustment and closure appears to be a lengthy period of political and media 'vigilantism'.

There are parallels with punitive theory in criminal law. The public were both confused and resentful in the wake of the 2007/8 financial crisis. This still remains true. The world of international banking, its language and levels of remuneration are beyond the experience of most people and the public reaction often expressed by the media and by politicians, generated views that the crisis was the result of 'dark forces'. The demands for the punishment of individuals represent an attack on the elites who are believed to have caused the collapse and reflects a high level of societal insecurity in the face of events which are difficult to comprehend. It may be that the reaction is based not simply on a 'Durkheimian problem of solidarity' but that the view is one of a Hobbesian break-down in financial order and security which requires Leviathan-like powers of retribution and punishment.[45]

In addition, in the face of public resentment and incomprehension, the regulators need to reassert their authority and display their 'power to punish'.[46] In the context of an analysis of the criminal law, the 'language of punitive discipline has ideologically cemented the political elite with the wider population into an often . . . emotional desire for inflicting vengeful retribution'.[47] This also reflects a rise in populism and a decline in the influence of the 'regulatory technocratic'.[48]

---

[40]   Emile Durkheim, *The division of labour in society* (first published 1893, Macmillan, London, 1984), 63.

[41]   Supra note 25 (Corlett), 222.

[42]   Supra note 38 (Hart), 235.

[43]   Joel Feinberg, 'The expressive function of punishment' (July 1965) The Monist, Vol. 49, No. 3, Philosophy of Law, 397–423, 403.

[44]   Steven Spitzer, 'Punishment and social organization: a study of Durkheim's "Theory of penal evolution"' (1975) Law & Society Review, Vol. 9, No. 4, 613–38, 634.

[45]   David Garland, *The culture of control* (Oxford University Press, Oxford, 2001), 102.

[46]   Richard Sparks, 'States of insecurity: punishment, populism and contemporary political culture' in Seán McConville (ed), *The use of punishment* (Willan, Cullompton, UK, 2003), 167.

[47]   Roy Coleman and Joe Sim, 'Contemporary statecraft and the "punitive obsession": a critique of the new penology thesis' in John Pratt and others (eds), *The new punitiveness: trends, theories and perspectives* (Willan, Cullompton, UK, 2005), 102.

[48]   Mick Ryan, 'Engaging with punitive attitudes towards crime and punishment: some strategic lessons from England and Wales' in *The new punitiveness*, ibid, 144.

In order for there to be public retribution there needs to be rules requiring individual accountability. The new regulation, as summarised in the next section, seeks to achieve this objective.

4.1   THE NEW SENIOR MANAGERS, CERTIFIED PERSONS AND INDIVIDUAL CONDUCT RULES REGIME

In March 2016, the new senior managers, certified persons and individual conduct rules regime, known collectively as the 'Senior Managers Regime' (SMR) came into force in the United Kingdom. The new regulations are derived from the Financial Services (Banking Reform) Act 2013.[49] The over-arching purpose of the new regime is to improve the culture in regulated firms by ensuring that individuals have clear areas of responsibility and are personally accountable to the regulators. It does this by requiring firms to have clear, delineated roles and to carry out regular assessments of individual fitness and properness – not just on appointment but throughout an individual's period in the post.

These changes replace the previous 'Approved Persons' regime. The new requirements initially applied only to banks, building societies, insurance companies and a few other large financial services firms but the rules were extended to all financial services businesses in 2019.[50] The Approved Persons regime required prior regulatory approval for individuals seeking appointment to one of a list of specified posts including 'those who exercise significant influence over' a firm, those carrying out a 'customer function' such as providing financial advice and those carrying out one of a number of specific functions such as money laundering reporting. Approval was based on the individual passing a regulatory 'fitness and properness' assessment. The Approved Persons regime was judged to have failed by the Parliamentary Commission on Banking Standards in its 2013 report. The reasons behind this view are central to this chapter and considered in detail later, but the next section summaries the four major elements of the changes: The SMR's statement of responsibilities, the responsibilities map, the certification regime and the individual conduct rules.

4.2   SENIOR MANAGERS REGIME

The new senior managers regime applies to individuals performing a senior management function ('SMF'). An SMF is a function that requires the person performing it to be responsible for managing one or more aspects of a firm's regulated affairs and those aspects that involve, or might involve, a risk of serious consequences for the relevant firm, or for business or other interests in the United Kingdom.[51] Individuals undertaking these roles require prior approval from the relevant regulator.[52] Besides these 'executive SMFs' the new rules also apply to non-executive board members who carry out specific oversight roles, including the chairman,

---

[49]   Ss 18–35, Financial Services (Banking Reform) Act 2013 amending the Financial Services and Markets Act 2000.

[50]   S 21, Bank of England and Financial Services Act 2016.

[51]   Ibid, s 19, Financial Services (Banking Reform) Act 2013.

[52]   Supra note 49, s 21.

senior independent director and the chairmen of sub-committees such as the risk and audit committees.[53] It is possible that SMF staff may be located outside the United Kingdom and be based in the parent and sister companies of the regulated entity.

4.2.1   Statements of Responsibilities

The new legislation includes a requirement that applications for approval as a senior manager of a regulated firm include a statement setting out the areas which the person concerned will be responsible for managing.[54] The 'Statement of Responsibilities' is a living document and must be resubmitted whenever there is a 'significant change' in the senior manager's responsibilities.[55]

The regulator can use the Statement of Responsibilities for enforcement action against individuals where there has been a regulatory breach in an area for which the individual was responsible. In assessing culpability, the regulators will apply an objective test of whether the senior manager failed to 'take such steps as a person in their position could responsibly be expected to take to avoid' the breach or its continuation.[56] For example, the FCA has issued guidance that 'a person will only be in breach of [the rules] . . . where they are personally culpable. Personal culpability arises where: either a person's conduct was deliberate; or the person's standard of conduct was below that which would be reasonable in all the circumstances.'[57] In determining whether the individual's conduct was reasonable 'the FCA would expect to take into account: whether they exercised reasonable care when considering the information available to them; whether they reached a reasonable conclusion upon which to act; and the knowledge they had, or should have had, of regulatory concerns, if any, relating to their role and responsibilities'.[58]

4.2.2   Responsibilities Map

A further significant change is the requirement for firms to prepare, maintain and update a 'Responsibilities Map' (i.e. a single document that describes the relevant firm's management and governance arrangements).[59] Such maps should also set out how responsibilities have been

---

[53]   Bank of England, Prudential Regulatory Authority, Supervisory Statement, SS28/15, 'Strengthening individual accountability in banking', September 2016 (updated January 2016), 7.

[54]   Supra note 49, s 20. See also FCA, 'CP15/22: 'Strengthening accountability in banking: final rules (including feedback on CP14/31 and CP15/5) and consultation on extending the certification regime to wholesale market activities' (July 2015).

[55]   Supra note 49, s 24.

[56]   Financial Conduct Authority, Consultation Paper CP16/26, 'Guidance on the duty of responsibility: amendments to the Decision Procedure and Penalties Manual', Guidance 6.2.9-A: amendments to the Decision Procedure and Penalties manual (DEPP) (September 2016). This reflects the wording of s 25 of the Bank of England and Financial Services Act 2016.

[57]   FCA Code of Conduct sourcebook (COCON), 3.1.3G.

[58]   Ibid (COCON), 3.1.5G. See also the FCA's Policy Statement PS17/9, 'Guidance on the duty of responsibility: final amendments (including feedback on CP16/26) to the Decision Procedure and Penalties Manual' (May 2017).

[59]   Ss 6.1–6.4, PRA Rulebook, 'Capital Requirement Regulation firms: individual accountability instrument', 2015 and FCA Rulebook, 'Senior Management Arrangements, Systems and Controls, (SYSC) 4.5, management responsibilities maps for UK relevant authorised persons.

allocated, including whether they have been allocated to more than one person. It is worth noting that the Financial Stability Board has announced that it will be undertaking work on 'responsibility mapping'.[60]

4.2.3   The Certification Regime

The new 'Certification Regime' is the third major change in addition to the Statement of Responsibilities and Responsibilities Map. The certification regime provides that firms will have to certify annually certain employees as being fit and proper to perform certain functions.[61] These are known as 'significant harm' functions.[62] A role will be designated as a significant harm function if the person performing it will be involved in aspects of the firm's affairs (so far as relating to a regulated activity carried on by the firm) that might involve a risk of significant harm to the firm or any of its customers or be a member of 'staff whose professional activities have a material impact on an institution's risk profile'.[63]

4.2.4   Conduct Rules

In addition, the regulators require that almost all employees, other than those outside the regulatory ambit such as receptionists, cleaners etc, are covered by a set of individual conduct rules derived from the regulatory Principles applicable to all regulated firms.[64] The new rules require these employees to act with integrity, due skill, care and diligence and to be open and cooperative with the regulators and, in addition, to pay due regard to the interests of customers and to treat them fairly and at the same time to observe proper standards of market conduct.[65]

In addition, senior management is subject to additional conduct rules requiring them to take reasonable steps to ensure: that the business of the firm, within their area of responsibility, is controlled effectively and complies with the relevant requirements and standards of the regulatory system; that any delegation is to 'an appropriate person'; and that the 'discharge of the delegated responsibility is effectively' undertaken and overseen by the responsible manager.[66] Finally, the rules require that the senior management 'disclose appropriately any information of which the [regulators] would reasonably expect notice'.[67]

The SMR is based on a series of assumptions about how organisations are structured and work. In practice, this approach may not accord with what actually happens. There are, additionally, a number of psychological and organisational factors which may operate against the successful application of the SMR. These are considered in the next section.

---

[60]   Financial Stability Board, 'FSB assesses implementation progress and effects of reforms', Press release, 28 February 2017.

[61]   Supra note 49, s 29, and FCA Source-book, SYSC 5.2.4, 5,2.11 and 5.2.12.

[62]   Ibid, SYSC 5.2.4.

[63]   Ibid, SYCS 5.2.42.

[64]   FCA, 'The principles for businesses' FCA website.

[65]   Ibid, Principles 5 and 6.

[66]   FCA Senior manager conduct rules and guidance, 2.2.3 and 4.2.17–24. PRC Rulebook: conduct rules, 3.3.

[67]   Ibid, 2.2.4 and 4.2.25–29, PRC Rulebook: conduct rules, 3.4.

5.1   FACTORS WHICH MIGHT UNDERMINE THE NEW APPROACH

There are a number of factors which may negate the acceptance of personal responsibility. These reasons encompass those that are related to business structures and the regulatory construct of organisational hierarchy. First, these include the fluid nature of allocated responsibilities, and hence accountability, within the larger organisations, and second, the confusing application of a management theory known as the 'three lines of defence'. Both of these issues are considered in more detail in the next section. Separately, there are also the human factors encompassing the failings of greed and hubris and lack of introspection on the part of individuals working within an organisation.

5.2   THE HIERARCHY CONCEPT

The SMR is based on a conceptual model in which financial firms are structured in the form of strict hierarchies with defined business areas operating as a highly structured bureaucracy. Some businesses may match this model. However, it is common for global firms to organise themselves with, for example, parallel reporting lines governing product groups and geographic locations. More generally, firms are much more fluid, operating through informal networks which frequently change, with responsibilities often moving depending on the task or issue in-hand. This poses issues for both regulators and firms since these undocumented arrangements are often not understood or appreciated by the regulated business and the regulator is too remote to comprehend what is opaque to the business itself.

In practice, organisations are 'complex and unpredictable' and based on a sense of reciprocity, and this fluidity centres on a 'system of dynamic functional relationships'.[68] This more anthropological approach is difficult to reconcile with organisational models based on hierarchical concepts. Coupled with this issue are the complexity of business operations and inter-dependence of roles within large businesses.

5.3   PERSONAL ACCOUNTABILITY: TOO ABSTRACT A CONCEPT?

Further, the application of the concepts 'responsibility' and 'accountability' produces a degree of abstraction which may be too difficult for individuals in a business to comprehend. The individual may be responsible for a particular area within the business and hence accountable if there is some serious regulatory failure exposing the individual to liability and regulatory sanction. However, this level of accountability is a construct which occurs within organisational and societal structures and hence the context may require explanation and the true position may be more complex.[69] For example, it is rare, in a business of any size for an individual to have control over all the key inputs required to operate all the necessary systems.

---

[68]   Supra note 9 (Painter-Morland and Werhane), 36–7.
[69]   Supra note 12 (Haines), 143–7.

The senior manager will have to rely on others. An individual's statement of responsibilities may, for example, include anti-money laundering arrangements. In banks, these will depend very heavily on IT, which in turn will depend on both budget allocations and work scheduling prioritisation. The staffing of all these areas is likely to depend on human resource department priorities and so on. There is, in practice, a complex mesh of accountabilities. The senior manager responsible for anti-money laundering may, thus, be responsible and hence be both accountable and liable to the regulator but many of the elements for success may be beyond their control. Many individuals will do the best they can in the circumstances, closing their mind to the personal conceptual risks they run as being too great and abstract to comprehend or they may resign from the role on the understanding that the task, subject to this level of accountability, is undoable.

5.4   'THREE LINES OF DEFENCE'

Second, the issues with corporate structures are compounded by a management theory, supported by the regulators, known as the 'three lines of defence', which has been widely adopted and is still prevalent in the financial services industry.[70] In essence, it divides the roles of ensuring control of risks and compliance into three, with the front-line business functions taking primary responsibility for risk management and regulatory compliance and with a second line of control functions, such as the compliance department, checking and reporting on the effectiveness of the first line backed up by the firm's internal audit function providing a third and final line of defence. The theory sounds conceptually attractive but it is difficult to operate successfully and has been described as providing 'a wholly misplaced sense of security . . . responsibilities have been blurred, accountability diluted, and officers in risk, compliance and internal audit have lacked the status to challenge front-line staff effectively. Much of the system became a box-ticking exercise whereby processes were followed, but judgement was absent.'[71]

The 'three lines of defence' model also promoted the use of an 'accountability firewall' which seems to have developed 'to prevent those in senior positions having a strong sense of personal engagement with and responsibility for failings and misconduct within their line of management'.[72]

There 'was a pervasive sense, reinforced by much of the evidence, that a culture exists in banking which diminishes a sense of personal responsibility'.[73] This issue is reinforced by a number of psychological factors, such as greed, hubris, 'tribal culture' and self-deception, that inhibit ethical behaviours and the acceptance of personal responsibility. These aspects are considered next.

---

[70]   Basel Committee on Banking Supervision, 'Guidelines: corporate governance principles for banks' (July 2015), 5, https://www.bis.org/bcbs/publ/d328.pdf.

[71]   Supra note 1 (PCBS report) 141.

[72]   Supra note 1 (PCBS report), 283.

[73]   Supra note 1 (PCBS report), 283.

5.5   GREED AND HUBRIS

Many of the problems evidenced in the recent financial crisis stemmed from board and senior executive objectives of rapid business growth and a desire to become the largest and most powerful of banks coupled with little or no appreciation of the risks being run. This is not new and could be seen, for example, in the last big bank run, prior to that on Northern Rock, on the well-respected bank of Overend & Gurney in 1866, and it is evident that 'money messes always start in the same way, when judgement is fuddled by greed, ambition and overweening self-confidence. Then when problems arise, there follows an obstinate refusal to admit mistakes or the imminence of disaster.'[74] A blind focus solely on the objective of winning without regard to the costs 'comes at a price: collateral issues of rivalry, arrogance, selfishness and a lack of humility and generosity'.[75] Salz describes investment bank leaders as having a high regard for their own 'cleverness' with a 'tendency to take robust positions with regulators, to determine [their] position by the letter rather than the spirit of the rules' and 'winning through intellectual power and single-mindedness'.[76] Consequently, a 'strong culture can easily become arrogant, inwardly focused and bureaucratic'.[77] The result may be the development of the attributes of a corrupt organisation including a focus on 'greed, arrogance, a sense of personal entitlement . . . and the inability to distinguish between organisational and personal ends' and a belief that 'laws and norms apply only to other, lesser mortals'.[78] These themes are developed later since they give some insight into the possible success of the SMR.

5.6   TRIBAL CULTURE

One of the potential issues with the application of the SMR is that it is predicated on the assumption that individuals are managed as part of an effective organisation. This can only work successfully if there is a high level of engagement between the individual and the organisation. However, this is not always the case, particularly in investment banking where individuals often stay with one firm for only a short period and then move to another; often moving from one jurisdiction to another. This often produces a 'tribal culture' with loyalty owned to the team leader and to other traders in other banks who all share a similar ethos with 'the internal culture . . . often based on patronage by individual senior bankers. This results in loyalty required to be shown to individuals rather than the organisation in order to achieve promotion (and pay).'[79] The Salz Review found that similar issues with individual loyalties owed 'to immediate superiors rather than to the whole organisation' had led to 'different sub-cultures' and that staff 'were likely to make their own decisions about values, based on

---

[74]   Geoffrey Elliott, *The mystery of Overend & Gurney* (Methuen, London, 2006), 10. See also Bank of England, 'The demise of Overend Gurney' (2016) Quarterly Bulletin Q 2, 94–106.

[75]   Supra note 30 (Carney).

[76]   Supra note 31 (Salz), 82.

[77]   Howard Rockness and Joanne Rockness, 'Legislated ethics: from Enron to Sarbanes-Oxley, the impact on corporate America' (2005) Journal of Business Ethics 57, 31–54, 51.

[78]   David Levine, 'The corrupt organization' (2005) Human Relations, Vol. 58, No. 6, 723–40, 724 and 731.

[79]   Written evidence from John Reynolds to the PCBS (22 August 2012) and supra note 1 (PCBS Report), 132.

what seemed to be important to their business unit head – or even the individual leaders to whom they reported'.[80]

5.7   MORAL BLINDNESS, SELF-DECEPTION AND NARCISSISM

In addition to the view that many bankers were motivated to err as a result of greed and hubris, there is also a perception that they suffered from a mix of moral blindness and self-deception. As described earlier, firms subject to a 'tribal culture' often celebrate the individual as some form of hero with a mythology of success.[81] It is a trope of fiction, whether film, book or play, on financial services.[82] This process may exacerbate the dulling of any form of moral assessment and increase the tendency towards self-deception. Moreover, the cultural focus on the individual may develop into a form of narcissism.

Business leaders are particularly prone to self-deception. In part, this is due to their close identification with the firm and a tendency to view everything through a business-centric lens.[83] This myopia is assisted by a process of 'ethical fading' as self-deception 'allows the businessman to behave self-interestedly while at the same time believing that he (and it almost always is a he) upholds his moral principles' based on a process which 'routinises decisions' and employs a 'language of euphemism'.[84] In common with any bureaucratic organisations, corporations have the ability, due to structure and the dynamics of their operations, to render normal the process of unreflective thinking. For example, Wells Fargo bank described its financial offering as 'solutions' to customer needs and not as 'products' to be sold, and a high-pressure sales campaign as 'a jump into January'.[85] In part, this is due to the employment of language which 'keep thoughts at bay'.[86]

The result can be a 'culture of optimism' where compliance and risk management constraints are seen as obstacles to be overcome and disconnected from those who believe in success and the business.[87] The process enables these individuals to rationalise 'wishful thinking' and to detach themselves 'from the emotions that would normally signify risks', adopting 'a semi-delusional state of mind (or a corrupt state of mind) in which, rather than admit responsibility ... rational logical arguments which explain [their] actions' are created.[88] The report on

---

[80]   Supra note 31 (Salz), 81–2.

[81]   Jasmin Mahadevan, 'Redefining organizational cultures: an interpretative anthropological approach to corporate narratives' (2009) Forum: Qualitative Social Research, 10(1), Art 44, para 49. See also Richard Gerrig, 'Moral judgments in narrative contexts', commentary on Cass Sunstein's, 'Moral heuristics' (2005) Behavioral and Brain Sciences, 28, 531–73, 550, 'moral judgments are affected by concomitants of narrative experiences' to the extent that listeners 'root for the bad guy'.

[82]   Norman Denzin, *Images of postmodern society* (Sage, London, 1991) ch. 6: 'Nouveau capitalists on Wall Street', 82–92.

[83]   Piet EenkHoorn and Johan Graafland, 'Lying in business: insights from Hannah Arendt's "Lying in politics"' (2011) Business Ethics: a European Review, Vol. 20, No. 4, 359–74, 371.

[84]   Ann Tenbrunsel and David Messick, 'Ethical fading: the role of self-deception in unethical behavior' (2004) Social Justice Research, Vol. 17, No. 2, 223–36, 224–5.

[85]   'Independent directors of the board of Wells Fargo & Company: sales practices investigation report' (April 2017), 22 and 23.

[86]   Harold Pinter, 'Art, truth and politics' (2005) Nobel Prize Lecture, Stockholm.

[87]   FSA, Bank of Scotland, Final Notice, 9 March 2012, 13, para 4.26.

[88]   Supra note 31 (Salz), 193.

the conduct failures at Wells Fargo bank notes a culture of senior management optimism in which problems are 'minimized'.[89] In a sense there is a 'breakdown in imagination'.[90]

The focus on the individual may 'create a collective dynamic which reinforces perverse behaviour through the process of turning a blind eye'.[91] It may produce what has been termed a 'corrupted herd' as the amoral approach becomes contagious and all individuals in the group may display the same 'illusory, self-deceptive . . . and exploitative' attitudes and the 'development and reward of narcissistic characteristics leads eventually to the creation of a perverse system'.[92] 'Guilt is a difficult emotion to acknowledge' and in order to maintain the appropriate self-image 'judgement is displaced . . . objectified and projected' onto imperfections in the 'market'.[93] Individual accountability is displaced by blame being attributed to 'the system' and ill-luck.

The extent of the self-deception is best summed up by the answer of one bank CEO: 'we thought that . . . we were on the side of the angels'.[94] Many of these issues are reflected in bank board failures.

5.8   STRATEGIC INCOMPETENCE

In all the financial problems and scandals there were significant failures at board level. Non-executive directors (NEDs) often lacked banking experience, did not understand the business and sometimes were subject to a dominating CEO. 'Chairmen proved weak; often they were too close to, and became cheerleaders for, the CEO. NEDs provided insufficient scrutiny of, or challenge to, the executive, and were too often advocates for expansion rather than cautioning of the risks involved.'[95]

There was insufficient focus by boards on bank culture. 'Some of the more qualitative information that could have alerted the Board to fundamental indications of cultural issues was not discussed.'[96] It was often the case that bad sub-cultures existed in specific important areas within the organisation. The information on these problems existed but was 'masked by higher-level annual staff opinion survey results and the board made no attempt to dig deeper into the statistics'.[97]

---

[89]   Supra note 85 (Wells Fargo),10.

[90]   Larry Hirschhorn, 'The financial crisis, exploring the dynamics of imagination and authority in a post-industrial world' in Susan Long and Burkard Sievers (eds), *Towards a socioanalysis of money, finance and capitalism: beneath the surface of the financial industry* (Routledge, London, 2012), 299–300.

[91]   Supra note 31 (Salz), 192.

[92]   Mannie Sher, 'Corruption: aberration or an inevitable part of the human condition? Insights from a "Tavistock' approach"' (2010) Organisational and Social Dynamics, Vol. 10, No. 1, 40–55, 45–6.

[93]   Alison Gill and Mannie Sher, 'Inside the minds of the money minders: deciphering reflections on money, behaviour and leadership in the financial crisis 2007–10' in *Towards a socioanalysis of money, finance and capitalism: beneath the surface of the financial industry*, supra note 90, 72.

[94]   Eric Daniels (former CEO of Lloyds Bank), oral evidence to the PCBS (14 February 2013) answer to question 4247.

[95]   Supra note 1 (PCBS report), 343.

[96]   Supra note 31 (Salz), 91.

[97]   Ibid.

The PRA has attempted to address the issue posed by the SMR to board collective actions and responsibilities by stating that 'the specific accountabilities of individual directors established by the [SMR] are additional and complementary to the collective responsibility shared by directors as members of the board . . . while the PRA recognises that culture is the collective responsibility of the board, it also requires the chairman to lead the development of the firm's culture and standards by the board as a whole.'[98] The PRA's Statement then goes on to focus on the collective role of the board 'to articulate and maintain a culture of risk awareness and ethical behaviour for the entire organisation to follow in pursuit of its business goals. The PRA expects the culture to be embedded with the use of appropriate incentives, including but not limited to remuneration, to encourage, and where necessary require, the behaviours the board wishes to see, and for this to be actively overseen by the board. The non-executives have a key role to play in holding management to account for embedding and maintaining this culture.'[99] This suggests that the board, collectively, has a set of responsibilities, but within that each individual on the board has their own individual regulatory role for which they will be held accountable. This may prove a challenge since it may require a level of personal introspection and insight not addressed by regulation and strength of character which was apparently absent in the failed banks in the 2007/8 financial crisis. By way of example these issues were manifest both in the period leading up to the collapse of Halifax Bank of Scotland (HBoS) and, apparently, subsequently.

5.9   AN EXAMPLE OF BOARD FAILURE: THE HALIFAX BANK OF SCOTLAND (HBOS) BOARD

Halifax Bank of Scotland (HBoS) failed in 2008. The causes behind its demise were examined by a sub-committee of the PCBS chaired by Lord McFall. The sub-committee found that 'the losses were caused by a flawed strategy, inappropriate culture and inadequate controls. These are matters for which successive chief executives and particularly the chairman and the board as a whole bear responsibility.'[100] The board set a strategy for 'aggressive, asset-led growth across divisions' and this 'strategy created a new culture in the higher echelons of the bank. This culture was brash, underpinned by a belief that the growing market share was due to a special set of skills which HBOS possessed and which its competitors lacked. The effects of the culture were all the more corrosive when coupled with a lack of corporate self-knowledge at the top of the organisation'. The board saw HBoS as 'a new force in banking' possessing special attributes, but this 'lack of corporate self-knowledge at the top of the organisation, enable[ed] the bank's leaders to persist in the belief, in some cases to this day, that HBOS was a conservative institution when in fact it was the very opposite'.[101]

---

[98]   PRA, 'Corporate governance: board responsibilities' (March 2016) Supervisory Statement, SS5/16, 5.

[99]   Ibid, 6.

[100]   Parliamentary Commission on Banking Standards '"An accident waiting to happen": The failure of HBOS', Fourth Report of Session 2012–13, Volume I: Report, together with formal minutes (HL Paper 144 HC 705 Published on 4 April 2013), 42.

[101]   Ibid ('Accident') 46. See also the oral evidence given by Paul Moore (former Head of Group Regulatory Risk, HBOS) to the PCBS on the 'culture of optimism' at HBoS (30 October 2012) answers

A few months before its collapse, Lord Stevenson, the chairman of HBoS, wrote to the Financial Services Authority about its preparations to weather the financial storm following the failure of Northern Rock by saying that 'without wishing to be complacent or hubristic, management has done a superb job . . . I and we sense a continual paranoia within the FSA about [HBoS's financial vulnerability]. I do believe that our management has done enough . . . to demonstrate its sense of responsibility and competence and that there could be some release of the FSA paranoia button!'[102]

This level of delusion persisted after the bank's collapse with Sir Ronald Garrick, who was a NED and the Senior Independent Director of HBoS from 2004. He gave evidence to the sub-committee's investigation stating that: 'I have no doubt that the HBOS Board was by far and away the best board I ever sat on. My recollection of the culture and characteristics of the Board was one of openness, transparency, high intellect, integrity, good working relationships between the chairman and chief executive, and a suitable diversity of backgrounds, mix of experience and expertise to maximise effectiveness [. . .] If with the benefit of hindsight I was asked if I wanted to sit on this board again I would be saying yes.'[103] The sub-committee's report on the demise of HBoS commented on the culture of the board and concluded it was 'shocked and surprised that, even after the ship has run aground, so many of those who were on the bridge still seem so keen to congratulate themselves on their collective navigational skills'.[104] The report summed up by saying that the board of HBoS 'represents a model of self-delusion, of the triumph of process over purpose'.[105]

Factors such as greed and hubris may undermine an individual's ability for self-reflection and introspection but over-arching everything is the culture of the organisation and the ethics of the individuals involved. These aspects are considered next.

6.1   THE ROLE OF BUSINESS CULTURE AND INDIVIDUAL ETHICS

The PCBS stated that public trust would only be restored 'when the deficiencies in banking standards and culture, and the underlying causes of those deficiencies, have been addressed'.[106] This is important since 'the relationship between ethics, culture and organisational purpose sets the individual within the business, the business within society and links the latter to the "good of society"'.[107]

The issues of poor culture are relevant to both investment and commercial banks. Many retail bank branches and telephony operations were driven by cross-selling targets. Daily, weekly and monthly competitions and relatively small rewards existed to encourage this behavior, with the underlying threat to an employee's job if they consistently failed to meet

---

to questions BQ95 and 96, Parliamentary Commission on Banking Standards – Minutes of Evidence, HL Paper 144/HC 705.

[102]   Supra note 100 ('Accident'), 34.
[103]   Ibid, 29.
[104]   Ibid, 31.
[105]   Ibid, 30.
[106]   Supra note 1 (PCBS Report), 104.
[107]   Josep Lozano, 'Ethics and corporate culture: a critical relationship' (1998) Ethical Perspectives Vol. 5, 53–70, 61.

sales demands. The New City Agenda report found, for example, that 'in one Halifax branch, there was a weekly "cash or cabbages day"'.[108] Employees who exceeded their sales were publicly rewarded cash. 'Those who missed their bonuses were given cabbages . . . Two tellers at branches of the bank in Glasgow and Paisley had the vegetables placed on their desks within full public view. In the first case, an 18-year-old male teller was said to be deeply upset by the cabbage put on his desk. In the second case . . . a 24-year-old had a cauliflower placed on her desk. She was apparently told she could only pass it on when someone opened an account.'[109] Following regulatory action these schemes were abolished but in many cases the culture behind them persisted.[110]

In parallel, regulators have also acted to change market structures to discourage price manipulation and mis-selling. These measures include, for example, the ban on commission payments for retail investment products.[111] There are issues with such measures which may lead to unintended consequences such as the growth of asset management 'platforms' operating under new fees arrangements which may compensate for the loss of commission income, and the use of 'activity' measures, mentioned earlier, to replace financial and sales targets.[112] Further, there has been a significant increase in regulation constraining variable pay and developing systems to 'clawback' elements of bonus payments as a result of regulatory breaches.[113]

There has also been discussion of introducing some form of 'banker oath' mirroring an arrangement instituted in the Netherlands.[114] It purportedly copies a doctor's 'Hippocratic oath'.[115] The Dutch affirmation is complex and it is unlikely to be instituted in the United Kingdom.[116] Some have cast doubt on the efficacy of a 'banker oath' without first building 'a more cohesive professional body and ethos . . . If you do it the other way around, it could just be hot air. If you have all bankers taking an oath and it is just words, and it is seen within six months to be flawed, I think you're in a worse place than you were before.'[117]

Nevertheless, regulating individual responsibility may have the effect of deterring 'conscious unethical behaviour', especially coupled with 'an increased risk of detection and personal sanction' and aided by encouraging 'whistleblowing programmes' which 'increase this risk substantially.'[118]

---

[108] André Spicer, 'A report on the culture of British retail banking' (2014) New City Agenda and Cass Business School, 21–2.

[109] The Guardian, 'Cabbage lands bank in the soup' (17 August 2005).

[110] For an example of regulatory action see the Financial Conduct Authority's Final Notice fining Lloyds Bank/Bank of Scotland for sales incentive arrangements (10 December 2013).

[111] Financial Services Authority Retail Distribution Review website.

[112] Financial Conduct Authority, 'Factsheet for firms who advise on or operate platforms: No. 11'.

[113] Bank of England, press release, 'Prudential Regulation Authority and Financial Conduct Authority announce new rules on remuneration' (23 June 2015).

[114] David Llewellyn, Roger Steare and Jessica Trevellick, 'Virtuous Banking: placing ethos and purpose at the heart of finance' (Res Publica, London July 2014), 14.

[115] Ibid, 14.

[116] Tuchtrecht Banken (The board enforces the ethical Code of Conduct for the Dutch banking industry enshrined in the Banker's Oath), website.

[117] City A.M., 'Sir Richard Lambert shoots down bankers' oath proposal as "hot air"' (30 July 2014).

[118] Supra note 77 (Rockness and Rockness), 49, quoting J. Kotter and J. Heskett, *Corporate culture and performance* (The Free Press, New York, 1992).

6.2   ETHICS AND INTROSPECTION

Central to holding an individual accountable is their ability for introspection. To be successful in encouraging individuals to do the right thing requires them to think about the issues and their role through a process of analysis and thought as well as the application of reason to act ethically. This is an Aristotelian approach since for Aristotle the choice of action is preceded by deliberation which involves both the application of reason and thought.[119] 'Virtue is not only a characteristic which is guided by the right reason but is united with the right reason and the latter, in moral matters, is practical wisdom.'[120]

However, it is likely that many people are more concerned with their every-day existence and have neutralised their introspective abilities. Locke sets a higher standard, particularly for those with positions of responsibility. While he expects people to live their lives with a level of moral introspection, he accepts that the extent to which this can be done depends on individual circumstances. 'Those whose lives are worn out only in the provisions of living' and whose life is drudgery have a very limited ability to live according to rational moral tenets.[121] However, those in positions of leadership have an opportunity to gain a clear perspective on their moral duty but may instead 'satisfy themselves with lazy ignorance' – this is a severe moral failing in itself.[122] Nevertheless, Hume is more sympathetic to those who act out of ignorance. For Hume the individual is only accountable for their actions where these 'proceed from thought and deliberation'.[123] The individual is not accountable for actions 'performed ignorantly or casually'.[124]

Again, as mentioned earlier, self-delusion, can have a significant effect on an individual's ability to analyse objectively and reflect on what to do. 'What suits our wish is fondly believed'.[125] Views which contradict or 'disturb' the perceived or prevailing position are kept out. Adam Smith was also concerned with the tendency towards self-deception and saw in this 'powerful forces' which need to be overcome.[126] It requires sufficient introspection to imagine how an 'autonomous impartial spectator' would view their actions in order to avoid the risk of self-deception.[127] The manager seeks not only praise but also to be 'praiseworthy', as measured by this inner impartial spectator.[128]

The additional counter to the risk of self-deception is the ability to 'imagine the other'.[129] This requires both self-understanding and an appreciation of the possible effect of one's

---

[119]   Supra note 11 (Ethics), 1139a22-35 (Penguin, 145–6).

[120]   Supra note 11 (Ethics) 1144b26-30 (Penguin, 165–6).

[121]   John Locke, *An essay concerning human understanding* (first published 1710, Thomas Tegg, London, 1846), Book IV, Chapter XX, 538.

[122]   Ibid, 541.

[123]   David Hume, *A treatise on human nature* (first published 1739–40, 2nd edn, Oxford University Press, Oxford, 1978), 412.

[124]   Ibid, 412.

[125]   Supra note 121 (Locke), 544.

[126]   Maria Pia Paganelli, 'Recent engagements with Adam Smith and the Scottish Enlightenment' (2015) History of Political Economy, Vol. 47, No. 3, 363–94, 369.

[127]   Jerry Evensky, *Adam Smith's moral philosophy, a historical and contemporary perspective on markets, law, ethics and culture* (Cambridge University Press, Cambridge, England, 2005), 44–5.

[128]   Ibid, 45.

[129]   April Capili, 'The created ego in Levinas' totality and infinity' (2011) Sophia, Vol. 50, No. 4, 677–92, 685 and 691.

actions on others and is central to being a 'just man'.[130] The difficulty of appreciating and understanding others and their perspective 'gives rise to ethics which goes beyond any form of self-fulfilment but is based on generosity, respect and humility'.[131] This inward mirror of conscience, 'turn'st mine eyes into my very soul'.[132] This process of self-enquiry provides a moral yard-stick against which to measure both one's actions and also self-respect which can be expressed as a 'moral law within me'.[133] 'Part of the process of reasoning should be based on an understanding of consequences . . . and this process should take account of causative responsibility and hence accountability . . . This chain of thinking requires the "faculty of imagination" and the ability to envisage something [or someone] who is not present' or 'representations of things which are not present'.[134] It is arguable that moral accountability cannot be applied to those who are so morally blind that they did not know what they were doing and are unable to envisage and assess any consequences.

6.3   ETHICS WITHIN A REGULATORY AND SOCIAL CONTEXT

Further, it may be that the process of moral reasoning and hence accountability is frustrated by the imposition of external rules and regulations. The 'use of coercion' is 'based on the assumption that individuals cannot be trusted to make good choices'.[135] These strictures set tramlines on which to act, and failing to follow them makes the action morally neutral, requiring only compliance without moral reflection and thus responsibility.[136] Nevertheless, the rules and regulations form part of the moral context in which the individual functions. 'The individual belongs to the ethical and social fabric' in which they live, and thus to a 'father seeking the best way to bring up his son, a Pythagorean, or some other thinker, replied, "Make him a citizen of a state which has good laws"'.[137] It is built on trust and faith.[138] The 'ethical life' ('*sittlichkeit*') is both a 'normative perspective' and one which takes account of 'the social context of an action'.[139]

Nevertheless, the risk remains, particularly in a complex system subject to considerable time pressures and not given to introspection, that the 'risk of being held accountable' will not deter 'individuals from . . . wrongdoing . . . . an individual never stops to deliberately ponder

---

[130]   Ibid, 685 and 691.

[131]   Carl Rhodes, 'Organizational justice' in Mollie Painter-Morland and René Ten Bos (eds), *Business ethics and continental philosophy* (Cambridge University Press, Cambridge, England, 2011) 141–61, 150–1.

[132]   William Shakespeare, 'Hamlet', Gertrude, Act III, Scene 3.

[133]   Immanuel Kant, *Critique of practical reason* (first published in 1788, Werner Pluhar (tr), Hackett, Indianapolis, 2002), Conclusion to Part II, line 162, page 203.

[134]   Hannah Arendt, *Responsibility and judgement* (first published in 1971, Shocken Books, New York, 2003), 139 and 189.

[135]   Zygmunt Bauman, *Postmodern ethics* (Blackwell, Oxford, 1993), 28–9.

[136]   Mollie Painter-Morland, 'Moral decision-making', supra note 131, 117–38, 138, quoting Zygmunt Bauman, *Postmodern ethics* (Blackwell, London, 1993) ch 5: 47.

[137]   Nathan Ross, 'Hegel on the place of corporations within ethical life' in *Cutting-edge issues in business ethics*, supra note 9, 48.

[138]   Georg Wilhelm Friedrich Hegel, *Philosophy of right* (T.M. Knox (tr), Oxford University Press, Oxford, 1942), Third Part, 'Ethical life', paras 147 and 153, pages 106 and 109.

[139]   Supra note 137 (Ross), 48.

the punitive consequences . . . .and calculate the risks.'[140] This lack of introspection coupled with a certain '*arbeitsfreude*', or satisfaction, in achievement in the task in hand is likely to reduce the effectiveness of the SMR regulations. In summary, there may be a 'mut[ing] of conscience'.[141] This issue is developed in the next section.

6.4   THE INSTRUMENTALISATION OF ETHICS

Antiphon, a Sophist, drew a distinction between 'nomos' – the formal laws and customs of a society – and 'physis' – those more internal, interior or private guides; truth towards oneself.[142] It may be possible to view 'physis' as part of the 'ethikos' or the moral character that underpins an individual. Consequently, there is a strong risk that a focus on regulatory compliance predominates and suppresses any attempt to 'inspire a true sense of ethical obligation'.[143] What is required is individual 'ethical reflection'.[144] A pure regulatory emphasis may well be counter-productive since the issue is 'how to prevent an "instrumentalization" of ethics' through 'window-dressing ethics'.[145] This adherence to the letter of the law and not its spirit is central to the issues of ethics and the SMR. The PCBS found evidence that 'rather than upholding high levels of professional standards, senior executive[s] pursued a box-ticking approach to compliance, adhering only to the specifics of their interpretation of the regulator's detailed rules'.[146]

The next section considers a range of actions which complement the SMR and may assist in improving the culture within financial services companies and the ethics and competence of individuals in this industry.

7.1   POSSIBLE REMEDIES

The starting point, in order to avoid the issues described earlier, is to determine a firm's purpose (not just to make money) to which its values, individual assessments and promotion and reward are linked.[147] It could be, for example, to provide money for individuals to buy their home and to create and grow their business.[148] The organisation's purpose needs to be clear

---

[140]   Supra note 9 (Painter-Morland and Werhane), 38.

[141]   Peter Gratton, 'An Arendtian approach to business ethics' in Painter-Morland and Werhane, supra note 9, 212.

[142]   Carroll Moulton, 'Antiphon the Sophist, on Truth' (1972) Transactions and Proceedings of the American Philological Association, Vol. 103, 329–66.

[143]   William Donaldson, 'Corporate governance' (2003) Business Economics, Vol. 38, No. 3, 16–21, 18.

[144]   Surendra Arjoon, 'Corporate governance: an ethical perspective' (2005) Journal of Business Ethics, Vol. 61, 343–52, 347.

[145]   Ronald Sims and Johannes Brinkmann, 'Enron ethics (or culture matters more than codes)' (2003) Journal of Business Ethics, Vol. 45, 243–56, 243 and 254.

[146]   Supra note 1 (PCBS report), 94.

[147]   Lynn Paine, 'Managing for organizational integrity' (1994) Harvard Business Review, Vol. 72, No. 2, 106–17, 115–16.

[148]   Onora O'Neill 'What is banking for?' Remarks at Federal Reserve Bank of New York, 20 October 2016, https://www.newyorkfed.org/medialibrary/media/governance-and-culture-reform/ONeill-Culture -Workshop-Remarks-10202016.pdf.

and known by all stakeholders, including the board, employees and customers. The need is for senior management to 'articulate a purpose for the bank that transcends business goals but also intersects with these goals'.[149] Everything must work towards this purpose. 'In the absence of a common purpose, shared culture and a set of values reinforced from the top, [Salz] found that Barclays' divisional leaders devised their own values frameworks.'[150]

In an organisation with the right culture individuals will assume personal responsibility and they will do all they can towards fostering the organisation's overall purpose, which, as mentioned earlier, is linked to the 'good of society'.[151] The 'creation and reinforcement of culture is the result of five primary mechanisms': senior management attention and focus, reaction to crises, acting as role models, how rewards are allocated and the criteria for hiring and firing.[152] There are also 'secondary articulations and reinforcement mechanisms' including: rites and rituals, organisational structures, the use of stories, processes and systems and formal codes of practice'.[153]

It is unlikely that law and regulation can engender ethical behaviour. 'Legal compliance is unlikely to unleash much moral imagination or commitment. The law does not generally seek to inspire human excellence or distinction.'[154] 'Those managers who define ethics as legal compliance are implicitly endorsing a code of moral mediocrity for their organizations.' As Richard Breeden, former chairman of the Securities and Exchange Commission, noted, 'It is not an adequate ethical standard to aspire to get through the day without being indicted.'[155] Much more is needed.

A possible approach is to consider the characteristics displayed by an organisation based on integrity.[156] These would include: a culture of openness and responsibility and the use of 'ethical language', 'structural supports and procedures that facilitate ethical decision-making (eg ability and willingness to raise issues)' and the valuing of professionalisation and thedevelopment of employees.[157]

As already mentioned, 'ethical business practices stem from ethical corporate cultures'.[158] Staff are always looking at their immediate managers and take their lead from them. The manager creates a 'shadow'. The 'management of meaning' creates important symbols which reflect the views of the senior management and strongly influence all those around them,

---

[149] Anjan Thakor, 'Corporate culture in banking' (August 2016) Federal Reserve Board of New York, Economic Policy Review, 13.

[150] Supra note 31 (Salz), 81.

[151] Supra note 107 (Lozano) 61.

[152] Edward Schein, *Organizational culture and leadership* (Jossey-Bass, San Francisco, 1985), 241–50.

[153] Ibid, 250–7.

[154] Ibid.

[155] Supra note 147 (Paine), 111.

[156] Gillian Guy, 'Voluntary action prompted by responsibility and integrity is far more effective – and results in a race to the top rather than bottom . . . It also puts the emphasis rightly on motivation rather than compliance' remarks at the British Bankers Association Retail Banking Conference, 29 June 2017, https://www.bankingstandardsboard.org.uk/gillian-guy-speaks-at-bba-retail-banking-conference-2017/.

[157] Christopher Kayes, David Stirling and Tjai Nielsen, 'Building organizational integrity' (2007) Business Horizons, 50, 61–70, 63.

[158] Patrick Murphy, 'Creating ethical corporate structures' (1989) Sloan Management Review, Vol. 30, No. 2, 81–7, 81.

throughout the business, and beyond.[159] It is possible that the 'language of accountability' ('responsibility', 'integrity' etc) present too many management problems to be wholly effective since the language is too complex in structure and content to be meaningful, with the result that it can be described as producing 'rhetoric-as-ritual', which become 'incantations' and submerge the 'moral' meaning of words.[160] This is an issue firms, especially the large ones, have since they need to use formalised rules to operate with any degree of consistency. This presents difficulties when applied to areas such as ethics and culture.

As mentioned earlier, ethics exist within a context and their application will depend on the situation, including the immediate issues, the organisational culture, the roles and related positioning of the individuals concerned, how the issues are presented or 'framed' and the potential harm and benefits, and the 'magnitude of the consequences'.[161] Indeed, it is possible to see corporate culture 'as a fundamental ingredient in institutionalizing ethics in organizations'.[162] Further shared ethics in an organisation can help to reduce operational costs since it allows coordination and cooperation to occur without recourse to an institutional structural mechanism (i.e. individuals work together through mutual trust rather than because they are ordered to do so).[163] It can also obviate the need to have recourse to regulation since there should be a 'congruence between an organization's beliefs' and the day-to-day experiences of its employees and the law.[164]

This is a special issue for banks since the trust placed by society in banks requires these organisations to respond and 'building an organisation's reputation for trustworthiness takes time and is founded on a robust ethical culture supported by leaders, systems and policies designed to foster and reinforce employee trustworthiness . . . Trust is also strongly related to fairness. Studies show that the experience of unfairness quickly erodes trust.'[165] It is unlikely that issues of trust and fairness can be directly regulated and, consequently, the following section looks at what banks can do themselves to improve culture and ethics both within their own organisations and across the industry.

7.2   CHANGING CULTURE

There are limits to what can be achieved by regulation. This is particularly an issue if the business leaders lack sound ethical principles and the firm operates with a deficient culture. Consequently, it is important 'that if we are to avoid a re-run of the financial crisis, it is vital to profoundly change the culture of banking'.[166] However, 'a new culture can't just be regulated

---

[159] Dan Gowler and Karen Legge, 'The meaning of management and the management of meaning: a view from social anthropology' in Michael Earl (ed), *Perspectives on management: a multidisciplinary analysis* (Oxford University Press, Oxford, 1983) 197–233.

[160] Ibid, 213–14 and 229–30.

[161] Jeri Beggs and Kathy Dean, 'Legislated ethics or ethics education? Faculty views in the post-Enron era' (2007) Journal of Business Ethics, Vol. 71, 15–37, 18.

[162] Supra, note 107 (Lozano), 55.

[163] Ibid, 57.

[164] Leonard Minkes, Michael Small and Samir Chatterjee, 'Leadership and business ethics: does it matter? Implications for management' (1999) Journal of Business Ethics, Vol. 20, 327–35, 330.

[165] Supra note 31 (Salz), 76.

[166] Supra note 108 (Spicer), 15.

into being. Rather, culture change is something banks themselves must take responsibility for and be held accountable for'.[167]

Following another recommendation by the PCBS, the chairmen of the major UK banks and building societies asked Sir Richard Lambert to review and report on what could be done in this area ,and his report in 2014 highlighted that the 'overriding responsibility for improving the behaviour of banks must lie with the leadership of the institutions themselves, operating within the framework set out by the regulators. It is for them to define the values and purpose of the banks which they lead, to appoint and promote people who are aligned with its values, to decide which types of business they are happy to accept and which to turn away, and to do everything in their power to make sure that the tone set at the top reaches all the way down through these often very large organisations.'[168]

While banks can do much to improve their culture and the ethics of their staff there is an important role for collective action since as with financial instability 'reputational damage is also contagious' and unethical behaviour and its consequences can 'flow across to others in the system'.[169] This is often due to 'individuals frequently mov[ing] from one firm to another' and spreading bad behaviours and the fact 'that dubious practices in the run-up to the crisis came to be justified as being the business norm'. To quote Warren Buffet: 'The five most dangerous words in business may be "everybody else is doing it". That was often the argument used, for example, to justify high-pressure sales techniques in retail branches, and it helped to encourage what has been described as a race to the bottom in the decades leading up to the crash.'[170]

The Lambert report recommended the establishment of a new body to help promote collective industry action, and in 2015 the banking industry came together to set up the Banking Standards Board (BSB), whose purpose is 'to promote high standards of behaviour and competence across UK banks and building societies'.[171] A significant part of the BSB's work is to support the SMR and the BSB has published a 'Statement of Good Practice' to aid firms implementing the certified persons regime and explain how to 'carry out a robust assessment of a person's . . . honesty and integrity, reputation etc' prior to their appointment to, and annually thereafter in, such a role.[172] Mikael Down, BSB's Director of Policy, described to the author that the BSB's intention is to encourage firms to go beyond the regulatory requirements and to treat the new regime as an opportunity to achieve high professional standards.

In addition, Lambert and the PCBS have recommended work to increase the level of professionalism in the financial services industry.[173]

---

[167] Ibid, 15.
[168] Richard Lambert, 'Banking standards review' (19 May 2014), 6.
[169] Ibid.
[170] Ibid.
[171] BSB website.
[172] Ibid.
[173] Supra note 168 (Lambert), 23–4, and supra note 1 (PCBS report), 363.

7.3   INCREASED PROFESSIONALISM AND THE ROLE OF PROFESSIONAL BODIES IN IMPROVING BEHAVIOUR IN BANKING

The SMR includes the need for senior managers and certified staff to be professionally competent to carry out their roles. This reflects the comments of the PCBS that senior bank staff should acquire 'appropriate banking qualifications' since it became clear in February 2009 that neither the chairmen nor the CEOs of the Royal Bank of Scotland or HBoS possessed a banking qualification.[174]

Consequently, there is a need for increased professionalism in financial services with both an increase both in competence to undertake the various roles and membership of authoritative professional bodies which set high standards of conduct and to whom their individual members are accountable. 'Robust forms of professional accountability might help re-establish a basis for placing or withholding trust intelligently' without the need for 'controls or proliferating sanctions'.[175] This view was supported by the PCBS, whose report stated that along with the regulatory changes, such as the SMR, 'the influence of a professional body for banking could assist the development of the culture within the industry by introducing non-financial incentives . . . such as peer pressure and the potential to shame and discipline miscreants. Such a body could, by its very existence, be a major force for cultural change.'[176]

There is still much that can be done both to improve bank board and senior executive competence and ethics. For example, following the 2007/8 financial crisis the Irish Institute of Banking, the professional body for those working in banking in the Republic of Ireland, developed a Board and Senior Executive Development Programme.[177] It includes both technical training and work on improving and developing business ethics using a process of self-evaluation and reflection. In parallel, for example, the Chartered Banker: Professional Standards Board operate a voluntary scheme to develop 'basic standards of competence and conduct' to 'promote higher standards of professionalism for those working in banking'.[178]

8.1   CONCLUSION

The changes brought into effect by the SMR will spread to all regulated financial services firms in 2019. The objects are both to change behaviour in these firms by clearly setting out regulatory expectations and making individuals personally accountable and to help assuage public anger by taking regulatory actions against those individuals who fail. However, due to individual psychological limitations and institutional structures it is questionable whether any regulations can make individuals act more ethically. However, the importance of satisfying

---

[174]   Supra note 1 (PCBS report), 297.

[175]   Onora O'Neill, 'Trust, trustworthiness and accountability' in Nicholas Morris and David Vines (eds), *Capital failure: rebuilding trust in financial services* (Oxford University Press, Oxford, 2014), 172–89, 188.

[176]   Supra note 1 (PCBS report), 363.

[177]   Institute of Banking website.

[178]   Chartered Banker: Professional Standards Board website, https://www.charteredbanker.com./the-institute.html.

public demands for retribution against individuals should not be neglected and the SMR will have an important role in this area.

Nevertheless, financial regulation will never be fully effective if there is no substantial change in the culture of financial services, with individuals gaining an ethical insight into their own actions. This requires leadership and action by both the regulators and, more, importantly the firms themselves. It requires a recognition of the need for change and a continual focus on bringing this about – it is not a project to be given to a business control function or human resources department to carry out. It requires an understanding of the purpose of the organisation in society, with everything designed to satisfy this objective to ensure the sustainability of the business. This is a function of both people and structures, including how the firm attracts individuals to join it, the recruitment process, induction, training and development, as well as the firm's management and leadership and its openness to raising concerns and following up. Equally important is the need for professionalism, which is an aid to both improving competence and to developing and sustaining ethical behaviour. All these aspects can be buttressed by the regulators but require firms in the industry to act themselves. Unethical behaviour does not happen somewhere else. It can permeate all firms and spread like a contagion. The remedy rests with the industry.

13. What makes deterrence credible?

Andromachi Georgosouli

1.   INTRODUCTION

According to current orthodoxy, deterrence is credible when it is visible and visibility calls for enforcement action that is harsh enough to be taken seriously so that it makes an impact on the behaviour of the industry.[1] In this chapter, I do not intend to doubt the role of enforcement in deterrence policy but to argue that the focus on enforcement is misplaced because, when it comes to the question of credibility, at best it tells half the story. The picture is far more complex. The credibility of deterrence is contingent on a multitude of factors. In this chapter, I consider three of them all of which are closely inter-related: The regulator's capacity to attain a congruence of *minds* and a congruence of *hearts* with the industry, and the regulator's ability to harness its profile as a credible enforcer. While the first and the second one refer respectively to the dialectical and moral dimensions of deterrence as regulatory strategy, the third one alludes to a non-exhaustive range of factors that impact on the psychology of the public and in particular on the confidence of the latter in the credibility of the FCA as enforcer.

It is a good time to consider this theme. In June 2015, the International Organisation of Securities Commissions (IOSCO) published a paper on 'Credible Deterrence in the Enforcement of Securities Regulation'. IOSCO identifies seven factors that make deterrence credible. These are the following: (a) legal certainty; (b) the capacity for being able to get the right information; (c) cooperation and collaboration; (d) investigation and prosecution of misconduct; (e) strong punishment through the imposition of sanctions; (f) promoting public understanding and transparency; and (g) good regulatory governance in order to deliver better enforcement. The IOSCO recommendations seem to be premised on the assumption that the credibility of deterrence can be strengthened as long as measures can be taken to improve the effectiveness of enforcement.[2] This chapter warns that improvements on enforcement do not necessarily have a positive impact on the credibility of deterrence. More generally, it is essential to keep in mind that the effectiveness of enforcement and the effectiveness of deterrence are not one and the same thing. The effectiveness of enforcement can be measured by the number of successful enforcement proceedings irrespective of whether enforcement inflicts behaviour modification. By contrast, a deterrence strategy is not successful, unless there is some evidence of long-term behaviour modification.

---

[1]   See notably, Gary Wilson and Sarah Wilson, 'The FSA, "Credible Deterrence, and Criminal Enforcement – a "haphazard pursuit"?' (2013) 21 (1) J Financ Crime 4–28; and Tracey McDermot (acting director of the Enforcement and Financial Crime Division) *Credible Deterrence: Here to Stay* (FSA Speech, FSA Enforcement Conference; 2 July 2012) http://www.fsac.org.uk/library/communication/speeches/2012/0702-tm.html accessed 15 October 2015.

[2]   IOSCO, *Credible Deterrence in the Enforcement of Securities Regulation* (June 2015) https://www.iosco.org/library/pubdocs/pdf/IOSCOPD490.pdf accessed 15 October 2015.

For expository purposes, I draw examples from the work of the Financial Conduct Authority (FCA) and, where appropriate, the work of the predecessor of the FCA, the Financial Services Authority (FSA) in deterring misconduct in the financial services sector.[3] This chapter does not offer a comprehensive account of all those market, institutional, legal, behavioural and cognitive conditions that make deterrence credible and it does not provide all the answers. However, it highlights certain determinants of deterrence, which point to pathways for reform and may even help put the IOSCO recommendations into perspective.[4]

Deterrence studies subscribe to the idea that prevention is better than cure and go hand in hand with regulatory scholarship on enforcement and compliance.[5] The chief objective of deterrence studies is the investigation and development of strategies that help in dissuading market actors from breaching the law in the future. Over the years, two schools of thought have influenced the relevant scholarship: On the one hand, those who believe that market actors will comply with the law only when confronted with tough sanctions and, on the other hand, those who believe that persuasion works better in securing long-term compliance. More recently, these strands of thought gave rise to hybrid accounts of deterrence strategies as it has been recognised that better results might be achieved when regulatory approaches combine elements of both.[6]

The deterrence policy of the FCA is an exemplary case of such a hybrid strategy, although currently there is a clear emphasis on enforcement.[7] Below, I put this enforcement-led approach to deterrence to the test and, progressively, I bring attention to certain other factors that impact on the credibility of deterrence. I conclude with a summary of the main points of this analysis and some tentative thoughts about the direction of future reform.

---

[3]   As of April 2013, the FSA was abolished and replaced by the Financial Conduct Authority (FCA) and the Prudential Regulation Authority (PRA), the latter being part of the Bank of England group. The FCA and the PRA are focus-specific public agencies with a separate set of statutory objectives to deliver. The strategic objective of the FCA is to ensure that financial markets function well (Financial Services Act 2012, section 1B(2) (amending Financial Services and Markets Act 2000)). To this effect, the FCA is responsible for consumer protection, market integrity, and competition in the interests of consumers (FSA 2012, sections 1B(2), 1(C), 1D, 1E). The PRA is the primary micro-prudential regulator and part of its mandate is to offer a helping hand to the Financial Policy Committee of the Bank of England in delivering its financial stability objective (FSA 2012 section 2B) ('The PRA's general objective'). For a general discussion, *see* further, Andromachi Georgosouli, 'The FCA-PRA coordination scheme and the challenge of policy coherence' (2013) 8 (1) CMLJ 62–76.

[4]   A critical appraisal of the IOSCO recommendations on credible deterrence falls beyond the scope of this chapter.

[5]   For an overview of the literature on compliance and enforcement, part of which is the theme of deterrence, *see* Bronwen Morgan and Karen Yeung, *An Introduction to Law and Regulation: Texts, Cases and Materials* (CUP, 2007) 151–217.

[6]   Hybrid strategies are considered to be pragmatic because the industry sometimes is motivated by making money and sometimes is motivated by a sense of social responsibility. For a general discussion, see John Braithwaite, *To Punish or Persuade: Enforcement of Coal Mine Safety* (State University of New York Press, 1985); and Bronwen Morgan and Karen Yeung, *An Introduction to Law and Regulation: Texts, Cases and Materials* (CUP, 2007) 194–5.

[7]   Roman Tomasic, 'The Financial Crisis and the Haphazard Pursuit of Financial Crime' (2011) 18 (1) J Financ Crime 7–31 (discussing the nature of the regulatory change by focusing on financial crime).

2.   THE DETERRENCE STRATEGY OF THE FINANCIAL CONDUCT AUTHORITY (FCA)

To understand the nature of the deterrence strategy of the FCA and, where relevant, of its predecessor the Financial Services Authority (FSA), it helps to draw a distinction between two different conceptions of deterrence: *Positive deterrence* and *negative deterrence*.

The distinctive feature of positive deterrence is its emphasis on voluntary adherence with regulatory stipulations. On this account, regulators and the regulatees do have their differences but nevertheless they are capable of forming harmonious relationships of trust and cooperation because in the long term they can work out a common view of key issues and priorities as, for example, with regards to measures that need to be taken in order to ensure that the provision of financial services corresponds with high standards of the conduct of business and professionalism. Positive deterrence comes hand in hand with forms of self-governance and soft law business ethics and culture.[8] Under this approach, enforcement is not precluded but it is nevertheless seen as a necessary evil.

Negative deterrence stands at the other side of the spectrum and it is associated with old school command and control schemes of regulation. This conception of deterrence depicts the nature of the relationship between regulators and regulatees as a relationship of insurmountable difficulties and perpetual conflict. On this account, the pursuit of a harmonious relationship as a prerequisite of voluntary adherence to regulatory stipulations is a utopian ideal. As such, it cannot offer any solution to real-life problems. Taking into account that regulators are under constant pressure to act swiftly in the public interest and indeed to do so in a hostile environment, the only strategy of deterrence that can actually work is a strategy that relies extensively on enforcement and the heavy hand of the law.

The UK regulator did not always give emphasis to negative deterrence strategies. Although there is no doubt that the entry into force of the Financial Services and Markets Act 2000 (FSMA) did mark an unequivocal departure from the traditional, and dominant until the late 1990s, self-regulatory approach to financial markets, it is interesting to note that initially the FSA worked very hard to assuage the regulatees that engagement with the industry and close cooperation would remain part and parcel of its approach to regulation. Nevertheless, more recently there has been a consistent and deliberate endeavour to forge the profile of the UK regulator as an enforcement-led regulator. The trend started off as early as 2007, when the FSA launched its so-called 'credible deterrence' strategy and it is continued today by the FCA.

At least on paper, the FCA enjoys a wider range of disciplinary and enforcement powers compared to its predecessor.[9] The FCA has, *inter alia*, the power to (a) impose administrative fines, (b) withdraw authorisation and permissions, (c) apply for injunctions and restitution

---

[8]   Howard S. Becker, 'Culture: A Sociological View' (1982) 71 Yale L Rev 513 (describing culture as shared understandings that permit a group of people to act in concert with each other); Justin O'Brien, George Gilligan and Seumas Miller, 'Culture and the Future of Financial Regulation: How to Embed Restraint in the Interests of Systemic Stability' (2014) 8 (2) LFMR 115, 126 (identifying five sources of cultures); Jasper Sorensen, 'The Strength of Corporate Culture and Reliability of Firm Performance' (2002) 47 (1) Admin Sci Q 70, 72 (offering a narrow definition of culture as a system of shared values).

[9]   Financial Services and Markets Act 2000, Part XI (Information Gathering and Investigations) and Part XIV (Disciplinary Powers) (as amended by the Financial Services Act 2012).

orders, and (d) prosecute certain criminal offences.[10] In addition, it is vested with a nuanced range of product intervention powers.[11] To ensure that the regulator's disciplinary action will be visible enough so that it has an impact on the conduct of market actors, new section 391(1ZB) also enables the FCA to publish information about warning notices in certain cases.[12]

There has been a notable increase in the rate of enforcement action over the past years. The imposition of record fines on Alliance and Leicester (A&L) for serious failings in the selling of Payment Protection Insurance (PPI) back in 2007 has been a milestone underlying a notable change of attitude, which crystallised over the subsequent years.[13] The *GMAC* is another case that offers a clear testament to this wind of change.[14] So does the impressive volume of Final Notices, Decision Notices, the number of prohibitions and criminal convictions during 2010–12 and reports about the aggregate amount of financial penalties imposed on individuals and firms during the same period of time.[15] More recently, the imposition of a record fine of

---

[10] *See* FCA, *Enforcement Information Guide* (2013) http://www.fca.org.uk/your-fca/documents/enforcement-information-guide accessed 15 October 2015.

[11] Financial Services Act 2012, new section 137D (FCA general rules: product intervention), new section 137R (Financial promotion rules), new section 137 S (Financial promotion: directions given by the FCA). With regards to the regulation of consumer credit, some of the FCA's key priorities at the time of writing this chapter include (a) the review of financial promotions, (b) the improvement of debt management standards, (c) considering the introduction of price caps on what payday lenders can actually charge, (d) assessing regularly how the industry treats financial difficulties, and (e) getting a better understanding of the economic behaviour of consumers. FCA, Business Plan 2014/15 (2014) http://www.fca.org.uk/static/documents/ corporate/business-plan-2014-2015.pdf accessed 15 October 2015. Product intervention powers are quite controversial but the regulator need not exercise these powers. Those powers are supposed to work like the proverbial musket in the closet. It suffices for the regulator to demonstrate a serious intention to resort to this arsenal of powers, if needed in the future, in view of repeated industry failings to provide products that are suitable to their clients.

[12] The FSA's use of these powers has already been challenged by way of judicial review and in the Upper Tribunal. *See R ex rel. S v X* [2011] EWHC (Admin) 1645, [4]–[10] (Eng.) (addressing the claimant's appeal of the FSA's decision notice to the Upper Tribunal and granting an interim injunction to restrain the FSA from publishing the notice); *R ex rel. Can. Inc. v FSA* [2011] EHWC (Admin) 2766 (Eng.).

[13] A&L was fined £7,000,000. Post crisis, financial firms were made to pay much higher fines. *See* FCA, *FCA Fines Lloyds Banking Group First a Total of £28,038,800 for Serious Sales Incentive Failings* (FCA Press Release; 12 November 2013), http://www.fca.org.uk/news/press-releases/fca-fines-lloyds-banking-group-firms-for-serious-sales-incentive-failings accessed 15 October 2015; FCA, *Final Notice from Financial Conduct Authority to Lloyds TSB Bank plc and Bank of Scotland plc* (10 December 2013) http://www.fca.org.uk/your-fca/documents/final-notices/2013/lloyds-tsb-bank-and-bank-of-scotland accessed 15 October 2015.

[14] GMAC was a non-bank lender in the prime, sub-prime and buy-to-let mortgage sectors. The disciplinary action focused on failures with respect to MCOB and the proper implementation of TCF. The GMAC failings included excessive and unfair charges for customers, proposing repayment plans that were not suitable, and starting repossession proceedings before considering other alternatives. Apart from having to pay a fine of £4m, like A&L, GMAC agreed to carry out a customer redress programme. *See* FSA, *Final Notice GMAC-RFC Ltd* (28 October 2009) http://www.fsa.gov.uk/pubs/final/gmac_rfc.pdf accessed 15 October 2015 and further, *Compliance Officer Bulletin* (Issue 76, May 2010).

[15] Tracey McDermot (acting director of the Enforcement and Financial Crime Division), *Credible Deterrence: Here to Stay* (FSA Speech, FSA Enforcement Conference; 2 July 2012) http://www.fsac.org.uk/library/communication/speeches/2012/0702-tm.html accessed 15 October 2015.

£284m on Barclays Bank plc has been celebrated as further cementing the role of the FCA as an enforcement-led regulator.[16]

These developments underscore an increasing belief in the potency of enforcement as a tool for credible deterrence. In the next section, I draw on the latest experience with the FCA to challenge this narrative.

3.   IS ENFORCEMENT MAKING DETERRENCE CREDIBLE?

A good starting point to consider this question is the experience with the imposition of the highest recorded fine on Barclays Bank in 2015. In relation to the FOREX scandal, Barclays continued to behave badly despite the fact that it had already paid a fine for a similar misconduct. Moreover, Barclays continued to misbehave while being subject to fresh investigations about its involvement in the LIBOR scandal. In the end, the FCA took into account the repeated compliance failings of Barclays as an aggravating factor and it increased the initial amount of the penalty but, at the same time, it was the first to admit that nobody appeared to have been deterred from anything let alone to have learnt any lesson.[17] In the case under examination, enforcement was eventually successful but deterrence was not. At best, the threat of huge fines went as far as to motivate Barclays to cooperate during investigations, hoping for an early settlement. This is not deterrence. It is perhaps more accurate to say that this is an arrangement whereby market actors buy out their freedom to continue misbehaving.

The use of Final Notices is closely connected with the FCA's enforcement strategy. The early publication of Final Notices is thought to be instrumental to the credibility of deterrence. On the one hand, it increases the visibility of the regulator's intended disciplinary and enforcement action. On the other hand, it sends an early message across that certain forms of misconduct will not be tolerated and that consequences will fall heavily on wrongdoers. In practice, Final Notices can backfire. The Court of Appeal's judgment in the *FCA v Macris* case illustrates this quite well.[18] The case concerns the giving of statutory enforcement notices to JP Morgan Chase Bank NA in relation to the involvement of the latter in 'London Wale' trades and the identification of Mr Macris. In agreement with the decision of the Upper Tribunal, the Court of Appeal ruled that the FCA should have treated Mr Macris as a third party for the purposes of section 393 of FSMA so that Mr Macris had availed himself with certain rights before the issue of the Final Notice. The Court of Appeal concluded that Mr Macris was entitled to refer the Final Notice to the Upper Tribunal for a hearing. On the FCA's appeal, the Supreme Court allowed the appeal on majority and declared that Mr Macris was not a third party for the

---

[16]   The fines that were imposed on Barclays relate to the LIBOR scandal and in particular to the involvement of Barclays in the Forex misconduct. Marcus Bonnell, 'Is credible deterrence really working? And other questions arising from a mixed week for the FCA' (*Financial Services Blog*, 28 May 2015) http://www.rpc.co.uk/index.php?option=com_easyblog&view=entry&id=1518&Itemid=133 accessed 15 October 2015.

[17]   Commenting on the recent FOREX investigations, Tracey McDermot declared that 'still lessons are not being learnt' '[a]nd there have been all too many examples – in both the retail and wholesale space – to reinforce that view'. T. McDermot, *Learning the Lessons of the Past as an Industry* (Speech, FCA Enforcement Conference: Our Part in Changing Culture, 2 December 2014) http://www.fca.org.uk/news/speeches/learning-the-lessons-of-the-past-as-an-industry accessed 15 October 2015.

[18]   *FCA v Macris* [2015] EWCA Civ 490 (19 May 2015).

purposes of section 393 of FSMA.[19] Even though this is a welcome development for the FCA, the history of this case reveals an embedded ambivalence in the application of the relevant legal test, which is unlikely to pass unnoticed by individuals asserting their third-party rights in the future.

Enforcement can also backfire in a different way, namely by creating bad press for the FCA. In virtually every attempt to ensure that imminent enforcement action is loud enough to be considered as a credible threat by the person under investigation (and by extension by their peers too), there is always the temptation to inflate the number of allegations against that person or even publish press statements that do not necessarily offer an accurate depiction of the case at stake. These scenarios do not lie in the sphere of fantasy. For example, in *Angela Burns v FCA*, the FCA was successful, however, the Upper Tribunal criticised the FCA for its unsatisfactory submissions on some points and for failing to reassess its position in the light of the fact that six out of its ten allegations had failed and out of the four allegations that were successful, three were upheld only to a limited extent.[20] In *Bayliss and Co (Financial Services) Ltd and Clive John Rosier v FCA*, the FCA was criticised *inter alia* about its handling of the press statement, which was sent to selected media outlets along with the decision notices issued to Bayliss and Mr Rosier.[21] The Upper Tribunal noted that the FCA press statement contained inaccuracies and that it failed *inter alia* to emphasise the tentative nature of those notices. Although the FCA was successful in both occasions, the rather poor handling of the enforcement procedure does not aid the good reputation of the FCA as a regulator whom the industry can trust and cooperate with. This is not a trivial matter as both trust and cooperation are key for industry enrolment and long-term behaviour modification.

A conclusion to be drawn out of the analysis so far is that the FCA is making itself more visible and loud but, at the same time, it exposes itself to legal risk and reputational costs, both of which are pervasively harmful to its credibility in the long term. Despite its increased visibility, it is doubtful whether the FCA is doing better in deterring future misconduct. Visibility is neither sufficient nor critical in securing the credibility of deterrence in the long term. Below, I consider three further aspects of regulatory strategy that impact on the credibility of deterrence in addition to enforcement: The regulator's ability to attain a congruence of minds and a congruence of hearts and its capacity to come across as a credible enforcer.

4. RETHINKING THE PARAMETERS OF CREDIBLE DETERRENCE

(a) Deterrence is Not Credible Unless there is a Congruence of Minds

Deterrence cannot render long-term results unless there is a congruence of minds between the regulator and the regulated industry about key problems and priorities. This idea is hardly new. In fact, it is embedded in the very nature of both positive and negative deterrence strategies.

---

[19] *Financial Conduct Authority v Macris* [2017] UKSC 19 (22 March 2017), [2017] WLR 1095, [2017] UKSC 19, [2017] 1 WLR 1095, [2017] Bus LR 643.
[20] *Angela Burns v FCA* [2015] UKUT 0252 (TCC) (FS/2012/0024).
[21] *Bayliss and Co (Financial Services) Ltd and Clive John Rosier v FCA* [2015] UKUT 0265 (TCC (fs/2013/0004 and 005).

While in the former case, this congruence of minds is the outcome of an effortless and voluntary endeavour to understand each other's rationalities, in the case of negative deterrence, this meeting of minds is (en)forced. Getting to congruence of minds calls for conversational capabilities and a focus on culture. The Treating Customers Fairly (TCF) Initiative is a good example of how the FCA and, before the FCA, the FSA have been trying to embed conversational regulation in their attempt to deter future misconduct.[22]

TCF asks the industry to work out what practices guarantee fair treatment for clients in a manner that is attuned to the policy goals and priorities of the regulator. These goals are encapsulated in the following six TCF outcomes:[23]

Outcome 1: Consumers can be confident that they are dealing with firms where the fair treatment of customers is central to the corporate culture.

Outcome 2: Products and services marketed and sold in the retail market are designed to meet the needs of identified consumer groups and are targeted accordingly.

Outcome 3: Consumers are provided with clear information and are kept appropriately informed before, during, and after the point of sale.

Outcome 4: Where consumers receive advice, the advice is suitable and takes account of their circumstances.

Outcome 5: Consumers are provided with products that perform as firms have led them to expect, and the associated service is of an acceptable standard.

Outcome 6: Consumers do not face unreasonable post-sale barriers imposed by firms to change product, switch provider, submit a claim, or make a complaint.

TCF is premised on the assumption that the members of the regulatory community are capable of working out for themselves the public standards that ought to govern their relationships. It is not a new set of secondary legislation. It is guidance, which embeds key elements of the UK regulator's strategy in the retail financial sector. Despite the apparently soft-law nature of this guidance, it is misleading to think that there are no legal consequences to follow. Most of the times, failure to deliver one or more of the TCF outcomes signals a failure to comply with Principle 6 and possibly other legally binding rules of the FCA Handbook.[24] The proactive and reactive nature of TCF measures have been discussed elsewhere and they will not be here

---

[22] For a classic exposition of the nature of conversational regulation as a dialectical practice, *see* Julia Black, 'Regulatory Conversations' (2002) J Law & Soc 163–96 and 'Talking about Regulation' (1998) PL 77–105. For a criticism *see* Andromachi Georgosouli, 'Regulatory Interpretation: Conversational or Constructive?' (2010) 30 (2) OJLS 361–84. On TCF *see* generally Andromachi Georgosouli, 'The FSA's "Treating Customers Fairly" (TCF) Initiative: What is So Good About It and Why It May Not Work' (2011) 38 (3) J Law & Soc 405–27.

[23] FSA, *Treating Customers Fairly – A Guide to Management Information* (2007) http://www.fca .org.uk/firms/being-regulated/meeting-your-obligations/fair-treatment-of-customers.pdf accessed 15 October 2015. *See* further, FCA Handbook of Rules and Guidance PRIN 2.1.1 (R) (enlisting all eleven principles for business) https://www.handbook.fca.org.uk/handbook/PRIN.pdf accessed 15 October 2015.

[24] Principle 6 (customers' interests) of the FCA Principles for Businesses stipulates that 'a firm must pay due regard to the interests of its customers and treat them fairly'.

reiterated.[25] Instead, the remainder of this section focuses on the dialectical practice that is embedded in these measures.

Long-term cultural change through behaviour modification is arguably impossible without industry engagement. The latter is deemed essential so that regulatees become more cognisant of their responsibilities and more sophisticated in sensing what TCF requires even in the presence of new or unforeseen circumstances. Regulatees who enjoy the discretion to decide how best to incorporate TCF into their business culture are believed to be more likely to view TCF as reasonable and thus worthy of compliance.[26] To encourage voluntary industry engagement during the supervisory process, tools like, for instance, the FCA's 'Culture Framework' (CF) and 'Management Information' (MI) are deployed to create a common dialectical space. The same tools are also instrumental for the organisation of ongoing regulatory conversations along the lines of key points of action, making it at the same time possible for the FCA to trace progress and to get a more accurate view of the firm's capacity to deliver the intended outcomes.[27]

Investigations and enforcement also provide channels of communication and in that sense they are instrumental in forging a congruence of minds. The FCA's enforcement strategy goes beyond penalising unacceptable forms of conduct. Being partly premised on negotiation, it creates opportunities for the alleged offender to deliberate with the regulator, remedy any wrongdoing, and revise its business practice where appropriate. A&L demonstrates this quite well. A&L was ordered to pay the biggest fine for serious failings in the selling of PPI pre-crisis. However, A&L also agreed to implement a customer contact programme overseen by third-party accountants. Under this programme, A&L undertook, amongst other things, to contact all customers who had purchased PPI in conjunction with an unsecured loan, to review its policy in respect of product information that was sent to these customers, to review any rejected complaints and claims, and to pay redress where appropriate.

Dialectical capabilities have their own limitations in promoting the required congruence of minds for behaviour modification and overall cultural change.[28] Their efficacy in part depends on the willingness of the industry to genuinely engage with the regulator and – when chal-

---

25   On TCF *see* generally Andromachi Georgosouli, 'The FSA's "Treating Customers Fairly" (TCF) Initiative: What is So Good About It and Why It May Not Work' (2011) 38 (3) J Law & Soc 405–27.

26   In the past (and to a large extent even today), the UK regulator encouraged this by offering to firms a 'regulatory dividend' in the form of less scrutiny, as an incentive to make them behave well, demonstrating essentially that customer interests were central to the corporate culture of the business in question. Like its predecessor, the FCA follows this approach but it does not rely entirely on the initiative of senior managers to ensure that the business culture of their firm is consistent with TCF. Andromachi Georgosouli, Costanza Russo and Phillip Rawlings, *Regulation of Financial Services: Aims and Methods* (CCLS Research Paper, April 2014) http://www.ccls.qmul.ac.uk/docs/research/138683.pdf accessed 15 October 2015 (noting that this policy reflected an assumption that the vast majority of firms had the intention to treat their customers fairly and that the majority were willing to engage openly and positively with the regulator, and arguing that both assumptions proved to be naive in reality).

27   FCA, *TCF Culture* (5 April, 2013) http://www.fca.org.uk/firms/being-regulated/meeting-your -obligations/fair-treatment-of-customers/Culture accessed 15 October 2015; FSA, *TCF – Towards fair outcomes for consumers* (2006) http://www.fca.org.uk/static/fca/documents/fsa-tcf-towards.pdf accessed 15 October 2015.

28   On the limitations of conversational regulation see Andromachi Georgosouli, 'The Revision of the FSA's Approach to Regulation: An Incomplete Agenda?' (2010) Issue 7 JBL 599, 604 and 'The Nature of the FSA's Approach to Regulation' (2008) 28 LS 119, 135.

lenged – to reflect on the soundness of existing business practices and to adjust those practices accordingly.[29] Financial firms are not charities working in the interests of customers. They are profit-driven institutions. Arguably, a business culture that ends up reflecting both the profit-driven character of the business and, at the same time, the firm's perceived commitment to public policy goals constitutes a contradiction in terms. One must take priority, and quite intuitively, this will have to be profit. This is not to say that no good can come out of regulatory conversation. It can, but only in the long run and in the form of outcomes, which are difficult to measure let alone causally attribute to measures that have been taken in the distant past. There are two other issues that are worth mentioning here in passing. The first one is that conversational practice breeds conditions of regulatory capture as a result of the close and ongoing interaction of the regulator with the regulated industry.[30] The second one is that regulatees tend to engage in creative compliance.[31]

To conclude, congruence of minds is good but not good enough. The credibility of deterrence requires more than getting the members of the regulatory community to reach out to each other's rationalities. As I argue below, it also calls for a congruence of hearts.

(b)   Deterrence is Not Credible Unless there is a Congruence of Hearts

The creation of a common language and increased familiarity with the rationalities of others are not enough to guarantee the genuineness of the industry's commitment to the promotion of the regulator's agenda. It may eventually lead to a meeting of minds, the avoidance of misunderstandings and overall procedural efficiency but it does not attain a meeting of hearts. The latter is crucial but very hard to achieve as this meeting of hearts presupposes that regulation is fair to all parties affected.[32] To be sure, one's view about the fairness (or otherwise) of a particular scheme of regulation is bound to manifest itself as a psychological reaction of some emotional sort. Nevertheless, getting regulatees to *feel* in a particular kind of way is not what a congruence of hearts is meant to describe here. Significantly, the latter alludes to the *reason-giving* capacity of the regulator and regulatees as moral agents and it is to be understood as an end point of a deliberative process where they reach a 'reflective equilibrium' about the fairness of a particular scheme of regulation as they go about trying to justify

---

[29]   Persistent industry regression leaves little scope for optimism in this regard. See discussion below at pages 309–10.

[30]   Although it is to be noted that not all instances of capture are socially wasteful. A distinction needs to be drawn here between positive and negative capture to connote the fact that on some occasions, capture can actually be instrumental in the promotion of the public interest. For a further discussion see, Daniel Carpenter and David A. Moss (eds), *Preventing Regulatory Capture: Special Interest Influence and How to Limit It* (CUP, 2014).

[31]   Doreen McBarnet and Christopher Whelan, 'The Elusive Spirit of the Law: Formalism and the Struggle for Legal Control' (1991) 54 (6) MLR 848–73.

[32]   For a classic account of the conceptual distinction between substantive fairness and procedural fairness in legal theory see Ronald Dworkin, *Law's Empire* (Hart Publishing 1998, reprinted 2007) 164–7.

themselves to each other.[33] With this in mind, it helps at this juncture to draw a conceptual distinction between procedural and substantive fairness.[34]

The regulator is arguably fair in the proceduralist sense of the term when procedural aspects of regulation correspond to constitutional principles of procedural due process and other widely accepted benchmarks of regulatory legitimacy.[35] At present, and subject to further empirical investigation, there is some evidence suggesting that although the FCA's policy of enforcement is compatible with constitutional principles, procedural fairness is under jeopardy. Specifically, quality assurance in the handling and effective execution of investigations and enforcement proceedings is an issue of concern.[36] The FCA must now manage a growing number of investigations and enforcements but, to the author's knowledge, resources have not been equally increased to match up with this trend.

The regulator is arguably fair in the substantive sense of the term when regulation delivers outcomes that are morally acceptable to all those it affects.[37] Substantive fairness is no less important in cementing the credibility of deterrence. Nevertheless, this is a bold and rather unpopular claim to make for at least two reasons: First, because of the presumably heavy demands of substantive fairness and, second, because fairness seems to be too elusive to measure. The ascription of a certain and definite meaning to substantive fairness is very difficult to pin down.[38] As it is commonly thought, fairness lacks a generally accepted definition

---

[33] Here, I loosely draw on the notion of reflective equilibrium as it is advanced by John Rawls in his theory of justice. *See*, John Rawls, *A Theory of Justice* (OUP 1971, revised edition 2000) 17–18 and 42–5.

[34] The importance of procedural fairness is well documented in the literature, especially in scholarly work on enforcement and compliance. For example, in her critique of responsive regulation, Karen Yeung argues that we should not overlook the constitutional values of proportionality and consistency in enforcement, which are themselves rooted in the right to a fair and equal treatment. With respect to enforcement, the principle of proportionality, for instance, requires that the regulator's action must be commensurate to the seriousness of the issue at hand. Crucially, the test of proportionality that Yeung proposes is not functional in nature. Rather, it is substantive in character, going beyond determinations that have as a point of reference the goal of effective future compliance without any due consideration to the nature and seriousness of the defendants' violation. Bronwen Morgan and Karen Yeung, *An Introduction to Law and Regulation: Texts and Materials* (CUP, 2007) 201–2. For a more comprehensive discussion, *see* Karen Yeung, *Securing Compliance* (OUP, 2004).

[35] Kristina Murphy, 'Procedural Justice and Its Role in Promoting Voluntary Compliance' in Peter Drahos (ed), *Regulatory Theory: Foundations and Applications* (ANU, 2017) 43, 46 (noting that '[i]n the socio-psychological literature, procedural justice is conceptualized as involving the quality of treatment and quality of decision-making received by an authority. It involves more than a regulator just being nice to people. Criteria typically used to define procedurally just treatment include respect, neutrality, trustworthiness and voice'). For a classic exposition of regulatory legitimacy, *see* Robert Baldwin, Martin Cave and Martin Lodge, *Understanding Regulation: Theory, Strategy and Practice* (OUP, 2nd edn, 2013) at 27 (identifying the following criteria of legitimacy: (a) legislative mandate, (b) accountability, (c) due process, (d) expertise, and (e) efficiency).

[36] *FCA v Angela Burns* [2015] UKUT 0252 (TCC), Case Number FS/2012/0024 and, in particular, paragraphs 15 and 16 http://www.tribunals.gov.uk/financeandtax/Documents/decisions/Burns-v-FCA-penalty.pdf accessed 15 October 2015.

[37] The importance of the distributional effect of regulation has already been noted in regulatory studies. *See*, for example, Justice Tankebe, 'Viewing Things Differently: The Dimensions of Public Perceptions of Police Legitimacy' (2013) 51 Criminology 103–35 (enlisting distributional justice as one of the components of legitimate regulation).

[38] Procedural fairness is not free from interpretive difficulties but compared to substantive fairness, it is easier to measure and to be accounted for.

and as a result it cannot be measured or accounted for in any tangible kind of way. This claim has a kernel of truth but it should be treated with caution.

Quite apart from the fact that it is premised on the absurd and, hence impractical, expectation that for every vague principle, norm or doctrine there must always be an *ex ante* and ideally universally accepted definition or it for otherwise public governance cannot work, this position also seems to downplay the fact that the members of the regulatory community are actually furnished with all the linguistic and interpretive tools that are necessary in order for them to make sense of abstract terms and thus to overcome any definitional difficulties in real-life situations.[39] Sometimes they get the interpretation of principles like fairness right. Sometimes they get it wrong. It may also be the case that they take advantage of this interpretive practice to manipulate it in a way that serves their own interests. The fact remains that although they tend to disagree on the best interpretation of fairness, they are still able to tell with some confidence when, in the circumstances, a particular market actor or a certain interest group has been fairly treated and when it has not. For instance, it is hard to argue that financial services providers are treated fairly when they do not have the chance to participate in public consultations about the introduction of substantial reforms to the existing regulatory framework, namely reforms that are going to have a major impact on them.

More generally, regulation promises benefits but comes with burdens. Experience suggests that the regulator's capacity to allocate burdens fairly goes a long way in getting regulatees to comply with relevant rules and guidance, assuming ownership of the delivery of certain desirable outcomes. Let's take the example of the recent financial mis-selling saga in the United Kingdom.[40] A closer look at the reaction of the industry reveals a more widely spread concern with the fairness of the way in which the regulation of financial mis-selling allocates burdens among financial services and products providers and their customers. Following the long British tradition of self-regulation as the main conduit of cultural change, the FSA initially internalised self-regulation into a government-based hybrid scheme of responsive regulation. It tried to engage with the industry in order to ensure that customers are treated fairly but the industry's commitment to attuning its business culture with the goals and priorities of the regulator's agenda was not genuine. The large number of Payment Protection Insurance (PPI) complaints about mis-selling practices that were referred to the Financial Ombudsman Service (FOS) and the significant discrepancy in outcomes between PPI complaints that were handled by firms (a majority of which were rejected) and those that were referred to the FOS gave a very disappointing picture of the industry's commitment.[41] More recently, this became

---

[39]   Andromachi Georgosouli, 'Regulatory Interpretation: Conversational or Constructive?' (2010) 30 (2) OJLS; 'Judgement-led regulation: Reflections on data and discretion' (2013) 14 JBR 209–20, 215 (providing brief examples). For a more comprehensive discussion in the literature of the philosophy of mind see notably Donald Davidson, 'What Thought Requires' Essay 9 in *Problems of Rationality* (OUP, 2004) 135 and 'Coherence Theory of Truth and Knowledge' Essay 10 in *Subjective, Intersubjective, Objective* (OUP, 2001)137, 138–40.

[40]   The articulation of the principles of fairness in regulation falls beyond the scope of this chapter, however, one possibility is to follow the contractualist tradition in moral philosophy and argue that burden sharing must adhere to principles of justice that regulatees are taken to be able to justify to each other. On the contractualist school of thought see notably Tim Scanlon, *What We Owe to Each Other* (Harvard University Press, 2000).

[41]   Andromachi Georgosouli, 'Payment Protection Insurance (PPI) Misselling: Some Lessons from the UK' (2014) 21 (1) Conn Ins L J 261–88; Ellis Ferran, 'Regulatory Lessons from the Payment Protection Insurance Mis-selling Scandal in the UK' (2012) 13 EBOLR 247.

evident in the industry's attempt to challenge the FSA's decision to take enforcement action in view of the industry's failure to take into account FOS decisions in handling customer complaints contrary to the regulator's expectation as it was communicated in a Policy Statement (PS).[42] The industry eventually lost its case, but, in the course of bringing the action, several firms put on hold the handling of nearly all PPI complaints. This caused significant delays in the processing of financial redress to the victims of financial mis-selling. Most importantly though, it aggravated the situation in the eyes of the UK regulator and eroded past attempts to build trust. The grounds of this deep resentment continue to gather momentum.[43]

Judging from the history of PPI mis-selling, it is clear that financial services providers fell short of complying with best practice in their dealings with customers. However, one should not be quick to vilify them or, indeed, to jump to the conclusion that their reluctance to commit to the FSA's agenda was capricious. A fundamental *reason* (and not emotion) for them to reject the FSA's policy regarding the tackling of financial mis-selling was the belief that the regulation of financial mis-selling was unduly burdensome to financial services providers. Indeed, for some financial firms, the burdens took the form of additional costs due to the legal uncertainty surrounding the informal nature of PSs through which the regulator communicated its expectations. For others, the burdens took the form of additional costs because of the eventual transformation of conduct of business requirements into a detailed set of legally binding rules – a development that also increased the risk of litigation. Yet for others, compliance with the relevant regulation meant investing time and resources to take action for matters that, in their view, were not their responsibility to pursue – most notably the review of complaints-handling policies even in relation to transactions for which they had never received customer complaints.

To conclude, the difficulties with attaching a fixed and unequivocal meaning to substantive fairness in regulation may explain why substantive fairness is omitted from textbook discussions and policy documents on what makes deterrence credible but, from this omission it does not follow that substantive fairness is irrelevant or that it is indeed of diminished significance as a parameter of credibility.

---

[42] *R ex rel. British Bankers Association v FSA* [2011] EWHC (Admin) 999. In its judicial review action the industry made three principal contentions. The first was that PRIN are not actionable at a suit by a private person in view of the wording of old section 150 of the FSMA 2000. Accordingly, they could not give rise to redress obligations. The second was that regulatory principles could not conflict with or augment specific rules. Finally, the third contention was that the existence of an alternative statutory collective redress scheme precluded the FSA from taking the action set out in the Policy Statement.

[43] For example, the length of time of the legal proceedings of the *Keydata Investment Services* case demonstrates the tendency of some members of the industry to cause delays and more generally derail the regulator's endeavours. *S.O. Ford, M.J. Owen, P.F Johnson v FCA* [2015] UKUT 0220(TCC) Case numbers FS/2014/0012, FS/2014/0013, FS/2014/0016 http://www.tribunals.gov.uk/financeandtax/ Documents/decisions/Ford-Owen-Johnson-v-FCA-decision.pdf accessed 15 October 2015. *See* further, FCA, 'The FCA has today published Decision Notices in respect of three former members of Keydata's senior management: Steward Ford (former chief executive), Mark Owen (Former Sales Director) and Peter Johnson (Former Compliance Office)' (*FCA Press Release*, 26 May 2015, last modified 2 June 2015) https://www.fca.org.uk/news/fca-published-decision-notices-three-former-members-keydatas -senior-management accessed 15 October 2015.

(c)   Deterrence is Not Credible Unless there is Public Confidence that the Regulator is a Credible Enforcer

It is not enough for the FCA to be a successful enforcer; the FCA must come across as a credible enforcer in the eyes of the beholder. It is naive to think that the increasing the volume of enforcement cases boosts the credibility of the FCA as an enforcer. In fact, the profile of the FCA as a credible enforcer can be diluted by several factors. One of them is certainly receiving bad press. As discussed in a previous section of this chapter, this is already concerning due to the FCA's perceived mishandling of some of the recent enforcement cases. Historically, however, bad press has been much more closely associated with the frequent resort to early settlement. Early settlement is time and cost efficient not only for the regulator and for the wrongdoer but also for the aggrieved party seeking financial redress or some other form of remedial action. Nevertheless, all these advantages are hardly registered in the collective memory. The lack of visibility that comes with early settlement fuels a sentiment that wrongdoers can get away with it because they can afford to pay the price of their wrong-doing.[44]

Experience in the United Kingdom suggests that the intensity of enforcement action varies and that it is by and large driven by the prevailing political climate.[45] For example, if we look back in time to a few years ago, the FSA's willingness to proceed to formal enforcement gained momentum during the recent financial turmoil, that is to say, at a time when there was great political pressure to bring cases to court. As the collective memory of the financial crisis of 2008 fades away, the regulator's commitment to formal enforcement is expected to recede. To the extent that this pattern can be attributed to political happenstance rather than a principled decision to adapt the strategy of deterrence in view of *inter alia* changes in the market environment, differences in the intensity of enforcement implies an inconsistent policy of deterrence. In the absence of a consistent strategy of deterrence, it hard to see how the FCA can possibly convey its seriousness of intention to pre-empt members of the industry from future misconduct.

It comes naturally to think that in the case of enforcement, the 'beholder' is the industry, since the industry provides the pool of future perpetrators of misconduct, namely the immediate target group of every deterrence strategy. This notwithstanding, the perceptions and attitudes of customers as future victims of misconduct matter too.[46] There is an important correlation between customers' attitudes towards enforcement and credible deterrence. On the one hand, active customer interest groups keep an eye on the regulator's acts and omissions and, depending on how they perceive the regulator's performance as an enforcer, they can

---

[44]   In fact, the industry is given several incentives to opt for early settlement, such as discounts and the reduction of financial penalties: FCA Handbook of Rules and Guidance, Decision procedure and penalties manual para 6.7 (2014) http://media.fshandbook.info/content/FCA/ DEPP.pdf accessed 15 October 2015.

[45]   Andromachi Georgosouli, Costanza Russo and Phillip Rawlings, *Regulation of Financial Services: Aims and Methods* (CCLS Research Paper, April 2014) paragraph 7.2.1 http://www.ccls.qmul .ac.uk/docs/research/138683.pdf accessed 15 October 2015.

[46]   A danger here, albeit a theoretical one, is that of a complacent regulator as there is no incentive to improve performance when the current and future victims of misconduct or perhaps other stakeholders no longer put pressure on the regulator to do a better job.

be instrumental in fortifying or otherwise challenging the regulator's reputation.[47] On the other hand, client awareness, consumer activism and the threat of private enforcement seem to bear the potential of deterring future misconduct alongside (albeit not in place of) public enforcement initiated by the regulator. So far, the correlation between customer attitudes and credible deterrence has not been comprehensively explored. Although financial literacy and other customer awareness initiatives are in place, these are neither explicitly nor fully incorporated into the FCA's strategy of deterrence. Moreover, it is uncertain whether this gap will ever be addressed in the future for mainly two reasons. First, because the enhancement of public awareness is not part of the FCA's list of statutory objectives after the amendments of the Financial Services and Market Act 2000 by the Financial Services Act 2012, and, second, because the FCA must now act in a time of financial austerity.[48]

5.   CONCLUSION

It is hard to argue against deterrence. Despite the fact that the implementation of deterrence strategies is a challenging ongoing process, everyone seems to accept that prevention is better than cure. Accordingly, the question to ask is how the regulator can do a better job in pre-empting future misconduct. In this chapter, I argued that, although enforcement (or rather the threat of it) is an undisputed incentive-modifying tool, the current focus on enforcement is misplaced. Credibility is not secured by simply scaring regulatees off in the gloomy prospect of tough consequences as a punishment for their misbehaviour. Deterrence is not credible, unless there is a congruence of minds and a congruence of hearts between the regulator and the industry. Moreover, credibility calls for measures that strengthen the profile of the regulator as a credible enforcer. The analysis above does not provide an exhaustive account of the factors that impact on the effectiveness of the FCA's strategy of deterrence. Nevertheless, it does demonstrate the complexity of deterrence strategy and highlights aspects that call for reform.

If the emphasis on enforcement is misplaced, as I have tried to argue, a question to ask is what is left to be done. Clearly, the FCA is not left without options. Perhaps a more promising way forward is to take a closer and more methodical look into the organisational structure of the financial services provider and its regime of corporate governance. This can be done through the development and implementation of ongoing incentive audits with respect to remuneration, executive compensation, accountability and legal liability in order to identify and monitor sources of conflicts of interest, moral hazard, organisational complexity, opacity and other features that affect the incentive structure that informs the setting of priorities and decision-making within these firms. Industry incentive audits are here recommended for an additional reason.[49] Culture cannot be enforced and is hard to regulate. Incentive audits can be

---

[47]   For a general discussion of public accountability in regulation, *see* Michael W. Dowdle, 'Public Accountability: Conceptual, Historical and Epistemic Mappings' in Peter Drahos (ed), *Regulatory Theory: Foundations and Applications* (ANU, 2017) 197–210.

[48]   Nevertheless, it is worth noting in passing that, as long as there is empirical evidence to support the view that financially literate consumers improve competition in the financial services sector, there is a window of opportunity to argue that financial literacy programmes and other relevant initiatives fall within the FCA's statutory mandate to promote competition in the interests of consumers.

[49]   The case for incentive audits in the context of financial regulation is closely linked with recent studies on the contribution of misaligned incentives to the outbreak of the recent financial crisis. The

the antidote to these difficulties because they promise to spot triggers of incentive misalignment at an early stage as these emerge.

Improving the substantive fairness of regulation is undoubtedly challenging but there are steps that can be taken towards this direction too. To return to the PPI mis-selling saga, obviously, the FCA need not agree with the industry's understanding of what would amount to fair burden allocation in the tackling of financial mis-selling practices as per the stipulations of the FCA. All the FCA needs to do, and in part already does, is to challenge industry perceptions about fair burden allocation in a structured, consistent, time-efficient and monitored fashion. This can be done by making more frequent use of 'comply or explain' rules and of *ad hoc* communications as part of the supervisory process. In addition, the FCA needs to communicate more effectively the steps that it has been taking to ensure that financial providers are not unduly burdened. Financial literacy can also reduce costs for financial services providers. Consequently, existing initiatives that aim to empower consumers and other financial customers should continue with greater intensity. The implementation of a comprehensive medium- and long-term 'follow up' process would also help. Specifically, it would make it possible for the FCA to return to former wrongdoers in order to monitor how well the latter are doing in adhering to rules post-enforcement. Moreover, the threat of shaming those who fail to see compliance as an ongoing commitment could be deployed in order to enhance the credibility of this follow-up process.[50]

The above tentative set of recommendations is not a panacea but it pledges to improve the incentive-realignment capabilities of the regulator by adding a more tangible and pragmatic dimension to the existing deterrence strategy. This is reason enough to merit consideration alongside, if not in priority, to enforcement.

---

relevant scholarship focuses on two inter-related issues. On the one hand, the impact of industry incentives when these are not aligned with those of the regulator and, on the other hand, the misalignment of regulators' incentives in various institutional settings. *See*, generally, Martin Cihak, Asli Demirguc-Kunt and Barry R. Johnston, 'Incentive Audits: A New Approach to Financial Regulation', *Policy Research Working Paper 6308* (The World Bank Development Research Group, Finance and Private Sector Development Team, January 2013) 12–13 (advocating for incentive-based regulation as a regulatory approach that pledges to be more dynamic and forward looking and to treat the underlying incentive issues that undermine regulatory effectiveness; not just the symptoms of regulatory failure).

[50]   For a classic exposition *see*, John Braithwaite, *Crime, Shame and Reintegration* (CUP, 1989). For a general discussion, *see* Nathan Harris, 'Shame in Regulatory Settings' in Peter Drahos (ed), *Regulatory Theory: Foundations and Applications* (NUA, 2017) 59–71.

14. Breaches of AML reporting requirements by UK bankers: Are effective enforcement choices being made by financial regulators?

Miriam Goldby

A.   INTRODUCTION

This chapter aims to analyse the way in which breaches of anti-money laundering (AML) reporting obligations by bankers have tended to be dealt with in the United Kingdom (UK). The need to ensure a high level of compliance with reporting requirements is key to the achievement of the objectives of AML legislation, namely to combat crime, in particular organised crime, through disrupting it, thus reducing it; to bring perpetrators of money laundering (and relevant predicate crimes) to justice; and to recover the proceeds of crime. As shall be discussed in this chapter, the sheer volume of funds that is estimated to be laundered through the UK financial system on an annual basis is worrying, and these estimates have not reduced since the large-scale reforms introduced with the Proceeds of Crime Act 2002 (PoCA). Neither is the amount of money being recovered reassuring.

As enforcement is a crucial aspect of compliance, a theoretical analysis and evaluation of enforcement decisions taken with respect to breaches of bankers' reporting obligations is essential. This chapter finds that, in spite of there being a variety of options for dealing with failure to report, the prosecution of individuals appears never to have been resorted to with respect to a banker since the Financial Services Authority (FSA) was established and since the coming into force of PoCA. While the banking sector files around 300,000 suspicious activity reports (SARs) annually, the high number of SARs does not necessarily indicate good overall compliance. The industry may be flooding the SARs system with 'noise' (indeed there are no statistics published on the quality of SARs submitted) or might be reporting suspicions relating to lower-value business and keeping quiet about suspicions relating to high-value, highly profitable client activity. The reason for the absence of prosecutions of individuals is more likely to be that authorities prefer to use alternative enforcement measures, usually against the institution rather than the individual committing the breach. The issue that this chapter seeks to highlight is that failure to use enforcement measures that involve criminal prosecution may be precluding the change in corporate culture required to reduce the prevalence of money laundering through the UK financial system.

In order to evaluate these enforcement decisions, the chapter examines where the powers and duties lie for investigating and prosecuting failure to report and what might be the reasons for the rarity of prosecutions of individuals operating in the financial sector. It argues that prosecution may be necessary to change corporate culture within banks, thereby improving compliance. In an institution where compliance is recalcitrant and where management will do as little towards compliance as they are able to get away with, law enforcers should ensure that they do not get away with failure to report, and that the full set of enforcement tools that the law makes available to them is put to use. It concludes by outlining the reasons why reform might be desirable as well as some possibilities for reform.

B.   REPORTING OBLIGATIONS UNDER ENGLISH LAW

Section 330 of PoCA lays down requirements applicable to the regulated sector which are complied with by filing a Suspicious Activity Report (SAR). There are four elements to the reporting requirement under s 330. First, s 330(2) states that where a person knows or suspects or has reasonable grounds for knowing or suspecting that another person is engaged in money laundering s/he should make a disclosure (by filing a SAR).[1] Secondly, the information on which the knowledge or suspicion is based (or gives reasonable grounds for such knowledge or suspicion to arise) must have come to that person in the course of a business in the regulated sector (s 330(3)). Thirdly, under s 330(3A) either s/he must be able to identify the whereabouts of the person or laundered money or s/he believes, or it is reasonable to expect her/him to believe, that the information may assist in identifying the person or the laundered property. Finally, s 330(4) requires the relevant person to make a disclosure as soon as it is reasonably practicable to do so. Thus, the first element, under s 330(2)(b), includes negligence-based liability, that is, liability for breach of s 330 may arise not only where a person knows or suspects and does not file a SAR but also where a person should have known or suspected, as there were reasonable grounds to do so.[2] This introduces an objective test of liability. Under s 334 PoCA, a person who fails to comply with reporting requirements under s 330 is liable (a) on summary conviction, to imprisonment for a term not exceeding six months or to a fine not exceeding the statutory maximum or to both, or (b) on conviction on indictment, to imprisonment for a term not exceeding five years or to a fine or to both.

Further requirements are found in the EU Funds Transfer Regulation 2015 (Funds Transfer Regulation),[3] with which payment service providers[4] established in the EU must comply in respect of transfer of funds[5] in any currency. Under Article 4, transfers of funds must be accompanied by certain information identifying payer and payee, and it is the obligation of a payee bank to detect missing information (Article 7) and 'to implement effective risk-based procedures for determining whether to execute, reject or suspend a transfer of funds lacking

---

[1]   This implements Article 33(1)(a) of Directive (EU) 2015/849 of the European Parliament and of the Council of 20 May 2015 on the prevention of the use of the financial system for the purposes of money laundering or terrorist financing, amending Regulation (EU) No 648/2012 of the European Parliament and of the Council, and repealing Directive 2005/60/EC of the European Parliament and of the Council and Commission Directive 2006/70/EC, OJ L 141/73 (hereinafter '4MLD'). 'Suspicion' is defined in *K Ltd v National Westminster Bank* [2007] 1 WLR 311, para 16 as 'a possibility which is more than fanciful that the relevant facts exist'.

[2]   PoCA, s 330(2).

[3]   Regulation (EU) 2015/847 of the European Parliament and of the Council of 20 May 2015 on information accompanying transfers of funds and repealing Regulation (EC) No 1781/2006, OJ L 141/1 (hereinafter 'Funds Transfer Regulation').

[4]   As defined in 4MLD (n 1), Art 3(5) by reference to Directive 2007/64/EC of the European Parliament and of the Council of 13 November 2007 on payment services in the internal market amending Directives 97/7/EC, 2002/65/EC, 2005/60/EC and 2006/48/EC and repealing Directive 97/5/EC, OJ L 319/1, Art 1(1). This includes credit institutions.

[5]   Defined in the Funds Transfer Regulation (n 3) Art 3(8) and (9).

the required complete payer and payee information or for taking the appropriate follow-up action' (Article 8). Steps that may be taken by the payee's payment service provider in response to failure to provide information include (i) asking for the missing information, (ii) rejecting the transfer (Article 8(1)), (iii) issuing warnings and deadlines, and (iv) rejecting any future transfers of funds from that payment service provider or restricting or terminating its business relationship with it (Article 8(2)). Importantly, the missing information must be taken into account in assessing whether that transfer of funds or any related transaction is suspicious for the purposes of complying with AML requirements (Article 9). Similar obligations apply to intermediary service providers (Articles 11–13). An important additional obligation for the purposes of reporting is found under Article 21(2) which provides as follows:

> Payment service providers, in cooperation with the competent authorities, shall establish appropriate internal procedures for their employees, or persons in a comparable position, to report breaches internally through a secure, independent, specific and anonymous channel, proportionate to the nature and size of the payment service provider concerned.

Where there is suspicion of money laundering, carrying out a transaction for a customer may involve committing a primary money laundering offence under PoCA, ss 327–329, in particular s 328 – entering into or becoming concerned in an arrangement which one knows or suspects facilitates (by whatever means) the acquisition, retention, use or control of criminal property by or on behalf of another person – unless consent to the transaction is first obtained under s 335.[6] In order to obtain such consent, the bank must make a disclosure by filing an SAR. Where consent is sought, the SAR is known as a defence against money laundering (DAML) request (previously known as a 'consent SAR').[7] The penalties for acting without consent are potentially very serious, if it is proven that the act constitutes a primary money laundering offence. Under s 334(1) a person committing such an offence would be liable, on summary conviction, to imprisonment for a term not exceeding six months or to a fine not exceeding the statutory maximum or to both, or, on conviction on indictment, to imprisonment for a term not exceeding 14 years or to a fine or to both.

C.   IS COMPLIANCE WITH REPORTING REQUIREMENTS BY THE UK BANKING SECTOR GOOD?

On the face of it, it would appear that there is no reticence about reporting suspicious activity in the UK banking sector. In the 18 months from October 2015 to March 2017 the banking sector filed 525,361 SARs, which constitutes 82.85 per cent of a total of 634,113 SARs filed in the

---

[6]   This implements 4MLD (n 1), Art 35(1).

[7]   Having made such disclosure, in order to carry out the transaction for its customer the relevant person must either receive explicit consent, or wait for the expiration of the notice period (s 335(3)) or, where consent is refused during the notice period, the expiration of the moratorium (s 335(4)). The notice period is seven working days (s 335(5)) and the moratorium period is 31 days (s 335(6)). If no consent is received and either the notice or the moratorium period (if applicable) has not passed, the relevant person can do nothing. If it acts, it may be liable for a primary money laundering offence, as provided by s 334(1). See *R (on the application of UMBS Online Ltd) v Serious Organised Crime Agency* [2008] 1 All ER 465 [51]–[52], per Ward LJ.

UK in that period.[8] Similarly, in the 12 months from October 2014 to September 2015, it filed 83.39 per cent of a total of 381,882 SARs filed in the UK (318,451)[9] and in the period between October 2013 and September 2014, it filed 82.18 per cent of 354,186 SARs (291,070).[10] These are very high numbers of SARs, especially when compared to other jurisdictions with important financial sectors. For example, in Switzerland which has a financial sector of comparable size to that of the UK,[11] banks filed only 2,159 SARs in 2015.[12]

The reason for the high number of SARs filed by banks in the UK is unclear, although it is believed that a substantial amount of reporting may be defensive.[13] It is however noteworthy that a much lower number of DAML requests or consent SARs (i.e. reports which request permission from the National Crime Agency (NCA) to carry out a transaction for a customer) are filed: in the 18-month period from October 2015 to March 2017 , the total was 27,471[14] and in the 12-month period from October 2014 to September 2015 it was 14,155.[15] Neither SARs Report specifies how many of these derived from the banking sector. For reasons which are evident, the UK Financial Intelligence Unit (FIU) gives priority to DAML requests (or consent SARs), and it would appear that non-consent SARs only tend to be examined closely if they come up in a database search undertaken by one of the Law Enforcement Agencies (LEAs) that have access to ELMER (the UK FIU's internal SARs database), i.e. if they have a connection with some other piece of evidence already in the hands of the relevant LEA.[16] In view of the numbers of SARs and how resource-intensive it would be to follow up on each one individually, this is not surprising, and very little information is available on the quality or usefulness of the non-consent SARs submitted.

There are, however, indications that the high number of SARs reported in the UK does not necessarily indicate good compliance by all banks. As discussed under heading D.1.2.3 below,

---

[8]   See National Crime Agency (NCA), *SARs Report 2017*, 11 October 2017 (hereinafter 'SARs Report 2017') available electronically at http://www.nationalcrimeagency.gov.uk/publications/ suspicious-activity-reports-sars/826-suspicious-activity-reports-annual-report-2017/file (accessed 3 March 2018), 12.

[9]   See National Crime Agency (NCA), *SARs Report 2015*, 24 March 2017 (hereinafter 'SARs Report 2015') available electronically at http://www.nationalcrimeagency.gov.uk/publications/suspicious -activity-reports-sars/677-sars-annual-report-2015/file (accessed 25 July 2017), 6 and 9.

[10]   See National Crime Agency (NCA), *SARs Report 2014*, 28 July 2015 (hereinafter 'SARs Report 2014'), available electronically at http://www.nationalcrimeagency.gov.uk/publications/suspicious -activity-reports-sars/464-2014-sars-annual-report/file (accessed 25 July 2017), 7 and 9.

[11]   See Bank of England, *EU Membership and the Bank of England*, October 2015, available electronically at http://www.bankofengland.co.uk/publications/Documents/speeches/2015/euboe211015.pdf (accessed 26 July 2017), Chart 1.10, 'The Size of the Financial System Excluding Derivatives'.

[12]   Federal Department of Justice and Police (FDJP), Federal Office of Police (Fedpol), *Report 2015: Annual Report by the Money Laundering Reporting Office Switzerland, MROS*, April 2016, available electronically at https://www.fedpol.admin.ch/dam/data/fedpol/kriminalitaet/geldwaescherei/jabe/jb -mros-2015-e.pdf (accessed 25 July 2017), 9.

[13]   House of Commons, Home Affairs Select Committee, Proceeds of Crime, Fifth Report of Session 2016–17, 1 July 2016 (hereinafter 'PoC HASC Report') available electronically at http://www .parliament.uk/business/committees/committees-a-z/commons-select/home-affairs-committee/inquiries/ parliament-2015/proceeds-of-crime/ (accessed 2 August 2017), [22]. See also M Goldby, 'Anti-Money Laundering Reporting Requirements Imposed by English Law: Measuring Effectiveness and Gauging the Need for Reform' [2013] *Journal of Business Law* 367, 375.

[14]   SARs Report 2017 (n 8), 6.

[15]   SARs Report 2015 (n 9), 6.

[16]   See PoC HASC Report (n 13), [22] and [24]. See also Goldby (n 13), 378.

the Financial Conduct Authority (FCA) and its predecessor the FSA have imposed fines of varying sizes on financial institutions for AML failures (see in particular Table 14.3).[17] In addition, it is worth observing that in the years since the enactment of PoCA, the FCA has uncovered numerous anti-money laundering control failings in banks operating in the UK on undertaking reviews. Most notably in the Anti-Money Laundering Annual Review of 2012–2013,[18] the FCA noted that:

> Our 2011 thematic review of Banks' management of high money laundering risk situations found that . . . [a]round a third of banks, including the private banking arms of some major banking groups, appeared willing to accept very high levels of money laundering risk if the immediate reputational and regulatory risk was acceptable . . . Around a third of them dismissed serious allegations about their customers without adequate review . . . Three quarters of the banks in our sample failed to take adequate measures to establish the legitimacy of the source of wealth and source of funds to be used in the business relationship. This was of particular concern where the bank was aware of significant adverse information about the customer's or beneficial owner's integrity . . . At more than a quarter of banks visited, relationship managers appeared to be too close to the customer to take an objective view of the business relationship. Many were primarily rewarded on the basis of profit and new business, regardless of their anti-money laundering performance. There were indications that some banks were willing to enter into very high risk relationships without adequate controls when there were large profits to be made.

Similar concerns were expressed in the Annual Review of the following year[19] as well as subsequent years.[20]

Finally, it is worth noting that it is reported on the website of the NCA that 'the NCA assesses that many hundreds of billions of pounds of international criminal money is laundered through UK banks, including their subsidiaries, each year'.[21] But if one considers that only £56,541,579 was recovered in the 18-month period from October 2015 to March 2017,[22] and that there were only 36 cases with arrests recorded in the same period,[23] this does raise questions regarding the diligence with which reporting obligations are being fulfilled, if so much allegedly dirty money is making its way through the financial system unhindered.

---

[17] For an overview, see A Ratan, *UK FCA AML Fines 2002 – 2015: Common and Recurring Themes: The 40-point Checklist*, Comply Advantage (undated), available electronically at https://complyadvantage.com/knowledgebase/anti-money-laundering/uk-fca-aml-fines-2002-2015/ (accessed 27 July 2017).

[18] FCA, *Anti-Money Laundering Annual Report 2012/13*, available electronically at https://www.fca.org.uk/publication/corporate/anti-money-laundering-report.pdf (accessed 27 July 2017), [6.2]–[6.5].

[19] FCA, *Anti-Money Laundering Annual Report 2013/14*, available electronically at https://www.fca.org.uk/publication/corporate/anti-money-laundering-annual-report-13-14.pdf (accessed 27 July 2017), [3.4].

[20] See FCA, *Anti-Money Laundering Annual Report 2015/16*, available electronically at https://www.fca.org.uk/print/anti-money-laundering-annual-report-2015-16 (accessed 27 July 2017), under Heading 3, Sub-heading: 'Findings'.

[21] See NCA, *Money Laundering*, available electronically at http://www.nationalcrimeagency.gov.uk/crime-threats/money-laundering (accessed 27 July 2017).

[22] SARs Report 2017 (n 8), 8. See also findings in K Bullock, 'Criminal Benefit, the Confiscation Order and the Post-conviction Confiscation Regime' (2014) 62 *Crime Law Soc Change* 45.

[23] SARs Report 2017 (n 8), 8. These figures relate to arrests pursuant to DAMT requests. No figures are provided for arrests pursuant to non-consent SARs.

1.   Analysis

If the estimate of money laundered is at all accurate, and if the failings in the banking sector are indeed as serious as the regulatory findings discussed above indicate, the argument that compliance by the UK financial system as a whole with reporting obligations is good is unpersuasive. While it may be true of a number of institutions, or certain departments within institutions, the indications are that there are ones where compliance is not thorough or conscientious. The evidence would suggest, with regard to some institutions or departments within institutions, either (a) failure on the part of bankers to report a number of suspicious transactions or (b) failure to file DAML requests (as distinct from non-consent SARs) with respect to them. In other words, while some (perhaps even the majority of) banks and bankers may be committed to fulfilling their obligations, it is unlikely that this is true of the industry as a whole.

The concern is that mid- to high-level managers within banks that liaise directly with high-value clients may be turning a blind eye to the activities generating the funds that they are being asked to manage for such clients, and that reporting is occurring mainly with respect to high-volume, low-value business where much of the processing is automated, where electronic monitoring can raise red flags with respect to unusual transactions and where the client account is not obtained and cultivated by clients through a business relationship with an individual bank representative. An illustration may be found in the FCA's report of a £1.88 billion transaction arranged and executed in 2011 and 2012 by Barclays Bank for clients who were Politically Exposed Persons (PEPs).[24] The FCA commented that, as the clients were PEPs, Barclays was 'required . . . to adhere to a higher level of due skill, care and diligence but Barclays failed to do this' and that:

> Barclays applied a lower level of due diligence than its policies required for other business relationships of a lower risk profile. Barclays did not follow its standard procedures, preferring instead to take on the clients as quickly as possible and thereby generated £52.3 million in revenue.

Further the FCA found that 'Barclays went to unacceptable lengths to accommodate the clients' and that due diligence records in their respect were kept only in hard copy and out of the electronic system (which presumably might have flagged up the transaction to the Money Laundering Reporting Officer (MLRO)).

Recent revelations involving the laundering of the proceeds of tax evasion[25] and corruption[26] indicate that the Barclays case is unlikely to be exceptional, and that the concern that some

---

[24]   See FCA, *FCA fines Barclays £72 million for poor handling of financial crime risks*, 26 November 2016, available electronically at https://www.fca.org.uk/news/press-releases/fca-fines-barclays-£72 -million-poor-handling-financial-crime-risks (accessed 27 July 2017). For another similar illustration see FCA, *Standard Bank Plc fined £7.6 million for failures in its anti-money laundering controls*, 23 January 2014, available electronically at https://www.fca.org.uk/news/press-releases/standard-bank-plc -fined-£76m-failures-its-anti-money-laundering-controls (accessed 27 July 2017).

[25]   See the revelations of the Mossack Fonseca papers (or 'Panama Papers') as reported in V Houlder, E Dunkley and R Atkins, 'Banks hatched shell companies with Panama law firm', *Financial Times*, 5 April 2016.

[26]   See HM Treasury and Home Office, *Action Plan for Anti-Money Laundering and Counter-Terrorist Finance*, April 2016 (hereinafter 'UK AP') available electronically at https://www.gov.uk/government/ uploads/system/uploads/attachment_data/file/517993/6-2118-Action_Plan_for_Anti-Money

bankers are colluding with criminals or at least turning a blind eye is founded. It appears that individuals who do turn a blind eye in order to secure lucrative accounts are not being pursued by the authorities for their breaches of s 330. Indeed, in the above given example, Barclays was fined over £72 million, but none of the individuals taking the relevant decisions appear to have been pursued, nor does the activity appear to have been subjected to a criminal investigation.[27] The problem with simply fining Barclays and not applying sanctions to individual decision-makers is that shareholders are penalised (and the companies' employees indirectly affected) while individuals within management remain unaccountable,[28] reinforcing the unethical corporate stance[29] and making it likely that any lower-level employee dissent on ethical grounds will (continue to) be suppressed[30] so that it is difficult for a change in corporate culture to be engendered.[31] The FCA report indicates that, in the Barclays case, the FCA '[made] no finding that the Transaction, in fact, involved financial crime', which begs the question, with so many palpable indications that the individuals responsible were turning a blind eye, why was a criminal investigation not launched? From the facts reported in the FCA's press release,

---

_Laundering__print_.pdf (accessed 30 July 2017), 28, [2.54]: 'Recent high profile international corruption cases have demonstrated that criminal funds were used to obtain real estate in the UK.'

[27]   As aptly noted by N Ryder, 'The Financial Services Authority and Money Laundering a Game of Cat and Mouse' (2008) 67 *Cambridge Law Journal* 635, 651–2, 'The FSA has concentrated upon its powers to impose financial sanctions upon the regulated sector as opposed to seeking prosecutions under the 2003 MLR.' The same would appear to apply to the FCA since it took over these functions.

[28]   This is an approach which has been prevalent in addressing various types of malpractice within the financial sector, but it is starting (rightly) to be viewed as objectionable. See for example the US case of Mr Eric Ben-Artzi, a risk officer who blew the whistle on Deutsche Bank to expose false accounting and then turned down his share of the $16.5 million payout, offered him by the US Securities and Exchange Commission, to register a protest against Deutsche Bank's shareholders being penalised rather than the bank's executives. See M Skapinker, 'Lessons from the Deutsche Bank Whistleblower Eric Ben-Artzi', *Financial Times*, 24 August 2016. As aptly noted by R Cheung, 'Money Laundering – A New Era for Sentencing Organisations' [2017] *Journal of Business Law* 23, 48, in the UK this issue has not been resolved by the Sentencing Council, *Fraud, Bribery and Money Laundering Offences: Definitive Guideline*, effective from 1 October 2014 (hereinafter 'SC Guideline') available electronically at https://www.sentencingcouncil.org.uk/wp-content/uploads/Fraud_bribery_and_money_laundering_offences_-_Definitive_guideline.pdf (accessed 28 July 2017), within which '[t]here is a tension between, on one hand, the Sentencing Council's desire to impose severe penalties to deter corporate crime, and, on the other hand, a recognition that severe penalties flow through the corporate shell and fall on the innocent corporate shareholders, employees and customers who bear the indirect burden of corporate penalties.' Neither does the Guideline provide for fine reductions where firms take measures to reform internal approaches to compliance (i.e. instil cultural changes) following a breach (Cheung, ibid, 44–7).

[29]   See M Kaptein, 'Understanding Unethical Behavior by Unraveling Ethical Culture' (2011) 64 *Human Relations* 843, 851: 'Reinforcement theory posits that the consequences of a decision made in the past influence decision-making in the future. Rewards will therefore lead to repetition and punishment to avoidance . . . [Research has found] a number of examples of unethical behavior that were preceded by similar forms of unethical behavior that were tolerated or even encouraged.'

[30]   See S M Croucher, C Zeng and J Kassing, 'Learning to Contradict and Standing up for the Company: An Exploration of the Relationship between Organizational Dissent, Organizational Assimilation and Organizational Reputation' [2016] *International Journal of Business Communication* 1, 5: 'high levels of tolerance of unethical behavior or illegal practices in organizations could diminish internal expressions of dissent, particularly those directed to management'.

[31]   It has been shown that employees often imitate the ethical or unethical behaviour of their superiors: see M Kaptein, 'Understanding Unethical Behavior by Unraveling Ethical Culture' (2011) 64 *Human Relations* 843, citing various studies at 848. See also ibid, 858.

it would appear that there were reasons for suspecting that the transactions involved criminal proceeds, and that therefore a duty to report in accordance with s 330 was triggered (whether they were in fact criminal proceeds or not). Yet the case appears to have been overlooked by criminal investigators. As shall be seen under section D below, this would seem to be in line with the general approach to addressing breaches of AML requirements by the banking sector.

D.   ENFORCEMENT OF FAILURE-TO-REPORT REQUIREMENTS

1.   The FCA's Powers to Investigate and Prosecute Breaches of s 330

1.1   Investigative powers
While the FCA (previously the FSA) has found many instances of banks and financial institutions failing to meet their AML obligations in the course of supervision, it is not completely clear whether the FCA has the power to investigate criminal breaches by individuals of reporting requirements laid down by s 330 PoCA.[32] In the main, the FCA's investigative powers are laid down in Part XI of the Financial Services and Markets Act 2000 (FSMA) on Information Gathering and Investigations (ss 165–177). The FCA may require any authorised person to provide it with 'information and documents reasonably required in connection with the exercise by [it] of functions conferred on it by or under [the FSMA]'.[33] Broad powers to investigate the nature, conduct or state of the business of authorised persons (i.e. regulated entities) or appointed representatives are granted by FSMA, s 167, which provides for the appointment of persons to carry out such investigations. Powers to investigate criminal conduct are granted by s 168, which refers specifically to the offences laid out in Table 14.1.

Section 168 thus makes no reference to money laundering offences, however powers similar to the ones granted by FSMA, s 165 are conferred by reg 66 of the Money Laundering Regulations (MLR) 2017,[34] regs 69 and 70 of which provide further powers to enter and search premises upon suspicion of a breach of the MLR themselves, the EU Fourth Money Laundering Directive (4MLD)[35] from which they derive or the EU Funds Transfer Regulation.[36] Interestingly, a breach of Part VII of PoCA by a regulated entity is not included in the list, although this may be said to derive from 4MLD,[37] rendering ambiguous the answer to the question whether the FCA may investigate such breaches.

---

[32]   See PoCA, s 378(4)–(6). While it is not entirely clear whether an investigation of a failure-to-report offence would constitute a 'money laundering investigation', as the definition of 'money laundering' under s 340 only refers to ss 327, 328 and 329, s 330 is considered a 'secondary' money laundering offence so it may be that an investigation into its breach would fall to be considered a 'money laundering investigation'. However, note that a s 330 offence is not covered by the SC Guideline (n 28), so it is not entirely clear where the powers to investigate its breach lie.

[33]   FSMA, s 165(4).

[34]   Money Laundering, Terrorist Financing and Transfer of Funds (Information on the Payer) Regulations 2017/692.

[35]   4MLD (n 1).

[36]   Funds Transfer Regulation (n 3).

[37]   See especially Arts 1, 33 and 35.

Table 14.1   *Investigative powers under FSMA*

Instrument	Offence
Financial Services and Markets Act 2000	Failure to comply with requirements to provide information upon request under ss 122B and 122C (s 122F)
	Failure to comply with requirements on Part XI on information gathering and investigations (s 177)
	Failure to comply with an obligation to notify the regulator under s 178(1) (acquisition or increase of control over UK authorised person) or s 191D (disposition of control over UK authorised person (s 191F))
	Provision of false or misleading information to auditor or actuary (s 346)
	Misleading the FCA (s 398(1))
	Failure to give written notice of intention to exercise Treaty rights (Schedule 4)
	Breach of general prohibition (s 19)
	Authorised person acting without permission (s 20)
	Breach of restrictions on financial promotion (s 21 and s 238)
	False claims to be authorised or exempt (s 24(1))
Financial Services Act 2012	Misleading statements and impressions (Part 7)
Criminal Justice Act 1993	Insider dealing (Part V)
Market Abuse Regulation 2014 (EU)	Insider dealing and unlawful disclosure of inside information (Article 14)
	Market manipulation (Article 15)

Therefore, there is uncertainty as to whether the duty to investigate potential breaches of s 330 by bankers lies with the FCA or with Law Enforcement Agencies (LEAs) empowered to investigate breaches of PoCA (i.e. police forces). There is no publicly available information about the frequency with which (if at all) the FCA liaises with LEAs with respect to evidence of criminal breaches by individuals uncovered by it in the performance of its supervisory functions. Nor does there seem to be in place any Memorandum of Understanding with respect to such exchange of information, although a search on the FCA website generates two examples of the Metropolitan Police assisting the FCA (and its predecessor the FSA) to address criminal breaches of laws prohibiting insider dealing.[38]

Therefore, although arguably it is the FCA which is best placed to investigate breaches of s 330,[39] it is unclear whether it has the formal power to do so. As the FCA is obliged to prioritise

---

[38]   See FCA, *Three Arrested in FSA Insider Dealing Investigation*, 27 February 2013, available electronically at https://www.fca.org.uk/news/press-releases/three-arrested-fsa-insider-dealing-investigation (accessed 31 July 2017) and FCA, *Four Arrested in FCA Insider Dealing Investigation*, 31 July 2013, available electronically at https://www.fca.org.uk/news/press-releases/four-arrested-fca-insider-dealing -investigation (accessed 31 July 2017).

[39]   See L E Dervan and E S Podgor, 'Investigating and Prosecuting White-Collar Criminals' Chapter 27 in S R Van Slyke, M L Benson and F T Cullen (eds), *The Oxford Handbook of White-Collar Crime* (OUP, 2016), 561–81, 565.

the use of its resources according to principles of good regulation, broadly construed,[40] it might be that the FCA considers that failure-to-report investigations should not take priority over other investigations (e.g. pertaining to the offences in Table 14.1), where its duty to investigate is clearly set out in the legislation and not ambiguous (as it is with respect to s 330 breaches).

1.2   Enforcement Action

1.2.1   The options

If evidence of failure to report is uncovered by the FCA, it has several options as to how to address it. Apart from taking persuasive measures, if the failure in question constitutes a breach of a 'relevant requirement', the FCA could impose civil penalties under MLR 2017, regs 76–85. The term 'relevant requirement' is defined under MLR 2017, Schedule 6. As indicated under section B above, some of these requirements relate to a bank's duties in relation to monitoring and reporting suspicions that may arise with respect to funds transfers that the bank might be asked to perform for a client. Breaching such requirements may lead to a fine being imposed by the FCA.

As Money Laundering Reporting is a Senior Management Function for the purposes of the Senior Managers Regime instituted on the basis of s 64A FSMA,[41] the FCA could also take disciplinary action against the designated person responsible for performing this function under s 66 FSMA provided the conditions listed in s 66A FSMA are satisfied.

While the breach of certain requirements would also constitute a criminal offence, as provided by MLR 2017 reg 86, the FCA is not among the entities empowered by reg 89 to institute a public prosecution against the offenders. However, among the FCA's powers to institute a public prosecution listed under FSMA s 402[42] are listed 'offences under prescribed regulations relating to money laundering'.[43] Although in spite of the apparent inconsistency, the FCA could in any case proceed by means of a private prosecution with respect to offences under MLR 2017 reg 86, there is a lack of clarity within the legislation as to where the *public* duty to prosecute lies. This is significant as an important distinction between public and private prosecutions is that with respect to the former, the decision *not* to prosecute is subject to judicial review.[44]

The FCA certainly does not have the power to initiate a public prosecution for breaches of PoCA s 330, as this offence lies outside the 'prescribed regulations relating to money laundering'. However, it would still have the option to initiate a private prosecution.[45] Alternatively,

---

[40]   FSMA, s 3B.

[41]   See FCA Handbook, SYSC 4.7 *Senior management responsibilities for UK relevant authorised persons: allocation of responsibilities*, SYSC 4.7.7 R, Table: FCA-prescribed senior management responsibilities, entry (4). See also SYSC 6.3.8 R and account of the parliamentary debates in S Kosmin, 'Ensuring Anti-Money Laundering Compliance Through the Senior Managers Regime of The Financial Services (Banking Reform) Bill: Hansard Brings Comfort' [2014] 3 *Journal of International Banking and Financial Law* 179.

[42]   This provision was interpreted in *The Queen on the application of Matthew Francis Uberoi, Neel Akash Uberoi v City of Westminster Magistrates' Court v The Financial Services Authority, HM Treasury* [2008] EWHC 3191 (Admin). See esp. [29].

[43]   See FSMA, s 402(1)(b) and MLR 2017, reg 2.

[44]   *R v DPP Ex p. Chaudhary* [1995] 1 Cr. App. R. 136; *R v DPP ex p. Manning* [2001] QB 330, 343–4.

[45]   *R v Rollins* [2010] UKSC 39.

the FCA could transfer evidence of wrongdoing to the relevant LEA for further investigation and eventual prosecution by the Director of Public Prosecutions (DPP).

1.2.2   Choosing among the options

Effective enforcement is vital to the implementation of legislation that is designed to achieve social objectives and address what are perceived to be harmful behaviours, and is therefore an essential facet of regulation and supervision. While it goes beyond the scope of this discussion to explore in detail the literature on enforcement strategy, it is helpful at this stage to make reference to some salient findings that have been made by researchers in recent times to give some context to the discussion below.[46] Recent scholarship has rejected the tenet that the regulatory enforcement strategy needs to choose between punishment and persuasion and has developed the concepts of 'responsive regulation'[47] and 'smart regulation'[48] to show that a more nuanced approach employing a variety of tools is likely to be more effective in terms of ensuring compliance than making the said stark choice.

If the aims of the enforcement strategy include deterrence, punishment may be an effective tool towards achieving compliance, however the research has found that its effectiveness will vary according to the motivations of the non-compliers to whom it is applied. If non-compliance is the result of simple incompetence or clumsy implementation (albeit in good faith), punishment is unlikely to lead to better compliance, and indeed may cause a negative reaction[49] (or even create a culture of 'regulatory resistance'[50]). But punishment may be a very effective deterrent with respect to those who are recalcitrant and grudging compliers[51] (i.e. 'amoral calculators'[52] who will deliberately fail to comply if they believe they can get away with it). In these circumstances, 'there is considerable evidence that cooperative approaches may actually discourage improved regulatory performance amongst better actors if agencies permit lawbreakers to go unpunished',[53] and a punitive sanction (whether disciplinary/administrative or criminal) can have a strong impact, even going so far as producing a 'sea change in attitudes'.[54] Indeed a study conducted in 2005 found that legal sanctions imposed against similar enterprises may motivate firms to review and strengthen their own compliance pro-

---

[46]   For a comprehensive albeit concise overview see N Gunningham, 'Enforcement and Compliance Strategies', Chapter 7 in R Baldwin, M Cave and M Lodge (eds), *Oxford Handbook of Regulation* (OUP, 2010), 120.

[47]   First put forward by I Ayres and J Braithwaite, *Responsive Regulation: Transcending the Deregulation Debate* (OUP, 1992).

[48]   First advocated by N Gunningham and P Grabosky, *Smart Regulation: Designing Environmental Policy* (OUP, 1998).

[49]   See S Shapiro and R Rabinowitz, 'Punishment Versus Cooperation in Regulatory Enforcement: A Case Study of OSHA' (1997) 14 *Administrative Law Review* 713, 718.

[50]   E Bardach and R Kagan, *Going by the Book: The Problem of Regulatory Unreasonableness* (Temple University Press, 1982).

[51]   See J Gilsinan et al., 'The Role of Private Sector Organizations in the Control and Policing of Serious Financial Crime and Abuse' (2008) 15 *Journal of Financial Crime* 111–23, esp. 114.

[52]   See analysis and findings in R A Kagan and J T Scholz, 'The "Criminology of the Corporation" and Regulatory Enforcement Strategies' in K O Hawkins and J M Thomas (eds), *Enforcing Regulation* (Springer, 1984), 67–96.

[53]   Gunningham (n 46), 125.

[54]   R Baldwin and J Anderson, *Rethinking Regulatory Risk* (DLA/LSE, 2002), 10.

gramme.[55] Thus in order to be 'credible', deterrents in the form of sanctions must be enforced where the occasion requires it, otherwise they will have no 'general deterrence' effect.[56]

It should be remembered here that punitive sanctions can be targeted at individuals as well as corporate entities, meaning that, where a breach occurs, judgment must be exercised by the regulator in determining not only whether it should stick to persuasive action without punishing either the corporation or the individual, but also, if alternatively it decides to resort to punitive sanctions, whether it will enforce them only against the corporation, only against the individual or against both the corporation and the individual. This makes it even more important to be able to identify the causes of the breach and attitudes underlying it. There is ample evidence that 'high monetary penalties may not deter large corporations'[57] and that, where individuals are not pursued, 'deterrence is limited because no one feels responsible for the infractions'.[58] It is interesting to note that a study by Paternoster and Simpson found that formal sanctions directed at firms were effective in deterring criminal conduct only when they were viewed as directly affecting the perceived costs for the individual.[59]

Research conducted in 2007 found that while '[m]oral values, overall, had the greatest impact on participants' choices of the ethical options',[60] 'severity of punishment had a significant, positive correlation with moral values'[61] and that 'the presence of punishment can encourage ethical decision making by giving more credence to people's moral values'.[62] Conversely '[w]hen other people are getting away with the unethical option and receiving personal gains, doing the right thing becomes harder'.[63] Another reason to ensure that individuals working within the financial industry take the threat of criminal sanctions seriously is the phenomenon of 'fear of falling', i.e. the trepidation of the personal losses that might ensue if

---

[55]   N Gunningham, R Kagan and D Thornton, 'General Deterrence and Corporate Behaviour' (2005) 27 *Law and Policy* 262.

[56]   See R Paternoster and S G Tibbetts, 'White-Collar Crime and Perceptual Deterrence', Chapter 30 in Van Slyke et al. (n 39), 622–40, who find that while white-collar criminals tend to act rationally in making their choices, in that 'they opt for the alternative that they perceive to have more rewards than costs' (ibid, 624), 'deterrence may be lacking not because white-collar offenders are not rational and cannot easily be deterred but because white-collar crimes are enforced with very low certainty and severity of punishment, or the anticipated benefits simply outweigh any possibly anticipated costs of crime' (ibid, 637, note 3).

[57]   P C Yaeger, 'The Elusive Deterrence of Corporate Crime' (2016) 15 *Criminology and Public Policy* 439, 443.

[58]   Yaeger (n 57), 443.

[59]   R Paternoster and S S Simpson, 'Sanction Threats and Appeals to Morality: Testing a Rational Choice Model of Corporate Crime' (1996) 30 *Law and Society Review* 549.

[60]   K Gurley, P Wood and I Nijhawan, 'The Effect of Punishment on Ethical Behavior when Personal Gain is Involved' (2007) 10 *Journal of Legal, Ethical and Regulatory Issues* 91, 97. The same finding was made in Paternoster and Tibbetts (n 56).

[61]   Gurley et al. (n 60), 97.

[62]   Gurley et al. (n 60), 97.

[63]   Gurley et al. (n 60), 97. See also Paternoster and Simpson (n 59), 580: 'our data suggest that an appeal to morality does not work for everyone. When morality weakens, compliance must be secured by legal threats . . . [T]he threat of legal sanctions is probably necessary to maintain the legitimacy of an extensive network of informal and normative controls. We have found that legal sanctions directed at the firm are a significant factor in supporting one's moral beliefs that corporate crime is wrong, a sense of shame if one were to commit it, and in strengthening the credibility of legal sanctions for the individual.'

certain choices were to be made. This phenomenon was first proposed in 1992 by Wheeler,[64] who suggested that individuals might commit 'white collar crime' in order to avert a loss of economic security, status and prestige. However, in 2012 Piquero found that fear of falling can also operate to the opposite effect: in her experiment, 'fear served to heighten the respondents' awareness of the risks of detection'[65] and also 'served to remind respondents about their moral stance against the commission of a crime'.[66] Of course this can only work if the risks to the individual of detection and punishment are high, and requires that deterrents in the form of sanctions against individuals be credible. All this points to the notion that in an environment of grudging compliance, if individuals are never pursued, the moral stance/climate within the corporation is unlikely to change,[67] and compliance will remain recalcitrant.

In light of the above, responsive regulation involves adopting different enforcement approaches depending upon the motivations and attitudes underlying the relevant non-compliance. The difficulty of course is establishing what those motivations are. Adoption of this approach is most likely to work in a regulatory landscape where the supervisor has repeated interactions with the individual regulated entities and is able, through such interactions, to gauge the motivations and attitudes underpinning their non-compliance.[68] Where this is possible, the responsive approach advocates moving up the 'enforcement pyramid'[69] in response to recurring failures and persistent non-compliance. The enforcement pyramid is reproduced in Figure 14.1.

The effectiveness of this approach depends on repeated interactions and a good flow of information between the supervisor and the supervisee. Information about the supervisee should prompt the enforcement choices of the supervisor. For example, it has been noted that 'if experience suggested that the very large majority of a sub-group of regulated enterprises was rationally recalcitrant then the bottom half of the pyramid response might be dispensed with in favour of deterrence'.[70]

The advocates of 'Smart Regulation' have similarly noted that a nuanced approach to making enforcement choices can lead to better compliance. They argue that in most circumstances better compliance will result from using multiple rather than single policy instruments and from engaging (to supplement state regulation) mechanisms of informal social control involving a broader range of actors, such as international standards organisations, trading partners, peer pressure (including self-regulation through industry associations) and civil society

---

[64]   S Wheeler, 'The Problem of White-Collar Motivation' in K Schlegel and D Weisburd (eds), *White-Collar Crime Reconsidered* (Northeastern University Press, 1992), 108–23, 116.

[65]   N L Piquero, 'The Only Thing We Have to Fear is Fear Itself: Investigating the Relationship Between Fear of Falling and White-Collar Crime' (2012) 58 *Crime & Delinquency* 362, 371.

[66]   Piquero (n 65), 372.

[67]   See discussion in B K Payne, 'Effects on White-Collar Defendants of Criminal Justice Attention and Sanctions' Chapter 29 in Van Slyke et al. (n 39), 603–21, esp. 604–6: '[For many] white-collar defendants . . . their behaviour is seemingly defined as normal in their business . . . More often than not, evidence of shame appears only after criminal justice attention or sanctioning.'

[68]   Of course, the downside of repeated interactions is the risk of regulatory capture (see D Carpenter and D A Moss (eds), *Preventing Regulatory Capture: Special Interest Influence and How to Limit It* (Cambridge University Press, 2014), in particular J Kwak, 'Cultural Capture and the Financial Crisis' Chapter 4 in Carpenter and Moss, ibid, 71–98), but it goes beyond the scope of this chapter to explore this aspect of repeated interactions.

[69]   Ayres and Braithwaite (n 47), 35–8.

[70]   Gunningham (n 46), 128, based on the findings of Kagan and Scholz (n 52).

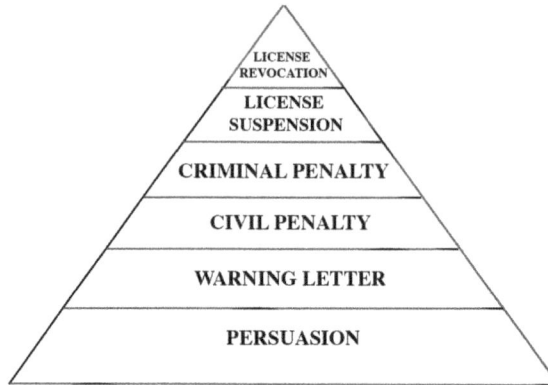

Figure 14.1   Enforcement pyramid

(including pressure groups), all of which can influence supervisees' behaviour.[71] Doing so adds further 'faces' to the pyramid so that a number of forces can work together at the lower levels towards achieving a higher degree of compliance, although only the state is able to invoke the higher rungs.

1.2.3   The UK financial regulator's choices

To come back to the issue at hand, i.e. an assessment of the enforcement action taken by the financial regulators in response to AML compliance failures, if one examines the enforcement action taken by the FCA and its predecessor the FSA with regard to AML breaches, there appears to be a notable preference for the three lower rungs of the pyramid.[72] Reported instances of the regulator choosing to proceed by way of criminal prosecution (whether in a public or private capacity) or to enlist the cooperation of LEAs and DPP appear rare. This author was able to find only two published cases[73] referring to a relevant private prosecution for money laundering offences brought by the FSA, and none by the FCA.[74]

Further, while the burden of proving breach of s 330 PoCA is relatively low, providing as it does the possibility of proving the necessary *mens rea* through an objective test (namely, that there were reasonable grounds for knowing or suspecting that a client, or prospective client, was engaged in money laundering[75]), use of it is rarely resorted to, as shown by the statistics reproduced in Table 14.2, which were released in response to a Freedom of Information Request in December 2014.[76]

---

[71]   Gunningham (n 46), 131.

[72]   In this regard see FCA, *Anti-Money Laundering Annual Report 2016/17*, available electronically at https://www.fca.org.uk/publication/annual-reports/annual-anti-money-laundering-report-2016-17.pdf (accessed 3 August 2017), 12.

[73]   *R v Rollins* [2010] UKSC 39; *In re M (Restraint Order)* [2009] EWCA Crim 997, [17].

[74]   The following two search terms were entered into the 'free text' search box on Westlaw on 1 August 2017: ['financial conduct authority' 'money laundering'] and ['financial services authority' 'money laundering' 'charge'].

[75]   PoCA, s 330(2)(b).

[76]   FOI Releases December 2014, *Conviction rates for 'failure to report' and "'tipping off' offences*, MS Word Document and MS Excel Spreadsheet, both available electronically at https://www.gov.uk/government/publications/foi-releases-for-december-2014 (accessed 25 July 2017). According to

Table 14.2   Conviction rates for 'failure-to-report' and 'tipping off' offences

Defendants proceeded against at magistrates courts and found guilty at all courts of offences under Sections 330 to 333 of the Proceeds of Crime Act 2002, England and Wales, 2003 to 2013										
Outcome	2003	2004	2005	2005	2007	2008	2009	2010	2011	2012	2013
Proceeded against	1	5	8	8	13	3	-	6	3	2	5
Found guilty	1	3	4	8	9	1	-	5	2	1	7
Conviction ratio	100%	60%	50%	100%	69%	33%	n/a	83%	67%	50%	140%

It should be noted that the figures reported do not relate exclusively to breaches of s 330, so it may be that not all of these prosecutions and convictions involved a failure-to-report offence. In addition, the statistics do not specify in which of the different regulated sectors the persons prosecuted were active at the time of breach. A survey over Westlaw of the published cases involving s 330[77] does not throw up a single case involving the prosecution of a banker under this provision. The same applies to prosecutions brought under ss 327, 328, 329 and 335.[78] This would indicate that not only does the financial regulator not tend to prosecute, but neither do relevant LEAs with the power to do so, where supervisory activity uncovers evidence of reporting failures.

Indeed, the enforcement record so far suggests that the financial regulator is much more likely to select enforcement methods which allow it to itself take persuasive action or, at most, disciplinary action against the institution rather than resort to prosecution of individuals for criminal breaches. Table 14.3 below[79] shows all AML fines imposed by the FSA and FCA on banks for AML breaches since the FSA took over conduct-of-business regulation of the financial sector.[80]

---

footnote (2): 'the figures given in the table relate to persons for whom these offences were the principal offences for which they were dealt with. When a defendant has been found guilty of two or more offences it is the offence for which the heaviest penalty is imposed. Where the same disposal is imposed for two or more offences, the offence selected is the offence for which the statutory maximum penalty is the most severe.'

[77]   The search was undertaken on 27 July 2017 and generated 23 results. This was a list of all cases citing s 330. Of these, 13 cases were not criminal cases. The remaining ten involved prosecutions, nine of them for failure to report under s 330, but none of these involved a banker.

[78]   The search was undertaken on 3 and 9 September 2017 and generated over 300 results. This was a list of all cases citing these provisions. Only one involved a banker who had himself stolen money out of his own parents' accounts. See *Regina v Sam Eason* [2013] EWCA Crim 143.

[79]   Information obtained at the time of writing online from FCA website: https://www.fca.org.uk/news/news-stories/2017-fines (accessed 27 July 2017) and archived FSA website: http://webarchive.nationalarchives.gov.uk/20130201213241/http://www.fsa.gov.uk/about/press/facts/fines/2013 (accessed 27 July 2017).

[80]   Interestingly the notorious HSBC scandal that occurred in 2012 led to the FSA 'requiring action' of the HSBC group although no fines were imposed. See FSA, *FSA Requires Action of HSBC Group*, 8 March 2013 available electronically at https://www.fca.org.uk/publications/documents/fsa-requires-action-hsbc-group (accessed 27 July 2017). For details on the scandal see US Senate, Permanent Subcommittee on Investigations, *US Vulnerabilities to Money Laundering, Drugs, and Terrorist Financing: HSBC Case History*, 17 July 2012, 3: 'In October 2010, the [Office of the Comptroller of the Currency] OCC issued a Cease and Desist Order requiring HSBC to strengthen multiple aspects of its AML program. The identified problems included a once massive backlog of over 17,000 alerts identifying possible suspicious activity that had yet to be reviewed; ineffective methods for identifying suspicious activity; a failure to file timely Suspicious Activity Reports with U.S. law enforcement; a failure to

Table 14.3   Fines imposed for AML breaches by financial regulators

DATE	INSTITUTION	FINE
17/12/2002	Royal Bank of Scotland	£750,000
04/08/2003	Northern Bank	£1,250,000
10/12/2003	Abbey National	£2,320,000
12/01/2004	Bank of Scotland	£1,250,000
05/04/2004	Raifaissen Zentralbank Österreich	£150,000
02/09/2004	Bank of Ireland	£375,000
26/03/2012	Coutts & Company	£8,750,000
15/05/2012	Habib Bank AG Zurich	£525,000
26/07/2012	Turkish Bank	£294,000
24/04/2013	EFG Private Bank	£4,200,000
23/01/2014	Standard Bank	£7,640,400
26/11/2015	Barclays Bank	£72,069,400
12/10/2016	Sonali Bank	£3,250,600
31/01/2017	Deutsche Bank	£163,076,224

Although occasionally Money Laundering Reporting Officers were also individually fined in connection with the institution's failings,[81] there is no indication of any fines being imposed on persons directly responsible for the client accounts in question.

Thus, in spite of the repeated AML failures which seem regularly to come to light,[82] escalation up the various rungs of the pyramid is not resorted to often and there is very little to suggest that the higher rungs are resorted to with any frequency. While they do represent the 'nuclear option' to which resort should only be had in extreme circumstances, in view of the priority that is being given by the UK government to the disruption of (organised) crime,[83]

---

conduct any due diligence to assess the risks of HSBC affiliates before opening correspondent accounts for them; a 3-year failure by HBUS, from mid-2006 to mid-2009, to conduct any AML monitoring of $15 billion in bulk cash transactions with those same HSBC affiliates, despite the risks associated with large cash transactions; poor procedures for assigning country and client risk ratings; a failure to monitor $60 trillion in annual wire transfer activity by customers domiciled in countries rated by HBUS as lower risk; inadequate and unqualified AML staffing; inadequate AML resources; and AML leadership problems. Since many of these criticisms targeted severe, widespread, and longstanding AML deficiencies, they also raised questions about how the problems had been allowed to accumulate and why the OCC had not compelled corrective action earlier.'

[81]   Specifically, in the case of Sonali Bank and in the case of Habib Bank AG Zurich.

[82]   See discussion under heading C supra. See also J Cotterill, M Arnold and C Binham, 'HSBC accused of "possible criminal complicity" in Gupta scandal', *Financial Times*, 1 November 2017 and T Hamblin, 'HSBC's sides must ache already – from laughing': Letter to the Editor, *Financial Times*, 10 November 2017 where the emissary, referring to the 'insignificant fine' HSBC could receive 'while avoiding prosecution', opined: 'Until there is an end to the cosy agreement that allows financial institutions to "pay off" prosecutors to avoid legal action, the credibility of the former will continue to erode from what is already a very thin base.' Indeed, the Gupta scandal did not affect the dismissal of HSBC's criminal charges in respect of which prosecution had been deferred in 2012. See M Arnold, 'US lifts threat of prosecution against HSBC', *Financial Times*, 11 December 2017.

[83]   Recent steps of particular note include the enactment of the Criminal Finances Act 2017 which received Royal Assent on 27 April 2017 and the adoption of the MLR 2017 on 22 June 2017. Also noteworthy is the creation of a new Office for Professional Body Anti-Money Laundering Supervision (OPBAS) (see announcement in HM Treasury, UK tightens defences against money laundering, 15 March 2017, available electronically at https://www.gov.uk/government/news/uk-tightens-defences -against-money-laundering (accessed 2 August 2017) and the proposed review of the Asset Recovery

and the large part that the financial system allegedly plays in facilitating it,[84] it is, to say the least, surprising, that it appears never to have been resorted to vis-à-vis bankers with respect to whom there is sufficient evidence of breach of PoCA s 330.[85]

There is also evidence that a culture of recalcitrant compliance is by no means absent from the financial industry. In a 2015 survey of the US and UK Financial Services Industries, 21 per cent of UK respondents stated that 'their company's confidentiality policies and procedures bar the reporting of potential illegal or unethical activities directly to law enforcement or regulatory authorities'[86] and 24 per cent found it 'likely that their employer would retaliate if they were to report wrongdoing in the workplace'.[87] The survey also found that 14 per cent of UK respondents experienced pressure at their companies to 'compromise ethical standards or violate the law', that 25 per cent had witnessed wrongdoing in their workplace[88] and that nearly 19 per cent of all respondents felt that 'misconduct is part of the recipe for success'.[89] Based on their findings, the researchers observed (referring to the investigation and prosecution of violations) that '[a]gainst the backdrop of a culture that effectively ignores – and perhaps even encourages – misconduct, enforcement may be the only way to create meaningful change'.[90]

As noted by this author in 2013,[91] because of the low burden of proof, s 330 encourages over-reporting from the ethically-minded and the risk-averse, but a lack of enforcement against bankers is likely to engender the perception in those who are amoral economic calculators that they are likely to get away with it, as, when considering whether to process a suspicious transaction without making a report, they will weigh up the potential profits against (a) the likelihood of being caught and (b) the likely consequences if they were to be caught.[92] This

---

Incentivisation Scheme (ARIS): see PoC HASC Report (n 13), [42]–[43] and [82]. See also UK AP (n 26), in particular the stated priority to 'bring those few companies who facilitate or enable money laundering to task' (ibid, 3). See also the establishment in December 2017 of a National Economic Crime Centre within the NCA: 'National Economic Crime Centre Announced' NCA Press Release, 11 December 2017, available electronically at http://www.nationalcrimeagency.gov.uk/news/1257-national -economic-crime-centre-announced (accessed 3 January 2018).

[84] It is estimated that at least £100 billion of criminal funds are being laundered through the UK every year. See PoC HASC Report (n 13), [60].

[85] See the Barclays example discussed under heading C.2 supra.

[86] A Tenbrunsel and J Thomas, *The Street, The Bull and The Crisis: A Survey of the US & UK Financial Services Industry* (University of Notre Dame and Labaton Sucharow LLP, 2015), (hereinafter '2015 Survey') available electronically at https://www.secwhistlebloweradvocate.com/pdf/Labaton -2015-Survey-report_12.pdf (accessed 9 August 2017), 3.

[87] 2015 Survey (n 86), 8.

[88] 2015 Survey (n 86), 5.

[89] 2015 Survey (n 86), 6.

[90] 2015 Survey (n 86), 8.

[91] In Goldby (n 13), 396–7.

[92] Indeed, white-collar criminals tend to act rationally by weighing the perceived costs and benefits of the proposed behaviour: see reference to Paternoster and Tibbetts (n 56). See also findings of Paternoster and Simpson (n 59) and P H Robinson and J M Darley, 'Does Criminal Law Deter? A Behavioural Science Investigation' (2004) 24 *Oxford Journal of Legal Studies* 173, 174: 'Even if [potential offenders] know the rules, the cost-benefit analysis potential offenders perceive – which is the only cost-benefit analysis that matters – commonly leads to a conclusion suggesting violation rather than compliance, either because the perceived likelihood of punishment is so small, or because it is so distant as to be highly discounted, or for a variety of other or a combination of reasons.'

is borne out by a survey conducted in 2005 which concluded that, in the eyes of the regulated, the likelihood of being caught is the biggest deterrent.[93]

It is worth noting here that the regulator's enforcement strategy has been found wanting in the past and has been criticised, with respect to the enforcement decisions it took in the wake of the failure of HBOS, by the House of Commons Treasury Select Committee. The committee criticised the regulator for, among other things, failing to consider for investigation 'the full range of relevant individuals . . . for whom the statutory threshold test for conducting an investigation had been satisfied'[94] and for adopting 'an approach where they "simply would not investigate unless they took the view that there was a very good chance of a successful outcome"'.[95] The committee also noted that 'there was at times a significant disconnect between the priorities set by senior management and actions taken by junior employees' so that although senior leadership declared that they 'expected, as is the statutory duty of the FSA, that any enforcement action that could be taken here should be taken',[96] this was not the approach that was eventually adopted.[97]

It is submitted that also of concern is the impression that the FCA's appetite for pursuing individuals for compliance failures does not seem to be increasing. The fact that the regulator did not oppose (and indeed appears to have downplayed[98]) the government's decision to remove the Presumption of Responsibility within the Senior Managers Regime,[99] putting the burden of proof on the regulator, in the event of a regulatory failure at a firm, to prove that a relevant senior manager failed to take reasonable steps to avoid or mitigate the effects of the issue concerned, could be symptomatic of a continued lack of appetite for pursuing individuals.

It should finally be noted that on 5 July 2017, the *Financial Times* remarked that the FCA had opened many investigations which it then dropped without taking action and that fines imposed by the regulator for criminal breaches were dipping sharply.[100] The same report questioned whether the strategy of opening more investigations had been adopted in response to the damning HBOS report.[101] It is unspecified what proportion of these investigations involve AML compliance breaches, in particular reporting failures.

---

[93]   see M Yeandle, M Mainelli, A Berendt and B Healy, *Anti-Money Laundering Requirements: Costs, Benefits and Perceptions*, City Research Series, Number Six, June 2005 (Corporation of London, 2005) available electronically at http://www.zyen.com/PDF/AMLR_FULL.pdf (accessed 28 July 2017), Section 3.5 'The likelihood of being caught is the biggest deterrent', 44–7.

[94]   House of Commons Treasury Select Committee, Review of the Reports into the Failure of HBOS, 22 July 2016 (hereinafter 'HBOS TSC Review') available electronically at https://publications .parliament.uk/pa/cm201617/cmselect/cmtreasy/582/58202.htm?utm_source=582&utm_medium= fullbullet&utm_campaign=modulereports (accessed 31 July 2017), [80].

[95]   HBOS TSC Review (n 94), [77].

[96]   A Green, *Report into the FSA's enforcement actions following the failure of HBOS*, Prudential Regulation Authority and FCA, November 2015 (hereinafter 'Green Report') available electronically at http://www.bankofengland.co.uk/pra/Documents/publications/reports/agreenreport.pdf (accessed 31 July 2017), 20.

[97]   HBOS TSC Review (n 94), [77]–[78].

[98]   See discussion in A Hayes, 'Responsibility and Accountability but Enforceability? The New Senior Managers Regime' [2016] 1 *Journal of International Banking and Financial Law* 29, 31.

[99]   The relevant amendment to s 66A of FSMA was made by the Bank of England and Financial Services Act 2016, s 25(2)(f) (10 May 2016).

[100]   See C Binham, 'FCA fines dip sharply despite record number of investigations', *Financial Times*, 5 July 2017.

[101]   Binham (n 100). The reference is to the Green Report (n 96).

E.   WHY DO THE LEAS NOT PROSECUTE BANKERS FOR BREACHES OF S 330?

It is important to understand the context within which the low number of prosecutions under s 330 subsists. On 24 July 2017, the *Financial Times* reported that '[i]n the white collar arena, there are worries that the prosecuting agencies are not adequately resourced for cases that typically require painstaking investigation over several years'.[102]

It is also worth noting that in the 2015 national risk assessment carried out by the Treasury and the Home Office,[103] it was found that '[t]he law enforcement response to money laundering has been weak for an extended period of time. It has not been a priority for most local police forces (although the metropolitan forces appear to provide a more effective response)'. It was also found that 'there is room for improvement across the board, including . . . in providing a credible deterrent'.[104] Accordingly, in their 2016 action plan,[105] they listed one of the results to be delivered as ensuring 'an effective multi-agency investigation response, drawing on private sector expertise, to target the most complex high-end money laundering cases', and creating 'a programme to upskill intelligence, analytical, investigative and legal staff to take on complex money laundering cases'.[106] The action plan also promises to consider 'whether all supervisors have and use appropriate incentives and powers, such as fines, disqualification, ability to impose changes to business models *and prosecution* to take effective, proportionate and dissuasive action against non-compliance'.[107]

It would thus appear that the drive is to place the bulk of these investigative and prosecutorial duties onto regulators rather than on traditional law enforcers. However, the recent reforms that led to the adoption of the Criminal Finances Act 2017 extend investigation powers to the FCA with respect to civil asset recovery investigations[108] but not investigations of breaches of s 330. It would appear that no thought was given to this question, perhaps because there is no perception of failure to report being an issue in the banking sector (indeed much of the discussion centres on how to address over-reporting), but as observed above, the high number of SARs does not necessarily mean good compliance across the board, so it is submitted that this is a missed opportunity by the legislator to improve deterrence in this area, as part of the effort to increase the effectiveness of the FCA's investigative function.

---

[102]   C Binham, 'White collar prosecutions plummet even as crime rises', *Financial Times*, 24 July 2017.

[103]   HM Treasury and Home Office, *UK national risk assessment of money laundering and terrorist financing*, October 2015 (hereinafter 'UK NRA') available electronically at https://www.gov.uk/government/uploads/system/uploads/attachment_data/file/468210/UK_NRA_October_2015_final_web.pdf (accessed 30 July 2017), 5.

[104]   UK NRA (n 103), 5.

[105]   UK AP (n 26).

[106]   UK AP (n 26), 5 and 19–20.

[107]   UK AP (n 26), 25, [2.47]. Emphasis added.

[108]   See Criminal Finances Act 2017, s 20. See also current public consultation by HM Treasury, *Proceeds of Crime Act 2002 and Anti-Terrorism, Crime and Security Act 2001: codes of practice*, 31 July 2017, in particular the draft *Code of Practice issued under s 377 of Proceeds of Crime Act 2002: Investigations*. All consultation documents available electronically at https://www.gov.uk/government/consultations/proceeds-of-crime-act-2002-and-anti-terrorism-crime-and-security-act-2001-codes-of-practice (accessed 3 August 2017).

Because LEAs explicitly empowered by PoCA to conduct money laundering investigations[109] are not likely to come upon evidence of breaches of s 330 by bankers without being alerted to it by regulators, before they are able to carry out their role they must be alerted to the fact that the breach of s 330 was/may have been committed. The extent to which LEAs such as the Metropolitan Police are receiving alerts from the financial regulator in relation to breaches of s 330 is not known.

F.   CONCLUSION: ADDRESSING THE INSTITUTIONAL GAPS WITH A VIEW TO MORE EFFECTIVE ENFORCEMENT

This chapter argues that in view of the type and degree of breaches of AML requirements within banking institutions in the UK uncovered by the financial regulator, the banking sector's compliance with reporting obligations must not be as good as the number of SARs filed may at first sight suggest. It also argues that the enforcement actions taken by the regulator to improve compliance may be insufficiently drastic. In particular, the tendency to target institutions rather than individuals may be precluding a change in corporate culture where compliance is grudging or recalcitrant and the tendency to impose civil sanctions rather than criminal ones may mean that criminal sanctions are not perceived as credible deterrents.

The ambiguity within the law with respect to the FCA's investigative powers in relation to breaches of s 330 may be a contributing factor to the regulator's lack of appetite to resort to criminal proceedings. There are a number of good reasons for considering seriously the option of removing these ambiguities. First of all, the FCA is an experienced investigator of certain types of financial offences in particular market abuse and insider dealing under Part 11 of the FSMA 2000, investigations which involve individuals. Secondly, in the course of conducting its supervisory role and/or any AML assessments it undertakes at institutional level, it is more likely to come across evidence of failure to report in the financial sector than LEAs, and to understand the motivations behind such failure. Thirdly, the FCA is arguably in a better position to dedicate resources to addressing this particular type of wrongdoing than LEAs, in view of the need to achieve its integrity objective,[110] its commitment to a credible deterrence approach[111] and the need to address criticisms it has faced for not pursuing individuals.[112]

In relation to money laundering breaches by the regulated sector more generally (including not just s 330 but also the primary money laundering offences in PoCA ss 327–329), more formal and binding mechanisms could be put in place to ensure the flow of information/ evidence as well as knowledge and skills between the FCA and those with the power to investigate and initiate a public prosecution. The instruments for strengthening the duty to investigate and clarifying its operation range from soft (e.g. MOUs) to hard (primary legislation).[113] Steps to ensure better communication and knowledge exchange could include for example second-

---

[109] See PoCA, s 378(4)–(6).

[110] FSMA, s 1D.

[111] See *Enforcement and credible deterrence in the FCA*, Speech by Tracey McDermott, FCA Director of Enforcement and Financial Crime, at the Thompson Reuters Compliance & Risk Summit, London, 18 June 2013, available electronically at https://www.fca.org.uk/news/speeches/enforcement -and-credible-deterrence-fca (accessed 3 August 2017).

[112] See Green Report (n 96) and HBOS TSC Review (n 94).

[113] A first step in this direction can be seen in MLR 2017, R 103.

ments of staff between the FCA and the Metropolitan Police Service or the City of London Police, and electronic information-sharing platforms.[114]

Arguably this would fit well with the reforms that have recently been adopted by the Treasury in setting up a new Office for Professional Body Anti-Money Laundering Supervision within the FCA, with an overarching responsibility to strengthen the UK's supervisory regime by improving coordination between AML supervisors and law enforcement agencies.[115] It would also contribute to the achievement of one of the aims of the NCA's High End Money Laundering Strategy, namely '[u]pskilling financial investigators to enable them to undertake complex and high end money laundering casework'.[116]

Finally, it is worth noting that said strategy also includes a new emphasis on sharing data with the financial sector.[117] The idea of intensifying engagement with the financial sector also comes up in the House of Commons Home Affairs Select Committee Report on Proceeds of Crime of 2016, which recommends enhancing cooperation with the private sector to improve the recovery of criminal proceeds, suggesting that 'the Government [create] a market for the private enforcement and collection of unpaid confiscation orders once they enter arrears, earning a fee from a portion of that order'.[118]

It is submitted that creating a financial incentive for more willing cooperation (rather than grudging compliance) by regulated entities may certainly be a positive step forward in achieving the aims of AML regulation, however, as argued in this chapter, improvement in compliance may be difficult to achieve unless a clear message is given that evasion of reporting requirements will not be tolerated and that sanctions will be imposed on individuals where appropriate. It is to be hoped that the recent efforts and reforms will encourage use by the FCA of its full range of enforcement tools in the future.

---

[114] This could be integrated with the measures on asset recovery data that are recommended in PoC HASC Report (n 13), [85].

[115] See Oversight of Professional Body Anti-Money Laundering and Counter Terrorist Financing Supervision Regulations 2017, SI 2017 No. 1301, which came into force on 18 January 2018, and FCA website page on the Office for Professional Body Anti-Money Laundering Supervision (OPBAS), available electonically at https://www.fca.org.uk/opbas (accessed 3 March 2018). See further HM Treasury, *Anti-Money Laundering Supervisory Regime Consultation*, 16 March 2017, available electronically at https://www.gov.uk/government/consultations/anti-money-laundering-supervisory-regime-response-and-call-for-further-information (accessed 3 August 2017), esp. Chapter 3 and HM Treasury, *Anti-Money Laundering Supervisory Review*, 20 July 2017, all documents available electronically at https://www.gov.uk/government/consultations/anti-money-laundering-supervisory-review (accessed 3 August 2017).

[116] NCA, *High End Money Laundering: Strategy and Action Plan*, December 2014 (hereinafter 'HEML 2014') available electronically at http://www.nationalcrimeagency.gov.uk/publications/625-high-end-money-laundering-strategy/file#page=3 (accessed 30 July 2017), [13]; [29]–[30].

[117] HEML 2014 (n 116), [20]–[22].

[118] PoC HASC Report (n 13), [50].

PART V

ARE FINANCIAL REGULATORS
ETHICAL?

15. Ethical culture and central banking[1]

Thomas C. Baxter, Jr.

This chapter will discuss ethical culture and central banking. In the first section, I examine whether central banks need to be mindful of their ethical culture. I conclude that they do need to be mindful of ethical culture and face significant adverse consequences if they reach a different conclusion. Like financial institutions of the garden variety, central banks from many and varied jurisdictions have periodically experienced situations where central bank officials have succumbed to ethical challenges. This should not be surprising because central banks, which may seem superhuman at times, are managed and operated by people. The words from the Lord's Prayer notwithstanding, people in every kind of organization are led into temptation. Central banks may have hallowed halls, but they are not monasteries.

After establishing the factual predicate that central bank officials do occasionally engage in misconduct, we turn to the related topic of central banks and legitimacy, and offer the view that the objective of legitimacy and the related need for public trust makes it especially important for central banks to pay careful attention to misconduct risk. Following the section discussing legitimacy, we identify some of the techniques that central banks use to mitigate misconduct risk, and the principal measures that may be employed to accomplish this objective. In the view of the author, one of the most important tools is fostering an ethical culture. I conclude with some forward-looking observations.

CENTRAL BANKS, LIKE ALL BANKS, SOMETIMES HAVE PERSONNEL THAT FACE ETHICAL CHALLENGES

The topic of ethics and central banking can generate strong views, particularly among the central bank community. Not long ago, when the ethics of central bankers first became a permitted topic for consideration, the subject matter generated considerable controversy. Some believed that if a person worked in a central bank that meant, as a matter of course, the behavior of that person should be presumed to be above reproach. How could service on behalf of the public be anything but ethical? And, fueling this delightfully naïve view, was a related belief that central bankers, as a class, were of a super human intellect and could do nothing but make the right choice every time.

Those who dared to dispute this view were often viewed like the skunk at a garden party – uninvited and unwanted. In the early days, this halcyon view of central banking was difficult to challenge because central banks had such a very impressive record. Among the diverse class of public organizations, central banks had been remarkably free of the kind of scandals that afflicted others (except, perhaps, for several salacious incidents involving extramarital affairs).

---

[1]   The author gratefully acknowledges receiving helpful commentary from his former colleagues at the Federal Reserve Bank of New York, Martin Grant and David Gross, and from a current colleague, Michael Wiseman, at Sullivan & Cromwell.

Cynics might look back to the period between 1925 and 1985 and opine that central bankers of that era were simply too boring to be mischievous. This could well be the counterpoint to the optimistic notion that central bankers of this era all possessed brilliant minds and white hearts. Another potential explanation is that central banks had a very different public profile – no one knew what they did and no one really cared.

A series of incidents during the last 35 years have dispelled the view that central bank officials never engage in misconduct. It appears that, today, the public's perception of central banks and the people who work in them has been re-cast. Without trying to be encyclopedic in our survey of examples of potential misconduct situations, we describe five different cases below, to demonstrate the point made in the opening – central banks are operated by people and people make mistakes. The review of the five cases is for the purpose of demonstrating this basic proposition. In describing the cases, we do not intend to disparage the people who found themselves in sensitive ethical situations. Their stories are only to underscore in concrete terms that people in a central bank can make the same mistakes made by people everywhere. Unfortunately, for each of the named officials, the increased public visibility of central banking makes the central bank an almost impossible place to hide questionable behavior. In this more transparent world, the behavior of central bank officials will continue to receive significant scrutiny, and a prudent central bank will respond to the trend with an energetic ethics program. There is a related point. Because the public profile of central banking has changed considerably, the central bank has become a focal point for the political class, and as seen in the survey, apparent central bank misconduct may become a political instrument.

The first case relates back to the late 1980s, and it concerns the conduct of a member of the board of directors of the Federal Reserve Bank of New York. The Federal Reserve Bank of New York is a key part of the US central bank, and the subject, Mr Robert Rough, was one director of a board of directors that, by statute, is composed of nine members. The Class A directors represent the shareholding member banks. The Class B directors represent the public, but they are drawn from the real economy – businesses that transact with banking organizations. The Class C directors are the most remote from the banking sector, and tend to be drawn from academia, organized labor, and the professional class (doctors, engineers, lawyers, etc.). Mr Rough was a Class A director, meaning he was a banker. Mr Rough was convicted of bank fraud, and his criminal conviction became a front-page headline in the *New York Times.* Mr Rough's criminal conviction arose directly out of his service as a Federal Reserve director. Mr Rough leaked confidential interest-rate information to a New Jersey securities dealer, and the dealer then traded in government securities with the intention of profiting on the communicated "inside" information.

To Mr Rough's credit, he did not dispute his conduct in appropriating confidential discount rate information and sharing it with his broker-dealer confederate. Consequently, he pleaded guilty to the criminal violation of defrauding the Federal Reserve of its confidential proprietary information concerning the discount rate. Mr Rough was sentenced by a United States District Court judge to a short term of imprisonment.

The misconduct of Mr Rough caused the Federal Reserve considerable reputational damage, which was undoubtedly compounded by the extensive media coverage. The case is an excellent illustration of what risk managers have come to characterize as "headline risk", a short-hand term for the damage that an organization may experience from an embarrassing situation, often involving staff misconduct and sometimes a violation of law. In the Rough case, the damage was somewhat mitigated by the fact that the Federal Reserve took an activist position in the case. It vigorously investigated the initial allegation that discount rate information had been leaked. The investigation generated evidence in the form of a "smoking gun", namely certain telephone records of calls made to the New Jersey government securities dealer from the directors' anteroom (with the calls being made immediately after board meetings). The telephone records were considered a "smoking gun" because they nicely corroborated testimony by a former principal in this broker-dealer that Mr Rough had been his source, and had telephoned him immediately after meetings of the board. Rather than try to downplay and "cover over" what Mr Rough had done, the Federal Reserve not only investigated his behavior aggressively and thoroughly, but it disclosed such highly incriminating evidence against Mr Rough to law enforcement.

This teaches at least two powerful lessons. The first concerns how to manage headline risk, and that is to work with the media rather than against it. The Federal Reserve did not fight the ugly fact that one of its directors had leaked confidential rate information to a trader, who used it in an attempt to receive financial gain. To the contrary, it worked hard to unmask the conduct and advocated that the Department of Justice bring criminal charges against Mr Rough. The second concerns the object lesson – using the publicity associated with Mr Rough's criminal conviction as a means to communicate that such behavior was offensive to the central bank.

The second case relates back to 2004, and concerns a very senior official of the Bundesbank, the central bank for the Federal Republic of Germany. Mr Ernst Welteke was the equivalent of a Governor and served on the Bundesbank's executive council. While serving in this senior position, he engaged in conduct that apparently did not violate German statutory law, but was seen as unethical. Mr Welteke resigned from the Bundesbank after the media reported he had accepted a four-night stay for him and his family at Berlin's luxurious Adlon Hotel. A German financial institution, Dresdner Bank, paid for the hotel stay. The Bundesbank had supervisory responsibility over Dresdner Bank. The Bundesbank board of directors issued a public statement accepting Welteke's resignation, and acknowledging that Welteke's resignation was "appropriate in view of the bank's reputation and the perception of its duties".

The Welteke case also illustrates a particular problem for those central banks that, like the Bundesbank, also have responsibility for banking supervision. This is the so-called "regulatory capture" problem. Regulatory capture is the term used to describe the risk that a supervised financial institution, or a class of supervised financial institutions, will "capture" the individuals charged with supervising them. Capture can occur when there is the prospect of some kind of reward flowing from the supervised bank to the supervisor, a *quid pro quo*. The reward could be in the form of a luxurious hotel stay, or it could be much more subtle, like the prospect of future, lucrative, employment in the supervised bank. In the Welteke case, the capture might be seen in Dresdner's payment of the Adlon bill. But whatever the reward, the concern is that a central bank official will take action out of self-interest and not in the public interest.

The third case occurred in 2012. Here, the central protagonist was not an official of a central bank, but rather was the spouse of a central bank official. Mr Phillip Hildebrand was the Governor of the Swiss National Bank and very highly regarded among the community of central banks. Mr Hildebrand's wife, a former hedge fund trader, engaged in a foreign exchange trade (Swiss francs against US dollars) several weeks before the Swiss National Bank took steps to counter the rise in value of the Swiss franc. After the Swiss National Bank's intervention, Mr Hildebrand's spouse sold the US dollars at a higher rate, thereby appearing to profit on the action taken by her husband's employer, the Swiss National Bank. The foreign exchange trade by Mr Hildebrand's wife was leaked to the Swiss media by someone associated with the Swiss People's Party, in what some have characterized as a targeted effort to discredit Mr Hildebrand.

The Swiss National Bank faced considerable public criticism over the incident. There was rampant speculation about Mrs Hildebrand's trading. Some speculated most cynically that she was acting as a proxy for Mr Hildebrand. Others speculated that she cleverly used information that she had learned from her husband. Many noted what is perhaps the most important point – there was no evidence that Mr Hildebrand disclosed to Mrs Hildebrand what her husband's employer was planning to do, and that it was completely unfair to draw the adverse inference.

The speculation eventually reached the point where it was too much. Mr Hildebrand concluded that he could not continue to serve as Governor. He said: "I have come to the conclusion that it is not possible to provide conclusive and final evidence that my wife did indeed initiate the foreign exchange transaction . . . without my knowledge." The statement evidences the impossible position in which Mr Hildebrand found himself. He needed to "prove a negative", namely that he did not share confidential rate information with his spouse, nor did he know his spouse was trading foreign exchange.

The situation that adversely affected Mr Hildebrand is why many central banks preclude their senior officials (and the officials' spouses) from trading foreign exchange. If foreign exchange trading is permitted, and an official makes an incredibly profitable trade because the official has correctly anticipated market direction, this official could be in a position similar to Mr Hildebrand. If the central bank has taken some action that has affected the profitability of the trade, the official will be placed in an impossible predicament – the natural tendency to draw the adverse inference will leave the central banker in the position of proving a negative. The official might be expected to prove he had no advance knowledge of the central bank's planned intervention. Alternatively, if the official did have advance knowledge, the official could be expected to try to show that the inside information had no impact on the profitability of the trade. To avoid such an impossible situation, some central banks have decided to avoid the situation entirely by precluding any personal foreign exchange trading by staff. Further, many central banks, including the Federal Reserve, have rules that also apply to spouses. These rules simply impute to the official whatever transaction the spouse engages in.

It is noteworthy that such a protective central bank rule is not without consequence. In Mrs Hildebrand's case, she was a trading professional, and one may question whether it is fair to force one spouse to sacrifice her profession because she is married to a central bank official.

The fourth case came to the public's attention in March of 2017, and it affected the newly appointed deputy governor of the Bank of England, Charlotte Hogg. Ms Hogg came under attack for what was perceived to be a material omission in her financial disclosure form. Ms Hogg omitted disclosing the fact that her brother was a senior executive at Barclays Bank. The mandatory disclosure form required officials to disclose relatives who occupied senior positions in supervised institutions. Like the situation involving Mr Hildebrand, there is some suggestion that politics played a role in the way Ms Hogg's omission was brought to public attention. In the face of headlines about her "failure" to reveal her brother's position, Ms Hogg decided to resign from the position of Deputy Governor, a position to which she had recently been appointed. She resigned over the objection of Mark Carney, the Bank of England's Governor, who looked at Ms Hogg's accusers as politically motivated. Ms Hogg admitted that she had made "an honest mistake" in leaving her brother's employment out of the required disclosure form. With that admission about the reason for the omission, Ms Hogg added that a central bank officer must nonetheless "exceed the standards we expect of others".

The incident involving Ms Hogg is distinctly different from the other incidents, in that Ms Hogg's conduct related to an omission (i.e., something she failed to do), where the others relate to commissions (affirmative conduct in which the officials or the spouse had actively engaged). In this connection, Mr. Hildebrand has stated that he did not know of his spouse's conduct, but if he is considered to be vicariously responsible for his spouse, then her commission becomes his. Further, Ms Hogg's omission seems to fall into the "harmless error" category, because nothing untoward resulted from it. It is not as if she failed to stop a bank from engaging in an unsafe and unsound practice that subsequently caused the bank to fail. To the contrary, Ms Hogg omitted a reference to her brother's employment, which was publicly known in the financial community and hardly a secret given the Hogg family's political profile. In some ways, the case affecting Ms Hogg may represent a new level in hypersensitivity about the conduct of central bank officials. We will return to this observation below. We note, here, that Ms Hogg's no-doubt-painful observation about exceeding the standard set for others seems especially astute. In the current environment, it is not sufficient that the behavior of central bank officials equal what is expected of other banking professionals. For central bank officials, the standard is set above that level. It is not at all clear just how much above the level is acceptable.

The fifth case became public in April of 2017, when Jeffrey Lacker, the President of the Federal Reserve Bank of Richmond, suddenly and unexpectedly resigned from his official position as President of the Federal Reserve Bank of Richmond. Mr Lacker admitted that he had broken the Federal Reserve's rules concerning disclosure of confidential information. He apparently violated the Federal Reserve's confidentiality rules by speaking with a financial analyst about confidential monetary policy deliberations. Further, Mr Lacker compounded the severity of what he had done by failing to admit the leak when he was questioned in the course of an internal investigation. His misconduct surfaced later during a different investigation of the same leak, this one conducted by law enforcement authorities. In connection with the termination of the criminal investigation, Mr Lacker said that he "deeply regretted the role I may have played."

There are two points to underscore in the discussion of Mr Lacker's resignation. First, the internal investigation was directed toward finding the source of an apparent leak of confidential information to a monetary policy tracking firm, Medley Global Advisors. Mr Lacker disputed that he was the source of the leak. However, he admitted that he had talked to a Medley employee in violation of Federal Reserve rules. The rules required that Mr Lacker, when responding to the Medley inquiry, state that he could not comment. He failed to make this required statement. This failure to state he was unable to comment was a rule violation. The second point demonstrates, once again, that the cover up is almost always worse than the underlying violation. When asked during the course of an internal investigation about contact with Medley, Mr Lacker did not reveal that he had a conversation with the Medley employee. Unlike Ms Hogg's conduct, involving forgetfulness, Mr Lacker's conduct shows he was untruthful in the course of the internal investigation.

What do these five cases show? In the view of the author, they show that the officials of a central bank are susceptible to the same kinds of transgressions that all employees face. It may well be that central banks are populated by officials with great minds. But this does not mean that central bank officials are immune from human fallibilities – some are forgetful, some make mistakes in judgments, and some violate legal restrictions. Motivation is complicated. It may result from the simple human need to be regarded as important. Alternatively, an individual simply might be forgetful, accepting Ms Hogg's characterization of her omission in the financial disclosure form. Without minimizing in any way the personal anguish that the individuals must have experienced, these situations are not unusual in the course of human experience. An official might be leaking information for personal gain, or perhaps simply because the official wants to appear important in the eyes of a reporter. The official may not have done anything other than be held vicariously responsible for the judgment of a spouse who, at a particular moment in time, acted to realize on a trading opportunity in the course of a marriage. What is noteworthy about these cases is not something odious about the behavior of the central bankers – the behavior is of a kind that is characteristically human. What is abnormal is the public attention that each of these events received.

CENTRAL BANKS, EVEN MORE THAN ORDINARY FINANCIAL INSTITUTIONS, HAVE A NEED FOR LEGITIMACY

In this section, we begin with Charlotte Hogg's astute observation that the central bank officer must "exceed the standards we expect of others". Ms Hogg did not explain her statement, and we will examine it here. Do central bankers need to exceed the standards expected of others? Are we not all the same in the eyes of the law? Does the public hold central bankers to a higher standard because of the perception that central banks have brilliant minds and white hearts, unlike ordinary humankind? And, if it is true that the public holds central bankers to a higher standard, is that right?

Perhaps one reason why central bankers should exceed the standards we expect of others relates to the important functions performed by central banks. All central banks make monetary policy, meaning they decide on a subject matter that impacts every citizen. For example, consider the situation when the Federal Reserve decides that monetary conditions need to be tightened to keep inflation well anchored. Interest rates are raised, and this action by the central bank affects every citizen. To earn its right to exercise such a sweeping power, the central bank needs to be perceived as legitimate. To be perceived as legitimate, there must be a general belief that the central bank is acting in the public interest and is putting the economic welfare of the people over all other interests.

When a central banker is seen to be trading on inside information, or revealing confidential information to augment his own importance, the public may start to doubt that the decision-makers in the central bank are prioritizing the public interest. Where there exists doubt regarding an official's motivation, this may lead to an erosion in the central bank's legitimacy. After all, a senior official has been revealed as acting in his personal interest rather than the public interest. The revelation of the real motive for official action can cause the central bank to lose legitimacy, and a loss of legitimacy might lead to other adverse actions with respect to central bank powers.

What are those potential adverse actions? Unlike the situation when the citizenry is displeased with the legislature, the citizenry cannot readily "throw the bums out" of a central bank. Unlike legislators, central bank officials are appointed and not elected. Typically, they are appointed by elected officials for a term, and can serve until the end of the term. As the cases reveal, it is possible that a central banker's term will be cut short by a resignation, perhaps a resignation inspired by the Damocles sword of adverse employment action – dismissal – if the official does not resign. And, this is all purposeful: the resignation is a statement by the official who accepts, through conduct, that the behavior is inconsistent with the central bank's values. Further, returning to the case involving Mr Rough, the central bank may even take on the mantle of the prosecutor, communicating the message that this is *not* who we are and this is how the central bank reacts when an official is faithless to the central bank's values.

The fact that central bankers are appointed and not elected does not mean that central bankers are unaccountable. They are typically called to account before legislative committees in an exercise of oversight. If a central banker has engaged in misconduct, whether a mistake in judgment or discretion, this is one place where the central banker will be answerable. Courts and public prosecutors also play a part. In the case involving Mr Rough, his guilty plea needed to be accepted by a Federal court judge. Before accepting such a plea, a Federal court judge needs to be comfortable that the defendant had admitted all of the elements of the crime charged. In Mr Rough's case, he admitted the elements of his offense in a Federal criminal proceeding known as an allocution.

In other cases, like the case of Mr Lacker, the accountability can be more subtle. Mr Lacker was not convicted of a criminal offense, so there was no allocution. But it was a criminal investigation of a leak that detected his wrongdoing, and triggered his resignation statement which included a recitation of what he had done wrong.

It is a reality of modern life that central bankers have great power. The need for the central bank to preserve and protect its legitimacy is derivative of the bank's desire to retain that power. Consequently, central bankers around the world feel the need to turn very straight corners. It is, in the author's view, the foundation for the belief that the central bank must adhere to a higher standard and eschew even the appearance of impropriety. Accordingly, when a central banker is seen as receiving a financial benefit (the payment of a luxury hotel bill) from a bank that he regulates, this endangers the legitimacy of the central bank. With respect to the Federal Reserve director who was sharing interest rate information with a securities broker-dealer, the fact that the director was compromised demonstrated that the director was not acting in the public interest. When events like this occur and are revealed in the media or at a Congressional hearing, they undermine the public's trust that the central bank is exercising its great power appropriately.

If a central bank were to lose legitimacy, its franchise is at risk. In the worst case, the people mount a challenge to the central bank through their elected representatives, and the elected representatives enact a law that takes the central bank's power away, or changes the power in a materially adverse manner.

A close cousin to the concept of legitimacy is trust. One of the post-crisis conditions that bankers are trying to change is a loss of public trust. In the pre-crisis period, the public tended to have much greater trust in financial institutions. With this greater degree of trust, financial institutions had far greater political power. The financial services industry could obtain prompt political attention to regulatory relief, and in fact generated sufficient support in 2006 to have a regulatory relief bill enacted by the Congress.

Today the situation is very different. Since the financial crisis, support from the financial services industry can be the kiss of death to prospective legislation. But even more worrisome is the effect of a loss of trust on business transactions. People enter into transactions not because of how they believe the transaction will fair if there should be litigation. They engage in transactions because of the belief that their counterparty will adhere to the promises it has made. It is trust, not courts, that enable the parties to conduct business. To be trusted, of course, you must be trustworthy. If you have a reputation for saying one thing and doing another, you will not have a trustworthy reputation.

A similar factor is at work in central banking. The public needs to trust the central bank to act in the public's interest. This is a part of the foundation of the central bank's power. If the central bank is seen to be acting in the individual interest of a central banker, the public loses trust in the central bank. Again, it is a close cousin to legitimacy but not the same concept.

If we accept that central bankers are expected to perform at a higher level, as Ms Hogg stated, we may ask the question whether this is right and fair? To many, the law should be blind to the position of the person who stands before her. It is a seminal principle of justice that we are all held to the same standard. This means that it is not right and it is not fair if central bankers are held to a higher standard.

Of course, this is the theoretical basis for answering the question. Yet, in practice, the theory seems to be a far cry from reality. The cases tend to show, in the author's view, that central bankers are held to a higher standard. While this might be unfair, it is merely one more manifestation that life is not fair. The reality of the situation is what must be addressed by the central bank. If its officials are not held to a higher standard, and this impacts the legitimacy that the central bank needs to effectively function, the central bank must deal with the condition.

INGREDIENTS TO FOSTER AN ETHICAL CENTRAL BANK CULTURE

Having demonstrated that central bankers can be led into temptation and commit the sins that afflict human kind, and given the enormous importance of central-bank legitimacy and public trust, are central banks in a position to take affirmative prophylactic actions to control their destiny? The key is to create an atmosphere that fosters and nurtures a strong ethical culture within the central bank. There are affirmative actions that central banks can take to nurture and protect legitimacy. Central banks are not helpless and can position themselves to control their own destiny. Without trying to be comprehensive, we will mention some of the techniques that central banks use to manage misconduct risk and the threat it poses to central bank legitimacy.

The Code of Conduct

The first action is to establish rules for the conduct of staff, typically in a written code of conduct. The "code of conduct" will often caution employees about taking any official action that might affect a personal financial interest. It will prohibit the staff from accepting gifts, or other favors, like a four-night stay at a luxury hotel. The code of conduct will often re-affirm rules that are embodied in statutory law.

Given what central banks do, and in an effort to avoid a situation where a central bank official will need to "prove a negative", many central banks have a code of conduct that contains investment restrictions. Typically, the central bank will restrict trading in financial instruments that are the subject matter of monetary policy, like foreign exchange and government securities. It is also customary for central banks to have rules limiting the trading that is done by officials with inside information. As noted above, there are times when central bank officials will possess material non-public information, and such officials cannot be in a position where such information is abused. For central banks with supervisory responsibility over banks, the code of conduct may preclude investments in bank stock. In some of the more advanced central banks, the staff will be required to have securities firms report their investments "on-line" to the central bank, and obtain prior approval of investments. Some conduct codes go further to prohibit actions that create an appearance of impropriety, something akin to what might be considered in the military to be conduct unbecoming an officer.

It is also typical for a central bank code of conduct to address what an official should do when he or she is in a position where there are conflicting interests. Most codes are designed to avoid conflicts of interests, but when they may not be avoided, the typical resolution is some type of official recusal.

The code of conduct should be much more than words on a printed page that no one pays attention to. When the code is violated, the central bank needs to take action against the violator, because it is the action that makes the words meaningful. Further, if a senior official violates the code of conduct, the central bank can use it defensively, as evidence that the official is a rogue. One of the worst mistakes that a central bank can make is to turn a blind eye to a notorious situation that the staff is speaking about in hushed tones. If some senior official has violated the code of conduct, and the central bank ignores it, then it will completely undermine the salutary effect of having a code. And, there are also those occasions when an investigation exonerates someone who has been wrongfully accused.

Training

The second action is training. The staff needs not only to know that there is a code of conduct, but they need to be educated about its importance and the types of behavior it regulates. The nature of the training can vary, but there should be an introductory course and a refresher. For efficiency purposes, in many central banks the training about the code of conduct may be done on-line. These training programs will also typically require the trainee to take a test at the conclusion. Often the on-line training will maintain an audit trail so that staff cannot later deny their knowledge of the behavioral restrictions within the code of conduct.

In many central banks, there will be staff dedicated to answering questions about the code of conduct. The better practice is to publish in some manner the generic questions that are being asked, and the answers to those generic questions. Another better practice is to keep a record of the types of inquiries that are being made. This record of queries will enable the central banks to detect trends. For example, if suddenly there are many questions about managed accounts, or the holding of common stock in a particular issuer, these specific questions may provide an early warning of a new problem. Perhaps there is confusion about whether an issuer is restricted, and some clarifying communication is needed by the staff. In the case of managed accounts, perhaps the central banker has concluded that having a person to manage the official's assets sufficiently insulates the official with inside information, and a proliferation of questions about managed accounts might suggest that there is a need for clarification. The catalog of questions may also be a leading indicator as to whether a particular training module is sufficient, and whether there is a need to cure some deficiency in the training, or in the words used in the Code of Conduct.

Communication and Shared Values

The third action is to foster and nurture a strong ethical culture by communicating effectively the pre-eminence of cherished norms and aligning institutional values to those norms. Having a cogent rule set is important, and so is a well-developed training program to assure that the staff understands the rules. But, in the view of the author, even more important than these foundational elements is the shared values that support the code of conduct and represent the culture of the central bank. These shared values should complement the detailed rules set forth in the code of conduct, and should provide a solid base on which the rules may stand. It is sometimes said that culture is what governs behavior when no one is watching. A variant on this view is that culture is what governs behavior, the rules notwithstanding.

One very important aspect is to safeguard against a situation where the rules require one type of conduct, but the values encourage another. There are some classical illustrations. One concerned a bank that had elaborate rules regarding how relationship managers could deal with their private wealth management customers, to comply with the laws of a particular jurisdiction. While the rules pushed in one direction, the values of the financial institution welcomed flight capital and placed great weight on customer service, features that were at the core of the organizational culture. Not surprisingly, staff tended to circumvent the rules and to follow the values.

Culture will be embedded through the tone at the top of the central bank, and with the appropriate support from above, culture will be reflected in the behavior of the staff. An organization's culture becomes visible both in a casual remark between staff members that "we don't do that here", and in the formality of a termination, when an offender is escorted out the door after committing an egregious violation of the code of conduct. Culture can also sometimes be evidenced dramatically in the last official act of a dedicated central banker. For example, when Mr Hildebrand resigned his position and said that he could not prove that he did not know of his spouse's trades, he was communicating a very powerful message. The message was that the central bank's credibility and legitimacy were *his* highest priority. When those were called into doubt, the central banker's personal interest had to be subordinated to the public interest, even if it meant the central bank would lose the dedicated service of a talented professional. Paradoxically, the act of resignation may turn into a final act vindicating the culture of the central bank. This may also be what Ms Hogg was illustrating when, on her way out, she said that central bankers need to exceed the standards set for others.

Speaking Up

A fourth action is to create mechanisms that encourage and enable the staff to report misconduct and to question behavior. Some central banks have anonymous hotlines where misconduct can be reported for investigation. It is better practice to have such hotlines staffed by an independent service, where the service provides reports to senior management and the board of directors about the kinds of things being revealed by callers. This is done by disclosing the general subject matter, taking care not to reveal personally identifiable information about the caller that might enable retaliation. There are also measures that can be taken to encourage employees to "feel free to speak", and to question the way that things are being done. All too often, serious misconduct occurs in an environment where employees are intimidated and afraid to confront the perpetrator.

Rules prohibiting retaliation against a person who speaks up are also essential. The process of socialization is strong in many organizations, including central banks. A group may have the ability to force conformity, and often that ability can be subtle but powerful. A person who is challenging the conventional wisdom will feel this power but may not even know from where it is directed. If the person challenging conventional wisdom is demoted or disparaged, the staff will play close attention. All of the nice words about feeling safe to speak will be lost if there is even one retaliatory episode.

There may also be appropriate limitations on the freedom to speak, and these limitations will typically reflect the culture and rules of the organization. Accordingly, while the organization will grant its staff the freedom to question objectionable conduct, they must speak respectfully and not disparage another staff member's race, religion, or sexual orientation ("we don't do that here"). Similarly, there is a point in time when discussion must stop but never a time when a cover-up should begin. No organization can function effectively as a perpetual debating society with no ability to reach decisions. The point is the organization can encourage its staff to speak up, but this must happen within the cultural norms established by the organization. Transparency around values and decisions concerning misconduct or impermissible behavior allow an institution's norms to be tested in a marketplace of ideas.

Discipline

A fifth type of action concerns how the central bank responds when staff fail to adhere to the required standard. There are some lessons from experience, both with respect to what to do and what not to do. In the author's experience, the staff is always watching and they will learn from the way the central bank responds to an event. If they know that a senior officer has been caught in a situation of fraud, waste or abuse, and there are no consequences, this will teach a powerful negative lesson. On the other hand, if a senior officer engages in significant wrongdoing, there will be no more powerful statement than the fact that the offender has been escorted off the premises. Further, it should not be done in a heartless, disrespectful manner. It should be done in a manner that communicates the message "we don't do that here".

Of course, the punishment should be proportional to the offense. The case involving Ms Hogg may be an example where a central bank official seemed to pay the ultimate price for being forgetful. In the eyes of many, it was too great a price for leaving your publicly-known brother's employment out of a compulsory form.

There are also powerful lessons as to what not to do. The worst mistake, as noted earlier, is to try to cover over the dereliction. The expression that the "cover up is worse than the underlying offense" applies in a central bank as it does in other organizations. Turning a blind eye to facts that cry out for investigation is always a mistake, especially when the object of investigation is a senior official. In the author's experience, investigating credible allegations of misconduct is always the right choice. If the allegations turn out to be unsubstantiated or vastly overblown, this is organizational "good news". If the allegations are substantiated, then the central bank can address a problem before the problem matures into a scandal. There is also a kind of "silver lining" in these situations, in that they provide a "teachable moment" when the central bank can re-affirm its value system in a way that is powerful and visible to the staff.

The lesson about covering up behavior is also applicable to officials. In the case of Mr Lacker, his failure to be truthful in the course of an internal investigation was worse than his failure to state "no comment" when he was communicating with the person from Medley.

There are other affirmative actions that a central bank can take to protect itself from official misconduct, and it is simply not possible to cover them all here. The point is that the destiny of the central bank is within its control.

CONCLUDING OBSERVATIONS

There may come a day when computers make monetary policy, and when central banks no longer need to be concerned about their ethical culture. But for as long as central banks are operated by humans, they will periodically face situations where a human has succumbed to temptation and engaged in misconduct. These situations may be restricted by the affirmative prophylactic measures summarized above, and when the prophylactic measures are well executed, the incidents of misconduct should be few and far between. But they will occur. When they do occur, the central bank should investigate thoroughly, respond appropriately and assuredly not resisting the teachable moment, and continue to work on strengthening its culture, values, and rules. In taking these affirmative steps, the central bank will maintain its legitimacy and the public's trust. Perhaps most importantly, it will *earn* legitimacy and the public's trust, and that is the secret to keeping it.

16. Central banks and ethics: the virtual paradox of transparency and confidentiality mandates
Manuel Monteagudo

INTRODUCTION

The emphasis on central bank independence, currently at the center of discussions on monetary and financial stability, brings up some issues regarding two ethical mandates: transparency and confidentiality of their traditional and less traditional functions and operations. Transparency is considered as a crucial component of central bank independence; i.e., as a means to make up for its "democratic deficit"; and central bank intervention during the global financial crisis has reinforced this general perception.[1] Insofar as central bank intervention in free markets is justified by public interest (monetary stability), international organizations such as the International Monetary Fund (IMF) and domestic legislation have developed transparency standards to communicate policy objectives and results,[2] in addition to a general evolution in favor of free access to the information in the hands of public bodies – an important development since the approval of the 1966 US Freedom of Information Act (FOIA)[3] during President Johnson's administration. In New Zealand, the stress on central bank transparency was part of a broader movement associated with the 1982 Official Information Act.[4]

The "transparency revolution" has not swept away central banks' confidentiality mandate, as stated expressly in legislation and statutes[5] based upon professional secrecy, private rights protection of privacy and trade secrecy, and the need to assure central banks' capacity to continue collecting statistical data (e.g., US case law related to the exemptions to FOIA).[6] The full disclosure of exceptional liquidity facilities that followed the international financial crisis opened a debate on the risk that it could create market misperceptions on financial stability.

Striking a balance between opponents (transparency and confidentiality) requires a fine assessment based on technical and ethical considerations. Central bank transparency has also

---

[1]   N. Nergiz Dincera and Barry Eichengreen, *Central Bank Transparency and Independence: Updates and New Measures*, 10 International Journal of Central Banking, 193 (March 2014).

[2]   On 26 September 1999 the IMF Interim Committee adopted the Code of Good Practices on Transparency in Monetary and Financial Policies: Declaration of Principles. *See* in http://www.imf.org/external/np/mae/mft/code/index.htm.

[3]   Freedom of Information Act, 5 U.S.C. § 552 (approved 4 July 1966).

[4]   N. Nergiz Dincera and Barry Eichengreen, *supra* note 1, at 190.

[5]   For example, Article 14.1 of the Code of Conduct for the Members of the Supervisory Board of the European Central Bank provides that "the Members of the Supervisory Board and other participants in Supervisory Board meetings shall take into account the requirements of professional secrecy in Article 37 of the Statute of the ESCB, Article 27(1) of Regulation (EU) No 1024/2013 and Article 23a of the Rules of Procedure of the European Central Bank, pursuant to which members are required not to disclose confidential information."

[6]   In section I.B.b. of this chapter we address some of the jurisprudential developments on the US FOIA exceptions.

been understood as a means of communication between independent central banks, markets and public opinion (as a foundation for their legitimacy and credibility).[7] In this context, exemptions to transparency based on confidentiality should be sufficiently founded in law and practice. This article reviews some of the main justifications for transparency and access to information (Section I) vis-à-vis confidentiality, in the search for a synthesis (Section II). For that purpose, we have selected some US and European regulations and cases that in the future will be part of new and complex developments in central banking and democracy. This article seeks to open avenues for a balanced assessment of two mandates, based not only on legal considerations, but also on ethical and human rights foundations. Money functioning is inherent to ethical and moral considerations for those who use it, but eventually more for those who define its value.[8]

In the exercise of power, there is a significant space for discretionary decision-making when positive legislation is not sufficient (which is evidently the case for central banks' activities). For an assessment of transparency vs. confidentiality in financial and monetary affairs, as proposed by William Blair, it is very relevant to consider that "many areas of corporate behavior are simply beyond the ability of the law to control, and we must rely on managers' ethical decision-making to achieve societal objectives" (quoting David Hess).[9]

I.   REASONS FOR CENTRAL BANK TRANSPARENCY

A.   Independence and Accountability

Independent central banks have sufficient administrative and operational (contractual) powers for allowing them to determine and execute monetary policy without the intervention of the government or Congress. They are even able to define what monetary stability means in quantitative and operational terms,[10] impose mandatory reserves on commercial banks, and participate in financial markets as any other participant, but using insight information and fiscal privileges.[11] All these powers are based on *classical* State monetary attributes (monetary

---

[7]   "... the prime task for central bank communication policy would consist of making its view of the world commonly understood and to make information available in a form (or language) that is *shared* with the public and understood *across* different segments of the public." Bernhard Winkler, ""Which kind of transparency? On the need for clarity in monetary policy-'making", Working Paper N° 26, 13, European Central Bank (Working paper series, August 2000).

[8]   *See* Hans Tietmeyer, *Economie Sociale De Marche Et Stabilite Monetaire*, Economica (1999). "'L'historien Karl Erich Born a écrit fort judicieusement que 'le rapport entre 'l'argent et la morale 'n'est pas véritablement un problème d''argent, mais un problème 'd'éthique pour ceux qui définissent la valeur de 'l'argent et pour tous ceux qui l''utilisent"'". *Ibid*, 148.

[9]   *See* William Blair, "Standards and the Rule of Law after the Global Financial Crisis" in M. Giovanoli and D. Devos (eds), *International Monetary and Financial Law: The Global Crisis*, 96 (Oxford 2010).

[10]   For example, on 13 October 1998 the Governing Council of the European Central Bank defined price stability (as its primary objective according to European treaties) "as a year-on-year increase in the Harmonised Index of Consumer Prices (HICP) for the euro area of below 2%." *See* ECB Press Release of 13 October 1998 http://www.ecb.europa.eu/press/pr/date/1998/html/pr981013_1.en.html.

[11]   In some countries, financial law excludes central bank's' operations from general requirements for private participants, leaving them to the provisions provided in their laws and statutes. That is the case

sovereignty) but allocated and concentrated into an independent public body, which is not subject to *classical* political scrutiny. Usually, independent central bank authorities (Executive Board members) cannot be subject to the impeachment of Congress for disagreements of the legislative with monetary policy. As they are not elected authorities, central banks remain as self-governed entities that in some jurisdictions even encompass, among their competences, the role of banking regulators.

It is in this institutional context that commentators refer to a "democratic deficit"[12] that must be "made up for" through accountability mechanisms tailored to central bank peculiarities, among them transparency. It is interesting that transparency, as the antidote to such a political claim (lack of democratic legitimacy), serves very well the search for monetary policy effectiveness. In 1999, the IMF approved its Code of Good Practices on Transparency in Monetary and Financial Policies (IMF Transparency Code), including a proposal to balance effectiveness and legitimacy as crucial benefits from central bank transparency: the case for transparency of monetary and financial policies is based on two main premises. First, the effectiveness of monetary and financial policies can be strengthened if the goals and instruments of policy are known to the public and if the authorities can make a credible commitment to meeting them. In making available more information about monetary and financial policies, good transparency practices promote the potential efficiency of markets. Second, good governance calls for central banks and financial agencies to be accountable; particularly where the monetary and

---

of article 25 of the Law MAF of 2 July 1996 in France. Being participants of financial markets, central banks also enjoy the capacity to require – under mandatory administrative provisions – economic and financial information from any person. Article 5 of the Statute of the European System of Central Banks and of the European Central Bank provides the capacity of the ESCB to "collect the necessary statistical information either from the competent national authorities or directly from economic agents." Fiscal exemptions for central banks are also provided in many local legislations (see as another example, article 23 of the Protocol of privileges and immunities of the European communities, modified by the Treaty of Amsterdam).

12   "The counterpose to independence is accountability. The central banks may be independent but they do not live on an island . . . They have to account for their policies and activities before the political organs in their jurisdiction. Furthermore, as repeatedly noted, they come under the scrutiny of the judiciary. The methods of subjecting central banks to public scrutiny differ greatly: there are central banks whose governing board members are to appear before the national parliament, while for others regular reporting on their activities is the means by which their accountability is assured." R. Smits, *The European Central Bank: Institutional Aspects*, 169–70 (J.J. Norton 1997). "Central banks are not majoritarian, democratic institutions. Central banks are, instead, technocratic bureaucracies, insulated from political control. This feature of central banks raises a basic issue in democratic legitimacy. However, the case for central bank independence can be reconciled, in general, with the theory of democratic self-determination. An analogy to the independent judiciary may be useful in this respect. Like central banks, the judiciary administers an institution (a nation''s laws) that goes to the core of a nation''s political identity. And like central bankers, judges, in general, are not popularly elected in liberal democracies." Rosa Lastra and Geoffrey Wood, *Constitutional approach to central bank independence*, 3 *Central Banking* Feb., 35 (2000). *See* also Manuel Monteagudo, "Neutrality of Money and Central Bank Independence" in *International Monetary and Financial Law the Global Crisis*, 500 (OUP 2010). "You cannot in a democratic society have an institution which is fully or partly dissociated from the electoral process and which has powers that central banks inherently have" (Alan Greenspan, 1994). KPMG Financial Services 2009 (David Schickner principal author), "Central bank accountability and transparency, a comparative study of financial reporting central bank practices" 8, 2009.

financial authorities are granted a high degree of autonomy."[13] The publication of precise goals of monetary policy (namely, inflation targets and interest rates) provides economic agents with a relevant degree of anticipation about macroeconomic and monetary performance. In fact, if monetary stability as a public good is expressed in objective terms, it can be easily judged by public opinion.[14] Such a double effect of transparency (effectiveness and legitimacy) was also identified by the Transparency International EU Report of 2017, which points out that, from an economic perspective, "central banks would have to communicate their goals transparently if they were to influence market outcomes in the desired direction" and from a political one "in order to compensate for their lack of democratic legitimacy, independent central banks would have to abide by a higher standard of transparency.[15]

During the last years, monetary policy transparency, as a source for effectiveness and legitimacy of independent central banks, has produced significant developments at the institutional, operative, and technical level. An example is that until January 2015, the European Central Bank did not publish the Governing Council minutes, as it was already the case in specific central bank legislation in countries like the United Kingdom, the United States, Japan, and Chile.[16] In principle, votes of Board members can reflect one or different perspectives of the economic evolution that favors the formation of expectations. However, the 1999 IMF transparency Code warned about the excess of information of internal deliberations of monetary decisions ("extensive disclosure requirements about internal policy discussion on money and exchange market operations might disrupt markets, constrain the free flow of discussion by policymakers, or prevent the adoption of contingency plans").[17] The ECB justified its opposition founded on two basic arguments: (1) disclosure of Council minutes could limit the depth of debates, as far as members would feel constrained by the public opinion in their own countries; and (2) disclosure of minutes does not ensure a better understanding of monetary decisions by the public.[18] However, on 16 December 2014 the ECB Governing Council decided to publish the regular accounts of its monetary policy discussions containing an overview of financial market, economic, and monetary developments. The Council emphasized that the "accounts will also include a summary of the discussion, in an unattributed form, on the

---

[13]   *See* paragraph 4 of the Introduction of the Code of Good Practices on Transparency in Monetary and Financial Policies http://www.imf.org/external/np/mae/mft/sup/part1.htm#appendix_I.

[14]   Banque de France, "Independence and accountability in central banking", in the Central Bank's Bicentennial celebrations, speaking notes, draft/ 24 May 2000, 1.

[15]   Transparency International EU, "Two sides of the same coin? Independence and accountability of the European Central Bank" 27–8 (2017) http://transparency.eu/wp-content/uploads/2017/03/TI-EU _ECB_Report_DIGITAL.pdf.

[16]   *See* Manuel Monteagudo, *La Independencia Del Banco Central*, 311–14 (Banco Central de Reserva del Perú, Universidad del Pacífico and Instituto de Estudios Peruanos 2010).

[17]   Paragraph 8 of the Declaration of Principles of the IMF Transparency Code that continues as follows: "Thus, it might be inappropriate for central banks to disclose internal deliberations and documentation, and there are circumstances in which it would not be appropriate for central banks to disclose their near-term monetary and exchange rate policy implementation tactics and provide detailed information on foreign exchange operations. Similarly, there may be good reasons for the central bank (and financial agencies) not to make public their contingency plans, including possible emergency lending'. IMF Transparency Code, *supra* note 2.

[18]   *See* "The 'ECB's monetary policy-accountability, transparency and communication'", presentation of Sirkka Hämäläien, in the Conference, Old Age, New Economy and Central Banking (CEPR/ESI and Suomen Pankki), 14 September 2001, Helsinki.

economic and monetary analyses and on the monetary policy stance. The accounts will offer a fair and balanced reflection of policy deliberations. The aim is to provide the rationale behind monetary policy decisions and enable members of the public to improve their understanding of the Governing Council's assessment of the economy and its policy responses in the light of evolving conditions."[19] While this ECB decision implied a political choice in favor of the independence of board members' judgment (beyond eventual national scrutiny), it also reinforced the will to communicate with public opinion.

In the general context of accountability, transparency also implies disclosing the economic and financial information used and managed by independent central banks for monetary policy purposes. Some central banks not only make statistical information available to the public, but prepared forecasts by board members and the staff for a variety of macroeconomic indicators, including those related with their own goals and objectives.[20] Dr Willem Duisenberg, the first ECB President, pointed out that monetary policy is well understood when economic information is made public by central banks, not only as a justification mechanism, but also as a judging instrument. In this regard, transparency is a central bank's "exercise of honesty."[21] This does not mean that an independent central bank must fully disclose its internal information, but that the reported information is a means of judgment instead of an artificial construction to justify policy decisions.

Along these lines, in 1996 the IMF established the *Special Data Dissemination Standard* (SDDS) to guide members seeking access to international capital markets in providing their economic and financial data to the public. The SDDS was amplified in 1997 by the General Data Dissemination System (GDDS) for member countries with less developed statistical systems and in 2012 by the SDDS as an upper tier of the IMF's Data Standards Initiatives to help address data gaps identified during the global financial crisis.[22]More than 97 percent of IMF member countries participate in the e-GDDS, SDDS, or SDDS Plus and adopt reporting obligations to the IMF regarding their implementation of standards. The basic purpose of these systems is to guide member countries in the dissemination of comprehensive, timely, accessible, and reliable economic and financial statistical data (SDDS focuses on real, fiscal, financial, and external data) in a context of increasing economic and financial integration. Even though these mechanisms correspond to more economic sectors than those exclusively concerned with monetary policy, they are part of the general trend of transparency and integrity of financial information.

---

[19]   *See* the details of ECB Governing Council in Press Release: ECB to publish accounts of monetary policy discussions from January 2015 https://www.ecb.europa.eu/press/pr/date/2014/html/pr141218.en.html.

[20]   In 2012, the US Federal Open Market Committee announced a plan to publish the predictions of Board members of the level of short-term interest rates. N. Nergiz Dincera and Barry Eichengreen, *supra* note 1, at 189–90. *See* also "Communication and Monetary Policy", Remarks by Ben S. Bernanke at the National Economists Club Annual Dinner, Herbert Stein Memorial Lecture, 5–6 (Washington, D.C. 19 November 2013).

[21]   W. F. Duisenberg, *From the EMI to the ECB,* speech delivered at the *Banque de 'France's Bicentennial Symposium,* Paris, 30 May 2000, www.ecb.int/press/key/date/2000/html/sp000530.en.html. Also *see* Manuel Monteagudo, "Neutrality of Money and Central Bank Independence", *supra* note 12, at 500.

[22]   See IMF, "The Special Data Dissemination Standard" and general information in http://dsbb.imf.org/Pages/SDDS/Home.aspx?sp=y.

However, the general trend of transparency is now more intense because it is expanded to demands of information regarding emergency lending and securities market intervention by monetary authorities in the context of the recent international financial crisis and auditing unconventional operations.[23] That is precisely the case of the United States, where the Government Accountability Office (GAO) audits the Term Asset-Backed Securities Loan Facility (TALF) and the performance of the Treasury's Troubled Asset Relief Program (TARP).[24] But the audit function does not cover "monetary policy deliberations and operations, including open market and discount window operations, and transactions with or for foreign central banks, foreign governments, and public international financial organizations."[25]

Finally, it should be noted that the efforts to harmonize central banks' accounting standards have also served to reinforce transparency for accountability purposes. Many central banks even try to follow the International Financial Reporting Standards (IFRS). This trend also admits the concurrence of specific rules for self-regulated and non-profit entities, as in the case of independent central banks.[26] For policy reasons, central banks may decide not to disclose certain information (for example, creditworthiness of individual commercial banks) which may be required under IRS regulations.[27]

B.   Right of Access to Information and Central Banks

(a)   Principles and rules

Some traces of a previous formulation of today's right of access to information guarded by government entities (in the context of accountability) can be found in article 15 of the 1789 *Declaration of the Rights of Man and of the Citizen* that provides that "Society has the right to call for an account of his administration by every public agent." In fact, the request of information that remains in the hands of public bodies implies a citizens' interest to know how public power is exercised and, therefore, it constitutes another form of transparency. The US FOIA establishes the obligation of federal agencies to *make available to the public* (publishing and making available for inspection and copying) information (documents and records) in their possession;[28] and an analogous principle is founded in European treaties as in many other

---

[23]   N. Nergiz Dincera and Barry Eichengreen, *supra* note 1, at 191.

[24]   D. L. Kohn, "Federal Reserve Independence" (Testimony by Mr Donald L. Kohn, Vice Chairman of the Board of Governors of the US Federal Reserve System, before the Subcommittee on Domestic Monetary Policy and Technology, Committee on Financial Services, US House of Representatives, Washington DC, 9 July 2009), 5–6 (https://www.bis.org/review/r090715d.pdf).

[25]   *Ibid.* In fact, the Emergency Economic Stabilization (EES) Act of 2008 (Pub. L. No. 110-343, 122 Stat. 3765) designated four TARP oversight bodies. Three of the oversight bodies are independent of Treasury: (i) the GAO, (ii) the newly created Special Inspector General for TARP "("SIGTARP""), and (iii) the newly created Congressional Oversight Panel "("COP""). Treasury and other government agencies sit on the fourth oversight body, the Financial Stability Oversight Board "("FSOB""), which is chaired by the Federal Reserve Chairman. James E. Kelly, *Transparency and Bank Supervision* 73 Alb. L. Rev. 426–7 (2009–10).

[26]   KPMG Financial Services 2009, *supra* note 12, at 32.

[27]   *Ibid.* at 36. In its financial statements the Bank of England states that it may not make full disclosures on contingent liabilities, indicating that this is due to its "lender of last resort" function. The Deutsche Bundesbank Act states that in the Deutsche Bundesbank's financial statements "the liability structure need not be disclosed". *Ibid.* at 40.

[28]   5 U.S.C. § 552 (a) (1)–(2) (2012).

national legislations. Articles 15.3 of the Treaty on the Functioning of the European Union (TFEU) and 42 of the Charter of Fundamental Rights of the European Union establish (with some slight differences) that "any citizen of the Union, and any natural or legal person residing or having its registered office in a Member State, shall have a right of access to documents of the Union's institutions."[29]

It can be easily imagined that not all information in the hands of the government should be authorized when private rights and the public interest are involved. In fact, the right to access of information legislation also establishes, under different formulations, some exemptions that are directly related to financial and monetary information with special significance in today's central bank activity. The US FOIA considers trade secrets, inter-agency and intra-agency memorandums and letters and information "contained in or related to examination, operating, or condition reports prepared by, on behalf of, or for the use of an agency responsible for the regulation or supervision of financial institutions" among the exemptions of the right to access of public information.[30] These exemptions have been precisely the object of substantial discussion in US Courts after the request of information by Bloomberg and Fox News of information on FED lending operations in the context of responses to the financial crisis, that we will comment on in the following paragraphs.

In the European Union, article 15.3 of the TFEU clarifies that general principles and limits on grounds of public or private interest governing this right of access to documents shall be determined by the European Parliament and the Council, by means of regulations, acting in accordance with the ordinary legislative procedure and in the specific case of the Court of Justice, the ECB and the European Investment Bank, they will be subject to this provision *only when exercising their administrative tasks*. The reference to administrative tasks in opposition to private or contractual tasks (which may include all the menu of financial operations and transactions of central banks) is also employed by the French Law No. 78753 of 17 July 1978, which excludes directly administrative documents that may affect *money* and *public credit*.[31] Regulation (EC) No. 1049/2001 of the European Parliament and of the Council of 30 May 2001 with the purpose of giving "the effect to the right of public access",[32] but admitting "that certain public and private interests should be protected by way of exceptions", [33] defines the principles, conditions and limits governing the right of access to Parliament, Council and Commission documents. Despite the fact that Regulation (EC) No. 1049/2001 is applicable to those Europeans institutions,[34] it authorizes them to refuse access to a document where disclosure would undermine the protection of "financial, monetary or economic policy of the community or a member State,[35] commercial

---

[29]   Article 42 of the Charter of Fundamental Rights of the European Union states the following: "Any citizen of the Union, and any natural or legal person residing or having its registered office in a Member State, has a right of access to documents of the institutions, bodies, offices and agencies of the Union, whatever their medium".

[30]   Exceptions 4, 5 and 8 of FOIA: 5. U.S.C. §552 (b) (4)–(5)–(8) (2012).

[31]   Article 6 (I) 2 (e) of the "Loi n° 78-753 du 17 juillet 1978 portant diverses mesures d'amélioration des relations entre l'administration et le public et diverses dispositions d'ordre administratif, social et fiscal". "Article 6 . . . I.-Ne sont pas communicables: . . . 2° Les autres documents administratifs dont la consultation ou la communication porterait atteinte: . . . e) A la monnaie et au crédit public".

[32]   Consideration (4) of Regulation (EC) No. 1049/2001.

[33]   Consideration (11) of Regulation (EC) No. 1049/2001.

[34]   Article 1 (a) of Regulation (EC) No. 1049/2001.

[35]   Article 4 (1) (a) of Regulation (EC) No. 1049/2001.

interests of a natural or legal person, including intellectual property,[36] or the purpose of inspections, investigations and audits".[37]

The Statute of the European System of Central Banks declares that, unless authorized by the Governing Council, the proceedings of the meetings shall be confidential[38] (a limitation that, as mentioned before, was modified by the Council in January 2015). A similar general principle was provided by article 23 of the Rules of Procedure of the ECB.[39] But the ECB, by the Decision of 4 March 2004 on public access to European Central Bank documents,[40] defined in a more specific way the *conditions and limits* according to which the ECB shall give public access to ECB documents, listing in article 4 the cases in which it can refuse access where disclosure would undermine the protection of public interest, privacy and the integrity of the individual, the confidentiality of information protected under Community law, commercial interests (including intellectual property), court proceedings and legal advice, the purpose of inspections, investigations and audits, opinions for internal use as part of deliberations, among others.[41] It should be noted that article 4(1)(a) of the Decision of 4 March 2004 understands public interests, as regards "the confidentiality of the proceedings of the ECB's decision-making bodies, the financial, monetary or economic policy of the Community or a Member State, the internal finances of the ECB or of the NCBs, protecting the integrity of euro banknotes, public security, and international financial, monetary or economic relations".

Even though both the *Rules of Procedure* and the ECB Decision of 4 March 2004 have a general principle providing that exceptions may apply for a period of 30 years unless specifically provided otherwise by ECB authorities (articles 23.3 and 4(6) respectively), the ECB Decision of 4 March 2004 considers two situations in which ECB discretionary power may continue refusing public access: when it is justified *on the basis of the document* and when it relates *to privacy or commercial interests.*[42]

(b)   Law in Action
The rationale for US FOIA exemptions related to central bank operations has been tested in courts since 2008, when exceptional liquidity facilities were accorded to banks in response to the international financial crisis and the FED refused Bloomberg and Fox News their requests for the names of institutions that had received last resort lending and "an accounting of the collateral provided by these institutions in exchange for the lending."[43] The main discussion in

---

[36]   Article 4 (2) of Regulation (EC) No. 1049/2001.
[37]   Article 4 (2) of Regulation (EC) No. 1049/2001.
[38]   Article 12.3 of the ESCB statute.
[39]   Decision of the European Central Bank of 19 February 2004 adopting the Rules of Procedure of the European Central Bank (ECB/2004/2) (2004/257/EC), ([2004] OJ L8/33).
[40]   Decision of the European Central Bank of 4 March 2004 on public access to European Central Bank documents (ECB/2004/3), (OJ L80, 18.3.2004, p. 42).
[41]   Article 4 of the ECB/2004/3.
[42]   The complete text of Article 4 (6) is as follows: "The exceptions as laid down in this Article shall only apply for the period during which protection is justified on the basis of the content of the document. The exceptions may apply for a maximum period of 30 years unless specifically provided otherwise by the 'ECB's Governing Council. In the case of documents covered by the exceptions relating to privacy or commercial interests, the exceptions may continue to apply after this period".
[43]   This was additionally requested by Fox News. *See* Samuel L. Zimmerman, *Understanding Confidentiality: Program Effectiveness and the Freedom of Information Act Exemption 4*, 53 WM. & Mary L. Rev. 1093–94 (2011–12).

both cases was the application of US FOIA Exemption 4 that justifies refusals in the case of "trade secrets and commercial or financial information obtained from a person and privileged or confidential". The FED claimed that the disclosure of information could in effect damage business operations of banks[44] and that Exemption 4 is precisely intended to protect a governmental interest in administrative efficiency and effectiveness,[45] pointing out that the requested information would impair the Board's ability: (i) to carry out its statutory responsibility "to promote effectively the goals of maximum employment, stable prices, and moderate long-term interest rates"; (ii) to utilize its authority to permit lending by the Reserve Banks to individuals, partnerships or corporations to address "unusual and exigent circumstances" in the domestic economy; and (iii) to utilize the discount window and TAF lending by the Reserve Banks as a safety valve.[46]

The FED emphasized that disclosure entities would subject the institutions to "stigmatization" and would discourage them from using the lender of last resort facilities, impairing the monetary authority's ability to maintain the basic stability of the payment system by supplying liquidity during times of systemic stress.[47] Supporting the FED's position, the Clearing House Association argued that that the disclosure of borrowers' use of the FED's emergency lending programs "marks them with a 'stigma' of financial weakness" and can have "severe adverse consequences for individual borrowers, including sparking bank runs."[48]

In the first instance, both cases produced opposite decisions. In *Bloomberg* the US District Court rejected the FED's arguments, ruling that the information was completely internal to the FED as a federal agency, and had not been obtained from commercial banks, which is necessary for Exemption 4 to apply.[49] To the contrary in *Fox News* the District Court *fully credited the Board's argument regarding the FED's statutory duties* and noted that "[t]he Board's concerns, that rumors are likely to begin and runs on banks are likely to develop, cannot be dismissed . . . The national economy is not so out of danger . . . as to make the Board's concern academic."[50] As Zimmerman comments, the Second Circuit Court of Appeals resolved the split, deciding the appeals of *Fox News* and *Bloomberg* on the same day,[51] in favor of disclosure.[52] The Court in *Bloomberg* did not accept to apply the so-called *effectiveness test* in favor of FED that would have justified refusal if disclosure (1) impairs government ability to obtain necessary information in the future; or (2) causes substantial harm to the competitive position of a person from whom the information is obtained.[53] On this issue, the Court "held that, although the arguments in favor of the program effectiveness test were 'plausible, and forcefully made,' adopting the test would give the agency an inappropriate degree of discre-

---

[44]   Benjamin W. Cramer and Martin E. Halstuk, *Crash and Learn: The Inability of Transparency Laws to Penetrate American Monetary Policy* 25 WM. & Mary Bill Rts. J., 211 (2016).

[45]   Samuel L. Zimmerman, *supra* note 43, at 1094.

[46]   *Ibid.* at 1095–6.

[47]   *Ibid.* at 1095.

[48]   James E. Kelly, *supra* note 25, at 443.

[49]   Benjamin W. Cramer and Martin E. Halstuk, *supra* note 44, at 211.

[50]   Samuel L. Zimmerman, *supra* note 43, at 1095.

[51]   *Ibid.* at 1096.

[52]   *Ibid.* See *Bloomberg, L.P. v. Bd. of Governors of the Fed. Reserve Sys.*, 601 F.3d 143 (2d cir. 2010) and *Fox News Network, LLC v. Bd. of Governors of the Fed. Reserve Sys.*, 601 F.3d 158 (2d cir. 2010). Zimmerman points out that the *Bloomberg* decision contains the court's analysis of the applicability of Exemption 4; *Fox News* only references the reasoning in *Bloomberg. Fox News, ibid.* at note 59.

[53]   Benjamin W. Cramer and Martin E. Halstuk, *supra* note 44, at 217.

tion and undermine FOIA's basic policy of disclosure."[54] In these cases, the Court privileged disclosure vis-à-vis a not sufficiently demonstrated damage of monetary policy effectiveness. For Karlson the data sought in *Fox News* and *Bloomberg* in practical terms did not violate the deliberative privilege because the disclosure of the records of the Central Bank's prior decisions would not result in premature disclosure or hamper open policy discussion.[55]

In 1999, the ECB confronted before the ECJ the challenge of its refusal to the request of Mr Athanasios Pitsiorlas, who, in the context of the preparation of his doctoral thesis, required the *Basle/Nyborg Agreement on the reinforcement of the European Monetary System (EMS)* endorsed by the Council of Economic and Finance Ministers at their informal meeting at Nyborg (Denmark) on 12 September 1987.[56] In fact, Mr Pitsiorlas requested (in his claim for re-examination of refusal) the reduction of the 30-year period of confidentiality that the Governing Council can accord in *special cases* under Article 23.3 of the ECB Rules of Procedure.[57] The Court of First Instance considered that the ECB refusal did not show any "assessment on the basis of wording of the documents"[58] and that "it is not clear from its decision that the applicant's interests had been weighed against the public interest constituted by monetary stability".[59] For the Court it was not until after the action for annulment had been brought that the ECB contended that the opinions expressed and the strategies analyzed in the documents constituting the Basle/Nyborg Agreement were still valid and could have implications for the current exchange rate mechanism and that, "in order to avoid any confusion of the markets," there were legitimate reasons for not making those documents public.[60] The Court concluded that ECB's refusal must be annulled "as not satisfying the obligation to give reasons, as laid down in Article 253 EC".[61] Article 253 EC and its current version in the TFEU establishes that legal acts shall state the reasons on which they are based.[62] It is very interesting to notice that in the *Bloomberg*, *Fox News* and *Pitsiorlas* cases the courts concluded that the damage and effect of monetary policy effectiveness of disclosure was not sufficiently evident to justify refusal.

As mentioned before, France's Law No. 78753 of 17 July 1978 excludes from the access to public information those administrative documents that may affect *money* and *public credit*.

---

[54]   Samuel L. Zimmerman, *supra* note 43, at 1096.

[55]   Kara Karlson, *Checks and Balances: Using the Freedom of Information Act to Evaluate the Federal Reserve Banks*, 60 Am. U. L. Rev. 219 (2010–11).

[56]   *Athanasios Pitsiorlas v. Council of the European Union and European Central Bank* (ECB). Joined Cases T-3/00 and T-337/04. Judgment of the Court of First Instance (Fifth Chamber), para 23, 27 November 2007-II 4784.

[57]   *Athanasios Pitsiorlas v. Council of the European Union and ECB*, para 29.

[58]   *Ibid.* para 267.

[59]   *Ibid.* para 271.

[60]   *Ibid.* para 277.

[61]   *Ibid.* para 279. The corresponding version of Article 253 EC is in Article 296 of the TFEU and states the following: "Where the Treaties do not specify the type of act to be adopted, the institutions shall select it on a case-by-case basis, in compliance with the applicable procedures and with the principle of proportionality. Legal acts shall state the reasons on which they are based and shall refer to any proposals, initiatives, recommendations, requests or opinions required by the Treaties. When considering draft legislative acts, the European Parliament and the Council shall refrain from adopting acts not provided for by the relevant legislative procedure in the area in question."

[62]   The appeal was dismissed by decision of 3 July 2008, Court of European Justice (Second Chamber).

Founded in that exclusion, in 2005 the Board of the *Commission d'accès aux documents administratifs* (Commission for the access to administrative documents) refused the request of the director of the *Centre de Recherche* "EDHEC Risk and Asset Management" for documents from the *Fonds de reserve pour les retraites* (the Pension Reserve Fund) that included financial strategies and investment choices by the Board.[63] The Commission considered that the disclosure of some requested documents had the risk of generating speculative movements that could damage the solvability of the Pensions Fund.[64]

Chile offers an interesting experience of a central bank that, based on its constitutional independence, is not in the sphere of the general legislation of access to public information; even if it preserves a special regime. In fact, the Central Bank of Chile is considered one of the most independent central banks in the emerging market world[65] and the Chilean Constitution, providing the basic principles of central bank independence, accords the status of *constitutional law* to its organic law.[66] This Law establishes that the Central Bank of Chile "shall, with regard to its duties and powers, be governed exclusively by the provisions of this Act and it shall not be bound for any legal purposes, by general or special provisions, present or future, enacted for the public sector".[67] This exclusive constitutional and legal regimen has made impossible the full application of the law on transparency and access of information to the Central Bank of Chile. The Constitutional tribunal accepted the argumentation of the Central Bank of Chile by its decision of 10 July 2008 and declared unconstitutional any interference of the Transparency Council over the Central Bank's Board regulations on access of information. In fact, the project of Law No. 20.285, submitted to the Constitutional Tribunal assessment, commanded the Central Bank of Chile *to adopt* regulations enacted by the Transparency Council, instead of what is provided by existing legislation that establishes that the Central Bank "would take into consideration" those regulations.[68]

---

[63]   Decision of Conseil 20051762 (session of 26/05/2005) *Commission d'accès aux documents administratifs*.

[64]   "Les documents relatifs à la politique de placement et d'investissement du fonds de réserve des retraites sont protégés par cette exception, eu égard aux montants élevés placés sur les marchés financiers et au risque de spéculation financière" (conseil n° 20051762 du 26 mai 2005).

[65]   J. I. Jácome, E. W. Niev and P. Iman, *Building Blocks for Effective Macroprudential Policies in Latin America: Institutional Considerations*, footnote 36, IMF Working Paper (July 2012).

[66]   Article 108 of the Constitution of Chile as follows: "There will be an autonomous organism, with its own patrimony, of technical character, denominated the Central Bank, whose composition, organization, functions and attributions will be determined by a constitutional organic law."

[67]   First paragraph of article 2 of the Constitutional Law of the Central Bank of Chile as follows: "The Bank shall, with regard to its duties and powers, be governed exclusively by the provisions of this Act and it shall not be bound for any legal purposes, by general or special provisions, present or future, enacted for the public sector. In the absence of regulatory provisions and provided the matter is within the scope of the Bank's duties and powers, provisions regulating the private sector shall apply".

[68]   *See* Pilar Arellano Gómez, *Jurisprudencia del Tribunal Constitucional Acerca del Artículo 8 de la Constitución Política: entre el Mandato Constitucional de Publicidad y las Causales de Reserva y Secreto*, 23–4, Estudios (Revista de Derecho Público) 80 (2014).

II.   REASONS FOR CENTRAL BANK CONFIDENTIALITY

Exemptions of the general principle of access to public information (provided by laws and regulations) are basically founded on the obligation of confidentiality in order to protect *private* and *public* interests. We have mentioned that the ECB decision of 4 March 2004 refers to the protection of privacy and integrity of the individual and intellectual property, and adds "court proceedings and legal advice, the purpose of inspections, investigations and audits, opinions for internal use as part of deliberations, among others".[69] However, in addition to these types of explicit protections, central bank employees are subject to the general commitment of confidentiality as part of the "requirement of professional secrecy".[70]

The plurality of sources of information protected by confidentiality in central banks is explained by the fact that the infringement of individual (and collective) rights can, at the same time, severely affect monetary policy effectiveness. Disclosure of protected personal information (for example, employees' health data) or the use of insight information for private interests (information on future foreign change intervention for personal investments) not only may cause individual injuries but also generate a serious reputational damage to central banks' authority. If, as mentioned before, monetary policy effectiveness and legitimacy benefit from transparency, they also benefit from confidentiality. Now, in extreme situations the infringement of rights seems to be clear enough and without the need to balance competing interests and rights. However, reality is never *Manichaean*[71] and real problems appear in the middle when it is necessary to discern when to be transparent and when confidential to keep reputation and credibility in a good standing. Schauer says that even though transparency can foster accountability and prevent the abuse of power, we celebrate the lack of transparency in issues of privacy, confidentiality, secrecy, and independence, with it becoming apparent that transparency, including transparency in and about the financial services industry, has its vices as well as its virtues.[72]

In the context of an incident in which potentially market-sensitive information appeared to have been disclosed to a limited audience by a senior official of the ECB in 2015, the ECB published new guiding principles for speaking engagements (*Guiding principles for external communication by members of the Executive Board of the European Central Bank*), specifying that no market-sensitive information should be divulged at non-public events or during bilateral meetings.[73] In fact, the guiding principles attempt to provide instructions to balance transparency and confidentiality (avoiding accusations of disclosing insight information). For instance, the first principle establishes that the "members of the Executive Board will safeguard confidential information in accordance with their obligations and apply utmost prudence in selecting speaking engagements at external events to avoid any appearance that potentially

---

[69]   *See* reference to ECB Decision of 4 March 2004 in section I.B.a.

[70]   Article 37 of the Statute of the ECB, Article 37 of the Bank Act.

[71]   Phrase usually attributed to André Malraux.

[72]   Frederick Schauer, *The Mixed Blessings of Financial Transparency* 31 Yale J. on Reg. 810–11 (2014).

[73]   *See* the text of the Guiding principles for external communication by members of the Executive Board of the European Central Bank (Guiding Principles) in http://www.ecb.europa.eu/ecb/orga/transparency/html/eb-communications-guidelines.en.html.

See also European Ombudsman, Annual Report for 2015 to the European Parliament, 8.

market-sensitive information may not be available to the widest possible public audience at the same time".[74]

Let us review some examples of how the protection of private rights and public interest has been conceptualized as an argument in favor of confidentiality to assess whether confidentiality is a real enemy of transparency.[75]

A.   Protecting Individual Rights and Avoiding Market Misrepresentation

A first solution to reconcile transparency with confidentiality in an institution that operates with banks and responds to the public for its performance, is assuming (as part of central banks' statistical activities) that transparency corresponds to aggregate information and confidentiality to individual data.[76] It is a worldwide practice recognized in law that central banks possess, as one of their most effective (*de jure*) instruments, the capacity to collect information from any economic agent (public or private) in order to measure economic activity, regulate liquidity provision and fully comply with the mandate to preserve stability of prices. In fact, monetary policy conduction needs such an *exorbitant* capacity to enter private information that is only comparable to public intrusion on taxation and recent developments in anti-money laundering legislation. Article 5 of the Statute of the European System of Central Banks and of the European Central Bank, besides making explicit this capacity over the whole Euro zone, provides that the Council defines "the confidentiality regime and the appropriate provisions for enforcement".[77] The obvious result is that monetary authority, jointly with an injunctive power to impose data a reporting obligation, is able to assure confidentiality to obligators. Precisely the IMF General Data Dissemination System prescribes under the *Principle of Integrity* the obligation of the dissemination of the terms and conditions under which official statistics are produced, "including those relating to the confidentiality of individually identifiable information".[78]

---

[74]   Guiding Principles, *supra* note 73.

[75]   *See* Frederick Schauer, *supra* note 72, at 815. Analyzing the willingness of individuals to be more open in private than in public, Schauer also suggests that the US First Amendment's protection of speaker anonymity can be described as a right against transparency. *Ibid.* at 818.

[76]   *Ibid.* at 816.

[77]   The full text of article 5 the Statute of the ESCB is as follows:

5.1. In order to undertake the tasks of the ESCB, the ECB, assisted by the national central banks, shall collect the necessary statistical information either from the competent national authorities or directly from economic agents. For these purposes it shall cooperate with the Union institutions, bodies, offices or agencies and with the competent authorities of the Member States or third countries and with international organizations.

5.2. The national central banks shall carry out, to the extent possible, the tasks described in Article 5.1.

5.3. The ECB shall contribute to the harmonization, where necessary, of the rules and practices governing the collection, compilation and distribution of statistics in the areas within its fields of competence.

5.4. The Council, in accordance with the procedure laid down in Article 41, shall define the natural and legal persons subject to reporting requirements, the confidentiality regime and the appropriate provisions for enforcement.

[78]   IMF, "The Special Data Dissemination Standard (Legal Text)", 9. *See* text in http://www.imf.org/external/np/pp/eng/2012/090712.pdf.

The *Bloomberg* and *Fox News* cases have opened in the United States the possibility to obtain information from the central bank about the liabilities of commercial banks as beneficiaries of monetary facilities in the context of the recent international financial crisis. However, US FOIA exemptions of the right to access of public information[79] remain in force to the benefit of monetary policy effectiveness and still of commercial banks' interests. Trade secrets, inter-agency and intra-agency memorandums and letters and information *contained in or related to examination, operating, or condition reports prepared by, on behalf of, or for the use of an agency responsible for the regulation or supervision of financial institutions* are considered among FOIA exemptions.

US Courts also recognize the "bank examination privilege," as it was formulated in 1992 by the Court of Appeals for the DC Circuit:[80] "The bank examination privilege is firmly rooted in practical necessity. Bank safety and soundness supervision is an iterative process of comment by the regulators and response by the bank. The success of the supervision therefore depends vitally upon the quality of communication between the regulated banking firm and the bank regulatory agency. This relationship is both extensive and informal." Even bank examination privilege is not absolute (for instance in cases of judicial process or government malfeasances),[81] it institutes the confidentiality of information to make effective the supervisory function. Something analogous happens with the exemption of disclosure of banks' investigations into financial crimes like money laundering and tax evasion.[82]

The US Congress approved in 2008 the "Emergency Economic Stability Act" that established its power to require the FED to periodically report to Congress on the status of monetary lending, the total value of the collateral, and the cost to the taxpayer, but it is very interesting to notice that this legislation provided that Congress may withhold all of these disclosures from the public at the request of the Board Chairman.[83] As already mentioned, limited access to information on central bank lending inspires legislation that does not expand the GAO audit function on "monetary policy deliberations and operations, including open market and discount window operations, and transactions with or for foreign central banks, foreign governments, and public international financial organizations".[84] In these cases, different from exclusive private interest protection, we are in the sphere of public interest in favor of governmental policy effectiveness (central banks authority) rather than exclusive private interest protection. Full disclosure of policy deliberations can produce a misrepresentation of monetary policy and of the evolution of the economy and finance. Sometimes, monetary policy decisions surprise markets, and may be an opportunity to influence the real economy.[85] Kelly quotes Judge Brennan's statement to illustrate the paradox of keeping information confidential for the good

---

[79]   Exceptions 4, 5 and 8 of FOIA: 5. U.S.C. §552 (b) (4)–(5)–(8) (2012).

[80]   James E. Kelly, *supra* note 25, at 439.

[81]   *Ibid.* at 441.

[82]   Benjamin W. Cramer and Martin E. Halstuk, *supra* note 44, at 209. According to the US Bank Secrecy Act this type of document can remain confidential and cannot be obtained via the FOIA, Exemption 3, which states that "[i]nformation that is prohibited from disclosure by another Federal law" can be withheld. 5 U.S.C. § 552(b) (3) (2012); 24 C.F.R. § 15.107 (2015). *Ibid.* at note 109.

[83]   Kara Karlson, *supra* note 55, at 223.

[84]   *See* Donald L. Kohn, *supra* note 24, at 5.

[85]   For Lucas the only opportunity of public powers to act and influence the real economy is to surprise them, even though temporarily because they will anticipate the next surprise attempts. *See* Banque De France, *Les fonctions de la banque centrale*, Bulletin de la Banque de France, 70, 80 (October 1999).

of the people: "to enable the government more effectively to implement the will of the people, the people are kept in ignorance of the workings of their government." [86]

B.   Is Confidentiality an Enemy of Transparency?

During his testimony before the Subcommittee on Domestic Monetary Policy and Technology, Committee on Financial Services of the US House of Representatives in July 2009, Mr Donald L. Kohn, Vice Chairman of the Board of Governors of the US FED, made a point about the possibility of removing statutory limits on GAO audits of monetary policy matters, making this entity able to produce judgments about policy actions. He expressed that such a new GAO competence would have undermined monetary independence because they could be used to influence monetary policy.[87] If eventually GAO audits were public, policymakers would be less willing to engage in the unfettered and wide-ranging internal debates that are essential to identifying the best possible policy options.[88] The main idea behind this warning was that full transparency would undermine central banks' independence, very well synthesized by Schauer: "If it is important that complex major macro-economic decisions with global and trillion dollar consequences not be made at the ballot box or on the front pages of the tabloids, then it may be just as important that those decisions remain independent from the kind of pressure that excess transparency might very well bring . . . it is important not to assume that transparency is necessarily for the better, even in the context of central banks and other financial institutions, but rather to recognize when and where this will be so and when and where it will not."[89]

Kelly highlights that right after the first signal of the financial international crisis in 2007, transparency was proposed as the basic antidote to improve the quality of banking regulation legislation of financial. TARP oversight bodies (GAO, the Special Inspector General of TARP, the Congressional Oversight Panel and the Financial Stability Oversight Board led by the FED) announced a "Transparency and Accountability Agenda" in the context of the expectation that Treasury resources invested in banks through TARP would result in increased lending by banks.[90] The Special Inspector General of TARP even recommended requiring TARP recipients to submit periodic reports on their uses of TARP funds such as lending, investments, and acquisitions, including "a description of what actions they were able to take that they would not have taken without TARP funding".[91] The Treasury declined to implement such a level of reporting and transparency, stating that this is a function of basic accounting principles and money is fungible; in fact, uses of money *cannot be said to be attributable to*

---

[86]   Kelly, *supra* note 25, at 441. *In re Franklin Nat'l Bank Sec. Litig.*, 478 F.Supp. 582 (quoting *Herbert v. Lando*, 441 U.S. 153, 196 (1979) (Brennan, J., dissenting)). *Ibid.*, citations of notes 89 and 90.

[87]   Donald L. Kohn, *supra* note 24, at 6. A similar objection was raised by Carney when the UK government tried to do the same. See: at footnote 107 of C. Russo, *The Ethics of Banking and Financial Regulatory Authorities: a study of the Bank of England, the Prudential Regulation Authority, the Monetary Policy Committee and the Financial Conduct Authority* (2016) https://www.gov.uk/government/uploads/system/uploads/attachment_data/file/554355/Ethics_of_Banking_and_Financial_Regulatory_Authorities_by_Dr_Costanza_Russo.pdf.

[88]   Donald L. Kohn, *supra* note 24, at 6.

[89]   Frederick Schauer, *supra* note 72, at 820–1.

[90]   *See* James E. Kelly *supra* note 25, at 426–32.

[91]   *Ibid.* at 433.

the TARP investment if the same expenditures would have been made from other sources in the absence of TARP funding.[92]

But even the over-expectation of transparency could be critical in the case of TARP-specific uses;[93] what did have a positive and immediate impact on private investor confidence was the *extraordinary* release of banks' stress test results on 7 May 2009 that were based on internal bank records which usually are subject to confidentiality protection under *bank examiner privilege*.[94] In other words, what in ordinary situations is considered private and confidential, in extraordinary circumstances should be subject to disclosure for the benefit of public interests and even for those whose confidential information is disclosed. Thus, there are no absolute rules on this matter. Full transparency in its role of *sunlight as the best of disinfectants*[95] could be well justified in extraordinary circumstances, but not every time.

Discernment on when to be transparent or confidential requires a high level of wisdom and proven experience; but, more than anything else, it requires a significant dose of *ethical* considerations. This dose should serve to determine when the public interest prevails over the private interest and to explain the reasons of one or another choice. The legislation and cases reviewed show that the assurance of monetary policy effectiveness (as a public interest) is one of the most relevant considerations in the balance between transparency and confidentiality.

From a legal perspective, it is necessary that discernment for a balancing test analysis is based on some legitimate source of law or standard. In fact, we started our analysis indicating that some traces of the citizen's claim for transparency can be found in article 15 of the 1789 *Declaration of the Rights of Man and of the Citizen* ("Society has the right to call for an account of his administration by every public agent"), because it seems that the whole exercise of balancing transparency and confidentiality corresponds to a due diligence exam for those who exercise power. Inflation is a monetary phenomenon but monetary policy implies an exercise of power[96] (extendedly increased during the last years), affecting different interests in different ways. Far from being irreconcilable enemies, transparency and confidentiality well justified can be complementary approaches.

CONCLUSION

The principles of transparency and confidentially are constitutive elements of central banks' independence and legitimacy, even in times of international financial crisis. The exercise of transparency for central banks can be an opportunity to give public opinion appropriate explanations of confidentiality on the basis of the need for protection of private and public interests.

---

[92] *Ibid.* at 434.

[93] "Transparency, though, may also be detrimental to the basic goals of a TARP like program with financial distributions that become politicized by making their existence and amount known to Congress, to the press, and to the public. Those distributions may become influenced by the vagaries and irrationalities of politics and political opportunism". Frederick Schauer, *supra* note 72, at 822.

[94] James E. Kelly *supra* note 25, at 436–7.

[95] Famous slogan in favor of openness and full disclosure and transparency. *See* Frederick Schauer, *supra* note 72, at 809 note 1 that refers to Louis D. Brandeis, "Other People's Money and How the Bankers Use it" 92 (1914).

[96] Wooley's statement in C. Aubin, *Les relations entre la Réserve fédérale et les différents pouvoirs économiques et politiques aux Etats-Unis*, 1976 Problemes Economiques, 9 (28/05/86).

However, even if a case-by-case approach will be better received than strict rules, recent case law and legislative experience reveals that, in extreme situations, it will be necessary to assess monetary policy effectiveness vis-à-vis private protection interests.

17. Enforcement, ethics and transparency: problems and perspectives[1]

Costanza A. Russo

INTRODUCTION

As in most countries, in the United Kingdom expectations of ethical behaviour placed upon regulatory authorities are traditionally well engrained in public law principles as well as in the statutory provisions that regulate their activities. By and large, these impose on regulators' duties of fairness, transparency, accountability, independence and impartiality.

A comprehensive assessment of whether financial regulators behave ethically, or whether they go beyond what is expected of them would be an extremely ambitious aim for a book chapter. This was the subject of a specific investigation by this author, at the request of a Cabinet Committee of the UK government,[2] and even in that inquiry certain issues could not be covered. Notably however, there is no body of literature that covers the issue of ethical behaviour of UK financial regulators and this chapter contributes to filling that gap.

A frank discussion is needed on what constitutes ethical behaviour in regulators. As mentioned, the law is already prescriptive in imposing ethical conduct upon them, which makes us question whether mere obedience to the law implies the realisation of such conduct. The answer to this should be in the negative. Law and regulations tend to set standards below which one must not fall[3] and as such these are minimum requirements. Ethical behaviour has a broader aspirational meaning, and should not equate with compliance-based practices. Therefore, to be considered genuinely ethical, regulatory activity should not merely fit within the legal perimeter but should strive to go beyond that minimum.

Expectations of ethical behaviour in public life are not only included in law, codes and regulations but also in standards. For instance, in the United Kingdom a set of high-level principles known as the Nolan Principles[4] elaborate on how public servants are expected to conduct their professional life. They include legally derived principles of objectivity and accountability as

---

[1] Last revised March 2018. The author would like to thank Philip Rawlings and Dalvinder Singh for useful comments. Any errors are her own.

[2] See Costanza Russo, The Ethics of Banking and Financial Regulatory Authorities: a study of the Bank of England, the Prudential Regulation Authority, the Monetary Policy Committee and the Financial Conduct Authority, Annex accompanying the commanding report of the Committee on Standards in Public Life, *Striking the Balance: Upholding the Seven Principles of Public Life in Regulation* (Sixteenth Report CM 9327) 2016 available at https://www.gov.uk/government/uploads/system/uploads/attachment_data/file/554355/Ethics_of_Banking_and_Financial_Regulatory_Authorities_by_Dr_Costanza_Russo.pdf.

[3] See Law and Ethics in Finance Project, *Submission to the FEMR*, para 9, available at www.bankofengland.co.uk/paper/2015/how-fair-and-effective-are-the-fixed-income-foreign-exchange-and-commodities-markets-responses.

[4] The Seven Principles of Public Life, available at www.gov.uk/government/publications/the-7-principles-of-public-life/the-7-principles-of-public-life--2.

well as others whose formulation is reminiscent of legal duties, such as integrity, honesty, and openness. Other principles like selflessness and leadership are somewhat loose or unclear, but nonetheless convey a message of good behaviour. Even though the principles are addressed to public servants, they are seen as applicable to public bodies more broadly.[5, 6]

The ability of authorities to go beyond the black letter of the law, holding themselves to the highest standards of behaviour may have three beneficial effects: (1) it would increase the level of trustworthiness of the regulator; and (2) it would reinforce its legitimacy, as well as (3) its credibility before regulatees and the public as a whole.

The problem is however how to fill these ethical commands with appropriate content, practices, and processes. This is all the more important if we consider that most regulators enjoy powers that are normally separated in democratic jurisdictions: legislative (as they have regulatory powers), executive (as they oversee the application of those regulations), and judicial powers (because of their enforcement and decision-making powers).

To this end, two factors come into play: (1) how regulators make use of their discretion and (2) how they improve legal requirements (namely, to what extent they set their own bar even higher). Under (2), matters that need consideration mostly relate to authorities' governance and quality of self-regulation.

There may be other factors too, relating to the existence, and possibly 'the quality of, policies related to whistleblowing, gender equality, career progression, bullying and harassing, creditors' payment, staff satisfaction surveys, and consideration for [the] personal privacy of employees',[7] their mental health, well-being and counselling. These are however more a matter of 'organisational integrity', and are not unique to the public sector.

As for UK financial regulators, extensive research has highlighted[8] how they seem to have reacted proactively to a string of allegations of unethical behaviour, or of lack of accountability. This has had an overall positive impact on their governance, self regulation, level of transparency and accountability towards the general public. For instance, in 2014 the Bank of England established an Independent Evaluation Office (IEO),[9] adopted the recommendations of different reviews,[10] and instated an 'open about our business' policy,[11] partially reflected in the 'One Bank' initiative. This latter is the strategic plan the Bank launched in 2014 to take full advantage of the expanded set of policy responsibilities within the central bank.[12] More recently, the Bank took sweeping action to remedy the impact of the Charlotte Hogg debacle by commissioning an independent review to assess lessons learned and review current

---

[5]   Despite, one could argue, that extending to legal persons duties specifically formulated for natural persons may well be a stretch, this chapter will take the applicability of the Nolan principles to the organisation as a whole as a given.

[6]   The business friendly Regulators' Code too reiterates the need for regulators to ensure that their approach is transparent. See Department for Business Innovation & Skills, *Regulators' Code*, para 6 April 2014, https://www.gov.uk/government/publications/regulators-code.

[7]   See Russo (n 2), 2.

[8]   See Russo (n 2).

[9]   The IEO is an independent committee within the Bank which evaluates its performance through in-depth reviews. See www.bankofengland.co.uk/independent-evaluation-office.

[10]   See Russo (n 2), 43.

[11]   See Minouche Shafik, *Goodbye ambiguity, hello clarity: the Bank of England's relationship with financial markets*, Speech delivered at the University of Warwick, 26 February 2015, available at www.bankofengland.co.uk/publications/Pages/speeches/default.aspx.

[12]   www.bankofengland.co.uk/news/2014/march/boe-launches-strategic-plan.

arrangements, and reconfiguring some of its reporting lines and internal structure.[13] The governance, transparency and accountability of the Bank of England were also strengthened with the enactment of the Bank of England and Financial Services Act 2016.[14] So, for instance, the Bank is now subjected to the scrutiny of the National Audit Committee that carries out 'value-for-money' reviews of the Bank. Also, the Prudential Regulation Authority and the Financial Policy Committee are now both committees of the Bank. The Membership of the governing body of the Bank, the Court, has also been changed and the latter has now been given broader oversight responsibilities.

The Financial Conduct Authority (FCA) improved its internal audit, established periodic governance reviews, and it is broadly more transparent.[15] Jointly with the Prudential Regulation Committee (PRC), it has also launched investigations into banking failures where supervision played a role.[16] The Bank, the PRC and the FCA seem to engage in a constructive dialogue with the Treasury Select Committee of the House of Commons (TC). To an extent, this means that authorities are increasingly demonstrating their intention to set higher standards of behaviour for themselves and to lead by example. For instance, both the Bank of England and the FCA applied the stringent Senior Mangers Regime to their own functions,[17] even though they were not legally required to do so.

In light of this, yet acknowledging the existence of still unresolved deficiencies[18] and of recent allegations of lack of transparency,[19] our focus will be on the one aspect of regulatory action which can be viewed as a litmus test to assess their behaviour, namely enforcement activities. The reason why enforcement is key to ethical behaviour is because this is an area where discretion is widely used and where subjects under investigation do not enjoy the same level of legal protection enjoyed in Courts. The process that leads to settlement or private

---

[13]   See Bank of England Response to the Resignation of Charlotte Hogg, available at www .bankofengland.co.uk/news/2017/march/boe-response-to-the-resignation-of-charlotte-hogg.

[14]   www.legislation.gov.uk/ukpga/2016/14/contents/enacted.

[15]   See Russo (n 2), 40, 41, 52.

[16]   See, FCA, PRA, *The Failure of HBOS plc (HBOS)*, November 2015, available at https://www .bankofengland.co.uk/-/media/boe/files/prudential-regulation/publication/hbos-complete-report.pdf?la= en&hash=35CB2876FD81928B886B1B30E0B0E9BB2D6B99BA.

[17]   See *SMR and the FCA*, available at www.fca.org.uk/publication/corporate/applying-smr-to-fca .pdf; and *PRA and the SMR*, December 2017, available at www.bankofengland.co.uk/-/media/boe/files/ about/human-resources/smr.pdf.

[18]   These have been highlighted both in Russo (n 2), and in the following joint report: New City Agenda and Cass Business School, *Cultural change in the FCA, PRA & Bank of England: Practising what they preach?*, 29 August 2016, available at https://newcityagenda.co.uk/wp-content/uploads/2016/ 10/NCA-Cultural-change-in-regulators-report_embargoed.pdf.

[19]   The FCA has been recently heavily criticised for refusing to make public a report on RBS mistreatment of thousands of small businesses by its Global Restructuring Group. The report was then handed over to the Parliament, see TC, *Treasury Committee has received RBS-GRG Report from FCA*, 16 February 2018, available at https://www.parliament.uk/business/committees/committees-a-z/commons -select/treasury-committee/news-parliament-2017/rbs-global-restructuring-group-report-received-17 -19/. See also the criticisms related to the delayed publication of the HBOS report which also led to a review of the so-called Maxwellisation process from the UK Parliament. See FT, *FCA bundles together two HBOS investigations after delay*, 18 July 2017, available at www.ft.com/content/5edf64e7 -64b9-32be-b7a4-f5e1636aa3bf and TC, *Maxwellisation inquiry*, available at www.parliament.uk/ business/committees/committees-a-z/commons-select/treasury-committee/inquiries1/parliament-2017/ maxwellisation-17-19/.

warning, part of enforcement activities, may lack transparency, both towards the public and towards the subjects investigated. Finally, enforcement also offers the chance to observe the inherent tensions between the different interests at stake when making a decision. These include, but are not limited to: the public interest in the exercise of justice and in the accuracy of administrative decision-making,[20] the interests of those under investigation in being treated fairly and impartially, the interest of the staff in a fair workload, the interest of the market in effective oversight, the interest of investors who rely on authorities' correct exercise of their functions, and the interest of regulators themselves in achieving enforcement objectives.

This chapter wants to explore how discretion is used in choosing the most appropriate action between supervision and enforcement. A further aim is to analyse the FCA's response to widespread criticisms of their use of enforcement powers to comment on whether the corresponding changes to the Handbook – a homage to fairness and transparency – can still expose the Authority to criticisms. Finally, the chapter critically reflects on the role of transparency in regulatory activities.

This work considers the FCA only. While there are instances where the PRC and the FCA have to cooperate on an investigation or where the PRC is the exclusively responsible regulator, the latter has not concluded any relevant enforcement investigation so far and is admittedly more focused on *ex ante* supervision, rather than on remedial action. Therefore, the experience of the PRC in the area is comparatively limited.

The chapter is organised as follows: it will first describe the drivers and tensions behind the use of enforcement versus supervisory powers, to move on to discuss the enforcement process and some ethical problems raised by enforcement action. The following sections consider the two most recent major reviews of enforcement at the FCA and how the Authority response may give rise to unintended criticisms. Finally, the chapter critically analyses whether transparency is a suitable tool to ensure the ethical behaviour and credibility of a regulator.

ENFORCEMENT OR SUPERVISION: HOW TO STRIKE THE RIGHT BALANCE?

Enforcement may not be the default option for the Authority to remedy possible regulatory infringements. It is a time-consuming, costly[21] and resource-intensive exercise, which starts with a forensic process.[22] The investigation may not necessarily lead to enforcement action. In fact, not even the latter may lead to the imposition of a penalty. In these cases, the investigation and enforcement process should not be seen as a 'wasted effort' *per se*, but as a useful exercise which 'can remove any suspicion that there is serious wrongdoing and exonerate those who might have been under suspicion. More particularly, the result of an investigation will produce

---

[20]   *Stephen Cooper v FCA* [2017] UKUT 428 (TCC) at para 80.
[21]   For instance, a recent FOI request to the FCA highlighted that during the first ten months of 2017, 108 investigations were initiated which ended with a 'no action' decision. The external cost (such as external contractors, counsel, experts and professional services) to the FCA for these investigations amounted to £794,779.03. See FOI 5448 available at www.fca.org.uk/publication/foi/foi5448-response .pdf.
[22]   See FCA, *Our Future Mission*, October 2016, at 44, available at www.fca.org.uk/publication/corporate/our-future-mission.pdf.

insight and learning that ought to be captured so as to be useful to the firm and . . . as an aid to better compliance'.[23] Overall, it could improve regulatory action and intelligence.

Given the efforts required however, the FCA will need to consider carefully if alternative options are available. Basically, the right balance has to be struck in choosing between supervisory and enforcement actions.

By focusing on the former, the regulator may impose certain requirements on a firm or prevent it from continuing a certain activity. It could also impose restrictions on the financial products offered, or make firms pay redress to consumers if harm to them has been ascertained. Ensuring that the most effective action is taken should not only consider FCA interests and the achievement of its statutory objectives, but also what would be fair for the subject(s) under investigation. Supervisory tools may be successful in achieving the same objectives sought by enforcement action. Deciding which option to choose however, leaves open the question of how much weight the FCA should give to the interests of those impacted by the action of the subject(s) under investigation and whether fairness towards the former would have to prevail in the regulator's overall assessment.

One should also acknowledge that the decision to use a supervisory tool rather than enforcement action could be influenced by the existence of possible conflicts between the two functions. Ongoing supervision is an activity that allows the supervisory team to develop a historical knowledge of the firm, to understand its dynamics, assess progress – where any – and to make a broader judgement on the firm's conduct. Its overall purpose is preventive and therefore focused on the effectiveness of *ex ante* action. As opposed to enforcement, supervision relies considerably on cooperation and on a good relationship with the firm.

The view of the enforcement team is arguably narrower in that it only looks at the specific case and it is less based on a rounded and more detailed evaluation of the firm due to their limited know-how. This is because the enforcement team is not involved in the day-to-day supervision of the firm. Enforcement is remedial in scope and driven by a disciplining objective.

Given that the decision to refer a case to the enforcement team is taken by the supervisory team and that the two are independent from each other, one can see how the different 'mind-sets' may come into play in deciding whether or not to make a referral. While the provision of the assistance of the supervisory team to the enforcement colleagues during the investigation[24] may reduce the information asymmetry, it does not eliminate the initial bias the supervisory team may have in making the referral decision.

By the same reasoning, it could be argued that the choice among these options has an impact on the type of deterrence effect sought. Also, one could speculate that a judgement-led risk-based regulator will pay greater attention to the *ex ante* aspects of supervision rather than to remedial action.

To mitigate this tension, it is possible that both supervisory and enforcement powers can be applied in the same case.

This balancing act between enforcement and supervision is reflected in the FCA approach to enforcement as included in their Enforcement Guide (EG). There are cases where enforcement is expected, as when the threshold conditions are no longer met. In this case however, firms

---

[23] See FCA, *Our Future Mission*, October 2016, at 46, available at www.fca.org.uk/publication/corporate/our-future-mission.pdf.

[24] EG [4.9].

will normally be given the opportunity to remedy the harm before formal proceedings are initiated.

In a case of suspected unauthorised activity the FCA would be expected to start proceedings due to the potential harm to consumers. But before that, the FCA will consider a broad range of factors that may tip the balance in favour of the use of other powers. So, for instance, the FCA will evaluate the elements of the breach, whether the person is willing to cooperate and whether the undertaking of remedial action has been offered.[25]

Another example comes from breaches of the listing regime, where supervisory tools are in fact limited. Or where there are instances of market abuse and other misconduct punishable with criminal sanctions. In most cases, the FCA will consider a non-exhaustive set of criteria in determining whether investigators should be appointed.

Finally, the FCA may be required by EU law to cooperate with foreign investigators, with the PRC investigations, which can indeed be joint, or to assist overseas investigations if requested.[26]

More generally, the FCA approach to enforcement gives consideration to certain facts or objectives when deciding between the two actions. For instance, the FCA will consider the existence of an open and cooperative relationship with its regulatees, but also the existence of a proactive supervision on its side; the need to use powers in a 'manner that is transparent, proportionate, responsive to the issue, and consistent with its publicly stated policies';[27] the need to ensure fair treatment of the subjects under investigation; the need to discourage future non-compliance by others; and the need to change the behaviour of the subject investigated as well as to remedy the harm caused by non-compliance whenever possible.[28]

Overall, enforcement is framed within the broader character of the FCA as a judgement-led risk-based regulator. As such, the decision to initiate an investigation will follow an assessment of priorities – also on the basis of the thematic reviews – and the severity of threats posed to FCA aims and objectives.

However, we should remember that enforcement is not only a tool to achieve statutory objectives or to exercise deterrence. It is also a means to raise awareness of regulatory standards[29] and to give teeth to the FCA Principles of Business, considering that their violation leads to investigations.

What are the elements that the FCA will take into account in deciding whether or not to take enforcement action? Referral criteria are actually framed as a set of questions which strive to comply with the overarching goal as to whether the investigation is likely to further the FCA's aims and statutory objectives.[30] To do so, the FCA will consider three aspects:[31] (1) evidence, proportionality and the impact of opening the investigation; (2) the final purpose or goal of the investigation; and (3) factors that needs assessing to ascertain whether the purpose of the investigation is met.

---

[25]   EG [2.4.3].

[26]   For an explanation of all those cases, see EG [2.2].

[27]   See EG [2.1.2 (2)].

[28]   See EG [2.1.2].

[29]   See EG [2.1.1].

[30]   See www.fca.org.uk/about/enforcement/referral-criteria.

[31]   See www.fca.org.uk/about/enforcement/referral-criteria.

With respect to evidence and proportionality the FCA will look at the strength of the evidence which is or may become available, and whether the enforcement action is proportionate to the seriousness of the failing, the amount and availability of resources needed, and the impact it may have on the subject of the investigation, especially if it is an individual. The FCA will also look at whether action is being taken by another authority or agency (in the United Kingdom or abroad).[32]

With regard to the final purpose and goal of the investigation, the FCA takes a 'strategic and risk based approach to enforcement.[33] This in practice means that the discretion used to decide whether to investigate will consider the deterrent effect, or lack thereof, enforcement action may have. Deterrence[34] is considered both at a general level (deterring others from offending, setting clear direction for the market and changing behaviour in the industry) and at a specific level (deterring the person from re-offending). Deterrence is also a specific objective for financial penalties.[35]

However, deterrence is not the only consideration that comes into play. Justice and protection are as important. Justice is achieved by inflicting proportionate penalties and sanctions on those responsible, whereas protection implies removing wrongdoers from the industry or the imposition of other restrictions as appropriate.[36]

Finally, the factors that need to be assessed to determine whether the purpose of the investigation is met are several and also articulated in the form of questions. These incorporate broader public, market and regulatory considerations relevant to the achievement of general and specific deterrence, justice and protection.[37]

The FCA therefore does not consider the evidentiary stage or whether it is likely to conclude successfully its disciplinary proceedings. However, the HBOS case highlighted that the FCA's predecessor, the FSA, had a recognised tendency not to investigate even when the threshold test was met and when there was public interest in enforcement because of a perceived fear of losing the case in court due to the evidence needed to prove personal culpability.[38] To an extent, it is still too early to assess whether the FCA will not succumb to the same fear.

---

[32]   In March 2017, the FCA came under the spotlight for not having investigated RBS and Standard Chartered over an alleged corruption episode. See https://www.ft.com/content/f4ec7648-23cf-11e8-add1 -0e8958b189ea#myft:saved-articles:page. Under FSMA [169], UK financial regulators should cooperate with overseas investigations if requested.

[33]   See www.fca.org.uk/about/enforcement/referral-criteria.

[34]   For a discussion on deterrence, see A Georgosouli, 'What makes deterrence credible?', Chapter 13 in this book.

[35]   See DEPP 6.1.2: 'The principal purpose of imposing a financial penalty or issuing a public censure is to promote high standards of regulatory and/or market conduct by deterring persons who have committed breaches from committing further breaches, helping to deter other persons from committing similar breaches, and demonstrating generally the benefits of compliant behaviour. Financial penalties and public censures are therefore tools that the FCA may employ to help it to achieve its statutory objectives.'

[36]   See FCA, Referral criteria (n 30).

[37]   The full list is available on the website, at www.fca.org.uk/about/enforcement/referral-criteria.

[38]   See Andrew Green, *Report into the FSA's enforcement action following the failure of HBOS*, November 2015, available at www.bankofengland.co.uk/-/media/boe/files/report/2015/ andrew-green-report-into-fca-enforcement-actions-following-failure-of-hbos.pdf?la=en&hash= 8A4DFC882AF297ADFCC2CA5E9E8941C1E064FB31p 12 (c).

The approach to enforcement and the referral criteria highlight how the FCA process is not judicial but administrative in nature.[39] By this, it is intended that public agencies such as the FCA, may not apply the same level of substantial fairness that is applied in courts. This consideration is relevant to determine the standard of procedural fairness expected from the regulator.

THE ENFORCEMENT PROCESS

The regulation of enforcement is included in the Financial Services and Markets Act (FSMA). FSMA however, covers only certain aspects of the enforcement cycle,[40] delegating the authorities to issue procedures and further rules on the matter. These are included in the supervisory Handbook, under 'Decision Procedure and Penalty Manual' (DEPP) and 'Enforcement Guide' (EG).[41] The FCA is fairly transparent on procedural aspects, publishing also an 'Enforcement Information Guide' and an 'Enforcement Annual Performance Account'. Information is also given on the composition of the Regulatory Decision Committee (RDC)[42] and on referral criteria.[43]

---

[39] For the two-prong test normally followed by public prosecutors (the evidence and the public interest test), see the Prosecutors Code and the DPP Guidance on Charging, available at www.cps.gov .uk/publication/full-code-test.

[40] Most notably: third party rights, statutory and related notices, right to have access to materials and its limitation, right to make representations, information gathering and investigators appointment, imposition of penalties.

[41] DEPP disciplines: statutory notices, the nature and process of the Regulatory Decisions Committee, the decisions by FCA staff under executive procedures, settlement decisions procedure, penalties, powers to impose a suspension, restriction, condition, limitation or disciplinary prohibition, statement of policies on interviews conducted on behalf of overseas and EEA regulators, and transitional provisions. EG covers: the FCA approach to enforcement, the use of information gathering and investigation powers, the conduct of investigation, settlement, publicity, financial penalty and other disciplinary functions, variation of firm's permission, prohibition order and withdrawal of approval, injunction, restitution and redress, prosecution of criminal offences, FCA approach in insolvency proceedings, exercise of powers in relation to Collective Investment Schemes, disqualification of auditors and actuaries, disapplication orders against members of the profession and enforcement of the Consumers Credit Act. DEPP and EG are available at www.handbook.fca.org.uk.

[42] The RDC is the independent decision-making body of the FCA. Technically it is a committee of the FCA Board, but it is operationally separate from the FCA. Only the Chair is employed directly by the FCA. It is also separate from 'the FCA Enforcement, Supervision and Authorisations teams that conduct investigations or consider applications for authorisation or approval', see www.fca.org.uk/about/ committees/regulatory-decisions-committee-rdc. The RDC includes practitioners and non-practitioners drawn from a variety of industry background. However, some members usually comes from a legal background with experience in litigation to contribute to the fairness of the process. To make the process fair, the RDC also has access to their own legal advisers and support staff. See www.fca.org.uk/ about/committees/rdc-members. The legal basis for the RDC, which insists on the independence of the decision-making body and which applies to the PRC too, is included in s 395 FSMA. For more details on the RDC see also DEPP [3].

[43] See www.fca.org.uk/about/enforcement/referral-criteria. Also, important information on the matter is included in EG 2 (The FCA's approach to enforcement), which covers 'Case selection and the use of enforcement powers' (EG 2.1) and 'Case selection and referral criteria' (EG 2.2).

The enforcement process works roughly as follows[44]: (1) FCA appoints internal investigators; (2) investigators scope the discussion with the firm and start the actual investigation; (3) following the investigation work, there is an internal legal review of the case by a lawyer who has not been part of the investigation;[45] (4) if appropriate, a Preliminary Finding Letter with an annexed Preliminary Investigation Report (PIR) is sent to the firm or the individual who has a reasonable time (usually 28 days) to respond; (5) if, following their investigation, it is believed that action is justified, investigators submit case papers to the RDC; (6) the RDC will decide whether it is appropriate to issue a Warning Notice informing the person of the FCA intention to take further action. The person will be given a reasonable time (usually 14 days) to make a written representation to the RDC; (7) if the RDC finds there is no case, either before or after representations, the FCA closes the investigation, issuing a notice of Discontinuance; (8) if the RDC thinks there is a role for enforcement, the enforcement process starts and terminates with a decision notice.[46] The FCA may close the investigation at any stage in the procedure.[47]

There are different options available to the firm or the individual (the person) under investigation before this reaches the RDC. For instance, having received the PIR the person may reach an agreement with the FCA. In what is called the early resolution stage, the parties may agree on all issues, or on issues of facts and liability and contest the penalty before the RDC or agree on the facts while contesting all or part of the liability and penalty. Should they reach an agreement in the early stage (also called stage 1),[48] the person can access a discount scheme. The scheme allows for a reduction of the financial penalty of up to 30 per cent.[49] The discount scheme applies also to suspensions, restrictions, conditions and disciplinary prohibitions imposed under s 123A FSMA.

Obviously, the person can contest all issues to the RDC. Since 2017, the person has also been able to refer the case directly to the Upper Tribunal following a 'fast track' procedure without making representations to the RDC.

---

[44]   For a more detailed explanation see FCA, *Enforcement Information Guide*, April 2017, available at www.fca.org.uk/publication/corporate/enforcement-information-guide.pdf.

[45]   The existence of a separate lawyer is one of the recommended actions of the 2005 Strachan Review, which is the first internal review of the recent past to question enforcement practices at the FSA, the FCA's predecessor. More information at FSA, *FSA publishes recommendations of enforcement process review*, FSA/PN/082/2005, 19 July 2005, available at www.fsa.gov.uk/library/communication/pr/2005/082.shtml. This requirement 'will help to ensure that there is consistency in the way in which our cases are put and that they are supported by sufficient evidence. A lawyer who has not been a part of the investigation team will also review warning notices before they are submitted to the settlement decision makers'. See EP [2.14.1].

[46]   See also Russo (n 2) at 51.

[47]   See FCA (n 44), 5.

[48]   'Stage 1 is the period from commencement of an investigation until the FCA has a sufficient understanding of the nature and gravity of the breach to make a reasonable assessment of the appropriate penalty (or suspension, restriction, condition or disciplinary prohibition, or combination thereof). The FCA, at stage 1, also needs to have communicated that assessment to the person concerned and allowed a reasonable opportunity to reach agreement as to the amount of penalty or the length of any suspension, restriction, condition or temporary disciplinary prohibition.' EG 5.5.2.

[49]   The Discount scheme works as follows: 30% of penalty discount for full agreement of facts, liability and penalty or for full agreement of facts and liability (but not penalty); 15-30% at the discretion of the RDC for full agreement of facts (but not liability or penalty); 0-30% at the discretion of the RDC in case of partial agreement as to facts, liability and penalty (leaving a narrow set of issues in dispute). See DEPP 6.7 3A and 5.1 and FCA (n 41), 4.

In cases where parties reach an early resolution agreement, even partial, the FCA will issue a focused resolution agreement followed by a Warning Notice. A warning notice will also be issued by the RDC if the case reaches it and the RDC finds it appropriate to take further action.

Finally, the person can also make oral representations before the RDC in a subsequent meeting, after having presented written statements.

After the decision notice has been issued, the person has 28 days to refer the case to the Upper Tribunal. The Tribunal will decide independently of the FCA and the person. In fact, the Upper Tribunal is an integral part of the 'regulatory scheme designed to produce quality decision making'[50] and to ensure regulatory action follows a fair process. After the decision of the Tribunal or if no referral is made, the FCA will issue a final notice. In the first case, the person could then appeal to the Court of Appeal.

The FCA retains discretion to publish information about certain warning notices and about the matter to which a decision or final notice relates as required or considered appropriate.

The person can bring claims to the Upper Tribunal against the decision included in the notice.

THE ETHICAL PROBLEMS RAISED BY ENFORCEMENT ACTIONS

Enforcement action and practices often give rise to discontent among the subjects of investigations. Lawsuits brought against the FCA show that claimants base their concerns on a perceived lack of fairness, on the use of disproportionate actions, or on the violation of human rights principles when action is directed against individuals (as opposed to the firm).

In the recent past, judges have partially sided with some of those claims, and either expressed 'wholesale disagreement'[51] at the financial penalty imposed by the supervisor, or accused the Authority of 'acting unreasonably'[52] in pursuing a certain allegation.[53] This also translated into the award of costs in favour of the claimant (against the Authority) despite ascertaining regulatory breaches.[54] In one case subsequently reversed on appeal, one judge found that the supervisor failed to give 'adequate reasons' in their decision notice.[55] In a few cases, judges considered whether the Authority had violated third party rights not to be identified in the final notice: courts reached different conclusions on one highly contested case,[56] highlighting the divergence of opinions on a matter which has issues of fairness at its core. In another case, one

---

[50] *Stephen Cooper v FCA* (n 20), at para 80.

[51] *Burns v FCA* [2015] UKUT 0252 (TCC) at para 16.

[52] *Burns v FCA* [2015] UKUT 0601 (TCC) at para 57.

[53] One judge refrained from agreeing with a claimant that accused the FCA of 'inconsistent and irrational decision making' in two related cased, but acknowledged that the disclosure of some of the evidence of the other case may be of some assistance to the claimant. *Hussein v Financial Conduct Authority* [2016] UKUT 549 (TCC) at paras 134 and 135.

[54] *Burns v FCA* [2017] EWCA Civ 2140 and [2015] UKUT 0601 (TCC).

[55] *R (on the application of C) v Financial Services Authority* [2012] EWHC 1417 (Admin). The decision has been overturned by [2013] EWCA Civ 677.

[56] *Macri v Financial Conduct Authority* [2015] EWCA Civ 490, where the Court of Appeal confirmed the Upper Tribunal decision in favour of the claimant that alleged to have been identified for the purposes of s 393 FSMA in a notice given to his employer, a bank. However, the decision was subsequently overturned by the Supreme Court although not unanimously. *FCA v Macris* [2017] UKSC 19.

judge expressed 'considerable sympathy'[57] with the claimant for the way the FCA had dealt with a Private Warning Notice.

Private Warning Notices, which can be issued to anyone and not just to approved persons, are at the fringes of enforcement action. These are not statutory notices and in principle a formal investigation is not a precondition for issuing the warning. However, these are a serious form of reprimand by the FCA and may give the recipient the impression that a formal investigation is or will soon be taking place. This is because a private warning 'tells the subject of the warning that the FCA has seriously considered formal steps to impose a penalty or censure'.[58] Yet the investigatory process that leads to the notice seems to be lacking transparency. Prior to issuing the warning, the FCA informs the person that it is 'minded to'[59] do it, and the person can offer their observations. The FCA will consider them carefully before deciding whether to issue the warning.[60]

However, anecdotal evidence reveals how subjects of the investigation perceive the warnings as an 'enforcement by the back door'.[61] Its fairness can also be questioned on the grounds that the issue is not covered by the same level of legal protection applicable to other statutory notices, yet the warning is not limited to cases of minor misconduct but can express more serious concerns.[62] This is exemplified both by the needed evidence and by the applicability of the same criteria included in the penalty manual to decide whether to issue the warning.[63]

The ability of the recipient to challenge the warning in front of the RDC appears to be hampered by the fact this is not a statutory notice issued within a formal enforcement procedure. One could argue that the warning can be challenged directly via judicial review, but this will make it public, perhaps exposing the person to outrage (for a breach that may not have occurred). It will also defeat the purpose of the warning which is meant as a private – not public – reprimand.

In 2016 the FCA consulted on,[64] among the other issues, on whether private warnings were consistent with the FCA's view on transparency. The question was part of a broader consultation on how the FCA regulates and on how they decide their priorities against a number of critical areas. At the time of writing, the FCA indicated its intention to commence an *ad hoc* consultation on private warnings.

In addition, there are two strong ethical concerns with these warnings. One is of a private nature and the other of a regulatory policy nature. The former relates to the weight they actually carry after being issued. Even though a private warning 'is not intended to be a determination by the FCA as to whether the recipient has breached the FCA's rules',[65] it nonetheless

---

One case relying on the judgment of the Supreme Court was subsequently withdrawn, *Martin-Artajo v Financial Conduct Authority* [2014] UKUT 340 (TCC).

57   *Stephen Cooper v FCA* (n 20), at para 124.
58   EG [7.6.2].
59   EG [7.8.1].
60   EG [7.8.1].
61   See FT, *City Watchdog in private warning blitz*, 19 October 2014, available at www.ft.com/content/b9ae4d2e-561c-11e4-bbd6-00144feab7de.
62   See for instance concerns related to the use of private warnings to settle possible disputes related to the rigging of LIBOR and FOREX discussed in FT (n 61).
63   DEPP [6].
64   FCA, *Our Future Mission* (n 22), 45.
65   EG [7.6.6].

will be in the compliance record of the person, its existence will be taken into account in future decisions to start investigations (even if the warning was issued long before), and it can also be an aggravating factor in determining the level of penalty. Its existence has to (and part of the warning may have to) be disclosed to future employers. Therefore, it is easy to understand why private warnings are a source of grievance for the recipients: they are a very powerful tool apt to cast a long shadow of suspicion on the person without necessarily being sustained by strong evidence.

From a policy perspective, the risk is that regulators may resort to private warnings because these are less onerous in terms of resources, level of investigation and – most strikingly – burden of proof required as opposed to what is needed to start full investigations. Eventually, the warning may have a considerable impact on the recipient both in terms of behavioural change and future career prospects, which is in line with the enforcement objective of deterrence. However, it would be unethical for the regulator to take shortcuts to achieve this, even when giving consideration to an authority's strained resources. It could be more appropriate for the regulator to ask for more resources and for a change in its own funding mechanisms. To this end, the provision that prohibits the FCA from using financial penalties towards its own budget seems overly cautious. While its rationale is clear, namely the need to avoid opportunistic behaviour on the part of the FCA when deciding the amount and/or the type of sanction to apply, it seems to denote a lack of trust in the regulator's fair use of powers. It is also unclear whether there is any demonstrable evidence of the existence of such opportunistic behaviour of the regulator.

The use of a shortcut will also seriously undermine the trust that regulatees have in the Authority, therefore affecting the cooperative relationship with them.

On the other hand, the alleged achievement of a deterrence effect via private warnings is a double-edged sword. The culpable recipient may interpret a possible lack of further enforcement action as a weakness on the regulator's side with a negative effect on the perceived credibility of the latter. This means that for the regulator to be credible, it will have to follow up with an investigation in all those cases where the breach may appear to be serious.

The settlement agreement during stage 1 may create ethical concerns too. As a reminder,[66] stage 1 covers the period of time 'from commencement of an investigation until the FCA has a sufficient understanding of the nature and gravity of the breach to make a reasonable assessment of the appropriate penalty', and where the FCA 'also needs to have communicated that assessment to the person concerned and allowed a reasonable opportunity to reach agreement as to the amount of penalty'.[67]

The person under investigation may have an incentive to settle[68] during this stage, for three reasons: (1) early settlement will close the matter swiftly without leaving the person entangled in the process for an undefinable period; (2) they may benefit from a penalty discount; and (3) settlement may give the person some (limited) negotiating powers as to the wording of the

---

[66]   See in this chapter, at n 48.

[67]   EG [5.5.2].

[68]   Settlement may be in the public interest too. As explained by the FCA 'Early settlement has many potential advantages as it can result, for example, in consumers obtaining compensation earlier than would otherwise be the case, the saving of FCA and industry resources, messages getting out to the market sooner and a public perception of timely and effective action. The FCA therefore considers it is in the public interest for matters to settle, and settle early, if possible'. EG [5.1.1].

facts stated in the final notice. The importance of this latter point can be fully appreciated if one considers that a person may be particularly minded of the reputational consequences of a full public disclosure.

Because of those incentives the person may indeed settle, however they would do so with only a limited amount of information at their disposal on the actual charges and the FCA evidence. At that stage even the start of a referral to the RDC cannot be taken for granted.

The amount of information shared by the FCA with the person is indeed relatively limited. There are two main documents issued to them at this stage: the so-called stage 1 letter and the PIR (mentioned above). As also mentioned, upon the appointment of investigators, the FCA holds a scoping meeting with the person under investigation. Its content is usually broad and mostly based on the procedural aspects of the investigation. Therefore, the amount of valuable information shared is not normally extensive.

The stage 1 letter is sent by the FCA to the person prior to deciding whether to refer the matter to the RDC and it normally includes the preliminary findings report. The person has 28 days to respond to the allegations therein. The EG covers the content of this letter very broadly,[69] merely recognising the useful role it has in focusing the decision making on the 'contentious issues in the case'[70] and that the letter 'will set out the facts which the investigators consider relevant to the matters under investigation'.[71] Firms have complained about having received knowledge of certain allegations and evidence against them only in the PIR[72] or that PIRs are not always provided and are instead substituted by a high level summary (probably because the production of a PIR is an onerous and costly process).[73] The ability of the person to rebut or clarify certain facts is normally limited to responding to the letter.

Following an HMT Review,[74] the FCA has agreed to widen the amount of information given at this stage to include the 'key factual and legal basis'[75] for their view so as to enable the person to understand the 'nature and the extent of the charges'.[76] Periodic updates on the investigation can now be expected. The content of scoping meetings has been widened to better reflect the understanding of the case by the FCA and a pre-stage 1 meeting has been introduced.

---

[69] EG [4.13].

[70] EG [4.13.2].

[71] EG [4.13.3].

[72] Linklaters, *HMT Review of enforcement decision-making at the financial services regulators*. Linklaters' response to the Call for Evidence, available at www.linklaters.com%2F-%2Fmedia%2Ffiles%2Flinklaters%2Fpdf%2Fpdfns%2F140704_client_version_response_to_hmt_call_for_evidence_10975.ashx%3Fla%3Dde-de%26rev%3Db24e9991-21e3-4640-aebe-290ce6c2e195%26hash%3D7B18F126F12D55BBC865C2E21CB63DC8C613B650&usg=AOvVaw2LpBI2tI3wSegG3-lOJjol at para 4.5, p 5. EG [5.5.2].

[73] HM Treasury, *Review of enforcement decision-making at the financial services regulators: final report*, December 2014, available at https://assets.publishing.service.gov.uk/government/uploads/system/uploads/attachment_data/file/389063/enforcement_review_response_final.pdf, at 5.8, p 29; Linklaters (n 72), at para 4.5, p 5.

[74] HM Treasury (n 73). The review is analysed in depth in the next section.

[75] EG [5.5.2].

[76] See FCA and PRA, *Implementation of the Enforcement Review and the Green Report*, Policy Statement FCA PS 17/1 PRA PS 2/17, February 2017, available at www.fca.org.uk/publication/policy/ps17-01.pdf, p 23.

In the most recent past, enforcement activities of the regulator have been under the lens of public scrutiny too. In the 2013 report of the Parliamentary Commission on Banking Standards (PCBS) on 'Changing Banking for Good' a section was dedicated to 'Sanctions and Enforcement'.[77] The PCBS commented on the record of regulatory enforcement against firms as 'patchy at its best'.[78] In December 2014, the UK Treasury issued its final report on the 'Review of enforcement decision making at the financial services regulators',[79] which followed a call for evidence issued by the Treasury a few months earlier. The call for evidence solicited views 'on the overall effectiveness of current enforcement decision making processes at the regulators' and 'on whether the processes and supporting institutional arrangements deliver an appropriate balance between fairness, transparency, speed and efficiency'.[80]

Enforcement practices at the then FSA were also the subject of a specific chapter of the 2016 final report of the Treasury Select Committee of the House of Commons (TC) into the failure of HBOS.[81] The report references the independent investigation carried out by Andrew Green at the request of the TC on the reasonableness of FSA's enforcement actions after the demise of HBOS (the Green Report).[82]

Among the concerns of the Committee was the unsatisfactory level of enforcement actions against individuals following the now well-documented cases of misconduct in the financial industry, such as the LIBOR and PPI scandals, or the bank failures propelled by mismanagement leading to the financial crisis. They also express outrage at the amount of fines issued as 'pitiful compared to the benefits banks gained through the misconduct'.[83]

Aside from those evaluations however, the Green Report and the HMT Review raise important issues worth considering here. Before moving on to their analysis, it is important to stress one caveat. The above analysis and the reported case law have mentioned that in certain cases enforcement action may lack aspects of procedural due process, which is indeed worrisome. However, one should keep in mind that the yardstick for evaluating regulators' actions is not the same of a Tribunal, where parties enjoy the highest standards of protection. This is not to imply of course that FCA standards can be lower. Quite the contrary in fact, considering that regulators act on behalf of and are the repository of the trust of society and are the guardians of market integrity. As said above, they are also extremely powerful in that they exercise functions which are normally separated. The point is that it would be unrealistic to expect no substantive mistakes by the regulators.

---

[77] See House of Lords and House of Commons, *Changing Banking for Good. Report of the Parliamentary Commission on Banking Standards*, Vol I and II, July 2013, available at www.parliament .uk/business/committees/committees-a-z/joint-select/professional-standards-in-the-banking-industry/ news/changing-banking-for-good-report/.

[78] See PCBS Report above, Vol II at para 1129.

[79] HM Treasury (n 73).

[80] See HM Treasury, *Review of enforcement decision-making at the financial services regulators: call for evidence*, available at https://www.gov.uk/government/consultations/review-of-enforcement -decision-makin.

[81] TC, *Review of the Reports into the Failure of HBOS*, HC 582, 26 July 2016, available at https:// publications.parliament.uk/pa/cm201617/cmselect/cmtreasy/582/582.pdf.

[82] PRA, FCA, *Report into the FSA's enforcement actions following the failure of HBOS* by Andrew Green QC November 2015, available at www.bankofengland.co.uk/-/media/boe/files/report/ 2015/andrew-green-report-into-fca-enforcement-actions-following-failure-of-hbos.pdf?la=en&hash= 8A4DFC882AF297ADFCC2CA5E9E8941C1E064FB31.

[83] PCBS (n 77), para 1132.

What should come into consideration is instead the governance mechanisms related to enforcement, how cases are being handled by staff, and the 'good faith', competence, and fairness in dealing with people under investigation. If those aspects are deficient, then mistakes or poor judgement have to be assessed more rigorously.

THE GREEN REPORT AND THE HMT REVIEW

In December 2014, the HMT issued their final report on the review of enforcement decision-making (HMT Review). The review focused on the following aspects: referral decision-making; cooperation between the regulators; subjects' understanding and representations; settlement; and contested case decision-making. The broad aim of the review was to ensure 'transparency, fairness, effectiveness and speed of enforcement decision-making at the financial regulators'.[84] Unsurprisingly, respondents to the preceding consultation focused their concerns mainly on the referral and the settlement decision-making strategy, while being broadly satisfied with 'current decision-making process and arrangements'.[85]

HMT made a set of recommendations aimed at 'taking the right action',[86] in relation to the alternative between tough enforcement actions or robust supervisory action; and at 'maintaining effective coordination between the FCA and the PRA',[87] in terms of increased transparency of the regulators' relationship in joint investigations and contested cases. Finally, recommendations focused on 'improving the process, enhancing capacity and creating a system which is fair for all'.[88] To this end, regulators were invited to provide more information, more often, to the subjects under investigation[89] and ensure that the members of the relevant decision-making committees (the RDC in the FCA case, referred to in the report as 'contested decision makers') regularly review the regulators processes in settled cases.[90] However, firms and individuals are also expected and encouraged to admit wrongdoing at an early stage.[91]

In terms of fairness, the latter should feel confident to challenge decisions in front of an objective and independent decision-maker, therefore HMT recommended the creation of an independent contested case decision-making committee at the PRC.[92] A further recommendation relates to the need to set up a fast-track procedure to allow individuals and firms to challenge regulators directly in front of a Tribunal, which has been implemented as mentioned above. Finally, to increase the accountability and efficiency of regulators in contested cases the HMT recommended a 'review and public reporting function', and if the Treasury Committee 'wishes, it should hold pre-commencement hearings for the chairs of the regulators' decision-makers'.[93]

---

[84]   HM Treasury (n 73), at para 1.7, p 3.
[85]   HM Treasury (n 73), at para 1.7, p 3.
[86]   HM Treasury (n 73), p 4.
[87]   HM Treasury (n 73), p 4.
[88]   HM Treasury (n 73), p 4.
[89]   HM Treasury (n 73), at para 1.14, p 4.
[90]   HM Treasury (n 73), at para 1.16, p 5.
[91]   HM Treasury (n 73), at para 1.15.
[92]   PRA decision-makers are chosen from within PRA staff, unlike the FCA RDC.
[93]   HM Treasury (n 73), at para 1.19.

With specific reference to referral decision-making, the recommendations took an overall balanced account of the suggestions of the respondents (which included law firms). These expressed the need to have clear guidance on the use of discretion in the choice of relevant action and on the referral criteria. Also, firms expressed concerns at the level of FCA transparency on enforcement activities. Despite existing FCA publications on thematic reviews, mission, annual reports and enforcement guidance, a number of respondents felt that more information could be published on 'why some cases were referred for investigation but others were not'.[94]

Therefore, the HMT recommended that the FCA (and the PRC) 'publish referral criteria which explicitly consider whether an enforcement investigation, rather than an alternative regulatory response is the right course in all of the circumstances'[95] and that 'the FCA should provide further examples of cases in which a firm's response to a breach of the regulatory requirement has been a factor in deciding not to take enforcement action'.[96] The referral criteria framework should also be reformed to give more weight to the reasoning behind the choice of regulatory action.

To enhance transparency, HMT also recommended that the FCA publish information on both formal enforcement outcomes and early intervention outcomes, on the enforcement actions taken in each priority area and on those related to thematic reviews. In this latter case, the FCA is asked to explain why certain cases were referred for investigation while others were not.[97]

To increase the amount of information provided to the subjects of an investigation and therefore to enhance fairness, HMT recommended a few changes in the way the FCA deals with these subjects, following suggestions from respondents. These can be grouped into five requests: (1) to release more information to the subjects at the outset of the investigation with a clear link to referral criteria and to promote early and constructive engagement at senior level; (2) to arrange scoping meetings once investigators are in a position to share the direction of their investigation; (3) there should be an enhanced dialogue and information sharing among the supervisory and the enforcement team in relation to the firm's business and relevant market practices; (4) to provide periodic (and detailed) updates to the investigated subjects; (5) as regards warning notices and PIR, regulators should consider, where appropriate, extending the period to respond to notices.[98]

The final review also includes a fair amount of recommendations on settlement procedures. These consider respondents' concerns in depth, and reflect some of their requests. In particular, HMT suggested amending procedures during stage 1, including 'without prejudice meetings', and actual settlement negotiations, discounts and ongoing review. In a nutshell, the HMT recommended an earlier notification of stage 1, the holding of preliminary 'without prejudice' meetings with the subjects to present the key legal and factual basis of the investigation (with the understanding that these can be subject to changes) as well as the key evidence at regulators' disposal. The 28 days post stage 1 investigations should be extended under certain circumstances. To enhance the consideration of the representations made by the subjects

---

[94]   HM Treasury (n 73), at para 2.22.
[95]   HM Treasury (n 73), Recommendation 1, at p 8.
[96]   HM Treasury (n 73), Recommendation 2, at p 9.
[97]   HM Treasury (n 73), Recommendations 6–8, at p 15.
[98]   HM Treasury (n 73), Recommendation 24 at p 26.

during settlement, the relevant Enforcement Head of Department should, where necessary, act as a 'suitably senior conduit'[99] between the case team and the Settlement decision-makers. The Head, or an appropriate substitute, should also attend a 'without prejudice' settlement meeting during stage 1.

The HMT also recommended that invited contested case decision-makers regularly review the regulators' processes in settled cases.[100] 'The review should include seeking comments from all or a sample of those who have settled FCA and PRA enforcement cases, and speaking with the relevant enforcement staff. The review should also monitor the effectiveness of the recommended changes to the settlement process.'[101]

Finally, to increase accountability HMT recommended an annual review of enforcement performance, which includes details of the annual operational review and of those of the settled cases. 'In addition, the TSC might consider requiring the attendance of future RDC and DMC Chairs on a pre-commencement basis.'[102]

The Green Report, issued in 2015, found the HBOS-related enforcement decision-making of the FSA unreasonable.[103] The report makes four recommendations to the FCA and the PRC to improve aspects of the process. These coalesce around: pre-referral decision-making; ongoing dialogue between enforcement and supervision during an investigation; information to share with subjects; and accuracy of executive committee meetings.[104]

It suggested a clearer identification of potential subjects at the pre-referral stage, and that one senior person should be in charge of the whole process. Regular and recorded meetings should take place among members of the supervisory and the enforcement team in relation to the scope of investigation and the possible need to expand the number of subjects on the basis of applicable referral criteria. Consistently with a similar HMT recommendation, the subject of the investigation should be given timely notice of the potential breaches they are going to be investigated for. Finally, minutes of the Executive committee meetings have to be properly reviewed and approved.[105]

BEING TOO RESPONSIVE OR BEING CREDIBLE? THAT IS THE MATTER

In 2016, the FCA and the PRA issued a Consultation Paper (CP)[106] followed by a Policy Statement (PS)[107] where they detail changes to the enforcement process following the Green

---

[99]   HM Treasury (n 73), Recommendation 31 at p 30.
[100] HM Treasury (n 73), Recommendation 33 at p 32.
[101] HM Treasury (n 73), at Recommendation 33 at p 32.
[102] HM Treasury (n 73), Recommendation 37 at p 39.
[103] See the Green Report (n 82), para 9 (a), at p 4.
[104] See the Green Report (n 82), para 356–64, at p 91–2.
[105] See Green Report (n 82), Recommendation 4, para 364 at p 92.
[106] FCA/PRA, *Proposed implementation of the Enforcement Review and the Green Report*, FCA CP 16/10 and PRA 14/16. As mentioned in the Policy Statement, regulators received 13 responses to the CP, from law firms (the majority), individuals, representative bodies and one from the Financial Services Consumer Panel.
[107] FCA/PRA, *Implementation of the Enforcement Review and the Green Report*, Policy Statement FCA PS 17/1 and PRA PS 2/17, February 2017, available at www.fca.org.uk/publication/policy/ps17-01 .pdf.

Report, the HMT Review and responses received to the CP. In 2017, they also described some of the adopted changes in the 'Our Mission'[108] document which was accompanied by a Feedback Statement (FS) on the previous consultation run by the FCA.[109]

Some of the changes to the referral criteria had been implemented before the HMT Review, specifically those related to the governance of the process and collaboration among teams.

In the PS, the FCA decided not to issue general guidance on how they use their discretion despite repeated requests from respondents, because such a guidance would necessarily have to be broad. They clarify however that the statutory test for referral 'is that the circumstances suggest that a potential breach of (for example) the FCA Principles for Business may have occurred'[110] and that further changes will be taken into consideration following responses to the CP. Those changes are mostly related to how the FCA holds discussions with firms on lessons learned from past enforcement actions.

The FCA committed to facilitate more formal discussion with firms, to engage more through a variety of events, such as the 'Live&Local' one,[111] and to investigate how lessons can be publicised more broadly.[112]

In terms of transparency and private warnings,[113] the FCA decided to take into due account the concerns of respondents and to launch a specific consultation in the future.

Other areas where there was broad agreement between FCA suggestions and respondents relate to cooperation among regulators, subjects' understanding and representations in enforcement investigations, and of course settlement and contested cases.

Within those areas, the FCA committed to investigate further certain concerns expressed by respondents. For instance, due to differences of opinion among respondents, the FCA decided to consult further on early settlement and partly contested cases. Also, while there was agreement on the need to increase cooperation and assistance among internal divisions, the FCA highlighted that what matters is the experience of the relevant staff rather than their level of seniority and also that there needs to be clarity on the internal division of responsibilities.[114]

Another area the FCA is willing to keep under review relates to the possibility of giving further guidance on PIR.[115] The penalty discount scheme will not be amended.

As for the RDC, as mentioned already a fast-track procedure has been instated, and a periodic review of its performance and activities will be made public.[116]

The resulting enforcement framework at the FCA reflects the efforts of the authority to be more fair and transparent towards subjects under investigation. In light of the discussed acceptance of most of the respondents' concerns during the public consultation process preceding the final recommendations of the HMT review and of the FCA PS, it also expresses the intention of the FCA to be responsive to public and private demands.

---

[108]   FCA (n 22).

[109]   See FCA, *Our Mission. Feedback Statement FS 17/1*, April 2017, available at www.fca.org.uk/publication/feedback/fs17-01.pdf.

[110]   FCA/PRA (n 107) 10.

[111]   See FCA, *Feedback Statement* (n 109), 39. For details on Live&Local activities, see: https://www.fca.org.uk/live-local-events.

[112]   FCA (n 111), 10.

[113]   FCA (n 111), p 40.

[114]   See FCA/PRA (n 107), at 4.22.

[115]   FCA/PRA, PS 17/1 (n 107), 21.

[116]   FCA/PRA, CP 16/10 (n 106), 39.

While this is certainly in line with principles of good regulation, and it follows in fact a well-established regulatory process, one may wonder whether the final result may expose the FCA to unintended consequences. Enforcement is an area where regulators and regulatees are doomed to clash. Each party brings opposite interests, especially when the subject under investigation is an individual.[117] Those may not necessarily be reconciled. The FCA should have fair and objective processes and governance mechanisms, but should also retain enough discretion and independence not to be unduly influenced by those investigated. Also, as mentioned before, the FCA is not a Tribunal. The same concept of 'acting fairly' doesn't necessarily imply equal treatment, but rather 'that certain cases will be subject to enforcement action and others not, even where they may be similar in nature or impact' depending on the need to ensure resources are used 'effectively and efficiently'.[118]

Yet the current framework seems to favour rigidity over discretion and flexibility of action.

One can interpret FCA reaction as an (understandable) attempt to show the public and the political arena their intent to remedy past poor practices.

However, there is a thin dividing line between transparency and openness as yardsticks of ethical and fair behaviour and exposure to an increased risk of regulatory capture. The fear is that the balance may tip towards the latter because of the enhanced dialogue between the parties, which in some cases will relate to the substance of the investigations at a time when the FCA staff are still forming their opinion.

Also, the FCA still seems to go through a process of identity formation. The regulator has been the subject of too much political attention, often with contrasting signals. A few years after its inception, the FSA was allegedly accused of inhibiting efficient business with their action and red tape. Post-FSA, the TC and the PCBS insisted on the inadequacy of the Authority's light touch approach, including in enforcement. Under the Wheatley leadership, the FCA embarked on an unprecedent wave of enforcement actions, only to come to a halt more recently, possibly as a consequence of a change in political climate which saw a desire

---

[117] When it is a firm instead, the same company management has an interest in proving its good intention to accept the consequences of wrongdoing, also as a way to change culture. Or to close the case as soon as possible to avoid further reputational damage, which is one of the incentives firms have to settle early. The professional consequences for a natural person may in a sense be more severe, as these may impact on their ability to continue working in the industry. Therefore, the latter is more likely to oppose the regulator's decision.

[118] See E.G 2.2.5.

for an end to the 'bashing the bankers' period.[119] The same CEO, Mr Martin Wheatley, was not confirmed at the helm of the Authority at the end of his mandate.[120]

Inevitably this may have an impact on staff morale and attitude. However, the current CEO of the Authority insisted on how the FCA is not going 'soft' on conduct as well as on Mifid II breaches (among the others) which may lead to enforcement actions.[121]

FCA efforts to be collaborative are necessary but are not the only condition for a trustworthy regulator. To deserve public trust, a regulator needs to be credible. If the FCA simply appears to allow interested parties to influence its policy in the way described above, or to be sensitive to political mood, it risks weakening its position as a credible regulator.

In the enforcement scenario, credibility tends to be linked to deterrence. Yet this belies the fact that a deterrence effect may only be temporary and that firms' approach to compliance may be influenced by external and political factors. In other words, unless the FCA is able to resist pressures, it will be difficult to establish a pattern where regulatees and the public as a whole hold trust and respect in the activities of the regulator in the long term. As mentioned, a component of credibility is the ability of an authority to use consistently and 'fearlessly' its unfettered judgement.

On the other hand, though, there seem to be elements within the legal system which run contrary to institutional support for trust in the FCA. For instance, the HMT recommendation that the TC holds pre-commencement hearings for the Chairs of the regulators' decision-makers[122] can be interpreted as a sign of wanting to intervene more stringently in the Authority's governance.

---

[119] See FT, *George Osborne to signal end to 'banker bashing'*, 5 June 2015, available at www.ft.com/content/eb8b6b1a-0b84-11e5-994d-00144feabdc0. More recently the FCA has been criticised for being 'soft' on enforcement in general, see FT, *FCA hands out fines totalling just 6.3m in its first half*, 28 December 2016, available at https://www.ft.com/content/38da3382-c863-11e6-9043-7e34c07b46ef; and FT, *Andrey Bailey insists FCA has not 'gone soft' on misconduct*, 19 March 2018, available at www.ft.com/content/9f5afd22-2946-11e8-b27e-cc62a39d57a0. And more specifically, for having merely fined the CEO of Barclays for trying to uncover the identity of a whistle-blower within the organisation. The FCA and the PRA found the CEO, Mr James Staley, in breach of Individual Conduct Rule 2 (Duty to act with due care, skill and diligence) but not of Individual Conduct Rule 1 (Duty to act with integrity). See FCA, *FCA and PRA jointly fine Mr James Staley £642,430 and announce special requirements regarding whistleblowing systems and controls at Barclays*, 11 May 2018, available at https://www.fca.org.uk/news/press-releases/fca-and-pra-jointly-fine-mr-james-staley-announce-special-requirements. See also FT, *Regulators need to show they care about whistleblowers*, 13 May 2018, available at www.ft.com/content/9fbe05cc-569e-11e8-bdb7-f6677d2e1ce8.

[120] See The Guardian, *City watchdog chief quits after George Osborne vote of no confidence*, 17 July 2015, available at www.theguardian.com/business/2015/jul/17/city-watchdog-chief-quits-fca-george-osborne and FT, *Martin Wheatley admits disappointment at leaving FCA*, 22 July 2015 available at www.ft.com/content/df262c4c-3056-11e5-91ac-a5e17d9b4cff.

[121] See FT, *Andrew Bailey insists FCA has not gone soft on misconduct*, available at www.ft.com/content/9f5afd22-2946-11e8-b27e-cc62a39d57a0 and FT Adviser, *FCA warns of enforcement on Mifid II breaches*, available at www.ftadviser.com/regulation/2018/06/14/fca-warns-of-enforcement-on-mifid-ii-breaches/.

[122] HM Treasury (n 73), para 1.19, at p 5.

Also, the existence of a 'Financial Regulators Complaint Commissioner'[123] allows anyone who is 'directly affected by the way in which regulators have carried out their functions'[124] to raise a complaint to express 'dissatisfaction about the manner in which the regulators have carried out, or failed to carry out, their relevant functions',[125] with the exclusion of the legislative ones.

Complainants can base their claim on lack of care, unprofessional behaviour, bias and lack of integrity, among others.[126] Claimants must be seeking a remedy for the inconvenience, distress or loss caused by the regulator's action or inaction. This may include an apology, taking steps to rectify errors or 'if appropriate, the offer of a compensatory payment on an *ex gratia* basis'.[127]

The complaint is first investigated by the FCA to evaluate whether it falls under the Scheme and, if so, whether it should be dealt with by the Area which is subject to the complaint (by a senior member of staff not involved in the case).[128] Claimants have the right to refer the complaint to the Commissioner if dissatisfied with the outcome. They can also refer the case directly to the Commissioner, however in this case the latter 'will consider whether it would be desirable to allow the relevant regulator'[129] the opportunity to carry out its own investigation before the Commissioner does.

At the end of each year the Commissioner issues a final report detailing the cases covered. This report is sent to the regulator, the HMT and Parliament, and it is published on the Commissioner's website.

The annual reports rarely depict a rosy picture of the FCA. In one year[130] the Authority issued a response addressing criticisms. However, in that document the FCA often merely apologises without offering an explanation as to why its performance was not satisfactory. Those reasons may be related to human errors made in good faith, to overload or to other organisational issues, and not necessarily to intentional lack of professionalism or worse, lack of integrity.

The problem with both the FCA response and the Commissioner's censure is that they may have the unintended effect of legitimising mistrust and fuelling further disenchantments with the regulator's activities. This in turns undermines the credibility of the FCA.

This conclusion is reinforced by the fact that the FCA has no other venue in which to challenge the Commissioner's decisions when they disagree with them. They can issue a report in response to criticisms, which is used to indicate how they have addressed problems internally,

---

[123] The Office of the Commissioner was originally included in FSMA 2000. The Commissioner issued its first annual report in 2002. The Scheme was recently amended by Part 6 'Investigation of Complaints against Regulators' of the Financial Services Act 2012, extending the scope of application to the PRA and the BoE. See also www.frccommissioner.org.uk.

[124] See PRA/FCA, *Complaints against the regulators, The Complaints Scheme*, Updated March 2016, available at www.fca.org.uk, at para 3.2.

[125] *Ibid* at para 2.1.(a).

[126] See PRA/FCA, *Complaints against the regulators* (n 124), para 3.1.(a)–(e).

[127] PRA/FCA, *Complaints against the regulators* (n 124), at para 6.6.

[128] PRA/FCA, *Complaints against the regulators* (n 124), at para 6.2.

[129] PRA/FCA, *Complaints against the regulators* (n 124), at para 6.12.

[130] See *The FCA's response to the Annual Report 2015/2016 of the Office of the Complaints Commissioner* (for the year ended 31 March 2016) available at www.frccommssioner.org.uk/publications/annual-reports.

but there is no third party to decide or comment on the validity of the criticisms made by the Commissioner. This gives an idea of the unilaterality of the process.

Furthermore, the existence of such a scheme – unheard of in continental European jurisdictions and not equally applicable to all UK regulated sectors – raises two interrelated questions.

The first is the extent to which the independence of the FCA is compromised by this further layer of accountability, which can be quite intrusive. And the other relates to its location in a jurisdictional order where the activities of an independent body should only be challenged before a Tribunal.

The Complaint Commissioner seems to be a hybrid figure as the ground for complaints are somewhat loose (being 'dissatisfied' with regulators' activities) and the whole scheme seems to express an institutional distrust in the ability of regulators to act fairly, or in their own internal mechanisms for dealing with complaints.

Therefore, while the rationale behind such a scheme is the legitimate need to make regulators more accountable, to give redress to entities being somehow mistreated by the regulator, to increase transparency, and to extend the public protection beyond the remit of ordinary justice, the consequences can be noticeable on both staff morale and public perceptions of the institution.

CRITICAL REFLECTIONS ON EXCESSIVE TRANSPARENCY

As discussed throughout the chapter, the current enforcement framework aims at increasing transparency. Transparency is not included among the Nolan principles. Yet it certainly falls under openness[131] and it is generally recognised as a basic principle of regulatory accountability and fairness. Therefore, transparency is also usually associated with ethical behaviour.

However, it is worth considering the drawbacks that may come with too much transparency, which could hinder regulatory action.

The first problem relates to an unintended effect of transparency. This was highlighted in a now seminal Reith Lecture by the eminent British moral philosopher Onora O'Neill.[132] The main thrust of that lecture is that openness and transparency have hugely flourished in the modern era. Part of the reason for this being the need to increase trust and trustworthiness in public life.

However, 'trust seemingly has receded as transparency has advanced',[133] and transparency and openness may not necessarily be the 'unconditional goods that they are fashionably

---

[131] 'Holders of public office should act and take decisions in an open and transparent manner. Information should not be withheld from the public unless there are clear and lawful reasons for so doing.' See CSPL, *Standards matter: A review of best practice in promoting good behaviour in public life*, January 2013, available at https://assets.publishing.service.gov.uk/government/uploads/system/uploads/attachment_data/file/348304/Standards_Matter.pdf, at p 25.

[132] See Onora O'Neill, The Reith Lectures: A Question of Trust, 04/2002, available at http://www.bbc.co.uk/radio4/reith2002/. See also, Minouche Shafik, In experts we trust?, 22 February 2017, available at https://www.bankofengland.co.uk/speech/2017/in-experts-we-trust; Onora O'Neill, Trust, Trustworthiness and Accountability, in *Capital Failure. Rebuilding Trust in Financial Services*, Nicholas Morris and David Vines (eds), OUP, 2014; and CSPL (n 131), paras 6.16 and 6.17.

[133] O'Neill. Reith Lectures (n 132) at min 9.18.

supposed to be'.[134] The lack of trust is fostered more by deception and lies than by secrecy. In a sense, transparency and openness do little to avoid the former, and can actually give incentives to people whose opinion is going to be in the public domain to 'massage the truth'[135] while 'public reports may underplay sensitive information and head teachers and employers may write blandly uninformative reports and references'[136] and 'evasive and uninformative statements may substitute for truth telling'.[137] This may be caused by the need of public bodies to be 'politically correct', while in fact what they are doing is 'self-censorship or deception'.[138]

At a time of unfavourable political climate, self-censorship is indeed a risk for the FCA.

The second problem is that empowering the general public with such a strong tool may increase suspicion rather than acting as a disinfectant. As it happens with too much information in securities regulation, the public may not be able to understand it, discern it, or to interpret it correctly.

In our case, the public may feel inclined to focus on relatively minor issues rather than on actual policies and practices. When the Bank of England decided to make public the Governor's expenses, it became inundated with FOI requests on who the Governor was having yoghurt with at the airport and whether he was staying in a single or double hotel room when travelling to a G20 meeting.[139]

Excessive public scrutiny then could lead to an unfounded erosion of credibility. Transparency certainly is a tool to make the regulator more accountable, as it should be.

However, an abuse of the tool may not be an effective way to guard against regulators' unfair behaviour, for excessive transparency per se is no panacea. A legal system should instead put a balanced weight on a broad variety of accountability mechanisms and should also rely on a cooperative relationship among public bodies which is respectful of their independence. To this end, one could argue that the current accountability framework in the United Kingdom does provide enough venues to ensure sufficient scrutiny of the FCA.

A third problem relates to expectations. As it emerged from the enforcement review, with the exception of statutory confidentiality, firms expect transparency on all fronts. This includes how regulators use discretion, which by definition implies independent judgement. It requires a strong and credible regulator to be able to resist these calls, while at the same time not being accused of lack of engagement with the stakeholders.

Expectations also relate to the ability of firms to anticipate the moves, decisions and actions of the regulator on the basis of what has been declared, consulted on, or otherwise made public. The possibility of firms gaming the rules or concentrating compliance efforts in an area they expect to be the focus of regulatory actions may be one of the unintended consequences of regulators' openness on thematic areas under review, for instance.

---

[134]   *Ibid* at min.11.20.
[135]   *Ibid* at min 15.28.
[136]   *Ibid* at min 15.38.
[137]   *Ibid* at min 15.42.
[138]   *Ibid* at min 16.00.
[139]   See FT, *BoE transparency culture stirs up yoghurt questions for Carney*, 24 May 2017, available at www.ft.com/content/a05746f2-406e-11e7-82b6-896b95f30f58.

There is no silver bullet to fully reconcile the role of transparency and openness as emblems of ethical behaviour[140] and the inherent risks they carry with them. However, actions could be taken to find a balance.

For instance, as mentioned already, what matters in enforcement is the existence of fair and objective procedural rules, as well as an internal governance mechanism that fosters independent judgement. *Ex ante* supervisory activity may prevent or reduce the risk of rules infringement by firms, therefore limiting FCA exposure to criticisms. *Ex ante* intervention, over enforcement, seems in fact to be the preferred option of the PRA.

Also, the applicability of the Senior Managers Regime to the FCA may be a step in the right direction. The allocation of responsibility to a specific member of staff may give them an incentive to ensure that due process is being respected throughout the enforcement cycle.

The focus should also be on the existing legal system of checks and balances which aims at making the regulator accountable. By relying on the correct functioning of these mechanisms, the question then moves from 'how much' is being published to 'how fairly' the regulator is behaving. However, that correct functioning requires objectivity and lack of bias on the political side too and we have discussed how this may not always be the case.

CONCLUSIONS

The current debate on ethics in finance is focused on the behaviour of firms. Little is being written or analysed on the behaviour of financial regulators. In the absence of an established body of literature on the matter, this chapter is a starting point for discussion. Enforcement activities are a key test to assess authorities' ethical behaviour because they require powers whose application needs a fair amount of discretion against a relatively lower amount of legal protection afforded to the subjects under investigation.

The quality of enforcement activities at the FCA has been under tight scrutiny in the recent past. Criticisms arose from both the public and the private sector. In some cases, FCA final notices attracted judicial admonition too. Yet enforcement is not a straightforward process and there may be a difficult balance to strike between different regulatory actions. Also, the level of discretion enjoyed by the regulator on the matter exposes it to the risk of being easily accused of acting unfairly or behind closed doors.

The current FCA regulatory enforcement framework has been repeatedly amended to reflect and address those concerns and its genesis has been discussed in this chapter.

After describing the enforcement cycle, the chapter analyses the ethical problems associated with enforcement, particularly with respect to settlement and private warnings. Some problems still remain despite the most recent reforms.

The chapter also argues that FCA efforts to be more transparent and to actively address criticisms certainly represent the right course of action. Regulators enjoy a vast amount of powers and discretion, and should be held tightly accountable. They should also be responsive

---

[140] For an analysis on ethical regulation see Christopher Hodges, *Ethical Business Regulation: understanding the evidence*, Better Regulation Delivery Office paper, February 2016, available at https://assets .publishing.service.gov.uk/government/uploads/system/uploads/attachment_data/file/497539/16-113 -ethical-business-regulation.pdf; Rodney Brooke, *Ethics and the Role of Regulators*, at Teaching Public Administration, 2003, 23:2, 1–19.

to well-founded concerns. However, there is a thin line between responsiveness and (public perception and risk of) regulatory capture, which in turn may have a negative impact on a regulator's credibility and the long-term effectiveness of their actions. Furthermore, even though transparency is widely – and in most cases rightly – seen as an indicator of ethical behaviour, doubts may arise as to its actual efficacy in delivering credibility. The latter also requires an institutional framework which is supportive of the efforts, of the activities and of the exercise of discretion by the regulator.

This chapter highlights for the first time how the legal framework surrounding regulators' activities may in itself have the unintended effect of hampering regulators' credibility if poorly constructed.

Index